Readings in Ethics

WAS HELFFEN FAKELN LICHT
ODER BRILN,
SO DIE LEVT NICHT SEHEN
WOLLEN.

Heinrich Khunrath, from his 1609 book *Amphi-theatrum Sapientiae Eternae* (The Amphitheatre of Eternal Wisdom). The German caption can be translated as follows: "What use are torches, light or glasses to people who do not want to see."

Readings in Ethics

MORAL WISDOM PAST AND PRESENT

EDITED BY
LOUIS F. GROARKE
PAUL V. GROARKE
PAOLO C. BIONDI

broadview press

BROADVIEW PRESS – www.broadviewpress.com
Peterborough, Ontario, Canada

Founded in 1985, Broadview Press remains a wholly independent publishing house. Broadview's focus is on academic publishing; our titles are accessible to university and college students as well as scholars and general readers. With 800 titles in print, Broadview has become a leading international publisher in the humanities, with world-wide distribution. Broadview is committed to environmentally responsible publishing and fair business practices.

Library and Archives Canada Cataloguing in Publication

Title: Readings in ethics : moral wisdom past and present / edited by Louis F. Groarke, Paul V. Groarke,
    and Paolo C. Biondi.
Other titles: Readings in ethics (Peterborough, Ont.)
Names: Groarke, Louis, editor. | Groarke, Paul, 1953- editor. | Biondi, Paolo C., 1964- editor.
Description: Includes bibliographical references.
Identifiers: Canadiana (print) 20210129972 | Canadiana (ebook) 20210129999 | ISBN 9781554813643
    (softcover) | ISBN 9781770486782 (PDF) | ISBN 9781460406342 (EPUB)
Subjects: LCSH: Ethics. | LCSH: Ethics—History. | LCSH: Ethics, Ancient.
Classification: LCC BJ1012 .R38 2021 | DDC 170—dc23

Broadview Press handles its own distribution in North America:
PO Box 1243, Peterborough, Ontario K9J 7H5, Canada
555 Riverwalk Parkway, Tonawanda, NY 14150, USA
Tel: (705) 743-8990; Fax: (705) 743-8353
email: customerservice@broadviewpress.com

For all territories outside of North America, distribution is handled by Eurospan Group.

Broadview Press acknowledges the financial support of the Government of Canada for our publishing activities.

Canada

Copy-edited by Robert M. Martin

Book design by Chris Rowat Design

PRINTED IN CANADA

This book is dedicated to
Ernie McCullough (†),
Ed Carty,
and Thomas De Koninck,
who have generously shared their wisdom
with students through generations.

Acknowledgments

The editors would like to thank Stephen Latta for his patience, support, and commitment to this project, Bob Martin for his careful copy editing, and Tara Trueman for managing the production of the book. We are also grateful to Meagan McCullagh and Francesca Biondi for photocopying the readings and copy editing early drafts of them, and to Leo Groarke for his wise guidance at various steps in the process.

CONTENTS

PART III MEDIEVAL SOURCES

PART IV MODERN SOURCES

Preface: For Instructors

This textbook is intended for post-secondary courses in moral philosophy, the meaning of life, and courses that introduce undergraduate students to the humanities. It will fit well into a course designed around the great books. It will also be of general interest to students who are beginning their studies in philosophy, and to teachers and faculty outside philosophy who are teaching interdisciplinary courses that touch upon the history of ideas. It will also appeal to anyone with a general interest in the development of ethics, the philosophical record, or the history of ideas.

We have followed a historically rigorous cosmopolitan approach, with a focus on wisdom. The wise individual makes good choices, understands happiness, makes sense of moral failure, maintains deep friendships, and so on. To use a stock phrase, morality is as much about discovering the "meaning of life" as it is about determining what we are permitted to do. The goal of morality is accordingly to live wisely. We believe that students will find much more room for thought in this broader approach, and hours of constructive and yet enjoyable reading.

As a result of the focus on wisdom, the selection of readings is much wider than the selection in most textbooks. Although the readings review the analytical tradition, and the logical arguments within it, they also include religious scriptures, political manifestos, fables, proverbs, letters, and epistles, which often reveal deep moral insights that need to be considered by anyone searching for a well-grounded ethics. We are certainly of the view, philosophically, that these texts deserve a more prominent place in the academic philosophical tradition.

The question we asked in choosing each reading was whether it reflects a significant view in the ethical record of humanity. This record contains historical writers who sometimes held views that are racist, sexist, or otherwise objectionable by today's standards. Though many of these writers had moral failings they nonetheless offer important moral insights today. We have occasionally included counter-readings; yet, the readings were edited in accordance with the pedagogical principle of charity, with the idea of providing the most cogent account of each school of ethics. The readings in different chapters nevertheless include some strong criticism of competing theories. This may be more significant in the case of modern thinkers, since the modern debate is unsettled.

The unsettled state of the modern debate is reflective, in part, of the increasing plurality and diversity of contemporary human societies living in a global village. Although none of the editors is of Indigenous, Muslim, Chinese, Indian, or any other non-Western cultural identity presented in the book, there are readings from these moral communities and traditions. It is our firm belief that hearing the variety of human voices about moral wisdom constitutes, potentially, a step towards acquiring it. True dialogue, and especially reconciliation with respect to past injustices, can only begin by first listening to each other. Our sincere hope is that instructors will view this anthology, during this time of heightened cultural sensitivities, as a small contribution to consciousness-raising in the efforts towards making us more enlightened moral beings.

The chapters of the book are arranged chronologically. The only real exception lies in those circumstances where a particular moral tradition—such as the proverb tradition, or the tradition of fables—has continued on, historically, beyond the period in which it flourished or became notable. For example, the story-telling tradition continues to live within some contemporary Indigenous cultures. These exceptions have not altered the character of the book, which is historically rigorous and charts the evolution of ethics through a number of discernible stages in its historical progression, right through to the contemporary era. Note, however, that "evolution" and "historical progression" refer simply to the adaptations made by human beings to the changes over time in social organization and cultural environment.

In the course of editing the readings, we naturally focused on the major contributions that a philosopher or a school has made to the history of ethics. We also tried to set out the most essential features of the relevant theory. We have excised a good deal of repetitious material, unnecessary asides, and technical fillips. Although some of the readings have been taken from familiar translations in the public domain, we have emended and updated them in order to make them more accessible to today's students.

Other matters aside, we place a high premium on provocative, well-edited selections that students will enjoy reading, without losing sight of the main outlines of each tradition. In spite of their brevity, the readings include interesting anecdotes, topical questions, memorable tropes, and provocative theoretical issues. We have also highlighted examples, cases, or issues that lend themselves to classroom discussion. All in all, we believe that this has produced abridged texts that are faithful to the original but eminently readable.

It will be evident to professors that there is enough material in the book for two or three courses in ethics. This gives an individual instructor wide leeway in choosing the readings for a particular course. Although most of the readings stand on their own, they can obviously be read in the company of other readings, or in a more selective arrangement, which focuses on specific issues. There is enough room here, for example, for professors to pick and choose among the readings, historically or thematically, in whatever manner suits their needs.

Pedagogical Features

The introductions to each reading are in keeping with the spirit of the book. Although they are brief, they contain biographical material, some explanation of relevant theories or schools, and a reference to the readings. They accordingly give the students some sense of the relevant philosopher's moral stance, as well as of the times in which the philosopher lived. We felt that an examination of the lives and times of these thinkers was particularly pertinent in a book that addresses the general question: "What kind of life should we live?" We also believe that philosophical theories cannot be fully understood outside their historical context, which always provides insight into the operation of the theory.

There are also a number of extra features. The timeline at the front of the book provides a quick chronological account of moral thinkers, authors, and texts. It contains sufficient material for an introductory overview of the historical development of ethics and provides a helpful source of information for examinations. We have also included an introduction for students. There is a list of questions at the end of each chapter, which occasionally raise new issues, and these questions are followed by suggestions for further readings. There is a substantial dictionary of important technical terms at the back of the book, some from classical or foreign languages and some in English.

The suggested readings, like the questions, expand the scope of the book well beyond the introduction and the readings in the relevant chapter. There are print and online sources, along with links to comprehensive bibliographies and helpful websites. Since we wanted to save space, preserve a readable narrative, and include as many references as possible, the references themselves are skeletal. This has allowed us to canvass a wide range of scholarship.

Introduction: For Students

"The first principle is that which is found in the connection subsisting between all the members of the human race." —Cicero

Moral philosophy may sound like a speculative and abstract subject. You may be thinking that it is an exercise in theory that is of little relevance to our busy lives.

This is not our view. As the readings in this anthology demonstrate, moral philosophy is everybody's business. It is something that everyone studies, inside or outside the classroom. Not everyone has to know about subatomic particle physics or the chemistry of photosynthesis. It is interesting, even fascinating, to discover how the Egyptian pyramids were built. But you are not obliged to know these things. It is a matter of personal inclination and vocation. You are obliged, however, to be moral. This is true, as a matter of personal principle and as a matter of social convention. Unless you come within a few exceptions—you are somehow incapacitated or too young to be reading these lines—we expect you to be moral.

Let us assume that you want to be a moral person. This merely means that you want to do the right thing. It follows that you need to know how to be moral. This requires contemplation and thought, and is something that—uniquely—you have to determine for yourself. This book accordingly provides you with a brief history of human ethics, so that you can figure out—for yourself—what it takes to be a moral person.

This book contains a diverse set of readings by some of the world's most celebrated thinkers. These philosophers speak to all of us. Ethics is not a passive activity, and as you go through the book, you may want to think of their arguments for one position or another as proposals for a given way of life. The ultimate choice as to the kind of life that you should lead must be left to you. It would nevertheless be foolish to ignore the advice of the wise men and women who have gone before us and mapped out the terrain.

The texts from which the readings are taken are part of a "wisdom literature." This term has a number of meanings and has been used, in a religious context, to identify those texts that pass on reliable moral and spiritual advice. The advice in the readings reaches out beyond any particular religious or cultural tradition, however, and speaks to all of us. The Stoics are notable because they subscribed to an early form of ethical "cosmopolitanism" and saw themselves as citizens of the world. The book in your hands is based on a new but similar form of cosmopolitanism, which spans many different cultures and traditions.

As you go through the historical traditions, you will discover that moral wisdom comes in many guises. Although professional philosophers are primarily interested in the development of theories and systems, theories are always incomplete and some of the most thought-provoking moral reflection can be found in written records of orally-transmitted stories and in literature, including everything from proverbs, poetry, and fables to letters, diaries, sermons, and so on. Perhaps it is obvious to say, but wisdom cannot be confined to an academic exercise and these forms of expression all deserve fair consideration. Moreover, it is possible for historical writers to offer important moral insights today all the while having sometimes held views that are racist, sexist, or otherwise objectionable by today's standards.

The ultimate aim of an ethics course is to give you the skills that you need to make insightful ethical decisions. Like anything else, this requires practice. Thomas Aquinas's notion of "equity" is one way of highlighting the importance of such a skill. What Aquinas means by "equity" here is not a kind of equality (as in modern usage). The Thomistic virtue of "equity" is a developed sense of right and wrong, which gives us the ability to pick through unusual or extreme circumstances and arrive at moral judgments that cohere with the spirit rather than the mere letter of the law. A good judge possesses a generalized wisdom and is able to adapt this general wisdom to unique particular circumstances. That is to say, a good judge exhibits "equity."

The realities of human life can be complicated. The increasing moral pluralism in our societies today introduces further complications. It is the wise person who has the ability to see through the complications, set aside extraneous factors, and come to sound decisions in the midst of confusing events and (sometimes conflicting) interpretations of their moral significance. The readings in this book should help you develop the "equity" that you need to find the right answer to difficult ethical questions. The ultimate aim is a working wisdom, which can make sense of life in logical and yet flexible ways.

This book is a starting point—a rather thorough starting-point—in the moral journey that everyone has to take, in school or out of it. As we have said, it gives you a good map of the route that wise people have taken up to this point in our ethical journey. We hope that you will cherish it as an affordable, all-in-one ethics library, which you can consult when you need to work through a pressing ethical issue or want a quick, authoritative explanation of an influential moral view.

General Questions

Each chapter ends with a set of questions that draws attention to some of the specific issues in that chapter's readings. There are also a number of general questions which you should consider while working through each of the readings.

The first set of general questions concerns the broader values underlying the reading:

- What values, or system of values, does the philosopher hold?

- What account of human achievement and failure does the reading contain?
- What is the end of human life, according to the reading?
- Where do we find happiness, in the view of the author?

The second set of general questions focuses on the behaviors that the writer condones or condemns:

- How do we determine the morality of an act, according to the philosopher?
- What kinds of behaviors are praised or condemned in the reading? Why?
- What duties do we have, according to the philosopher?
- What virtues does the reading promote? What vices should we avoid?
- Discuss the philosopher's view of what is admirable, noble, good, beautiful, or heroic.
- Does the reading contain social criticisms? If so, what is being criticized? Why? What is the moral rationale behind the criticism?

The third set of general questions concerns omissions or biases:

- What does this philosopher leave out?
- Do the philosopher's views reflect any sort of gender bias?
- Do the philosopher's views reflect any sort of cultural or racial bias?

The fourth set of general questions concerns your assessment of the reading:

- Discuss an example that the philosopher uses. Do you agree with the philosopher's analysis of the example?
- Provide a contemporary example (or an example from your own life, or the life of your friends) to illustrate or criticize the theory in the reading.
- Provide an example that seems to raise difficulties for the theory in the reading.

These suggestions naturally supplement the specific questions already provided at the end of each chapter.

A note on footnotes: The original sources (or editions or translations thereof) from which the readings in this book are excerpted are listed as the first footnote for each reading. Almost all the footnotes for the readings have been added by the editors of this volume. The very few that were written by the authors and carried over here are indicated by the insertion of "[Author's Note]."

Historical Timeline of Ethical Theories

Earliest Times		Key Associations
Pre-tribal traditions	From before time immemorial	Varied ethical traditions, often based on consensus and a respect for local customs and cosmologically enshrined relationships
African tribal traditions	From time immemorial	Varied ethical traditions, some of which emphasize the development of good character (e.g., *suban*), which rests on one's ability to act in accord with moral judgment
Indigenous traditions around the world	From time immemorial	Varied ethical traditions, many of them continuing today in Indigenous cultures
Epic of Gilgamesh	Compiled from early sources before it was written down in 2100 BCE	Babylonian Myth
Hammurabi, King of Babylon	c. 1792–1750 BCE	Known for his "code" of Babylonian Law
Vedas (वेद), from 'véda,' "knowledge"	Mid-2nd to mid-1st millennium BCE, Hindu scriptures	Religious ethic resting on the idea of *dharma* (a central and multifaceted term, like *dao*), which includes the idea of self-realization and a strong concept of personal and social duty within it
Moses (מֹשֶׁה)	1400–1300 BCE (Rabbinic calendar: 1393–1273 BCE)	Judaism

Fall of the city of Ilium (Ἴλιος), also known as Troy (Τροία), the subject of the *Iliad*	1300–1200 BCE	
Solomon (הַמֶּלֶךְ)	975–926 BCE	Judaism, wisdom tradition
Iliad, *Odyssey*, historically attributed to Homer (Ὅμηρος)	900–800 BCE	Greek tribal ethics; warrior ethics
Oral Shinto tradition	Before the 6th century and from time immemorial	Emphasized inner and outer purity, sincerity
Ancient		
The written *Torah* (הַרוֹת, which means "teaching" or "instruction"), which contains the Mosaic law	Probably after the 5th century BCE (though this is disputed)	Scripture containing the prescriptive Jewish ethical tradition based on obedience to the revealed wisdom of God and written law
Aesop (Αἴσωπος)	c. 620–560 BCE	Greek tribal ethics; Fables
"TEN PRECEPTS" in *Setting the Will on Wisdom* (part of the Daoist canon)	First half of the 5th century BCE	One of a number of Daoist consolidations of ethical injunctions, emphasizing compassion and temperance
Laozi (also Lao-tzu, "Old Master," 老子)	Sixth century BCE, born c. 601	The seminal figure in classical Daoism and the reputed author of the *Dao de jing*, usually identified as an "older contemporary" of Kongzi
Kongzi (孔子, meaning Master Kong), also known as Kong Fu Zi (Grand Master Kong, 孔夫子) and thus Confucius	551–479 BCE	Confucianism: a conservative ethical system based on loyalty (*zhong*) to a moral hierarchy and reciprocity (*shu*), emphasizing *li* (rites, proper conduct), *ren* (human feeling), and *yi* (right)
Buddha (Siddhartha Gautama)	c. 563 BCE–483 BCE (the dates are disputed)	Buddhism
Bhagavad Gita (भगवद् गीता)	c. 500–200 BCE	Hindu ethics; warrior ethics; deontological
Heraclitus of Ephesus (Ἡράκλειτος)	c. 535–c. 475 BCE	Pre-Socratic Philosophy

Protagoras (Πρωταγόρας)	c. 490–c. 420 BCE	Greek Sophists
Mozǐ (墨子), who rejected the teachings of Kongzi	c. 480–392(?) BCE	Postulated a collective notion of "universal love" recognizing self-interest and emphasizing action for mutual benefit; defense in war
Diogenes of Sinope, Διογένης (Diogenes in Greek, Diogenes the Cynic), known for choosing to live in a barrel	c. 404–323 BCE	Cynicism; ethical naturalism, following nature rather than convention; Ascetism (*askēsis*)
(The) Zhuangzǐ (莊子), a text traditionally attributed to Master Zhuang (Zhuangzǐ 莊子; also known as Zhuang Zhou [Chuang Chou], 莊周), a follower of Laozi	Late 4th century BCE, but probably compiled in the 3rd century CE	Late early Daoism; Skeptical teachings emphasizing ethical naturalism and inactivity over social convention, culminating in an emptying of the mind and mystic dissolution of the self
Socrates (Σωκράτης)	469–399 BCE	Virtue Ethics; Teleological Ethics based on knowledge of the good and human flourishing
Democritus (Δημόκριτος)	c. 460–c. 370 BCE	Atomism; Hedonism
Hippocrates (Ἱπποκράτης) / Hippocratic Oath	c. 450–380 BCE	Greek Medicine; Professional Ethics based on self-government
Plato (Πλάτων)	427–347 BCE	Platonism; Mysticism; Virtue Ethics
Callicles (Καλλικλῆς) (who may be a fictional character)	c. 484–late 5th century BCE	Greek Sophists; a warrior ethic within society; "might is right"
Aristotle (Ἀριστοτέλης) / *Nicomachean Ethics*	384–322 BCE	Virtue Ethics; Eudaimonism
Mengzi (孟子), a follower of Kongzǐ and opponent of Mozǐ	371–289 BCE	Emphasized the goodness of human nature and the development of natural feelings like *ts'e yin* (commiseration) and *hsiu wu* (shame)
Pyrrho of Ellis (Πύρρων)	c. 360–270 BCE	Ancient Skepticism (Pyrrhonism)
Epicurus (Ἐπίκουρος)	341–271 BCE	Epicureanism
Zeno of Citium (Ζήνων ὁ Κιτιεύς)	334–c. 262 BCE	Considered the founder of Stoicism
Book of Job, Ecclesiastes, Song of Songs, Proverbs	3rd–2nd centuries BCE	Wisdom Tradition; Judaism

Dao de jing (道德經), honorifically attributed to Laozi, who reputedly lived in the 6th century BCE	late 4th century BCE	Daoism: a syncretic compilation (perhaps agglomeration) of earlier views based on a cosmological ethic that emphasizes ethical naturalism, praises the virtue of not acting, and counsels emptying the mind
Xunzi (劝学, also Hsun-tzu)	312–210 BCE	Confucianism; Realism; argues (against Mengzi) that human nature is bad and goodness requires deliberate effort; moral teachings, *li*, and punishments are needed to reform our original nature
Han Fēizǐ (韓非)	280–233 BCE	Chinese Legalism, based on an empirical recognition of self-interest and the need for social correction; Realism
Cicero (Marcus Tullius Cicero)	106–43 BCE	Roman Stoicism
Lucretius (poet)	99–55 BCE	Epicureanism
Jesus	b. 7 BCE–3 CE d. 27–36	Christian ethics, based on love
(Saint) Paul the Apostle (Paul [or Saul] of Tarsus, Παῦλος)	5–67	Christian ethics; Epistles (New Testament)
New Testament	50–110	Christian Revelation; an ethics of love
Epictetus (Ἐπίκτητος), whose teachings are found in *Discourses*, *Enchiridion*, a handbook by Arrian	55–135	(Roman) Stoicism
Seneca (Lucius Annaeus Seneca or Seneca the Younger)	c. 4–65	(Roman) Stoicism
Marcus Aurelius (Emperor Marcus Aurelius Antoninus Augustus)	121–180	(Roman) Stoicism
Sextus Empiricus, a physician who saw philosophy as a kind of medicine	2nd–3rd centuries	Ancient Skepticism (Pyrrhonism)
Diogenes Laertius (Διογένης Λαέρτιος) *Lives of Eminent Philosophers*	3rd century	Contains the most influential biographies of previous philosophers (e.g., Diogenes of Sinope); Laertius sees philosophy—the pursuit of wisdom—as a way of life and ethical practice

Plotinus (mystic, philosopher)	204–270	Neoplatonism
(Saint) Anthony of the Desert	c. 251–356	Christian ethics; Asceticism; Anchoritism
Desert Fathers and Mothers	c. 250–9th century	Christian ethics; Asceticism; Anchoritism
(Saint) Jerome (Eusebius Sophronius Hieronymus) / *Vulgate* (Latin translation of Bible)	347–420	Christian ethics, ethics based on Revelation
Medieval		
(Saint) Augustine (of Hippo)	354–430	Christian ethics; Neoplatonism
Boethius (Anicius Manlius Severinus Boëthius) / *The Consolation of Philosophy*	c. 480–524	Neoplatonism; Christian ethics
Qur'an (The *Koran*, literally "the recitation")	644–656 (the traditional dates)	Islamic Revelation
Al-Ghazali, (الغزالي محمد ابن محمد ابو حامد), the author of *Tahafut al-Falasifa* (*The Incoherence of the Philosophers*)	1056–1111	Islamic Theology; Entelechy; *riyâdat al-nafs*
Zhou Dunyi (周敦頤)	1017–1073	Early Neo-Confucianism; Daoism, a cosmological grounding of ethics in metaphysics of yin-yang (the *Taijitu*) and inactivity (e.g., loved his grass and ethically refused to cut it); sincerity is the basis of our moral nature
Peter Abelard (Petrus Abaelardus)	1079–1142	Theologian; philosopher; Intentionalism
Moses Maimonides, author of *Guide for the Perplexed* (c. 1190)	1138–1204	Judaism; The Mean; "Therapeutic" Philosophy
(Saint) Francis of Assisi	1182–1226	Asceticism; Franciscanism; *imitatio Christi*
(Saint) Bonaventure	1221–1274	Christian Theology; Franciscanism
(Saint) Thomas Aquinas (Tommaso d'Aquino) / *Summa Theologiae*	1225–1274	Thomism; Natural Law; Virtue Ethics; "Theological" Ethics

Dante Alighieri (Durante degli Alighieri) / *Divine Comedy* (*Divina Commedia*)	1265–1321	Poet; Christian ethics; Thomism
William of Ockham	1287–1347	Voluntarism; Franciscanism
Saint Catherine of Siena	1347–1380	Christian Mysticism
Wáng Yáng-míng (王陽明) also known by his birth name, Wang Shourén (王守仁)	1472–1529	Neo-Confucianism, believing in the unity of knowledge of the good and action; "acting and knowing is one thing"
Modern		
Yi Hwang (이황), pen name T'oegye	1501–1570	Korean ethics; Sung Confucianism; rejected Wáng Yáng-míng's "unity of knowledge and action"; instead, he proposed that "knowledge precedes action" and argued for the innateness of rational ethical norms
The Society of Jesus (the Jesuits) founded by Ignatius of Loyola, who became its first Superior General	1541	Known for its devotion to education; Casuistry
Thomas Hobbes *Leviathan*	1588–1679	Liberalism; Contractarianism; Social Contract Theory
Bernard (de) Mandeville	1670–1733	Realism; Philosophical Immoralism; Libertinism
(Bishop) Joseph Butler	1692–1752	Judaeo-Christian ethics; Rational Christian ethics
David Hume	1711–1776	Emotivism; Mitigated Skepticism
Jean-Jacques Rousseau	1712–1778	Communitarianism
Adam Smith	1723–1790	Sentimentalism
Immanuel Kant	1724–1804	Deontological ethics; Kantianism
Mary Wollstonecraft	1759–1797	Early Liberal Feminism; Virtue Ethics
Jeremy Bentham	1784–1832	Utilitarianism

William Godwin	1756–1836	Utilitarianism; "Fire Cause"; each individual has an obligation to produce as much happiness in the world as he/she is able
United States Constitution	September 17, 1787	Republicanism
Déclaration des droits de l'homme et du citoyen	August 26, 1789 (*Assemblée nationale constituante* of France)	Recognized the "natural rights" of the individual; Human Rights; Egalitarianism
La Déclaration des droits de la femme et de la citoyenne, written by Olympe de Gouges (1748–1793)	1791	Feminism; Egalitarianism; a response to the *Déclaration des droits de l'homme et du cityoyen* by substituting the feminine wherever the masculine is found in the text
Sojourner Truth	c. 1797–1883	Early Feminism; Egalitarianism
Arthur Schopenhauer	1788–1860	Nihilism; Pessimism; Buddhism; Asceticism
On Liberty by John Stuart Mill (1806–1873)	1859	Liberalism; Utilitarianism; Egalitarianism
Søren Kierkegaard	1813–1855	Christian Existentialism
Karl Marx	1818–1883	Marxism
Communist Manifesto (Karl Marx and Friedrich Engels)	1848	Socialism; Communism; Ethics of revolution
Friedrich Nietzsche	1844–1900	Nihilism; Philosophical Immoralism; Social Darwinism
William James	1842–1910	American Pragmatism
Yan Fu (嚴復)	1853–1921	Chinese scholar and translator who introduced western philosophy to China
John Dewey	1859–1952	American Pragmatism; Social Democracy based on a rejection of individualistic (i.e., Liberal) utilitarianism
Ethical Studies by F.H. Bradley (1846–1924)	1876	British Idealism; like the Pragmatists, he rejected the utilitarian notion of self and argued that the moral self was essentially "social"; advocated a religious ethics

Prolegomena to Ethics by T.H. Green (1836–1882)	1883	British Idealism; advocated self-realization on the basis that the moral ideal can only be realized in a social whole
Contemporary		
Mohandas Karamchand (Mahatma) Gandhi	1869–1948	Indian political ethicist
Bertrand Arthur William Russell	1872–1970	English philosopher, logician, popular moralist
George Edward Moore	1873–1958	Intuitionism; Analytic Philosophy
Martin Buber	1878–1965	Austrian, Palestinian/Jewish, Israeli popular existentialist moralist
Jacques Maritain	1882–1973	Neo-Thomism; Natural Law
Watsuji Tetsur	1889–1960	Japanese ethics, which rejects abstract individualism; *Ningen sonzai, Rinri*
Jean-Paul Sartre	1905–1980	Existentialism; Marxism; Secular Humanism
Ayn Rand	1905–1982	Russian-American popular novelist; libertarian
Simone de Beauvoir	1908–1986	Feminism; Feminist Existentialism
Albert Camus	1913–1960	Existentialism; an Ethics of the Absurd
World War I	1914–1918	The scale of the war promoted the idea that there must be ethical limits on war
Iris Murdoch	1919–1999	Neoplatonism
Gertrude Anscombe	1919–2001	Virtue Ethics; Neo-Aristotelianism
Libertarianism: A Political Philosophy for Tomorrow by John Hospers (1918–2011)	1971	Libertarianism
A Theory of Justice by John Rawls (1921–2002)	1971	Contractarianism; Liberalism; Social contract
Lawrence Kholberg	1927–1987	Neo-Kantianism; Liberalism; Theory and Stages of Moral Development

Gustavo Gutiérrez	1928–	Liberation theology (*Teología de la liberación*); an ethics emphasizing a) the "dignity of the poor" and b) the obligation to change "social structures"
(Rev.) Martin Luther King (Jr.)	1929–1968	Natural Law; Egalitarianism; Civil Rights
Nel Noddings	1929–	"Second Wave" Feminism; Female Essentialism
After Virtue, by Alasdair MacIntyre (1929–)	1981	Virtue Ethics; Communitarianism
Charles Taylor	1931–	Communitarianism; Substantive Liberalism
Richard Rorty	1931–2007	Neo-Pragmatism; Skepticism; Post-Modernism
Carol Gilligan	1936–	Feminism; Female Essentialism
Jan Narveson	1936–	Libertarianism; Contractarianism
John Kekes	1936–	Conservativism; Communitarianism
World War II	1939–1945	War Crimes; Crimes against humanity (crimes against civilian populations)
Margaret Sommerville	1942–	Natural Law
Robert Solomon	1942–2007	Existentialism
The Nuremberg Trials	1945–1946	Natural Law Jurisprudence; recognition of crimes against humanity, which "shock the conscience of mankind"
Universal Declaration of Human Rights	1948	Liberalism; Egalitarianism; an idea of individual human rights emanating from philosophers like John Locke and Immanuel Kant
Martha Nussbaum	1947–	Neo-Aristotelianism; Virtue Ethics
Establishment of the People's Republic of China by Mao Zedong (1893–1976) and the Chinese Communist Party	1949	Communism; state-sanctioned Marxism, which brought in a general rejection of traditional Chinese philosophy
Peau noire, masques blancs by Frantz Fanon (1925–1961)	1952	Black existentialism (under the influence of Jean-Paul Sartre); Africana ethics, which gave rise to a "decolonial" ethic justifying the use of violence

Invisible Man by Ralph Ellison (1913–1994)	1952	Black existentialist novel
Christine Korsgaard	1952–	Neo-Kantianism
The Ethics of Psychoanalysis by Jacques Lacan (1901–1981)	*Séminaires* in 1959–60, Paris	Replaces the "sovereign good" and the hedonistic concept of pleasure in the ethics of psychiatry with psychological desire
Animal Liberation by Peter Singer (1946–)	1975	A popular declaration of animal rights, following Jeremy Bentham (Benthamite); Utilitarianism
Hunhuism or Ubuntuism by Stanlake J. W.T. Samkange (1922–1988)	1980	Ubuntu; African Humanism; a Communitarian view that rejects individualist ethics: "A person is a person through other people"

PART I

EARLY SOURCES

Cosmological Ethics. The Tribal Origins of the Wisdom Tradition

To properly appreciate the origins of the wisdom tradition, it is perhaps beneficial to bear in mind a few features of human history, which is thought to have begun 200,000 years ago. (The evolution of the hominid/hominine family from which modern human beings come measures 7 million years.) The evidence for agrarian societies places their appearance at 10,000 years, with the first cities and city-states arising 5,000 years ago. This span of time shows that for much of human history, the origins of the wisdom tradition had its roots in distant clans and tribes, the earliest forms of human social organization regardless of geographical location.[1]

Throughout this period of time, there were a number of interconnected lines of transition worth noting as well: from the less settled and more nomadic mode of life to the more settled lifestyle of city dwellers; from living with those who are familiar (the clan and tribe based on kinship) to living with unfamiliar strangers (unrelated members of a city); from the social mechanism of decision-making by consensus to the political mechanism based on the rule of law; from an oral to a written transmission of (moral) culture and wisdom; and finally, from a communal identity of the individual to the emergence of an individual identity.

---

1 When we use the terms 'tribe' and 'tribal' in this text, we are referring to all societies organized around these smaller social groups, not those of any specific cultures or regions.

Those of us who study moral philosophy often fail to recognize the full moral significance of this very early wisdom tradition and its development. It developed in conjunction with the development of the human brain as it adapted to living in social groups, that is, adapted to the human and cultural—as distinct from the merely natural and physical (or geographical)—environment. The tribal traditions pre-date the formal philosophical tradition, from the dawn of human history to the beginnings, circa 500 BCE, of the classical Chinese tradition and to the awakening of philosophy among the Greeks that culminated in the Golden Age of Athens.

The wisdom tradition was originally oral: the teaching of elders was transmitted by stories and sayings. These stories or "folktales" were intended for adults although they could be used in a pedagogical manner when instructing youth. Proverbs were prized, not only for the wisdom they contained, but also because they provided an economical and memorable means of passing on knowledge. The tradition was a didactic tradition, and a source of practical wisdom, which was based on the experience of previous generations.

Even when civilizations began to attach names such as Homer, Aesop, Confucius, or King Solomon to texts, it was often the case that these names refer to the personification of a living oral tradition rather than to a single author in the modern sense. No one knows who invented, altered, recorded, and embellished the moral proverbs, stories, and anecdotes that early tribal societies carefully guarded and cherished as their main source of moral wisdom. Customs, rules, poems, stories, myths, and proverbs were passed down from generation to generation without much emphasis being placed on any rigorous or precise identification of individual authors. We have here a repository of wisdom in collective memory.

The debate about how humans were organized during the very early periods of human civilization is complicated by many factors. Although the twentieth-century Viennese anthropologist Bertha Eckstein-Diener[1] famously argued that all human societies were, at their origins, matriarchal, this view has been largely discounted. Scholars distinguish between matriarchal, matristic, matrilineal, matrilocal, and matrifocal societies, but we cannot explore these distinctions here. Suffice it to say that although masculine names are attached to traditional texts at this stage of history during which the oral tradition slowly gave way to the written word, this is often a case of communal authorship rather than texts written by specific living individuals.

It is important to keep in mind that we tend to misunderstand the belief systems of these tribal societies because of the contemporary liberal emphasis on individualism. The contribution of individual women, specifically to written, technical moral philosophy, keeps on increasing as we head into the modern age. Still, the small number of written records attributed to women philosophers in the early tribal, ancient, and medieval eras isn't likely proportionate to women's actual contributions within the moral communities of those peoples. Early peoples often placed female goddesses and female priestesses at the very center of their religious traditions, and wisdom was typically portrayed as a woman.

---

1 Eckstein-Diener (1874–1948) is also known by her American pseudonym, Helen Diner.

The success of the early system of ethics rested on the individual's internalization of the customs and practices of the clan or tribe. For these early people, wisdom lay in custom, which was later enshrined in customary law. The tribal traditions are, however, perennial, living traditions and still contribute to the moral character of our intuitive moral notions and everyday conduct. These traditions continue in every human society to some degree, as they account for many of our deepest ethical instincts as social beings.

Chapter 1

The Wisdom in Customary Laws

The ethics of the tribal traditions, which were based on custom, found expression in many cultures as *customary* laws. These laws probably reflect the social changes that came about with settled agrarian life. The customary laws had a religious and a secular facet and, in the Babylonian case, provide a remote but recognizable example of civil government. The primary impetus for a formal apparatus of government appears to come from the development of cities, which conceptually take the form of collections of strangers (i.e., unfamiliar people). This is important because it means that the people in cities are not bound together by the ties and obligations of family (i.e., familiar people). Nor is there the same "internalization" of the moral law.

This makes cities inherently unruly, and calls for the development of other ethical mechanisms that restrict personal conduct. The concept of a citizen—a later word, which refers to the inhabitant of a city—may have provided a convenient receptacle for some of the elements of the tribal identity. The primary development, however, was customary laws, which were based on the establishment of kings and rulers. The invention of writing was instrumental in this development.

It is difficult to say exactly how notions of the gods developed in these societies, but this was also significant since it often gave specific divine personalities a legal and ethical jurisdiction, which could then be transferred to a delegate. This is represented by the figures at the top of the stele containing the law of Hammurabi: they show a standing King receiving the law—represented by a measuring rod and tape—from Shamash, the Babylonian god of justice, who is seated on a throne.

The Babylonian king or ruler was not seen as a person with a law-making power. The function of the ruler was to see that the existing ethical order, which was found in tribal customs, was respected and enforced. The common law developed in a similar manner. The so-called *Code of Hammurabi* is accordingly a collection of legal decisions, like the reports of decisions in the common law. It is not a "code," a term which refers specifically to a legislative compilation of laws that obtains its authority from a recognized political source. Hammurabi's collection of decisions follows the example of older compilations, such as the (so-called) *Code of Ur-Nammu* (2100–2050 BCE) and the *Laws of Eshnunna* (c. 1930 BCE).

Hammurabi was the sixth Amorite king of Babylon from 1792 to 1750 BCE. He ruled for 42 years, an extremely long period, and was reportedly respected for putting "order and righteousness in the land." As King, he held the chief judicial office, and the decisions that have come down to us may represent decisions of his court, rather than personal decisions. They may also represent decisions on appeal, which he had approved or somehow confirmed and which were intended to provide precedents for judicial officers trying specific cases.

The decisions that we have were carved on slabs of black basalt and placed essentially in city squares, where they provided a public record of the case law. This satisfied the legal requirement of notice, which is still required by the law, and informed the people of the decisions of the court. The carving was apparently difficult and the steles themselves were designed to convey the majesty and power of the King. They were clearly designed to demonstrate the wisdom and justice of the King and naturally served a political purpose. The King had fulfilled the responsibilities of his office, as required by God.

It will be clear to any student of the common law that the inscriptions on the stele are essentially head-notes, which provide the essential facts and *ratio decidendi* (reason for the decision) in individual cases. Ethically, the issue of dishonesty seems to be the primary concern. This gave rise to the need for proof. Thus, Hammurabi requires the existence of a contract—or witnesses—to establish that one has obtained the property legally. Annotation seven, for example, states that if "any one buy from the son or the slave of another man, without witnesses or a contract... he is considered a thief and shall be put to death." As a result, archaeologists have discovered many clay tablets in the form of receipts and contracts, with witnesses, which must have been used to attest to commercial transactions.

Hammurabi's decisions focus on the civil, rather than the criminal, law, which deals with the social relations between those people with a recognized legal status in the system. The cases provide us with considerable insight into the values of Babylonian society. The importance of agriculture can be seen in the decision that a man who steals an ox must pay back thirty times its value. The cases deal with family matters, professional contracts, public censure, and general issues of liability.

The laws of Hammurabi also contain penalties. A citizen who knocked out the teeth of an equal must have his own teeth knocked out, though many wrongdoers undoubtedly negotiated settlements with the victim in order to avoid the actual infliction of the penalty. A citizen who knocked out the teeth of someone below him in rank would simply pay compensation. Husbands and wives were the subject of particular attention, and were legally required to conduct themselves in a way that honored the marriage contract. Tavern-keepers were under strict restrictions.

One of the interesting features of Hammurabi's laws is their concern with personal fault and moral excuses, which reflects our own law of torts. This is the part of the early law that ultimately gave rise to the criminal law, which is the most prominent holdover of the oral law. It is significant that this concern with personal fault seems to reflect a new and enhanced sense of individuality that presages later developments.

The Mosaic collection of laws, found in the *Torah*, is from the same geographical area and in spite of much controversy contains many parallels. The religious aspects of the customary law nevertheless come to the fore in the *Torah*, which represents a somewhat different development: from a cosmological to a religious framework of morality and law. This is evident in the *Torah*'s persistent emphasis on the religious covenant between the Israelites and Yahweh.

There is a debate in Judaism as to the status of the *Torah*. The conventional contemporary position is that the *Torah* was not revealed by God in the traditional sense but was a product of the social customs of ancient Israel. Maimonides (whose work appears in a later chapter) emphasized the rational aspects of the work. Like many Jewish commentators, he saw it as a rejection of idolatry, though his understanding of idolatry was more abstract and philosophical than that of his contemporaries.

The tendency in the *Torah* is to equate ethical thought with moral action. Wisdom in the Mosaic tradition is seen as a practical rather than a theoretical kind of knowledge, firmly embedded in the ordinary responsibilities of life. This is a point that is worth bearing in mind when reviewing the modern tradition. Ethical ideas and theories are not sufficient in themselves.

READING 1A

The Decisions of Hammurabi[1]

(c. 1780 BCE)

Preamble

Hammurabi, the prince… am I,… the royal scion of Eternity, the mighty monarch, the sun of Babylon, whose rays shed light over the land…

When Marduk[2] sent me to rule over men, to give the protection of law to the land, I did [law] and righteousness [impose upon the land], and brought about the well-being of the oppressed.

Cases of False Testimony

1. If anyone ensnare another, putting a ban upon him, but he cannot prove it, then he that ensnared him shall be put to death.

2. If anyone bring an accusation against a man, and the accused go to the river and leap into the river, if he sink in the river his accuser shall take possession of his house. But if the river prove that the accused is not guilty, and he escape unhurt, then he who had

---

1 "Laws of Hammurabi," from *The Code of Hammurabi* (1780 BCE), translated by L. [Leonard] W. King (with an introduction by Charles F. Horne dated 1915, but without a location, publisher or date), which is available at http://avalon.law.yale.edu/ancient/hamframe.asp.

2 The head of the Babylonian pantheon of gods and patron deity of the city of Babylon.

brought the accusation shall be put to death, while he who leaped into the river shall take possession of the house that had belonged to his accuser.

3. If anyone bring an accusation of any crime before the elders and does not prove what he has charged, he shall, if it be a capital offense charged, be put to death.

Of Theft

6. If anyone steal the property of a temple or of the court, he shall be put to death, and also the one who receives the stolen thing from him shall be put to death.

8. If anyone steal cattle or sheep, or an ass, or a pig or a goat, if it belong to a god or to the court, the thief shall pay thirtyfold; if they belonged to a freed man of the king he shall pay tenfold; if the thief has nothing with which to pay he shall be put to death.

9. If anyone lose an article, and find it in the possession of another: if the person in whose possession the thing is found say "A merchant sold it to me, I paid for it before witnesses," and if the owner of the thing say, "I will bring witnesses who know my property," then shall the purchaser bring the merchant who sold it to him, and the witnesses before whom he bought it, and the owner shall bring witnesses who can identify his property. The judge shall examine their testimony—both of the witnesses before whom the price was paid, and of the witnesses who identify the lost article on oath. The merchant is then proved to be a thief and shall be put to death. The owner of the lost article receives his property, and he who bought it receives the money he paid from the estate of the merchant.

Protecting Houses

21. If anyone break a hole into a house [to steal something], he shall be put to death before that hole and be buried.

22. If anyone is committing a robbery and is caught, then he shall be put to death.

25. If fire break out in a house, and someone who comes to put it out cast his eye upon the property of the owner of the house, and take the property of the master of the house, he shall be thrown into that self-same fire.

Protecting Fields and Gardens

53. If anyone be too lazy to keep his dam in proper condition, and does not so keep it; if then the dam break and all the fields be flooded; then shall he in whose dam the break occurred be sold for money, and the money shall replace the corn which he has caused to be ruined.

54. If he be not able to replace the corn, then he and his possessions shall be divided among the farmers whose corn he has flooded.

59. If any man, without the knowledge of the owner of a garden, fell a tree in a garden he shall pay half a mina[1] in money.

Regulating Taverns

108. If a woman tavern-keeper does not accept corn according to gross weight in payment of drink, but takes money, and the price of the drink is less than

---

1 An Ancient Near-Eastern unit of weight and currency. The unit of weight was divided into 50 shekels and was equal to 1.25 pounds.

that of the corn, she shall be convicted and thrown into the water.

109. If conspirators meet in the house of a tavern-keeper, and these conspirators are not captured and delivered to the court, the tavern-keeper shall be put to death.

110. If a "sister of a god"[1] open a tavern, or enter a tavern to drink, then shall this woman be burned to death.

Bailment

120. If anyone store corn for safe keeping in another person's house, and any harm happen to the corn in storage, or if the owner of the house open the granary and take some of the corn, or if especially he deny that the corn was stored in his house: then the owner of the corn shall claim his corn before God,[2] and the owner of the house shall pay its owner for all of the corn that he took.

122. If anyone give another silver, gold, or anything else to keep, he shall show everything to some witness, draw up a contract, and then hand it over for safe keeping.

123. If he turn it over for safe keeping without witness or contract, and if he to whom it was given deny it, then he has no legitimate claim.

Concerning Husbands and Wives

127. If anyone "point the finger" at a sister of a god or the wife of anyone, and cannot prove it, this man shall be taken before the judges and his brow shall be marked.[3]

128. If a man take a woman to wife, but have no intercourse with her, this woman is no wife to him.

129. If a man's wife be surprised with another man,[4] both shall be tied and thrown into the water, but the husband may pardon his wife and the king his slaves.

130. If a man violate the wife of another man, who has never known a man, and still lives in her father's house, and sleep with her and be surprised, this man shall be put to death, but the wife is blameless....[5]

148. If a man take a wife, and she be seized by disease, if he then desire to take a second wife he shall not put away his wife, who has been attacked by disease, but he shall keep her in the house which he has built and support her so long as she lives....

Punishing Incest

154. If a man be guilty of incest with his daughter, he shall be driven from the place.

157. If anyone be guilty of incest with his mother after his father, both shall be burned.

---

1 Presumably a nun.
2 To claim before God is to assert something under oath.
3 To point the finger at is to sexually slander someone. The brow is marked by cutting the skin or perhaps the hair.
4 I.e., caught in the act of sexual intercourse.
5 The case concerns a betrothed or child-wife.

Protecting Inheritance

168. If a man wish to put his son out of his house,[1] and declare before the judge: "I want to put my son out," then the judge shall examine into his reasons. If the son be guilty of no great fault, for which he can be rightfully put out, the father shall not put him out.

169. If he be guilty of a grave fault, which should rightfully deprive him of the filial relationship, the father shall forgive him the first time; but if he be guilty of a grave fault a second time the father may deprive his son of all filial relation.

Cases Setting Penalties and Compensation

192. If a son of a paramour or a prostitute say to his adoptive father or mother: "You are not my father, or my mother," his tongue shall be cut off.

193. If the son of a paramour or a prostitute desire his father's house, and desert his adoptive father and adoptive mother, and goes to his father's house, then shall his eye be put out.

195. If a son strike his father, his hands shall be hewn off.

196. If a man put out the eye of another man, his eye shall be put out.

197. If he break another man's bone, his bone shall be broken.

200. If a man knock out the teeth of his equal, his teeth shall be knocked out.

201. If he knock out the teeth of a freed man,[2] he shall pay one-third of a gold mina.

202. If anyone strike the body of a man higher in rank than he, he shall receive sixty blows with an ox-whip in public.

209. If a man strike a free-born woman so that she lose her unborn child, he shall pay ten shekels[3] for her loss.

210. If the woman die, his daughter shall be put to death.

Cases Concerning Physicians and Other Occupations

215. If a physician make a large incision with an operating knife and cure it, or if he open a tumor [over the eye] with an operating knife, and saves the eye, he shall receive ten shekels in money.

218. If a physician make a large incision with the operating knife, and kill him, or open a tumor with the operating knife, and cut out the eye, his hands shall be cut off....

224. If a veterinary surgeon perform a serious operation on an ass or an ox, and cure it, the owner shall pay the surgeon one-sixth of a shekel as a fee.

225. If he perform a serious operation on an ass or ox, and kill it, he shall pay the owner one-fourth of its value.

229. If a builder build a house for someone, and does not construct it properly, and the house which he

---

1 I.e., to deprive him of his inheritance.
2 I.e., someone who is below his rank.
3 See p. 44, note 1.

built fall in and kill its owner, then that builder shall be put to death.

230. If it kill the son of the owner, the son of that builder shall be put to death.

235. If a shipbuilder build a boat for someone, and do not make it tight, if during that same year that boat is sent away and suffers injury, the shipbuilder shall take the boat apart and put it together tight at his own expense. The tight boat he shall give to the boat owner.

Other Liabilities and Exclusions

247. If anyone hire an ox, and put out its eye, he shall pay the owner one-half of its value.

266. If the animal be killed in the stable by God, or if a lion kill it, the herdsman shall declare his innocence before God, and the owner shall bear the cost.

267. If the herdsman overlook something, and an accident happen in the stable, then the herdsman is at fault for the accident which he has caused in the stable, and he must compensate the owner for the cattle or sheep.

Epilogue

Laws of justice which Hammurabi, the wise king, established.

Hammurabi, the protecting king am I. . . .

That the strong might not injure the weak, in order to protect the widows and orphans, I have in Babylon . . . set up these, my precious words . . .

By the command of Shamash, the great judge of heaven and earth, . . . let the oppressed, who has a case at law, come and stand before this [stone and read the inscription, which] . . . will explain his case to him; he will find out what is just, and his heart will be glad . . .

[This is followed by a curse:]

If a succeeding ruler . . . destroy the law which I have given . . . may Anu, the Father of the gods . . . break his scepter, curse his destiny. . . .

May Nergal, the might among the gods, whose contest is irresistible . . . in his great might burn up his subjects like a slender reed-stalk, cut off his limbs with his mighty weapons, and shatter him like an earthen image. . . .

Excerpts from the written *Torah*[1]

(fifth century BCE)

Leviticus

CHAPTER 5

20. And the LORD spoke unto Moses, saying:

21. If anyone sin, and commit a trespass against the LORD, and deal falsely with his neighbor in a matter of deposit, or of pledge, or of robbery, or have oppressed his neighbor;

22. or have found that which was lost, and dealt falsely therein, and swear to a lie; in any of all these that a man does, sinning therein;

23. then it shall be... that he shall restore that which he took...

24. and anything about which he has sworn falsely, he shall even restore it in full, and shall add the fifth part more thereto.

25. And he shall bring his forfeit unto the LORD, a ram without blemish out of the flock, according to your valuation, for a guilt-offering unto the priest.

CHAPTER 14

33. And the LORD spoke unto Moses and unto Aaron, saying:

34. [If] I put the plague of leprosy in a house of the land of your possession;

35. then he that owns the house shall come and tell the priest, saying: 'There seems to me to be as it were a plague in the house.'

36. And the priest shall command that they empty the house... and afterward the priest shall go in to see the house.

37. ... and, behold, if the plague be in the walls of the house with hollow streaks, greenish or reddish, and the appearance thereof be lower than the wall;

38. then the priest shall go out of the house to the door of the house, and shut up the house seven days.

39. And the priest shall come again the seventh day, and shall look; and, behold, if the plague be spread in the walls of the house;

40. then the priest shall command that they take out the stones in which the plague is, and cast them into an unclean place outside the city.

41. And he shall cause the house to be scraped within round about, and they shall pour out the mortar that they scrape off outside the city into an unclean place.

42. And they shall take other stones, and put them in the place of those stones; and he shall take other mortar, and shall plaster the house.

---

1 Excerpts from the book of Leviticus and the book of Deuteronomy, part of the *Torah*, are from the Jewish Publication Society's 1917 edition of *The Hebrew Bible in English, The Holy Scriptures According to the Masoretic Text: A New Translation with the Aid of Previous Versions and with Constant Consultation of Jewish Authorities* (Philadelphia: The Jewish Publication Society of America, 1917). Available at http://www.mechon-mamre.org/e/et/et0.htm.

43. And if the plague come again, and break out in the house,

44. then the priest shall come in and look; and, behold, if the plague be spread in the house, it is a malignant leprosy in the house: it is unclean.

45. And he shall break down the house, the stones of it, and the timber thereof, and all the mortar of the house; and he shall carry them forth out of the city into an unclean place....

54. This is the law for [the leprosy of a house]...

CHAPTER 19

1. And the LORD spoke unto Moses, saying:

2. Speak unto all the congregation of the children of Israel, and say unto them: You shall be holy; for I the LORD your God am holy.

3. You shall fear [your mother and your father], and you shall keep My Sabbaths: I am the LORD your God.

4. Turn you not unto the idols, nor make to yourselves molten gods: I am the LORD your God....

11. You shall not steal; neither shall you deal falsely, nor lie one to another.

12. And you shall not swear by My name falsely, so that you profane the name of your God: I am the LORD.

13. You shall not oppress your neighbor, nor rob him...

14. You shall not curse the deaf, nor put a stumbling-block before the blind, but you shall fear your God: I am the LORD.

15. You shall do no unrighteousness in judgment; you shall not respect the person of the poor, nor favor the person of the mighty; but in righteousness shall you judge your neighbor.

16. You shall not go up and down as a talebearer among your people...

17. You shall not hate your brother in your heart; you shall surely rebuke your neighbor, and not bear sin because of him.

18. You shall not take vengeance, nor bear any grudge against the children of your people, but you shall love your neighbor as yourself: I am the LORD.

26. You shall not eat with the blood; neither shall you practice divination nor soothsaying.

29. Profane not your daughter, to make her a harlot, lest the land fall into harlotry, and the land become full of lewdness.

32. You shall rise up before the hoary head, and honor the face of the old man, and you shall fear your God: I am the LORD.

33. And if a stranger sojourn with you in your land, you shall not do him wrong.

CHAPTER 20

Cursing a father or mother

9. [and] whatsoever man there be that curses his father or his mother shall surely be put to death.

Adultery

10. And the man that commits adultery with another man's wife, even he that commits adultery with his

neighbor's wife, both the adulterer and the adulteress shall surely be put to death....

13. And if a man lie with mankind, as with womankind, both of them have committed abomination: they shall surely be put to death; their blood shall be upon them....

CHAPTER 23

1. And the LORD spoke unto Moses, saying...

Keeping the Sabbath

3. Six days shall work be done; but on the seventh day is a Sabbath of solemn rest, a holy convocation; you shall do no manner of work; it is a Sabbath unto the LORD in all your dwellings....

CHAPTER 24

Blasphemy and injury

13. And the LORD spoke unto Moses, saying:

14. Bring forth him that has cursed outside the camp; and let all that heard him lay their hands upon his head, and let all the congregation stone him....

17. And he that smites any man mortally shall surely be put to death.

18. And he that smites a beast mortally shall make it good: life for life.

19. And if a man maim his neighbor; as he has done, so shall it be done to him:

20. breach for breach, eye for eye, tooth for tooth; as he has maimed a man, so shall it be rendered unto him.

21. And he that kills a beast shall make it good; and he that kills a man shall be put to death....

CHAPTER 26

3. [And the Lord said:] If you walk in My statutes, and keep My commandments, and do them;

4. then I will give your rains in their season, and the land shall yield her produce, and the trees of the field shall yield their fruit.

6. And I will give peace in the land, and you shall lie down, and none shall make you afraid; and I will cause evil beasts to cease out of the land, neither shall the sword go through your land.

7. And you shall chase your enemies, and they shall fall before you by the sword.

9. And I will have respect unto you, and make you fruitful, and multiply you; and will establish My covenant with you.

14. But if you will not hearken unto Me, and will not do all these commandments;

15. and if you shall reject My statutes, and if your soul abhor My ordinances, so that you will not do all My commandments, but break My covenant;

16. I also will do this unto you: I will appoint terror over you, even consumption[1] and fever, that shall make the eyes to fail, and the soul to languish; and you shall sow your seed in vain, for your enemies shall eat it.

17. And I will set My face against you, and you shall be smitten before your enemies; they that hate you shall rule over you; and you shall flee when none pursues you.

---

1 The historical name given for tuberculosis due to the weight loss associated with the illness.

[This is followed by escalating warnings.]

27. And if you will not for all this hearken unto Me, but walk contrary unto Me;

28. then I will walk contrary unto you in fury...

29. And you shall eat the flesh of your sons, and the flesh of your daughters shall you eat.

31. And I will make your cities a waste, and will bring your sanctuaries unto desolation...

33. And I will scatter you among the nations, and I will draw out the sword after you; and your land shall be a desolation, and your cities shall be a waste.

44. And yet for all that... I will not reject you, neither will I abhor you, to destroy you utterly, and to break My covenant with you; for I am the LORD your God.

Deuteronomy

CHAPTER 14

3. You shall not eat any abominable thing.

4. These are the beasts which you may eat: the ox, the sheep, and the goat,

5. the hart, and the gazelle, and the roebuck, and the wild goat, and the pygarg,[1] and the antelope, and the mountain-sheep.

6. And every beast that parts the hoof, and has the hoof wholly cloven in two, and chews the cud, among the beasts, that you may eat.

7. Nevertheless these you shall not eat of them that only chew the cud, or of them that only have the hoof cloven: the camel, and the hare, and the rock-badger, because they chew the cud but part not the hoof, they are unclean unto you;

8. and the swine, because he parts the hoof but chews not the cud, he is unclean unto you; of their flesh you shall not eat, and their carcasses you shall not touch.

9. These you may eat of all that are in the waters: whatsoever has fins and scales may you eat;

10. and whatsoever has not fins and scales you shall not eat; it is unclean unto you.

11. Of all clean birds you may eat.

12. But these are they of which you shall not eat: the great vulture, and the bearded vulture, and the osprey;

13. and the glede, and the falcon, and the kite...

14. and every raven...

18. and the stork, and the heron... and the hoopoe, and the bat.

19. And all winged swarming things are unclean unto you; they shall not be eaten.

20. Of all clean winged things you may eat.

21. You shall not eat of anything that dies of itself; you may give it unto the stranger that is within your gates... or you may sell it unto a foreigner; for you are a holy people unto the LORD your God. You shall not seethe a kid in its mother's milk.[2]

---

1 I.e., "white-rumped," so probably a deer of some sort.
2 To seethe is to boil or to be hot.

CHAPTER 20

19. When you shall besiege a city a long time, making war against it, you shall not [wield an axe against the fruit-bearing trees thereof]; for you may eat of them, but shall not cut them down; for is the tree of the field [a] man, that it should be besieged by you?

CHAPTER 22

5. A woman shall not wear that which pertains unto a man, neither shall a man put on a woman's garment; for whosoever does these things is an abomination unto the LORD your God.

6. If a bird's nest chance to be before you in the way, in any tree or on the ground, with young ones or eggs, and the dam[1] sitting upon the young, or upon the eggs, you shall not take the dam with the young;

7. you shall in any wise let the dam go...

Questions

1. The Babylonian law has a secular and a religious/cosmological source, though it is the religious/cosmological source that gives it the character of law. Explain.
2. One of the principal concerns in the Babylonian law is dishonesty. This was partly a product of the rise of cities, which weakened the hold of tribal customs. What is your solution? Mention the Babylonian law.
3. The giving of false testimony was essentially unforgivable in the Babylonian and Hebrew legal systems. Why?
4. The Hebrew tradition was based on the idea that there is a "covenant" between Yahweh and his chosen people. What was the most fundamental term of such a contract and the consequences of violating it?
5. The moral idea that things are "clean" or "unclean" in the *Torah* comes out of the tribal tradition and the idea of taboos. Discuss.
6. Note two or three laws from the *Torah* to which you have heard people make reference today. Note two or three laws to which you have never heard people refer. Why do you think that is the case?
7. Our abstract conception of God would have made no sense to early peoples, who believed that the gods are angry when we act improperly. They may accordingly intervene. Defend the position of early peoples.

---

1 I.e., the mother.

Suggested Readings[1]

The decisions of King Hammurabi were carved into steles (stone pillars) for display, one of which can be seen at louvre.fr, with brief comments and a bibliography, mostly in French. L.W. King's translation of Hammurabi's law is at the website of *The Avalon Project* at Yale Law School, with commentary. There are sources on the *Torah* in chapter 19. For general historical material, see Martha Roth, *Law Collections from Mesopotamia and Asia Minor* (1997). William Robson engages in a rare philosophical discussion of the early manifestations of law in *Civilization and the Growth of Law* (1935). The early issues of *The Monist* contain a discussion of the relationship between the Babylonian law and the *Torah*. For a more recent discussion, see David Wright, *Inventing God's Law* (2009), and for contemporary academic work on the *Torah*, see, for example, Laura Weed, "Freud and the Torah" (1995).

---

1 Note to students: For the sake of brevity, the suggested readings do not provide full bibliographical references. Book titles are italicized; book chapters and journal articles are placed within quotation marks, and in such cases the book or journal title is not provided. The only other information provided is the name of the author(s) and publication year. Students may copy the author and title, and use online search tools available through their library or else Google search to find the full reference.

Chapter 2

The Wisdom in Proverbs

Proverbs are one of the main repositories of the early ethical traditions. The prominence of proverbs in these early oral traditions reflects the fact that before writing was invented, they served as a kind of mnemonic,[1] which preserved and passed on the ethical insights of the people. Commentators like Roman Jakobson and Jeremy Driscoll have accordingly argued that proverbs function in many respects like poetry. The use of colorful language and oral techniques such as recognizable rhythms, internal rhyme, and figurative devices all provide a means of remembering.

The study of proverbs is called paremiology, from the obsolete Greek word παροιμία or *paroimía*, proverb. It comes as no surprise that paremiologists have experienced many difficulties in trying to define a proverb, since proverbs are semantically loose and allusive, and have few formal requirements other than brevity of expression. This does not prevent their successful use. In the *ABC Dictionary of Chinese Proverbs*, John Rohsenow relates the proverb of Duke Mu: "A leaky bag can still hold things."

The proverb traditions are didactic. Proverbs usually capture a significant truth or shrewd observation that expresses the wisdom of the people. This wisdom usually has ethical implications. Although most tribal sources naturally contain proverbs and sayings, their full realization as relatively independent traditions appears to come later. They can generally be thought of as verbal formulas, which identify a rational proposition that explains a particular set of circumstances. This is related to the development of the early forms of argument in Aesop's fables and the conventional idea that a fable has a moral. Earlier forms of proverbs appear to be less overtly propositional and often contain bare observations.

Proverbs usually come, one way or the other, from the popular tradition. They are made to be spoken and repeated, often in colloquial guise. There are nevertheless exceptions to this pattern, such as the *Ad Monachos*, a collection of 137 proverbs written by Evagrius Ponticus (345–399), which were written in a style that consciously imitates the proverb literature of the Bible, but for the purposes of meditation rather than popular use.

One of the main technical features of proverbs is parallelism, a kind of linguistic and

---

1 I.e., a technique for remembering something.

conceptual pairing. The Biblical *Book of Proverbs* provides many examples. Although there are many forms of parallelism, three forms are easily discerned. In synonymous parallelism, a second thought restates a first thought using different words. Thus, we read: "Pride goes before destruction / And a haughty spirit before a fall." In antithetic parallelism, the second of two thoughts supplies a contrasting truth. Thus, "He who has a slack hand becomes poor / But the hand of the diligent makes rich." And, lastly, in synthetic parallelism, a second thought develops an earlier proposition, such as: "The eyes of the Lord are in every place / Keeping watch on the evil and the good."

Proverbs are particularly difficult to date, since they are adapted and modified over time, and often change their linguistic clothes. One of the deficiencies in the academic literature is the general failure of paremiologists to provide chronological collections that include an accurate account of their historical development. All that can be said in the current context is that many of the proverbs contained in the following readings have their provenance in much older oral traditions.

Paremiologists agree that the historical proverb tradition declined in modern Europe. It is clear that the Enlightenment introduced a scientific element—and a level of abstraction—into European thinking that did not favor the retention of proverbs as a conduit of ethical wisdom. In "Proverbs and Social History," James Obelkivitch has argued that this reflects changes in the ethical foundations of Western society. Proverbs, he writes, have gone out of favor because they "put the collective before the individual, the recurrent and stereotyped before the unique, external rules before self-determination, common sense before the individual vision, survival before happiness."

The historical proverb traditions, like the traditions of fables, nevertheless had an important place in the history of Western philosophy. This is because the Western philosophical tradition, like Western languages, is inherently propositional. Proverbs provide part of the history by which thinkers slowly came to formulate and recognize logical propositions, which can be examined and verified internally. In spite of their decline, proverbs are a living part of any linguistic culture, and have persisted, to some extent, in legal and ethical maxims, simple rhymes, musical lyrics, familiar sayings (which we often dismiss as clichés), and other forms of popular expression.

The readings contain examples of proverbs from three proverb traditions. The wisdom literature in the *Torah* and the Bible is based heavily on the proverb traditions. The sayings of the wise, who see into the true nature of things and succeed at difficult tasks, became part of the sacred literature. As a result, the *Book of Proverbs*, *Ecclesiastes*, and the *Song of Solomon* were honorifically attributed to King Solomon, in much the same way in which early kings like Hammurabi, for example, were associated with the customary law.

The Hebrew tradition is also significant because so many of its proverbs were formalized, whether in the law or the written historical record. The *Book of Proverbs* (יְלִשְׁמ in Hebrew, or *Mish'ley*) is in fact a highly refined poetic exercise that makes use of wise sayings that had been collected over hundreds and probably thousands of years. In an imaginative turn, the Hebraic authors of *Proverbs* extol wisdom, personified as a woman, as a prize to be won. She stands in stark contrast to "Dame Folly," who leads men to their doom.

The historical proverb tradition may have reached its height in China. As Arthur Smith wrote in one of the collections in the readings, a full catalogue of Chinese proverbs would require an encyclopedia rather than a dictionary. This is still true today, though less so than in the past. The prevalence of Chinese proverbs appears to have been related to the reliance on rote learning[1] in classical Chinese culture. As the passages in one of the readings demonstrate, proverbs accordingly became a convenient means of keeping the extensive cultural literature alive. Many of the earliest Chinese proverbs transmit the practical wisdom associated with an early peasant society. Others are more overtly philosophical and raise religious or cosmological issues, which often express themselves in terms of fate.

The proverbs from Bihar, a state in north-eastern India, have a similar provenance to many of the early Chinese proverbs. In his introduction to these proverbs, John Christian comments on their ethical realism, which "would help us rather to meet and combat the acuteness and cunning that pass for wisdom in the world than to shun them as artifices unworthy of us." There are many echoes of very early views in these proverbs. Thus, one proverb merely comments sardonically on bad conduct: "In the wedding of the sickle, the song of the hoe!" This refers literally to a time when a sickle or a hoe was formally "married" to a field, with the idea that the union of the two would thus produce agricultural offspring such as corn.

READING 2A

Ancient Jewish Proverbs[2]

The Human Condition

Falsehood is common [and truth uncommon].

[But] truth survives; falsehood does not survive.

The dog in his hunger swallows dung.

Two kabs of dates—one kab of stones and more.[3]

Poverty befits the Jew as a red leather trapping on a white horse.

Better on the dunghills of Matha Mehasya, and not in a palace at Pumbeditha.[4]

---

1 I.e., a memorization technique based on repetition.

2 Rev. A. Cohen, *Ancient Jewish Proverbs* (London: John Murray, 1911). Available online at archive.org. We have edited and modified the text where appropriate.

3 Biblical or Talmudic measures are a matter of some historical speculation: a "kab" is thought to have been 1/18 of a basket (an ephah).

4 Two Babylonian municipalities with Rabbinic academies. There are two familiar interpretations of the proverb: (1) that Matha Mehasya was a better school and so it was better to be a student there even if poverty-stricken; (2) that, as Matha Mehasya escaped political persecution during ancient times, it is better to be poor but safe than rich but in danger.

Should the castle totter, its name is still castle; should the dunghill be raised, its name is still dunghill.

In the place where the master of the house once hung up his weapons, there the shepherd hangs up his scrip.[1]

Seven years lasted the pestilence, but not a man died before his year.

Hang the heart of a palm-tree[2] around a pig and it will trample it in filth.

When the ox falls, everyone sharpens their knives.

When the ox falls, its slayers are many.[3]

In the hour of distress, a vow; in the hour of release, forgetfulness.[4]

They make an elephant pass through the eye of a needle.[5]

A woman accustomed to miscarriages is no longer troubled by them.[6]

Tobiah sinned and Sigud is beaten.[7]

Dishonesty and Insincerity

Even those who hire false witnesses despise them.[8]

Money

Man is never shown a golden date-palm.[9]

Who has not worked shall not eat.

Flay a carcass in the street and earn a living, and say not, I am a great man and the work is below my dignity.[10]

Loosen your purse-strings; then open the sack [with your goods].[11]

Bullying

A proud man is unbearable, even in his own household.

"Every dog is a lion at home."[12]

If the body is taken away, of what use is the head?[13]

---

1 I.e., a small bag or pouch.
2 I.e., a rare dainty.
3 A Palestinian proverb.
4 Cf. "Vows made in storms are forgotten in calms."
5 Applied to philosophers, who are masters of dialectic. Hence the reference in the New Testament: "It is easier for a camel to go through a needle's eye" (Matt. xix. 24).
6 I.e., even troubles and misfortunes are lightened by frequent occurrence.
7 I.e., life is fundamentally unfair. A Babylonian proverb.
8 This is a historical refrain. Elsewhere it is said that "A false witness is worthy of being cast to the dogs."
9 I.e., money does not grow on trees.
10 Said with particular reference to Rabbis, who historically worked as shoemakers, carpenters, smiths, builders, bakers, etc.
11 I.e., take payment before giving someone your goods.
12 See the Hindi proverbs below.
13 Said to criticize those whose power or riches have made them arrogant. The welfare of the higher classes depends upon the lower classes.

People

Many a good cow has a bad calf.[1]

From the thorn-bush comes the rose.[2]

Should there be two dry logs and a fresh one together, the dry logs set the fresh one on fire.[3]

Moral Observations

Bad acts harm those who do them.

When two quarrel, he who keeps silence first is more praiseworthy.[4]

Receive the goods from the thief and you too have a taste.[5]

What is hateful to yourself, do not to your fellow-man.[6]

He who gives vent to his wrath destroys his house.[7]

It is not enough to give [the poor] to eat and drink; you must accompany them on their way.

Either friendship or death.[8]

Either friends like Job's or death.[9]

A myrtle standing among reeds is still a myrtle.[10]

Practical Advice

Learn first; then form your opinions.

In the time of rejoicing, rejoicing; in the time of mourning, mourning.

He who hears something unpleasant and preserves silence wards off what would prove still more objectionable.

Even a fool, when he holds his peace, is counted wise. (Prov. xvii. 28)

When in the city, conform to its laws.

Have spoiled your work, take up a needle and sew.[11]

Better one bird tied up than a hundred flying.

Should there be a hanging in a family, do not say to him: "Hang up this fish."

Your friend has a friend and your friend's friend has a friend.[12]

---

1 The bad son of a good father is described as "Vinegar, the son of wine."
2 Good children of a bad father. Cf. "You are a lion, the son of a fox."
3 I.e., wicked companions demoralize the good.
4 A Palestinian saying.
5 I.e., the receiver of stolen goods is also a thief.
6 This negative form of the Golden Rule (cf. Matt. vii. 12) is ascribed in the *Talmud* to Hillel, who gave it to the would-be proselyte who wanted to be taught the whole of the Law while he stood on one foot.
7 Another saying is: "The wrathful man is subject to all kinds of tortures."
8 Ibn Gabirol says: "A friendless man is like a left hand without a right hand."
9 Job's friends visited him in the time of his trouble. Cf. "He that makes many friends does it to his own destruction: but there is a friend that sticks closer than a brother" (Prov. xviii. 24).
10 A later Jewish moralist, quoted by Dukes, declares: "The wise man is honored even if his family is despised."
11 Said metaphorically. If you have acted morally badly, repair the damage.
12 So no secret can be kept for long. "The sage was asked: How do you keep a secret? He replied, I make my heart its tomb."

Do not become intoxicated and you shall not sin.[1]

In the city my name, out of the city my dress.[2]

If a man of Naresh has kissed you, count your teeth.[3]

Lessons

With two dogs they killed the wolf.[4]

The ass came and kicked away the lamp.[5]

A scorpion met a camel, who pushed it aside with her heel. Whereupon the scorpion cried, "By your life, I [hope next time] to reach your head!"[6]

Sarcasm

[Even a dog] attaches itself to someone who throws it a piece of meat.[7]

READING 2B

Historical Chinese Proverbs[8]

Very Early Proverbs

Pride invites calamity, humility reaps its reward.

Men at their birth are by nature good.

People have approximately the same nature, but diverge widely in practice.

Unworked gems are of little use.

Without learning, men do not know what is proper.

---

1 Cf.: "Wine leads both man and woman to adultery"; "Enter wine, exit the secret"; "Wine ends in blood"; "Wine is the devil's ambassador." It should not be inferred, however, that abstinence was commended. Why, ask the Rabbis, was the Nazirite commanded to bring a sin-offering? Because he imposed upon himself the oath to abstain from wine, which is one of God's gifts to man.

2 In the place I live my name is sufficient to command respect, but in other places I am judged by my clothes. Cf. "For man looks on the outward appearance" (1 Sam. xvi. 7).

3 The town of Naresh in Babylonia had a bad reputation. Beware of a deceitful man, especially when he greets you effusively.

4 The proverb relates the following fable: Two dogs were once quarrelling, and suddenly one of them was attacked by a wolf. Then said the other to himself, 'If I do not help him now, the wolf will kill him and then turn his attention to me.' So they both assailed the wolf and slew him.

5 A reference to another fable, in which a dishonest judge was presented with a golden lamp by one litigant and a Libyan ass—which was very highly prized—by the other. The verdict went in favor of the ass and the proverb is a warning against bribery—because there is always the danger of being outbid.

6 Another reference to a fable, suggesting that the camel should have killed the scorpion and saved herself from the possibility of revenge. The disdainful neglect of something deemed at the time insignificant may later on have serious consequences.

7 Said of someone whose friendship is based on self-interest.

8 Arthur H. Smith, *Proverbs and Common Sayings from the Chinese, together with much related and unrelated matter, interspersed with observations on Chinese things-in-general* (new and revised edition) (Shanghai: American Presbyterian Mission Press, 1902). Available online at archive.org. We have edited and modified the text where appropriate.

A father who rears children without educating them has failed as a father.

A teacher who is lenient is merely lazy.

Without learning, men are worse than the brutes.

There is no remedy for bad luck.

When the heron and the oyster seize each other, the fisherman reaps the benefit.[1]

It is like running against the claws—madness and chaos.[2]

Proverbs that allude to historical or mythical persons

It is the fox, arrogating the tiger's power.[3]

It is like Chiang Tai K'ung fishing—only those that are willing are taken.[4]

Chu Mao Ch'en divorcing his wife—spilled water is hard to gather up.[5]

Han Hsin, though defeated a hundred times, by a single battle established his merit. Pa Wang, though a hundred times victorious, ruined his country and lost his life in a single battle.

It was not the will of Heaven that Ssu Ma-I should perish.[6]

The feathers of the Phoenix are of no assistance if you have the liver of a chicken.[7]

Begging with a silver bowl.[8]

---

1 A very old proverb, derived from a fable, in which a bird sticks its beak into an open oyster—and the oyster closes its shell on the bird's beak. During the ensuing argument, the fisherman seizes both of them.

2 According to folklore, the five animals—foxes, weasels, hedgehogs, snakes, and rats, who were able to make themselves invisible—had a fondness for wine and had an unfortunate habit of sleeping it off in the middle of the road. Anyone who stepped on their claws at such times was bewitched. A person of uprightness and integrity, however—hence the moral point—would escape the bewitching.

3 Supposedly said to the King of Ch'u by Chuang Yi, one of his ministers, who was describing the actions of Chou Hsi Hsu, whose approach inspired terror in the people of the north. "A tiger who happened to be preceded by a fox was greatly astonished to see all the animals running away from the fox, little suspecting that their terror was inspired by himself."

4 Chiang Tai Kung (c. 12th century BCE) had an eccentric habit of angling with a straight iron rod, thus offering as little inducement as possible to the fishes, who were—therefore—only attracted by his virtue.

5 Chu Mao Ch'en was a scholar who was very poor. In spite of his entreaties, his wife insisted that he release her from the marriage. Later, when he was highly successful, she implored him to remarry her. He replied by telling her to pour water on the ground—and then told her that he would marry her after she had gathered it up. The saying probably goes back much further and is still used in China, where a divorced woman may be referred to, simply, as "spilled water."

6 Ssu Ma-I was a famous general at the time of the Three Kingdoms. He was once hard pressed by his distinguished antagonist K'ung Ming, who hemmed him in within a deep valley, where it was impossible to advance or to retreat. Fire was then set to the underbrush, so that the horses all perished, as well as all the men, with the exception of Ssu Ma-I and his two sons, who embraced each other with tears in momentary expectation of destruction. At this critical juncture, a heavy rain fell, which extinguished the fire. His adversary dared not disobey the mandate of heaven and allowed his prisoners to escape. The saying is used in reference to any signal providential intervention to save life.

7 This saying was made at the expense of Yuan Shao, a decorated general who was unsuccessful in his military adventures.

8 This refers to the story of Yen Sung, a wicked minister, who was guilty of many crimes. The Emperor, wishing to punish him, gave him a silver bowl and commanded him to go out among the people and beg for food. Since the people, who hated him, refused to give him anything, he subsequently starved, while retaining the silver bowl, since no one would dare to purchase the Emperor's bowl. The expression is used of valuable things that are of no use.

Names or Sayings that Preserve Local History

Like Hsiao Pai Lien Tzu—never seen.[1]

Like Liu Kao Shou curing a malady.[2]

Lessons

Rhetorically: "Although Teng Tung had a money mountain, he died of starvation."[3]

Additional Traditional Chinese Proverbs[4]

The Human Condition

Men are one in heart; their hearts are in principle one.

Who but the sages are free from faults?

It is easier to fill up a ravine than the wants of a man.

The four seas: all within it are brothers.

A person's life is like a candle in the wind.

Abroad, it is clothes they see; at home, the man himself.

The road to heaven shines bright [i.e., is easy to find]; but the multitude does not follow it.

The heart is like a horse on a flat plain; easily started, hard to stop.

Disease may be cured; but not fate.

If your fate is only to have eight-tenths of a pint of rice, you won't get the full pint.

A man in luck is like a boat with a favorable wind.

Good swimmers sometimes drown.

No medicine can cure the disease of vulgarity.

---

1 A reference to a famous thief who was never caught.

2 A man was wounded by an arrow that passed through his temple and came out the other side. The physician Liu Kao Shou supposedly cut off the end of the arrow close to the man's head and put a plaster over the wound. When the family objected that he had not extracted the body of the arrow, he replied: "External medicine has nothing to do with internal complaints."

3 It is related that Teng Tung, a favorite of the Emperor, was told by a fortune teller that he would die of starvation. When he asked if there was any way to escape his fate, he was told that the only way to avert it was to cultivate virtue. Teng Tung did not believe the prophecy and told the Emperor, who gave his favorite a furnace for coining cash—in other words a small mint—so that he could lay up a "money mountain." Now, he said, we shall see if you will starve. As fate would have it, however, the minister later suffered from a stricture in the gullet; unable to eat, he eventually died of starvation.

4 William Scarborough, *A Collection of Chinese Proverbs, Translated and Arranged* (Shanghai, American Presbyterian Mission Press, 1875). Available online at https://archive.org. We have edited and modified the text where appropriate.

Dishonesty and Insincerity

Strike a man dead and you must forfeit your life; kill him by guile and you do not have to forfeit your life.

Money and Poverty

Great riches depend upon fate.

What cat does not go after rats?[1]

The less conscience, the more wealth.

One may know the law; but poverty is hard to bear [and therefore leads to crime].

The poorer one is, the more devils he meets.

Poverty destroys relationships.

Bullying

Heaven is high and the emperor far away.[2]

People

Inferior in youth, [he will be] useless in age.

Old trees are empty inside; old men see things clearly.[3]

Nine women in ten are jealous.

He who is inhospitable to guests is probably a fool.

[The stingy man] expects his donkey to run and not eat food.

Moral Observations

Everyone can distinguish between right and wrong.

Rivers and hills are easily altered; but a man's natural disposition is difficult to change.

Kindness is bigger than law.

When the hare dies, even the fox [his enemy] mourns.

When people come face to face, their disagreements disappear.

Rather than light up a seven story pagoda[4] [which is showing off], it is better to light one lamp in a dark place.

People will not be good without being exhorted to do so, as a bell will not ring without being struck.

One good act will correct a thousand misdeeds.

Filial piety moves heaven and earth.

Virtue is the [true] foundation of happiness.

Good and evil have their reward; the question is merely when it comes.

[A teacher who teaches] without rigor is merely indolent [i.e., lazy].

---

1 An idiomatic phrase meaning "Who doesn't want money?"
2 So the bully does what he likes.
3 The proverb requires seeing old men as being "empty" like old trees. The Daoist and the Buddhist want to be empty, for emptiness brings wisdom.
4 I.e., a Hindu or Buddhist temple or sacred building, typically a tower with many tiers.

If there is no punishment above,[1] there will be no law below.

To an evil man, reproof is [merely] a breath of wind.

[Roughly:] Someone who forgets the favors that he has received is merely a brute.

Let there be plenty of food and clothing, and propriety and righteousness will flourish.

Practical Advice

Do not adjust your hat under a plum tree.[2]

When the mountains have tigers, wait for the tigers to leave.

He who wakens a sleeping tiger runs the risk of harm.

He who rides a tiger is afraid to get off.

Adapt yourself to circumstances.

If you want dinner, do not offend the cook.

Do not mix with violent men.

Be—medium—honest.

Do not say what you see.

Too much politeness covers deceit.

If someone offends you, you must tell him the reason.

Do not neglect your own field to weed your neighbor's.

Stopping one moment of anger may save you a hundred days of sorrow.

It is easy to avoid a spear in daylight; but it is difficult to guard against an arrow in the dark.[3]

It is best to row with the stream in doing a favor.[4]

In plenty, think of want.

In good weather, carry an umbrella.

Sarcasm

He who has an iron mouth and bean-curd feet will not be able to escape trouble.[5]

---

1 I.e., if the judges do not punish.
2 Because it looks suspicious: someone may think you are stealing the plums.
3 This proverb is said of slander.
4 So, for instance, if someone is a reader, buy him a book.
5 Because his words do not match his actions.

Rural Hindi Proverbs[1]

The Human Condition

Though the trees in the orchard have not been planted yet, the woodworms have settled down to wait.

Someone who is dependent on others knows no happiness.

Faith makes god of a stone.

Dishonesty and Insincerity

After eating nine hundred rats the cat is now going on a pilgrimage.[2]

After eating the whole of the cucumber he pretends the end of it is bitter!

She styles herself a *saiyad*, but she is capable of stealing a nose stud.[3]

Money

Never mind religion and brothers, it is the rupee[4] that matters.

Bullying

The *situa* is sharp enough for the pumpkin.[5]

A dog is brave at his own door. An equivalent saying in Urdu is: *Ghar ka kutta sher*, "A dog is brave as a lion at his own door!"[6]

The anvil bears the missing stroke.[7]

The rage of the cunning man is vented on the weak.[8]

The fallen are cudgeled repeatedly.[9]

People

The [tattle-tale] who tells the secrets of the house will bring it down.[10]

---

1   John Christian, *Behar Proverbs: Classified and Arranged According to Their Subject-Matter, etc., With Notes, Appendix and Two Indexes* (London: K. Paul, Trench, Trübner, 1891). Available online at archive.org. We have edited and modified the text where appropriate.

2   An Urdu proverb. The idea is that a person on pilgrimage will stop eating meat. Said of a wicked man who pretends to become virtuous after countless acts of sin.

3   A *saiyad* is a member of the highest class, the priestly class, whereas a nose stud is a trifle.

4   I.e., money, since the rupee is the basic monetary unit of India and several other nearby countries.

5   The *situa* is a blunt spoon, so the proverb is a derisive reference to someone who bullies the weak. The bully is no better than the *situa*.

6   The proverb is said derisively of someone who is a local bully.

7   Said when someone habitually vents his anger on a person who is weaker than himself, rather than the person who has angered him.

8   I.e., on those unable to resist it.

9   I.e., those who are (already) down are kicked.

10   The proverb implicitly refers to Bibhikhan, a figure in Hindu mythology, who caused the downfall of Lanka.

Even if it has been fed milk all its life, the viper spits out venom when it bites.[1]

In the friendship of the ass you can expect constant kicks.

An old parrot can never be tamed.[2]

One with a wax nose is easily led.[3]

He has a bamboo nail-cutter.[4]

A fool's property is the prey of all.

When a fool's buffalo is in milk, everyone runs to him with milk pails.

A fool's property is enjoyed by the cunning.

Moral Observations

Having neither mother-in-law nor sister-in-law, she is happy in her house.[5]

The rope burns, but not the twist [which can be seen in the ashes]. And to the same effect: The dog's tail, even if buried for twelve years, will remain as crooked as ever.[6]

Practical Advice

Better to endure the pain than the remedy![7]

If the eye is blind, what is the use of applying an ointment?

There is no point in crying in front of a blind man.[8]

If you speak the truth, even a friend will be angry with you.

Lessons

Rhetorically: "Why did the *Teli* feed his bullock on oilcakes?"[9]

---

1 Said of a person who is inherently ungrateful.
2 Said when an old person is ungrateful.
3 Whichever side you bend a wax nose, it bends. Thus, someone with a weak will is a tool in the hands of others.
4 Said of inexperienced people, who do not know that nail-cutters are never made of bamboo.
5 I.e., it is better not to have a mother and a sister-in-law, who will—unjustly—criticize the wife of their son and brother.
6 Said in reference to habits that cannot be broken.
7 Naturally said when the remedy is worse.
8 Said metaphorically of someone who has no sympathy.
9 The *Teli* is a villager. An ironic proverb reflecting the view of ordinary people that those in authority are merely there to fleece them. The fable is that a villager, who has lost his bullock (i.e., steer), goes to complain to the police, hoping that they will help him find it. The "Red Book" (which contains the law) is brought out. The daroga (i.e., chief officer or inspector) gravely turns the pages one by one, and then pronounces judgment in the following words: "Hear you Teli, it is thus found in the Red Book: You are really at fault, why did you feed your bullock on oilcakes? Of course as a consequence he became unmanageable and ran away. You are therefore clearly to blame, and must pay a fine."

Sarcasm

It is just as well that my husband has been carried away by a tiger; now he won't have to do the chores.[1]

If all the dogs go on a pilgrimage to Benares, who will search the pots and pans for food?[2]

Questions

1. Proverbs seem to fit more comfortably into rural rather than city life. Why?
2. As the introduction states, the proverb traditions died in Western Europe but survived in Asia. Why? What is different about the societies in these regions?
3. How would you characterize the moral views in the various proverb traditions? What is wisdom? What constitutes a good life?
4. Compare the proverbs in the readings from different cultural traditions. Can you find any differences?
5. The Hebrew proverbs are part of the Biblical tradition. What does this tell you about the Bible and its philosophical orientation?
6. The semantic structure of many proverbs rests on parallelism. Identify three forms of parallelism in the readings and provide examples.
7. Can you find any phrases, slogans, or sayings on the internet or social media that qualify as proverbs? What is it that makes them proverbs?
8. Your sister has unfortunately fallen in love with someone who is morally bad. And when she lets her new heart-throb drive your parents' car, there is naturally an accident. Your parents have now discovered that your sister was lying when she said that she was driving the car. Can you come up with a proverb that covers the situation?

Suggested Readings

The cloudy origins of many proverbs may account for the dearth of academic work that clearly traces their historical provenance. George Barton's *Archaeology and the Bible* contains a few Babylonian proverbs (1600 BCE), which can be found in Fordham University's *Ancient History Sourcebook*. There was a vogue for collecting proverbs in the nineteenth and early twentieth centuries, which gave rise to collections such as Reverend P. Percival's *Tamil Proverbs... Containing upwards of Six Thousand Proverbs* (1874), which is one of many sources available at archive.org. William Scarborough's *Collection of Chinese Proverbs* (1875; 1926) and Abraham Cohen's *Ancient Jewish Proverbs* (1911) are helpful because they are thematically organized. General sources include Hrisztalina Hrisztova-Gotthardt and Melita Aleksa Varga, eds., *Introduction to Paremiology: A Comprehensive Guide to Proverb Studies* (2014), and James Obelkevitch, "Proverbs and Social History," in Burke and Porter,

---

1 Said sarcastically of someone who tries to minimize calamity.
2 This is a familiar formula that takes many guises and is used to deride someone who has over-reached himself. For example, "If everybody takes to the learned professions, who will attend to the agriculture of the country?"

eds., *The Social History of Language* (1987). For more specific sources, see J.M. Thomson, *Form and Function of Proverbs in Ancient Israel*, and the scholar's edition of Chinese proverbs, *ABC Dictionary of Chinese Proverbs*, by John S. Rohsenow (2001), which contains a helpful if limited introduction.

For a discussion of the mechanics of proverbs, see Neal Norrick, *How Proverbs Mean* (1985), and, in another vein, Frank Nuessel's discussion of the semiotics of proverbs in "Proverbial Language as Applied Metaphor" (2009).

Chapter 3

The Wisdom in the Warrior Ethic

Homer (Ὅμηρος [Homeros]) probably lived in the eighth or seventh century BCE. He was traditionally depicted as a blind bard who wandered about and told stories. He is known as the author of the *Iliad* and the *Odyssey*. However, this ascription is inherently misleading since it is evident that these works, like other early works, were the product of a long oral tradition, which was passed on and embellished from generation to generation.

We are accordingly dealing with an oral wisdom tradition in Homer. The *Iliad* and the *Odyssey* represent a sophisticated, highly developed literary exposition of a warrior ethic that is nevertheless a direct product of tribal life in early Greece. Both works see the ideal warrior, who is held up as the epitome of manly virtue, as a praiseworthy figure.

The highest achievement in the Homeric ethic is heroism. The warrior ideal, which is still a part of military tradition, glorifies bravery, strength, loyalty, and other military virtues. It also cherishes a sense of honor and a related notion of dignity, which take on larger-than-life dimensions, since the theater in which the warrior ethic comes into play is the theater of death. Mastery in war is physically, intellectually, and morally difficult, particularly when it is accomplished in accordance with the kind of stern ethical code that the battlefield demands.

Many early cultures appear to have seen war, in many regards, as the ultimate test of virtue. This is, in part, as the later moral tradition recognizes, because it placed the interest of one's tribe and people above one's personal and selfish interests. It accordingly brought into play a certain kind of military altruism and provided a kind of proving-ground, in which the morally virtuous could establish their moral merits.

There are specific virtues associated with the warrior ideal, which include loyalty, courage, obedience, and strength of character. Homer's ethical interests are well-developed and more personal than in most other tribal traditions since his primary focus is on the proper attitude of the moral hero towards his own death. The depiction of the warrior in the Homeric works is reflective and, like the Greek tradition generally, distinctly philosophical. This heralds the coming of a philosophical age.

It is evident from the historical record that the Greek public had a signal reverence for Homer's works, much to the dismay of many Greek philosophers, who often disapproved of the violence in his text, his depiction of the gods, and the dishonest and unethical behavior of many of his central characters. This difference in taste between different elements in Greek society reflects the emergence of a new, incipiently modern ethic, based on personal and rational foundations. The conventional view is that this new ethic rejects many of the social and cosmological elements in the earlier Greek tribal culture. It is a harbinger of our own view of the world, which is usually seen as a product of the Greek philosophical tradition.

Although the conventional view has considerable merit, it is probably more accurate to see the work of Homer—like the work of the early Greek philosophers—as a very late bridge between the early tribal world and the ancient era, which contains the formal beginnings of our own philosophical tradition. This tradition has generally failed to recognize that the thought of such figures as Socrates and Plato also has its origins in the thinking of their tribal ancestors, which was still a part of the common memory.

It is notable that the ideal warrior in Homer is also intelligent and extremely shrewd. The ideal Greek hero is a realist, who understands that the route to success in war, and life more generally, sometimes requires cunning. Thus, in the *Odyssey*, it is Odysseus who is seen as the archetypal hero, rather than the *Iliad*'s Achilles, who is honorable rather than intelligent. Thus, both are deserving of immortal fame, but for different virtues.

The *Iliad* tells the story of the Trojan War.[1] The war occurred because Paris, one of the princes of Troy, had abducted Helen, the most beautiful woman in the world and the Queen of Sparta. As a result, the Greeks (the Achaeans) laid siege against the city of Troy. The conventions of the time included the taking of hostages and women. The hero Achilles, a Greek soldier, accordingly wins himself the maiden Briseis, a prize of war, which Agamemnon, the Greek commander, then takes for himself.

Stung by the actions of Agamemnon, Achilles refuses to enter into battle. However, Achilles has a male lover, Patroclus, who cannot bear to see the Greeks defeated and dons Achilles's armor. This trick changes the course of the battle, until the ruse is discovered and Hector—Paris's brother and the son of Priam, Troy's King—slays Patroclus. Achilles then returns to the battlefield, seeking vengeance against Hector, who has killed his friend and lover.

As Achilles—who is feared by the Trojans—approaches Hector, the Trojan warrior balks at the idea of entering the city gates for fear of the disgrace that comes with it. He then considers offering Achilles a ransom (a recognized practice at the time) but rejects it as dishonorable. These are moral choices. Homer's depiction of the event is multifaceted and captures the complexities of war. All the characters have a variety of competing motivations, good and bad. The ethical difficulty of the situation is compounded by the fact that Achilles bears at least some of the blame for Patroclus's death.

The prominence of fate in Homer's narrative is a reflection of larger cosmological forces, which are personified in the character of individual gods (and goddesses). These deities intervene in human affairs in partisan and ethically dubious ways that humans are pow-

---

1   The war pitted the Greeks (which included the Achaeans, Spartans, and other Greek city-states) against the Trojans (of Troy, also known as Ilius or Ilium).

erless to oppose. The goddess Athena, who champions the Greek forces, deceives Hector and covertly aids Achilles so he can kill his opponent. The right ethical response is to act bravely in the face of death and maintain one's honor, in spite of the overwhelming forces opposed against one.

The elements in Homer's narrative include prophecy, which gives us direct access to a larger cosmological order, and a kind of universal justice, which provides the foundations for the idea of a natural law. The hero aimed to accomplish great military feats that would be commemorated, honored, and celebrated after his passing. This confers a kind of immortality on the hero.

The idea of a larger and more universal ethic can be seen in Homer's concern with the treatment of the dead. After Patroclus's death, Achilles and the Greeks retrieve his body so that he can be given the proper funeral rites. Achilles nevertheless dishonors the body of Hector, dragging it through the dirt behind his chariot, allowing his fellow soldiers to mutilate it, and leaving it to rot in the open, unprotected from dogs and carrion birds. This is implicitly immoral.

There is nevertheless a moment of ethical recovery. At the end of the *Iliad*, Priam, Hector's father, begs for the body of his son, so that it can be brought back to Troy and receive the proper funeral rites. In a moment of moral illumination, Achilles relents and allows him to reclaim the body of his son.

READING 3

The Iliad, Book 22[1]

(seventh or eighth century BCE)

With fell intent Achilles made towards the city, and as the winning horse in a chariot race strains every nerve when he is flying over the plain, even so fast and furiously did the limbs of Achilles bear him onwards. King Priam was first to note him as he scoured the plain, all radiant as the star which men call Orion's Hound, and whose beams blaze forth in time of harvest more brilliantly than those of any other that shines by night; brightest of them all though he be, he yet bodes ill for mortals, for he brings fire and fever in his train—even so did Achilles' armour gleam on his breast as he sped onwards. Priam raised a cry and beat his head with his hands as he lifted them up and shouted out to his dear son, imploring him to return; but Hector still stayed before the gates, for his heart was set upon doing battle with Achilles.

The old man reached out his arms towards him

---

1   Homer, Book XXII of the *Iliad* (probably written down c. 760 BCE, but from a much earlier oral tradition describing the fall of Troy, 1300–1200 BCE) from Samuel Butler, trans., *The Iliad of Homer* (London: Longmans, Green, & Co., 1898). Available at http://classics.mit.edu/Homer/iliad.22.xxii.html.

and bade him for pity's sake come within the walls. "Hector," he cried, "my son, stay not to face this man alone and unsupported, or you will meet death at the hands of the son of Peleus,[1] for he is mightier than you. Monster that he is; would indeed that the gods loved him no better than I do, for so, dogs and vultures would soon devour him as he lay stretched on earth, and a load of grief would be lifted from my heart, for many a brave son has he reft from me, either by killing them or selling them away [into slavery] in the islands that are beyond the sea: even now I miss two sons…Lycaon and Polydorus…. Should they be still alive and in the hands of the Achaeans, we will ransom them with gold and bronze, of which we have store…

"Come, then, my son, within the city, to be the guardian of Trojan men and Trojan women, or you will both lose your own life and afford a mighty triumph to the son of Peleus. Have pity also on your unhappy father…after I have seen my sons slain and my daughters hauled away as captives, my bridal chambers pillaged, little children dashed to earth amid the rage of battle, and my sons' wives dragged away by the cruel hands of the Achaeans; in the end fierce hounds will tear me in pieces at my own gates after some one has beaten the life out of my body with sword or spear…. When a young man falls by the sword in battle,…there is nothing unseemly;…all is honourable in death, but when an old man is slain there is nothing in this world more pitiable…"

The old man tore his grey hair as he spoke, but he moved not the heart of Hector. His mother hard by wept and moaned aloud as she bared her bosom and pointed to the breast which had suckled him. "Hector," she cried, weeping bitterly the while, "Hector, my son, spurn not this breast, but have pity upon me too: if I have ever given you comfort from my own bosom, think on it now, dear son, and come within

the wall to protect us from this man; stand not without to meet him. Should the wretch kill you, neither I nor your richly dowered wife shall ever weep, dear offshoot of myself, over the bed on which you lie, for dogs will devour you at the ships of the Achaeans…."

Thus did the two with many tears implore their son, but they moved not the heart of Hector, and he stood his ground awaiting huge Achilles as he drew nearer towards him. As a serpent in its den upon the mountains, full fed with deadly poisons, waits for the approach of man—he is filled with fury and his eyes glare terribly as he goes writhing round his den—even so Hector leaned his shield against a tower that jutted out from the wall and stood where he was, undaunted.

"Alas," said he to himself in the heaviness of his heart, "if I go within the gates, Polydamas will be the first to heap reproach upon me, for it was he that urged me to lead the Trojans back to the city on that awful night when Achilles again came forth against us. I would not listen, but it would have been indeed better if I had done so. Now…I dare not look Trojan men and Trojan women in the face, lest a worse man should say, 'Hector has ruined us by his self-confidence.' Surely it would be better for me to return after having fought Achilles and slain him, or to die gloriously here before the city. But what, again, if I were to lay down my shield and helmet, lean my spear against the wall and go straight up and negotiate with the noble Achilles?

"What if I were to promise to give up Helen, who was the cause of all this war, and all the treasure that Alexandrus[2] brought with him in his ships to Troy, [yes], and to let the Achaeans divide the half of everything that the city contains among themselves?…But why argue with myself in this way? Were I to go up to him he would show me no kind of mercy; he would kill me then and there as easily as though I were a woman, when I had off my armour.

---

1 I.e., Achilles.
2 Another name for Paris.

There is no parleying with him from some rock or oak tree, as young men and maidens prattle on with one another. Better fight him at once, and learn to which of us Zeus will vouchsafe victory."

Thus did he stand and ponder, but Achilles came up to him as if it were Mars[1] himself, plumed lord of battle. From his right shoulder he brandished his terrible spear of Pelian ash, and the bronze gleamed around him like flashing fire or the rays of the rising sun. Fear fell upon Hector as he beheld him, and he dared not stay longer where he was but fled in dismay from before the gates, while Achilles darted after him at his utmost speed. As a mountain falcon, swiftest of all birds, swoops down upon some cowering dove—the dove flies before him but the falcon with a shrill scream follows close after, resolved to have her—even so did Achilles make straight for Hector with all his might, while Hector fled under the Trojan wall as fast as his limbs could take him.

On they flew along the waggon-road that ran hard by under the wall, past the lookout station, and past the weather-beaten wild fig-tree, till they came to two fair springs which feed the river Scamander.... Past these did they fly, the one in front and the other giving chase behind him: good was the man that fled, but better far was he that followed after, and swiftly indeed did they run, for the prize was no mere beast for sacrifice or bullock's hide, as it might be for a common foot-race, but they ran for the life of Hector. As horses in a chariot race speed round the turning-posts when they are running for some great prize—a tripod or woman—at the games in honour of some dead hero, so did these two run full speed three times round the city of Priam. All the gods watched them...[2]

Thus did Athena inveigle him by her cunning, and when the two were now close to one another great Hector was first to speak. "I will no longer fly from you, son of Peleus," said he, "as I have been doing hitherto. Three times have I fled round the mighty city of Priam, without daring to withstand you, but now, let me either slay or be slain, for I am in the mind to face you. Let us, then, give pledges to one another by our gods, who are the fittest witnesses and guardians of all covenants; let it be agreed between us that if Zeus vouchsafes me the longer stay and I take your life, I am not to treat your dead body in any unseemly fashion, but when I have stripped you of your armour, I am to give up your body to the Achaeans. And do you likewise."

Achilles glared at him and answered, "Fool, prattle not to me about covenants. There can be no covenants between men and lions, wolves and lambs can never be of one mind, but hate each other out and out and through. Therefore, there can be no understanding between you and me, nor may there be any covenants between us, till one or other shall fall and glut grim Mars with his life's blood. Put forth all your strength; you have need now to prove yourself indeed a bold soldier and man of war. You have no more chance, and Pallas Minerva[3] will forthwith vanquish you by my spear: you shall now pay me in full for the grief you have caused me on account of my comrades whom you have killed in battle."

He poised his spear as he spoke and hurled it. Hector saw it coming and avoided it; he watched it and crouched down so that it flew over his head and stuck in the ground beyond; Minerva then snatched it up and gave it back to Achilles without Hector's seeing her; Hector thereon said to the son of Peleus, "You have missed your aim, Achilles, peer of the gods, and Zeus has not yet revealed to you the hour of my doom, though you made sure that he had done so. You were a false-tongued liar when you deemed that I should forget my valour and quail

---

1 I.e., the god of war.
2 At this point the goddess Athena enters the battle, tricking Hector into standing his ground against Achilles by taking the form of Hector's favorite brother, Deiphobus, and pretending that she has come to stand by him.
3 An epithet for Athena.

before you. You shall not drive spear into the back of a runaway—drive it, should heaven so grant you power, drive it into me as I make straight towards you; and now for your own part avoid my spear if you can—would that you might receive the whole of it into your body; if you were once dead the Trojans would find the war an easier matter, for it is you who have harmed them most."

He poised his spear as he spoke and hurled it. His aim was true for he hit the middle of Achilles' shield, but the spear rebounded from it, and did not pierce it. Hector was angry when he saw that the weapon had sped from his hand in vain, and stood there in dismay for he had no second spear. With a loud cry he called Deiphobus and asked him for one, but there was no man; then he saw the truth and said to himself, "Alas! the gods have lured me on to my destruction. I deemed that the hero Deiphobus was by my side, but he is within the wall, and Minerva has inveigled me; death is now indeed exceedingly near at hand and there is no way out of it—for so Zeus and his son Apollo the far-darter have willed it, though heretofore they have been ever ready to protect me. My doom has come upon me; let me not then die ingloriously and without a struggle, but let me first do some great thing that shall be told among men hereafter."

As he spoke he drew the keen blade that hung so great and strong by his side, and gathering himself together he sprang on Achilles like a soaring eagle which swoops down from the clouds on to some lamb or timid hare—even so did Hector brandish his sword and spring upon Achilles. Achilles mad with rage darted towards him, with his wondrous shield before his breast, and his gleaming helmet, made with four layers of metal, nodding fiercely forward. The thick tresses of gold with which Vulcan had crested the helmet floated round it, and as the evening star that shines brighter than all oth-

ers through the stillness of night, even such was the gleam of the spear which Achilles poised in his right hand, fraught with the death of noble Hector. He eyed his fair flesh over and over to see where he could best wound it, but all was protected by the goodly armour of which Hector had stolen from Patroclus after he had slain him, save only the throat where the collar-bones divide the neck from the shoulders, and this is a most deadly place: here then did Achilles strike him as he was coming on towards him, and the point of his spear went right through the fleshy part of the neck, but it did not sever his windpipe so that he could still speak.

Hector then fell, headlong, and Achilles vaunted over him saying, "Hector, you deemed that you should come off scatheless when you were spoiling Patroclus, and reckoned not of myself who was not with him. Fool that you were: for I, his comrade, mightier far than he, was still left behind him at the ships, and now I have laid you low. The Achaeans shall give him all due funeral rites, while dogs and vultures shall work their will upon yourself."

Then Hector said, as the life ebbed out of him, "I pray you by your life and knees, and by your parents, let not dogs devour me at the ships of the Achaeans, but accept the rich treasure of gold and bronze which my father and mother will offer you, and send my body home, that the Trojans and their wives may give me my dues of fire[1] when I am dead."

Achilles glared at him and answered, "Dog, talk not to me neither of knees nor parents; would that I could be as sure of being able to cut your flesh into pieces and eat it raw, for the ill you have done me, as I am that nothing shall save you from the dogs—it shall not be, though they bring ten or twenty-fold ransom and weigh it out for me on the spot, with promise of yet more hereafter. Though Priam son of Dardanus should bid them offer me your weight in gold, even so your mother shall never lay you out

---

1 I.e., cremation by funeral pyre. More broadly, it is a recognition of the importance of performing the time-honored rituals for the deceased.

and make lament over the son she bore, but dogs and vultures shall eat you utterly up."

Hector with his dying breath then said, "I know what you are, and was sure that I should not move you, for your heart is hard as iron; look to it that I bring not heaven's anger upon you on the day when Paris and Apollo,[1] valiant though you be, shall slay you at the Scaean gates."[2]

When he had thus said, the shrouds of death enfolded him, whereon his soul went out of him and flew down to the house of Hades,[3] lamenting its sad fate that it should even in youth and strength no longer be. But Achilles said, speaking to the dead body, "Die; for my part I will accept my fate whenever Zeus and the other gods see fit to send it."

As he spoke he drew his spear from the body and set it on one side; then he stripped the blood-stained armour from Hector's shoulders while the other Achaeans came running up to view his wondrous strength and beauty; and no one came near him without giving him a fresh wound. Then would one turn to his neighbour and say, "It is easier to handle Hector now than when he was flinging fire on to our ships." And as he spoke he would thrust his spear into him anew.

When Achilles had done spoiling Hector of his armour, he stood among the Argives and said, "My friends, princes and counsellors of the Argives, now that heaven has vouchsafed us to overcome this man, who has done us more hurt than all the others together, consider whether we should not attack the city in force, and discover in what mind the Trojans may be. We should thus learn whether they will desert their city now that Hector has fallen, or will still hold out even though he is no longer living. But why argue with myself in this way while Patroclus is still lying at the ships unburied and unmourned—he whom I can never forget so long as I am alive and

my strength fails not? Though men forget their dead when once they are within the house of Hades, yet not even there will I forget the comrade whom I have lost. Now, therefore, Achaean youths, let us raise the song of victory and go back to the ships taking this man along with us; for we have achieved a mighty triumph and have slain noble Hector to whom the Trojans prayed throughout their city as though he were a god."

On this he treated the body of Hector with [contempt]: he pierced the sinews at the back of both his feet from heel to ankle and passed thongs of ox-hide through the slits he had made: thus he made the body fast to his chariot, letting the head trail upon the ground. Then when he had put the goodly armour on the chariot and had himself mounted, he lashed his horses on and they flew forward nothing loth. The dust rose from Hector as he was being dragged along, his dark hair flew all abroad, and his head once so comely was laid low on earth, for Zeus had now delivered him into the hands of his foes to do him outrage in his own land.

Thus was the head of Hector being dishonoured in the dust. His mother tore her hair and flung her veil from her head with a loud cry as she looked upon her son. His father made piteous moan, and throughout the city the people fell to weeping and wailing. It was as though the whole of frowning Ilius was being smirched with fire. Hardly could the people hold Priam back in his hot haste to rush outside the gates of the city. He grovelled in the mire and besought them, calling each one of them by his name. "Let be, my friends," he cried, "and for all your sorrow, suffer me to go single-handed to the ships of the Achaeans. Let me beseech this cruel and terrible man, if maybe he will respect the feeling of his fellow-men and have compassion on my old age. His own father is even such another as

---

1 (At the time of the *Iliad*) the god of healing and also the bringer of disease and death with his arrows. Many other functions were assigned to him over time.

2 One of the gates of Troy.

3 I.e., the Greek underworld, where souls go after death.

myself—Peleus, who bred him and reared him to be the bane of us Trojans, and of myself more than of all others. Many a son of mine has he slain in the flower of his youth, and yet, grieve for these as I may, I do so for one—Hector—more than for them all, and the bitterness of my sorrow will bring me down to the house of Hades. Would that he had died in my arms, for so both his ill-starred mother who bore him, and myself, should have had the comfort of weeping and mourning over him."

Thus did he speak with many tears, and all the people of the city joined in his lament. Hecuba[1] then raised the cry of wailing among the Trojans. "Alas, my son," she cried, "what have I left to live for now that you are no more? Night and day did I glory in you throughout the city, for you were a tower of strength to all in Troy, and both men and women alike hailed you as a god. So long as you lived you were their pride, but now death and destruction have fallen upon you."

Hector's wife had as yet heard nothing, for no one had come to tell her that her husband had remained outside the gates. She was at her loom in an inner part of the house, weaving a double purple web, and embroidering it with many flowers. She told her maids to set a large tripod on the fire, so as to have a warm bath ready for Hector when he came out of battle; poor woman, she knew not that he was now beyond the reach of baths, and that Minerva had laid him low by the hands of Achilles. She heard the cry coming as from the wall and trembled in every limb; the shuttle fell from her hands and again she spoke to her waiting-women. "Two of you," she said, "come with me that I may learn what it is that has befallen; I heard the voice of my husband's honoured mother; my own heart beats as though it would come into my mouth and my limbs refuse to carry me; some great misfortune for Priam's children must be at hand. May I never live to hear it, but I greatly fear that Achilles has cut off the retreat of brave Hector

and has chased him on to the plain where he was singlehanded; I fear he may have put an end to the reckless daring which possessed my husband, who would never remain with the body of his men, but would dash on far in front, foremost of them all in valour."

Her heart beat fast, and as she spoke she flew from the house like a maniac, with her waiting-women following after. When she reached the battlements and the crowd of people, she stood looking out upon the wall, and saw Hector being borne away in front of the city—the horses dragging him without heed or care over the ground towards the ships of the Achaeans. Her eyes were then shrouded as with the darkness of night and she fell fainting backwards. She tore the tiring from her head and flung it from her.... Her husband's sisters and the wives of his brothers crowded round her and supported her, for she was fain to die in her distraction...

[And] when she again presently breathed and came to herself, she sobbed and made lament among the Trojans saying... "Hector, you are now going into the house of Hades under the secret places of the earth, and you leave me a sorrowing widow in your house. The child, of whom you and I are the unhappy parents, is as yet a mere infant. Now that you are gone, O Hector, you can do nothing for him nor he for you. Even though he escape the horrors of this woeful war with the Achaeans, yet shall his life henceforth be one of labour and sorrow, for others will seize his lands. The day that robs a child of his parents severs him from his own kind; his head is bowed, his cheeks are wet with tears, and he will go about destitute.... You, O Hector, were the only defence of the Trojan gates and battlements. The wriggling writhing worms will now eat you at the ships, far from your parents, when the dogs have glutted themselves upon you. You will lie naked, although in your own house you have fine and goodly raiment made by hands of women. This will

---

1 King Priam's wife.

I now burn; it is of no use to you, for you can never again wear it, and thus you will have respect shown you by the Trojans both men and women."

In such a way did she cry aloud amid her tears, and the women joined in her lament.[1]

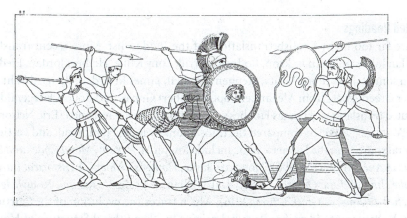

Plate 22, from *The Iliad of Homer*: Engraved by John Piroli from the compositions of John Flaxman, Sculptor (1795). Copper plate engraving. Fighting for the body of Patroclus.

Questions

1. Death on the battlefield is a noble and illustrious end in Greek culture. Discuss the philosophy of life behind such a view.
2. The Greeks saw trickery as a part of war. Patroclus tricks the Trojans into thinking he is Achilles. Athena tricks Hector (who killed Patroclus) into thinking that she is his brother. Is cunning morally permissible in warfare? Defend your position.
3. Was Hector wrong to run away from Achilles, who was larger and a better fighter, at the beginning of the battle? Why, why not? What are the limits of courage?
4. Why did Achilles desecrate the body of Hector? How would you defend him, if you were asked to do so? What should be the rules of war, on this?
5. Homer suggests that Achilles has become a better, wiser man, when he allows Priam to bring Hector's body back for a proper funeral. Do you agree? Why?
6. Although fate plays a major role in Homer's world, it often creates conditions in which personal heroism is possible. This seems to be the real focus of Homer's work. Discuss. Can you think of a contemporary analogy?

---

1 As noted in the Introduction, Achilles does eventually release Hector's body to his father Priam so that he may receive the requisite funeral rites.

7. It has been argued that in many ways sports have taken the place of war in contemporary culture, since they provide an opportunity to display physical prowess, courage, and tactical insight. Comment.

Suggested Readings

There are far too many English translations of the *Iliad* to list. More recent translators include Ian Johnston, John Jackson, Rodney Merrill, Tony Kline, Herbert Jordan, Frederick Light (in sonnets), Anthony Verity, Stephen Mitchell, James Muirden, Richard Whitaker, and Peter Green. Poets from Alexander Pope to Robert Graves and Robert Fitzgerald have contributed translations. Thomas Hobbes's translation has been re-issued (Eric Nelson, ed.; 2008); P.V. Jones (2003) has compared the translations by Rieu, Hammond, and Lattimore.

General sources on the Homeric ethic include Joseph M. Bryant, *Moral Codes and Social Structure in Ancient Greece* (1996); Howard Clarke, *Homer's Readers. A Historical Introduction to the Iliad and the Odyssey* (1981); and William J. Prior, *Virtue and Knowledge: An Introduction to Ancient Greek Ethics* (2016), which traces the evolution of the "virtue" of wisdom. K. Yamamoto identifies its tribal origins in "The Ethical Structure of Homeric Society" (2002).

The commentary on the *Iliad* includes Hektor K.T. Yan, "Morality and Virtue in Poetry and Philosophy: A Reading of Homer's *Iliad* XXIV" (2003); Graham Zanker, *The Heart of Achilles: Characterization and Personal Ethics in the Iliad* (1996); and Dean Hammer, "The *Iliad* as Ethical Thinking: Politics, Pity, and the Operation of Esteem" (2002). Students may want to consult Ian Johnston's webpage at viu.ca.

Chapter 4

The Wisdom in Indigenous Stories

The ethical history of many tribally organized societies can be found in the stories of their oral traditions. These stories, often called folktales, are part of a "wisdom tradition" and are fundamentally didactic. They usually contain some account of the origins of the tribe, its history and customs, and provide examples of good and bad behavior, along with the cosmological consequences of such behavior.

The readings in this chapter come from four Indigenous traditions—two from North America, one from Africa, and one from Australia—in which story-telling is still a valued means of transmitting wisdom. As the unit introduction suggests, Indigenous peoples do not exhaust the tribal tradition, and story-telling is not the only method employed in the oral wisdom tradition. It is the fact that the method of recounting folktales is still alive, and valued, in many Indigenous communities that makes them an eminently suitable source of readings. The readings constitute an initial step in the direction of providing a more comprehensive account of the varied ethical traditions of the world's Indigenous cultures.

The initial reading demonstrates the altruistic and collective principle at the heart of many tribal ethics. The warrior maiden sacrifices her life in order to save her people from starvation. Nor is this a simple ethical matter: she displays intelligence, trickery in the service of tribal interests, and physical bravery when she is tortured. These are all attributes of moral behavior in this culture. Through the act of telling her story over the generations, she also secures a place in the collective memory of the people. In this manner, she will be forever with her people.

As the next two readings demonstrate, hospitality and "reciprocal giving" are also fundamental in many tribal traditions. The greedy man who slaughters his fat ox, on the pretext that he is leaving his kraal, has made an exception to the rule and breached his obligation to share the meat with other villagers. Nature itself is offended at his act of self-ishness and avenges his immoral conduct by visiting misfortune upon him. Much of Little Rabbit's messianic violence, which has a cosmological theme, is a similar response to the failure of the people he meets to treat him generously, in accordance with tribal customs.

The final brief tale from Australia illustrates the role of sexual taboo in some tribal cultures. A man's own genitalia rebel against him, because he has breached the natural order by having intercourse with his mother-in-law.

One valuable piece of wisdom that we can draw from the Indigenous stories of a wide range of cultures concerns the broader cosmological dimension of an ethics grounded in kinship within a tribe. Thus, some of the stories, myths, legends, and folktales teach us that almost all of the entities of the universe are persons with whom we have kin relations. Such tales speak eloquently on behalf of our ailing environment.[1]

"The Warrior Maiden,"[2] from the Oneida[3]

Long ago, in the days before the white man came to this continent, the Oneida people were beset by their old enemies, the Mingoes. The invaders attacked the Oneida villages, stormed their palisades, set fire to their longhouses, laid waste to the land, destroyed the cornfields, killed men and boys, and abducted the women and girls. There was no resisting the Mingoes, because their numbers were like grains of sand, like pebbles on a lake shore.

The villages of the Oneida lay deserted, their fields untended, the ruins of their homes blackened. The men had taken the women, the old people, the young boys and girls into the deep forests, hiding them in secret places among rocks, in caves, and on desolate mountains. The Mingoes searched for victims, but could not find them. The Great Spirit[4] himself helped the people to hide and shielded their places of refuge from the eyes of their enemies.

Thus the Oneida people were safe in their inaccessible retreats, but they were also starving. Whatever food they had been able to save was soon eaten up. They could either stay in their hideouts and starve, or leave them in search of food and be discovered by their enemies. The warrior chiefs and sachems met in council but could find no other way out.

Then a young girl stepped forward in the council and said that the good spirits had sent her a dream showing her how to save the Oneida. Her name was Aliquipiso and she was not afraid to give her life for her people.

Aliquipiso told the council: "We are hiding on top of a high, sheer cliff. Above us the mountain is covered with boulders and heavy sharp rocks. You warriors wait and watch here. I will go to the Mingoes and lead them to the spot at the foot of the cliff where they all can be crushed and destroyed."

---

1 The editors wish to acknowledge Dr. Mary Ann Corbiere, Associate Professor of Indigenous Studies at the University of Sudbury and highly-respected linguist of the Ojibwe (Nishnaabemwin) language, for her kindly advice and guidance on how to present this material in a respectful manner.

2 "The Warrior Maiden," an Oneida story in Richard Erdoes and Alfonso Ortiz, eds., *American Indian Myths and Legends* (New York: Pantheon Books, 1984).

3 Oneida means "the People of the Upright Stone or Standing Stone." They are a First Nations people indigenous to North America originally located in the area of modern-day central New York State. The Mingo lived in neighboring regions. Both tribes spoke languages rooted in the Iroquois language.

4 Or Great Mystery; the name refers to the supreme being or universal spiritual force. This conception is common to several North American Indigenous peoples.

The chiefs, sachems, and warriors listened to the girl with wonder. The oldest of the sachems honored her, putting around her neck strands of white and purple wampum.[1] "The Great Spirit has blessed you, Aliquipiso, with courage and wisdom," he said. "We, your people, will always remember you."

During the night the girl went down from the heights into the forest below by way of a secret path. In the morning, Mingoe scouts found her wandering through the woods as if lost. They took her to the burned and abandoned village where she had once lived, for this was now their camp. They brought her before their warrior chief. "Show us the way to the place where your people are hiding," he commanded. "If you do this, we shall adopt you into our tribe. Then you will belong to the victors. If you refuse, you will be tortured at the stake."

"I will not show you the way," answered Aliquipiso. The Mingoes tied her to a blackened tree stump and tortured her with fire, as was their custom. Even the wild Mingoes were astonished at the courage with which the girl endured it. At last Aliquipiso pretended to weaken under the pain. "Don't hurt me anymore," she cried, "I'll show you the way!"

As night came again, the Mingoes bound Aliquipiso's hands behind her back and pushed her ahead of them. "Don't try to betray us," they warned. "At any sign of it, we'll kill you." Flanked by two warriors with weapons poised, Aliquipiso led the way. Soundlessly the mass of Mingoe war- riors crept behind her through thickets and rough places, over winding paths and deer trails, until at last they arrived beneath the towering cliff of sheer granite. "Come closer, Mingoe warriors," she said in a low voice, "gather around me. The Oneidas above are sleeping, thinking themselves safe. I'll show you the secret passage that leads upwards." The Mingoes crowded together in a dense mass with the girl in the center. Then Aliquipiso uttered a piercing cry: "Oneidas! The enemies are here! Destroy them!"

The Mingoes scarcely had time to strike her down before huge boulders and rocks rained upon them. There was no escape; it seemed as if the angry mountain itself were falling on them, crushing them, burying them. So many Mingoe warriors died there that the other bands of Mingoe invaders stopped pil- laging the Oneida country and retired to their own hunting grounds. They never again made war on Aliquipiso's people.

The story of the girl's courage and self-sacrifice was told and retold wherever Oneidas sat around their campfires, and will be handed down from grandparent to grandchild as long as there are Onei- das on this earth.

The Great Mystery changed Aliquipiso's hair into woodbine,[2] which the Oneidas call "running hairs" and which is a good medicine. From her body sprang honeysuckle, which to this day is known among her people as the "blood of brave women."[3]

---

1 A traditional shell bead, often kept on strings. It could be used as a form of gift exchange or serve other purposes, such as story- telling and recording important treaties.

2 Woodbine and honeysuckle (in the next sentence) are shrubs native to the Northern Hemisphere.

3 The original editors of this text say it is based on the version told by W.W. Canfield in 1902.

"The Greed of the Old Man and His Wife," a Masai Tale[2]

There was once upon a time an old man who lived in a kraal[3] with his neighbors. And this old man had a wife and a small child, and he possessed a very fine ox.

One day he said to himself, "How shall I slaughter my ox?" And he said aloud to his wife, "My child! I will call the men and tell them that I am going to move. We can then slaughter our ox all by ourselves."

His wife agreed and, in the evening, the old man blew his horn as a signal to his friends that he had something to tell them. His neighbors came together, and he told them that he wished to move, as the air did not agree with him. The others consented, and in the morning he saddled his donkeys, separated his cattle from the rest, and started off, accompanied by his wife, who was carrying the child.

When they had gone some distance, they halted and erected their kraal, after which they rested.

At dawn on the second day the old man called his wife and asked her why they had not yet slaughtered their ox. The woman replied, "My husband! How shall we manage to slaughter the ox? There are two things to be considered—the first is that we have no herdsman and the second that I am carrying the baby."

The old man then said, "Oh, I know what we will do. I will stab the ox in the neck, then I will leave you to skin it, and I will carry the child to the grazing ground. But when you have skinned the animal, roast some meat so that it will be ready on my return."

The old man then killed the ox, after which he picked up his bow and quiver, put the child on his back, and drove the cattle to the grazing ground where he herded them.

In the afternoon, as the child was asleep, the old man put it down in the grass, and went to drive back the cattle, for they had wandered far. But when he returned to the spot where he had left the child, he was unable to find it, so he decided to set fire to the grass. "When the fire reaches the child, it will cry," he thought, "and I will run to the place and pick it up before it is burned."

He made a fire with his fire-sticks, and the fire traveled to where the child was. He ran to the spot, but when he reached it, he found that the child was dead.

The old man had left his wife in the morning skinning the ox. And while she was skinning it— she had just reached the dewlap[4]—the knife slipped, and she stabbed herself in the eye. She went and lay down, and the birds came and finished the meat.

After the child was burned, the old man drove the cattle to the kraal, and when they were opposite to the gate, he heard his wife weeping, and saying, "Oh, my eye!" He therefore asked her who had told her the news.

"What news?" she inquired.

"The child has been burned," he replied.

The woman exclaimed, "Oh, my child!"

The old man then asked where his meat was, and his wife informed him that the birds had eaten it, whereupon he cried out, "Oh, my meat!"

They both wept, the old man crying, "Oh, my

---

1 "The Greed of the Old Man and His Wife," in Paul Radin, ed., *African Folktales*, Bollingen Series (n.p.: Princeton University Press, [1964] 1970).

2 The Masai are an ethnic group indigenous to the region of Africa where modern-day southern Kenya and northern Tanzania are located.

3 I.e., an enclosure for cattle or sheep.

4 I.e., the flap of skin that hangs beneath the neck or lower jaw of many vertebrates.

meat!" and the woman, "Oh, my child! Oh, my eye!"

Look well at these people. It was for their greed that they were punished. They lost their child and their ox, the woman lost her eye, and they had to return in shame to their former home.

"Little Rabbit Fights the Sun,"[1] from the Ute[2]

Ta-vwots, the Little Rabbit, was sleeping with his back to the sun. He got burned. His children saw that his back was smoking and cried: "Father, what is happening to your back?"

Little Rabbit woke up with a start. "Children," he rumbled, "why do you wake me up?"

"Father, your back is covered with sores. It has holes in it," cried his children.

Then Little Rabbit knew that it was Ta-vi, Sun, who had burned him. He got very angry. "My children," he said, "I must go and fight Sun." He left right away.

On his way to fight Sun, Little Rabbit came into a beautiful valley and in its middle stood a cornfield with the ears ready for roasting. Little Rabbit had never seen corn before. He looked at the ears of corn and saw that they were covered with beautiful, silky hair. He opened one husk and inside found white grains covering the cobs in rows. Then he knew that this was corn and that it was good to eat. He roasted an armful of ears over a fire and ate until his belly was full. Then it occurred to him that the cornfield might belong to somebody and that he had been stealing. So he dug a hole in which to hide himself.

Now, Cin-au-av, the owner of the cornfield, noticed that his corn had been stolen and right away guessed who had been the guilty one. The owner got very angry and cried: "I will kill this thieving Rabbit, I will kill him!" He called all his warriors together and began looking for the thief, but could not find him, because Little Rabbit had gone underground. At last they found Rabbit's hole and shot arrows into it. But Little Rabbit blew them back. Cin-au-av's people were enraged and shot more arrows at Little Rabbit, but with his mighty breath he blew them all back against them.

Then they ran to grab him with their hands, but he nimbly sidestepped them so that they only caught each other's fists. Then they said: "Let's dig him out!" And they dug in a frenzy, but Little Rabbit had an escape hole through which he slipped out. From the top of a rock he watched Cin-au-av's people dig deeper and deeper until they almost vanished from sight. Then Little Rabbit hurled a magic ball, which he always carried with him, at the ground above the diggers. It made the earth cave in on top of them, and they were buried.

Little Rabbit said: "Why did these foolish people get in my way? I am in a killing mood; I am going to fight the Sun. I'll make an end of anyone trying to stop me!"

Then he saw two men making arrowheads out of

---

1   "Little Rabbit Fights the Sun," a Ute tale in Richard Erdoes and Alfonos Ortiz, eds., *American Indian Trickster Tales* (Penguin Books: 1998, 1999).

2   The Ute are an Indigenous North American tribe now living primarily in Utah and Colorado.

hot rocks. He watched them for a while from behind a tree. Then he went up to them, saying: "Let me help you." He looked at the rocks, which were glowing red-hot, and said: "These rocks will not burn me."

They laughed at him, calling him a fool, saying: "Maybe you are some kind of a ghost?"

"I am not a ghost," said Little Rabbit, "but I am more powerful than you. Put me on these red-glowing rocks and if I do not burn you must let me do the same to you."

"This fellow is really a fool," thought the two men. Aloud they said: "We agree." They put Little Rabbit on the sizzling rocks, but he cooled them with his magic breath and did not burn.

Little Rabbit said: "Brothers, now it's your turn." He seized them and held them down on the red-hot stones, and they were consumed by heat and fire until only their ashes remained. "Lie there," said Little Rabbit, "until you can get up again!" He laughed, saying: "This is good practice for fighting Sun!" He went on, uttering fierce war cries.

Next day he came upon two women gathering berries in baskets. He sat down and the women brought him a basket of berries to eat. He saw that there were many thorns among the berries, and told the women: "Blow these thorns into my eyes, because it will make them feel good!" They did as told, thinking to blind him, but he blew the thorns away with his magic breath.

Then the women asked: "Are you a ghost?"

"I am not a ghost," he answered. "I am just an ordinary, everyday fellow. I guess you know that thorns cannot hurt your eyes. Let me show you." They agreed and he made them blind. "That will teach you offering a guest berries mixed with thorns," said Little Rabbit, and knocked them dead. "Aha," he said, "I am learning how to kill. This is good practice. I am going to kill Sun." He went on, whooping and hollering.

The next day he saw some women standing on the top of a high cliff. They saw him coming. "It is Little Rabbit," they said to each other. "Let us kill him by hurling rocks at his head as he passes." He heard them. He stopped a little short of them, took some dried meat mixed with chokecherries. He ate some of it with great relish.

The women on the cliff became curious. "What have you got there?" they asked him.

"Something very sweet and good-tasting. Come to the edge and I will throw some of it up to you."

The women went to the brink of the cliff. Little Rabbit threw lumps of the jerk meat up to them, but so that they could not quite reach them. He kept throwing it up again and again, until the women came to the cliff's very edge, leaning way over trying to catch the meat. They leaned so far over that they toppled from the cliff and fell to their deaths. "You got what you deserved for your greed," said Little Rabbit. "I am on my way to kill Sun." He went on, uttering war cries.

The day after, Little Rabbit saw two women making willow baskets lined with pitch. He was still a good way off, but he heard them talking, for he had a wonderful ear. He heard them saying: "Here comes that no-good Rabbit. Let's kill him."

He went up to them and said: "What were you talking about?"

"Oh, we were only saying: 'Here comes that good-looking grandson of ours.'"

"Is that so? Well, let's see whether I can fit into one of your water baskets." He got in. "Now braid the neck," he told them.

"Gladly," they said. They wove the basket's neck really small, thinking: "Now he's trapped. He can't get out." But with his magic breath Little Rabbit burst the basket open, and stood there smiling.

"You must surely be a ghost," said the women.

"I am no ghost," he said, "just a common little no-account Rabbit. But why do you wonder? Don't you know that such a basket can hold water, but never a human being?"

"You are smart and know everything," said the women.

"Try it out for yourselves," he told them. They

jumped into the baskets lined with pitch and got stuck. "Why don't you jump out?" he taunted them. Then he rolled them around, and kicked them about, and made fun of them. Finally, he killed them with his magic ball. "I am getting better and better at this killing business," said Little Rabbit. "I am going to fight Sun." He uttered a war cry and went on.

The next day Little Rabbit came upon Kwiats, the Great Bear. Kwiats was digging in the ground, making a huge hole. "What are you doing?" asked Little Rabbit.

"Brother, I am digging a hole so that I can hide myself from Little Rabbit, the Great Slayer of all who stand in his way."

"What a coincidence," exclaimed Little Rabbit, "I am trying to hide myself from this same terrible killer. Let us dig together." While Kwiats scooped out huge amounts of earth, Little Rabbit quickly made himself a secret passage out of this den. He slipped out. After a while, Kwiats wondered where his companion had gone. "I wonder where the little fellow is at?" Kwiats grumbled. He found the secret passage all the way to the exit, but he could not get through because he was much too big. He could only squeeze his head through. At the exit Little Rabbit was waiting. He shattered Kwiats's skull with his magic ball. "I am really getting the hang of it now," said Little Rabbit. "Now I go on to fight Sun." He uttered a war whoop and continued his journey.

Next, Little Rabbit came across Tarantula. Taran-tula was very smart. He had already heard about Little Rabbit and his deeds. Tarantula had a magic club that could not hurt him, but could hurt others. "I shall be using it to kill Little Rabbit," Tarantula said to himself. Aloud he said: "Brother, I have a terrific headache. It is caused by an evil spirit inside my skull. Please beat it out of me with this club."

Little Rabbit pounded Tarantula's head with the club but could not hurt him. Little Rabbit was smarter than Tarantula. He figured out what Tarantula was up to. He quickly exchanged the club for his magic ball and with it pounded Tarantula's head to bits. "I am on my way to kill Sun," Little Rabbit cried. "Now I know I can do it!" He uttered his piercing war cry.

Little Rabbit came to the edge of the world in the east. He was careful not to fall over the edge into bottomless nothingness. He waited for Sun to come up. As soon as Sun did, Little Rabbit shattered the Sun's face into a thousand fragments. They were scattered all over the world, setting the earth on fire. The flames burned Little Rabbit's toes, then his legs, body, and arms, until only his head was left. It rolled on all by itself until the terrible heat burst his swollen eyes, which exploded in a flood of tears that covered the whole earth and put out the fire. It took a long time until Sun and Little Rabbit had re-created themselves. "It seems killing is not the answer," said Little Rabbit.

"Incestuous Dangidjara"[1] (Australia)[2]

Dangidjara was a *djagamara* man.[3] From Njinyir-awurul, east of Yabuna near Lake Mackay, on his way to Windal claypan, he came to Munggug-adja rockhole where he camped. Later he went on to Bulgal rockhole and then to Yumari rockhole. Here Magindi, a *nangala* woman, was camping: she was related to Dangidjara as a mother-in-law (*yumari*)[4] … 'He couldn't help it. He copulated with her!' He camped with her for some time. He walked all around the place and speared kangaroos, removing their entrails; there is a soak[5] where he did this. He returned to Yumari now and then to supply Magindi with meat. She became pregnant, and eventually gave birth to a *djabaldjari* son.

Leaving his *yumari* and his son, Dangidjara went on to Nundjil. Here he slept in a big rockhole, but while he was sleeping, ants bit his testes so severely that they fell off and 'ran away by themselves!' He went on to Malga, where there is a big rockhole, and camped there. His testes had gone in the opposite direction. His penis too, as a result of the ant bites, had dropped off and gone in another direction. In the morning he called out for his testes and penis— but they did not return. He walked on southward, and camped—but they did not come back to him. It was not until he reached Lungulurul swamp that his testes and penis rejoined him.

Dangidjara continued to Bugudi swamp, where he camped, and tied up his hair into a *bugudi* bun. He walked on to Wila-duludjara where there is another swamp. He was tired. He turned back to Yugala, where he camped for a while to recover his strength, then went on to Baldjaga swamp and camped, and to Mandan-gunda where there is a hole, but no water. Living in the lake area nearby were Munga-munga people—'wild' people, who were looking for him. Seeing them, he 'dived into' the hole at Mandan-gunda. The Munga-munga blocked the entrance to it. However, he came out at another place, Djindara, after having traveled underground. They continued looking for him at Mandan-gunda. He called out to them from Djindara, 'teasing' them, then ran away to Njiringgi soak. The Munga-munga followed him. He went on to Gunawiri soak. It was there that they found him. They encircled him. He dodged between them and escaped. He placed his sacred boards in a tree nearby and, standing on one leg, gathered together all the Munga-munga people and put them into Gunawiri soak. As he stood there on one leg, he turned himself into a rock. All of them 'finished up' at that place.[6]

---

1 "Incestuous Dangidjara," in Ronald M. Berndt and Catherine H. Berndt, *The Speaking Land: Myth and Story in Aboriginal Australia* (Rochester, VT: Inner Traditions International, 1988, 1994).

2 The Indigenous people of this myth speak Gugadja (or Kukatja). The names of the places mentioned in the text are located in the north of Western Australia.

3 *Djagamara* (as well as *nangala* and *djabaldjari*) designate categories within the kinship system found in many Australian Indigenous cultures. A person's position within this system of social organization determines their prescribed and prohibited behaviors in relation to people in other categories.

4 In the Indigenous language of this text, mother-in-law is *yumari*, hence the place name, Yumari rockhole. It signifies a taboo relationship.

5 I.e., a source of water in Australian deserts.

6 The original editors of this text note: "A version of this myth is contained in R. Berndt (1970: 231–32); it is part of a much larger cycle, some of which (not this) is secret-sacred. The point made in this section of the myth is that punishment inevitably follows an act of incest."

Questions

1. The warrior maiden has a dream that tells her how to defeat the Mingoes. What role do you think dreams play in this culture? Why?
2. What moral lessons do we learn from the greed of the old man and his wife? From Little Rabbit's encounters?
3. The modern view of the world comes out of the sciences and entails a "reductive materialism" that explains everything in physical terms. Does this capture everything? Do other traditions, such as the story-telling traditions of some Indigenous cultures, offer explanations that go beyond what science can tell us? Discuss.
4. Based on the small sample of stories presented here, can you think of a way in which the wisdom contained in Indigenous stories speaks to us today? Is it any different than the moral wisdom contained in the sacred Scriptures of the three monotheistic religions of Judaism, Christianity, and Islam? In a spirit of reconciliation, speak with an Indigenous person or elder about the importance to them of their stories.

Suggested Readings

The original accounts of Indigenous tradition are in the anthropological literature. Students can find original sources online in the Memoirs of the American Folklore Society at archive.org. Students may want to consult the volumes from which the readings were taken, or read the "Bungling Host" stories in Morris Edward Opler, *Myths and Tales of the Chiricahua Apache Indians* (1942). In more recent work, Natalia Grincheva examines the epistemology behind many Indigenous traditions in "Scientific Epistemology versus Indigenous Epistemology" (2013). The African work also deserves attention. Kwame Gyekye's *Tradition and Modernity: Philosophical Reflections on the African Experience* (1997) argues that the concept of "ubuntu" finds political expression in a "moderate communitarianism." In "A Continuing Study on Sage Philosophy" (2002), Peter Ogola Onyango writes that African sage philosophy is part of a living tradition based on the "expressed thought" of the wise members of the community. For a review of some of the issues raised by Indigenous traditions in applied ethics, see, for example, G. Garvey et al., "Is There an Aboriginal Bioethic?" (2004).

PART II
ANCIENT SOURCES

The Rise of Philosophical and Religious Ethics

In the Greek and Roman world at least, the ancient period was an age of philosophy. With Athens, the turn was towards the theoretical and, then, in Roman times, towards the primarily practical. In moving from the tribal era, the shift from an oral to a written tradition, the rise of the first universities, and the development of systems of logic, formal argument, and the art of rhetoric gave rise to an academic tradition. At times, this shifted the ethical discussion from the earlier wisdom tradition with its focus on practical wisdom to theoretical wisdom.

The Greek philosophical tradition relied heavily on the use of logic and the idea that we can know the good. This "epistemological" approach reached its height in Plato, who argued that we can ascend to an ineffable or speechless contemplation of the Good. The mystic and transcendent implications of Plato's position were nevertheless elaborated in Neo-Platonism, which continued all the way into the medieval period and found its way into several religious traditions, including Christianity.

Greek philosophy was highly diverse. Alongside Plato's sometimes dissenting pupil Aristotle, a series of moral schools developed, often taking inspiration from the life and heroism of Socrates. The often-competing philosophical systems of Sophism, Skepticism, Cynicism, Stoicism, and Epicureanism, as well as Platonism and Aristotelianism, along with the folk-moralism of Aesop's fables, added depth and scope to the range of moral speculation.

In the East, the classical Chinese tradition continued to be a product of a well-developed academic tradition based on the received wisdom of the past, and lingering cosmological beliefs, which still saw moral conduct as a matter of acting in accordance with a larger universal order. Daoism contained a mix of religious and philosophical elements, which flowered in a dissident anti-realism, on one side, and in a highly influential Confucianism, on the other. Buddhism became a central religious and moral force in India.

It is hard to generalize about an entire age, but one observes material advances in society and increasing social differences that motivate people to seek personal advancement and promote their self-interest. This is a feature of many fables, and later enters, in a more philosophical guise, for example into Stoicism and Epicureanism. There is a corresponding emphasis on moderation, which finds expression in Aristotle's golden mean and in the "middle way" in China. The development of a recognized aristocracy contributed to the idea that the higher individual lives above narrow self-interest. People who cultivate virtue and ethical judgment are happier because of it.

The idea of dignity was still pivotal and an individual's ethical obligations are still grounded on membership in a family and community. Rather than accept exile, Socrates chooses to die as a citizen of Athens. This idea, like the notion of honor, was carried over into the Roman tradition, and persisted, in spite of the development of a more individualistic ethics.

The ancient period was also a time of religious conversion, which probably reflected, in part, a reaction to the changes in the material structure and organization of society. There was a slow, cumulative elaboration of a theological ethics based on faith and revelation, which built upon the earlier wisdom tradition and on newer philosophical sources supplemented by the teaching of charismatic figures such as Jesus and the Buddha.

Chapter 5

Early Daoism

Laozi (老子 Laozi—"Old Master," also Lao-tzu), was a Chinese philosopher who lived in the sixth century BCE, and was probably a much older contemporary of Kongzi (Confucius). Although he has regularly been described—rather simplistically—as the "founder" of Daoism, the Daoist tradition goes much further back, and is far too complex and untidy to be attributed to individual figures. It is more accurate to say that he was the major figure in the early philosophical tradition that we know as Daoism, which later became institutionalized in a somewhat different guise as a religion.

Laozi apparently was born in the state of Chu and became the historiographer (the official responsible for the imperial library, which kept the official records) for the Zhou Dynasty. The position of historiographer was a weighty responsibility, since the official historians were in some sense responsible to heaven and posterity rather than the Emperor. Since Laozi was the official librarian, he was familiar with the protocols of the time and was supposedly consulted by a younger Kongzi on the rites, who said: "today, I have met a dragon!"

Laozi and Kongzi lived during the late Spring and Autumn Period, a period of turbulent change, and looked at the near-distant past as a time of stability and social harmony. After the death of King Jing in 516 BCE, a civil war broke out and the collections of the Zhou library were removed by one of the warring princes. Laozi then renounced the life of an official, and decided to become a hermit. When he arrived at the western gate of the kingdom, Yinxi, the keeper of the gate, refused to allow him to pass until he had written down his wisdom.

The story has it that Laozi then wrote the collection of teachings known as the *Laozi* in China, which is known to western readers as the *Tao Te Ching* or *Dao de jing*. This book is in fact composed of two works, the *Book of Dao* and the *Book of De* (or *Te*, virtue), which have been excerpted in the readings. The standard version of the *Laozi* was compiled by Wang Bi (226–249 BCE), a Confucian commentator, and contains a recognized canon of Daoist teachings, rather than the work of a single author, supplemented by commentaries from later scholars.

The term "Daoism" refers to a loose body of metaphysical and cosmological tenets, a rather vague philosophical school and a specific religious tradition. It is nevertheless the concept of the *Dao* which distinguishes these different strands of belief. The Chinese character for *Dao*, 道, is essentially a pictograph of a walking foot and originally referred to a road or path. Later it became a term of general application and is usually translated as "the way." There are many *Dao*s. There is the "little *dao*," which refers to the moral path of a particular individual. There is also the "great" (literally, the "big") *Dao*, which expresses the cosmic order and universal will.

The philosophical framework in the *Dao de jing* comes out of earlier cosmological theories. The great *Dao* is associated with the *yuan qi*—the vital breath—in the originally existing state before things came into being. This *Dao* was apparently associated with the relative non-being, out of which things were created. The suggestion in early Chinese metaphysics is that non-being is primary, and thus it is the formless and the nameless, the *Dao*, that completes all things.

The moral aspects of the "mighty *Dao*" come from the fact that it explains both the unity of things, the unity behind *ying* and *yang*, and the existence of the multitude of discrete things. In chapter 25 of the *Laozi*, the narrator says that he has chosen to call the formless entity, the mother of all things, the *Dao*, but that it could also be called "greatness." In chapter 40 of the *Laozi*, we read that being is born from non-being.

This seems to be the philosophical source of the ethics of not acting, which has intrigued western commentators. The phrasing of such a dynamic is important: metaphysically, the *Dao* is the state or condition, essentially, which allows myriad things to come into being; and if we wish to follow the *Dao*, as it manifests itself, morally, we allow ourselves—and therefore all things—to be what they are. Thus, virtue lies in *wuwei*, inaction or not doing—in the sense of not striving—which became the staple principle of early Daoist thought. Laozi openly rejects the new sense of individualism and competition that had come out into the open during the period.

As a result of the collapse of the political order in the Spring and Autumn Period, the philosophy of the time is preoccupied with moral and political theory, which was nevertheless inherently cosmological. To Laozi and Kongzi, it seemed, quite literally, that society had somehow lost its "way." The rulers in the ideal past had scrupulously followed the *Dao*, which found expression in the customs that were to be followed by those in official positions. The disintegration of society was accordingly attributed to "the collapse of propriety [i.e., rites] and music." Music is significant because it played an official role in the life of the state.

There is a deep moral issue here. The character for "propriety" refers both to the rituals themselves and, more philosophically, to the internal ordering of the individual in accordance with the *Dao*. The ethical argument is accordingly that the rites mean nothing, without a sincere commitment. The changes in society had led to a loss of authenticity, which had been replaced with personal ambition and political calculation. The rulers and ministers no longer internalized the rites. Chapter 38 of the *Laozi* says that propriety—the rites—was only brought in because the righteousness underlying the rites had been lost. This was already too late.

The concept of *de* or *te* (virtue) in the *Laozi* is similar to our own concept. In chapter

38, Laozi contrasts "superior" and "inferior" virtue. Wang Bi says that the man of inferior virtue seeks to "complete things through repeated efforts and propaganda." He is looking for a reputation and wishes to "gain the name of virtue." Like later Chinese philosophers, such as Zhou Dunyi, Laozi suggests that it is our lack of sincerity—our lack of authenticity—that explains why the way does not prevail in the world. The man of superior virtue, on the other hand, follows the *Dao* alone.

The solution to the world's corruption lies in the appearance of the sage, who is the embodiment of the "mighty *Dao*" and the "mystical virtue," which Laozi associates, in chapter 51, with complete unselfishness. Without thinking, without trying or "acting," the sage follows the *Dao* and the universal moral order. He rules without—in any explicit sense—ruling. Things therefore come to fruition. Simply by being, without "acting," he transforms the world. His virtue is the virtue inherent in the whole of nature. He is therefore one with all things.

The pessimism in the *Laozi* is easily misunderstood. The Daoist view is that people are good, and Laozi is merely rejecting the philosophical, scientific, and technological advances in society. This rejection is fundamentally epistemological: the people are better when they are left in ignorance. Much of the social deterioration in the world is ascribed to ideas, and the development of language, which have a structure of their own. Instead of using our intellectual faculties to see things as they are, we use them to re-configure reality, so that it meets the outline of our ideas. This is a very modern, even post-modern idea. The person who practices *wuwei* leaves language behind.

READING 5

Excerpts from the *Lǎozǐ* (*Dào dé jīng* 道德經)[1]

(uncertain date: sixth century BCE or earlier)

Book 1 *dao jing* (The classic of the *dao*)

CHAPTER 1

The dao [the way or road] that can be trodden is not the enduring and unchanging dao. The name that can be named is not the enduring and unchanging name.

Having no name, it is the Originator of heaven and earth; Having a name, it is the Mother of all things.

Therefore it is always from the Being-without-form that the subtlety of the dao can be contemplated;

---

1 This is an original translation by Paul Groarke. There are different systems for "Romanizing" Chinese names—that is, for rendering them into the alphabet English-speakers use. During the 1980s, one system, called pinyin, was recognized as standard, and we will use these spellings. Pinyin includes diacritics—little marks above vowels showing what "tone" should be used in their pronunciation. Most often, however, the diacritics are omitted in English writing, and we will follow this practice; but for the sake of scholarly completeness, we will show that version once for each name.

Similarly it is always from the Being-within-form that the manifestation of the dao can be perceived.

Under these two aspects, it is really the same; but receives the different names. Together we call them the Mystery. Where the Mystery is the deepest is the gate of all that is subtle and wonderful.

CHAPTER 2

Therefore the sage manages affairs without doing anything, and conveys his instructions without the use of speech.

He allows all things to spring up, and there is not one which declines to show itself; they grow, and he claims no ownership; they go through their processes, and there is no expectation.

It is because he takes no credit that his accomplishment stays with him forever.

CHAPTER 3

Do not value and employ men of superior ability and the people will not compete; do not prize articles that are difficult to procure and they will not become thieves; do not show them what is likely to excite their desires and they will not be disturbed.

Therefore the sage, in the exercise of his government, empties their minds, fills their bellies, weakens their wills, and strengthens their bones.

He constantly keeps them innocent of knowledge and desires; and makes those who have knowledge afraid to act. When there is this abstinence from action, good order is universal.

CHAPTER 5

Heaven and earth are not benevolent [humane]. They treat all things as if they were straw dogs.

The sages are not humane. They regard the common people as if they were straw dogs.

The spirit of the valley dies not and is always the same. It is the subtle and profound female. The gate of the subtle and profound female is the root from which grew heaven and earth.

CHAPTER 7

The reason why heaven and earth are able to endure and continue long is because they do not live of, or for, themselves.

Therefore the sage puts himself in the back; and yet is found in the front. He treats his person without regard; and yet his person is preserved. Is it not because he has no personal and private ends that his ends are realised?

CHAPTER 8

The highest excellence is like water. Water benefits all things and occupies, without striving, the low place that all men dislike. Hence its way is like the dao.

When one (with the highest excellence) does not compete (accepts his low position), there is no fault.

CHAPTER 9

When the work is done, and one's name is becoming distinguished, to withdraw into obscurity is the way of Heaven.

CHAPTER 10

In loving the people and ruling the state, can you proceed without any (purpose of) action?

In the opening and shutting of the gates of heaven, can you do so as the female?

(The dao) gives birth but does not possess.

This is called 'the mysterious Quality' (of the dao).

CHAPTER 11

Thirty spokes meet in the hub of a wheel; but it is on the space in the center [i.e., where the axle goes] that the usefulness of the wheel depends.

Clay is molded into a pot; but it is in the emptiness inside it that the usefulness of the pot depends.

Door and windows are cut out to form a room; but it is on the emptiness inside the room that the usefulness of the room depends.

Therefore it is what has a positive existence that can be profitably adapted; but what has a negative existence that can be used.

CHAPTER 15

The skilful masters (of the dao) in old times, with a subtle and exquisite penetration, comprehended its mysteries.

Shrinking they looked like those who wade through a stream in winter; irresolute like those who are afraid of all around them; grave like a guest in awe of his host; evanescent like melting ice; unpretentious as unworked wood; and dull like muddy water.

They who preserve this method of the dao do not wish to be full; it is in not being full that they are renewed.

CHAPTER 17

In the highest antiquity, the people did not know that there were rulers. In the next age they loved them and praised them. In the next they feared them; in the next they despised them. Thus it was that when the rulers lost faith in the dao, the people lost faith in the rulers.

How cautious did those earliest rulers appear, and reticent in giving orders. Their work was done and their undertakings were successful, while the people all said, 'We are as we are, of ourselves!'

CHAPTER 18

When the great Dao ceased to be observed, benevolence [ren] and righteousness [yi] came into vogue. Then appeared knowledge and shrewdness, and with it, hypocrisy.

When harmony no longer prevailed, filial sons found their manifestation; when the state fell into disorder, loyal ministers appeared.

CHAPTER 19

If we could renounce our sageness and discard our cleverness, it would be better for the people a hundredfold.

If we could renounce our benevolence [ren, humanity; a Confucian virtue] and discard our righteousness, the people would again become filial and kindly.

If we could renounce the crafty and discard profit, there would be neither thieves nor robbers.

Since these three principles are insufficient to prove a social doctrine, we urge the following: manifest the plain; embrace simplicity. Reduce selfishness and desires; abolish learning and there will be no worries.

CHAPTER 21

The character of the great de [virtue] comes only from dao.

CHAPTER 22

The sage holds on to the one thing (humility), and manifests it to all the world. Since he does not cling to his ideas, he can see clearly. Since he does not claim to be right, he can distinguish right from wrong. Since he does not boast, his merit is acknowledged. Since he does not consider himself superior, he acquires superiority.

It is because he does not compete that no one in the world can compete with him.

Because he yields, he shall be preserved intact.

CHAPTER 31

1. Now arms, however beautiful, are instruments of evil omen; hateful, it may be said, to all creatures. Therefore they who have the dao do not like to employ them.

Calm and repose are what the superior man prizes; victory by force of arms is to him undesirable.

He who has killed multitudes of men should weep for them with the bitterest grief; and therefore the victor in battle has [traditionally] been given the position of mourning when the rites are held.

CHAPTER 32

The dao, unchanging, has no name.

Though it is simple and seems diminutive, nothing under heaven can subordinate it. The whole world dares not deal with (one embodying) it as a minister. If a prince or king could maintain it, the people and myriad creatures would spontaneously submit to him.

Book II. *De jing* (The classic of *de* [virtue])

CHAPTER 38

The man of highest virtue [*de*] is not conscious of his virtue and therefore possesses it. The man of inferior virtue never loses sight of it, and therefore does not possess it.

The man of highest virtue does nothing, and thus nothing is left undone. The man of inferior virtue is always doing and therefore leaves things undone.

[Now the subsequent rulers] who possessed the highest benevolence [*ren*, humanity] were (always seeking) to carry it out, when [as we have seen] they had no need to be doing so. [The subsequent rul-

ers who] possessed the highest righteousness were (always seeking) to carry it out, when they had no need to do so.

[Similarly, those rulers who] possessed the highest propriety were always seeking to show it, and when men did not respond to it, they bared their weapons and coerced them.

Thus it was that when the dao was lost, *de* [virtue] appeared; when *de* was lost, benevolence [*ren*, human feeling] appeared; and when benevolence was lost, righteousness [*yi*] appeared; and when righteousness was lost, propriety appeared.

Now propriety is the mere form of loyalty and good faith, and the source of disorder; knowledge is (only) a flower of the dao, and the beginning of ignorance.

Thus the great man abides by the highest virtue [literally, the virtue (*de*) that is solid or thick] and not by its form [which is thin or flimsy]; dwells with the fruit [of the dao] and not with its flower.

CHAPTER 41

When scholars [*shi*] of the highest class hear about the dao, they earnestly carry it into practice.

When scholars of the middle class hear about the dao, they seem now to keep it and now to lose it.

When scholars of the lowest class have heard about it, they laugh greatly at it. If they did not laugh at it, it would not be fit to be the dao.

CHAPTER 42

What other men teach, I also teach. The violent and strong [i.e., tyrants] do not die their natural death. I will make this the foundation of my teaching.

CHAPTER 43

The softest thing in the world [water] rushes easily over the hardest.

That which has no physical substance [e.g., a

magnetic force] can enter that which has physical substance, even if there is no crack [i.e., without doing anything].

I therefore know that not doing has the advantage.

There are few who can grasp the teaching which has no words and the advantage of not doing.

CHAPTER 46

When the dao prevails in the world, they send back their war horses to provide the dung [the fertilizer] for the dung-carts. When the dao is disregarded, even the breeding horses in the border lands must serve.

There is no wrong greater than to applaud ambition; no calamity greater than to be discontented; no fault greater than the desire for gain.

He who finds sufficiency in knowing contentment will always be content.

CHAPTER 47

Without going out the door, one can understand all that takes place under the sky. Without looking out of the window, one can see the dao of Heaven. The farther one goes, the less one knows.

Therefore the sages [became wise] without journeys; were able to name things correctly without seeing them; and accomplished their aims without effort.

CHAPTER 48

He who devotes himself to learning seeks from day to day to increase his knowledge; he who devotes himself to the dao seeks from day to day to diminish his doing.

He diminishes it again and again, till he arrives at inaction [*wuwei*; doing nothing, acting without doing]. Having arrived at inaction, there is no action which is not done.

CHAPTER 49

The sage has no mind of his own; he makes the mind of the people his mind.

To those who are good, I am good. To those who are not good, I am also good;—thus goodness is attained.

To those who are sincere, I am sincere. To those who are not sincere, I am also sincere;—thus sincerity is attained.

The sage appears indecisive, with no will of his own, and returns all to simplicity. The people fix their eyes and ears on him, like children, and forget their desires.

CHAPTER 51

All things are produced by the dao and nourished by *de*. Substance gives them form; circumstances complete them.

Therefore all things without exception honour the dao, and honour *de*.

Thus it is that the dao produces them and makes no claim to the possession of them; it carries them through their processes and does not vaunt its ability in doing so; it brings them to maturity and exercises no control over them;—this is called mysterious *de*.

CHAPTER 55

He who has in himself abundantly the attributes of the dao is like an infant. Poisonous insects will not sting him; fierce beasts will not seize him; birds of prey will not strike him.

The infant's bones are weak and its sinews soft; yet its grasp is firm. It has yet to know the union of male and female, and yet its penis may become erect;—showing the perfection of its physical essence. It may cry all day without its throat becoming hoarse;—because its constitution is in perfect harmony with the dao. To know this harmony is to know the secret of the unchanging dao. And in this knowledge to be wise.

The desire to make life more by controlling the vital breath [the *qi*] by the mind is a mistake; it requires force. When things have become strong, they become old, which may be said to be contrary to the dao. Whatever is contrary to the dao soon ends.

CHAPTER 56

He who knows the dao does not care to speak of it; he who is ready to speak about it does not know it.

He who knows it will keep his mouth shut and close the portals (of his nostrils). He will blunt his sharp points and unravel the complications of things; he will temper his brightness, and bring himself into agreement with the obscurity of others.

This is called 'the Mysterious Agreement.'

Such an individual cannot be treated familiarly or distantly; he is beyond all considerations of profit or injury; of honour or debasement:—therefore he is esteemed by all under heaven.

CHAPTER 57

A state should be ruled in the expected way; an army should be deployed craftily; but the world is won over by inaction [i.e., by cultivating emptiness].

How do I know that it is so?

By these facts:

In the kingdom the multiplication of prohibitions increases the poverty of the people;

the more implements that they have to add to their profit, the greater the disorder in the state and clan;

the more contraptions [products of craft and technology] that men possess, the more vicious things there will be;

the more the criminal law is emphasized, the more thieves and robbers there are.

Therefore a sage has said:

'When I do nothing [*wuwei*], the people transform themselves;

When I keep still, they correct themselves.

When I do not interfere, they prosper;

It is because I have no ambition that the people become [simple, like raw wood].'

CHAPTER 60

Governing a great state is like cooking small fish.

Let the kingdom be governed according to the dao and the spectres will not exercise their supernatural powers.

It is not that the spectres do not have supernatural power; it is that it will not be employed to hurt men.

It is that it will not be employed to hurt men; and that the sage [and ruler] does not harm them.

Since they do not harm men, and men do not harm them, they run together in the virtue (of the dao).

CHAPTER 61

What makes a great state is that it is low-lying and down-flowing;—therefore it is like an estuary, into which the small states, like rivers and streams, naturally flow. It is the point where all converge.

It is the female of the world.

CHAPTER 62

The dao has of all things the most honoured place.

(Its) admirable words can purchase honour; (its) admirable deeds can raise their performer above others. Even men who are not good are not abandoned by it.

Therefore when the sovereign has occupied his place as the Son of Heaven, and has appointed his three ministers, though (a prince) were to send him a jade disk as wide as the span of both hands, and a four-horse chariot, it would be better to get down on his knees and learn this dao.

Why was it that the ancients prized this dao so much? Was it not because it was available to those who sought it, and the guilty could escape (from the stain of their guilt) by it? This is the reason why all under heaven consider it the most valuable thing.

CHAPTER 63

It is the way of the dao to consider what is small as great, and few as many; and to recompense injury with kindness.

As a rule, the most difficult things begin easy; the greatest things begin small. Hence, the master deals with things which are difficult while they are easy, and things which are great while they are small.

He who is continually thinking things easy is sure to find them difficult. Therefore the sage sees difficulty even in what seems easy and is able to accomplish the greatest things.

CHAPTER 64

Deal with things before they happen. Secure order before disorder has begun.

The tree as large as the circumference of your arms grew from the tiniest sprout; the tower of nine stories rose from a (small) heap of earth; the journey of a thousand *li* began with a single step.

He who acts for his own purposes [out of self-interest] does harm; he who takes hold of a thing loses his hold. The sage does not do so, and therefore does no harm;—neither does he lay hold of a thing; therefore he does not lose his hold.

Thus the sage helps the natural development of all things and does not dare to act for his own purposes.

CHAPTER 65

The ancients who showed their skill in practicing the dao did so, not to enlighten the people, but to make them simple and ignorant.

The difficulty in governing the people arises from their having too much [cleverness, craftiness]. Therefore he who (tries to) govern a state by his [cleverness, craftiness] is a scourge; while he who does not (try to) do so is a blessing.

CHAPTER 66

That whereby the rivers and seas are able to receive the homage and tribute of all the valley streams, is their skill in being lower than they;—thus they are the kings of them all.

So it is that the sage (and ruler), if he wishes to be above men, puts himself below them in his words; if he wishes to be in front of them, he places his person behind them.

In this way, though he is above them, they do not feel his weight; though he is in front of them, they are not offended.

Therefore all in the world delight to praise him and do not weary of him. Because he does not strive, no one finds it possible to strive with him.

CHAPTER 67

I have three precious things which I prize and hold fast. The first is gentleness; the second is economy; and the third is shrinking from taking precedence over others.

With gentleness I can be bold; with economy I can be generous; shrinking from taking precedence over others, I can become a vessel of the highest honour.

Nowadays they give up gentleness and are all for being bold; they give up economy, and are all for being liberal; they give up the hindmost place, and seek only to be foremost;—the end of which is death.

Gentleness is sure to be victorious even in battle, and firmly to maintain its ground. Heaven will save its possessor, by his (very) gentleness protecting him.

CHAPTER 69

There is no calamity greater than lightly engaging in war. To do that is near losing (the gentleness) which is so precious. Thus it is that when opposing armies clash, he who deplores (the situation) conquers.

CHAPTER 73

He whose bravery lies in daring (to defy the laws) is put to death; he whose bravery lies in not daring (to do so) lives on. Of these two cases, the one appears to be advantageous, the other injurious.

CHAPTER 75

The people suffer from famine because of the multitude of taxes consumed by those who govern. It is through this that they suffer famine.

The people are difficult to govern because they are [over-regulated] by those who govern them. It is through this that they are difficult to govern.

CHAPTER 78

There is nothing in the world more soft and weak than water, and yet for overcoming things that are firm and strong there is nothing that can take precedence over it.

Everyone in the world knows that the soft overcomes the hard, and the weak the strong, but no one is able to carry it out in practice.

It is the [apparently] paradoxical that is true.

CHAPTER 79

The dao of Heaven does not play favourites [i.e., there are no exceptions]: it always takes the side of the good man.

CHAPTER 80

In a little state with a small population, I would have it, that individuals with the abilities of ten or a hundred men should not be employed. I would have the people, while looking on death as a grievous thing, not move elsewhere to avoid it.

Though they had boats and carriages, they should have no occasion to ride in them; though they have buff coats and sharp weapons, they should have no occasion to don or use them.

I would have the people return to using knotted cords instead of written characters.

Let them enjoy their food, beautify their clothing, find rest in their homes, and take pleasure in their simple ways.

Though there should be a neighbouring state within sight, and the people should hear the crowing of their cocks and barking of their dogs, I would have the people live to old age, even death, without meeting its people.

CHAPTER 81

Sincere words are not fine; fine words are not sincere. Those who are skilled in the dao do not dispute about it; the disputatious are not skilled in it. Those who know the dao are not extensively learned; the extensively learned do not know it.

The sage does not accumulate (for himself). The more that he expends for others, the more does he possess of his own; the more that he gives to others, the more does he have himself.

Questions

1. Victor H. Mair has described the *Dao de jing* as a collection of "proverbial wisdom." Identify three or four proverbs and discuss them in the context of the proverb tradition. Refer to chapter 2.
2. It is clear that Laozi associates the great Dao with non-being, which "nourishes all things." If morality consists of following this Dao, how do we follow it?
3. There is the "big" and the "little" *dao*. The "little" *dao* determines how a particular person should act, morally and ethically. Where does your *dao* lie?
4. Try to sum up the moral teaching of Laozi in one or two sentences. Do you agree with his teaching? Why, why not?
5. How does *wuwei* fit into the scheme of practical ethics? Can you provide an example from your life or that of your friends?
6. Laozi is a conservative. What is it that he finds so appealing in early agricultural society, which he saw as a kind of golden age? What is he rejecting in his own age?
7. The *Dao de jing* identifies selfishness and "striving" (competition) as the source of disorder in society. The sage is selfless and acts in accordance with the universal order. How can we encourage people to act selflessly? What does Laozi say?

Suggested Readings

General Chinese Sources

The most accessible bilingual source for canonical Chinese philosophical works is probably the Chinese Text Project at ctext.org, though the translations are old and the *Dao de jing* (and "Daoism") is indexed inappropriately. Derk Bodde's lucid translation of Fung Yu-lan's *History of Chinese Philosophy* (1937; 1952) is still the best introduction to classical Chinese philosophy. Feng's *A Short History of Chinese Philosophy* (1948) is also available in paperback. In spite of its inexplicable lack of Chinese characters, the *Encyclopedia of Chinese Philosophy* (Routledge, 2003) provides a convenient introduction to recognized topics and bibliographical sources. Students may wish to consult bilingual Chinese textbooks, such as Gao Huaping's *Laozi* (2010), which is part of a larger series from Nanjing University. The brusque style and literal tone of these texts is typical in the Chinese tradition and philosophers like Fung (*Hall of the Three Pines*) and Liang Shuming (*Has Man a Future?*) have complained about the abstract wanderings of contemporary western philosophers.

Daoism

The *Dao de jing* is available in a bewildering number of translations, many of which are available online. The Chinese Text Project uses James Legge's 1891 edition, which is "Orientalist" and over-precise, like most translations, but academically sound. A well-respected translation by D.C. Lau is available at terebess.hu, along with dozens of other translations.

The philosophical study of Daoism is complicated by the fact that there is no clean division between the philosophical and religious aspects of the Daoist tradition. A reasonable starting place, philosophically, is the entry on Daoism in the *Stanford Encyclopedia of Philosophy* at plato.stanford.edu. Another starting point is Herrlee Glessner Creel's *"What Is Taoism?"* (1970). Although there is a two-volume *Encyclopedia of Taoism*, edited by Fabrizio Pregadio (Routledge, 2008), its focus is not philosophical.

In *Taoism: The Enduring Tradition* (2004), Russell Kirkland argues that the distorted understanding of Daoism in the west was implicitly promoted by Confucians. See also Hans-Georg Moeller, *The Philosophy of the Daodejing* (2006). For ethical sources, see Russell's "Self-Fulfillment through Selflessness: The Moral Teachings of the *Dao de Jing*" (2002), and Livia Kohn, *Cosmos and Community: The Ethical Dimension of Daoism* (2004). For comparative studies, see Jiyuan Yu, "Moral Naturalism in Stoicism and Daoism" (2016), and Vincent Shen, "Thomas's Natural Law and Laozi's Heavenly Dao" (2013).

Chapter 6

Confucius

Kongzi (孔子 Kǒng zǐ, 551–479 BCE), known as Confucius in English,[1] is generally considered the most eminent thinker in the classical Chinese tradition. The character for "Kong" is a surname; "zi" is an honorific that has traditionally been applied to venerable thinkers, such as Laozi and Zhuangzi as well as Kongzi. The name "Kongzi" is usually translated as "Master Kong."

Kongzi was born in the kingdom of Lu, in the Spring and Autumn Period, a period in which the "warring states" fought for control of the central plains of China. This period in Chinese history was marked by ferocious violence and general upheaval. Like Laozi, Kongzi was profoundly affected by the disorder of the time and wanted to recover the peace and stability of the idealized past. Kongzi's father, an impoverished noble, took a fifteen-year-old girl as a second wife when he was over seventy because he wanted a male heir. This was considered the first and foremost responsibility of a male at the time, since without a son there would be no family to pay proper respects to one's ancestors.

Kongzi began his career as a minor official, supervising public granaries and then managing public fields and lands. He later became a judicial officer. At some point, relatively early in his adult life, he devoted his time to a study of the classics and to teaching. In this regard, he is a representative of a larger movement, known as "the *ru*," the school of scholars. He taught from a defined curriculum, which included propriety (*li*, the "rites"), music making, archery, charioteering, writing, and mathematics. The focus was nevertheless on the cultivation of moral character, which was believed to be more essential than practical skills.

From our perspective, Kongzi was essentially someone who believed in a liberal arts education. By studying the ancient classics—and history, literature, philosophy, and the rites—students become moral individuals and good citizens. Like other classical Chinese philosophers, he was particularly interested in social and political theory. Like Plato, however, he wished to see his political views put into practice. In his early fifties, he accordingly

---

1 "Kongfuzi" is another honorific term meaning *Master Kong*, and the name 'Confucius' is thought to be the Latin version of that name produced by seventeenth-century Jesuit missionaries. You may find Kongzi's name also spelled "Kong Zi" or even "K'ung-tzu."

left his home state accompanied by a group of loyal students with the intention of offering his advice to the ruler of a state.

Although Kongzi failed to find a satisfactory position, his influence grew. At the end of his life, he returned to Lu and compiled the "Five Classics": the *Book of Documents*, which contains a chronicle of the sage-kings, Yao and Shun; the *Book of Odes*; the *Book of Rites*; the famous *I Ching*, a manual of divination; and a history of the state of Lu, the *Spring and Autumn Annals*. The Confucian canon can be found in the Five Classics and the "Four Books"—the *Great Learning*, the *Analects*, the *Mencius*, and the *Doctrine of the Mean* (also known as "Maintaining the Proper Balance").

This canon later became the basis of the civil examination system in Han China, which gave Confucianism the status of a state doctrine. Candidates were tested on their knowledge of the classics and literary style, and implicitly on their ethical and cultural understanding, rather than on their technical or political knowledge. This reflects the Confucian ideal of the sage, whose role is to bring the world into alignment with the *Dao*.

Philosophically, Kongzi was working within the Daoist tradition, which had retained its early elements. The entire cosmological order is a unity and includes our natural ethical inclinations. Moral conduct consists of acting in accordance with the *Dao*, 道, in accordance with the universal order, which is disrupted by immoral conduct. This also explains why Kongzi and other thinkers in the Daoist tradition are so comfortable with the inclusion of mountains and water, for example, in their ethical schemes. All things are brothers.

The political system functions within this larger universal order. The fundamental obligation of the ruler is to follow the *Dao*, which finds expression in the rites. This is a form of *wuwei*: Kongzi says that a ruler, merely by facing south, the direction that a ruler was ritually obliged to face, will restore the *Dao*. Thus he obtains the confidence of the people. It follows that virtue is the most important ingredient in successful government. A ruler who relies solely on coercion and punishment to enforce his commands will not succeed.

It follows from the Daoist cosmology that people are naturally good. Morality is therefore a matter—as in Laozi—of recovering our natural selves. Kongzi begins his ethical analysis with the family and clan, which is "the basic unit of humanity." The central virtue is filial piety. The ethical goal of living is to achieve and maintain harmony between the various members of the family and the wider community by properly following established social roles. This extends, ultimately, to society, the state, and all humanity.

Although Kongzi is inherently conservative, he shares the modern interest in personal ethics. In moral and political theory, this means observing *li*, the rites. This is a general term, related to our notion of dignity, which includes the correct performance of sacrifices; acting properly in public with the right demeanor; proper hygiene, and so on. Like Aristotle, Kongzi subscribed to a doctrine of the "Mean" or "middle," which poet Ezra Pound translated as the "unwobbling pivot." Thus he quotes the ancient Chinese proverb: "going too far is as bad as not going far enough." He also suggests that *shu*, 恕 (reciprocity), treating others as we would like to be treated, provides the basic ethical rule.

Kongzi's moral theory is imbued with a strong sense of duty. He urges us to become *junzi* (literally, the son of a noble), a term which he uses to describe "the (morally) superior man," "the gentleman," or the man "of authoritative conduct." Kongzi distinguishes between the *junzi* and the "little man," the petty individual, who is preoccupied with his own self-interest. The *junzi* is never partisan—he does not join factions or play politics—and keeps his desires in harmony.

The *junzi* has *ren*, 仁, human-heartedness, which is often translated as "benevolence" or "humanity" and which makes us human. This is the key Confucian virtue: the man with *ren* is morally and emotionally in accord with all things. Like Laozi, Kongzi sees an over-developed sense of self—which is artificial in the Daoist scheme—as the source of bad behavior. The man with virtue (*de* or *te*) is *yi*, upright, and naturally influences others. Thus the sage, who is sincere and selfless, transforms the people.

Before dealing with the readings, it is important to say something about the problems of translation. For example, there is no capitalization in the Chinese language, though we have made a concession in the case of personal names. The more important observation is that it is probably impossible to capture the bluntness and compactness of the Chinese unless we abandon the grammar and conventions of English. Students should accordingly appreciate that the original texts leave far more to the reader and translator—the Chinese language has been compared to very loose clothing—than western languages.

The first reading is from the *K'ung Tzu Chia Yu*, the "school sayings" or "teachings" of Kongzi. The term "sayings" is implicitly misleading, however, and the Chinese term refers merely to "what is (or was) said," or "talk," and not to "sayings" in the English sense. Although the *Teachings* have a recognizably academic tone, they have received relatively little attention, mostly because they were traditionally believed to have been compiled fraudulently in the third century. Recent archaeological finds have established that this cannot be the case, and R.P. Kramers was clearly right in concluding that the text is authentic.

The second reading is taken from the *Lunyu*, which consists primarily of a collection of pedagogical statements made by Kongzi, along with examples of his exchanges with his students. Again, these are often described as "sayings." It is nevertheless true that, at this early stage in our philosophical history, these succinct and sometimes cryptic entries serve the same kind of purpose as proverbs or fables in the western tradition. They utter a proposition or make a point.

The major difficulty for a western reader in the case of the *Lunyu* is that the book is in fact a series of different collections, preserved by different students, and was not designed as a single book. As a result, the text is unsystematic and even discordant. The book also assumes that the reader is familiar with the fundamentals of the classical Chinese tradition. In spite of these difficulties, the book provides a convenient starting place for those wishing to understand the classical Chinese tradition.

Kǒng zǐ, *K'ung Tzǔ Chia Yü (The School Sayings of Confucius)*[1]

(fifth or sixth century BCE)

Book I

SECTION 2: FIRST PUNISHMENT

[Shao-cheng Mao]

1. When Confucius had become Lu's Great Director of Crimes...

he punished the *shao-cheng* Mao, a great-officer who threw the government into confusion: he had him executed at the foot of the Twin Watchtowers, and had his body exposed in court for three days.

Tzu-kung came forward and said: "This *shao-cheng* Mao was a well-known man in Lu, and now in performing your office, Master, you start with punishing him. Could this possibly be a mistake?"

Confucius said: "Sit down, and I will tell you the reason for this. In the world there are five great evils [in a man], not including theft and robbery. The first is called a heart which is dangerous in rebelliousness..., the second a conduct which is persistent in its depravity, the third a speech which is eloquent in its falsehood, the fourth a comprehensive memory for wicked matters, the fifth an obedience to wrong [principles] extending its influence. When of these five there is one in a man, then [already] he cannot escape punishment by a noble man, but the *shao-cheng* Mao had them all combined.

His [standing in] private life was sufficient to gather followers and constitute a faction. His speeches and talk were sufficient to dissimulate his depravity and deceive the masses. His strength and obstinacy

were sufficient to go against the right and stand alone. This man, in short, was the leader of the seditious among men, and he could not but be eliminated...."

2. When Confucius [is criticized for refusing to execute a man who is unfilial, he responds:]...

"Alas! That a ruler,... falling short of the Way,... should kill his subjects [for falling short], is contrary to reason. Without educating [the people] in filial piety [and then] judge [as] criminal[s]...,—this means to kill the innocent... [I]f the ruler's teaching is not put into effect, the guilt is [with the ruler, and] not with the people. Now to be lax in giving orders... but diligent in punishment,—this means injury. Collecting taxes [outside] the proper season,—this means oppression. Without warning beforehand...to demand the completion [of tasks],—this means cruelty. [It is o]nly when a government lacks these three [evils], that punishments may be effected. In the *Documents* it is said: '[Let there be] just punishments and just executions, and do not make use of them to suit your own heart....' It means that one has to teach [first] and only then to punish..."

SECTION 3

The ruler's goodness

Confucius said: "...[Let the ruler] first establish Goodness (*jên*) within himself; only then the great-officers will be loyal, the knights dependable, the people sincere, their customs simple, the men guileless and the women chaste. [This is] where the teachings

---

1 Kongzi, *Kongzi Jiayu*; "Teachings"; excerpts (updated and adapted) from the *Kongzi Jiayu*, trans. R.P. Kramers, *K'ung Tzu Chia Yu: The School Sayings of Confucius: Introduction, Translation of Sections 1–10 with Critical Notes* by Dr. R.P. Kramers (Leiden: E.J. Brill, 1950).

lead…Stratify [them] through the rites (*li*), establish them through justice (*i*), and practice them through accommodation (*shun*), and the people will throw off wickedness as if hot water were poured on snow".…

Confucius said: "…There is still more to it. In ancient times,…[the King's officials] promoted and employed the worthy and good, and degraded…the unworthy…They had pity [and compassion.]…The people cherished [the ruler's] Virtue; those nearby gladly submitted themselves, those afar came to [show their] adherence.…

Thus it is said [that if the King] has much honesty and little simulation, his ritual rules may be maintained, his words may be repeated, his footsteps may be followed.… [That the people regard such a King as if he were next-to-them, even when he is far away] is not [because…] [they are near the *dao*] but because they see [his] enlightened Virtue (*te*). Therefore, without moving his weapons he is held in awe; without distributing goods and advantages he is held dear.… When the enlightened Kings defended [their country], they broke down the [enemy] battering-rams a thousand miles away" [because the people in the most remote parts of the kingdom cherished their King and defended him].

Tsêng-tzu [asked about the "three perfections"].…

Confucius said: "…[1] In goodness (*jen*) nothing is greater than to love others. [2]] In wisdom (*chih*) nothing is greater than to perceive the worthy. [3]] In governing nothing is greater than to give office to the able. When the rulers over territory try to acquire these three [things], then within the four seas [all] will obey their commands without fail.…"

SECTION 7

The five grades

1.…The Duke said: "May I ask what [you call] a common man?"

Confucius said: "What I call a common man…[is not] heedful of his [purpose].… Following…things as if floating along, he does not know what to grasp. This, then, is a common man."

The Duke said: "What do you call a knight?" Confucius said: "What I call a knight, in his heart he has [a {fixed} purpose]…, in his plans [he upholds principles]. Though he may not be able to penetrate to the roots of the [*dao*] and the arts, he [has] guidance [in them]…[He abides by his principles and will not swerve for] life and limbs.… This, then, is a knight."

The Duke said: "What do you call a noble man?"

Confucius said: "What I call a noble man…is always loyal and truthful, in his [speech. He has] Goodness…and justice…in his person…[His thought] is penetrating and clear…He walks in uprightness and speaks in truthfulness, and never rests from exerting himself. He is inconspicuous as if he could be surpassed, but he can never be reached. This, then, is a noble man."

The Duke said: "What do you call a [valuable] man?"

Confucius said: "What I call a [valuable] man,… his spiritual power [(virtue, *de*) is such that he stays within the moral] bounds…His words are sufficient to be taken as a law unto the world…His [*dao*] is sufficient to be felt as a transforming power by the people…When he is rich, then there will be no [hoarding] of riches…When he spreads [his mercies], then the world will not suffer from poverty. This is a [valuable man]."

The Duke said: "What do you call a sage?"

Confucius said: "What I call a sage,…his spiritual power [(*de*)]…is in harmony with Heaven and Earth.… He harmonizes the natural course of all the classes [of things]. He spreads his great [*dao*] and in consequence completes…[… all things]. His brilliance is equal—to sun and moon. His transforming activity is like [that of] the spirits.… This is called a sage".…

Book II

SECTION 8

Chi-kao

4. When Chi-kao had become judge of Wei, he...cut off a man's feet. [Then s]uddenly...in Wei [there were] the disorders of K'uai-wai. Chi-kao fled from there and ran to the gate in the outer city wall. The man with the cut-off feet guarded the gate there. He said to Chi-kao: "Over there is a gap." Chi-kao said: "A noble man does not pass through it." Again he said: "Over there is a hole." Chi-kao said: "A noble man does not pass through it." [Perhaps because it is wrong for an official to leave the city and thus his post.] Again he said: "Here is a house." Chi-kao then entered it.

When the pursuers had desisted, Chi-kao...said to the man with the cut-off feet: "I have not been able to set aside the laws of the ruler and have personally cut off your feet. Now I was in [desperate] straits, and this was just the time for you to avenge your grudge; but [instead] three times you [wished to] make me escape; why?"

The man with the cut-off feet said: "The cutting off of my feet was my fault, and nothing could be done about it. Prior to this, my lord [tried to] rectify me according to laws and decrees... [This was part of the ancient judge's role.] When the trial was decided and the crime fixed, and when it came to the moment of deciding the punishment, my lord grew pale and was not [happy]; I saw it on my lord's face, so I knew...again [that it was my fault; there was nothing that the judge could do except apply the law;] why should my lord have been partial to me? When Heaven gives birth to a noble man his [dao] certainly is so. That is why I made my lord escape."

When Confucius heard this, he said: "Good! In acting as an official, [one must apply] the law [impartially and consistently], [but] [merely] by thinking of goodness and altruism [an official] plants Virtue [(de);]...by [callously] inflicting severity and cruelty [he] plants hatred...."

The waterfall

14. When Confucius returned from Wei to Lu, he rested his horses at Ho-liang and looked at [the dam]. There was a cascade thirty jen [high] and a whirling stream ninety miles [long]. Fish and pieh turtles could not go there, yuan turtles and crocodiles could not stay in it, [but] there was a man who was just going to ford it. Confucius sent someone to go along the shore and stop him, [saying]: "In this cascade of thirty jen and this whirling stream of ninety miles fish and pieh turtles, yuan turtles and crocodiles cannot stay. I think it can hardly be forded." The man did not pay any attention to him, forded [the river] and came out.

Confucius asked him: "How skillful! You [must] have ways and arts. What is [the art] by which you can enter [this stream] and come out [of it]?"

The man answered: "When first I go in, I put sincerity and faith first, and when I come out, I still continue with sincerity and faith. With sincerity and faith I entrust my body to the waves and the stream, and I do not dare to use selfishness. That is why I am able to enter and come out again."

Confucius said to his disciples: "My children, mark this. Even with water you can, with sincerity and faith, perfect yourself and win it. How much more with man!"...

SECTION 9

Water

5. Confucius was contemplating a stream flowing eastwards. Tzu-kung asked: "Why does a noble man always contemplate a great stream whenever he sees one?" Confucius answered: "Because it never rests; also, it gives everywhere [of its power] to all living

things without [acting. I.e., it follows the principle of *wuwei*, not doing.]

"Now water resembles spiritual power [or virtue:] When it flows it tends downwards, straight or winding: it always follows the natural course. This resembles justice. It is endlessly vast and there is no time when it will [ever] be exhausted. This resembles the [*dao*]. While flowing on it runs into ravines a hundred *jen* [deep] and it is not afraid. This resembles courage. Coming to concavities it always brings them on a level [with the ground]. This resembles law. When [it fills] up [the concavities], it does not require a levelling stick. This resembles correctness. Being soft and pliable, it penetrates [into the smallest things]. This resembles scrutiny. Setting out from its source it always goes east. This resembles purpose. Coming in and out of it, all things [are cleaned, purified] thereby. This resembles the aptitude for transforming. The power [or virtue, *de*] of water has such [qualities]. Therefore [the] noble man…always contemplates it."

Remonstration

9. Tzu-kung[1] asked Confucius: "When a son obeys his father's commands, is [he not] filial? When a minister obeys his ruler's commands, is [he not] faithful?"…

Confucius said: "How stupid! Ssu, you do not understand it. Formerly, under the enlightened Kings, in [a] state of ten thousand war chariots there were seven remonstrating ministers, so the ruler had

no faults to be corrected. In a state of a thousand war chariots there were five remonstrating ministers, so the altars of the soil and the millet were not in danger. A House of a hundred war chariots had three remonstrating ministers, so its revenue and position were not discontinued. If a father has a remonstrating son, he does not fall into incorrect behavior. If a knight has a remonstrating friend, he does not act in an unjust way.

"Therefore, when a son [simply] obeys his father's commands, how [can] he be [called] filial? And when a minister [simply] obeys the commands of his ruler, how [can] he be [called] faithful? Now when you are able to reflect upon [the {commands}] which you obey, that is called filial piety, and that is called faithfulness"….

SECTION 10

Noble men

5. Tzu-lu in warrior's clothes visited Confucius. Pulling out his sword, he brandished it. He said: "The noble men of antiquity surely protected themselves with swords?"

Confucius said: "The noble men of antiquity considered loyalty their base, and Goodness their guard…. When there were bad men, then they transformed them by loyalty. When there were invaders or oppressors, they fortified themselves against them with Goodness. Why should they handle a sword?"…

---

1 Tuan-mu Ssu, Tzu-kung.

Kongzi, *the Lunyu* (論語 the *Analects*)[1]

(fifth or sixth century BCE)

Usually called the *Analects* (the "gleanings") in English, and which contains "talk and conversations" (i.e., what he said in exchanges with his students and others) compiled after his death in 479 BCE.

Book 1

3. THE MASTER SAID: Clever words and an insinuating manner seldom exist in the truly benevolent.

9. ZHENG ZI SAID: Perform the proper rites for the ancestors, and the virtue of the people will be renewed.

Book 2

1. THE MASTER SAID: A Chief Minister with virtue may be compared to the North Star, which stays in place, and which other stars follow.

3. THE MASTER SAID: Lead them by decree, threaten them with punishment, and the people will leave the path and have no shame. Lead them by virtue, order them by propriety [*li*, rites], and they will have shame and reform themselves.

4. THE MASTER SAID: At fifteen, I set my purpose on learning. At thirty, I stood firmly [in the rites]. At forty, I had no doubts. At fifty, I knew the order of Heaven. At sixty, I heard it willingly. At seventy, I could follow my heart [my feelings and thoughts] without stepping outside the square.

12. THE MASTER SAID: The *junzi* is not a tool.

17. THE MASTER SAID: Know when you know. [Know] when you do not know. That is wisdom.

Book 4

2. THE MASTER SAID: Without *ren*, a person cannot bear poverty or good fortune [without a loss of character]. A benevolent person is content with benevolence; a knowing (shrewd) person is benevolent because it is advantageous.

3. THE MASTER SAID: Only the person with *ren* can find [things to] love and hate in others.

5. THE MASTER SAID: Wealth and rank are desirable, but a man should not keep them if they compromise him morally. Poverty and obscurity are to be hated, but if a man cannot avoid them rightfully, he should accept them.

9. THE MASTER SAID: The scholar who sets his mind on the *dao* and is ashamed of bad clothing and food is not worth talking to.

10. THE MASTER SAID: The *junzi*'s position in the world is not simply for or against [i.e., he does not take sides].

11. THE MASTER SAID: The *junzi* cherishes virtue; the small man cherishes his property. The *junzi* cherishes justice; the small man cherishes profit.

---

1 Kongzi, *Lunyu*, "Sayings and Conversations." This is an original translation by Paul Groarke.

12. THE MASTER SAID: He who constantly seeks his own profit will incur animosity.

15. THE MASTER SAID: Shen! [i.e., Zeng, to whom he is speaking] My way has one thread [one string] that runs right through it.

MASTER ZENG SAID: Yes.

WHEN the Master had gone out, the disciples asked: what did he mean?

MASTER ZENG said: The Master's way is only: trying to do one's best; and reciprocity.

[The metaphor used by Kongzi refers to Chinese coins, which had a hole in the center, so that they could be carried on a string. The role of Master Zeng in this exchange is merely an attempt by his followers to promote his reputation.]

24. THE MASTER SAID: The *junzi* wishes to be slow in speech but quick in action.

Book 6

30. ZIGONG SAID: Suppose the case of a man giving plentifully to the people, and able to relieve others, what about such a person? Might he be called benevolent?

THE MASTER SAID: Why say simply that he is benevolent? Certainly he is also a sage. Even Yao and Shun [legendary leaders] were unable to do this much. Now the benevolent man, wishing to establish himself, also establishes others; wishing to advance, advances others. To be able to judge [others] by what is in yourself, this may be called the prescriptive method of benevolence.

Book 7

7. THE MASTER SAID: Whatever the voluntary payment [whether dried meat or more], I have never refused to instruct anyone [i.e., because he would not pay].
[Dried meat—jerky—was a trivial form of payment in ancient China.]

8. THE MASTER SAID: [If a student is] not eager, [I do] not explain. Not speak, not help. [If I] hold up one corner, [and he does] not return [the other] three, not repeat.

12. THE MASTER SAID: If it was [morally permissible to devote oneself exclusively to the search for wealth]; even if I had to hold a whip for a gentleman [i.e., become a groom], I would do it. Since it is not morally permissible, I shall follow my own interests.

21. THE MASTER did not talk of ghost stories, feats of strength, public disturbances, or spirits.
[This is in contrast to the Masters in competing schools, who taught students about these matters.]

22. THE MASTER SAID: Even with three of us, strolling, I can learn. I learn to follow the good in them, avoid the bad.

25. THE MASTER taught four things: letters [arts] and ethics [proper conduct], devotion [sincerity in doing, which was associated with loyalty], and truthfulness.

27. FISHING, the Master did not use a net. Hunting, he did not shoot at nesting birds.

35. WHEN THE MASTER was gravely ill, Zilu asked leave to offer prayers for him.

THE MASTER SAID: Is this done?

ZILU REPLIED: It is. The Eulogies says: pray to the gods above and below.

THE MASTER SAID: My prayer began long ago.

[Kongzi sees the attempt to live a virtuous life (to follow the *dao*) as a prayer.]

Book 8

9. THE MASTER SAID: The people can be made to follow the *dao*; they cannot be made to know it.

10. THE MASTER SAID: A brave man who suffers poverty will be a source of disorder.

13. THE MASTER SAID: When the country respects the *dao*, be seen. When it is disordered, stay concealed. It is shameful to be poor and of low rank when the *dao* prevails, but it is shameful to be wealthy and of high rank when it does not.

Book 11

24. JI ZIRAN ASKED WHETHER Zhong You and Ran Qiu [ministers who served the Ji clan rather than the ruler] could be called great ministers.

THE MASTER SAID: I thought you would ask about some extraordinary individuals, and you only ask about You and Qiu! A great minister follows the *dao* [right principles] in serving his lord, and when he cannot, he leaves office. Now as to You and Qiu, they may be considered ordinary ministers.

JI ZIRAN ASKED: Then they will always follow the orders of their superiors?

THE MASTER SAID: To kill their own fathers and kill the ruler—no, they would not follow orders, no!

[The final sentence refers to the specific possibility that the Ji clan may be planning to assassinate the ruler, the Duke of Lu.]

Book 12

1. YAN YUAN ASKED ABOUT *ren* [benevolence, also translated as goodness or humanity].

THE MASTER SAID: To restrain one's self and return to propriety [*li*, the rites] is benevolence. If you can for one day restrain yourself and observe the proprieties, all under heaven will return to *ren* [benevolence]. However, the conduct of benevolence comes from oneself, not from others.

YAN YUAN SAID: May I ask you for details?

THE MASTER REPLIED: [If it is an impropriety, literally not *li*,] do not look. Improper, do not listen. Improper, do not say. Improper, do not touch.

YAN YUAN SAID: Although I am not clever, I ask to work on this.

5. SIMA NIU grieved, saying: Alas! Everyone else has younger and older brothers. I alone have none!

ZIXIA SAID: I have heard the saying 'Death and life are fate, wealth and rank depend on Heaven.' If a *junzi* is attentive and not negligent, if he behaves with courtesy to others and observes propriety, then all within the Four Seas are his brothers. How, then, can the superior man grieve that he is without brothers?

7. ZIGONG asked about governing.

THE MASTER SAID: Enough food, enough weapons, trust in the government.

ZIGONG SAID: If there is no choice but to give up one, which of the three must be put aside?

THE MASTER SAID: Put aside the weapons.

ZIGONG SAID: If there is no choice but to give up one, which of the two must be put aside?

THE MASTER SAID: Put aside food. From old, death has been the lot of men. But without trust the state will not survive.

19. JI KANGZI asked Kongzi about government, saying: What about killing those who have left the *dao*, for the sake of those who follow it?

KONGZI ANSWERED: Sir, in governing, why must you kill? Let it be shown that you desire what is morally good, and the people will be morally good. A *junzi*'s virtue is like the wind. Small men are like the [tall] grasses. Grass below the wind will bend.

22. THE MASTER SAID: Raise the straight [the upright] above the crooked. This will make the crooked straight.

Book 13

6. THE MASTER SAID: If a person is [morally] upright, he will act properly, even without orders. If a person is not upright, even with orders, he will not comply.

9. WHEN the Master went to Wei, Ran You drove him.

THE MASTER SAID: So many people!

RAN YOU SAID: Since they are already so many, what can be added?

THE MASTER SAID: Enrich them.

RAN YOU SAID: Since they are already rich, what can be added?

THE MASTER SAID: Teach them.

18. THE DUKE OF SHE SAID TO KONGZI: In my country there is an upright man. His father stole a sheep and he testified against him.

KONGZI SAID: In my country, the upright are different. A father will conceal his son, a son a father. There is a kind of uprightness here, too.

Book 15

17. THE MASTER SAID: Those who would spend all day demonstrating how clever they are without ever touching on the subject of morality are difficult to teach.

18. THE MASTER SAID: The *junzi* is fundamentally moral. He puts this into practice... [modestly, by following the rites] completes it by being true to his word.

19. THE MASTER SAID: The *junzi* is troubled by his own lack of ability, not by the failure of others to acknowledge him.

21. THE MASTER SAID: What the *junzi* seeks, he seeks within himself; what the small man seeks, he seeks in others.

24. ZIGONG asked: Is there one saying that one can act upon all day and every day?

THE MASTER SAID: It is *shu* [reciprocity]. What you do not want done to you, do not do to others.[1]

36. THE MASTER SAID: In benevolence [goodness, humanity], do not yield, even to one's teacher.

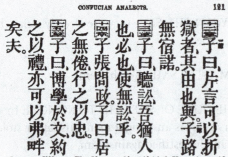

A sample page from the first edition of James Legge's *Chinese Classics* (1861), which contains the most influential translation of the *Lunyu* in English. The excerpt is from Book XII. Students might note that the Chinese is read from right to left and up to down.

Questions

1. There is a strong element of Daoism in Confucian thought. What is new in Kongzi? What does he take from the earlier tradition?

2. Discuss the qualities of a sage, referring to Laozi and/or Kongzi. Who would you call a sage, and why?

3. It has been suggested that Confucianism is like "virtue ethics" in the Western tradition,

---

1   This is a version of the so-called "Silver Rule," the negative version of the Golden Rule, "Do onto others as you would have them do onto you."

which is discussed in chapter 13. Do you think Kongzi's moral and political ideas can be applied successfully in Western society. Why, why not?

4. Kongzi believed that virtue lies in following *li*, the rites, moral and religious protocols which were well developed among the ancient Chinese. Do you agree? Can you think of any customs in contemporary society that might qualify as rites?

5. What is *ren*? Describe the *junzi*, who has *ren* and whose conduct is in accordance with the *Dao*.

6. In spite of his aversion to killing, Kongzi felt that execution was necessary in certain circumstances. Why? What should be done in the case mentioned in the reading?

7. Kongzi believes that the chief requirement of a successful ruler is personal virtue. Discuss, with reference to the readings.

8. The classical Chinese tradition is openly patriarchal. What are the limits on filial piety? What if your father wants to do something wrong?

Suggested Readings

All of the English translations of the *Lunyu* are over-precise and fail to catch the bluntness of the Chinese. This raises hermeneutical issues. The friendliest translation for students is probably the bilingual interface at ctext.org, which uses James Legge's 1861 translation. Although every translation raises questions, *The Analects of Confucius: A Philosophical Translation*, translated by Roger Ames and Henry Rosemont Jr., includes a helpful introduction and recent corrections to the text. Philip Ivanhoe's *Confucian Moral Self Cultivation* (2000) provides a convenient introduction to the Confucian tradition. The Routledge *Encyclopedia of Chinese Philosophy* has twenty entries on Confucianism, including articles on Confucian ethics and the tradition outside China.

There is an extensive comparative literature on Confucianism. Philosophers such as May Sim (*Remastering Morals with Aristotle and Confucius*), Yu Jiyuan (*The Ethics of Confucius and Aristotle*), and Bryan Van Norden (*Virtue Ethics and Consequentialism in Early Chinese Philosophy*) have stressed that both Confucianism and virtue ethics rely upon example and practice. Others, like Alasdair MacIntyre ("Once More on Confucian and Aristotelian Conceptions of the Virtues," 2004), have argued that Confucianism is culturally *sui generis*. See Van Norden's helpful review of Sim's *Remastering Morals* in *Dao* (2009) 8:109–11. See also Richard N. Stichler, "Interpreting the Zhongyong: Was Confucius a Sophist or an Aristotelian?" (2004).

Chapter 7

Mencius

Mengzi (孟子, 371–289 BCE), also known as Mèng zǐ, "Master Meng" is very often called Mencius in English; this again is a seventeenth-century Latin version of his Chinese name. Mencius was born in the kingdom of Zhou (Zou) and supposedly studied under Zisi, the grandson of Confucius. This may have been said to establish his scholarly credibility, since he claimed explicitly to be a follower of the school. He has commonly been called the "Second Sage" (after Confucius) by the Confucians.

We know little about the details of Mencius's life. He apparently became a teacher and a minister in the State of Qi, a scholar-official, who may have been associated with the Jixia Academy, which formulated and proposed policy for the government. Mencius also traveled extensively, like Confucius and many other itinerant scholars (called *shi*), offering his advice and counsel to the princes in various states. The *shi* were usually men of noble origins, who retained a deep knowledge of etiquette and protocol—Confucius's *li*, or "rites"—and served as professional administrators in the retinue of local rulers. They were also historians.

Mencius lived during the Warring States period, when the Chinese social and political order finally collapsed in chaos, warfare, and devastation. The decline of the Zhou Dynasty eroded the authority of the central government, allowing lesser states and principalities to vie with each other for power. To the thinkers of the time, these struggles suggested that the Zhou rulers had lost the mandate of heaven. This loss was attributed to a more general loss of virtue, which Laozi and Confucius, before Mencius, had already lamented.

The pressing question for Mencius and other Confucians was how to retrieve the old order and recover the stability of the past. In the thinking of the time, this was a matter of rediscovering the *Dao*, which needed to be restored. Like Plato, and like other scholars of his time, Mencius believed that the existing order could be redeemed and hoped to find a ruler who would put his moral and political theories into practice. The realities of the time were against him, however, and he eventually despaired of political reform, withdrawing into private life.

Mencius's teachings have been preserved in the *Mengzi*, or *Mencius*, a collection of exchanges probably compiled by Mencius and his students, and then edited, augmented, and rearranged after his death. The standard edition was edited and abridged by Zhao

Qi, who added commentary, several centuries later. The *Mengzi* became one of the "Four Books" in the Confucian canon and is regarded as a definitive source of doctrine. It provides us with a more developed moral theory than we find in the relatively scattered exchanges in the *Lunyu* and is more reminiscent of the *K'ung Tzu Chia Yu*.

The text of the *Mengzi* contains conversations between the philosopher and various rulers, with sustained philosophical arguments. The Warring States Period was a time of intellectual ferment, and in the book, Mencius is competing with a number of other moral philosophers. His two most influential opponents were Mozi and Yang Zhu. Mozi was a social reformer and radical who preached "universal love" and therefore neglected filial piety. Yang Zhu, on the other hand, adopted a liberal interpretation of the *Dao* that justified a narrow self-interest. Mencius rejects the position of both philosophers and complains in the reading that "profit" is not a legitimate criterion in the ethical analysis.

Mencius is often called a moral "idealist," though the word is used in a popular rather than a philosophical sense in this context. The term merely indicates that he believes it is possible for people to become better and more virtuous. Historically, it is evident that the moral concept of the *Dao* narrowed over time, and by the time of Mencius, it refers principally to the cultivation of personal virtue. The idea of the *Dao* nevertheless retains its social and cosmological significance.

There is, in spite of this idealism, a pragmatic side to Mencius's ethics, which can be seen in his political realism. Thus, his theory of benevolent government includes an implicit right of revolution. A ruler who does not respect the principle of reciprocity in his dealings with the people is no longer *wangdao*, i.e., he is not following the "way of the virtuous king" and is therefore no longer a legitimate ruler. Thus the killing of Zou, the last king of the Shang, was not regicide—the killing of a king—since Zou had lost the mandate of heaven and was no longer a legitimate ruler. It is notable that western philosophers like Aquinas have taken much the same position.

The so-called "idealism" in Mencius's theory is more a matter of optimism, which can be traced to the ancient Chinese idea that human beings are innately good. It follows that acting ethically is ultimately a matter of acting in accordance with our natures. This idea explains why sincerity is the sign of the sage. It is by introspection, by reflecting on one's feelings and experiences that one comes to know, not merely one's nature, but also heaven. This is similar to the Stoic conceptual parallel between microcosm and macrocosm. Looking into ourselves, we find the universe.

Although Mencius's concept of human nature, *renxing*, includes our natural appetites, it is nonetheless a moral concept. The character for *renxing*, 人性, is a pictograph that depicts a person whose heart is "alive." This reflects the ancient Chinese belief that the heart is the seat of thinking as well as feeling. As a result, Mencius locates moral understanding in the heart, *xin* (心), sometimes called the "heart-mind," which harbors ethical feelings. It is our ethical discrimination, which includes our instinctive empathy for all things, that makes us human.

Mencius argues that, just as the body has four external limbs, the mind-heart possesses four beginnings or "sprouts of virtue." Under proper moral guidance, these sprouts grow into the four most important Confucian virtues: an innate sense of sympathy produces *ren*

(仁); *yi* (易), a feeling of shame produces moral rightness; *li* (禮), the rites; and *zhi* (智), the moral and practical wisdom that derives ultimately from our capacity to distinguish between right and wrong.

The main point, however, is that the moral sensitivities that reside within every human heart can be developed, through education and training, into a stable, virtuous character. This is a matter of habit. The assiduous individual may become a *junzi*, and in the ultimate self-realization, a sage. This has been described by many philosophers as a kind of virtue ethics. There is a psychological and even physiological side to Mencius's view. Mencius's ethical practices extend to quasi-mystical disciplines such as meditation. The heart-mind, *xin*, can be developed and must undergo training, at its highest level, to produce "the flood-like *qi* (*chi*)," which characterizes the morally enlightened and, ultimately, the sage.

The figure of the sage is prominent in Mencius. This is probably because the sage has the power to transform the world. Mencius lived in desperate times and felt literally that society could only be redeemed by a savior. At the end of the *Mengzi*, he asks plaintively: "Where is the sage? Where is he?" It is notable, however, that the figure of the sage has become a moral rather than a political exemplar—Confucius has become a sage. This view might be extended, outside the classical Chinese tradition, to religious figures like the Buddha and Jesus Christ.

The reading from the *Mengzi* is an original translation guided by James Legge's translation, which is the standard English translation, and includes passages on benevolent government and the art of ruling, which were central to his teaching, along with some of his characteristic comments on justice, sage-hood, and our moral nature.

Mencius, *The Mengzi* (孟子)[1]

(371–289 BCE)

Book 1, Part 1

CHAPTER 2

1. Mencius, another day, saw King Hûi of Liang. The king went and stood with him by a pond, and, looking round at the large geese and deer, said: "Do wise and good princes also find pleasure in these things?"

2. Mencius replied: "Being wise and good, they have pleasure in these things. If they are not wise and good, though they have these things, they do not find pleasure."

CHAPTER 4

1. King Hui of Liang said: "I wish quietly to receive your instructions."

---

1 This is an original translation by Paul Groarke.

2. Mencius replied: "Is there any difference between killing a man with a stick and with a sword?" The king said: "There is no difference!"

3. "Is there any difference between doing it with a sword and with the style of government?" "There is no difference," was the reply.

4. Mencius then said: "In your kitchen there is fat meat; in your stables there are fat horses. But your people have the look of hunger, and in the wilderness there are the bodies of those who have died of famine. This is leading the wild animals to devour the bodies of the people.

5. "The wild animals devour one another, and men hate them for doing so. When a prince, being the parent of his people, administers his government in a way that leads the wild animals to devour the bodies of the people, in what sense can he be said to be the parent of the people?"

Book 1, Part 2

CHAPTER 8

1. King Hsuan of Chi asked Mencius: "Was it so, that Tang banished Chieh, and that King Wu smote Chau?"[1] Mencius replied: "The records say so."

2. The King said: "May a minister then put his sovereign to death?"

3. Mencius said: "He who outrages the benevolence proper to his nature, is called a robber; he who outrages righteousness, is called a ruffian. The robber and ruffian we call a mere fellow. I have heard that they cut the head off that fellow Chau, but I have not heard that it was putting the sovereign to death."

---

1 I.e., wicked rulers.

CHAPTER 12

1. There had been a brush between Tsau and Lu, when the duke Mu asked Mencius, saying, "Of my officers there were killed thirty-three men, and none of the people would die in their defense. Though I sentenced them to death for their conduct, it is impossible to put such a multitude to death. If I do not put them to death, then there is the crime unpunished of their looking angrily on at the death of their officers, and not saving them. How are the needs of this case to be met?"

2. Mencius replied: "In calamitous years and years of famine, the old and weak of your people, who have been found lying in the ditches and water-channels, and the able-bodied who have been scattered about to the four quarters, have amounted to several thousands. All the while, your granaries, O prince, have been stored with grain, and your treasuries and arsenals have been full, and not one of your officers has told you of the distress. Thus negligent have the superiors in your State been, and cruel to their inferiors. The philosopher Tsang said: 'Beware, beware. What proceeds from you, will return to you again.' Now at length the people have paid back the conduct of their officers to them. Do not you, O prince, blame them.

3. If you will put in practice a benevolent government, this people will love you and all above them, and will die for their officers."

Book 2, Part 1

CHAPTER 3

2. When one by force subdues men, they do not submit to him in heart. They submit, because their strength is not adequate to resist. When one subdues men by virtue, in their heart's core they are

pleased, and sincerely submit, as was the case with the seventy disciples in their submission to Confucius. What is said in the Book of Poetry,

> From the west, from the east,
> From the south, from the north,
> There was not one who thought of refusing
> submission,

is an illustration of this.

CHAPTER 6

1. Mencius said: "All men have a mind which cannot bear to see the sufferings of others."

2. The ancient kings had this commiserating mind, and they, as a matter of course, had likewise a commiserating government. When with a commiserating mind was practiced a commiserating government, to rule the kingdom was as easy a matter as to make anything go round in the palm.

3. When I say that all men have a mind which cannot bear to see the sufferings of others, my meaning may be illustrated thus: even nowadays, if men suddenly see a child about to fall into a well, they will without exception experience a feeling of alarm and distress. They will feel so, not as a ground on which they may gain the favor of the child's parents, nor as a ground on which they may seek the praise of their neighbors and friends, nor from a dislike to the reputation of having been unmoved by such a thing.

4. From this case we may perceive that the feeling of commiseration is essential to man, that the feeling of shame and dislike is essential to man, that the feeling of modesty and complaisance is essential to man, and that the feeling of approving and disapproving is essential to man.

5. The feeling of commiseration is the principle of benevolence. The feeling of shame and dislike is the principle of righteousness. The feeling of modesty and complaisance is the principle of propriety. The feeling of approving and disapproving is the principle of knowledge.

6. All men have these four principles just as they have their four limbs. When men, having these four principles, yet say of themselves that they cannot develop them, they play the thief with themselves, and he who says of his prince that he cannot develop them plays the thief with his prince.

CHAPTER 7

1. Mencius said: "...Now, benevolence is the most honorable dignity conferred by Heaven, and the quiet home in which man should dwell. Since no one can hinder us from being so, if yet we are not benevolent;—this is being not wise.

3. "From the want of benevolence and the want of wisdom will ensue the entire absence of propriety and righteousness—

5. "The man who would be benevolent is like the archer. The archer adjusts himself and then shoots. If he misses, he does not murmur against those who surpass himself. He simply turns round and seeks the cause of his failure in himself."

Book 4, Part 1

CHAPTER 9

1. Mencius said: "Chieh and Chaus[1] lost the throne because they lost the people, and to lose the people means to lose their hearts. There is a way to get the

---

1 Both were famously wicked rulers.

kingdom: get the people, and the kingdom is got. There is a way to get the people: get their hearts, and the people are got. There is a way to get their hearts: it is simply to collect for them what they like, and not to lay burdens on them that they dislike.

2. "The people turn to a benevolent rule as water flows downwards, and as wild beasts fly to the wilderness.

3. "Accordingly, as the otter aids the deep waters, by driving the fish into them, and the hawk aids the thickets, by driving the little birds to them, so these wicked rulers aided Tang and Wu,[1] driving the people to them.

4. "If among the present rulers of the kingdom, there were one who loved benevolence, all the other princes would aid him, by driving the people to him. Although he wished not to become sovereign, he could not avoid becoming so."

CHAPTER 12

2. Sincerity is the way of Heaven. To think how to be sincere is the way of man.

3. Never has there been one possessed of complete sincerity, who did not move others. Never has there been one who had not sincerity who was able to move others.

CHAPTER 17

1. Shun-yu Kwan said: "Is it the rule that males and females shall not allow their hands to touch in giving or receiving anything?" Mencius replied: "It is the rule." Kwan asked, "If a man's sister-in-law be drowning, shall he rescue her with his hand?" Men-

cius said: "He who would not stretch out his hand to a drowning woman is a wolf."[2]

CHAPTER 18

2. Mencius said: "The circumstances of the case forbid a father from teaching his son. This is because the teacher must inculcate what is correct. When he inculcates what is correct, and his lessons are not practiced, he follows them up with being angry. When he follows them up with being angry, then, contrary to what should be, he is offended with his son.

3. "The ancients exchanged sons, and one taught the son of another.

4. "Between father and son, there should be no reproving admonitions to what is good. Such reproofs lead to alienation, and there is nothing more inauspicious than alienation."

Book 4, Part 2

CHAPTER 5

Mencius said: "If the sovereign is benevolent, all will be benevolent. If the sovereign is righteous, all will be righteous."

CHAPTER 11

Mencius said: "The great man does not plan [how he is going to speak and act, so that he appears sincere and resolute]—he simply speaks and does what is right."

---

1 Both were good rulers.
2 I.e., the enemy of man.

CHAPTER 12

Mencius said: "The great man is he who does not lose his child's-heart."

CHAPTER 24

2. The people of Chang sent Tsze-cho Yu to make a stealthy attack on Wei, which sent Yu-kung Sze to pursue him. Tsze-cho Yu said: "Today I feel unwell, so that I cannot hold my bow. I am a dead man!"

At the same time he asked his driver, "Who is it that is pursuing me?" The driver said: "It is Yu-kung Sze," on which he exclaimed, "I shall live!" The driver said: "Yu-kung Sze is the best archer of Wei, why do you say I shall live?" Yu replied: "Yu-kung Sze learned archery from Yin-kung To, who learned it from me. Now, Yin-kung To is an upright man, and [those he chose to teach must be upright]."

When Yu-kung Sze came up, he said: "Master, why are you not holding your bow?" Yu answered him, "Today I am feeling unwell and cannot hold my bow." On this Sze said: "I learned archery from Yin-kung To, who learned it from you. I cannot bear to injure you with your own science. The business of today, however, is the prince's business, which I dare not neglect." He then took his arrows, knocked off their steel points against the carriage-wheel, discharged four of them, and returned.

Book 5, Part 2: Wan Chang

CHAPTER 3

1. Wan Chang asked Mencius, saying, "I venture to ask the principles of friendship." Mencius replied: "Friendship should be maintained without any presumption on the ground of one's superior age, or station, or the circumstances of his relatives. Friendship with a man is friendship with his virtue, and does not admit of assumptions of superiority.

2. "Mang Hsien was the chief of a family with a hundred chariots. He had five friends. With those five men Hsien maintained a friendship, because they thought nothing of his family's wealth. If they had thought about his family's wealth, he would not have maintained his friendship with them."

CHAPTER 8

1. Mencius said to Wan Chang: "The scholar whose virtue is most distinguished in a village shall make friends of all the virtuous scholars in the village. The scholar whose virtue is most distinguished throughout a State shall make friends of all the virtuous scholars of that State. The scholar whose virtue is most distinguished throughout the kingdom shall make friends of all the virtuous scholars of the kingdom.

2. "When a scholar feels that his friendship with all the virtuous scholars of the kingdom is not sufficient to satisfy him, he proceeds to ascend to consider the men of antiquity. He repeats their poems, and reads their books, and as he does not know what they were as men, to ascertain this, he considers their history. This is to ascend and make friends of the men of antiquity."

Book 6, Part 1

CHAPTER 7

2. Mencius said: "Consider barley—Let it be sown and covered up; the ground being the same, and the time of sowing likewise the same, it grows rapidly up, and, when the full time is come, it is all found to be ripe. Although there may be inequalities of produce, that is owing to the difference of the soil, as rich or poor, to the unequal nourishment afforded by the rains and dews, and to the different ways in which man has performed his business in reference to it.

3. "Thus all things which are the same in kind are like to one another;—and why should we doubt this, in regard to the nature of man, as if he were a solitary exception to this? The sage and [the rest of us] are the same in kind...

8. "What is it then of which [we all] approve? I say that it is the principles of our nature, and the determinations of righteousness. The sages merely apprehended before me that which my mind already approves, along with other men. Therefore, their determinations of righteousness are agreeable to my mind, [just as they are to other people]..."

CHAPTER 10

1. Mencius said: "I like fish, and I also like bears paws. If I cannot have the two together, I will let the fish go, and take the bears paws. So, I like life, and I also like righteousness. If I cannot keep the two together, I will let life go, and choose righteousness.

2. "I like life indeed, but there is that which I like more than life, and therefore, I will not seek to possess it by any improper ways. I dislike death indeed, but there is that which I dislike more than death, and therefore there are occasions when I will not avoid danger....

5. "[This is true of all men.]

6. "Imagine a small basket of rice and a platter of soup, and a case in which the getting them will preserve life, and the want of them will be death;—if they are offered with an insulting voice, even a tramp will reject them; if you walk on them, even a beggar will refuse them."

CHAPTER 18

1. Mencius said: "Benevolence subdues its opposite just as water subdues fire. But those who practice benevolence these days do it [meanly, without gen-

erosity,] as if they could extinguish a whole wagon-load of fuel which was on fire with one cup of water. And when the flames are not extinguished, they say that water cannot subdue fire. This conduct merely encourages those who are not benevolent."

Book 6, Part 2

CHAPTER 2

Mencius said: "The way of truth is like a great road. It is not difficult to know it. The evil is only that men will not seek it."

CHAPTER 4

1. Sung Kang being about to go to Chû, Mencius met him in Shih-chiû.

2. "Master, where are you going?" asked Mencius.

3. Kang replied: "I have heard that Chin and Chu are fighting together, and I am going to [try and persuade the kings of Chu and Chin] to cease hostilities..."

4. Mencius said: "I will not venture to ask about the particulars, but I should like to hear [how you will] try to persuade them?" Kang answered, "I will tell them how unprofitable their course is to them." "Master," said Mencius, "your aim is great, but your argument is not good.

5. "If you, starting from the point of profit, [convince the kings] to stop the movements of their armies, then all belonging to those armies will rejoice in the cessation of war, and find their pleasure in the pursuit of profit. Ministers will serve their sovereign for the profit of which they cherish the thought; [and the same will be true of father and sons and brothers]:—and the issue will be, that,

abandoning benevolence and righteousness, sovereign and minister, father and son, younger brother and elder, will carry on all their intercourse with this thought of profit cherished in their breasts. But never has there been such a state of society, without ruin being the result of it.

6. "[If, on the other hand, you start] from the ground of benevolence and righteousness, offer your counsels to the kings of Chin and Chu, and if those kings are pleased with the consideration of benevolence and righteousness so as to stop the operations of their armies, then all belonging to those armies will rejoice in the stopping from war, and find their pleasure in benevolence and righteousness. Ministers will serve their sovereign, cherishing the principles of benevolence and righteousness; sons will serve their fathers, and younger brothers will serve their elder brothers, in the same way:—and so, sovereign and minister, father and son, elder brother and younger, abandoning the thought of profit, will cherish the principles of benevolence and righteousness, and carry on all their intercourse upon them. But never has there been such a state of society, without the State where it prevailed rising to the royal sway. Why must you use that word 'profit'?"

Book 7, Part 1

CHAPTER 3

Virtue is sure to be found if we seek it, unlike riches and external things.

CHAPTER 5

Mencius said: "To act without understanding, and to do so habitually, without examination, pursuing the proper path of life without knowing its nature;—this is the way of the multitudes."

CHAPTER 7

1. Mencius said: "The sense of shame is of great importance.

2. "Those who are skilled in devising the most artful political strategies do not allow their sense of shame to come into action."

3. "Now when someone distinguishes himself in this way, and loses his sense of shame, how can he be said to be one of us?"

CHAPTER 13

1. Mencius said: "Under a true sovereign, the people have an air of deep contentment....

3. "Wherever the superior man passes through, transformation follows; wherever he abides, he has a spiritual influence. His influence flows abroad, above and beneath, like [water, like the spiritual powers] of Heaven and Earth."

CHAPTER 24

1. Mencius said: "Confucius ascended the eastern hill, and Lu appeared to him small. He ascended the Tai mountain, and all beneath the heavens appeared to him small. So he who has contemplated the sea, finds it difficult to think anything of other waters, and he who has entered the gate of the sage [and heard his words], finds it difficult to think anything of the words of others."

CHAPTER 26

1. Mencius said: "The principle of the philosopher Yang was 'Each one for himself.' Though he might have benefited the whole kingdom by plucking out a single hair, he would not have done it.

2. "The philosopher Mo loves all equally. If by rubbing all of the hair off his body from the crown to the heel, he could have benefited the kingdom, he would have done it.

3. "Tsze-mo holds a medium between these. By holding the mean, he is nearer the right. But by holding it without leaving room for the exigencies that may arise in circumstances, he is like them in holding to one point.[1]

4. "The reason why I hate holding to one point is the injury it does to [other principles, which may intervene in a particular case, and dictate a different position.] It takes up one point and disregards a hundred others."

CHAPTER 37

1. Mencius said: "To feed a scholar and not love him is to treat him as a pig. To love him and not respect him is to keep him as a domestic animal.

2. "Honoring and respecting must exist before any offering of gifts.

3. "If there be the show of honoring and respecting without the reality of them, a superior man is not bound by such empty demonstrations."

Book 7, Part 2

CHAPTER 15

Mencius said: "A sage is the teacher of a hundred generations:—this is true of Po-i and Hui of Liu-Hisa. Therefore, when men now hear about the character of Po-i, the corrupt become pure, and the weak acquire determination. When they hear about the character of Hui of Liu-Hsia, the mean become generous, and the niggardly become liberal. Those two made themselves distinguished a hundred generations ago, and after a hundred generations, those who hear of them, are all moved in this manner. Could they have such an effect upon people, if they had not been sages?"

CHAPTER 25

1. Ha-shang Pu-hai asked, saying, "What sort of man is Yo-chang?" Mencius replied: "He is a good man, a true man."

2. What do you mean by "A good man," "A true man?"

3. The reply was,

1. A man that we approve is what is called a good man.

2. He whose goodness is part of himself is called a true man.

3. He whose goodness has been filled up is called beautiful man.

4. He whose completed goodness is brightly displayed is what is called a great man.

5. When this great man exercises a transforming influence, he is called a sage.

6. When the sage is beyond our knowledge, he is called a spirit-man.

CHAPTER 32

3. The disease of men is this: firstly, that they neglect their own fields,[2] and go to weed the fields of others;[3] and secondly, that what they require from others is great, while what they lay upon themselves is light.

---

1 I.e., being too rigid.

2 I.e., their own character.

3 I.e., criticize the character of others.

CHAPTER 35

Mencius said: "To nourish the mind there is nothing better than to make the desires few. Here is a man whose desires are few: in some things he may not be able to keep his heart, but they will be few. Here is a man whose desires are many: in some things he may be able to keep his heart, but they will be few."

CHAPTER 37

11. Mencius said: "If you wish to criticize [the respectable men in the village], you find nothing to criticize. It is because they agree with the current customs. They consent [to the views of] an impure age. As a result, their principles have the appearance of right-heartedness and truth. Their conduct has the appearance of disinterestedness and purity. All men are pleased with them, and they think themselves right, so it is impossible to teach them the principles of the sages. On this account they are called 'The thieves of virtue.'"

12. Confucius said: "I hate the appearance which is not the reality. I hate the darnel, lest it be mistaken for the corn. I hate glib-tonguedness, lest it be mistaken for righteousness. I hate sharpness of tongue, lest it be mistaken for sincerity. I hate your good careful men of the villages, lest they be mistaken for the truly virtuous."

Questions

1. Compare one of Mencius's teachings about what virtue consists in with one from Laozi or Confucius in the Chinese tradition; or with one of the Buddhist teachings on virtue.
2. The idea that feelings and thoughts reside in the heart gave classical Chinese philosophy a different orientation than Western philosophy, which tends to separate ideas and feelings. The western position is arguably a mistake. Discuss.
3. Mencius holds that the distinguishing characteristic of humanity is *ren*, which James has been translated as 'benevolence.' Even the worst among us have it. Do you agree with Mencius? Are we born good, and then deviate? Or not? Provide examples, and justify your position.
4. The Confucians believed that the success of government lies in the moral character of the ruler. Why does Mencius think that oppression never succeeds in the long term? Is he right?
5. Mencius says that the sage is the teacher of a hundred generations. What distinguishes the sage's teaching? Who, outside the Chinese tradition, would you consider a sage? Why?
6. Mencius suggests that the inner life of the sage essentially merges with the *Dao* and the rules of propriety. Discuss the significance of this claim.
7. How does the principle of exigency operate? Provide examples.
8. The Chinese moral tradition rests on correction. Scholars and ministers, sons and brothers, should "remonstrate" with those who act without virtue. How important is this in morality?

Suggested Readings

The Chinese Text Project uses Legge's 1895 (Oxford) translation of the *Mengzi*. For a recent translation of the more celebrated passages, along with an introduction, a bibliography, and a translation of the historical commentary by Zhu Xi (1130–1200), see Bryan Van Norden, *Essential Mengzi* (2009).

For general sources, see Kwang-loi Shung, *Mencius and Early Chinese Thought* (1997); Liu Xiusheng and Philip J. Ivanhoe, eds., *Essays on Mencius' Moral Philosophy* (2002); and Alan K.L. Chan, ed., *Mencius: Contexts and Interpretations* (2002). In "The Natural Law Philosophy of Mencius" (1957), Paul Sih draws attention to the ascendancy of the law over politics in the Confucian tradition. Lee H. Yearley makes the conventional connection between virtue ethics and Confucianism in *Mencius and Aquinas: Theories of Virtue and Conceptions of Courage* (1990). James Ryan disputes this connection and surveys the academic literature in "A Moral Philosophy and Moral Psychology in Mencius" (1998). In an interesting twist, Jung Lee explores the idea of moral exemplars in "The Moral Power of Jim: A Mencian Reading of *Huckleberry Finn*" (2009). Cecilia Wee argues that the Confucian position can be expanded to include the relations between human beings and the natural world in "Mencius and the Natural Environment" (2009).

Chapter 8

Buddhism

Siddhartha Gautama (also Gotama; fifth century BCE; but his dates are disputed), known as the Buddha, was the son of an Indian king. He was born in what is now Nepal, and traveled and taught throughout eastern India. A mystic and a prophet rather than a philosopher, he taught a way of life, relying on his own spiritual experience. He has been variously considered as a manifestation of the divinity, a spiritual leader, a saint, and a sage.

The traditional stories about Siddhartha's life have come down to us essentially as parables. Since it had been prophesied that he would become the Buddha, and had an inclination for meditation, his father surrounded him with pleasures to try and dissuade him from entering a religious life. In spite of this, on three successive days, when he was (c.) twenty-nine, he saw an old man, a sick man, and a corpse, and thus learned that all men must suffer and die. On the fourth day he saw an ascetic and understood that the way of overcoming suffering was to give up worldly pleasures.

The next day, it is said, Gautama left his kingdom, his wife, and newborn son, in search of the path that leads to the cessation of suffering. For the next six years, he lived the life of an ascetic, studying, fasting, and meditating, but was never fully satisfied. Finally, on the point of starvation, he realized that extreme physical deprivations do not provide the path to enlightenment, symbolically accepting a bowl of rice gruel from a herdswoman. He then followed a "middle" practice that avoided such extremes.

When Siddhartha was (c.) thirty-five, he made himself a seat of "auspicious grass" under a pippala tree, later called the "Bodhi" tree, and meditated for forty-nine days, attaining *Bohdi*, supreme or complete enlightenment. The term 'Buddha' refers to one who has attained *Bodhi*, the highest state of intellectual and ethical perfection that can be achieved through human means. The term 'Buddha' means 'Enlightened' or 'Awakened' one, someone who knows, and refers to someone who is beyond suffering.

After his enlightenment, the Buddha devoted himself to teaching the *Dhamma* (*Dharma*), up until his death at eighty years of age. In the current context, this consisted of the Middle Path or "Way," the way of right conduct, which leads to enlightenment, but also provides a practical code for living an ethical life. There are affinities with the concept of *Dao* here, which have not been recognized in the literature. The theology of Buddhism has a complicated history. The Buddha nevertheless saw religion as a pragmatic solution to the problem of human suffering and death. He emphasized experience over doctrine.

The metaphysics of Buddhism also includes a "middle path" between the view that things exist and the view that things do not exist. Reality is a kind of illusion or projection, which has no hold on someone who sees it accurately. We are released from suffering by developing an awareness of reality (mindfulness), which sees reality as it is, and is called developing the Right View. The immediate cause of our suffering arises from our attachment to an illusory self, which is only a happenstance bundle of different, changing things. The Buddhist who attains enlightenment dissolves this ephemeral self (thus disbanding the compounded), and enters into ultimate emptiness. This results in nirvana, a state of peaceful annihilation that frees the soul from the effects of karma and from bodily existence.

The content of the Buddha's teaching has been summarized in the Four Noble Truths. The first Noble Truth (*dukkha*) is the suffering of all existence. The second (*samudaya*) is that suffering is caused by our craving for externals and attachments, which can never satisfy our desires. Much like the Stoics, the Buddha taught us that we must give up our attachment to these externals. The third Noble Truth (*nirhodha*) is that suffering can be extinguished with diligent practice and enlightenment, which frees us from self-hood. The fourth Noble Truth (*magga*) is that the correct method of salvation is embodied in the (Noble) Eightfold Path (again, the middle path or way), which consists of following the Right View, Right Intention, Right Speech, Right Action, Right Livelihood, Right Effort, Right Mindfulness, and Right Concentration.

Historically, Buddhism was only one of many schools of "anti-Brahmanic" thought which arose in reaction to the Brahmanist orthodoxy in India. We now know this tradition as Hinduism. Despite rejecting the caste system, Brahmanic ritual, and the emphasis on the Vedas (scriptures), Buddhism is like Hinduism in teaching that the world is mostly illusion, that our senses and desires chain us to a painful cycle of birth and death (the turbulent whirlpool of *samsara*), that souls migrate through higher or lower levels of existence, and that liberation is possible through enlightenment.

The concepts of karma and reincarnation are common to both bodies of doctrine. The karma that attaches to our acts has inevitable consequences. Good consequences *must* follow good acts and bad consequences *must* follow bad acts, either immediately, in the future, or in another lifetime. Like reincarnation, this is an older idea, and provides a mechanism, much like hell, for the punishment of wrongdoers. The fool "who has given himself over to misconduct of body, speech, and mind" may reappear as an animal that feeds on grass; or in the company of animals that feed on dung; or in the company of maggots and flies. The wise man "who has given himself over to good conduct" reappears "in a happy destination, even in heaven."

The main difference between Buddhism and Hinduism is that the Buddha does not posit an eternal, unchanging soul or a separate, transcendent God, independent from the rest of the universe. Critics complain that Buddhism rests on a worldview that is too negative, too selfless, and too passive. The larger moral issue posed by Buddhism, like the turn to religion and mysticism in the middle ages, lies in its rejection of ordinary being. This is philosophically challenging. The renunciation of ordinary life has never prevented

Buddhist monks, however, from expressing themselves on moral, social, and sometimes political issues.

Other matters aside, the Buddhist tradition sets out a comprehensive system of practical ethics, inside and outside the monastic life (the *Sangha*), which emphasizes four "all-embracing virtues": charity, kindly speech, service to the public, and equality. It also condenses its basic moral teaching into a number of specific precepts, which apply to everyone. The first five precepts advise us to: 1) refrain from harming living beings, 2) refrain from what is not freely given, 3) refrain from engaging in sexual misconduct, 4) refrain from using false speech, and 5) refrain from using intoxicating drinks and drugs. The majority of Buddhist ethics involves the practice of *ahimsa* or non-violence, an extension of the first precept. There are additional precepts that apply to ascetics and monks.

The readings contain excerpts from a number of *suttas*, or discourses, found in several collections of texts published in *The Teachings of the Buddha Series*. The collections ostensibly record the Buddha's teachings and sermons. The material in these discourses was originally preserved in the oral tradition and was probably polished and embellished over time. They are nevertheless believed, like other texts in the *Buddhavacana* (the works of the Buddha), to contain an accurate record of his teaching. The discourses include poems, parables, and stories that contain moral instruction, insight into the process of spiritual release, and theological teachings and rules regarding the proper behavior of monks.

Siddhartha Gautama, the Buddha, Discourses from the *Sutta Pitaka*[1]

(fifth century BCE)

Part One. The Root Fifty Discourses[2]

1. THE DIVISION OF THE DISCOURSE ON THE ROOT

MN 9[3]

[The Venerable Sāriputta, the Buddha's chief disciple, is addressing his fellow monks:]

14. "When, friends, a noble disciple understands suffering, the origin of suffering, the cessation of suffering, and the way leading to the cessation of suffering, in that way he is one of right view, whose view is straight, who has perfect confidence in the Dhamma and has arrived at this true Dhamma.

15. "And what is suffering, what is the origin of suffering, what is the cessation of suffering, what is the way leading to the cessation of suffering? Birth is suffering; ageing is suffering; sickness is suffering; death is suffering; sorrow, lamentation, pain, grief, and despair are suffering; not to obtain what one wants is suffering; in short, the five aggregates affected by clinging are suffering. This is called suffering.

16. "And what is the origin of suffering? It is craving, which brings renewal of existence, is accompanied by delight and lust, and delights in this and that; that is, craving for sensual pleasures, craving for existence, and craving for non-existence. This is called the origin of suffering.

17. "And what is the cessation of suffering? It is the remainderless fading away and ceasing, the giving up, relinquishing, letting go, and rejecting of that same craving. This is called the cessation of suffering.

18. "And what is the way leading to the cessation of suffering? It is just this noble eightfold path; that is, right view, right intention, right speech, right action, right livelihood, right effort, right mindfulness, and right concentration. This is called the way leading to the cessation of suffering."

3. THE DIVISION OF SIMILES

MN 21

10. "A monk may be extremely gentle, extremely meek, extremely peaceful, so long as disagreeable courses of speech do not touch him. But it is when disagreeable courses of speech touch him that it can

---

1 The excerpts come from three collections in *The Teachings of the Buddha Series: The Middle Length Discourses of the Buddha: A Translation of the Majjhima Nikāya*, translated by Bhikkhu Ñāṇamoli, ed. and rev. by Bhikkhu Bodhi, 4th ed. (Somerville, MA: Wisdom Publications, [1995]; 2015); *The Numerical Discourses of the Buddha: A Translation of the Aṅguttara* Nikāya, translated by Bhikkhu Bodhi (2012); *The Connected Discourses of the Buddha: A Translation of the Saṃyutta* Nikāya, translated by Bhikkhu Bodhi (2003). Revisions in terminology for this publication made by Bhikkhu Bodhi (2021). The editors wish to thank Bodhi for his helpful suggestions in the selection of reading passages. *Sutta* or *Sutra* means a discourse, or sayings or aphorisms; *Pitaka*, a basket.

2 The reading excerpts from Part One and Part Two (below) come from *The Middle Length Discourses of the Buddha*.

3 In the headings of this reading, *Majjhima Nikāya* is abbreviated as MN, *Aṅguttara Nikāya* as AN, and *Saṃyutta Nikāya* as SN. Chapter number is then provided, followed by sutta number for some excerpts.

be understood whether that monk is really kind, gentle, and peaceful.

12. "Monks, suppose a man came with a hoe and a basket and said: 'I shall remove this great earth.' He would dig here and there, saying: 'Go away earth, go away earth!' What do you think, monks? Could that man remove this great earth?"—"No, sir." "Why is that? Because this great earth is deep and immense; it is not easy to remove it. Eventually the man would reap only weariness and disappointment.

13. "So too, monks, there are these five courses of speech that others may use when they address you: their speech may be timely or untimely, true or untrue, gentle or harsh, connected with good or with harm, spoken with a mind of loving-kindness or with inner hate. [No matter how others speak to you], monks, you should train thus: 'Our minds will remain unaffected, and we shall utter no evil words; we shall abide compassionate for their welfare, with a mind of loving-kindness, without inner hate. We shall abide pervading that person with a mind imbued with loving-kindness, and starting with him, we shall abide pervading the entire world with a mind imbued with loving-kindness, abundant, exalted, immeasurable, without hostility and without ill will.' That is how you should train, monks.

20. "Monks, even if bandits were to sever you savagely limb by limb with a two-handled saw, he who gave rise to a mind of hate towards them would not be carrying out my teaching. Herein, monks, you should train thus: 'Our minds will remain unaffected, and we shall...abide pervading them with a mind imbued with loving-kindness; and starting with them, we shall abide pervading the entire world with a mind imbued with loving-kindness, abundant, exalted, immeasurable, without hostility and without ill will.' That is how you should train, monks.

21. "Monks, if you keep this advice on the simile

of the saw constantly in mind, do you see any course of speech, trivial or gross, that you could not endure?"—"No, sir."—"Therefore, monks, you should keep this advice on the simile of the saw constantly in mind. That will lead to your welfare and happiness for a long time."

MN 22

THE SIMILE OF THE RAFT

13. "Monks, I shall show you how the Dhamma is similar to a raft, being for the purpose of crossing over, not for the purpose of grasping.

"Suppose a man in the course of a journey saw a great expanse of water, whose near shore was dangerous and fearful and whose further shore was safe and free from fear, but there was no ferryboat or bridge for going to the far shore. To get across, the man would collect grass, twigs, branches, and leaves and bind them together into a raft, and supported by the raft and paddling with his hands and feet, he would safely reach the far shore. He might then think 'This raft has been very helpful to me, since supported by it, I have safely reached the far shore. Suppose I were to hoist it on my head or load it on my shoulder, and then go wherever I want.' Now, monks, what do you think? By doing so, would that man be doing what should be done with that raft?"

"No, sir."

"[What, then,] should be done with that raft? Here, monks, when that man has reached the far shore, he would haul it onto the dry land or leave it in the water, and then go wherever he wants. That is what should be done with the raft. So I have shown you how the Dhamma is similar to a raft, being for the purpose of crossing over, not for the purpose of grasping.

14. "Monks, when you know the Dhamma to be similar to a raft, you should abandon even the teachings, how much more so things contrary to the teachings."

Part Two. The Middle Fifty Discourses

1. THE DIVISION ON HOUSEHOLDERS[1]

MN 51

3. "In this Sangha [community] of monks there are monks who are arahants[2] with taints destroyed, who have lived the holy life, done what had to be done, laid down the burden, reached the true goal, destroyed the fetters of existence, and who are completely liberated through final knowledge."

12. "Here, monks, a Tathāgata arises in the world, accomplished, fully enlightened, perfect in true knowledge and conduct, sublime, knower of worlds, incomparable leader of persons to be tamed, teacher of gods and humans, enlightened, blessed. He teaches the Dhamma good in the beginning, the middle, and the end, with the right meaning and phrasing, and he reveals a holy life that is utterly perfect and pure.

13. "A householder or householder's son hears that Dhamma and acquires faith in the Tathāgata. Based on that faith, he...shaves off his hair and beard, puts on the ochre robe, and goes forth from the home life into homelessness.

14. "Having thus gone forth, he follows the monastic training and way of life. Abandoning the killing of living beings, he abstains from killing living beings; with rod and weapon laid aside, gentle and kindly, he abides compassionate to all living beings. Abandoning the taking of what is not given, he takes only what is given, expecting only what is given; by not stealing he abides in purity. Abandoning sexual activity, he observes celibacy, living apart, abstaining from the vulgar practice of sexual intercourse.

"Abandoning false speech, he speaks truth, adheres to truth, is trustworthy and reliable, one who is no deceiver of the world. Abandoning malicious speech...harsh speech...gossip, he abstains from gossip; at the right time he speaks such words as are worth recording, reasonable, moderate, and beneficial.

"He abstains from injuring seeds and plants. He eats only one meal a day, abstaining from eating at night and outside the proper time. He abstains from dancing, singing, music, and theatrical shows.... He abstains from buying and selling. He abstains from wounding, murdering, binding, brigandage, plunder, and violence.

15. "He becomes content with robes to protect his body and with almsfood to maintain his stomach, and wherever he goes he sets out taking only these with him. Just as a bird, wherever it goes, flies with its wings as its only burden, so too, the monk becomes content with robes to protect his body and with almsfood to maintain his stomach. Possessing this aggregate of noble virtue, he experiences within himself a bliss that is blameless.

16. "On seeing a form with the eye, he does not grasp at its signs and features. On hearing a sound with the ear...On smelling an odour with the nose...On tasting a flavour with the tongue...On touching a tangible with the body...On cognizing a mind-object with the mind, he does not grasp at its signs and features. Since, if he left [these faculties] unguarded, evil unwholesome states of covetousness and grief might invade him, he practises the way of [their] restraint. Possessing this noble restraint of the faculties, he experiences within himself a bliss that is unsullied.

17. "He becomes one who acts in full awareness when going forward and returning; when looking ahead and looking away; when flexing and extending his limbs; when wearing his robes and carrying his outer

---

1 The Blessed One addressed Kandaraka the wanderer and the monks, saying what follows.

2 I.e., "perfected persons" who have attained nirvana.

robe and bowl; when eating, drinking, consuming food, and tasting; when defecating and urinating; when walking, standing, sitting, falling asleep, waking up, talking, and keeping silent.

18. "Possessing this aggregate of noble virtue, and this noble restraint of the faculties, and possessing this noble mindfulness and full awareness, he resorts to a secluded resting place: the forest, the root of a tree, a mountain, a ravine, a hillside cave, a charnel ground, a jungle thicket, an open space, a heap of straw.

19. "On returning from his almsround, after his meal he sits down, folding his legs crosswise, setting his body erect, and establishing mindfulness before him. (1) Abandoning craving for the world, he abides with a mind free from craving; he purifies his mind from craving. (2) Abandoning ill will and hatred, he abides with a mind free from ill will, compassionate for the welfare of all living beings. (3) Abandoning sloth and torpor, he abides free from sloth and torpor. (4) Abandoning restlessness and remorse, he abides unagitated with a mind inwardly peaceful. (5) Abandoning doubt, he abides free from doubt.

20. "Having thus abandoned these five hindrances, imperfections of the mind that weaken wisdom, quite secluded from sensual pleasures, secluded from unwholesome states, he enters upon and abides in the first *jhāna*, which is accompanied by applied and sustained thought, with rapture and pleasure born of seclusion.

21. "Again, with the stilling of applied and sustained thought, he enters upon and abides in the second *jhāna*, which has self-confidence and singleness of mind without applied and sustained thought, with rapture and pleasure born of concentration.

22. "Again, with the fading away as well of rapture, he abides in equanimity, and mindful and fully

aware, still feeling pleasure with the body, he enters upon and abides in the third *jhāna*, on account of which noble ones announce: 'He has a pleasant abiding who has equanimity and is mindful.'

23. "Again, with the abandoning of pleasure and pain, and with the previous disappearance of joy and grief, he enters upon and abides in the fourth *jhāna*, which has neither-pain-nor-pleasure and purity of mindfulness due to equanimity.

24. "When his concentrated mind is thus purified, bright, unblemished and attained to imperturbability, he directs it to knowledge of the recollection of past lives. He recollects his manifold past lives: 'There I was so named, of such a clan, with such an appearance, such was my nutriment, such my experience of pleasure and pain, such my life-term; and passing away from there, I was reborn elsewhere.' Thus with their aspects and particulars he recollects his manifold past lives.

25. "When his concentrated mind is thus purified, bright, unblemished...and attained to imperturbability, he directs it to knowledge of the passing away and rebirth of beings. With the divine eye, which is purified and surpasses the human, he sees beings passing away and reappearing, inferior and superior, fair and ugly, fortunate and unfortunate and understands how beings pass on according to their actions (*kamma*) thus: 'These beings who behaved badly by body, speech, and mind have been reborn in a bad destination, even in hell; but these beings who behaved well by body, speech, and mind have been reborn in a good destination, even in the heavenly world.'

26. "When his concentrated mind is thus purified, bright, unblemished, rid of imperfection, malleable, wieldy, steady, and attained to imperturbability, he directs it to knowledge of the destruction of the taints. He understands as it actually is [suffering,

its origin, its cessation, and the way to its cessation. He understands the taints, their origin, their cessation, and the way to their cessation].

27. "When he knows and sees thus, his mind is liberated from the taint of sensual desire, the taint of [craving for] existence, and the taint of ignorance. When it is liberated there comes the knowledge: 'It is liberated.' He understands: 'Birth is finished, the holy life has been lived, what had to be done has been done, there is no more coming to any state of being.'

28. "This, monks, is called the kind of person who does not torment himself and who does not torment others. He is one who here and now is hungerless, extinguished, and cooled, and abides experiencing bliss, having himself become holy."

5. THE DIVISION ON BRAHMINS[1]

MN 96

12. "I, brahmin, 'declare the noble supramundane Dhamma' as a person's own wealth. But recollecting his ancient maternal and paternal family lineage, he is reckoned according to wherever he is reborn.

13. "If, brahmin, anyone from a clan of nobles goes forth from the home life into homelessness, and after encountering the Dhamma and Discipline proclaimed by the Tathāgata, he abstains from killing living beings, from taking what is not given, from sexual activity, from false speech, from malicious speech, from harsh speech, and from gossip, and is uncovetous, has a mind without ill will, and holds right view, he is one who is accomplishing the true way, the Dhamma that is wholesome.

"If, brahmin, anyone from a clan of brahmins or a clan of merchants or a clan of workers goes

forth from the home life into homelessness, and after encountering the Dhamma and Discipline proclaimed by the Tathāgata [follows it in the same way], he is one who is accomplishing the true way, the Dhamma that is wholesome.

14. "What do you think, brahmin? Is only a brahmin capable of developing a mind of loving-kindness towards a certain region, without hostility and without ill will, and not a noble, or a merchant, or a worker?"

"No, Master Gotama. Whether it be a noble, or a brahmin, or a merchant, or a worker—those of all four castes are capable of developing a mind of loving-kindness towards a certain region, without hostility and without ill will."

15. "What do you think, brahmin? Is only a brahmin capable of taking a brush and bath powder, going to the river, and washing off dust and dirt, and not a noble, or a merchant, or a worker?"

"No, Master Gotama. Whether it be a noble, or a brahmin, or a merchant, or a worker—those of all four castes are capable of taking a brush and bath powder, going to the river, and washing off dust and dirt."

"So too, brahmin, if [any of these go] forth...(*doing as above*)...he is one who is accomplishing the true way, the Dhamma that is wholesome."

The Good and the Bad[2]

AN 10:178

"Monks, I will teach you what is good and what is bad. Listen and attend closely. I will speak."

"Yes, sir," those monks replied. The Blessed One said this:

"And what is bad? The destruction of life, taking what is not given, sexual misconduct, false speech,

---

1 Brahmins are the priestly caste.
2 Excerpt from *The Numerical Discourses of the Buddha*.

divisive speech, harsh speech, idle chatter, longing, ill will, and wrong view. This is called bad.

"And what is good? Abstention from the destruction of life, abstention from taking what is not given, abstention from sexual misconduct, abstention from false speech, abstention from divisive speech, abstention from harsh speech, abstention from idle chatter, non-longing, good will, and right view. This is called good."

Moral Reasoning as a Basis for Ethics[1]

SN 55:7

The householders of Bamboo Gate said to the Blessed One: "Please teach us how we might dwell happily at home and after death be reborn in a good destination, in a heavenly world."

"I will teach you, householders, a doctrine that is applicable to yourselves. Here, householders, a noble disciple reflects thus: 'I am one who wishes to live, who does not wish to die; I desire happiness and am averse to suffering. Since that is so, if someone were to take my life, that would not be pleasing and agreeable to me. Now if I were to take the life of another— of one who wishes to live, who does not wish to die, who desires happiness and is averse to suffering— that would not be pleasing and agreeable to the other. What is displeasing and disagreeable to me is displeasing and disagreeable to the other too. How can I inflict upon another what is displeasing and disagreeable to me?' Having reflected thus, he himself abstains from the destruction of life, exhorts others to abstain from the destruction of life, and speaks in praise of abstinence from the destruction of life. Thus this bodily conduct of his is purified in three respects.

"Again, householders, a noble disciple reflects

thus: 'If someone were to take from me what I have not given, that is, to commit theft, that would not be pleasing and agreeable to me. Now if I were to take from another what he has not given, that is, to commit theft, that would not be pleasing and agreeable to the other. What is displeasing and disagreeable to me is displeasing and disagreeable to the other too. How can I inflict upon another what is displeasing and disagreeable to me?' Having reflected thus, he himself abstains from taking what is not given, exhorts others to abstain from taking what is not given, and speaks in praise of abstinence from taking what is not given. Thus this bodily conduct of his is purified in three respects."[2]

The Ethical Dimensions of Meditative Training[3]

MN 7

2. "Monks, suppose a cloth were defiled and stained, and a dyer dipped it in some dye or other, whether blue or yellow or red or pink; it would look poorly dyed and impure in colour. Why is that? Because of the impurity of the cloth. So too, when the mind is defiled, an unhappy destination may be expected. Monks, suppose a cloth were pure and bright, and a dyer dipped it in some dye or other, whether blue or yellow or red or pink; it would look well dyed and pure in colour. Why is that? Because of the purity of the cloth. So too, when the mind is undefiled, a happy destination may be expected.

3. "What, monks, are the imperfections that defile the mind? Covetousness and unrighteous greed is an imperfection that defiles the mind. Ill will... anger ... resentment ... contempt ... insolence ...

---

1 Excerpt from *The Connected Discourses of the Buddha.*

2 The same kind of reasoning is then used to justify abstinence from sexual misconduct and false speech.

3 Excerpt from *The Middle Length Discourses of the Buddha*, Part One: The Root Fifty Discourses; 1 The Division of the Discourse on the Root; the Simile of the Cloth.

envy...avarice...deceit...fraud...obstinacy...rivalry...conceit...arrogance...vanity...negligence is an imperfection that defiles the mind.

4. "Knowing that covetousness and unrighteous greed is an imperfection that defiles the mind, a monk abandons it. Knowing that ill will...negligence is an imperfection that defiles the mind, a monk abandons it."

Removing the Roots of Conflict and Disputes[1]

AN 6:36

"Monks, there are these six roots of disputes. What six? (1) Here, a monk is angry and hostile, (2) a denigrator and insolent, (3) envious and miserly, (4) crafty and hypocritical, (5) one who has evil desires and wrong view, (6) one who adheres to his own views, holds to them tenaciously, and relinquishes them with difficulty. A monk [with any of these faults] dwells without respect and deference toward the Buddha, the Dhamma, and the Sangha, and he does not fulfill the training. He creates a dispute in the Sangha that leads to the harm of many people, to the unhappiness of many people, to the ruin, harm, and suffering of gods and humans. If, monks, you perceive any such root of dispute either in yourselves or in others, you should strive to abandon this evil root of dispute, and practice so that this evil root of dispute does not emerge in the future. In such a way this evil root of dispute is abandoned and does not emerge in the future."

Principles for Establishing Harmony within the Sangha[2]

AN 6:12

"Monks, there are these six principles of cordiality that create affection and respect and conduce to concord and unity. What six?

(1) "Here, a monk maintains bodily acts of loving-kindness toward his fellow monks both openly and privately.

(2) "Again, a monk maintains verbal acts of loving-kindness toward his fellow monks both openly and privately.

(3) "Again, a monk maintains mental acts of loving-kindness toward his fellow monks both openly and privately.

(4) "Again, a monk shares without reservation any righteous gains that have been righteously obtained, including even the contents of his alms-bowl, and uses such things in common with his virtuous fellow monks.

(5) "Again, a monk dwells both openly and privately observing the pure precepts in common with his fellow monks.

(6) "Again, a monk dwells both openly and privately in common with his fellow monks holding a view that is noble and emancipating, which leads to the complete destruction of suffering.

"These, monks, are the six principles of cordiality that create affection and respect and conduce to concord and unity."

---

1 Excerpt from *The Numerical Discourses of the Buddha*.
2 Excerpt from *The Numerical Discourses of the Buddha*.

Questions

1. What are the origins of suffering in the Buddhist view, and how do we rid ourselves of it? Do you agree with the Buddhist view?

2. The Buddha promotes a life of renunciation. What role do you think renunciation should play in ethics?

3. The Buddha taught mindfulness, even in bodily functions like urinating and defecating. What is mindfulness? Is it a part of morality? Why, why not?

4. Buddhism emerged from a well-developed Indian tradition, which included a belief in reincarnation. Do you believe in it? Discuss the Buddhist teaching that we can escape the cycle of reincarnation.

5. The Buddha says that a monk should maintain a mind of loving-kindness, even towards someone who viciously attacks him. Do you agree with this teaching, or feel we must strike back? Why, why not?

6. One of the important philosophical developments in Buddhism is the idea that people are equal. Are people equal? Why did earlier people hold different views?

7. The five excerpts at the end of the reading express a number of moral principles that Buddhist monks and householders are to live by. What kind of community and society would be built from such principles? Would you like to live in such a community? Why, why not?

Suggested Readings

The *Sutta Pitaka* and other Buddhist scriptures are available at accesstoinsight.org. There are innumerable sources on the history and development of Buddhism. Donald Mitchell's *Buddhism: Introducing the Buddhist Experience* (2002) reviews the life of Buddha, the early scriptures, and the historical dissemination of Buddhism around the world.

Like Catholicism, Buddhism mixed successfully with earlier religions and there are many cultural traditions. Zhao Puchu's *Essentials of Buddhism: Questions and Answers*, for example, contains a lucid account of the Buddhist tradition in China as well as India. Zen Buddhism began as "Chan" Buddhism in China, which John McRae discusses in *The Northern School and the Formation of Early Chan Buddhism* (1986). For the developments in Japan, see vol. 2 of Heinrich Dumoulin, *Zen Buddhism: A History* (1988), and Daisetz Teitaro Suzuki's *Introduction to Zen Buddhism* (1961), which is easily available. Jacob Dalton's rather uneven *Taming of the Demons: Violence and Liberation in Tibetan Buddhism* (2011) raises ethical issues concerning killing, violence, and death in the Tibetan tradition.

Ian Harris (*Buddhism in a Dark Age: Cambodian Monks under Pol Pot*, 2012) and Katarina Plank ("Living Torches of Tibet—Religious and Political Implications of the Recent Self-Immolations," 2013) discuss the ethical response of Buddhism to drastic social and political realities.

Chapter 9

Aesop's Fables

This chapter is concerned with fables, rather than the work of a particular figure. Aesop has nevertheless come to be seen, in some mythical capacity, as the recognized father of fables. As in the case of many early figures—such as Solomon, in the case of proverbs, or Laozi in the Daoist tradition—this was a convenient way of both honoring a seminal figure in the tradition and creating an official canon of relevant material.

Although the historical record is uncertain, there are references to Aesop in relatively early ancient sources, which seem to verify that he was a slave in the sixth century BCE, who was supposedly sold to a philosopher called Xanthus on the island of Samos. The sources agree that Aesop ultimately obtained his freedom by his skill in telling stories. Even these minimal facts suggest that he had the kind of intellectual resourcefulness that the Greeks admired.

There is a *Life of Aesop*, which is included in the readings. This account of Aesop's legendary life contains wild and obscene elements, along with plenty of satire. It must have found a ready audience with the rowdier elements in Greek and Roman society. Although the work was frequently ascribed to Maximus Planudes, a monk of Constantinople in the fourteenth century, scholars have now discovered earlier accounts, which can be traced back as far as the fifth and sixth centuries BCE. This suggests that there is considerable reality behind the stories, though the description of Aesop's death at Delphi is clearly fictional.

The history of fables can be traced to the early ethical tradition, which depended heavily on the use of stories and folktales. These stories also make use of the animal and natural world for didactic purposes, though the fables clearly come from a later society in which the focus has moved to the relations between people. The point of view in the fables nevertheless reflects the early view, which did not separate the human, natural, and supernatural worlds. The eagle in the reading, for example, which drops the ring with the town seal in the bosom of a slave, is a token that indicates that the natural order of things has been threatened.

The "fabulist" tradition is fluid and amorphous, and defies simple classification. Any definition of a fable is accordingly open to debate and adjustment. The tradition extended well into the middle ages, though it eventually deteriorated into the rather precious children's stories that we know today: they were intentionally "bowdlerized"—re-written to eliminate their possibly offensive content, or unsuitability for children—and fail to capture both the liveliness or philosophical penetration of the original versions. In spite of their decline, some of the narrative elements in fables made their way into a Rabelaisian tradition of "*contes*" in the French language.

The reading from *The Life of Aesop* is instructive because it demonstrates the way in which fables were used, essentially as metaphors, to unlock the deeper significance of notable events. Although this was done in a homely and remarkably robust manner, it also required considerable insight into the nature of things. Aesop's fame seems to have rested on the appositeness of the fables that he told. They seemed, at least in the minds of his listeners, to have been unerringly accurate. In modern parlance, we might say that they somehow catch "the truth" of things.

We can go further. It is evident that fables were not merely metaphors; they were moral metaphors, which gave the listener a better grasp of life and its ethical profile. In that sense, they fit naturally into the wisdom tradition. As we see in Aesop's final fable, which is addressed to the mob that is about to kill him, they provided a powerful means of passing ethical judgment on people and their actions. The force of this should not be overlooked. There are clear parallels between fables and the parables and "similes" in the eastern and western religious traditions, which explain the true significance of human actions by some homely analogue.

The logical side of the fabulist tradition also deserves mention. The early moral tradition culminated in the idea that stories and tales contain ethical propositions. They function in many ways like a moral case law, which draws appropriate principles drawn out of a recitation of facts. This was part of a slow and increasingly explicit historical development, which gave rise in Greece to a tradition—related to the proverb tradition—of collecting *logoi* (λόγος) composed of short pithy sayings and aphorisms, inside and outside the moral tradition. Aesop's fables were originally compiled by sophist philosophers (see chapter 12), who used them as a vehicle for philosophy.

Although there is a literary side to the fables, the significant point is that they contain some lesson or insight that is easily rendered in propositional form. Like a homespun tale told by a lawyer to a jury, they provided a means of persuading the reader that a particular point of view was correct. Thus many *logoi*—like so many proverbs—sum up the "point" of a particular fable. These formulations were treated as early examples of arguments and were accordingly associated with the development of rhetoric. It is significant that Demetrius of Phalerum, who studied with Aristotle and became an important proponent of Aristotelian rhetoric, was probably the most important collector of the early fables.

Morally, the historical canon of western fables—called "Aesopia" or "Aesopica"—gives expression to an early ethic, which has been neglected by philosophers. The fables are often rude, bawdy, and grim, and were seen as honest accounts of the moral realities of life, itself often brutal and grim, and the politics of the animals—there is an incipient political science in the fables—is usually based on power and the threat of violence. The ancient fables counsel us to be shrewd and wary in our dealings with others. Like many of the rural proverbs, the lessons they teach are often ambiguous and suggest that success—or even survival—requires deft behavior, canny deliberation, and a willingness to exploit the weaknesses of others, if not outright trickery.

As Leo Groarke writes, at aesopfables.com:

> In ancient times, fables are not designed as moral tales for children. Some are versions of famous fables we all know ("The Tortoise and the Hare," "The Ant and the Grasshopper," "The Boy Who Called Wolf," etc.), but early fables are more frequently designed to explain the causes of natural phenomena, and ancient fables are characterized by a hard-nosed realism which is at odds with the view of the world that contemporary authors put in the mouth of Aesop. The wisdom associated with the ancient fable is the kind of wisdom evident in Aesop's explanation of the frustrating fact that weeds seem to grow more vigorously than the seeds we plant…

The explicit moral aphorisms that we now associate with Aesop were a later addition, which seemed to find favor in the middle ages. This can be seen in the illustrated examples in the readings, which have been put in verse, and which conclude with the kind of encomiums with which we are familiar. It was apparently Robert L'Estrange, the translator of *The Life of Aesop*, who conceived the idea that fables might be used to teach children some sense of duty. Since fables are didactic by nature, they were well suited to such a purpose, though they lost most of their original "bite" in the process.

The fables in the readings are taken from the general canon. Students can find many other examples from the Greek, Roman, and medieval sources at mythfolklore.net/aesopica.

The Life of Aesop by Roger L'Estrange[1]

Chapter I

Aesop was by birth, of Ammorius, a town in the Greater Phrygia…of a mean condition, and in his person deformed to the highest degree: flat-nosed, hunch-backed, blobber-lipped, a long misshapen head; his body crooked all over, big-bellied, baker-legged, and his complexion so swarthy that he took his very name from it. For, Aesop is the same with Aethiop.[2] And he was not only unhappy in the most scandalous figure of a man that ever was heard of, but he was in a manner tongue-tied too, by such an impediment in his speech that people could very hardly understand what he said.[3]

Chapter V

Some two or three days after [being purchased], Xanthus took Aesop along with him to a garden to buy some herbs. The gardener seeing him in the habit of a philosopher told him the admiration he was in, to find how much faster those plants shot up that grow of their own accord than those that he set himself, though he took never so much care about them. Now you that are a philosopher, pray will you tell me the meaning of this? Xanthus had no better answer at hand than to tell him that Providence would have it so. Whereupon Aesop broke out into a loud laughter. "Why how now you slave you," says Xanthus, "what do you laugh at?" Aesop took him aside and told him, "Sir, I laugh at your master that taught you no better: for what signifies a general answer to a particular question? And it is no news either that Providence orders all things. But if you'll turn him over to me, you shall see I'll give him another sort of resolve."

Xanthus told the gardener that it was below a philosopher to busy his head about such trifles; but says he, "If you have a curiosity to be better informed, you should do well to ask my slave here, and see what he will say to you." Upon this, the gardener put the question to Aesop, who gave him this answer. "The earth is in the nature of a mother to what she brings forth of herself out of her own bowels. Whereas she is only a kind of a stepmother in the production of plants that are cultivated and assisted by the help and industry of another. So, it's natural for her to withdraw her nourishment from the one towards the relief of the other." The gardener, upon this, was so well satisfied that he would take no money for his herbs, and desired Aesop to make use of his garden for the future, as if it were his own.[4]

Chapter XIV

Now it came to pass, upon a very solemn day, the ring that had the town-seal upon it was laid somewhere in the open when an eagle came down upon it, took it up in the air, and dropped it into the bosom

---

1 Anonymous, *The Life of Aesop*, from Roger L'Estrange, *Fables of Æsop and Other Eminent Mythologists* (1692), which is available at wikisource.org.

2 I.e., Ethiopia.

3 Chapter III recounts how, after being sent to Ephesus as a slave, Aesop is sold to Xanthus, a philosopher.

4 In the following chapters, the history relates a number of episodes in Aesop's life, such as Aesop's preparation of the best and worst of feasts for a gathering of philosophers—in both cases, a feast including dishes of animal tongues, since "the tongue be the key that leads us into all knowledge" but also provides the necessary means of planning the worst of crimes.

of a slave. The Samians[1] took this for a foreboding that threatened some dismal calamity to the state, and in a general consternation they presently called a council of their wise men.[2]

"You have here before you," says Aesop, "an ungracious figure of a man, which has nothing to do with the business before us. I ask you, did you never taste delicious drink out of an ugly-looking vessel? Or wine that was vapid, or eager, out of a vessel of gold?[3]

"Now the eagle is a royal bird, and signifies a great king; that the dropping of the ring into the bosom of a slave that has no power over himself, portends the loss of your liberties, if you do not look to yourselves in time; and that some potent prince has a design upon you."

This inflamed the Samians.... And some short time after, there came ambassadors from Croesus, the King of Lydia,[4] to demand a tribute[5]...and threatened the Samians with a war in case of a refusal. This affair came to be debated in the council, where the majority was rather for peace with slavery than for running the risk of a dispute. But after consulting Aesop, all declared that they would follow the path of liberty...[6]

"In old times, when some beasts talked better sense than many men do nowadays, there happened to be a fierce war between the wolves and the sheep. And the sheep, by the help of the dogs, had rather the better of it. The wolves, upon this, offered the sheep a peace on condition only that they might have their dogs for hostages. The silly credulous sheep agreed to it, and as soon as they had parted with the dogs, the wolves broke in upon them, and destroyed them at pleasure."

The Samians quickly smelled out the moral of this fable and cried out, one and all, that they would not part with Aesop. But this did not hinder Aesop from putting himself aboard a ship and taking a passage for Lydia with the ambassadors.

Chapter XV

Immediately upon Aesop's arrival in Lydia, he presented himself before the King, who looked upon him with contempt, hatred, and indignation. Aesop paid no mind; and then with a reverence after the Lydian fashion, delivered what he had to say.

"I am here, Great King, without compulsion and come to lay myself at your Majesty's feet, and with this only request, that you will vouchsafe me the honor of your Royal ear and patience but for a few words.

"There was a boy hunting of locusts, and he had the fortune to take a grasshopper. She found he was about to kill her and pleaded after this manner for her life. 'Alas (says she) I never did anybody an injury, and never had it either in my will or in my power to do it. All my business is my song; and what will you be the better for my death?' The youth's heart relented and he set the simple grasshopper at liberty.

"Your Majesty has now that innocent creature before you: there's nothing that I can pretend to but my voice, which I have ever employed so far as in

---

1 I.e., people from or of Samos.
2 Aesop advises Xanthus to tell the council that he has a servant who can explain the riddle. At the sight of Aesop, however, they all burst out laughing, to which Aesop replied the following.
3 Having convinced the council, Aesop agrees to interpret the portent, but states that it would be improper "to take the opinion of a slave into your councils." By this means, he persuades the council to set him free, and after being set free, he accordingly states the following.
4 Lydia was a kingdom located in modern-day western Turkey.
5 I.e., a payment given to another as a sign of respect, or more often, of submission or allegiance.
6 When Croesus hears of these events, he offers to put a stop to the war, if only the Samians would send him Aesop. The latter was willing to go, but only after telling the Samians one story before he left them.

me lay to the service of mankind." The King was so tenderly moved with the modesty and prudence of the man that he did not only give him his life, but ordered him to ask anything further that he had a mind to, and it should be granted him. "Why then," says Aesop (with that veneration, gratitude and respect that the case required), "I do most humbly implore your Majesty's favour for my countrymen the Samians." The King granted him his request, and confirmed it under his seal…

Aesop, soon after this, returned to Samos with the news of the peace, where he was welcomed with all the instances of joy and thankfulness imaginable…Afterwards, he returned to Croesus, composed some of his famous fables, and from there, travelled out of curiosity to Greece and eventually Babylon.

Chapter XVI

In Babylon, Aesop adopted a son, Ennus, who betrayed him. Aesop nevertheless took his son back, instructing him.

Chapter XVII

"My son (says he) do not worship God as if that divine name and power were only an invention to frighten women and children, but know that God is omnipresent, true and almighty.

"Have a care even of your most private actions and thoughts, for God sees through you, and your conscience will bear witness against you.

"It is according to prudence, as well as nature, to pay that honor to your parents that you expect your children should pay to you.

"Do all the good you can to all men, but in the first place to your nearest relations, and do no hurt whatever, where you can do no good.…

"Follow the dictates of your reason.… Our minds must be cultivated as well as our plants. The improvement of our reason makes us like angels, whereas the neglect of it turns us into beasts.

"There is no permanent and inviolable good but wisdom and virtue, though the study of it signifies little without the practice.

"Do not think it impossible to be a wise man, without becoming sour. Wisdom makes men severe, but not inhumane.

"It is virtue not to be vicious.

"Keep faith with all men…

"Take delight in and frequent the company of good men, for it will give you a tincture of their manners too.…

"Have a care of luxury and gluttony, but of drunkenness especially; for wine as well as age makes a man a child.

"Love and honor Kings, Princes and Magistrates, for they are the bands of society, in punishing the guilty, and protecting the innocent."

Chapter XVIII

After many successes, Aesop went to Delphos, either for the oracle's sake, or for the sake of the wise men that frequented the place.[1] But when he came there…he found the Delphians proud and avaricious, and in consequence of this, delivered his opinion of them under this fable:

"I find (says he) the curiosity that brought me here to be much the case of people at the seaside that see something come hulling toward them a great way

---

1 Delphos is the name of the person from whom the town of Delphi was believed to have derived its name. The town was considered by the Greeks to be the navel, or center, of the world. The oracle refers to the Pythia, the High Priestess of the Temple of Apollo located there. She was consulted by numerous people seeking advice on all sorts of matters.

off at sea and take it at first to be some mighty matter, but upon driving nearer and nearer the shore, it proves at last to be only a heap of weeds and rubbish."

The magistrates of the place took infinite offence at this liberty and presently entered into a conspiracy against him. They secretly placed a golden cup from a temple into his baggage. He was accordingly no sooner out of the town than he was pursued and taken upon the way by officers, and charged with sacrilege…[1]

"There was an old fellow (says he) that had spent his whole life in the country without ever seeing the town. As he found himself weak and decaying, nothing would serve, but his friends had to show him the town once before he died. Since their asses were very well acquainted with the way, they caused them to be made ready, and turned the old man and the asses loose without a guide to try their fortune. They were overtaken upon the road by a terrible tempest so that what with the darkness and the violence of the storm, the asses were beaten out of their way and tumbled with the old man into a pit. He had only

time to deliver his last breath with this exclamation. 'Miserable wretch that I am to be destroyed, since die I must by the basest of beasts: by asses.' And that's my fate now in suffering by the hands of a barbarous sottish people that understand nothing either of humanity or honor; and act contrary to the ties of hospitality and justice. But the gods will not suffer my blood to lie unrevenged, and heaven will punish you…"

He was speaking on, but they pushed him off headlong from the rock, and he was dashed to pieces with the fall. And indeed, the Delphians were soon visited with famine and pestilence to such a degree that they went to consult the oracle of Apollo to know what wickedness it was that had brought these calamities upon them. The oracle gave them this answer: that they were to expiate for the death of Aesop. They therefore erected a pyramid to his honor. Afterwards, a great many of the most eminent men among the Greeks went to Delphos to learn the truth of the history, and found upon enquiry the principal conspirators and laid violent hands upon them.[2]

---

1 The Delphians will not listen to Aesop's fables. Falsely convicted, he takes refuge at an Altar, where they seize him. When Aesop found that neither the holiness of the place nor the clearness of his innocence was sufficient to protect him, he gave them yet one fable.

2 I.e., they killed them (as a punishment for what they had done).

READING 9B

Aesop, Selected Fables and *logoi*[1]

The Boy Who Cried 'Wolf'

There was a boy tending the sheep who would continually go up to the embankment and shout, 'Help, there's a wolf!' The farmers would all come running only to find out that what the boy said was not true. Then one day there really was a wolf, but when the boy shouted, they didn't believe him and no one came to his aid. The whole flock was eaten by the wolf....

The Fox and the Raven

... The raven seized a piece of cheese and carried his spoils up to his perch high in a tree. A fox came up and walked in circles around the raven, planning a trick. 'What is this?' cried the fox. 'O raven, the elegant proportions of your body are remarkable, and you have a complexion that is worthy of the king of the birds!

If only you had a voice to match, then you would be first among the fowl!' The fox said these things to trick the raven and the raven fell for it: He let out a great squawk and dropped his cheese. By thus showing off his voice, the raven let go of his spoils. The fox then grabbed the cheese and said, 'O raven, you do have a voice, but no brains to go with it!'...

The Fox and the Stork

... The fox is said to have started it by inviting the stork to dinner and serving a liquid broth on a marble slab which the hungry stork could not so much as taste. The stork, in turn, invited the fox to dinner and served a narrow-mouthed jug filled with crumbled food. The stork was able to thrust her beak inside and eat as much as she wanted, while her guest was tormented with hunger. As the fox was licking the neck of the jug in vain, the stork is supposed to have said, 'When others follow your example, you have to grin and bear it.'...

---

1   The translations are by Laura Gibbs, published in *Aesop's Fables* (Oxford: Oxford University Press, 2002, 2008). Illustrations are by Francis Barlow, in *Aesop's Fables with his Life: in English, French and Latin* (London: H. Hills jun., 2nd ed., 1687). Short poems in English by Aphra Behn and longer Latin and French versions of the fables accompany the illustrations. Online at https://luna.folger.edu/luna/servlet/view/search?q=call_number=%22A703%22; and also at https://archive.lib.msu.edu/DMC/aesopsfables/aesopsfableslife.pdf.

The Wolf and the Lion

A wolf had seized a young pig and was carrying it away when he ran into a lion. The lion immediately took the pig away from him. After having to surrender the pig, the wolf said to himself, 'I wondered myself how what I acquired by theft could possibly have stayed with me.'...

The Wolf and the Lamb

A wolf once saw a lamb who had wandered away from the flock. He did not want to rush upon the lamb and seize him violently. Instead, he sought a reasonable complaint to justify his hatred. 'You insulted me last year, when you were small,' said the wolf. The lamb replied, 'How could I have insulted you last year? I'm not even a year old.' The wolf continued, 'Well, are you not cropping the grass of this field which belongs to me?' The lamb said, 'No, I haven't eaten any grass; I have not even begun to graze.' Finally, the wolf exclaimed, 'But didn't you drink from the fountain which I drink from?' The lamb answered, 'It is my mother's breast that gives me my drink.' The wolf then seized the lamb, and as he chewed he said, 'You are not going to make this wolf go without his dinner, even if you are able to easily refute every one of my charges!'...

The Monkeys and the Two Men

There were two men travelling together: One was a liar and the other always told the truth. Their journey led them to the land of the monkeys. There was a whole crowd of monkeys there and one of them noticed the travelers. The monkey who was clearly their leader ordered that the men be detained. Since he wanted to know what the men thought of him, he commanded all the rest of the monkeys to stand before him in a long line to his right and to his left, while a seat was prepared for him to sit on (this monkey had once seen the emperor, so he was ordering his monkeys to line up for him in the same way). The men were then told to come forward into the midst of the monkeys. The chief monkey said, 'Who am I?' The liar said, 'You are the emperor!' Then the monkey asked, 'And those whom you see standing before me: who are they?' The man answered, 'They are your noble companions, your chancellors, your officials and the commanders of your armies!' Because these lies flattered the monkey and his troops, he ordered that the man be showered with presents. All the monkeys were fooled by his flattery. Meanwhile, the man who always told the truth thought to himself, 'If that liar received such rewards for telling lies, then surely I will receive an even greater reward for telling the truth.' The chief monkey said to the second man, 'Now you tell me who I am, and who are these whom you see standing before me?' And the man who always loved the truth and never lied said to the monkey, 'You are simply a monkey, and all of these similar simians are monkeys as well!' The chief monkey immediately ordered the monkeys to attack the man with their teeth and claws because he had spoken the truth....

The Ant and the Cricket

During the wintertime, an ant was living off the grain that he had stored up for himself during the summer. The cricket came to the ant and asked him to share some of his grain. The ant said to the cricket, 'And what were you doing all summer long, since you weren't gathering grain to eat?' The cricket replied, 'Because I was busy singing I didn't have time for the harvest.' The ant laughed at the cricket's reply, and hid his heaps of grain deeper in the ground. 'Since you sang like a fool in the summer,' said the ant, 'you better be prepared to dance the winter away!'...

The Wolf and the Shepherd

A wolf followed along after a flock of sheep without doing them any harm. At first the shepherd kept his eye on the wolf as a potential enemy to the flock and never let him out of his sight. But as the wolf continued to accompany the shepherd and did not make any kind of attempt to raid the flock, the shepherd eventually began to regard the wolf more as a guardian of the flock than as a threat. Then, when the shepherd happened to have to go to town, he commended the sheep to the wolf in his absence. The wolf seized his chance and attacked the sheep, slaughtering most of the flock. When the shepherd came back and saw that his flock had been utterly destroyed, he said, 'It serves me right! How could I have ever trusted my sheep to a wolf?'...

The Dog and the Hare

A dog was running after a hare, and when he caught him he would alternately bite the hare and then lick the blood that flowed from the wound. The hare thought that the dog was kissing him, so he said, 'You should either embrace me as a friend, or bite me like an enemy.'...

The War between the Beasts and the Birds

The birds were at war with the beasts, and it was impossible to tell which side was winning and which was losing. Afraid to find himself on the losing side, the bat kept switching to the other side as soon as he thought it was going to prevail. Peace was eventually restored, and both the birds and the beasts realized that the bat had been a traitor. Found guilty of such a dastardly crime, the bat fled from the light and concealed himself in the dark shadows of the night....

The Dog, the Meat and the Reflection

A dog seized some meat from the butcher shop and ran away with it until he came to a river. When the dog was crossing the river, he saw the reflection of the meat in the water, and it seemed much larger than the meat he was carrying. He dropped his own piece of meat in order to try to snatch at the reflection. When the reflection disappeared, the dog went to grab the meat he had dropped but he was not able to find it anywhere, since a passing raven had immediately snatched the meat and gobbled it up. The dog lamented his sorry condition and said, 'Woe is me! I foolishly abandoned what I had in order to grab hold of a phantom, and thus I ended up losing both that phantom and what I had to begin with.'...

Questions

1. The protagonist in many fables and tribal tales is often a trickster. Why is trickery such an integral part of the early moral tradition? What does this tell us about the human condition? About wisdom?

2. Why is there such a close association between animals and people in fables, proverbs, and tribal tales? Why do you think we lost that part of the moral tradition?

3. Fables provided an engaging way of dealing with serious social and political issues. What does the fable of the wolf and the crane tell us about (Greek) politics? About life?

4. Explain the meaning behind three of the fables in your own words.

5. Find two contemporary stories—about politicians or celebrities, for example—that provide the same kind of moral service as fables. Explain their significance.

6. Aesop's fables were part of the development of explicit forms of argument in the history of philosophy. What is the *argument*, then, in two fables?

7. Is the Aesop in the *Life of Aesop* a wise man, a man of moral courage, or simply someone with a shrewd grasp of language and reason? Defend your view.

8. What is the general philosophy of life behind Aesop's fables? What would a good human life consist of from such a perspective?

Suggested Readings

Although Aesop appears to have been a real historical figure, with a knack for *logoi*, the fables attributed to him are the product of a tradition rather than a single author. These fables, sometimes labeled *Aesopica*, are widely available in print and online. Excellent collections can be found at aesopfables.com and mythfolklore.net, which has a detailed index, facsimiles of many editions, and hundreds of sources. Many of the fables were rewritten (particularly in the Victorian Age) with a children's audience in mind. See, for example, George Townsend's *Three Hundred Aesop's Fables* (1867), and the discussion in Lloyd Daly's *Aesop without Morals* (1961).

General sources include Edward Clayton, "Aesop, Aristotle, and Animals: The Role of Fables in Human Life" (2008), and Anthony Skillen, "Aesop's Lessons in Literary Realism" (1992). C.A. Zafiropoulos deals explicitly with ethical issues in *Ethics in Aesop's Fables*

(2001). Lester H. Hunt ("Literature as Fable, Fable as Argument," 2009) and Leo Groarke ("The Life of Aesop: Rhetoric and the Philosophical Life," 2010) discuss the use of fables as rhetorical devices. Mark L. McPherran ("Socrates and Aesop in Plato's *Phaedo*," 2012) and Todd Compton ("The Trial of the Satirist: Poetic Vitae as Background for Plato's Apology," 1990) discuss the significance of the story of Aesop in the subsequent philosophical tradition.

Chapter 10

Socrates

Socrates lived during the Golden Age of Athens. It is very difficult to separate the reality of his life from the mythology that grew up around him. He was notorious in Athens for his ugly or comical appearance, his physical fortitude, and his lack of worldly aspirations. We know that he was a stonemason by trade and spent much of his time discussing philosophy with his aristocratic male friends, in their homes, in gymnasia, in the marketplace, or on street corners. This apparently left his wife Xanthippe unhappy.

When the oracle at Delphi pronounced that there was "no one wiser," Socrates stated that this reflected the fact that we are all ignorant. Some later commentators have argued that such self-deprecating remarks—which are consistent with skepticism, but inconsistent with many of his philosophical comments—were merely a sly way of defending himself against the accusations of hubris that were typically made against the philosophers.

Socrates wrote no works and spent his philosophical life in exchanges with his peers and students. This recalls the early Chinese tradition, which was also oral. It was Socrates's student, Plato, who recorded these debates in his famous dialogues. Although the veracity of Plato's account is difficult to determine, he has left us a lively account of the practice of philosophy in Athens. Scholars generally agree that the dialogues progress, chronologically, from relatively short, inconclusive conversations between Socrates and others (the "aporetic" dialogues) to longer, more thorough discussions that contain Plato's answers to deeper philosophical questions.

We now tend to focus on the philosophical arguments in the dialogues. Socrates sets out an epistemological ethics, which sees the good as a subject of knowledge, and therefore open to rational inquiry. Earlier philosophers, however, saw Socrates primarily as an example of how we should live: in fact, at seventy he was charged with corrupting the youth of Athens, ostensibly for practicing philosophy. Rather than go into exile, as he was urged to do, he accepted a fatal cup of hemlock, a common mode of execution for Athenian nobles. His resoluteness and equanimity in the face of death had a deep effect on later philosophers.

Socrates was primarily interested in moral inquiry, famously claiming that the unexamined life is not worth living. He believed that ignorance is the cause of vice, and that philosophy—the vigorous search for knowledge—is the best way to achieve virtue. This search for knowledge was based on a method of examination, called *elenchus*, which brought out the different, often inconsistent, positions of the interlocutors in the dialectic. When pressed, Socrates supposedly claimed that he had never taught anyone anything, and merely served like his mother, a midwife, to bring the ideas of his interlocutors to birth. This is selective, however, and evasive.

Although many Athenians considered Socrates a Sophist (see chapter 12), he did not ask for money from his interlocutors (a rather technical distinction) and insisted that he was interested in philosophy—rational argument—rather than rhetoric (persuasion). Plato is clearly biased and was siding with Socrates, who had defended himself by asserting— precisely—that there was a clear demarcation between the philosophers and Sophists. The situation is unclear, however, since there are many elements of rhetoric and "sophistry" in the dialogues. There is plenty of evidence that Socrates associated with the Sophists. David Corey, for example, has drawn attention to Prodicus, a Sophist who taught Socrates. Then there is the fact that Socrates employed a skeptical methodology, which consisted of prolonged questioning.

There are differences, however. The main point in a moral context has to be that Socrates seems to have consistently disputed the Sophists' epistemological relativism. Even if he used sophistic tricks and strategies to win an argument, he takes the position that we can make definite statements about virtue and ethics that are not merely culturally—and personally—relative. This commitment to ethical values and beliefs set him apart from the Sophists.

These issues are addressed in the reading from the *Gorgias*, which contains a conversation between Socrates and Callicles, a student of Gorgias, a well-known Sophist or rhetorician. It is notable that Callicles originally accuses Socrates of slyness, suggesting that he has purposely confused the two meanings of "justice" in order to confound those who argue against him. Later, he describes Socrates as a splitter of words, another sophist criticism, and derides philosophy as a frivolous amusement.

The exchange nevertheless seems to set sophistry and philosophy against each other. Callicles takes a pre-Socratic or sophistic position, which holds that nature (*physis*) is supreme. This position, which contains elements of the warrior ideal, reflects the state of constant warfare that had subsumed ancient Greece. Callicles, a realist in the fabulist tradition, believes in a "lion-like natural justice" that favors the stronger. Hercules can take what he wants.

Socrates objects that Callicles's position, however, is inconsistent with his desires. This is because Callicles is an honor-seeker and honor is based on the esteem of other people. It therefore lies outside nature, in *nomos* (custom), which is conventional. There is a sexual subtext, since Callicles has two beloveds—not only demos, the people, but also a man, Demos. Both need to be flattered. We cannot force other people to love us.

Some philosophers have argued that the right response to Socrates is to recognize that there are two kinds of sophisms: a *physis* (or nature) sophism that views human life as a competitive struggle between the weak and the strong and a *nomos* (or conventional) sophism that emphasizes the importance of custom and law as the final arbiter of human action. One has to choose between these two alternatives; both cannot be justified. The discussion breaks off, however, when Socrates (who also has a male lover, Alcibiades) accuses Callicles of being a catamite—the young male sexual companion of an older man. This looks like an *ad hominem*, an attack on the person as a substitute for rational argument critique, another maneuver that we might expect from the Sophists.

The second reading is from Plato's *Apology*, which contains an account of Socrates's trial. The title refers to an "apologetics" (or polemics): an argument in support of a cause. There were three allegations: that Socrates corrupted the young; that he had taught rhetoric, making the weaker argument seem stronger (and was therefore a Sophist); and that he promoted a nature philosophy which did not acknowledge the gods the city acknowledges. Scholars have suggested that the real source of the charges was political. Ancient Athens was full of conflict, intrigue, and political manipulation. Socrates was associated with the "thirty tyrants," who had brought in a reign of terror in establishing an oligarchy. Meanwhile his trial took place during the democracy that was restored once the oligarchs were ousted.

Socrates flatly denies the charges. He is composed during the trial, if indignant, and avoids the displays of emotion and flattery—the democratic and rhetorical ploys—that were commonly used to obtain the sympathy of the jury. He describes himself as a philosophical gadfly, whose bite keeps the dozy Athenian stallion alert and focused. The decisive consideration in sentencing appears to be his refusal to bow to the authority of the jury. Once a person was convicted, it was customary to then determine the punishment, and Socrates suggests—impudently—that he should be rewarded with free meals in the town hall, a courtesy that was extended to Olympic victors. He then suggests a small fine, at the urging of his friends. But the jury returns with the death penalty.

There is a new individualism here, with its psychological accoutrements. Socrates asserts the primacy of his own moral views over the popular will and accuses those who turn their back on his arguments of misology: a hatred of reason. Whatever death may be, he says, nothing can harm a good man. He tells the jury that his mantic sign—a friendly demon and tribal hold-over, like a guardian angel and perhaps a conscience—has not opposed his conduct. There is accordingly something right in his conduct.

Plato, *Gorgias*[1]

(c. 380 BCE, but referring to earlier events)

CALLICLES: O Socrates, you are a regular declaimer...For the truth is, Socrates, that you, who pretend to be engaged in the pursuit of truth, are appealing now to the popular and vulgar notions of right, which are not natural, but only conventional. Convention and nature are generally at variance with one another...

The difference between these notions of right, as I conceive it, is that the makers of laws are the majority, who are weak; and they make laws and distribute praises and censures with a view to themselves and to their own interests; and they want to terrify the stronger sort of men, and those who are able to get the better of them in order that they may not get the better of them; and they say, that dishonesty is shameful and unjust; meaning, by the word injustice, the desire of a man to have more than his neighbors...

And therefore the endeavor to have more than the many, is conventionally said to be shameful and unjust, and is called injustice, whereas nature herself intimates that it is just for the better to have more than the worse, the more powerful than the weaker; and in many ways she shows, among men as well as among animals, and indeed among whole cities and races, that justice consists in the superior ruling over and having more than the inferior....

The most famous men are the men who act according to nature. Yes, by Heaven, and according to the law of nature. Not, perhaps, according to that artificial law, which we invent and impose upon...the best and strongest from their youth upwards, and tame them like young lions,—charming them with the sound of the voice, and saying to them, that...the equal is the honorable and the just.

But if there were a man who had sufficient force, he would shake off and break through, and escape from all this. He would trample under foot all our formulas and spells and charms, and all our laws which are against nature: the slave would rise in rebellion and be lord over us, and the light of natural justice would shine forth. And this I take to be the sentiment of Pindar...who says that Heracles[2] carried off the oxen of Geryon, according to the law of natural right, and that the oxen and other possessions of the weaker and inferior properly belong to the stronger and superior.

And this is true, as you may ascertain, if you will leave philosophy and go on to higher things: for philosophy, Socrates, if pursued in moderation and at the proper age, is an elegant accomplishment, but too much philosophy is the ruin of human life.... For a man who carries philosophy into later life is necessarily ignorant of all those things which a gentleman and a person of honor ought to know; he is inexperienced in the laws of the State, and in the language which ought to be used in the dealings of man with man, whether private or public, and utterly ignorant of the pleasures and desires of mankind and of human character in general....

And I have the same feeling about students of philosophy; when I see a youth thus engaged—the study appears to me to be in character, and becoming a man of liberal education, and him who neglects philosophy I regard as an inferior man, who will

---

1 Conversation between Socrates and Callicles (484–? BCE) in Plato's *Gorgias* (c. 380 BCE, but dealing with events before the trial and death of Socrates in 399 BCE) in Benjamin Jowett, trans., *The Dialogues of Plato* (3rd revised and corrected ed.), vol. 2 (Oxford University Press, 1892). Available at http://oll.libertyfund.org/titles/766.

2 Or Hercules. The reference to the oxen is to one of his "Twelve Labors."

never aspire to anything great or noble. But if I see him continuing the study in later life, and not leaving off, I should like to beat him, Socrates; for, as I was saying, such a one, even though he have good natural parts, becomes effeminate....

Now, Socrates, though I am very well inclined towards you, I am obliged to say that you,

Who have a soul so noble, are remarkable for
a puerile exterior;
Neither in a court of justice could you state a
case, or give any
reason or proof, offer valiant counsel on
another's behalf....[1]

For suppose that someone were to take you, or anyone of your sort, off to prison, declaring that you had done wrong when you had done no wrong, you must allow that you would not know what to do. There you would stand giddy and gaping, and not having a word to say; and when you went up before the Court, even if the accuser were a poor creature and not good for much, you would die if he were disposed to claim the penalty of death....

Cease, then, emulating these paltry splitters of words, and emulate only the man of substance and honor, who is well to do....[2]

CALLICLES: I have already told you that I mean those who are wise and courageous in the administration of a state. They ought to be the rulers of their states, and justice consists in their having more than their subjects.

SOCRATES: But whether rulers or subjects, will they or will they not have more than themselves, my friend?

CALLICLES: What do you mean?

SOCRATES: I mean that every man is his own ruler; but perhaps you think that there is no necessity for him to rule himself. He is only required to rule others?

CALLICLES: What do you mean by his "ruling over himself"?

SOCRATES: A simple thing enough: just what is commonly said, that a man should be temperate and master of himself, and ruler of his own pleasures and passions.

CALLICLES: What innocence! You mean those fools—the temperate?

SOCRATES: Certainly. Anyone may know that to be my meaning.

CALLICLES: Quite so, Socrates; and they are really fools, for how can a man be happy who is the servant of anything? On the contrary, I plainly assert that he who would truly live ought to allow his desires to wax to the uttermost and not to chastise them; but when they have grown to their greatest he should have courage and intelligence to minister to them and to satisfy all his longings. And this I affirm to be natural justice and nobility....

For if a man had been originally the son of a king, or had a nature capable of acquiring an empire or a tyranny or sovereignty, what could be more truly base or evil than temperance—to a man like him, I say, who might freely be enjoying every good, and has no one to stand in his way, and yet has admitted custom and reason and the opinion of other men to be lords over him? Must not he be in a miserable plight whom the reputation of justice and temperance hinders from giving more to his friends than to his enemies, even though he be a ruler in his city?

---

1 Callicles is citing or paraphrasing lines from Euripides's play *Antiope*.

2 In reply to Callicles's speech, Socrates asks him to tell him once and for all whom Callicles affirms to be the better and superior and in what they are better.

No, Socrates, for you profess to be a votary of the truth, and the truth is this: that luxury and intemperance and license, if they be provided with means, are virtue and happiness. All the rest is a mere bauble, agreements contrary to nature, foolish talk of men, worth nothing.

SOCRATES: There is a noble freedom, Callicles, in your way of approaching the argument; for what you say is what the rest of the world think, but do not like to say. And I must beg of you to persevere, that the true rule of human life may become manifest. Tell me, then: you say, do you not, that in the rightly-developed man the passions ought not to be controlled, but that we should let them grow to the utmost and somehow or other satisfy them, and that this is virtue?

CALLICLES: Yes; I do.

SOCRATES: Then those who want nothing are not truly said to be happy?

CALLICLES: No indeed, for then stones and dead men would be the happiest of all....

SOCRATES: Let me request you to consider how far you would accept this as an account of the two lives of the temperate and intemperate in a figure. There are two men, both of whom have a number of casks; the one man has his casks sound and full, one of wine, another of honey, and a third of milk, besides

others filled with other liquids. And the streams which fill them are few and scanty, and he can only obtain them with a great deal of toil and difficulty. But when his casks are once filled he has no need to feed them anymore, and has no further trouble with them or care about them. The other, in like manner, can procure streams, though not without difficulty; but his containers are leaky and unsound. And night and day he is compelled to be filling them, and if he pauses for a moment, he is in an agony of pain. Such are their respective lives. And now would you say that the life of the intemperate is happier than that of the temperate? Do I not convince you that the opposite is the truth?

CALLICLES: You do not convince me, Socrates, for the one who has filled himself has no longer any pleasure left; and this, as I was just now saying, is the life of a stone: he has neither joy nor sorrow after he is once filled. But the pleasure depends on the superabundance of the influx.

SOCRATES: But the more you pour in, the greater the waste; and the holes must be large for the liquid to escape.

CALLICLES: Certainly.

SOCRATES: The life which you are now depicting is not that of a dead man, or of a stone, but of a cormorant[1]...

---

1 I.e., a bird of messy habits.

Plato, *Apology*[1]

(an account of the trial of Socrates, written in the decade after Socrates's death in 399 BCE)

One of you might perhaps interrupt me and say: "But Socrates, what is your occupation? From where have these slanders come? For surely if you did not busy yourself with something out of the common, all these rumours and talk would not have arisen unless you did something other than most people. Tell us what it is, that we may not speak inadvisedly about you." Anyone who says that seems to be right, and I will try to show you what has caused this reputation and slander.

Listen, then. Perhaps some of you will think I am jesting, but be sure that all that I shall say is true. What has caused my reputation is none other than a certain kind of wisdom. What kind of wisdom? Human wisdom, perhaps. It may be that I really possess this, while those whom I mentioned just now are wise with a wisdom more than human; else I cannot explain it, for I certainly do not possess it, and whoever says I do is lying and speaks to slander me....

[Perhaps then s]omeone might say: "Are you not ashamed, Socrates, to have followed the kind of occupation that has led to your being now in danger of death?" However, I should be right to reply to him: "You are wrong, sir, if you think that a man who is any good at all should take into account the risk of life or death; he should look to this only in his actions, whether what he does is right or wrong, whether he is acting like a good or a bad man."...

This is the truth of the matter, gentlemen of the jury: wherever a man has taken a position that he believes to be best, or has been placed by his commander, there he must I think remain and face danger, without a thought for death or anything else,

rather than disgrace. It would have been a dreadful way to behave, gentlemen of the jury, if, at Potidaea, Amphipolis and Delium, I had, at the risk of death, like anyone else, remained at my post where those you had elected to command had ordered me, and then, when the god ordered me, as I thought and believed, to live the life of a philosopher, to examine myself and others, I had abandoned my post for fear of death or anything else.... To fear death, gentlemen, is no other than to think oneself wise when one is not, to think one knows what one does not know. No one knows whether death may not be the greatest of all blessings for a man, yet men fear it as if they knew that it is the greatest of evils. And surely it is the most blameworthy ignorance to believe that one knows what one does not know. It is perhaps on this point and in this respect, gentlemen, that I differ from the majority of men, and if I were to claim that I am wiser than anyone in anything, it would be in this that as I have no adequate knowledge of things in the underworld, so I do not think I have. I do know, however, that it is wicked and shameful to do wrong, to disobey one's superior, be he god or man. I shall never fear or avoid things of which I do not know, whether they may not be good rather than things that I know to be bad. Even if you acquitted me now and did not believe Anytus, who said to you that either I should not have been brought here in the first place, or that now I am here, you cannot avoid executing me, for if I should be acquitted, your sons would practise the teachings of Socrates and all be thoroughly corrupted; if you said to me in this regard: "Socrates, we do not believe Anytus now;

---

1   Plato, *The Apology* from *The Apology and Related Dialogues*, ed. Andrew Bailey, trans. Cathal Woods and Ryan Pack (Broadview Press, 2016).

we acquit you, but only on condition that you spend no more time on this investigation and do not practise philosophy, and if you are caught doing so you will die"; if, as I say, you were to acquit me on those terms, I would say to you: "Gentlemen of the jury, I am grateful and I am your friend, but I will obey the god rather than you, and as long as I draw breath and am able, I shall not cease to practise philosophy, to exhort you and in my usual way to point out to anyone of you whom I happen to meet: Good Sir, you are an Athenian, a citizen of the greatest city with the greatest reputation for both wisdom and power; are you not ashamed of your eagerness to possess as much wealth, reputation and honours as possible, while you do not care for nor give thought to wisdom or truth or the best possible state of your soul?" Then, if one of you disputes this and says he does care, I shall not let him go at once or leave him, but I shall question him, examine him and test him, and if I do not think he has attained the goodness that he says he has, I shall reproach him because he attaches little importance to the most important things and greater importance to inferior things. I shall treat in this way anyone I happen to meet, young and old, citizen and stranger, and more so the citizens because you are more kindred to me. Be sure that this is what the god orders me to do, and I think there is no greater blessing for the city than my service to the god. For I go around doing nothing but persuading both young and old among you not to care for your body or your wealth in preference to or as strongly as for the best possible state of your soul, as I say to you: "Wealth does not bring about excellence, but excellence makes wealth and everything else good for men, both individually and collectively."

Now if by saying this I corrupt the young, this advice must be harmful, but if anyone says that I give different advice, he is talking nonsense. On this point I would say to you, gentlemen of the jury: "Whether you believe Anytus or not, whether you acquit me or not, do so on the understanding that this is my course of action, even if I am to face death

many times." Do not create a disturbance, gentlemen, but abide by my request not to cry out at what I say but to listen, for I think it will be to your advantage to listen, and I am about to say other things at which you will perhaps cry out. By no means do this. Be sure that if you kill the sort of man I say I am, you will not harm me more than yourselves. Neither Meletus nor Anytus can harm me in any way; he could not harm me, for I do not think it is permitted that a better man be harmed by a worse...

Indeed, gentlemen of the jury, I am far from making a defence now on my own behalf, as might be thought, but on yours, to prevent you from wrongdoing by mistreating the god's gift to you by condemning me; for if you kill me you will not easily find another like me. I was attached to this city by the god—though it seems a ridiculous thing to say—as upon a great and noble horse which was somewhat sluggish because of its size and needed to be stirred up by a kind of gadfly. It is to fulfill some such function that I believe the god has placed me in the city. I never cease to rouse each and every one of you, to persuade and reproach you all day long and everywhere I find myself in your company.

Another such man will not easily come to be among you, gentlemen, and if you believe me you will spare me. You might easily be annoyed with me as people are when they are aroused from a doze, and strike out at me; if convinced by Anytus you could easily kill me, and then you could sleep on for the rest of your days, unless the god, in his care for you, sent you someone else. That I am the kind of person to be a gift of the god to the city you might realize from the fact that it does not seem like human nature for me to have neglected all my own affairs and to have tolerated this neglect now for so many years while I was always concerned with you, approaching each one of you like a father or an elder brother to persuade you to care for virtue... Now if I profited from this by charging a fee for my advice, there would be some sense to it, but you can see for yourselves that, for all their shameless accusations, my accusers have not been able in their impudence to bring forward a witness to say that I have ever received a fee or ever asked for one. I, on the other hand, have a convincing witness that I speak the truth, my poverty.

It may seem strange that while I go around and give this advice privately and interfere in private affairs, I do not venture to go to the assembly and there advise the city. You have heard me give the reason for this in many places. I have a divine or spiritual sign which Meletus has ridiculed in his deposition. This began when I was a child. It is a voice, and whenever it speaks it turns me away from something I am about to do, but it never encourages me to do anything. This is what has prevented me from taking part in public affairs, and I think it was quite right to prevent me. Be sure, gentlemen of the jury, that if I had long ago attempted to take part in politics, I should have died long ago, and benefited neither you nor myself. Do not be angry with me for speaking the truth; no man will survive who genuinely opposes you or any other crowd and prevents the occurrence of many unjust and illegal happenings in the city. A man who really fights for justice must lead a private, not a public, life if he is to survive for even a short time....

[The jury now gives its verdict of guilty, and Meletus asks for the penalty of death.]

... He assesses the penalty at death. So be it. What counter-assessment should I propose to you, gentlemen of the jury? Clearly it should be a penalty I deserve, and what do I deserve to suffer or to pay because I have deliberately not led a quiet life but have neglected what occupies most people: wealth, household affairs, the position of general or public orator or the other offices, the political clubs and factions that exist in the city? I thought myself too hon-est to survive if I occupied myself with those things. I did not follow that path that would have made me of no use either to you or to myself, but I went to each of you privately and conferred upon him what I say is the greatest benefit, by trying to persuade him not to care for any of his belongings before caring that he himself should be as good and as wise as possible, not to care for the city's possessions more than for the city itself, and to care for other things in the same way. What do I deserve for being such a man? Some good, gentlemen of the jury, if I must truly make an assessment according to my deserts, and something suitable. What is suitable for a poor benefactor who needs leisure to exhort you? Nothing is more suitable, gentlemen, than for such a man to be fed in the Prytaneum, much more suitable for him than for anyone of you who has won a victory at Olympia with a pair or a team of horses.[1] The Olympian victor makes you think yourself happy; I make you be happy. Besides, he does not need food, but I do. So if I must make a just assessment of what I deserve, I assess it at this: free meals in the Prytaneum....

Perhaps someone might say: But Socrates, if you leave us will you not be able to live quietly, without talking? Now this is the most difficult point on which to convince some of you. If I say that it is impossible for me to keep quiet because that means disobeying the god, you will not believe me and will think I am being ironical. On the other hand, if I say that it is the greatest good for a man to discuss virtue every day and those other things about which you hear me conversing and testing myself and others, for the unexamined life is not worth living for man, you will believe me even less.

What I say is true, gentlemen, but it is not easy to convince you. At the same time, I am not accustomed to think that I deserve any penalty. If I had money, I would assess the penalty at the amount I could pay, for that would not hurt me, but I have

---

1   The Prytaneum was an important building on the Acropolis of Athens where, among other things, dignitaries and civil servants were fed. Olympic winners were awarded meals there.

none, unless you are willing to set the penalty at the amount I can pay, and perhaps I could pay you one mina of silver. So that is my assessment.

Plato here, gentlemen of the jury, and Crito and Critobulus and Apollodorus bid me put the penalty at thirty minae, and they will stand surety for the money.[1] Well then, that is my assessment, and they will be sufficient guarantee of payment.

[The jury now votes again and sentences Socrates to death.]

... I am saying this not to all of you but to those who condemned me to death, and to these same

jurors I say: Perhaps you think that I was convicted for lack of such words as might have convinced you, if I thought I should say or do all I could to avoid my sentence. Far from it. I was convicted because I lacked not words but boldness and shamelessness and the willingness to say to you what you would most gladly have heard from me, lamentations and tears and my saying and doing many things that I say are unworthy of me but that you are accustomed to hear from others. I did not think then that the danger I ran should make me do anything mean, nor do I now regret the nature of my defence. I would much rather die after this kind of defence than live after making the other kind....

Questions

1. How do the moral views in Homer and the ethical realism in Aesop's fables find expression in Callicles's arguments?

2. Many people would say—privately, at least—that most of us want riches and power. So Callicles may be right. Can you think of someone who has openly subscribed to Callicles's moral philosophy? Defend their actions against moral criticism.

3. Explain Callicles's distinction between natural and conventional justice. What does his position say about morality more generally?

4. Describe the different kinds of life that Callicles and Socrates promote. Which is the better life, and why? Which is the happier life, and why?

5. Socrates says he would rather face death than commit a wrong or an act of injustice. Would you make the same choice? Why, why not?

6. Socrates invites us to live an examined life, which involves the wisdom of not pretending to know what is unknown. What are the implications of living this way?

7. Socrates says that he is like a gadfly, which keeps the steed of Athens lively and aware. Do you agree? Can you think of someone who has performed a similar service? Explain.

8. Socrates makes it clear to the jury that he will not stop searching for knowledge. Is he a moral hero, who refuses to compromise, even in the face of death? Or is he a troublemaker, who refuses to submit to the public will?

---

1 This was a relatively large sum of money; according to one estimate, the equivalent of eight-and-a-half years' salary.

Suggested Readings

For the Sophists, see the suggested readings in chapter 12. Although Socrates left no writings, his life and martyrdom had such a significant effect on Plato and the Hellenistic schools that their writings could all be said to be those of a Socratic school.

The standard English translations of the Socratic dialogues are included in the suggested readings for chapter 11. Other translations of *Gorgias* include those by Donald Zeyl, Robin Waterfield, W.R.M. Lamb, and Walter Hamilton. For alternative translations of the *Apology* see those by G.M.A. Grube, Reginald Allen, Thomas and Grace West, and F.J. Church. For historical accounts of Socrates's trial, see C.D.C. Reeve, ed., *The Trials of Socrates: Six Classic Texts* (2002), which includes Plato's four dialogues (*Euthyphro*, *Apology*, *Crito*, and *Phaedo*), Aristophanes's *Clouds*, and Xenophon's *Socrates' Defense to the Jury*. The contrasting portraits of Socrates by these three authors make for interesting reading. A more exhaustive treatment of the trial may be found in Thomas Brickhouse and Nicholas Smith, *Socrates on Trial* (1989, 2002).

Other sources include David C. Corey, *The Sophists in Plato's Dialogues* (2015), Sarah Broadie, "The Sophists and Socrates" (2003), David Lewis Schaefer, "Was Socrates a Corruptor?" (1992), and the older paper by A.K. Rogers, "The Ethics of Socrates" (1925).

Chapter 11

Plato

Plato (427 BCE–347 BCE) was a student of Socrates. His birth name was Aristocles and as a young man he supposedly aspired to be a poet. After hearing Socrates arguing in the marketplace, however, he was so taken by what he said that he went home, burned his poems, and decided to devote the rest of his life to philosophy. The name "Plato" (Greek for "broad") is a nickname that was awarded to him either because he was broad-shouldered, had a broad forehead, was broad in the torso (i.e., overweight), or had a broad knowledge of philosophy.

Unlike Socrates, Plato came from a noble Athenian family, which had become embroiled in the political troubles of the time. One of his uncles, Charmides, was one of the "thirty tyrants" who ruled the city at the end of the Peloponnesian War. These associations undoubtedly played a role in the conviction and execution of Socrates, who was associated with the aristocratic faction in the city.

After Socrates's death, Plato left Athens, meeting other thinkers and traveling through Attica, Cyrene, Italy, Sicily, and even Egypt. When he returned to Athens, in about 387 BCE, he instituted what is widely regarded as the first university, called the Academy, which was situated on a wooded site, named after the mythological hero *Akademos*, about a mile or so outside the city walls. Since Plato, who was influenced by the teachings of Pythagoras, believed that rigorous mathematics (geometry) provided the best preparation for logical argument, he had, apparently, the motto "Let None but Mathematicians Enter Here" carved over the gateway to the school.

Plato stayed at the Academy for the rest of his life, except for two ill-fated trips to Sicily. Invited to Syracuse to put his theory of government into practice, he was caught up in political intrigues. On both occasions his life and liberty were put at risk, but he managed to escape. He then returned to Athens and took up residence at the Academy, where he taught and wrote for the last thirteen years or so of his life. Ancient sources suggest that he was buried on the Academy grounds. Although the philosophical orientation of the school shifted decisively towards skepticism after Plato's death, it reputedly survived until 86 BCE, when it was destroyed in a Roman military campaign.

Although Plato does not appear in the dialogues, it is evident that he often uses the voice of Socrates, particularly in the later dialogues, to express his own views. As we have already seen, the earlier dialogues often pit Socrates against the Sophists, who argue that morality is conventional and therefore relative. Socrates rejects their arguments and consistently maintains that virtue has some objective basis, which can be grasped through the exercise of reason. Socrates's practical views seem in keeping with the practical wisdom tradition.

Plato's wisdom-interests lie in theory. In the later dialogues, he sets out an extensive metaphysical system that sees material objects as imperfect reflections of divine, eternal, unchangeable ideas called "forms" (*eidos* in the singular and *eidē* in the plural). The "idealism" in his system reflects the influence of the pre-Socratic philosophers such as Pythagoras, Heraclitus, and Parmenides, and sharply distinguishes intellectual from physical sorts of experience. Plato believes that our ideas are more real than material objects. The summit of morality accordingly lies in the intellectual experience of the highest idea of all, a divine archetype, which Plato calls the form of the good (the *agathon,* ἀγαθόν). It is only reason, logic, and argument that can lead us to the knowledge of this ultimate metaphysical and moral principle.

Morality and immorality are products of our knowledge or ignorance, respectively, of the form of the good, which we perceive imperfectly. Since our physical appetites distract us from the hard work of acquiring such knowledge, the route to virtue accordingly lies in philosophy, and a theoretical wisdom, which provides the necessary corrective. As one might expect from someone with his metaphysical views, Plato believes that the human soul is eternal and divine. There is therefore life after death, and the gods use reincarnation to reward the good and punish the bad, a view very much in line with the Eastern idea of karma.

The first two readings are from the *Republic,* which has become Plato's most widely read work. The book takes the form of a dialogue between Socrates and a group of young men, who discuss the meaning of justice. It sets out Plato's mature views on politics and morality. These subjects overlap in the mind of the ancient Greeks, who did not conceive of the moral person outside society and believed that the good state produces good persons.

Early in the dialogue, after a famous exchange with Thrasymachus—who, like Callicles, believes that might is right—Plato's older brother, Glaucon, relates the fable-myth of Gyges, who found a ring that made him invisible and used it to kill the king and take his kingdom. Glaucon declares that any rational person would take full advantage of such a situation. People are only moral because they are afraid of being caught and punished.

Socrates disagrees. In order to demonstrate that morality is valuable for its own sake, he draws an analogy between the city and the individual. In the ideal city, he argues, there are three classes. There is the gold caste, the philosopher kings (called Guardians), who rule benevolently with the help of the silver caste, the military and police (called Auxiliaries). The lowest bronze caste comprises artisans, menial workers, and the general masses who provide for the physical needs of everyone. Plato is not an egalitarian. Since philosophy is the route to virtue, he assumes that the state should be run by those educated in philosophy, who must therefore be the most virtuous.

Plato then takes the position that there are three parts to the human soul, just as there are three parts to the city: the mind (*logistikon*), a source of intelligence and reason which Socrates figuratively represents as a man; the spirited part (*thymos*), which controls enthusiasm and will, which Socrates represents as a lion; and the appetites (*epithymia*), the source of biological drives and sensual desires, which Socrates represents as a hungry hydra, a many-headed monster capable of growing new heads (and mouths) at will.

These three parts of the soul are in harmony in the just individual, whose mind makes use of the spirited part to restrain the appetites. To put it metaphorically, the interior man, with the help of the lion, rules over the hydra so as to ensure a life of law-abiding moderation (*sophrosune*). When the appetites rebel and seize control, the hydra fights with the lion, enslaving the interior man. The disorder is tyranny. It follows that the unjust individual mirrors the unjust city; in both cases, the worst rules the best, which leads inevitably to chaos and disaster.

In establishing this general position, Plato broaches many other topics. In one digression (the second reading below), he sketches out the Analogy of the Cave, which depicts ordinary people as unthinking prisoners looking at shadows on a wall which they mistake for reality; in another, he proposes using noble lies (i.e., propaganda) for the sake of promoting public loyalty; in another he argues for censorship of the arts; in yet another he argues that women are the intellectual equals of men. Plato criticizes democracy as a form of government, perhaps thinking of Athens, on the basis that it leads to tyranny, which is the worst form of government.

The last reading is an excerpt from the Seventh Letter, the authenticity of which has been disputed by some scholars. It nevertheless expresses the mystical element in Plato's work, and his view that the highest wisdom belies human expression. Philosophy, properly practiced and studied, leads us to the contemplation of goodness in itself, a truth so elevated that it cannot be expressed in words. This mystical vein was mined by Plotinus and other Neoplatonists several centuries later.

READING 11A

Plato, "The Rational Self and Tripartite Soul"[1]

from the *Politeia* (usually known in English as the *Republic*, 380–360 BCE)

Book IV

SOCRATES: First let us complete the old investigation, which we began, as you remember, under the impression that if we could previously examine justice on the larger scale, there would be less difficulty in discerning her in the individual. That larger example appeared to be the State, and accordingly we constructed as good a one as we could, knowing well that in the good State justice would be found.

---

1   Plato, "The Rational Self and Tripartite Soul," from *The Republic*, Book IV, in Benjamin Jowett, trans., *The Dialogues of Plato* (2nd ed.), vol. 3 (Oxford: Clarendon Press, 1875). Available at http://classics.mit.edu/Plato/republic.html.

Let the discovery which we made be now applied to the individual...

The just man then, if we regard the idea of justice only, will be like the just State?

GLAUCON: He will....

SOCRATES: And a State was thought by us to be just when the three classes in the State severally did their own business; and also thought to be temperate and valiant and wise by reason of certain other affections and qualities of these same classes?

GLAUCON: True.

SOCRATES: And so of the individual. We may assume that he has the same three principles in his own soul which are found in the State; and he may be rightly described in the same terms because he is affected in the same manner?

GLAUCON: Certainly....

SOCRATES: Must we not acknowledge that in each of us there are the same principles and habits which there are in the State; and that from the individual they pass into the State?—how else can they come there? Take the quality of passion or spirit. It would be ridiculous to imagine that this quality, when found in States, is not derived from the individuals who are supposed to possess it, e.g. the Thracians, Scythians, and in general the northern nations; and the same may be said of the love of knowledge, which is the special characteristic of our part of the world,...

But the question is not quite so easy when we proceed to ask whether these principles are three or one. Whether, that is to say, we learn with one part of our nature, are angry with another, and with a third part desire the satisfaction of our natural appetites; or whether the whole soul comes into play in each sort of action—to determine that is the difficulty.

GLAUCON: Yes, there lies the difficulty.

SOCRATES: Then let us now try and determine whether they are the same or different....

The same thing clearly cannot act or be acted upon in the same part or in relation to the same thing at the same time, in contrary ways; and therefore whenever this contradiction occurs in things apparently the same, we know that they are really not the same, but different....

For example, can the same thing be at rest and in motion at the same time in the same part?

GLAUCON: Impossible....

SOCRATES: Then the soul of the thirsty one, in so far as he is thirsty, desires only drink; for this he yearns and tries to obtain it?

... And if you suppose something which pulls a thirsty soul away from drink, that must be different from the thirsty principle which draws him like a beast to drink; for, as we were saying, the same thing cannot at the same time with the same part of itself act in contrary ways about the same....

And might a man be thirsty, and yet unwilling to drink?

GLAUCON: Yes, it constantly happens....

SOCRATES: Would you not say that there was something in the soul bidding a man to drink, and something else forbidding him, which is other and stronger than the principle which bids him?

... And the forbidding principle is derived from reason, and that which bids and attracts proceeds from passion and disease?

GLAUCON: Clearly.

Then we may fairly assume that they are two, and that they differ from one another. The one with which man reasons, we may call the rational principle of the soul; the other, with which he loves and hungers and thirsts and feels the flutterings of any other desire, may be termed the irrational or appetitive, the ally of sundry pleasures and satisfactions?

GLAUCON: Yes, we may fairly assume them to be different.

SOCRATES: Then let us finally determine that there are two principles existing in the soul. And what of passion, or spirit? Is it a third, or akin to one of the preceding?

GLAUCON: I should be inclined to say—akin to desire.

SOCRATES: Well, there is a story which I remember to have heard, and in which I put faith. The story is that Leontius, the son of Aglaion, coming up one day from the Piraeus, under the north wall on the outside,[1] observed some dead bodies lying on the ground at the place of execution. He felt a desire to see them, and also a dread and abhorrence of them. For a time he struggled and covered his eyes, but at length the desire got the better of him; and forcing them open, he ran up to the dead bodies, saying, Look, you wretches, take your fill of the fair sight....

The moral of the tale is that anger at times goes to war with desire, as though they were two distinct things....

GLAUCON: Yes, that is the meaning....

SOCRATES: But a further question arises: Is passion different from reason also, or only a kind of reason; in which latter case, instead of three principles in the soul, there will only be two, the rational and the appetitive; or rather, as the State was composed of three classes, traders, auxiliaries, counsellors, so may there not be in the individual soul a third element

which is passion or spirit, and when not corrupted by bad education is the natural auxiliary of reason?

GLAUCON: Yes, there must be a third.

SOCRATES: Yes, if passion, which has already been shown to be different from desire, turns out also to be different from reason.

GLAUCON: But that is easily proved. We may observe even in young children that they are full of spirit almost as soon as they are born, whereas some of them never seem to attain to the use of reason, and most of them late enough.

SOCRATES: Excellent, and you may see passion equally in brute animals, which is a further proof of the truth of what you are saying....

And so,...we are fairly agreed that the same principles which exist in the State exist also in the individual, and that they are three in number.

GLAUCON: Exactly.

SOCRATES: Must we not then infer that the individual is wise in the same way, and in virtue of the same quality which makes the State wise?

GLAUCON: Certainly.

SOCRATES: Also that the same quality which constitutes courage in the State constitutes courage in the individual, and that both the State and the individual bear the same relation to all the other virtues?

... And the individual will be acknowledged by us to be just in the same way in which the State is just?

GLAUCON: That follows, of course.

---

1 The Piraeus is the port harbor of the city of Athens. There was a wall, approximately 12 kilometers long, along the road that connected Athens to the Piraeus, which served as the naval base during Athens's period of dominance.

SOCRATES: We cannot but remember that the justice of the State consisted in each of the three classes doing the work of its own class? ...

GLAUCON: Yes, we must remember that too.

SOCRATES: And ought not the rational principle, which is wise, and has the care of the whole soul, to rule, and the passionate or spirited principle to be the subject and ally?

GLAUCON: Certainly....

SOCRATES: And these two, thus nurtured and educated, and having learned truly to know their own functions, will rule over the appetitive, which in each of us is the largest part of the soul and by nature most insatiable of gain; over this they will keep guard, lest, waxing great and strong with the fullness of bodily pleasures, as they are termed, the appetitive soul, no longer confined to her own sphere, should attempt to enslave and rule those who are not her natural-born subjects, and overturn the whole life of man? ...

GLAUCON: True.

SOCRATES: And he is to be deemed courageous whose spirit retains in pleasure and in pain the commands of reason about what he ought or ought not to fear?

... And him we call wise who has in him that little part which rules, and which proclaims these commands; that part too being supposed to have a knowledge of what is for the interest of each of the three parts and of the whole?

GLAUCON: Assuredly.

SOCRATES: And would you not say that he is temperate who has these same elements in friendly harmony, in whom the one ruling principle of reason, and the two subject ones of spirit and desire are equally agreed that reason ought to rule, and do not rebel?

GLAUCON: Certainly, that is the true account of temperance whether in the State or individual....

SOCRATES: If the case is put to us, must we not admit that the just State, or the man who is trained in the principles of such a State, will be less likely than the unjust to make away with a deposit of gold or silver? Would any one deny this?

GLAUCON: No one.

SOCRATES: Will the just man or citizen ever be guilty of sacrilege or theft, or treachery either to his friends or to his country?

GLAUCON: Never.

SOCRATES: Neither will he ever break faith where there have been oaths or agreements?

GLAUCON: Impossible.

SOCRATES: No one will be less likely to commit adultery, or to dishonor his father and mother, or to fail in his religious duties?

GLAUCON: No one.

SOCRATES: And the reason is that each part of him is doing its own business, whether in ruling or being ruled?

GLAUCON: Exactly so.

Plato, "The Allegory of the Cave"[1]

from the *Republic* (380–360 BCE)

Book VII

SOCRATES: And now, let me show in a figure how far our nature is enlightened or unenlightened. Behold! human beings living in an underground den, which has a mouth open towards the light and reaching all along the den. Here they have been from their childhood, and have their legs and necks chained so that they cannot move, and can only see before them, being prevented by the chains from turning round their heads. Above and behind them a fire is blazing at a distance, and between the fire and the prisoners there is a raised pathway; and you will see, if you look, a low wall built along the way, like the screen which marionette players have in front of them, over which they show the puppets...

And do you see...men passing along the wall carrying all sorts of vessels and statues and figures of animals made of wood and stone and various materials, which appear over the wall? Some of them are talking, others silent.

GLAUCON: You have shown me a strange image, and they are strange prisoners.

SOCRATES: Like ourselves; and they see only their own shadows, or the shadows of one another, which the fire throws on the opposite wall of the cave. ... And of the objects which are being carried in like manner they would only see the shadows.... And if they were able to converse with one another, would they not suppose that they were naming what was actually before them?

GLAUCON: Very true.

SOCRATES: And suppose further that the prison had an echo which came from the other side, would they not be sure to fancy when one of the passers-by spoke that the voice which they heard came from the passing shadow? ... To them...the truth would be literally nothing but the shadows of the images.

GLAUCON: That is certain.

SOCRATES: And now look again, and see what will naturally follow if the prisoners are released and disabused of their error. At first, when any of them is liberated and compelled suddenly to stand up and turn his neck round and walk and look towards the light, he will suffer sharp pains. The glare will distress him, and he will be unable to see the realities of which in his former state he had seen the shadows. And then conceive someone saying to him, that what he saw before was an illusion, but that now, when he is approaching nearer to being and his eye is turned towards more real existence, he has a clearer vision—what will be his reply? And you may further imagine that his instructor is pointing to the objects as they pass and requiring him to name them—will he not be perplexed? Will he not fancy that the shadows which he formerly saw are truer than the objects which are now shown to him?

GLAUCON: Far truer.

SOCRATES: And if he is compelled to look straight

---

1 Plato, "The Allegory of the Cave," from *The Republic*, Book VII, in Benjamin Jowett, trans., *The Dialogues of Plato* (2d ed.), vol. 3 (Oxford: Clarendon Press, 1875). Available at http://classics.mit.edu/Plato/republic.html.

at the light, will he not have a pain in his eyes which will make him turn away and take in the lower objects of vision which he can see, and which he will conceive to be in reality clearer than the higher things which are now being shown to him?

... And suppose once more, that he is reluctantly dragged up a steep and rugged ascent, and held fast until he's forced into the presence of the sun himself, is he not likely to be pained and irritated? When he approaches the light his eyes will be dazzled, and he will not be able to see anything at all of what are now called realities....

He will require to grow accustomed to the sight of the upper world. And first he will see the shadows best, next the reflections of men and other objects in the water, and then the objects themselves; then he will gaze upon the light of the moon and the stars and the spangled heaven; and he will see the sky and the stars by night better than the sun or the light of the sun by day.

...Last of all he will be able to see the sun, and not mere reflections of him in the water, but he will see him in his own proper place, and not in another; and he will contemplate him as he is.

GLAUCON: Certainly.

SOCRATES: He will then proceed to argue that this is he who gives the season and the years, and is the guardian of all that is in the visible world, and in a certain way the cause of all things which he and his fellows have been accustomed to behold?

GLAUCON: Clearly... he would first see the sun and then reason about him.

SOCRATES: And when he remembered his old habitation, and the wisdom of the den and his fellow-prisoners, do you not suppose that he would congratulate himself on the change, and pity them?

GLAUCON: Certainly, he would.... I think that he would rather suffer anything than entertain these false notions and live in this miserable manner.

SOCRATES: Imagine once more, such an one coming suddenly out of the sun to be replaced in his old situation; would he not be certain to have his eyes full of darkness?

GLAUCON: To be sure.

SOCRATES: And if there were a contest, and he had to compete in measuring the shadows with the prisoners who had never moved out of the den, while his sight was still weak, and before his eyes had become steady (and the time which would be needed to acquire this new habit of sight might be very considerable) would he not be ridiculous? Men would say of him that up he went and down he came without his eyes; and that it was better not even to think of ascending; and if any one tried to unchain another and lead him up to the light, let them only catch the offender, and they would put him to death....

This entire allegory you may now append, dear Glaucon, to the previous argument.[1] The prison-house is the world of sight, the light of the fire is the sun, and you will not misapprehend me if you interpret the journey upwards to be the ascent of the soul into the intellectual world according to my poor belief, which, at your desire, I have expressed whether rightly or wrongly, God knows. But, whether true or

---

1 The reference is to two other images and analogies Plato presented and explained just before this allegory. In the analogy of the sun, the sun is an image for the Form of Good (or Goodness), whose light makes truth intelligible and knowable. In the analogy of the divided line, the vertical line is divided into the world of sight and the intellectual world. Both worlds are further subdivided into two sections: the first into sensible objects and images, and the second into forms (or ideas) and numbers, both of which have real being. The ascent out of the cave further clarifies both analogies together by showing how the philosopher-king is to go through the four sections of the line to reach the highest sort of intellectual truth about the Good.

false, my opinion is that in the world of knowledge the idea of good appears last of all, and is seen only with an effort; and, when seen, is also inferred to be the universal author of all things beautiful and right, parent of light and of the lord of light in this visible world, and the immediate source of reason and truth in the intellectual; and that this is the power upon which he who would act rationally, either in public or private life, must have his eye fixed....

But then, if I am right, certain professors of education must be wrong when they say that they can put a knowledge into the soul which was not there before, like sight into blind eyes.... our argument shows that the power and capacity of learning exists in the soul already; and that just as the eye was unable to turn from darkness to light without the whole body, so too the instrument of knowledge can only by the movement of the whole soul be turned from the world of becoming into that of being, and learn by degrees to endure the sight of being, and of the brightest and best of being, or in other words, of the good....

Then, the business of us who are the founders of the State will be to compel the best minds to attain that knowledge which we have already shown to be the greatest of all. They must continue to ascend until they arrive at the good. But when they have ascended and seen enough we must not allow them to do as they do now....

I mean that they remain in the upper world, but this must not be allowed. They must be made to descend again among the prisoners in the den, and partake of their labors and honors, whether they are worth having or not.

GLAUCON: But is not this unjust? Ought we to give them a worse life, when they might have a better?

SOCRATES: You have again forgotten, my friend, the intention of the legislator, who did not aim at making any one class in the State happy above the rest; the happiness was to be in the whole State. And he held the citizens together by persuasion and necessity, making them benefactors of the State, and therefore benefactors of one another. To this end he created them, not to please themselves, but to be his instruments in binding up the State.

Plato, *Seventh Letter*[1]

(353 BCE)

Plato to the kindred and friends of Dion[2]—Prosperity

Thus much I can say about all who either have written, or shall write, and state that they know about what things I am occupied. Whether they have heard from myself or others, or have discovered themselves, it is not possible for them to know anything about my opinions upon the matter. For there is not, and never will be, any writing of mine about them. For a matter

---

1 Plato, "The Seventh Letter" (353 BCE), trans. by George Burges, 1851. Available at https://en.wikisource.org/wiki/Epistles_(Plato)/Seventh_Letter.

2 Dion was tyrant of Syracuse and for a brief period a student of Plato's.

of that kind cannot be expressed by words, like other things to be learned; but by a long intercourse with the subject and living with it, a light is kindled suddenly, as if from a leaping fire, and being generated within the soul, feeds itself upon itself.

Thus much I know, however, that what has been written or said by me, has been said in the best manner; and moreover, that what has been written badly, does not pain me in the least. But if it had appeared to me that such matters could be written or spoken of sufficiently before the masses, what could have been done by us more beautiful in life than to impart a great benefit to mankind, and to bring nature to light before all? I think, however, that the attempt in favor of such things being promulgated, would not be beneficial except to a few, who are able with a little showing to make discoveries for themselves. But of the rest, some it will fill with a mistaken contempt by no means reasonable, and others with a lofty and vain hope, as if they had learned something solemn.

And it has now come into my mind to say something further still. For perhaps by what I am about to say a portion of what has been said will become more clear. For a certain true account is the antagonist of him who dares to write anything whatever about matters of this kind. Although it has been stated by me frequently before, it seems it must be stated on the present occasion, too.

There are three things, acting like instruments, through which it is necessary for knowledge (or science) to be produced. The fourth thing is the knowledge itself. And the fifth is the thing itself that is known and exists truly. Of these things, the first is its name; the second its definition; the third its resemblance; and the fourth its knowledge.

Now if you desire to understand what has been just now asserted, take one example, and imagine that this is so in all cases. A circle is called something to which there is the name we have just mentioned. Its definition is the second thing, composed of nouns and verbs. For that which is everywhere equally distant from the circumference to the middle, would be the definition of that to which is given the name of 'round,' and 'annular,' and 'circle.' But the third is the circle, drawn or blotted out, or made on a lathe or destroyed. The circle itself is none of these accidental features or properties, which, being of a different nature, are affected and are predicated of the circle. The fourth thing is the knowledge and intelligence and correct opinion about these things. And the whole of this must be laid down as one thing, which exists neither in voice, nor in a corporeal figure, but is in the soul. By this example it is manifest that there is something different from the nature itself of the circle, and the three previously mentioned instruments. But among these four things, knowledge and intelligence, by its relation and similitude, approaches the nearest to the fifth, while the rest are more remote from it.

The same is the case with respect to a thing straight, and circular things, and with figure, and with color, and of a thing good, and beautiful, and just, and of every body whether fashioned by the hand or produced according to nature, and of fire, and water, and all things of that kind, and of every animal, and of character in souls, and of all actions and things suffered.

For unless a person does, after a certain manner, understand all four of these things, he will never perfectly participate in the knowledge relating to the fifth. Moreover, on account of the weakness of language, these four no less endeavor to show forth the quality (or likeness) than the being of each thing that exists truly. On this account, no one possessing a mind will ever dare to place the things, which are perceived by the soul and mind, under the same view as those four things that are represented by figures and in language, and especially in language which, once written, remains fixed and is never to be changed.

Questions

1. The Greek tradition originated in tribal sources. The philosophical nature of Plato's moral theory is relatively different and new, however. In what ways does it depart from the tribal view?

2. Explain the analogy that Socrates draws between the "just" individual and the just State. Do you agree with the analogy?

3. Briefly describe the three parts of the soul and their hierarchical order. What are the four virtues of the soul and how do they correspond to its parts?

4. Answer either question. On the basis of the allegory of the cave, what would you expect Plato's philosophy of education to be? What would you expect his political philosophy to be?

5. In the Seventh Letter, Plato says there are three instruments by which we can know things. He then adds that there is knowledge and the thing known. Discuss. What is Plato's principal point?

6. Commentators have argued that the Seventh Letter draws our attention to a mystical element in wisdom, which transcends ordinary language and may be compared to a flame leaping from one soul to another. What do you make of such a claim?

7. Based on the readings, what would you say is the ultimate purpose of life and morality? What role does the idea of the good play in our private and public lives? How does virtue fit into this?

Suggested Readings

There are numerous English translations of Plato's works available in print and online. A standard English translation containing all twenty-eight of Plato's dialogues today is that by J.M. Cooper, ed., *Plato: Complete Works* (Hackett, 1997). The previous standard was Benjamin Jowett, ed., *The Dialogues of Plato* (Oxford University Press, 1871, 1875, 1891). The latter translation is available in the Online Library of Liberty, at oll.libertyfund.org; at The Internet Classics Archive, classics.mit.edu; and in English and Greek at the Perseus Project, perseus.tufts.edu.

Although many of Plato's dialogues touch on ethical themes, those with a predominantly ethical theme include *Euthyphro, Apology, Crito, Charmides, Laches, Protagoras,* and *Gorgias.* The authenticity of the letters attributed to Plato is disputed. There are also issues regarding Plato's own beliefs and views, which are invariably presented through the opinions and arguments of the characters in the dialogues. A list of readings providing various interpretive strategies may be found in the bibliography at plato.stanford.edu. See also Terence Irwin, *Plato's Ethics* (1995), J.M.E. Moravcsik, "Plato and Platonism: Plato's Conception of Appearance and Reality in Ontology, Epistemology, and Ethics" (1992), and, more generally, Gail Fine, ed., *Plato, Volume 2: Ethics, Politics, Religion and the Soul* (1999).

Chapter 12

The Greek Sophists

We know the early Sophist tradition only in skeletal form. The term 'Sophist' was nevertheless taken, like the word 'philosophy,' from *sophia* (σοφία), the Greek word for wisdom. Although the distinction between these two branches of the wisdom inquiry is often quite nebulous, Sophistry gave rise to rhetoric, which developed independently of philosophy. Sophism is nevertheless significant, like philosophy, because it introduced a rational and theoretical component into the wisdom tradition, which hitherto had concerned itself primarily with practical wisdom.

The later Sophist tradition is familiar to us through Plato and Aristotle. By Socrates's time, the Sophists had become itinerant teachers, who went from one Greek city-state to another, teaching 'higher education,' i.e., an education beyond the rudimentary education common in Greek societies at the time. This met a growing need in the Greek city-states and particularly in Athens, which was going through fundamental social changes at the time. This probably reflected a change to a money economy and was similar to the changes that led to the introduction of professional teaching in China.

The stability of the older, class-based system was threatened by the new realities, which favored personal opportunity and upward mobility. The aristocratic elites, whose wealth was hereditary and based on the ownership of land, found themselves in competition with a new class of nouveaux riches, who had become wealthy through commerce and trade. It was the newer class especially that sought out instruction from Sophists, who promised to teach them the skills required to succeed in the legal and political arena. These skills included grammar, rhetoric (use of language to persuade others), and oration (delivery of speeches).

The Sophists claimed to teach *aretē* (ἀρετή), virtue, which was also a term of general application and in popular usage meant "excellence." As a result of the changes in society, the newer class saw "excellence" as a political as well as a moral quality. This changed the fundamental understanding of virtue, which had previously been seen as a function of character. The reaction of some aristocrats was predictably indignant: they bridled at the idea that the Sophists were selling 'virtue,' something traditionally won on the battle field at the risk of losing one's own life for the safety and good of community.

The traditional notion of virtue was also connected to citizenship, which had come out of the earlier ideas of clan and tribe, and the new ideas must have seemed radically democratic, superficially valuable but really not. The Greeks were keenly aware of the possibilities for manipulation in the new legal and political order. In spite of this, it was evident that young men were willing to pay high fees in order to acquire the skills that they thought would advance them in their political careers and improve their social status.

The Sophists taught public speaking and debate, and introduced dialectic, the art of discussion, which was supposedly invented by Zeno the Eleatic. The focus was on argument and persuasion. It was the substantive philosophical views behind their teaching, however, that seemed to threaten the established order. The Sophists argued that knowledge, in the strict sense, was not available to us, since we are always at the mercy of our senses. This leaves us only with opinion, which prompted Protagoras to make the famous remark: "Man is the measure of all things; of the things that are, that they are; of the things that are not, that they are not."

There are academic issues here. Although some commentators have disputed the "commonplace" that the Sophists were relativists, this is merely a matter of emphasis. In point of fact, the Sophists were very mitigated—i.e., qualified—relativists. They avoided extreme positions and accepted that we have a common fund of experience which permits us to enter into a meaningful exchange of ideas. Indeed, in many ways their epistemological position resembles our scientific approach, since it pointed to the need to supply evidence in support of propositions.

The ethical relativism and agnosticism of the Sophists nevertheless challenged the foundations of the popular beliefs of the time. Protagoras did not deny the gods: he merely stated that he could not say whether they existed, or what form they took. This must have shaken the popular mind to its core, for it is plain where it leads. Philosophically, the Sophists held that moral beliefs were a matter of convention and implicitly questioned their authority. This was the deeper ethical controversy that led to the charges against Socrates.

The conventional view of the Sophists is mostly a product of Plato's dialogues, which clearly make an effort to distinguish the Sophists from Socrates, who seems to endorse many of the Sophists' views. This is buttressed by some of the scholarly evidence: in the Socratic dialogues, there are many Sophists, either in the audience or participating in the dialectic. Plato often mentions their (self-proclaimed) logical, technical, or pedagogical abilities; and we can glean from the setting of the dialogues that Socrates taught in the same places where the Sophists taught. It is also evident that Socrates uses the arguments of the Sophists against them, as if he had been schooled, himself, in their methods.

The charge that Socrates had corrupted the youth was, indeed, an accusation that he was a Sophist, who had encouraged the youth to question the orthodoxies of the time, both by teaching rhetoric and by promoting a nature philosophy that left out the gods. Plato's position is easily explained by the fact that he was essentially forced—in defense of Socrates—to take the position that he was not a Sophist. It is impossible to resolve these issues here, but the dialogues are, in many ways, a response to Sophists such as Protagoras, Hippias, Gorgias, Prodicus, and Thrasymachus and their students.

It is evident that first Plato, and then Aristotle, typically portray the Sophists in a negative light. Their use of the term 'philosophy' is itself an attempt to contrast the legitimate pursuit of this new theoretical wisdom with its illegitimate counterpart. According to both the philosophers, the Sophists, in their report of the school, make endless distinctions about 'names' and the meanings of words. Their arguments are designed to win at any cost; they flaunt *dissoi logoi* (double arguments, which argue both sides of an issue); they are skeptical or indifferent towards truth claims and uncommitted in ethical matters.

For the most part, Plato and Aristotle seem to be reacting to the Sophists' moral relativism, which comes out of their epistemological position. Plato plainly believed that it was the self-interested pursuit of power and the permissive, anything-goes morality of the Sophists that lead to the downfall of Athens and the unjust execution of Socrates. The matter is complicated, however, by the fact that the skeptical elements in Sophistry made them socially conservative, since they generally adopted the moral beliefs that were popular in whichever city-state they happened to be.

The first reading contains a classic compendium of early Sophist arguments, which reflects their technical interest in the formulation of arguments. Such collections recall their habit of collecting *logoi* and fables. The reading from Antiphon provides an example of a discussion concerning the nature of the customary law (based on *nomos*, custom) and the law of nature (*physis*, i.e., the "natural law"), which is the same for all human beings. The next two readings provide an account of Protagoras, from Diogenes Laertius and the Platonic dialogue *Protagoras*. There is also a reading from Plato's dialogue *Gorgias*, named after a contemporary of Protagoras whose teaching focused on rhetorical skills. It is up to his students to decide how they will make use of skills he imparts.

Anonymous, *Dissoi Logoi: Two-Fold or Contrasting Arguments*[1]

(c. 425 BCE)

2. On seemly and shameful

(1) Contrasting arguments are also put forward on what is seemly and shameful. For some say that what is seemly and what is shameful are two different things; as the name differs, so likewise does the reality. Others, however, say that the same thing is both seemly and shameful. (2) For my part, I shall attempt an exposition of the matter along the following lines: for example, it is seemly for a boy in the flower of his growth to gratify a respectable lover, but it is shameful for a handsome boy to gratify one who is

---

1 Anonymous, "Dissoi Logoi: Two-Fold or Contrasting Arguments" (c. 425 BCE), in T.M. Robinson, trans., *Contrasting Arguments: An Edition of the Dissoi Logoi* (New York: Arno Press, 1979). Available at http://www.constitution.org/gr/dissoi_logoi.html.

not his lover.[1] (3) And it is seemly for women to wash indoors, but shameful to do it in a wrestling school; but for men it is seemly to wash in a wrestling-school or gymnasium. (4) And to have sexual intercourse with one's husband in private, where one will be concealed from view by walls, is seemly: to do it outside, however, where somebody will see, is shameful. (5) And it is seemly to have sexual intercourse with one's own husband, but very shameful with someone else's. Yes—and for the husband too it is seemly to have sexual intercourse with his own wife, but shameful with someone else's. (6) And for the husband it is shameful to adorn himself and smear himself with white lead and wear gold ornaments, but for the wife it is seemly. (7) And it is seemly to treat one's friends kindly, but shameful to treat one's enemies in such a way.... (9) However, I shall go on to what cities and nations consider shameful. To Spartans, for example, it is seemly that girls should exercise naked or walk around bare-armed or without a tunic, but to Ionians this is shameful. (10) And [in Sparta] it is seemly that boys should *not* learn arts or letters, but to Ionians it is shameful not to know all these things. (11) Among Thessalians it is seemly for a man first to select the horses from the herd and then train them and the mules *himself*, and seemly for a man first to select a steer and then slaughter, skin, and cut it up *himself*; in Sicily, however, such activities are shameful, and the work of slaves. (12) To Macedonians it appears to be seemly that girls should love and have intercourse with a man [i.e., another man] before marrying a man, but shameful to do this once they are married. To Greeks both practices are shameful. (13) The Thracians count it an adornment that their girls tattoo themselves, but in the eyes of everyone else tattoo-marks are a punishment for wrong-doers.... (14) Massagetes[2] cut up their parents and then eat them, and it seems to them an especially seemly form of entombment to be buried inside one's children; if a person did this in Greece he would be driven out of Greece and die a miserable death for doing things that are shameful and horrible.... (16) Again, to Lydians it appears seemly that girls should prostitute themselves to earn money, and in that way get married; among the Greeks no one would be willing to marry any such girl.... (18) I think that if one were to order all mankind to bring together into a single pile all that each individual considered shameful, and then again to take from this mass what each thought seemly, nothing would be left, but they would all, severally, take away everything. For not everyone has the same views.... (20) To put the matter generally, all things are seemly when done at the right moment, but shameful when done at the wrong moment. What then have I managed to do? I said I would demonstrate that the same things are shameful and seemly, and I demonstrated it in all the above-mentioned cases.

---

1 Note that the lover in question is an adult male. Greek culture generally accepted certain homosexual relations between an adult male and an adolescent male. It was an educational institution for the inculcation of moral and cultural values as well as a form of sexual expression.

2 An ancient Iranian nomadic tribe.

Antiphon, *Truth*[1]

(between 430 and 400 BCE)

Justice, then, is not to transgress that which is the law of the city in which one is a citizen. A man therefore can best conduct himself in harmony with justice, if when in the company of witnesses, he upholds the laws, and when alone without witnesses he upholds the edicts of nature. For the edicts of the laws are imposed artificially, but those of nature are compulsory. And the edicts of the laws are arrived at by consent, not by natural growth, whereas those of nature are not a matter of consent.

So, if the man who transgresses the legal code evades those who have agreed to these edicts, he avoids both disgrace and penalty; otherwise not. But if a man violates against possibility any of the laws which are implanted in nature, even if he evades all men's detection, the ill is no less, and even if all see, it is no greater. For he is not hurt on account of an opinion, but because of truth. The examination of these things is in general for this reason, that the majority of just acts according to law are prescribed contrary to nature. For there is legislation about the eyes, what they must see and what not; and about the ears, what they must hear and what not; and about the tongue, what it must speak and what not; and about the hands, what they must do and what not; and about the feet, where they must go and where not. [And] the law's prohibitions are in no way more agreeable to nature and more akin than the law's [requirements]. But life belongs to nature, and death too, and life for them is derived from advantages, and death from disadvantages. And the advantages laid down by the laws are chains upon nature, but those laid down by nature are free. So that the things

which hurt, according to true reasoning, do not benefit nature more than those which delight; and things which grieve are not more advantageous than those which please; for things truly advantageous must not really harm, but must benefit....

(*According to law, they are justified*) [those] who having suffered defend themselves and do not themselves begin action; and those who treat their parents well, even though their parents have treated them badly; and those who give the taking of an oath to others and do not themselves swear.[2] Of [the many provisions in law], one could find many which are hostile to nature; and there is in them the possibility of suffering more when one could suffer less; and enjoying less when one could enjoy more; and faring ill when one need not. Now if the person who adapted himself to the provisions of the law received support from the laws, and those who did not, but who opposed them, received damage, obedience to the laws would not be without benefit; but as things are, it is obvious that for those who adapt themselves to the law the justice proceeding from law is not strong enough to help, seeing that first of all it allows him who suffers to suffer,...and does not prevent the sufferer from suffering or the doer from doing. And if the case is brought up for punishment, there is no advantage peculiar to the sufferer rather than to the doer. For the sufferer must convince those who are to inflict the punishment, that he has suffered; and he needs the ability to win his case. And it is open to the doer to deny, by the same means...and he can defend himself no less than the accuser can accuse, and persuasion is open to both parties, being a matter of technique....

---

1 Antiphôn, *Truth* (usually said to have been written between 430 and 400 BCE), in Kathleen Freeman, *Ancilla to the Pre-Socratic Philosophers: A Complete Translation of the Fragments in Diels,* Fragmente der Vorsokratiker (Oxford: Basil Blackwell, 1948).

2 Thus the person accepts the requirement to be truthful requested by another without asking for the same in return.

"Protagoras" from Diogenes Laertius, *Lives of Eminent Philosophers*[1]

(481–411 BCE)

Protagoras was the first to maintain that there are two sides to every question, opposed to each other, and he even argued in this fashion, being the first to do so. Furthermore, he began a work thus: "Man is the measure of all things, of things that are, that they are, and of things that are not, that they are not." He used to say that soul was nothing apart from the senses, as we learn from Plato in the *Theaetetus*, and that everything is true. In another work he began thus: "As to the gods, I have no means of knowing either that they exist or that they do not exist. For many are the obstacles that impede knowledge, both the obscurity of the question and the shortness of human life." ...

He was the first to exact a fee of a hundred minae[2] and the first to distinguish the tenses of verbs, to emphasize the importance of seizing the right moment, to institute contests in debating, and to teach rival pleaders the tricks of their trade. Furthermore, in his dialectic he neglected the meaning in favor of verbal quibbling, and he was the father of the whole tribe of eristical[3] disputants now so much in evidence ...

He too first introduced the method of discussion which is called Socratic.... [H]e was the first to use in discussion the argument of Antisthenes which strives to prove that contradiction is impossible, and the first to point out how to attack and refute any proposition laid down ... He was the first to mark off the parts of discourse into four, namely, wish, question, answer, command ...

Plato, *Protagoras*[4]

(399–387 BCE, but dealing with earlier events)

SOCRATES: I must explain that my friend Hippocrates is a native Athenian. He is the son of Apollodorus, and of a great and prosperous house, and he is himself in natural ability quite a match for anybody of his own age. I believe that he aspires to political eminence; and thus he thinks that conversation with you is most likely to procure this for him.... he would like to know what will happen to him if he associates with you....

---

1 "Protagoras," Book IX, chapter 8 of Diogenes Laertius, *Lives of Eminent Philosophers*, trans. by Robert Drew Hicks, Loeb Classical Library No. 184 (Cambridge: Harvard University Press, 1925).

2 In Ancient Greece, 1 mina = 70 drachmae, and the daily wage of a skilled worker was 1 drachma.

3 I.e., the argument technique of question and answer.

4 Plato, *Protagoras*, in Benjamin Jowett, trans., *The Dialogues of Plato* (2nd ed.), vol. 1 (Oxford: Clarendon Press, 1875).

PROTAGORAS (answered): Young man, if you associate with me, on the very first day you will return home a better man than you came, and better on the second day than on the first, and better every day than you were on the day before.

SOCRATES (upon hearing this, said): Protagoras, I do not at all wonder at hearing you say this; even at your age, and with all your wisdom, if any one were to teach you what you did not know before, you would become better no doubt: but please answer in a different way...

When you say that on the first day on which he associates with you he will return home a better man, and on every day will grow in like manner—in what, Protagoras, will he be better? and about what?

When Protagoras heard me say this, he replied: You ask questions fairly, and I like to answer a question which is fairly put. If Hippocrates comes to me he will not experience the sort of drudgery with which other Sophists are in the habit of insulting their pupils; who, when they have just escaped from the arts, are taken and driven back into them by these teachers, and made to learn calculation, and astronomy, and geometry, and music (he gave a look at Hippias as he said this). But if he comes to me, he will learn that which he comes to learn. And this is prudence[1] in affairs private as well as public; he will learn to order his own house in the best manner, and he will be able to speak and act for the best in the affairs of the state.

SOCRATES: Do I understand you; and is your meaning that you teach the art of politics, and that you promise to make men good citizens?

PROTAGORAS: That, Socrates, is exactly the profession which I make.... Education and admonition commence in the first years of childhood, and last to the very end of life. Mother and nurse and father and tutor are vying with one another about the improvement of the child as soon as ever he is able to understand what is being said to him: he cannot say or do anything without their setting forth to him that this is just and that is unjust; this is honorable, that is dishonorable; this is holy, that is unholy; do this and abstain from that. And if he obeys, well and good; if not, he is straightened by threats and blows, like a piece of bent or warped wood.

At a later stage they send him to teachers, and enjoin them to see to his manners even more than to his reading and music; and the teachers do as they are desired. And when the boy has learned his letters and is beginning to understand what is written, as before he understood only what was spoken, they put into his hands the works of great poets, which he reads sitting on a bench at school; in these are contained many admonitions, and many tales, and praises, and encomia[2] of ancient famous men, which he is required to learn by heart, in order that he may imitate or emulate them and desire to become like them....

When they have done with masters, the state again compels them to learn the laws, and live after the pattern which they furnish, and not after their own fancies... the city draws the laws, which were the invention of good lawgivers living in the past. These are given to the young man, in order to guide him in his conduct whether he is commanding or obeying; and he who transgresses them is to be corrected, or, in other words, called to account, which is a term used not only in your country, but also in many others, seeing that justice calls men to account. Now when there is all this care about virtue private and public, why, Socrates, do you still wonder and doubt whether virtue can be taught? Cease to wonder, for the opposite would be far more surprising.... And this is true of virtue or of anything else.

---

1 I.e., practical wisdom.

2 I.e., a speech or writing that highly praises someone.

If a man is better able than we are to promote virtue ever so little, we must be content with the result. A teacher of this sort I believe myself to be, and above all other men to have the knowledge which makes a man noble and good. And I give my pupils their money's-worth, and even more, as they themselves confess.

Plato, *Gorgias*[1]

(c. 380 BCE, but dealing with events before the trial and death of Socrates in 399 BCE)

SOCRATES: I would still beg you briefly and clearly, Polus...to say what this art is, and what we ought to call Gorgias. Or rather, Gorgias, let me turn to you, and ask the same question, what are we to call you, and what is the art which you profess?

GORGIAS: Rhetoric, Socrates, is my art.

SOCRATES: Then I am to call you a rhetorician?

GORGIAS: Yes, Socrates, and a good one too, if you would call me that which, in Homeric language, "I boast myself to be."...

SOCRATES: And are we to say that you are able to make other men rhetoricians?

GORGIAS: Yes, that is exactly what I profess to make them, not only at Athens, but in all places....

SOCRATES: Very good then. As you profess to be a rhetorician, and a maker of rhetoricians, let me ask you, with what is rhetoric concerned?...

GORGIAS: With discourse....

SOCRATES: Well, then, let me now have the rest of my answer. Seeing that rhetoric is one of those arts which works mainly by the use of words, and there are other arts which also use words, tell me what is that quality in words with which rhetoric is concerned...

GORGIAS: To the greatest, Socrates, and the best of human things.

SOCRATES: That again, Gorgias is ambiguous. I am still in the dark: for which are the greatest and best of human things?...What is that which, as you say, is the greatest good of man, and of which you are the creator?...

GORGIAS: That good, Socrates, which is truly the greatest, being that which gives to men freedom in their own persons, and to individuals the power of ruling over others in their several states.

SOCRATES: And what would you consider this to be?

GORGIAS: What is there greater than the word which persuades the judges in the courts, or the

---

1 Plato, *Gorgias*, in Benjamin Jowett, trans., *The Dialogues of Plato* (2nd ed.), vol. 2 (Oxford: Clarendon Press, 1875).

senators in the council, or the citizens in the assembly, or at any other political meeting? If you have the power of uttering this word, you will have the physician your slave, and the trainer your slave, and the money-maker of whom you talk will be found to gather treasures, not for himself, but for you who are able to speak and to persuade the multitude.

SOCRATES: Now I think, Gorgias, that you have very accurately explained what you conceive to be the art of rhetoric; and you mean to say, if I am not mistaken, that rhetoric is the artificer of persuasion, having this and no other business, and that this is her crown and end. Do you know any other effect of rhetoric over and above that of producing persuasion?

GORGIAS: No: the definition seems to me very fair, Socrates; for persuasion is the chief end of rhetoric....

SOCRATES: And I am going to ask: what is this power of persuasion which is given by rhetoric, and about what?

GORGIAS: ... I answer, Socrates, that rhetoric is the art of persuasion in courts of law and other assemblies, as I was just now saying, and about the just and unjust....

SOCRATES: And which sort of persuasion does rhetoric create in courts of law and other assemblies about the just and unjust, the sort of persuasion which gives belief without knowledge, or that which gives knowledge?

GORGIAS: Clearly, Socrates, that which only gives belief.

SOCRATES: Then rhetoric, as would appear, is the artificer of a persuasion which creates belief about the just and unjust, but gives no instruction about them?

GORGIAS: True.

SOCRATES: And the rhetorician does not instruct the courts of law or other assemblies about things just and unjust, but he creates belief about them; for no one can be supposed to instruct such a vast multitude about such high matters in a short time?

GORGIAS: Certainly not.

SOCRATES: Come, then, and let us see what we really mean about rhetoric; for I do not know what my own meaning is as yet. When the assembly meets to elect a physician or a shipwright or any other craftsman, will the rhetorician be taken into counsel? Surely not. For at every election he ought to be chosen who is most skilled. And, again, when walls have to be built or harbors or docks to be constructed, not the rhetorician but the master workman will advise. Or when generals have to be chosen and an order of battle arranged, or a proposition taken, then the military will advise and not the rhetoricians. What do you say, Gorgias? Since you profess to be a rhetorician and a maker of rhetoricians, I cannot do better than learn the nature of your art from you....

GORGIAS: A marvel, indeed, Socrates, if you only knew how rhetoric comprehends and holds under her sway all the inferior arts. Let me offer you a striking example of this. On several occasions I have been with my brother Herodicus or some other physician to see one of his patients, who would not allow the physician to give him medicine, or apply a knife or hot iron to him; and I have persuaded him to do for me what he would not do for the physician just by the use of rhetoric. And I say that if a rhetorician and a physician were to go to any city, and had there to argue in the Council or any other assembly as to which of them should be elected state-physician, the physician would have no chance; but he who could speak would be chosen if he wished. And in a contest with a man of any other profession the rhetorician more than anyone would have the power of getting himself chosen, for he can speak more persuasively to the multitude than any of them, and on any subject. Such is the nature and power of the art of rhetoric.

And yet, Socrates, rhetoric should be used like any other competitive art, not against everybody. The rhetorician ought not to abuse his strength any more than a pugilist or pancratiast[1] or other master of fence; because he has powers which are more than a match either for friend or enemy, he ought not therefore to strike, stab, or slay his friends. Suppose a man to have been trained in the gymnasium and to be a skillful boxer—he in the fullness of his strength goes and strikes his father or mother or one of his familiars or friends. But that is no reason why the trainers or fencing-masters should be held in detestation or banished from the city—surely not. For they taught their art for a good purpose, to be used against enemies and evil-doers, in self-defense not in aggression, and others have perverted their instructions and turned to a bad use their own strength and skill. But not on this account are the teachers bad, neither is the art in fault, or bad in itself. I should rather say that those who make a bad use of the art are to blame.

And the same argument holds good of rhetoric; for the rhetorician can speak against all men and upon any subject. In short, he can persuade the multitude better than any other man of anything which he pleases, but he should not therefore seek to defraud the physician or any other artist of his reputation merely because he has the power. He ought to use rhetoric fairly, as he would also use his athletic powers. And if after having become a rhetorician he makes a bad use of his strength and skill, his instructor surely ought not on that account to be held in detestation or banished. For he was intended by his teacher to make a good use of his instructions, but he abuses them. And therefore he is the person who ought to be held in detestation, banished, and put to death, and not his instructor....

SOCRATES: Let me tell you then, Gorgias, what surprises me in your words. Though I dare say that you may be right, and I may have understood your meaning....

SOCRATES: Then, when the rhetorician is more persuasive than the physician, the ignorant is more persuasive with the ignorant than he who has knowledge? Is not that the inference?

GORGIAS: In the case supposed: Yes.

SOCRATES: And the same holds of the relation of rhetoric to all the other arts. The rhetorician need not know the truth about things; he has only to discover some way of persuading the ignorant that he has more knowledge than those who know?

GORGIAS: Yes, Socrates, and is not this a great comfort?—not to have learned the other arts, but the art of rhetoric only, and yet to be in no way inferior to the professors of them?

Questions

1. Although the Sophists were teachers, who focused on the skills that were needed for success in public life, their epistemological stance shares some similarities with that of the Buddha. Explore.

---

1 I.e., an athlete that participates in a pancratium, a wrestling and boxing contest.

2. Explain the double arguments on the seemly and the shameful in the *Dissoi Logoi*. What are the deeper implications, morally?

3. Antiphon is a limited relativist. Although he describes justice as obedience to human law, he also refers to the laws of nature. What is the relationship between these two kinds of laws? Suppose they conflict? Provide examples.

4. Explain the moral doctrine that derives from Protagoras's famous statement that man is the measure of all things. Is the Sophist doctrine helpful in today's world? Or does it undermine our moral beliefs? Use examples.

5. What did a) Protagoras and b) Gorgias say that they were teaching? Discuss their understanding of these disciplines and the larger moral and philosophical implications.

6. Sophists like Antiphon and Gorgias recognized that the success of rhetoric does not depend upon its veracity. How do we deal with the troubling consequences of this in fields like politics, where rhetoric seems of pivotal importance?

7. What kind of human life do the Sophists seem to promote? How do morality, knowledge, and wisdom come into such a life?

Suggested Readings

Very few written texts from the Sophists have survived. As a result, their philosophical views must be drawn from fragments and second-hand testimony. For an English translation of this material, see Rosamond Kent Sprague, *The Older Sophists: A Complete Translation* (revised, 1972), and Robin Waterfield, *The First Philosophers: The Presocratics and Sophists* (2009). Patricia O'Grady's *The Sophists: An Introduction* (2008) provides a readable and scholarly survey of the main figures in the Sophistic tradition. See also Rachel Barney, "The Sophistic Movement," in Gill and Pellegrin, eds., *A Companion to Ancient Philosophy* (2006).

The negative depiction of Sophistry in Plato's dialogues, such as the *Apology* and the *Sophist*, has greatly influenced our perception of the practice. The dialogues nevertheless contain a rich source of relevant material. The eponymously named dialogues portraying Sophists include the *Gorgias*, the *Protagoras*, the *Greater Hippias* (which is of disputed authorship) and the *Lesser Hippias*. Other Sophists or students of Sophists mentioned in the Platonic corpus include Thrasymachus (a Sophist) in Book I of *Republic*, Meno (a pupil of Gorgias) in the *Meno*, and Euthydemus and his older brother Dionysodorus (Sophist imitators) in *Euthydemus*. All these texts are easily available online. G.B. Kerferd ("Socrates and the Sophists," 1972; *The Sophistic Movement*, 1981) has attempted to rehabilitate the Sophists and restore their philosophical reputation.

Chapter 13

Aristotle

Aristotle (384–322 BCE) was born in Stagira, Northern Greece, the son of a doctor to the Macedonian court. His family was wealthy and well-connected. At eighteen, he traveled to Athens, became a student of Plato, and spent twenty years at the Academy. He then traveled again, becoming a tutor to the young Alexander the Great (who was a Macedonian prince), before returning to Athens, where he founded a university, the Lyceum.

Aristotle's intellectual interests were extensive. His academic works range from biology to physics, theology, logic and rhetoric, ethics, politics, history, and psychology. Many of his manuscripts have been lost. Much of what is left are lecture notes, kept by his students and colleagues, which were pieced together and compiled by editors at a much later date. As one might expect, these notes are often cryptic, repetitious, and unpolished. These blemishes do not detract from their significance.

Aristotle was also a scientist. The interest in science during his era reflects the increasing influence of the skepticism in the Sophist tradition, which challenged the authority of mere statements of opinion. It followed that evidence was needed in support of philosophical claims. Aristotle's work was accordingly empirical. Philosophically, he took the position that observation was the beginning of knowledge. Alexander the Great supposedly provided him with many slaves, so that he could collect zoological specimens for physical study.

Aristotle's followers were known as Peripatetics (Greek for "walkers" or "wanderers") because Aristotle taught while walking through the gardens of the Lyceum, his students following behind. With the death of Alexander in 323 BCE, and rising anti-Macedonian sentiment, he fled Athens in fear of his life, saying that he would not allow the Athenians, who had executed Socrates, to sin twice against philosophy.

Aristotle's philosophy is rigorous and sophisticated, but common sense, i.e., in keeping with our common-sense perceptions of the world. He is fundamentally a "realist" and became a rival of Plato, whose idealism he disputed. His work frequently surveys the theories of previous thinkers and provides us with a compendium of the ancient Greek tradition. In moral philosophy, he is still considered the major western philosopher in "virtue ethics." Many philosophers have found parallels between his work in ethics and the work of Confucius and Mencius in the Chinese tradition.

The historical record suggests that Aristotle was moderate, gracious, and generous in his private life and, like Confucius and Mencius, placed enormous value on being a "gentleman," i.e., a noble. His account of magnanimity (*megalopsychia*, "greatness of soul"), the "crowning virtue" in his moral system, has been criticized as haughty, but most of the criticism reflects the changes in our social attitudes. Aristotle sees the magnanimous man as someone who is openly wealthy and powerful, and recognizes his superiority over other people. He is nevertheless socially responsible and a public benefactor, using his money, power, and prestige for the common good of the city as a whole.

Most scholars believe that Aristotle's *Nicomachean Ethics*, which was named after his son Nicomachus, contains his central contribution to ethics. There is also a *Eudemian Ethics*, which includes some of the same material. These works consolidate the conventional ethical views of aristocratic Greek culture in a formidable philosophical theory. Unlike Plato, Aristotle does not set out to describe a perfect society. Instead, he makes penetrating observations about how people actually act, develops a scientific account of human nature on the basis of these observations, and then comes to conclusions about how we should ideally act.

Like earlier Greek thinkers, Aristotle conceives of moral virtue (*aretē*, "excellence") as a sign of character. The way to flourish as human beings is to develop the praiseworthy traits that characterize noble human beings. When virtues such as honesty, fairness, generosity, and courage become natural and reliable aspects of our characters, practiced in the right way for the right reasons, we enjoy the self-esteem that naturally accompanies the successful achievement of the good. The highest moral good and the surest path to happiness are found in the cultivation and continual improvement of our individual talents.

Aristotle believes, like other ancients, that morality and politics overlap. This view comes out of the tribal tradition. We are inherently social animals and do not exist in the full human sense outside human society. His moral philosophy is organized around three major principles. First, he maintains that we all strive for happiness, which he calls *eudaimonia* (εὐδαιμονία) or "good fate." This happiness is not the same as mere pleasure and includes the sense of fulfillment and self-esteem that accompanies moral conduct.

Second, Aristotle argues that we cannot achieve happiness without virtue. Happiness requires that we strive to improve ourselves—to pursue excellence in worthwhile endeavors. The virtuous person, who has developed good habits, can be proud of their accomplishments. This is the best form of happiness.

Third, Aristotle believes that morality requires a special type of knowledge, which he calls "practical wisdom" (*phronēsis*). This wisdom is the kind of wisdom that we find expressed in the proverbs and aphorisms, for example, in the original wisdom tradition. Morality is not a theoretical or speculative endeavor but a form of (intelligent) behavior. The source of moral knowledge can be found in an intuition that discerns the difference between right and wrong. Later philosophers have often translated Aristotle's Greek term *phronêsis* as "prudence."

The *Nicomachean Ethics* also sets out Aristotle's doctrine of the mean—the "Golden Mean"—which holds that our behavior is virtuous when it achieves a "happy medium" between an excess and a deficiency of particular human qualities. Aristotle gives us the example of healthy eating. We can eat too little and suffer malnutrition, or eat too much and suffer from obesity. In order to live a healthy life—which is part of the moral life—we need to eat moderately, in accordance with our natural size and lifestyle.

This view of morality may seem counter-intuitive in the case of virtues like honesty, but it is clearly possible to be too truthful or not truthful enough. Naturally we are not truthful enough when we tell lies. But we can be *too* truthful if we tell secrets or refuse to respect the legitimate conventions that make it impolite to speak openly in certain situations. Aristotle, like Confucius, recognizes that the Mean has to be adjusted to maintain the right fit between actions and circumstances.

The text of the *Nicomachean Ethics* broaches many other moral questions. Aristotle argues, for example, that the contemplative life of study is best (because thinking is literally divine), that the political life is noble but second-best, and that a life devoted exclusively to amusement is beneath human dignity. He identifies various intellectual virtues such as scientific knowledge (*epistēmē*), philosophical wisdom (*sophia*), and art (*technē*). He also claims that friendship is a necessary part of happiness. Lastly, he emphasizes the importance of childhood upbringing and finishes the book by explaining the role that the state should play in moral education.

The reading, from the *Nicomachean Ethics*, briefly covers a variety of foundational issues, discusses virtue, and sets out his theory of happiness. It also includes a discussion of Aristotle's theory of friendship.

READING 13

Aristotle, *Nicomachean Ethics*[1]

(350 BCE)

Book I.

1. Every art and every kind of inquiry, and likewise every act and purpose, seems to aim at some good: and so it has been well said that the good is that at which everything aims.... Now since there are many kinds of actions and many arts and sciences, it follows that there are many ends also;...

2. If then in what we do there be some end which we wish for on its own account, choosing all the others as means to this, but not every end without exception as a means to something else (for so we should go on ad infinitum, and desire would be left void and objectless),—this evidently will be the good or the best of all things. And surely from a practical point

---

1 Aristotle, *Nicomachean Ethics* (350 BCE), from Aristotle, *The Nicomachean Ethics of Aristotle*, trans. F.H. Peters, M.A., 5th edition (London: Kegan Paul, Trench, Trübner & Co., 1893). Available at http://oll.libertyfund.org/titles/903.

of view it much concerns us to know this good; for then, like archers shooting at a definite mark, we shall be more likely to attain what we want.

If this be so, we must try to indicate roughly what it is, and first of all to which of the arts or sciences it belongs. It would seem to belong to the supreme art or science, that one which most of all deserves the name of master-art or master-science.

Now politics seems to answer to this description.... Since then it makes use of the other practical sciences, and since it further ordains what men are to do and to refrain from doing, its end must include the ends of the others, and must be the proper good of man. For though this good is the same for the individual and the state, yet the good of the state seems a more perfect thing both to attain and to secure; and glad as one would be to do this service for a single individual, to do it for a people and for a number of states is nobler. This then is the aim of the present inquiry, which is a sort of political inquiry....

4. Since all knowledge and every purpose aims at some good, what is this which we say is the aim of politics; or, in other words, what is the highest of all realizable goods? As to its name, I suppose nearly all men are agreed; for the masses and the men of culture alike declare that it is happiness, and hold that to "live well" or to "do well" is the same as to be "happy." But they differ as to what this happiness is, and the masses do not give the same account of it as the philosophers....

5. It seems that men not unreasonably take their notions of the good or happiness from the lives actually led, and that the masses who are the least refined suppose it to be pleasure, which is the reason why they aim at nothing higher than the life of enjoyment.

For the most conspicuous kinds of life are three: this life of enjoyment, the life of the statesman, and, thirdly, the contemplative life. The mass of men show themselves utterly slavish in their preference for the life of brute beasts, but their views receive consideration because many of those in high places have the tastes of Sardanapalus.[1]

Men of refinement with a practical turn prefer honor; for I suppose we may say that honor is the aim of the statesman's life. But this seems too superficial to be the good we are seeking: for it appears to depend upon those who give rather than upon those who receive it; while we have a presentiment that the good is something that is peculiarly a man's own and can hardly be taken away from him....

The third kind of life is the life of contemplation: we will treat of it further on.

As for the money-making life, it is something quite contrary to nature; and wealth evidently is not the good of which we are in search, for it is merely useful as a means to something else....

7. If then there be one end of all that man does, this end will be the realizable good,—or these ends, if there be more than one...

We see that there are many ends. But some of these are chosen only as means, as wealth, flutes, and the whole class of instruments.... Now that which is pursued as an end in itself is more final than that which is pursued as means to something else, ... and that is strictly final which is always chosen as an end in itself and never as means. Happiness seems more than anything else to answer to this description: for we always choose it for itself, and never for the sake of something else; while honor and pleasure and reason, and all virtue or excellence, we choose partly indeed for themselves..., but partly also for the sake of happiness, supposing that they will help to make us happy. But no one chooses happiness for the sake of these things, or as a means to anything else at all....

The final good is thought to be self-sufficing. In

---

1 Sardanapalus (c. seventh century BCE) was a king of Assyria whose decadence became legendary.

applying this term, we do not regard a man as an individual leading a solitary life, but we also take account of parents, children, wife, and, in short, friends and fellow-citizens generally, since man is naturally a social being. Some limit must indeed be set to this; for if you go on to parents and descendants and friends of friends, you will never come to a stop....

But perhaps the reader thinks that though no one will dispute the statement that happiness is the best thing in the world, yet a still more precise definition of it is needed. This will best be gained, I think, by asking, What is the function of man? For as the goodness and the excellence of a piper or a sculptor, and generally of those who have any function or business to do, lies in that function, so man's good would seem to lie in his function, if he has one...

The function of man, then, is the exercise of his faculties of soul[1] involving reason.... Man's function then being a kind of life—that is to say, exercise of his faculties and action of various kinds with reason—the good man's function is to do this well and nobly. But the function of anything is done well when it is done in accordance with the proper excellence of that thing. If this be so the result is that the good of man is exercise of his faculties involving reason in accordance with excellence or virtue, or, if there be more than one, in accordance with the best and most complete virtue.

But there must also be a complete span of life for this exercise; for one swallow or one fine day does not make a spring, nor does one day or any small space of time make a blessed or happy man.

This, then, may be taken as a rough outline of the good....

13. Since happiness is an exercise of the faculties of soul in accordance with perfect virtue or excellence, we will now inquire about virtue or excellence; for this will probably help us in our inquiry about happiness.

And indeed the true statesman seems to be especially concerned with virtue, for he wishes to make the citizens good and obedient to the laws.... The virtue or excellence that we are to consider is, of course, the excellence of man;.... And by the excellence of man I mean excellence not of body, but of soul; for happiness we take to be an activity of the soul....

Two parts of the soul are distinguished, an irrational and a rational part....

Of the irrational part, again, one division seems to be common to all things that live, and to be possessed by plants—I mean that which causes nutrition and growth;...But there seems to be another vital principle that is irrational, and yet in some way partakes of reason. In the case of the continent and of the incontinent man alike we praise the reason or the rational part, for it exhorts them rightly and urges them to do what is best; but there is plainly present in them another principle besides the rational one, which fights and struggles against the reason....

The irrational part, then, it appears, is twofold. There is the vegetative faculty, which has no share of reason; and the faculty of appetite or of desire in general, which in a manner partakes of reason or is rational as listening to reason and submitting to its sway,...But all advice and all rebuke and exhortation testify that the irrational part is in some way amenable to reason.[2]

Now, on this division of the faculties is based the

---

1 For Aristotle, the soul is the principle of life present in all living beings, and it is the cause of the various life functions (or vital activities) they are capable of performing through different faculties or powers, such as the faculties of reproduction, of sensation, and, in human beings, of thinking.

2 Aristotle is saying that the soul may be divided into three faculties or powers: 1) the vegetative, which is completely irrational; 2) reason, which is completely rational; and 3) the appetitive (or desire), which can be irrational when it disobeys reason and rational when it obeys reason. He will next say that intellectual virtue is the excellence of reason and moral virtue is the excellence of desire when it obeys reason.

division of excellence; for we speak of intellectual excellences and of moral excellences; wisdom and understanding and prudence we call intellectual, liberality and temperance we call moral virtues or excellences. When we are speaking of a man's moral character we do not say that he is wise or intelligent, but that he is gentle or temperate. But we praise the wise man, too, for his habit of mind or trained faculty; and a habit or trained faculty that is praiseworthy is what we call an excellence or virtue.

Book II.

1. Excellence, then, being of these two kinds, intellectual and moral, intellectual excellence owes its birth and growth mainly to instruction,...while moral excellence is the result of habit or custom.... From this it is plain that none of the moral excellences or virtues is implanted in us by nature; for that which is by nature cannot be altered by training.... The virtues, then, come neither by nature nor against nature, but nature gives the capacity for acquiring them, and this is developed by training (or habituation)....

Again, both the moral virtues and the corresponding vices result from and are formed by the same acts; and this is the case with the arts also. It is by harping that good harpers and bad harpers alike are produced.... And it is just the same with the virtues also. It is by our conduct in our interactions with other men that we become just or unjust, and by acting in circumstances of danger, and training ourselves to feel fear or confidence, that we become courageous or cowardly.... In a word, acts of any kind produce habits or characters of the same kind.

Hence we ought to make sure that our acts be of a certain kind; for the resulting character varies as they vary. It makes no small difference, therefore, whether a man be trained from his youth up in this way or in that, but a great difference, or rather all the difference.

2. But our present inquiry has not, like the rest, a merely theoretical aim; we are not inquiring merely in order to know what excellence or virtue is, but in order to become good; for otherwise it would profit us nothing. We must ask therefore about these acts, and see of what kind they are to be....

First of all, then, we must observe that, in matters of this sort, to fall short and to exceed are alike fatal. This is plain (to illustrate what we cannot see by what we can see) in the case of strength and health. Too much and too little exercise alike destroy strength, and to take too much meat and drink, or to take too little, is equally ruinous to health, but the fitting amount produces and increases and preserves them. Just so, then, is it with temperance also, and courage, and the other virtues. The man who shuns and fears everything and never makes a stand, becomes a coward; while the man who fears nothing at all, but will face anything, becomes foolhardy. So, too, the man who takes his fill of any kind of pleasure, and abstains from none, is a profligate, but the man who shuns all (called a "boor") is devoid of sensibility. Thus temperance and courage are destroyed both by excess and defect, but preserved by moderation....

4. The virtues are not in this point analogous to the arts. The products of art have their excellence in themselves, and so it is enough if when produced they are of a certain quality; but in the case of the virtues, a man is not said to act like a just or temperate man if what he does merely be of a certain sort—he must also be in a certain state of mind when he does it: first of all, he must know what he is doing; secondly, he must choose it, and choose it for itself; and, thirdly, his act must be the expression of a formed and stable character. Now, of these conditions, only one, the knowledge, is necessary for the possession of any art; but for the possession of the virtues knowledge is of little or no avail, while the other conditions that result from repeatedly doing what is just and temperate are not a little important, but all-important.

The thing that is done, therefore, is called just or temperate when it is such as the just or temperate man would do; but the man who does it is not just or temperate, unless he also does it with the character of the just or the temperate man. It is right, then, to say that by doing what is just a man becomes just, and temperate by doing what is temperate, while without doing thus he has no chance of ever becoming good.

But most men, instead of doing thus, fly to theories, and fancy that they are philosophizing and that this will make them good....

6. The proper excellence or virtue of man will be the habit or trained faculty that makes a man good and makes him perform his function well. How this is to be done we may exhibit by inquiring what the nature of this virtue is.

Now, if we have any quantity, whether continuous or discrete, it is possible to take either a larger (or too large), or a smaller (or too small), or an equal (or fair) amount, and that either absolutely or relatively to our own needs. By an equal amount I understand a mean amount, or one that lies between excess and deficiency. By the absolute mean, or mean relatively to the thing itself, I understand that which is equidistant from both extremes, and this is one and the same for all. By the mean relatively to us I understand that which is neither too much nor too little for us; and this is not one and the same for all.

For instance, if ten be too large and two be too small, if we take six we take the mean relatively to the thing itself (or the arithmetical mean); for it exceeds one extreme by the same amount by which it is exceeded by the other extreme: and this is the mean in arithmetical proportion. But the mean relatively to us cannot be found in this way. If ten pounds of food is too much for a given man to eat, and two pounds too little, it does not follow that the trainer will order him six pounds: for that also may perhaps be too much for the man in question, or too little.... And so we may say generally that a master

in any art avoids what is too much and what is too little, and seeks for the mean and chooses it—not the absolute but the relative mean.

If, then, every art or science perfects its work in this way, looking to the mean and bringing its work up to this standard..., it follows that moral virtue also must aim at the mean; for it has to do with passions and actions, and it is these that admit of excess and deficiency and the mean. For instance, it is possible to feel fear, confidence, desire, anger, pity, and generally to be affected pleasantly and painfully, either too much or too little, in either case wrongly; but to be thus affected at the right times, and on the right occasions, and towards the right persons, and with the right object, and in the right fashion, is the mean course and the best course, and these are characteristics of virtue. And in the same way our outward acts also admit of excess and deficiency, and the mean or due amount.

Virtue, then, has to deal with feelings or passions and with outward acts, in which excess is wrong and deficiency also is blamed, but the mean amount is praised and is right.... Virtue, then, is a kind of moderation, inasmuch as it aims at the mean or moderate amount....

Virtue, then, is a habit or trained faculty of choice, the characteristic of which lies in moderation or observance of the mean relatively to the persons concerned, as determined by reason, i.e. by the practical reason by which the prudent man would determine it. And it is a moderation, firstly, inasmuch as it comes in the middle or mean between two vices, one on the side of excess, the other on the side of defect; and, secondly, inasmuch as, while these vices fall short of or exceed the due measure in feeling and in action, it finds and chooses the mean....

But it is not all actions nor all passions that admit of moderation; there are some whose very names imply badness, as malevolence, shamelessness, envy, and, among acts, adultery, theft, murder.... It is impossible therefore to go right in them; they are always wrong....

9. And on this account it is a hard thing to be good; for finding the middle or the mean in each case is a hard thing,... Thus any one can be angry—that is quite easy; any one can give money away or spend it: but to do these things to the right person, to the right extent, at the right time, with the right object, and in the right manner, is not what everybody can do, and is by no means easy; and that is the reason why right doing is rare and praiseworthy and noble....

Book VI.

5. And in fact statesmanship[1] and prudence are the same faculty, though they are differently manifested....

But it is when applied to the individual and to one's own affairs that this faculty is especially regarded as prudence or practical wisdom... Knowing one's own good, then, would seem to be a kind of knowledge (though it admits of great variety), and, according to the general opinion, he who knows and attends to his own affairs is prudent or practically wise....

Book VIII.

1. After the foregoing, a discussion of friendship will naturally follow, as it is a sort of virtue, or at least implies virtue, and is, moreover, most necessary to our life. For no one would care to live without friends, though he had all other good things.... Again, it seems that friendship is the bond that holds states together, and that lawgivers are even more eager to secure it than justice....

2. In order to be friends, then, they must be well-wishers one of another, i.e. must wish each other's good from one of the three motives above mentioned,[2] and be aware of each other's feelings.

3. The kinds of friendship accordingly are three, being equal in number to the motives of love; for any one of these may be the basis of a mutual affection of which each is aware....

Those, therefore, whose love for one another is based on the useful, do not love each other for what they are, but only in so far as each gets some good from the other.

It is the same also with those whose affection is based on pleasure; people care for a wit,[3] for instance, not for what he is, but as the source of pleasure to themselves.

Those, then, whose love is based on the useful care for each other on the ground of their own good, and those whose love is based on pleasure care for each other on the ground of what is pleasant to themselves, each loving the other, not as being what he is, but as useful or pleasant. These friendships, then, are "accidental"; for the object of affection is loved, not as being the person or character that he is, but as the source of some usefulness or some pleasure. Friendships of this kind, therefore, are easily dissolved, as the persons do not continue unchanged; for if they cease to be pleasant or useful to one another, their love ceases.

But the perfect kind of friendship is that of good men who resemble one another in virtue. For they both alike wish well to one another as good men, and it is their essential character to be good men. And those who wish well to their friends for the friends' sake are friends in the truest sense; for they have these sentiments towards each other as being what

---

1 As Aristotle's description of prudence will implicitly show, statesmanship is knowing what is good for one's state or country, i.e., the affairs of the state or the public good.

2 Aristotle previously argued that friendship involves something loveable in the friend, and that the lovable is either good or pleasant or useful. Whichever of these three is loveable thus becomes the motive for the friendship.

3 I.e., a witty person, someone who is clever and humorous.

they are, and not in an accidental way: their friendship, therefore, lasts as long as their virtue, and that is a lasting thing. Again, each is both good simply and good to his friend; for it is true of good men that they are both good simply and also useful to one another. In like manner they are pleasant too; for good men are both pleasant in themselves and pleasant to one another.... This kind of friendship, then, is lasting, as we might expect, since it unites in itself all the conditions of true friendship.... and so it is between persons of this sort that the truest and best love and friendship is found.

Book X.

7. But if happiness be the exercise of virtue, it is reasonable to suppose that it will be the exercise of the highest virtue; and that will be the virtue of the best part of us. Now, that part or faculty—call it reason or what you will—which seems naturally to rule and take the lead, and to apprehend things noble and divine, the exercise of it, in its proper excellence, will be perfect happiness. That this consists in reflection or contemplation we have already said....

If, then, the life of ... the exercise of the reason seems to be superior in seriousness (since it contemplates truth), and to aim at no end beside itself, and to have its proper pleasure..., and further to be self-sufficient, and leisurely, and inexhaustible..., and to have all the other characteristics that are ascribed to happiness, it follows that the exercise of reason (i.e., intellectual virtue) will be the complete happiness of man, i.e. when a complete life span is added....

But a life which realized this idea would be something more than human; for it would not be the expression of man's nature, but of some divine element in that nature—the exercise of which is as far superior to the exercise of the other kind of virtue

(i.e., moral or practical virtue), as this divine element is superior to our compound human nature.[1] If then reason be divine as compared with man, the life which consists in the exercise of reason will also be divine in comparison with human life. Nevertheless, instead of listening to those who advise us as men and mortals not to lift our thoughts above what is human and mortal, we ought rather, as far as possible, to put off our mortality and make every effort to live in the exercise of the highest of our faculties; for though it be but a small part of us, yet in power and value it far surpasses all the rest....

Again, we may apply here what we said above—for every being the best and pleasantest is that which is naturally proper to it. Since, then, it is the reason that in the truest sense is the man, the life that consists in the exercise of the reason is the best and pleasantest for man—and therefore the happiest.

8. The life that consists in the exercise of the other kind of virtue is happy in a secondary sense; for the manifestations of moral virtue are emphatically human. Justice, I mean, and courage, and the other moral virtues are displayed in our relations towards one another by the observance, in every case, of what is due in contracts and services, and all sorts of outward acts, as well as in our inward feelings. And all these seem to be emphatically human affairs.

Again, prudence is inseparably joined to moral virtue, and moral virtue to prudence, since the moral virtues determine the principles of prudence, while prudence determines what is right in morals. But the moral virtues, being bound up with the passions, must belong to our compound nature; and the virtues of the compound nature are emphatically human. Therefore, the life which manifests them, and the happiness which consists in this, must be emphatically human.

---

1 The compound human nature refers to Aristotle's view that a human being is composed of a soul and a body. Since reason is one faculty of the soul, and its highest faculty, it is seen as something "divine," something beyond human.

Questions

1. Discuss the development of the Greek moral tradition, with reference to Socrates, Plato, and Aristotle. Or compare the Greek and Chinese traditions. Include some reference to Aristotle's idea of happiness.
2. At the beginning of the *Nicomachean Ethics*, Aristotle seems to see politics as the natural realm of ethics. Why do we find this difficult to accept? What has changed?
3. How does Aristotle explain happiness (*eudaimonia*)? What distinguishes happiness from other goods? Do you agree with Aristotle's understanding? Would you add anything?
4. How does Aristotle define virtue? How does the mean and the concept of vice operate in this context? Include an example from your own life.
5. Explain the kinds of virtue. Where does moral virtue originate, in Aristotle's view? What does nature have to do with it?
6. Aristotle thinks moral virtue requires the exercise of practical reason. What is prudence (or practical wisdom), and how does it function in morality?
7. Aristotle describes friendship as a virtue. Discuss the three kinds of friendship, with particular emphasis on the nature of "perfect" friendship.
8. In the *Nicomachean Ethics*, Aristotle says the life of reflection—which requires the contemplative use of reason (i.e., intellectual virtue)—is the happiest life for a human being. Do you agree? Or is his view self-serving?

Suggested Readings

The standard scholarly translation of Aristotle's complete works into English is Jonathan Barnes, ed., *The Complete Works of Aristotle: The Revised Oxford Translation*, 2 vols. (1984). The original *Oxford Translation* includes introductions and additional material. The *Nicomachean Ethics* has been translated by Irwin, Reeve, Crisp, Sachs, Ostwald, and others. In addition to the *Nicomachean Ethics*, Aristotle also wrote the *Eudemian Ethics* and the *Politics*, which he saw as a subdivision of ethics. A minor work called the *Magna Moralia* (a Latin rather than a Greek name, meaning "Great Ethics") may have been written by a student of Aristotle. Aristotle explores the idea of human nature behind his moral views in *On the Soul (De Anima)*. There are bilingual editions of Aristotle on Perseus at perseus.tufts.ed.

For secondary sources, see the annotated bibliography at ethikseite.de. The commentary includes W.F.R. Hardie, *Aristotle's Ethical Theory*, second edition (1980), and J.L. Ackrill et al., *Aristotle's Ethics: Critical Essays* (1998). For comparisons between Plato and Aristotle, see Robert Heinaman, ed., *Plato and Aristotle's Ethics* (2003), and A.W. Price, *Virtue and Reason in Plato and Aristotle* (2011). Daniel P. Mayer has written on Aristotle's idea of friendship in "Contemplative Friendship in *Nicomachean Ethics*" (2012) and "Friendship and Teaching Philosophy in *Nicomachean Ethics* IX.1" (2013). Students may wish to search for the terms "*akrasia*" and "happiness."

In applied ethics, see Robert Solomon, "Corporate Roles, Personal Virtues: An Aristotelian Approach to Business Ethics" (1992), and "Aristotle, Ethics and Business Organizations" (2004).

Chapter 14

Skepticism

The Hellenistic period (referring to the "Hellenes," the Greeks) in antiquity is usually said to have extended from the reign of Alexander the Great (356–323 BCE) to the end of the second century CE, when the Roman Empire entered its decline. Although Rome came to dominate the ancient world with its military might, its intellectual culture derived largely from the Greeks.

After the death of Plato and Aristotle, the focus of philosophical inquiry shifted to moral philosophy. This philosophical shift reflects social and political changes, which had nurtured a growing sense of individualism but left people disconnected from their older beliefs. There was uncertainty and a rising sense of moral dissatisfaction. A number of competing schools of philosophy sprang up, each teaching a different way of life. The Platonists, Aristotelians (known as Peripatetics), Cynics, Stoics, Epicureans, and Skeptics all vied for pre-eminence.

There are at least two sides to the developments within moral philosophy. The first is personal, emotional, and psychological. The central aim of those who practiced philosophy during the Hellenistic period was to achieve *ataraxia* (αταραξία, "unperturbedness," "freedom from disturbance," inner tranquility). There was also a practical side that raised a wide variety of issues about the way that we should conduct ourselves inside and outside civil society. During the Hellenistic period each of the schools developed one or both of these sides to varying degrees.

Ancient skepticism grew along two main branches. The first and most celebrated is Pyrrhonian skepticism, which has a long historical pedigree and is the focus of the current chapter. The second branch grew within Platonism and is usually described as "Academic" skepticism. It was developed by Arcesilaus and other members of Plato's Academy in the second century BCE, who concluded that Socrates and Plato were "proto-Skeptics" and did not believe that anything could be known with certainty. Another academician, Carneades of Cyrene (c. 213 to 129 BCE), developed a variety of techniques that could be used to argue both sides of an argument. He, like the Academic Skeptics in general, felt that the purpose of Socrates's *elenchus* (question/answer technique) was to establish that others did not know what they professed to know. This would make Socrates a Skeptic. The best account of the academic tradition is in Sextus Empiricus's *Outlines of Pyrrhonism* (*Pyrrhoniae Hypotyposes*).

Pyyrhonian skepticism derives from Pyrrho, who lived from about 360 to 270 BCE. Like Socrates, Pyrrho wrote nothing but was plainly charismatic and inspired those who followed him. Diogenes Laertius tells us that he became a Skeptic as a result of meeting some "naked wise men" (*gymnosophistai*) in India. After Pyrrho's death, the school lapsed and was apparently "revived" by Aenesidemus, in the first century BCE, who developed the "tropes" or "modes" listed by Sextus Empiricus in his *Outlines of Pyrrhonism*, which recounts the history of the school.

Although there is a strong strain of cultural relativism in the Pyrrhonian tradition, it is, however, the subjective concerns in Greek moral philosophy that set it apart from the earlier tradition, which was essentially collective. The Skeptics focused on the inside, as it were, of our experience, and at least implicitly rejected the objective reality of the world. It follows that Pyrrho may also have been attracted to the anti-materialism in the Vedic tradition.

The philosophical origins of ancient skepticism nevertheless lie in epistemology. As we have seen, the Greeks were interested in questions such as "What is knowledge?" and "How do we know?" The term 'skeptic' comes from the Greek word *skepsis* (σκέψις), meaning 'investigation.' The Skeptics, then, were investigating the question of whether we know. The primary tool that they used in such an investigation was doubt. This was a major innovation and constitutes their major contribution to philosophy.

The deeper issue behind the epistemological concerns was certainty. The Greeks believed that the distinguishing feature of knowledge, which sets it apart from mere opinion, is that it is true. This is a condition of knowing: a person cannot know something unless he or she is certain that it is true. The Skeptics rejected the possibility that such a condition could be met—without committing themselves to any position—and maintained a storehouse of examples to demonstrate that neither perception nor reason provides us with an account of reality that is necessarily true.

In philosophy, skepticism refers to the practice of methodically questioning—doubting—anything that we purport to "know" about the world. This includes moral values and principles. When we do so, the Skeptics say, we inevitably discover that there is some level of uncertainty in what we say. Neither science nor philosophy provide the certainty that we are looking for in the pursuit of knowledge. We are accordingly left with appearances and mere opinion.

There are many aspects to the skeptical investigation. The primary interest of the Skeptics, however, was with the subjective aspects of experience, rather than the state of external phenomena. They believed that peace of mind (*ataraxia*) is the fundamental goal of human life. Their principal concern, then, was that the endless search for certitude leaves us unhappy. The right response in the face of our persistent doubts is to recognize that it is not available and, in the accepted terminology, suspend belief. We then cease to trouble ourselves about the matter.

The goal of Pyrrhonian skepticism, which was seen as a therapeutic practice rather than a philosophical position, was therefore tranquility. Sextus Empiricus saw the Skeptic as a kind of physician, who administers doubt to cure the ills that flow from our mistaken commitment to appearances. There is a dialectical side to such a position, which became the focus of the skeptical tradition. Sextus describes skepticism as a skill in argument, which gives the practitioner the logical and rhetorical skills to neutralize virtually any argument. The result is *epochê* or suspension of judgment, which brings us tranquility.

The major criticism of ancient skepticism was that it reduces us to inaction. The Skeptics accordingly looked for some means of making the decisions that are necessary for the purpose of living our lives. The criterion that they settled on was called the practical criterion, which simply held that we should follow whatever course of conduct seems appropriate in the circumstances.

Thus, the Pyrrhonians advise us to accept appearances, whether they consist of our perceptions or the customs of the society in which we live, albeit tentatively, without dogmatism or any epistemological commitment. The moral standard that emerges here is usefulness. The Skeptics reject the theoretical wisdom sought by philosophers, who see wisdom as a kind of knowledge, which is simply not available to us. In spite of this rejection of philosophy, however, they seem comfortable with the "realist" elements in the original wisdom tradition, which provide us with a set of useful and practicable rules for living our lives.

The first reading is from Diogenes Laertius's life of Pyrrho. The overriding impression in the historical sources is that he was widely admired for his equanimity. As Aristocles of Messene tells us, his student Timon, a well-known satirist, described him as having a "god-like" calm.

The second reading is from Aristocles, a little known Peripatetic (i.e., an Aristotelian) in the first century CE, who criticized competing schools. He has become important in recent years principally because his polemic against the Pyrrhonians has given scholars considerable assistance in reconstructing Pyrrho's original teaching. The parental consternation in Aristocles's tone reflects the exasperation of many philosophers, who found themselves at a loss to respond to the Skeptics.

The third reading is from *Outlines of Pyrrhonism* (sometimes called *Outlines of Skepticism*), which identifies five distinct skeptical schools of thought. It was written by Sextus Empiricus (160–210 CE), a medical doctor, who was called "Empiricus" because he belonged to the "empirical" school of medicine. Sextus distinguishes between dogmatists, who believe that the truth is available to us, the Academic Skeptics—who take the position that the truth is not available to us—and the Pyrrhonian Skeptics, who continue to investigate, without subscribing to either view. In his work, he formulates objections to the Stoics, the Epicureans, and the Peripatetics, who maintained that there is an "art of living" (in Latin, *ars vivendi*), and competed with each other in articulating the principles of such an art. Sextus raises doubts about the idea that there is such an art.

READING 14A

"Pyrrho" from Diogenes Laertius, *Lives of Eminent Philosophers*[1]

(c. 360–270 BCE)

Pyrrho of Elis...was first a painter.... Afterwards he joined [the philosopher] Anaxarchus, whom he accompanied on his travels everywhere so that he even met with the Indian Gymnosophists and with the Magi.[2] This led him to adopt a most noble philosophy...taking the form of agnosticism and suspension of judgement. He denied that anything was honourable or dishonourable, just or unjust. And so, universally, he held that there is nothing really existent, but custom and convention govern human action; for no single thing is in itself any more this than that.

[Pyrrho] led a life consistent with [this suspension of judgement, refusing to accept that what we perceive exists and]...taking no precaution, but facing all risks as they came, whether carts, precipices, dogs or what not...but he was kept out of harm's way by his friends, who...used to follow close after him. But Aenesidemus says that it was only his philosophy that was based upon suspension of judgement, and that he did not lack [practical prudence] in his everyday acts. He lived to be nearly ninety....

[One author says that he] would [remain calm and composed] at all times, so that, even if you left him when he was in the middle of a speech, he would finish what he had to say with no audience but himself, although in his youth he had been hasty. Often, our informant adds, he would leave his home and, telling no one, would go roaming about with whomsoever he chanced to meet. And once, when Anaxarchus fell into a [swamp], he passed by [indifferently] without giving him any help, and, while

others blamed him, Anaxarchus himself praised his indifference and [calmness]....

[Pyrrho] lived...in piety with his sister, a midwife,...now and then even taking things for sale to market, poultry maybe or pigs, and he would dust the things in the house, quite indifferent as to what he did. They say he once showed his indifference by washing a [pig]. Once he got enraged in his sister's cause (her name was Philista), and told the man who criticized him [for it] that it was not over a weak woman that one should display indifference. When a [stray dog] rushed at him and terrified him, he answered his critic that it was not easy entirely to strip oneself of human weakness [and the resulting belief that appearances are real]; but that one should strive with all one's might against circumstances by deeds if possible, and if not, in word.

They [also say, however,] that, when septic salves and surgical and caustic remedies were applied to a wound he had sustained, [which must have hurt very much,] he did not so much as frown.... Philo of Athens, a friend of his, used to say that he...[would repeat all the Homeric] passages...on the unstable purpose, vain pursuits, and childish folly of man.

Posidonius, too, [tells us that when Pyrrho's] fellow-passengers on board a ship were all unnerved by a storm, he kept calm and confident, pointing to a little pig in the ship that went on eating, and telling them that such was the unperturbed state in which the wise man should keep himself.

[Pyrrho had several pupils, who] were called Pyrrhoneans after the name of their master, but

---

1 "Pyrrho," Book IX, chapter 11 of Diogenes Laertius, *Lives of Eminent Philosophers*, trans. by Robert Drew Hicks, Loeb Classical Library No. 184 (Cambridge: Harvard University Press; 1925, 1972). Available at http://www.perseus.tufts.edu/hopper/text?doc=Perseus:text:1999.01.0258; also: wikisource.org/wiki/Lives_of_the_Eminent_Philosophers.

2 I.e., Hindu ascetics and Persian wise men, respectively.

[also]...Zetetics or seekers because they were forever seeking truth, [and] Skeptics or [investigators] because they were always looking for a solution and never finding one, Ephectics or doubters because of their state of mind,...and finally Aporetics or those in perplexity...

The Skeptics...were constantly engaged in overthrowing the dogmas of all schools, but enunciated none themselves;...they themselves laid down nothing definitely, not even the laying down of nothing. So much so that they even refuted their laying down of nothing...but put forward...theories only for the purpose of [defeating them]...

[The Skeptics held that every saying[1] has its corresponding antithesis, which is equally true—and readily acknowledged that this proposition, too, has its antithesis—so that after destroying all other propositions, "it turns round and destroys itself, like a medical purge which drives the substance out and then in its turn is itself eliminated and destroyed." This leaves the suspension of judgement and vacancy of mind that they were striving for.]

[The Pyrrhonean method was to present anomalous and confusing facts, and show that everything is relative, so that the probabilities for and against any proposition are equal.]

These perplexities they distinguished under ten different modes....

The *first* mode relates to the differences between living creatures in respect of those things which give them pleasure or pain, or are useful or harmful to them.... [S]o to the goat vine-shoots are good to eat, to man they are bitter [i.e., so we cannot say they are "good" or "bad" to eat]...

The *second* mode has reference to the natures and idiosyncrasies of men; for instance, Demophon, Alexander's butler, used to get warm in the shade and shiver in the sun.... and the same ways of life

are injurious to one man but beneficial to another...

The *third* mode depends on the differences between the sense-channels in different cases...An object of the same shape is made to appear different by differences in the mirrors reflecting it. Thus it [is no more one shape than the other]...

The *fourth* mode [depends upon the changes due to] health, illness, sleep, waking, joy, sorrow, youth, old age, courage, fear,...to say nothing of breathing freely and having the passages obstructed. The impressions received thus appear to vary according to the nature of the conditions....

The *fifth* mode is derived from customs, laws, belief in myths, compacts between nations and dogmatic assumptions...Obviously the same thing is regarded by some as just and by others as unjust.... Persians think it not unnatural for a man to marry his daughter; to Greeks it is unlawful.... In burying their dead, the Egyptians embalm them; the Romans burn them; the Paeonians throw them into lakes. As to what is true, then, let suspension of judgement be our practice.

The *sixth* mode relates to mixtures and participations, by virtue of which nothing appears pure in and by itself, but only in combination with air, light, moisture, solidity, heat, cold, movement, exhalations and other forces.... [A] rock which in air takes two men to lift is easily moved about in water, either because, being in reality heavy, it is lifted by the water or because, being light, it is made heavy by the air....

The *seventh* mode has reference to distances, positions, places and the occupants of the places. In this mode things which are thought to be large appear small [from certain vantage points],...straight things to be bent.... Since, then, it is not possible to observe [things, other than from a particular vantage point,] their real nature is unknowable.

The *eighth* mode is concerned with quantities and qualities of things... [So, for example,] wine taken

---

1 I.e., every proposition.

in moderation strengthens the body, but too much of it is weakening, [so we cannot say definitively that wine strengthens or weakens the body]...

The *ninth* mode has to do with perpetuity, strangeness, or rarity. Thus earthquakes are [surprising if you have not experienced them, but no surprise to those who live where they constantly take place]...

The *tenth* mode rests on inter-relation, e.g. between light and heavy, strong and weak, greater and less, up and down. Thus that which is on the right is...so understood in virtue of its position with respect to something else; for, if that change its position, the thing is no longer on the right....

[A]ll demonstration, [the Skeptics] say, is constructed out of things either already proved or [unproven]. If out of things proved, those things too will require some [further proof], and so on *ad infinitum*; if out of things [unproved], then...the whole is [unproved]....

We must not assume that what convinces us is actually true.... Persuasiveness sometimes depends...on the reputation of the speaker, on his ability as a thinker or his artfulness [rather than on the truth of what he or she is saying]...

[The Skeptics hold that t]he end to be realized [is the tranquility that comes from] suspension of judgement...And when the dogmatists argue that [the Skeptic]...would not shrink from killing and eating his own father...the Skeptic replies that he [merely suspends his judgement and is stating that we cannot know—definitively—whether something is inherently good or bad,]...but not in matters of [daily] life...Accordingly [skepticism does not prevent us from choosing a thing]...by habit, [or from observing] rules and customs. According to some authorities the end proposed by the Skeptics is...gentleness....

<hr>

READING 14B

Aristocles of Messene, *Peri philosophias* (*On Philosophy*)[1]

(first century CE)

Against Pyrrhonian Sceptics also called Ephectics, who affirm that nothing is apprehensible

2....Pyrrho of Elis...was emphatic in this opinion, [though] he himself has left nothing in writing[.] [We must therefore rely on his pupil Timon, who] says that the man who means to be happy must consider these three things: first, how things are by nature; secondly, what attitude we should take

towards them; finally, what advantage will come to those who are in this disposition.

3. Things, [Pyrrho declared, are by nature] equally undifferentiated, unstable, and indeterminate; therefore, neither our sense-perceptions nor our opinions are true or false. For this reason, then, we must not trust them, but be unopinionated, unwavering, and unshaken, saying about every single thing that it no

1   Maria Lorenza Chiesara, *Aristocles of Messene: Testimonies and Fragments* (Oxford: OUP, 2001). The reading comes from "Against Pyrrhonian Sceptics also called Ephectics Who Affirm that Nothing is Apprehensible," in *Peri philosophias* (On Philosophy), Book 8 (14.18.1–5), which gives us an account of Pyrrho's views (late 1st century BCE), from F[ragment] 4, in Chiesara.

more is than is not, or that it both is and is not, or that it neither is nor is not.

4. To those who are in this disposition, says Timon, will come first speechlessness and then imperturbability; Aenesidemus says pleasure.

5. Now these are the main points of their arguments; let us consider whether they are right. Since then they say that all things are equally undifferentiated, and for this reason require us to incline to nothing and to have no opinion, one could reasonably ask them, I think, whether those who think that things differ are in error or not.... So they [will be] forced to say that there are some people who have false opinions about things; and they themselves would be those who say the true things; but [then] there would be something true and something false....

8. And those who affirm that everything is obscure must do one of two things, be mute or state and say something. If they were silent, clearly there would be no arguing with such folk; but if they make statements, in every way and absolutely they [must] either affirm that something [is] or that it [is] not...

9.... [And if they] should say that the same thing is and is not, first the same thing will be true and false, and secondly he will say and not say something...and further, while admitting that he speaks falsely, he will [be forced to] say that we should believe him....

11. And when Aenesidemus in his *Outlines* goes through the nine tropes..., shall we say that he spoke of things he knew or of which he was ignorant?...

12.... It would be a pleasure, I tell you, to ask the fellow who was making such fine speeches whether he was speaking in full knowledge that things were in this way or in ignorance of it; for if he did not

know, [why] could we believe him? but if he knew, he was an utter idiot, [since his thesis was that we do not know]...

17.... [A]nd if there is no use in words, why do they bother us?...

20. [And when they say] that one ought to live in accordance with nature and custom, and yet assent to nothing, they are naive in the extreme. For one must assent to that, even if to nothing else, and assume that it is so. And why should we follow nature and custom more than not, if we know nothing and have nothing by which to judge?

21. For it is absolutely silly when they say that just as cathartic drugs bring about their own excretion together with the superfluities, in the same way the argument that maintains that all things are obscure also nullifies itself together with everything else. For if it refutes itself, those who use it would talk nonsense. It would be better for them to keep quiet and not open their mouths at all.

22. But indeed there is no similarity at all between the cathartic drug and their argument. For the drug is excreted and does not remain in the body, while the [skeptical] argument must stay in the mind, where it remains the same and is always believed; for this is the only thing that would keep people from [assenting to their sense-perceptions]...

26. [That it is against nature to philosophize in the way of the Skeptics is evident from] the following fact: Antigonus of Carystus, who lived at about the same time and wrote about their life, says that Pyrrho, being pursued by a dog, escaped up a tree and, when laughed at by those who stood by, said that it was difficult to put off human nature. And when his sister Philista was to offer a sacrifice, and one of their friends promised what was necessary for the sacrifice but did not provide it, Pyrrho bought it and showed

his annoyance; and when the friend said that his acts were not in accord with his words nor worthy of his freedom from passions, he replied: 'In the case of a woman, at any rate, what need is there to produce any proof of it?' But his friend might fairly have answered: 'Fool,...if there is any good in these arguments of yours[, they must apply in every case.]'...

28. [And it is worth knowing both who were those who admired him.] Timon of Phlius was his pupil,

who...after coming across him wrote offensive and vulgar parodies, in which he reviled all the philosophers who ever lived....

30. It is evident that no one in his right mind would approve such a sect or school or however and whatever one cares to call it. For I think we should not call it philosophy at all, for it takes away the basis of philosophy....

READING 14C

Sextus Empiricus, *Pyrrhoniae Hypotyposes* (*Outlines of Pyrrhonism*)[1]

(sometimes called *Outlines of Skepticism*; second or third century CE)

Book I.

CHAPTER III. OF THE NOMENCLATURE OF SKEPTICISM

The skeptic school, then, is also called "zetetic" from its activity in investigation and inquiry, and "ephectic" or suspensive from the state of mind produced in the inquirer after his search, and "aporetic" or dubitative either from its habit of doubting..., or from its indecision as regards assent and denial,[2] and "Pyrrhonean" [because Pyrrho was such a conspicuous figure in the tradition].

CHAPTER IV. WHAT SKEPTICISM IS

Skepticism...opposes appearances to judgements [i.e., uses appearances to raise doubts about our judgements], with the result that, owing to [the equal weight of the opposing appearances], we are brought firstly to a state of mental suspense and next to a state of "unperturbedness" or quietude....

CHAPTER VI. OF THE PRINCIPLES OF SKEPTICISM

The originating cause of skepticism is, we say, the hope of attaining quietude.... The main basic principle of the skeptic system is that of opposing

---

1 Sextus Empiricus, *Outlines of Pyrrhonism* (*Pyrrhoniae Hypotyposes*, probably the 2nd century CE) from Sextus Empiricus, *Outlines of Pyrrhonism*, trans. R.G. Bury (Amherst, NY: Prometheus Books, 1990).

2 "Zetetic" derives from a Greek adjective "ζητητικός" (*zētētikos*) meaning "inquisitive or keen." "Ephectic" derives from the Greek adjective "ἐφεκτικός" (*ephektikos*) meaning "to suspend judgment." The Skeptics called themselves "those who suspend judgment" (*ephektikoi*). "Aporetic" derives from the Greek "ἀπορητικός" (*aporētikos*)—"at a loss"—in this case, inclined to doubt or to raise objections.

to every proposition an equal proposition; for we believe that as a consequence of this we end by ceasing to dogmatize.

CHAPTER VII. DOES THE SKEPTIC DOGMATIZE?

... (... [T]he skeptic gives assent to feelings which are the necessary results of sense impressions, and he would not, for example, say when feeling hot or cold "I believe that I am not hot or cold");[1] but we say that "he does not dogmatize"[2] ... [T]he skeptic does not posit ... formulae in any absolute sense; for he conceives that, just as the formula "All things are false" asserts the falsity of itself as well as of everything else, ... so also the formula "No more" asserts that itself, like all the rest, is "No more (this than that)," and thus cancels itself along with the rest. ...

CHAPTER X. DO THE SKEPTICS ABOLISH APPEARANCES?

Those who say that "the skeptics abolish appearances," or phenomena, seem to me to be unacquainted with the statements of our school. For, as we said above, we do not overthrow the affective sense impressions [the perceptions] which induce our assent involuntarily ... And when we [Skeptics] question whether the underlying object is such as it appears, ... our doubt does not concern the appearance itself but the [explanation] given of that appearance. For example, honey appears to us to be sweet ... but whether it is also sweet in its essence[3] is for us a matter of doubt, since this is not an appearance but a judgement regarding the appearance. ...

CHAPTER XII. WHAT IS THE END OF SKEPTICISM?

[The Skeptic, by suspending his judgement and giving up the idea that anything is by nature good or bad] neither shuns nor pursues anything eagerly; and, in consequence, he is unperturbed. ...

[Although the Skeptic is still troubled by certain unavoidable discomforts:] for we grant that he is cold at times and thirsty, ... even in these cases, ... [he escapes] with less discomfort, [since he does not suffer the additional affliction of thinking that these conditions are inherently evil.]

CHAPTER XIII. OF THE GENERAL MODES LEADING TO THE SUSPENSION OF JUDGEMENT

[S]uspension of judgement ... is the result of setting things in opposition. ... For instance, we oppose appearances to appearances when we say "The same tower appears round from a distance, but square from close at hand." ... And thoughts we oppose to appearances, as when Anaxagoras countered the notion that snow is white with the argument, "Snow is frozen water, and water is black; therefore, snow also is black." ...

CHAPTER XIV. CONCERNING THE TEN MODES

The usual tradition amongst the older skeptics is that the "modes" by which "suspension" is supposed to be brought about are ten in number; ... the first, based on the variety in animals; the second, on the differences in human beings; the third, on the different structures of the organs of sense; the fourth, on the circumstantial conditions; the fifth,

---

1 So the Skeptic does dogmatize in the broader sense of giving approval of a thing, and does not refrain from doing this.

2 I.e., the Skeptic does not dogmatize in the sense of assenting to something non-evident, a non-evident object of scientific inquiry.

3 I.e., its underlying nature.

on positions and intervals and locations; the sixth, on intermixtures; the seventh, on the quantities and formations of the underlying objects; the eighth, on the fact of relativity; the ninth, on the frequency or rarity of occurrence; the tenth, on the disciplines and customs and laws, the legendary beliefs and the dogmatic convictions....

[The] *tenth mode,*... is mainly concerned with ethics, being based on rules of conduct, habits, laws, legendary beliefs, and dogmatic conceptions.... And each of these we oppose now to itself, and now to each of the others....

CHAPTER XXII. OF THE EXPRESSION "I SUS-PEND JUDGEMENT"

[We adopt t]he phrase "I suspend judgement"...in place of "I am unable to say which of the objects[1] presented I ought to believe and which I ought to disbelieve," indicating that the objects appear to us equal as regards credibility and incredibility.... [T]he term "suspension" is [used because] the mind [is thus] "suspended," so that it neither affirms nor denies anything...

CHAPTER XXVIII. SUPPLEMENTARY NOTES ON THE SKEPTIC EXPRESSIONS

[It should also be noted that the Skeptics' prop-ositions] themselves are included in the things to which their doubt applies, just as aperient drugs do not merely eliminate the humours from the body, but also expel themselves along with the humours....

Book III.

CHAPTER XXIV. WHAT IS THE SO-CALLED ART OF LIVING?

[Sextus rejects the Stoic belief that there is a specific "art of living," since nothing is "naturally" good or evil, and then demonstrates that our] notions con-cerning things shameful and not shameful, unholy and not so, laws and customs, piety towards the gods, reverence for the departed, and the like [are relative]....

For example, amongst us sodomy is regarded as shameful or rather illegal, but by the Germani, they say, it is not looked on as shameful but as a custom-ary thing.... and some [thus explain] the burning love of Achilles for Patroclus....

And with us it is sinful to marry one's mother or one's own sister; but the Persians, and especially those of them who are reputed to practice wisdom—namely, the Magi,—marry their mothers; and the Egyptians take their sisters in marriage...

[Indeed], Zeno of Citium says that it is not amiss for a man to rub his mother's private part with his own private part, just as no one would say it was bad for him to rub any other part of her body with his hand. Chrysippus, too, in his book *The State* approves of a father getting children by his daughter, a mother by her son, and a brother by his sister....

Moreover, the eating of human flesh is sinful with us, but indifferent amongst whole tribes of barbar-ians. Yet why should one speak of "barbarians" when even Tydeus is said to have devoured the brains of his enemy, and the Stoic school declare that it is not wrong for a man to eat either other men's flesh or his own?...

And the Amazons[2] used to maim the males amongst their offspring so as to make them incapable of...warfare; [whereas we regard war as the province

---

1 I.e., propositions.
2 In Greek mythology, they were a tribe of women warriors.

of men]. The Mother of the gods[1] also approves of effeminates, and the goddess would not have decided thus if unmanliness were naturally a bad thing....

Around all matters of religion and theology also, there rages violent controversy. For while the majority declare that gods exist, some deny their existence...Epicurus [maintains that God] is anthropomorphic, Xenophanes that he is an impassive sphere. Some, too, hold that he cares for human affairs, others that he does not so care...

[T]he rituals of worship [also], exhibit great diversity.... Thus, for example, no one would sacrifice a pig to Sarapis, but they sacrifice it to Heracles and Asclepius.... To Poseidon they sacrifice a horse; but to Apollo...that animal is an abomination....[2]

[There are similar examples] in the religious observances with regard to human diet.... [Amongst the Egyptians, for example, some of the] sages believe it is sinful to eat an animal's head, others the shoulder, others the foot, others some other part.... [I]n some cults they abstain from mint...And some declare that they would sooner eat their fathers' heads than beans....

A similar account may be given of reverence towards the departed.... The fish-eating tribes of the Ethiopians cast [the dead] into the lakes...the Hyrcanians expose them as prey to dogs, and some of the Indians to vultures.... Some burn the dead; and of these some recover and preserve their bones, while others show no care but leave them scattered about....

Accordingly, the skeptic, seeing so great a diversity of usages, suspends judgement as to the natural existence of anything good or bad or (in general) fit or unfit to be done, [and abstains from dogmatism, nevertheless following—undogmatically—the ordinary rules of life in his society]...

Questions

1. Compare skepticism with the Daoism in Laozi. What are the similarities, the differences?

2. Ancient skepticism was more philosophical than modern skepticism, which is often associated with religious and even political views. What was the principal idea in ancient skepticism and how does it translate into concrete moral principles?

3. Pyrrho taught by example and did not leave any writings. Provide a character sketch of Pyrrho in one paragraph. Add another paragraph, describing his good and bad points. Do you think he would be a good friend or mentor?

4. According to legend, Pyrrho used to argue aloud with himself. Why does this make some sense, from a skeptical perspective? How does the skeptical form of argument differ from other forms of argument?

5. Sextus saw the Skeptics as physicians, dispensing medicine to patients, who have become too attached—dogmatically attached—to appearances. How would Sextus diagnose and treat fanaticism? A broken heart? That feeling that you must have a new phone?

---

1 In Greek mythology, this would refer to Rhea, the mother by Kronos of the first generation of the Olympian gods (Hestia, Demeter, Hera, Hades, Poseidon, and Zeus).

2 These are names of various gods or heroes (demi-gods) of Greek mythology. Animal sacrifices made to them and others was customary religious practice in Greek (and Roman) (pagan) culture.

6. The "dogmatists" alleged that the Skeptics contradicted themselves by affirming certain things. Whose side are you on? Explain your position, with examples.
7. How do the Skeptics know that they do not know? Or do they?
8. Do you think skepticism is a helpful attitude in a high school teacher? A police officer? A politician? A judge? Why, why not?

Suggested Readings

The major ancient source for Pyrrho's life and philosophy is Diogenes Laertius's *Lives of Eminent Philosophers*, from which the first reading is taken. There are short passages on Pyrrho in Aristocles of Messene and various other authors. Sextus Empiricus left a substantial body of written work, which includes the *Outlines of Pyrrhonism* and a series of "Againsts," including *Against the Ethicists* and *Against the Professors*. There is an older translation of the *Outlines* by R.G. Bury and a variety of more recent translations. Benson Mates's *The Skeptic Way* (1999) includes a translation, introduction, and commentary.

Some of the importance of skepticism derives from its place in the development of Greek and Roman (and therefore western) ethics. Students may accordingly want to consult the entries on "Ancient Ethical Theory" and "Ancient Ethics" in the *Stanford Encyclopedia of Philosophy* and the *Internet Encyclopedia of Philosophy*. The philosophical literature focuses on the Skeptics' epistemological position. For an account of the development of skepticism, see Harald Thorsrud, *Ancient Scepticism* (2009, 2014). King's College, London has an accessible lecture on Pyrrho in its history of philosophy series of podcasts at historyofphilosophy.net. The sources on skeptical ethics include Hayden Weir Ausland, "On the Moral Origin of the Pyrrhonian Philosophy" (1989); Tad Brennan, *Ethics and Epistemology in Sextus Empiricus* (1999); and G. Striker, "Ataraxia: Happiness as Tranquility" (1990, 1996).

Chapter 15

Epicureanism

Epicurus (341–270 BCE) was a controversial figure with fervent disciples and many detractors. As a result, piecing together a fair account of his life is a daunting task. The basic outline of his life is nevertheless clear.

Epicurus was born on the island of Samos, of modest parents. His father was a school teacher; his mother was a priestess, or fortune-teller. After his compulsory service in the Athenian military, he probably worked as a teacher in remoter settlements, while studying philosophy. When he was thirty-five, he moved to Athens, which was the center of the philosophical world. With the aid of influential benefactors, he bought a house in the city and a garden on the outskirts, where he gathered together a small but devoted group of followers. As far as we are aware, he never married and had no children.

Epicurus's garden community—loosely referred to as a "school"—had members from different economic and social classes, women, and even slaves. They seem to have lived quietly together, following a communal way of life, while eschewing any involvement in the politics of the city. Inside the school, Epicurus was referred to as "the wise man"; his followers were known as "seekers." Decisions were made in a hierarchical manner, with Epicurus having complete authority over other members, who were divided into associate leaders, assistants, and pupils. Although individual members did not share their belongings, they were expected to help one another financially.

According to a legend reported by Seneca, there was an inscription over the gate to the Garden that read: "Stranger, here you will do well to tarry; our highest good is pleasure." This is probably a fiction, but captures the attitude of the school. Although the members of the group ostensibly lived on plain food and meager drink, preferring the intellectual pleasures of philosophical conversation and calm friendship over sensuous indulgence, their critics accused them of gluttony, drunkenness, luxurious living, and orgies. We can only assume that this was calumny.

Epicurus had administrative gifts and established a network of similar communities throughout the region, which survived until the end of the Roman Empire. Epicurus encouraged the cult that grew up around him and declared himself a god. The Garden probably contained a statue of him and there was a monthly celebration in his name, an ancient practice reserved for divinities. On his deathbed, Epicurus wrote a letter in which he cheerfully mentions the great sufferings caused by his physical ailments. Critics have, perhaps unfairly, derided the letter as "theatrics."

Most of our information about Epicurean doctrines comes from Diogenes Laertius's life of Epicurus and the poem *On the Nature of Things* (*De rerum natura*) by the Roman poet Titus Lucretius Carus in the first century BCE. We know very little about Lucretius's life. Saint Jerome says that he was driven mad by a love potion, that he suffered from bouts of insanity, and that he committed suicide. Jerome would have seen him as an enemy, however, for his religious views. Modern scholars tend to dismiss these reports as unreliable rumors or outright fabrication. The poem nevertheless provides some evidence, at least, that Lucretius was prone to excesses of emotion.

We also have two compilations of Epicurean aphorisms: *Principal Doctrines* and the *Vatican Sayings* (so-named because they come from a book in the Vatican Library). Archaeologists have also discovered a large number of scrolls that were buried in ash when Mount Vesuvius erupted in ancient times. Scholars are now trying to decipher these charred texts.

Laertius tells us that Epicurus wrote three hundred scrolls. This may be so, since they would have included many lesser works, such as his critiques (diatribes) against competing schools, lectures for his inner circle, philosophical epistles (letters) that were sent out to other communities, and lists of slogans for students to memorize. The style of prose in the work that we have is simple and direct.

The Epicureans were hedonists, a term of description that derives from the Greek *hēdonē* (ἡδονή), "pleasure." Like the Skeptics, they were primarily concerned with the personal and subjective aspects of experience. They nevertheless described the experience of pleasure negatively, not as sensual stimulation, but as the absence of pain. According to their analysis, pleasure consists of the state of rest or satisfaction that arises when we remove physical and mental distress. Like the Skeptics and Stoics, they accordingly made *ataraxia*, mental tranquility or "unperturbedness," their goal.

Epicurean philosophy was a kind of rational materialism. Like Democritus, Epicurus believed that the world was composed of atoms. He was also an empiricist, who accepted that the experience of our five senses gives us reliable information about reality. Sensation is therefore an arbiter of pleasure. In the Epicurean view, no pleasure is intrinsically bad, and pleasure is only to be avoided when it leads to a greater pain. Pain is to be avoided unless it leads to a greater pleasure. Happiness can be found in a simple life, quiet friendship, and the practice of philosophy, which arises when we are calm and untroubled.

Since the experience of pleasure is fundamentally subjective, the Epicureans focused on the management of our personal desires. Epicurus distinguishes between 1) natural necessary desire, 2) natural unnecessary desire, and 3) vain empty desire. The first set of desires includes, for example, our experience of hunger and thirst. These desires are natural and cannot be eliminated. They should accordingly be satisfied. The second set might include a desire for a particular food or drink, which we may occasionally indulge, but which is largely superfluous to happiness.

The third set of desires includes the desire for immortality, wealth, fame, or political power. Such desires can never be satisfied. We will never be immortal, and no matter how much wealth, fame or power we acquire, it will never be enough to satisfy the unbridled, uncritical human appetite for such things. These kinds of desires should accordingly be eliminated. Not desiring such things is, in large part, the secret to happiness. If we desire very little, we will be readily satisfied.

Since the Epicureans were seeking tranquility, one of their chief aims was to calm our fears. Thus, though the gods exist, they do not meddle in human affairs, since that would disturb their own tranquility. Nor is there any reason for the materialist to fear death. Epicurus believes that when we die, the atoms that compose us disperse. We therefore cease to exist. It follows that our fear of death is unwarranted, since it is illogical to suppose that something untoward can happen to us when we no longer exist. Lucretius also raises a "symmetry argument": since we are not distressed by the fact that we did not exist before birth, why should we be distressed by the fact that we will not exist after death?

The first reading is from Epicurus's *Letter To Menoeceus*, which Diogenes Laertius includes in his *Life*. It contains a summary of Epicurus's ethical doctrines. As one might expect, from someone who believed that personal pleasure is the highest good, Epicurus took a liberal and individualistic stance in matters of practical morality. Thus he sees justice, for example, as an agreement between individuals "neither to harm nor be harmed."

The second reading is a brief excerpt from Lucretius's poem *On the Nature of Things*, which contains the best exegesis that we have of Epicurean physics. Lucretius discards the superstitions of religion and replaces them with a scientific cosmology. He thereby derives the principles of morality from the material existence of the world. As Cyril Bailey, the translator of the poem, puts it: pain is the "dislocation of atomic arrangements and motions; pleasure, their readjustment and equilibrium." The highest pleasure—and it is interesting that it is, in theory, a material pleasure—is found in philosophy and the pursuit of knowledge.

READING 15A

"Epicurus" from Diogenes Laertius, *Lives of Eminent Philosophers*[1]

(341–270 BCE)

[Diogenes gives us a letter from Epicurus to Menoeceus:]

Epicurus to Menoeceus, greeting.

"Let no one be slow to seek wisdom when he is young nor weary in the search thereof when he is grown old. For no age is too early or too late for the health of the soul. And to say that the season for

---

1 "Epicurus," Book X of Diogenes Laertius, *Lives of Eminent Philosophers*, trans. by Robert Drew Hicks, Loeb Classical Library No. 184 (Cambridge: Harvard University Press; 1925, 1972). Available at http://www.perseus.tufts.edu/hopper/text?doc=Perseus: text:1999.01.0258 and en.wikisource.org/wiki/Lives_of_the_Eminent_Philosophers.

studying philosophy has not yet come, or that it is past and gone, is like saying that the season for happiness is not yet or that it is now no more.... So we must exercise ourselves in...happiness since, if that be present, we have everything...

"Those things which...I have declared unto [you], those do, and exercise [yourself] therein, holding them to be the elements of right life. First believe that God is a living being immortal and blessed, according to the notion of a god indicated by the common sense of mankind; and so believing, [you] shall not affirm of him [anything] that is foreign to his immortality or that agrees not with blessedness, but shalt believe about him whatever may uphold both his blessedness and his immortality. For verily there are gods, and the knowledge of them is manifest; but they are not such as the multitude believe, seeing that men do not steadfastly maintain the notions they form respecting them.... For the utterances of the multitude about the gods are not true preconceptions but false assumptions; hence it is that the greatest evils happen to the wicked and the greatest blessings happen to the good from the hand of the gods, seeing that they are always favorable to their own good qualities and take pleasure in men like unto themselves, but reject as alien whatever is not of their kind.

"Accustom yourself to believe that death is nothing to us, for good and evil imply sentience, and death is the privation of all sentience; therefore, a right understanding that death is nothing to us makes the mortality of life enjoyable, not by adding to life an illimitable time, but by taking away the yearning after immortality. For life has no terrors for him who has thoroughly apprehended that there are no terrors for him in ceasing to live. Foolish, therefore, is the man who says that he fears death, not because it will pain when it comes, but because it pains in the prospect. Whatsoever causes no annoyance when it is present, causes only a groundless pain in the expectation. Death, therefore, the most awful

of evils, is nothing to us, seeing that, when we are, death is not come, and, when death is come, we are not. It is nothing, then, either to the living or to the dead, for with the living it is not and the dead exist no longer. But in the world, at one time men shun death as the greatest of all evils, and at another time choose it as a respite from the evils in life. The wise man does not deprecate life nor does he fear the cessation of life. The thought of life is no offence to him, nor is the cessation of life regarded as an evil. And even as men choose of food not merely and simply the larger portion, but the more pleasant, so the wise seek to enjoy the time which is most pleasant and not merely that which is longest. And he who admonishes the young to live well and the old to make a good end speaks foolishly, not merely because of the desirableness of life, but because it is the same exercise of philosophy [that teaches us] to live well and to die well....

"We must remember that the future is neither wholly ours nor wholly not ours, so that neither must we count upon it as quite certain to come nor despair of it as quite certain not to come.

"We must also reflect that of desires some are natural, others are groundless; and that of the natural some are necessary as well as natural, and some natural only. And of the necessary desires some are necessary if we are to be happy, some if the body is to be rid of uneasiness, some if we are even to live. He who has a clear and certain understanding of these things will direct every preference and aversion toward securing health of body and tranquility of mind, seeing that this is the sum and end of a blessed life. For the end of all our actions is to be free from pain and fear, and, when once we have attained all this, the tempest of the soul is laid; seeing that the living creature has no need to go in search of something that is lacking, nor to look for anything else by which the good of the soul and of the body will be fulfilled. When we are pained because of the absence of pleasure, then, and then only, do we feel the need of pleasure. Wherefore we call pleasure the alpha and omega of a blessed life. Pleasure is our first and kindred good. It is the starting-point of every choice and of every aversion, and to it we come back, inasmuch as we make feeling the rule by which to judge of every good thing. And since pleasure is our first and native good, for that reason we do not choose every pleasure whatsoever, but oftentimes pass over many pleasures when a greater annoyance ensues from them. And oftentimes we consider pains superior to pleasures when submission to the pains for a long time brings us as a consequence a greater pleasure. While therefore all pleasure because it is naturally akin to us is good, not all pleasure is choiceworthy, just as all pain is an evil and yet not all pain is to be shunned.

"It is, however, by measuring one against another, and by looking at the conveniences and inconveniences, that all these matters must be judged. Sometimes we treat the good as an evil, and the evil, on the contrary, as a good. Again, we regard independence of outward things as a great good, not so as in all cases to use little, but so as to be contented with little if we have not much, being honestly persuaded that they have the sweetest enjoyment of luxury who stand least in need of it, and that whatever is natural is easily procured and only the vain and worthless hard to win. Plain fare gives as much pleasure as a costly diet, when once the pain of want has been removed, while bread and water confer the highest possible pleasure when they are brought to hungry lips. To habituate one's self, therefore, to simple and inexpensive diet supplies all that is needful for health, and enables a man to meet the necessary requirements of life without shrinking...

"When we say, then, that pleasure is the end and aim, we do not mean the pleasures of the prodigal or the pleasures of sensuality, as we are understood to do by some through ignorance, prejudice, or willful misrepresentation. By pleasure we mean the absence of pain in the body and of trouble in the soul. It is not an unbroken succession of drinking-bouts and of revelry, not sexual love, not the enjoyment of the fish and other delicacies of a luxurious table, which produce a pleasant life; it is sober reasoning, searching out the grounds of every choice and avoidance, and banishing those beliefs through which the greatest tumults take possession of the soul. Of all this the beginning and the greatest good is prudence. Wherefore prudence is a more precious thing even than philosophy. From it spring all the other virtues, for it teaches that we cannot lead a life of pleasure which is not also a life of prudence, honor, and justice; nor lead a life of prudence, honor, and justice, which is not also a life of pleasure. For the virtues have grown into one with a pleasant life, and a pleasant life is inseparable from them.

"Who, then, is superior in judgement to such a man? He holds a holy belief concerning the gods, and is altogether free from the fear of death. He has diligently considered the end fixed by nature, and understands how easily the limit of good things can be reached and attained, and how either the duration or the intensity of evils is but slight. Destiny, which some introduce as sovereign over all things, he laughs to scorn, affirming rather that some things happen of necessity, others by chance, others through our own agency. For he sees that necessity destroys responsibility and that chance or fortune is inconstant; whereas our own actions are free, and it is to them that praise and blame naturally attach. It were better, indeed, to accept the legends of the gods than to bow beneath that yoke of destiny which the natural philosophers have imposed. The one holds out some faint hope that we may escape if we honor the gods, while the necessity of the naturalists is deaf to all entreaties.[1] Nor does he hold chance to be a

---

1   The necessity of the naturalists refers to a form of material determinism, i.e., everything that happens in the universe is determined by the properties of the matter that composes all existing things.

god, as the world in general does, for in the acts of a god there is no disorder...

"Exercise [yourself] in these and kindred precepts day and night, both by [yourself] and with him who is like unto [you]. Then never, either in waking or in dream, [will you] be disturbed, but will live as a god among men...."

[Diogenes then lists the "Sovereign Maxims," which contain Epicurus's Principal Doctrines (*kuriai doxai*)]

1. A blessed and eternal being has no trouble himself and brings no trouble upon any other being; hence he is exempt from movements of anger and partiality, for every such movement implies weakness.[1]...

2. Death is nothing to us; for the body, when it has been resolved into its elements, has no feeling, and that which has no feeling is nothing to us.

3. The magnitude of pleasure reaches its limit in the removal of all pain. When pleasure is present, so long as it is uninterrupted, there is no pain either of body or of mind or of both together.

4. Continuous pain does not last long in the flesh; on the contrary, pain, if extreme, is present a very short time, and even that degree of pain which barely outweighs pleasure in the flesh does not last for many days together. Illnesses of long duration even permit of an excess of pleasure over pain in the flesh.

5. It is impossible to live a pleasant life without living wisely and well and justly, and it is impossible to live wisely and well and justly without living pleasantly. Whenever any one of these is lacking, when, for instance, the man is not able to live wisely, though

he lives well and justly, it is impossible for him to live a pleasant life.

6. In order to obtain security from other men, any means whatsoever of procuring this was a natural good.

7. Some men have sought to become famous and renowned, thinking that thus they would make themselves secure against their fellow-men. If, then, the life of such persons really was secure, they attained natural good; if, however, it was insecure, they have not attained the end which by nature's own prompting they originally sought.

8. No pleasure is in itself evil, but the things which produce certain pleasures entail annoyances many times greater than the pleasures themselves.

9. If all pleasure had been capable of accumulation—if this had gone on not only by recurrence in time, but all over the frame or, at any rate, over the principal parts of man's nature, there would never have been any difference between one pleasure and another, as in fact there is.

10. If the objects which are productive of pleasures to profligate persons really freed them from fears of the mind—the fears, I mean, inspired by celestial and atmospheric phenomena, the fear of death, the fear of pain; if, further, they taught them to limit their desires, we should never have any fault to find with such persons, for they would then be filled with pleasures to overflowing on all sides and would be exempt from all pain, whether of body or mind, that is, from all evil....

12. It would be impossible to banish fear on matters of the highest importance, if a man did not know

---

1 Regarding the gods, elsewhere Epicurus says that they can only be discerned by reason; elsewhere again, he says that the physical appearance of the gods is an illusion, resulting from the continuous influx of similar images directed to the same spot.

[the physical nature of the universe] but lived in dread of what the [myths about gods and religious beliefs] tell us....

14. When tolerable security against our fellow-men is attained, then on a basis of power sufficient to afford support and of material prosperity arises in most genuine form the security of a quiet private life withdrawn from the multitude.

15. Nature's wealth at once has its bounds and is easy to procure; but the wealth of vain fancies recedes to an infinite distance.

16. Fortune but seldom interferes with the wise man; his greatest and highest interests have been, are, and will be, directed by reason throughout the course of his life.

17. The just man enjoys the greatest peace of mind, while the unjust is full of the utmost disquietude.

18. Pleasure in the flesh admits no increase when once the pain of want has been removed; after that it only admits of variation. The limit of pleasure in the mind, however, is reached when we reflect on the things themselves and their congeners[1] which cause the mind the greatest alarms.

19. Unlimited time and limited time afford an equal amount of pleasure, if we measure the limits of that pleasure by reason.

20. The flesh receives as unlimited the limits of pleasure; and to provide it requires unlimited time. But the mind, grasping in thought what the end and limit of the flesh is, and banishing the terrors of futurity, procures us a complete and perfect life [without the need] of unlimited time. Nevertheless, it does not shun pleasure, and even in the hour of death, when

ushered out of existence by circumstances, the mind does not lack enjoyment of the best life.

21. He who understands the limits of life knows how easy it is to procure enough to remove the pain of want and make the whole of life complete and perfect. Hence he has no longer any need of things which are not to be won save by labor and conflict.

22. We must take into account as the end all that really exists and all clear evidence of sense to which we refer our opinions; for otherwise everything will be full of uncertainty and confusion.

23. If you fight against all your sensations, you will have no standard to which to refer, and thus no means of judging even those judgements which you pronounce false....

25. If you do not on every separate occasion refer each of your actions to the end prescribed by nature, but instead of this in the act of choice or avoidance swerve aside to some other end, your acts will not be consistent with your theories....

27. Of all the means which are procured by wisdom to ensure happiness throughout the whole of life, by far the most important is the acquisition of friends.

28. The same conviction which inspires confidence that nothing we have to fear is eternal or even of long duration, also enables us to see that even in our limited conditions of life nothing enhances our security so much as friendship....

30. Those natural desires which entail no pain when not gratified, though their objects are vehemently pursued, are also due to illusory opinion; and when they are not got rid of, it is not because of their own nature, but because of the man's illusory opinion.

---

1 I.e., a thing of the same kind.

31. Natural justice is a symbol or expression of expediency, to prevent one man from harming or being harmed by another.

32. Those animals which are incapable of making covenants with one another, to the end that they may neither inflict nor suffer harm, are without either justice or injustice. And those tribes which either could not or would not form mutual covenants to the same end are in like case.

33. There never was an absolute justice, but only an agreement made in reciprocal intercourse in whatever localities now and again from time to time, providing against the infliction or suffering of harm.

34. Injustice is not in itself an evil, but only in its consequence, [namely,] the terror which is excited by apprehension that those appointed to punish such offences will discover the injustice.

35. It is impossible for the man who secretly violates any article of the social compact to feel confident that he will remain undiscovered, even if he has already escaped ten thousand times; for right on to the end of his life he is never sure he will not be detected....

38. Where without any change in circumstances the conventional laws, when judged by their consequences, were seen not to correspond with the notion of justice, such laws were not really just; but wherever the laws have ceased to be expedient in consequence of a change in circumstances, in that case the laws were for the time being just when they were expedient for the mutual intercourse of the citizens, and subsequently ceased to be just when they ceased to be expedient.

39. He who best knew how to meet fear of external foes made into one family all the creatures he could; and those he could not, he at any rate did not treat as aliens; and where he found even this impossible, he avoided all intercourse, and, so far as was expedient, kept them at a distance.

40. Those who were best able to provide themselves with the means of security against their neighbors, being thus in possession of the surest guarantee, passed the most agreeable life in each other's society; and their enjoyment of the fullest intimacy was such that, if one of them died before his time, the survivors did not lament his death as if it called for commiseration.

Lucretius, *De rerum natura* (*On the Nature of Things*)[1]

(first century BCE)

[In the Proem in Book I, Lucretius describes the victory of Epicurus over the monster Superstitious Religion. He urges us not to give in to our fear of death and the threats of the seers, and instead pursue philosophy. He then continues:]

---

1   Titus Lucretius Carus, *On the Nature of Things*, trans. Cyril Bailey (Oxford: Clarendon Press, 1910), with minor revisions.

This terror then, this darkness of the mind, must needs be scattered not by the rays of the sun and the gleaming shafts of day, but by the outer view and the inner law of nature; whose first rule shall take its start for us from this, that nothing is ever begotten of nothing by divine will....

For if things came to being from nothing, every kind might be born from all things, nothing would need a seed. First men might arise from the sea, and from the land the race of scaly creatures, and birds burst forth from the sky.... Nor would the same fruits stay constant to the trees, but all would change: all trees might avail to bear all fruits....

This establishes the existence of fundamental matter in the form of particles.

Then follows this, that nature breaks up each thing again into its own first-bodies, nor does she destroy anything into nothing. For if anything were mortal in all its parts, each thing would on a sudden be snatched from our eyes and pass away. For there would be no need of any force, such as might cause disunion in its parts and unloose its fastenings. But as it is, because all things are put together of ever-lasting seeds,[1] until some force has met them to batter things asunder with its blow, or to make its way inward through the empty voids and break things up, nature suffers not the destruction of anything to be seen....

There is a void, or empty space.

And yet all things are not held close pressed on every side by the nature of body; for there is void in things.... mere space untouchable and empty.

For if there were not, by no means could things move; for that which is the office of body, to offend and hinder, would at every moment be present to all things; nothing, therefore, could advance, since nothing could give the example of yielding place....[2]

Then, too, neighbors began eagerly to form friendship one with another...and they commended to mercy children and the race of women, when with cries and gestures they taught by broken words that it is right for all men to have pity on the weak....[3]

It is the glory of Athens to have produced Epicurus. In time gone by Athens, of glorious name, first spread among struggling mortals the fruits that bear corn, and fashioned life afresh, and enacted laws; she, too, first gave sweet solace for life, when she gave birth to the man gifted with the great mind, who once poured forth all wisdom from his truthful lips...He saw that men, in spite of all outward advantages, were miserable, for when he saw that mortals had by now attained well-nigh all things which their needs crave for subsistence, and that...their life was established in safety, that men abounded in power through wealth and honors and renown...and yet not one person for all that had at home a heart less anguished...he then did understand that it was the vessel itself which wrought the disease, and that by its disease all things were corrupted within...

And so with his discourse of truthful words he purged the heart and set a limit to its desire and fear. He purged the heart and taught it the path to the highest good, and the means of meeting the ills of life, and set forth what is the highest good, towards which we all strive, and pointed out the path...he showed that what there is of ill in the affairs of mortals everywhere, coming to being and flying abroad in diverse forms, be it by the chance or the force of nature, is there because nature had so brought it to pass...

Thus, he taught us that the darkness of the mind must be dispelled by knowledge. For even as children tremble and fear everything in blinding darkness, so we sometimes dread in the light things that are no

---

1 I.e., atoms.

2 In the rest of the poem, Lucretius shows that "everything else is either a property or accident of these two, atoms and void." In Book V, he recounts the beginnings of civilization, the establishment of marriage, family, and ethical conventions.

3 Eventually, men invented the gods, which caused misery. "True piety," Lucretius writes, "consists not in worship, but the peaceful mind." Then in the Introduction to Book VI, Lucretius writes that human happiness lies, as Epicurus taught, in philosophy and science.

whit more to be feared than what children shudder at in the dark and imagine will come to pass. This terror then, this darkness of the mind, must needs be scattered not by the rays and the gleaming shafts of day, but by the outer view and the inner law of nature.

Questions

1. Compare Epicureanism and Skepticism. Are they compatible?
2. What is the secret to happiness in Epicurus's judgment? How do we put ourselves in the proper position to achieve mental tranquility and enjoy pleasure? How would you apply Epicurus's view to your own life?
3. The Epicurean conception of happiness was revived in the modern era by the Utilitarians. It seems clear, however, that Aristotle would find Epicurus's conception of happiness too narrow. Why? What does it leave out?
4. How does Epicurus explain the desire for pleasure? Draw up a list of things that might be included under Epicurus's three types of desire. Do you think the Epicurean model is helpful in teaching us how to control our desires?
5. What is the Epicurean position regarding the gods and religious beliefs? Do you agree with it? Why, why not?
6. What is the theory behind the Epicurean view of friendship? Which type of desire would having a friend satisfy? Do you agree with the Epicurean theory of friendship?
7. What is the Epicurean view of participating in public life and politics? Explain Epicurus's understanding of justice.
8. Describe Lucretius's view of the physical world. How does it fit into Epicureanism? Where does wisdom lie, if he is right?

Suggested Readings

Epicurus was a voluminous writer. Diogenes Laertius provides a list of works that includes *Letter to Menoeceus,* which summarizes his ethics. Very little of his writing has come down to us, however, and our understanding of his teaching comes primarily from the later writers of Antiquity, especially Lucretius, the Roman politician Cicero, and the Platonist Plutarch. The accounts of Cicero and Plutarch must nevertheless be treated with caution, since they were opposed to Epicureanism and may have misrepresented it. There are many English translations of Lucretius's *On the Nature of Things* (sometimes rendered as *The Universe*). The contemporary translation by R.E. Latham in the Penguin edition (1951, 1967) is readily available and friendly.

As in the case of skepticism, students will want to consult the entries on "Ancient Ethical Theory" and "Ancient Ethics" in the *Stanford Encyclopedia of Philosophy* and the *Internet Encyclopedia of Philosophy.* For ethical sources, see Phillip Mitsis's *Epicurus' Ethical Theory: The Pleasures of Invulnerability* (1988). Mitsis shows that the Epicurean notion of pleasure differs from the modern utilitarian conception. For specific sources, see James Warren, *Facing Death: Epicurus and His Critics* (2004), which deals with the central argument in Epicureanism. In "The Moral Virtues and Instrumentalism in Epicurus" (2010), Kristian Urstad responds to the argument that the Epicureans saw virtue as a part of happiness. And for a comparative analysis, see Adam Barkman, "Was Epicurus a Buddhist?" (2008).

Chapter 16

Stoicism

As already noted, the philosophical schools that arose during the Hellenistic period tended to have at least two sides to their philosophy. The first was concerned with the personal, emotional, and psychological dimension of human experience, and the second dealt with the practical question of how we ought to conduct ourselves inside and outside civil society. The school that was most successful at addressing both sides of the moral inquiry is, arguably, Stoicism, which held sway for about five hundred years until it was finally supplanted by Christianity.

The origins of Stoicism can be traced to the third century BCE, when the followers of Zeno of Citium (c. 334–262 BCE) congregated at the "*Stoa Poikilē*" (or "Painted Porch") in the Athenian marketplace. They were therefore called "Stoics." Zeno taught that virtue consists of living in accordance with nature. We should accordingly resign ourselves to the ways of providence. At Zeno's death, his student Cleanthes, a boxer turned philosopher, took charge of the school, later passing the leadership to Chrysippus of Soli (c. 279–c. 206 BCE). Chrysippus was a prolific writer in logic, epistemology, ethics, and physics, and was sometimes called the second founder of Stoicism.

Scholars divide the history of Stoicism into three phases: the early Stoa, which saw the establishment of the school in Athens; the middle Stoa, which saw the export of Stoic doctrines to Rome under the influence of thinkers such as Diogenes of Babylon and Panaetius of Rhodes; and the late Stoa, after the school had become popular among the Roman elites and found expression in the political and ethical writings of Cicero, and even in Virgil's long poem *Aeneid*.

One of the most celebrated Stoics in Rome was Lucius Annaeus Seneca (4 BCE–65 CE), known as Seneca the Younger, who was an advisor of the Emperor Nero. Although Seneca was an influential man of letters, who wrote a wide variety of Stoic works, he has been traditionally criticized on the grounds that he did not live up to his ideals. This is a devastating criticism for a Stoic, since Stoicism rests on the strength of our commitment to our ethical beliefs. At the end of his life, Seneca was allowed to commit suicide as a punishment for his alleged part in an assassination attempt against Nero. The evidence suggests that he was innocent.

The most eminent Stoic philosopher was probably Epictetus (55–135 CE), a freed slave, who was known for his simple, rugged way of life. Epictetus was banished from Rome, along with other philosophers, by the Emperor Domitian around 90 CE. He then started a famous school in Nicopolis, Greece, which was apparently visited by Hadrian, a later emperor. The most well-known Stoic, however, was undoubtedly the Emperor Marcus Aurelius (121–180 CE), who kept a famous philosophical diary, familiarly known as the *Meditations.* Aurelius's ethical outlook is characterized by humility, self-mastery, and a Spartan sense of duty.

We know the central features of academic Stoicism in spite of the deficiency of written texts. The Stoics divided philosophy into three subject-areas: logic, physics, and ethics. The study of logic and physics was considered preparatory. Once we master logic, we can obtain reliable knowledge about the nature of the cosmos, and once we obtain reliable knowledge about the nature of the cosmos, we can determine how we should behave.

The Stoics were materialists but also pantheists, and thought of Zeus as a primordial fire that regulates and organizes the cosmos on a rational basis. Wise individuals respectfully submit to his divine providence. The most engaging feature of Stoic ethics, however, in contemporary terms, was the cosmopolitanism of its ethics, which saw all human beings as children of Zeus and citizens of the world, regardless of their ethnic background or social position. Virtue is essentially the same for everyone, everywhere.

The mechanics of this cosmopolitanism is significant. Although individual human beings are perishable, there is a divine spark, a rational seed (*logos spermatikos*) inside each human mind. This develops, as we mature, and gives us a feeling that we are one with the sense of orderly purpose that fills the universe. Through our experience of this "cosmic belonging" (*oikeiōsis*) and the rational process, we move beyond our childhood attachments to family members and see all other human beings as equals. There is a strong element of the natural law behind this. Acting ethically is a matter of acting rationally, in accordance with human nature and the will of the cosmos.

On the personal side, the Stoics make a distinction between what is in our power and what is beyond our power. Basically what is in our power is inside the mind, which we can control: our beliefs, attitudes, choices, and emotions. What is beyond our power is outside the mind. We cannot control external realities such as fame, fortune, political power, popularity, health, and death. The secret to happiness—and virtue—is to properly manage what is in our control and resign ourselves to whatever is beyond our control.

The management of our desires nevertheless requires training. The Stoics taught their followers to steel themselves in a military fashion against the inevitable disappointments of life through the practice of asceticism (*askēsis*). We should habitually relinquish comforts and enjoyments, and harden ourselves to physical and mental discomfort. The Stoics also recommended spiritual exercises, which included edifying dialogue, reminders of death, regular examination of conscience, and a meditative focus on the present moment. We should cultivate a "stoic apathy" (*apatheia*, ἀπάθεια), "without passion"), an objective state of mind, unclouded by emotion, that is able to judge rightly in accordance with the will of the universe.

The Stoics contend that virtue is good and vice bad; everything else is "indifferent." They nevertheless distinguished three types of 'indifferents': the preferred, the dis-preferreds, and the absolute indifferents. Preferred indifferents include matters such as wealth, health, life, technical expertise, and good reputation. Dis-preferred indifferents include poverty, illness, death, and so on. Absolute indifferents include trivial matters which are of no moral consequence. We may prefer the preferred indifferents, as long as we do not let our preference interfere with the practice of virtue.

The virtuous person possesses the four cardinal virtues: wisdom, justice, courage, and temperance. Moral individuals aim at "appropriate acts" and fulfill the responsibilities that come with their station in life. Like Socrates, the Stoics maintained that immorality results from human ignorance. They also held that we should avoid anger or even jealousy when confronting evil-doers; rather, we should pity them for their plight.

The first reading contains an excerpt from Diogenes Laertius's account of the life of Zeno of Citium (c. 334–c. 262 BCE), the Hellenistic philosopher who provided a model of behavior for those who followed him. The second reading is from Epictetus, whose lectures and remarks were collated by his student Arrian in the *Discourses* and the *Enchiridion*, or handbook. The *Enchiridion* provides a manual, as it were, for those who aspire to be Stoics. The third reading is from the diary of Marcus Aurelius, which gives us insight into the internal life of a distinguished Stoic.

READING 16A

"Zeno of Citium" from Diogenes Laertius, *Lives of Eminent Philosophers*[1]

(c. 334–c. 262 BCE)

Zeno, the son of Mnaseas (or Demeas), was a native of Citium in Cyprus, a Greek city which had received Phoenician settlers.... Apollonius of Tyre says he was lean, fairly tall, and swarthy—hence someone called him an Egyptian vine-branch...They say he was fond of eating green figs and of basking in the sun....

He was a pupil of Crates...[and] attended the lectures of Stilpo and Xenocrates for ten years...

[When] at last he left Crates,...

[H]e used to discourse, pacing up and down in the painted colonnade...of Pisianax [in the Stoa]...[Hence people came to the Stoa] to hear Zeno, and this is why they were known as men of the Stoa, or Stoics; and the same name was given to his followers, who had formerly been known as Zenonians....

Zeno himself was sour and of a frowning countenance. He was very cheap too, clinging to a miserliness unworthy of a Greek, on the plea of economy.

---

1   "Zeno of Citium," Book VII, chapter 1 of Diogenes Laertius, *Lives of Eminent Philosophers*, trans. by Robert Drew Hicks, Loeb Classical Library No. 184 (Cambridge: Harvard University Press; 1925, 1972). Available at www.perseus.tufts.edu/hopper/text?doc= Perseus:text:1999.01.0258 88 and en.wikisource.org/wiki/Lives_of_the_Eminent_Philosophers.

If he pitched into anyone[1] he would do it concisely, and not effusively, keeping him rather at arm's length.... When his pupil Ariston argued with him in...a headstrong and over-confident way. "Your father," said Zeno, "must have been drunk when he begat you."...

There was [also a glutton] so greedy that he left nothing for his table companions. A large fish having been served, Zeno took it up as if he were about to eat the whole. When the other looked at him, [Zeno said,] "What do you suppose,...those who live with you feel every day, if you cannot put up with my gluttony in this single instance?"...

He said that when conversing we ought to be earnest and, like actors, we should have a loud voice and great strength; but we ought not to open the mouth too wide, which is what your senseless chatterbox does.... [T]he hearer should be so absorbed in the discourse itself as to have no leisure even to take notes....

Nothing, he declared, was more unbecoming than arrogance, especially in the young. He used also to say that it was not the words and expressions that we ought to remember, but we should exercise our mind in [using] what we hear, instead of, as it were, tasting a well-cooked dish or well-dressed meal....

Again he would say that if we want to master the sciences there is nothing so fatal as conceit, and again there is nothing we stand so much in need of as time.... When Dionysius the Renegade asked, "Why am I the only pupil you do not correct?" the reply was, "Because I mistrust you."...

A dialectician once showed him seven logical forms concerned with the sophism known as "The Reaper,"

and Zeno asked him how much he wanted for them. Being told a hundred drachmas, he promptly paid two hundred...They say too that he first introduced the word 'duty' and wrote a treatise on the subject. It is said, moreover, that he corrected Hesiod's[2] lines, thus:

He is best of all men who follows good advice: good too is he who finds out all things for himself....

When he was asked why he, though so austere, relaxed at a drinking-party, he said, "Lupins[3] too are bitter, but when they are soaked become sweet."...

He showed the utmost endurance, and the greatest frugality; the food he used required no fire to dress,[4] and the cloak he wore was thin....

And in very truth in this species of virtue and in dignity he surpassed all mankind,...and in happiness; for he was ninety-eight when he died and had enjoyed good health without an ailment to the last.... The manner of his death was as follows. As he was leaving the school he tripped and fell, breaking a toe. Striking the ground with his fist, he quoted the line from the Niobe:[5]

I come, I come, why do you call for me?

and died on the spot through holding his breath.[6]

Philosophic doctrine, say the Stoics, falls into three parts: one physical, another ethical, and the third logical....

Philosophy, they say, is like an animal: Logic corresponding to the bones and sinews, Ethics to the fleshy parts, Physics[7] to the soul. Another simile

---

1 I.e., criticized or vigorously dealt with someone.
2 Hesiod was a Greek poet who was active at around the same time as Homer.
3 Lupins are a kind of bean.
4 I.e., the food required no cooking.
5 The Niobe could be a reference to a play by Sophocles or by Aeschylus. The story of Niobe, who had many children and boasted about that fact, is a stock type for mourning. In fact, since she boasted about her many children compared to Leto, a goddess with only two children, Leto became indignant at Niobe's show of hubris and had all of her children killed.
6 Diogenes then discusses the views of the Stoics.
7 I.e., science.

they use is that of an egg: the shell is Logic, next comes the white, Ethics, and the yolk in the center is Physics. Or, again, they liken Philosophy to a fertile field: Logic being the encircling fence, Ethics the crop, Physics the soil or the trees. Or, again, to a city strongly walled and governed by reason.

No single part, some Stoics declare, is independent of any other part, but all blend together....

The ethical branch of philosophy they divide as follows: (1) the topic of impulse; (2) the topic of things good and evil; (3) that of the passions; (4) that of virtue; (5) that of the end; (6) that of primary value and of actions; (7) that of duties or the befitting; and (8) of inducements to act or refrain from acting....

As for the assertion made by some people that pleasure is the object to which the first impulse of animals [such as man] is directed, it is shown by the Stoics to be false. For pleasure,...they declare to be a by-product, which never comes until nature by itself has sought and found the means suitable to the animal's existence or constitution...

This is why Zeno was the first...to designate as the end [or the goal of life, to be] "life in agreement with nature" (or living agreeably to nature), which is the same as a virtuous life, virtue being the goal towards which nature guides us....

Amongst the virtues some are primary, some are subordinate to these. The following are the primary: wisdom, courage, justice, temperance.... And wisdom they define as the knowledge of things good and evil and of what is neither good nor evil...

Further, they hold that the vices are forms of ignorance of those things of [which] the corresponding virtues are the knowledge....

Good in general is that from which some advantage comes, and more particularly what is either identical with or not distinct from benefit....

Another particular definition of good which they give is "the natural perfection of a rational being *qua*[1] rational."...

[T]hey [also] characterize the perfect good as beautiful [since] it has...perfect proportion....

And they say that only the morally beautiful is good....

Befitting acts are all those which reason prevails with us to do...Unbefitting, or contrary to duty, are all acts that reason deprecates, e.g., to neglect one's parents, to be indifferent to one's brothers, not to agree with friends, to disregard the interests of one's country, and so forth....

Nor indeed will the wise man ever feel grief; seeing that grief is [an] irrational contraction of the soul...

They are also, it is declared, godlike; for they have something divine within them; whereas the bad man is godless....

It is one of their tenets that sins are all equal... For he who is a hundred furlongs from Canopus[2] and he who is only one furlong away are equally not in Canopus, and so too he who commits the greater sin and he who commits the less are equally not in the path of right conduct....

Again, the Stoics say that the wise man will take part in politics, if nothing hinders him...since thus he will restrain vice and promote virtue...At the same time [the wise] are not pitiful and make no allowance for anyone; they never relax the penalties fixed by the laws, since indulgence and pity and even equitable consideration are marks of a weak mind...

Friendship, they declare, exists only between the wise and good, by reason of their likeness to one another.... They argue that a friend is worth having for his own sake...But among the bad there is, they hold, no such thing as friendship, and thus no bad man has a friend....

The world, in their view, is ordered by reason and providence...Thus, then, the whole world is a living

---

1 *Qua*: insofar as it is considered as...
2 An ancient Egyptian city.

being, endowed with soul and reason, and having aether[1] for its ruling principle…

The deity, say they, is a living being, immortal, rational, perfect or intelligent in happiness…taking providential care of the world and all that therein is…

Also they hold that there are [spirits[2]] who are in sympathy with mankind and watch over human affairs. They believe too in heroes, that is, the souls of the righteous that have survived their bodies….

READING 16B

Epictetus, *Enchiridion*[3]

(135 CE)

1. Some things are in our control and others not. Things in our control are opinion, pursuit, desire, aversion, and, in a word, whatever are our own actions. Things not in our control are body, property, reputation, command, and, in one word, whatever are not our own actions….

The things in our control are by nature free, unrestrained, unhindered; but those not in our control are weak, slavish, restrained, belonging to others. Remember, then, that if you suppose that what belongs to others is your own, then you will be hindered. But if you suppose that only to be your own which is your own, then no one will ever compel you or restrain you. Further, you will find fault with no one or accuse no one. You will do nothing against your will….

Work, therefore to be able to say to every harsh appearance, or circumstance, "You are merely an appearance." And then examine it by those rules which you have, and first, and chiefly, by this:

whether it concerns the things which are in our own control, or those which are not; and, if it concerns anything not in our control, be prepared to say that it is nothing to you.

5. Men are disturbed, not by things, but by the principles and notions which they form concerning things. Death, for instance, is not terrible, else it would have appeared so to Socrates. But the terror consists in our notion of death that it is terrible. When therefore we are hindered, or disturbed, or grieved, let us never attribute it to others, but to ourselves.

7. Consider when, on a voyage, your ship is anchored. If you go on shore to get water you may along the way amuse yourself with picking up a shellfish, or an onion. However, your thoughts and continual attention ought to be bent towards the ship, waiting for the captain to call on board. You must then immediately leave all these things, otherwise you

---

1 I.e., the incorruptible material, the substance constituting the stars and planets.

2 The Greek word is *daimōn*, meaning something like guardian angel.

3 Epictetus, *The Enchiridion* (135 CE) from Elizabeth Carter, trans., *The Moral Discourses of Epictetus* (London and New York: J.M. Dent, E.P. Dutton [1910]). Available at http://classics.mit.edu/Epictetus/epicench.html. *Enchiridion* means handbook or manual.

will be thrown into the ship, bound neck and feet like a sheep. So it is with life. If, instead of an onion or a shellfish, you are given a wife or child, that is fine. But if the captain calls, you must run to the ship, leaving them, and regarding none of them. But if you are old, never go far from the ship: lest, when you are called, you should be unable to come in time.

8. Don't demand that things happen as you wish, but wish that they happen as they do happen, and you will go on well.

9. Sickness is a hindrance to the body, but not to your ability to choose, unless that is your choice. Lameness is a hindrance to the leg, but not to your ability to choose....

10. With every accident, ask yourself what abilities you have for making a proper use of it. If you are attracted to a person, you will find that self-restraint is the ability you have against your desire. If you are in pain, you will find fortitude. If you hear unpleasant language, you will find patience....

14. If you wish your children, and your wife, and your friends to live forever, you are stupid; for you wish to be in control of things which you cannot, you wish for things that belong to others to be your own. So likewise, if you wish your servant to be without fault, you are a fool; for you wish vice not to be vice, but something else.... Exercise, therefore, what is in your control. He is the master of another person who is able to confer or remove whatever that person wishes either to have or to avoid. Whoever, then, would be free, let him wish nothing, let him decline nothing, which depends on others, or else he must necessarily be a slave.

15. Remember that you must behave in life as at a dinner party. Is anything brought around to you? Put out your hand and take your share with moderation. Does it pass by you? Don't stop it. Is it not yet come? Don't stretch your desire towards it, but wait till it reaches you. Do this with regard to children, to a wife, to public posts, to riches, and you will eventually be a worthy partner of the feasts of the gods. And if you don't even take the things which are set before you, but are able even to reject them, then you will not only be a partner at the feasts of the gods, but also of their empire.

17. Remember that you are an actor in a drama, of such a kind as the author pleases to make it. If short, of a short one; if long, of a long one. If it is his pleasure you should act a poor man, a cripple, a governor, or a private person, see that you act it naturally. For this is your business, to act well the character assigned you; to choose it is another's....

22. If you have an earnest desire of attaining to philosophy, prepare yourself from the very first to be laughed at, to be sneered by the multitude, to hear them say, "He is returned to us a philosopher all at once."

33. Don't allow your laughter to be much, nor on many occasions, nor profuse. Avoid swearing, if possible...In parties of conversation, avoid a frequent and excessive mention of your own actions and dangers. For, however agreeable it may be to yourself to mention the risks you have run, it is not equally agreeable to others to hear your adventures. Avoid, likewise, an endeavor to excite laughter. For this is a slippery point, which may throw you into vulgar manners.

50. Whatever moral rules you have deliberately proposed to yourself, abide by them as they were laws, and as if you would be guilty of impiety by violating any of them. Don't regard what anyone says of you, for this, after all, is no concern of yours.

51. The first and most necessary topic in philosophy is that of the use of moral theorems, such as, "We ought not to lie"; the second is that of demonstrations, such

as, "What is the origin of our obligation not to lie"; the third gives strength and articulation to the other two, such as when we ask, "What is a valid demonstration?" "What is logical consequence?" "What contradiction?" "What truth?" "What falsehood?" The third topic, then, is necessary on the account of the second, and the second on the account of the first. But the most necessary, and that whereon we ought to rest, is the first.

And yet we act just on the contrary. For we spend all our time on the third topic, and employ all our diligence about that, and entirely neglect the first. Therefore, at the same time that we lie, we are immediately prepared to show how it is demonstrated that lying is not right.

READING 16C

Marcus Aurelius, *Meditations*[1]

(167 CE)

Book Four

Men seek retreats for themselves, houses in the country, seashores, and mountains; and you too are wont to desire such things very much. But this is altogether a mark of the most common sort of men, for it is in your power whenever you shall choose to retire into yourself.

For nowhere either with more quiet or more freedom from trouble does a man retire than into his own soul, particularly when he has within him such thoughts that by looking into them he is immediately in perfect tranquility; and I affirm that tranquility is nothing else than the good ordering of the mind. Constantly then give to yourself this retreat, and renew yourself; and let your principles be brief and fundamental, which, as soon as you shalt recur to them, will be sufficient to cleanse the soul completely, and to send you back free from all discontent with the things to which you return....

Book Five

That which does no harm to the state, does no harm to the citizen. In the case of every appearance of harm apply this rule: if the state is not harmed by this, neither am I harmed. But if the state is harmed, you must not be angry with him who does harm to the state. Show him where his error is.

Let the part of your soul which leads and governs be undisturbed by the movements in the flesh, whether of pleasure or of pain; and let it not unite with them, but let it circumscribe itself and limit those affects to their parts.

Live with the gods. And he does live with the gods who constantly shows to them, his own soul is satisfied with that which is assigned to him, and that it does all that the spirit wishes, that spirit which Zeus has given to every man for his guardian and guide, a portion of himself. And this spirit is every man's understanding and reason....

---

1   Marcus Aurelius, *Meditations* (167 CE), originally from George Long, trans., *The Thoughts of the Emperor Marcus Aurelius Antoninus* (London: Bell & Daldy, 1862) and re-published in many editions. Available at http://classics.mit.edu/Antoninus/meditations.html.

Book Six

Let it make no difference to you whether you are cold or warm, if you are doing your duty; and whether you are drowsy or satisfied with sleep; and whether ill-spoken of or praised; and whether dying or doing something else....

If you had a step-mother and a mother at the same time, you would be dutiful to your step-mother, but still you would constantly return to your mother. Let the court[1] and philosophy now be to you step-mother and mother. Return to philosophy frequently and repose in her, through whom what you meet with in the court will be tolerable to you.

Strive to continue to be such as philosophy wished to make you. Reverence the gods, and help men. Short is life. There is only one fruit of this earthly life, a pious disposition and social acts.

Adapt yourself to the things with which your lot has been cast: and the men among whom you have received your portion, love them, but do it truly, sincerely....

Book Seven

Let the body itself take care, if it can, that it suffer nothing, and let it speak, if it suffers. But the soul itself, that which is subject to fear, to pain, which has completely the power of forming an opinion about these things, will suffer nothing, for it will never deviate into such a judgement....

The universal nature out of the universal substance, as if it were wax, now molds a horse, and when it has broken this up, it uses the material for a tree, then for a man, then for something else; and each of these things subsists for a very short time. But it is no hardship for the vessel to be broken up, just

as there was none in its being fastened together....

Retire into yourself. The rational principle which rules has this nature, that it is content with itself when it does what is just, and so secures tranquility.

Wipe out the imagination. Stop the pulling of the strings. Confine yourself to the present. But remember your last hour. Let the wrong which is done by a man stay there where the wrong was done....

Adorn yourself with simplicity and modesty...

Love mankind. Follow God. The poet says that Law rules all. And it is enough to remember that Law rules all....

Look round at the courses of the stars, as if you were going along with them; and constantly consider the changes of the elements into one another; for such thoughts purge away the filth of the earthly life.

Look within. Within is the fountain of good, and it will ever bubble up, if you will ever dig.

Book Eight

It is satisfaction to a man to do the proper works of a man. Now it is a proper work of a man to be benevolent to his own kind...

Speak both in the senate[2] and to every man, whoever he may be, appropriately, not with any affectation: use plain discourse....

Receive wealth or prosperity without arrogance; and be ready to let it go....

Neither in your actions be sluggish nor in your conversation without method, nor wandering in your thoughts, nor let there be in your soul inward contention nor external effusion, nor in life be so busy as to have no leisure.

---

1 I.e., public life.
2 A political institution in ancient Rome.

Book Nine

He who acts unjustly acts impiously. For since the universal nature has made rational animals for the sake of one another to help one another according to their deserts, but in no way to injure one another, he who transgresses her will, is clearly guilty of impiety towards the highest divinity.

And he too who lies is guilty of impiety to the same divinity; for the universal nature is the nature of things that are... And this universal nature is named truth, and is the prime cause of all things that are true. He then who lies intentionally is guilty of impiety inasmuch as he acts unjustly by deceiving; and he also who lies unintentionally, inasmuch as he is at variance with the universal nature....

He who does wrong does wrong against himself. He who acts unjustly acts unjustly to himself, because he makes himself bad.

He often acts unjustly who does not do a certain thing; not only he who does a certain thing....

Your present opinion founded on understanding, and your present conduct directed to social good, and your present disposition of contentment with everything which happens—that is enough.

Wipe out imagination: check desire: extinguish appetite: keep the ruling faculty[1] in its own power....

It is your duty to leave another man's wrongful act there where it is.

Book Ten

When you have assumed these names, good, modest, true, rational, a man of equanimity, and magnanimous, take care that you do not change these names; and if you should lose them, quickly return to them. For to continue to be such as you have been thus far, is the character of a very stupid man and one overly fond of his life, and like those half-devoured fighters with wild beasts, who though covered with wounds and gore, still entreat to be kept to the following day, though they will be exposed in the same state to the same claws and bites....

Book Eleven

The man who is honest and good ought to be exactly like a man who smells strong, so that the bystander as soon as he comes near him must smell whether he choose or not. But the affectation of simplicity is like a crooked stick. Nothing is more disgraceful than a wolfish friendship.[2] Avoid this most of all. The good and simple and benevolent show all these things in the eyes, and there is no mistaking....

Questions

1. What kind of person was Zeno of Citium? Do not hesitate to be critical.
2. The Stoics compared philosophy to an egg. The shell is Logic; the white is Ethics; and the yolk Physics, or science. What does this say about these disciplines? Can you think of another metaphor that captures the role of morality in philosophy?
3. Epictetus begins his *Enchiridion* with the fundamental principle "Some things are in our control and others not." What follows from this principle, morally? How does it affect his view of death?

---

1 I.e., reason.
2 I.e., a false friendship.

4. What is the goal of philosophy for the Stoics? Why does Epictetus say that philosophers usually go wrong in discussing lies? How does this compare with the view of Confucius?

5. Marcus Aurelius was known for his remarkable sense of duty. But there is also a strong sense of honor in his work. Discuss how this fits into his philosophy and the relationship between honor and duty.

6. Many readers find the Stoics rather cold emotionally. In spite of this, they were famous for their idea of friendship. What would you expect of a Stoic friend?

7. Do you think the Stoics were happy? Why or why not? Do you think that you could live a Stoic life? Why, why not?

8. The opponents of Stoicism criticized their fatalism, on the basis that it left them disinclined to change anything for the better. What do you think?

Suggested Readings

The standard primary source of Stoic writings is A.A. Long and D.N. Sedley, *The Hellenistic Philosophers*, Volume 1 (1987), which contains readings with commentaries on Epicureanism, Stoicism, Pyrrhonian Skepticism, and the Academics (the successors of Plato's Academy). The Loeb Classical Library includes two volumes on Epictetus, *Discourses, Manual and Fragments* (translated by W.A. Oldfather, 1925) and a single volume on *Marcus Aurelius* (translated by C.R. Haines, 1930).

Material on several Stoic philosophers, including Zeno, Cleanthes, and Chrysippus, can be found in Book VII of Diogenes Laertius's *Lives of Eminent Philosophers*. Other works of note include Cicero's *On Duties* (*De Officiis*) and *On Ends* (*De finibus bonorum et malorum*, "Of the best goods and worst evils"). The University of Chicago Press has recently begun publishing a series entitled *The Complete Works of Lucius Annaeus Seneca*.

Long has given us a readable introduction to the three Hellenistic schools in *Hellenistic Philosophy: Stoics, Epicureans, Sceptics* (1986). In *The Stoic Life: Emotions, Duties, and Fate* (2005), Tad Brennan "explains how to live the Stoic life." The *Cambridge Companion to the Stoics* (2003) devotes two chapters to ethics, "the heart and soul of the Stoics' system." Students may want to look for sources on the grounding of the Stoics' ethical views in the natural order and, therefore, the study of physics. There are also sources on the stoic conception of freedom.

Chapter 17

Jesus of Nazareth

Jesus of Nazareth (7/2 BCE–30/36 CE) is more familiar in the Christian tradition as Jesus Christ and, simply, "Jesus." In the Jewish and Islamic traditions, he is seen as a Jewish prophet and healer. In the Christian tradition, he is considered as the Messiah and Savior, whose death has redeemed us.

The artificial separation between the religious and moral traditions has obscured the importance of religious figures in moral philosophy. Like the Buddha or Muhammad, Jesus is an esteemed moral teacher, who tells us how we should live our lives. The importance of his teaching also derives, however, from its influence on the Western tradition. It is probably impossible to disentangle the Christian elements from many of the ethical theories presented in the rest of this book.

The historical Jesus was an itinerant teacher, prophet, and healer from Galilee, who lived in the late Roman Empire. He was reportedly baptized by John the Baptist, had a "ministry" that spanned ancient Israel, and was crucified in Jerusalem under Pontius Pilate, the Roman governor of Judaea. The events of his life are recorded in the four gospels, by Matthew, Mark, Luke, and John, which provide the seminal sources of the Christian tradition.

There are many cosmological remnants in the gospel narrative. There were portents of Jesus's birth, an ancient sign of divinity, and he was the son of God, conceived by a Virgin herself conceived immaculately.[1] These kinds of motifs have historical antecedents. At the age of 30, perhaps, he began to preach and perform miracles, gathering disciples around him. After his death on the cross, he is said to have risen from the dead and ascended into heaven, leaving his disciples to deliver his message to the world.

Biblical scholars have argued that the teachings of Christ are a fusion of the prophetic Jewish tradition and the philosophical tradition, particularly as it found expression in Cynicism. The religious elements are foremost in his teaching, and morality, which includes prayer, is only possible with divine aid. It is faith that heals the sick and saves the fallen. There is also an idea of atonement: Jesus is someone who provides expiation for the sins of others, by sacrificing himself, and repairs our relationship with God. This became the central motif in the Christian moral tradition.

---

1 I.e., without transmission of original sin.

The early origins of the Jewish ethical tradition are reflected in Jesus's use of the devices that we find in proverbs and fables, such as parallelism and paradox. He speaks in metaphors, parables, and even poetry, and constantly alludes to the Jewish wisdom tradition, rather than the logical arguments that we find in the rationalistic Greek tradition. His miracles have a cosmological character, which brings nature and the cosmos—now under the authority of God—into the moral exercise.

The philosophical side of such a fusion comes from the Greek and Roman philosophers called Cynics. These thinkers were notoriously called "dogs"—the word 'cynic' comes from *kynikos*, meaning 'dog-like.' This was a term of derision, which referred to the fact that they lived on the streets, flagrantly rejecting the manners of the time—satisfying their bodily functions and even gratifying themselves sexually, in public, like dogs. In spite of their indecency, however, the Cynics were moralists and ascetics, who believed that the path to virtue lay in returning to nature. They were rejecting the kind of artificial morality that makes us ashamed of natural acts, and yet permits dishonesty to flourish.

The Stoics recognized the value of the cynical teachings and saw Cynicism as a "shortcut" to virtue. The most famous Cynic is Diogenes of Sinope (c. 412–323 BCE), who spoke bluntly about the hypocrisies of the time. The Cynics were also evangelical, like Christ, and had occasionally been martyred for questioning the authority of those in power. They had the same concerns of conscience that Jesus seems to have had, and it has been argued that the Q document, a hypothetical collection of material that may have provided the source of the gospels, contains teachings from the Cynics.

There are, in addition, Aristotelian and Stoic elements in Jesus's philosophy, which find expression in a cosmopolitanism that focuses on our relations with other people. The central ethical rule is the so-called "Golden Rule." In the gospel of Matthew, Jesus declares: "So in everything, do to others what you would have them do to you, for this sums up the Law and the Prophets" (Matthew 7:12). This principle of reciprocity has many precedents, but the firmness and prominence of the obligation in Jesus's formulation is new. We must love even our enemies.

The general emphasis on personal experience is also Hellenistic. When Jesus is asked which commandment is the most important, he responds that the first commandment is to love God; the second commandment is to love one's neighbor as oneself (Mark 12:28–31). He accordingly shifts the focus of the ethical inquiry from the strict observance of a complex body of customary law to the subjective character of our will and actions. This kind of development has an Aristotelian facet and can be seen as a version of virtue ethics.

Although some of Jesus's statements seem to reject the customary law, these statements seem to be directed against the empty obedience to the form rather than the actual substance of the law. Jesus consistently emphasizes the spirit over the letter of the law, claiming that a tax collector's abject plea for mercy (because tax collectors were despised) is more worthwhile than the boastful prayer of a Pharisee, or that the good Samaritan (an outcast) is more worthy than a Levite.

Like the Cynics, Jesus embraces poverty and rejects the corrupting influence of power and wealth, standing outside society. Unlike the Cynics, however, he formulates ethics in terms of our relationship with God, and through God, with other people. The renunciation in his teaching is offset by a heroic altruism, which counsels us to love other people. The virtuous are rewarded in heaven. There is a last judgment and punishment in another life for those who act wickedly. It is better, Jesus says, to cut off a sinful hand, than to abandon ourselves to sin and eternal punishment.

The apocalyptic tone in Jesus's teaching is notable. He explicitly declares: "Do not suppose that I have come to bring peace to the earth. I did not come to bring peace, but a sword" (Matthew 10:34–36). Jesus makes a whip out of ropes and drives the money-changers and their livestock from the temple. Citing Isaiah, he says that he has come to proclaim liberty to captives and to set the oppressed free (Luke 4:18). Although such passages seem to foretell a moral rather than a civil revolution, they probably reflect a general resentment of the abuses that the public suffered under the power of those in positions of authority.

The first reading is from the gospel of Matthew and contains the Sermon on the Mount, in which Jesus identifies himself with those on the margins of society and emphasizes the virtues of charity, humility, and forgiveness. In spite of his apocalyptic statements and references to overthrowing the old order, the gospels tell us to refrain from violence and accept the authority of government. One question this raises is whether the concept of a just war is consistent with Christianity.

The second reading recounts the story of the widow's mite as found in Mark's gospel.

The final reading is from St. Paul's "First Letter to the Corinthians." St. Paul, a Roman convert to Christianity, influenced the development of Christianity. He wrote a series of letters in the middle of the first century CE, providing advice and religious counsel to Christian communities in the Middle East. Aside from institutional issues, these letters stress the importance of religious faith and Christian love, implicitly rejecting the approach in the philosophical tradition.

Jesus of Nazareth, "The Sermon on the Mount" and Other Excerpts from the Gospel of Matthew[1]

(first century)

Chapter 5

And having seen the multitudes, [Jesus] went up to the mount, and his disciples came to him. He, having sat down and having opened his mouth, was teaching them, saying:

Blessed[2] the poor in spirit—because theirs is the reign of the heavens.

Blessed the mourning—because they shall be comforted.

Blessed the meek—because they shall inherit the land.

Blessed those hungering and thirsting for righteousness—because they shall be filled.

Blessed the kind—because they shall find kindness.

Blessed the clean in heart—because they shall see God.

Blessed the peacemakers—because they shall be called Sons of God.

Blessed those persecuted for righteousness' sake—because theirs is the reign of the heavens.

Blessed are you whenever they may reproach you, and may persecute and may say any evil thing against you falsely for my sake—rejoice and be glad because your reward is great in the heavens, for thus did they persecute the prophets who were before you.

You are the salt of the land, but if the salt may lose savor, in what shall it be salted? For nothing is it good from then on, except to be cast out and to be trodden down by men.

You are the light of the world; a city set upon a mount is not able to be hidden. Nor do they light a lamp and put it under the basket, but on the lampstand; and it shines to all those in the house. So let your light shine before men, that they may see your good works, and may glorify your Father who is in the heavens.

Do not suppose that I came to throw out[3] the law or the prophets—I did not come to take apart, but to fulfill.[4] For, verily I say to you, till that the heaven and the earth may pass away, one iota[5] or one tittle may not pass away from the law, till all may come to pass.... For I say to you, that if your righteousness may not abound above that of the scribes and Pharisees, you may not enter to the reign of the heavens.

You heard that it was said to the ancients: You shall not kill, and whoever may kill shall be in danger

---

1 "The Sermon on the Mount" and other excerpts from the Gospel of Matthew in The New Testament (written in the first century, on the basis of accounts of the life of Jesus very early in that century). Matthew 5:1–18, 20–24, 27–29, 31–46, 48; 6:1–15, 19–34; 7: in toto; 13:18–32. The Bible text designated *Youngs-Literal-Translation* is from the 1898 *Young's Literal Translation* by Robert Young who also compiled *Young's Analytical Concordance to the Bible*. This is an extremely literal translation that attempts to preserve the tense and word usage as found in the original Greek and Hebrew writings. The text was scanned from a reprint of the 1898 edition as published by Baker Book House, Grand Rapids Michigan. The book is still in print and may be ordered from Baker Book House. Obvious errors in spelling or inconsistent spellings of the same word were corrected in the computer edition of the text. Found at https://www.biblegateway.com/versions/Youngs-Literal-Translation-YLT-Bible/.

2 I.e., happy.

3 "Throw out" could mean abolish, annul, demolish, destroy, disunite, put down, take apart, or weaken.

4 "Fulfill" could mean bring to fullness, complete, fill up, or make full.

5 Iota is the smallest Hebrew letter; a tittle is any small stroke or dot used in writing or printing. Nowadays 'jot,' equivalent to 'iota,' is in the phrase meaning the smallest possible amount.

of the judgment; but I—I say to you, that everyone who is angry at his brother without cause, shall be in danger of the judgment. And whoever may say to his brother, "Empty fellow!" shall be in danger of the sanhedrin,[1] and whoever may say, "Rebel!" shall be in danger of the gehenna of the fire.[2] If, therefore, you bring your gift to the altar, and there remember that your brother has anything against you, leave your gift before the altar, and go—first be reconciled to your brother, and then having come bring your gift....

You heard that it was said to the ancients: You shall not commit adultery; but I—I say to you, that everyone who is looking on a woman to desire her, did already commit adultery with her in his heart. But if your right eye does cause you to stumble, pluck it out and cast from you, for it is better that one of your members perish than your whole body be cast to gehenna. And, if your right hand causes you to (morally) stumble, cut it off, and cast from you, for it is better that one of your members perish than your whole body be cast to gehenna....

And it was said: That whoever may put away his wife, let him give to her a writing of divorce; but I—I say to you, that whoever may put away his wife, except for the matter of prostitution, does make her to commit adultery; and whoever may marry her who has been put away does commit adultery.

Again, you heard that it was said to the ancients: You shall not swear falsely, but you shall pay to the Lord your oaths; but I—I say to you, not to swear at all; neither by the heaven, because it is the throne of God, nor by the earth, because it is His footstool, nor by Jerusalem, because it is a city of a great king, nor by your head may you swear, because you are not able to make one hair white or black; but let your word be, Yes, Yes, No, No, and that which is more than these is of the evil.

You heard that it was said: Eye for eye, and tooth for eye; but I—I say to you, do not resist evil, but whoever shall slap you on your right cheek, turn to him also the other; and whoever is willing to take you to law, and take your coat—give him also the cloak. And whoever shall impress you one mile, go with him two, to him who asks of you, be giving, and him who is willing to borrow from you, you may not turn away.

You heard that it was said: You shall love your neighbor, and shall hate your enemy; but I—I say to you, love your enemies, bless those cursing you, do good to those hating you, and pray for those accusing you falsely and persecuting you; that you may be sons of your Father in the heavens, because the sun He does cause to rise on evil and good, and He does send rain on righteous and unrighteous. For, if you may love those loving you, what reward have you? Do not also the tax-gatherers do the same?...

And if you do this, you shall therefore be perfect, as your Father who is in the heavens is perfect.

Chapter 6

Take heed not to do your kindness before men to be seen by them [or] reward you have not from your Father who is in the heavens.

Whenever, therefore, you may do kindness, you may not sound a trumpet before you as the hypocrites do in the synagogues and in the streets, that they may have glory from men; verily I say to you—they have their reward! But you, doing kindness, let not your left hand know what your right hand does, that your kindness may be in secret, and your Father who is seeing in secret Himself shall reward you openly.

And when you may pray, you shall not be as the hypocrites, because they love in the synagogues and in the corners of the broad places—standing—to pray, that they may be seen of men; verily I say to you, that they have their reward. But you, when you may pray, go into your chamber, and having shut

---

1 I.e., the supreme council of the Jewish people. It functioned as a judicial body and administrative council.
2 I.e., hell.

your door, pray to your Father who is in secret, and your Father who is seeing in secret shall reward you openly.

And praying—you may not use vain repetitions like the nations, for they think that in their much speaking they shall be heard. Be you not therefore like them, for your Father does know those things that you have need of before your asking him. Thus therefore pray:

Our Father, who is in the heavens, hallowed be Your name!
Your reign come: Your will come to pass, as in heaven also on the earth.
Our appointed bread give us today.
And forgive us our debts, as also we forgive our debtors.
And may You not lead us to temptation, but deliver us from the evil, because Yours is the reign, and the power, and the glory—to the ages. Amen.
For, if you may forgive men their trespasses He also will forgive you—your Father who is in the heavens; but if you may not forgive men their trespasses, neither will your Father forgive your trespasses....

Treasure not up to yourselves treasures on the earth, where moth and rust disfigure, and where thieves break through and steal; but treasure up to yourselves treasures in heaven, where neither moth nor rust does disfigure, and where thieves do not break through nor steal, for where your treasure is, there will be also your heart.

The lamp of the body is the eye, if, therefore, your eye may be perfect, all your body shall be enlightened, but if your eye may be evil, all your body shall be dark. If, therefore, the light that is in you is darkness—the darkness, how great!

None is able to serve two lords, for either he will hate the one and love the other, or he will hold to the one, and despise the other. You are not able to serve God and Mammon.[1] Because of this I say to you, be not anxious for your life, what you may eat, and what you may drink, nor for your body, what you may put on....

Look to the birds of the sky, for they do not sow, nor reap, nor gather into storehouses, and your heavenly Father does nourish them; are not you much better than they? And who of you, being anxious, is able to add to his age one cubit?[2] And about clothing why are you anxious?

Consider well the lilies of the field; how do they grow? They do not labor, nor do they spin. And I say to you that not even Solomon in all his glory was arrayed as one of these. And if the herb of the field, that today is and tomorrow is cast to the furnace, does not God so clothe you much more, O you of little faith? Therefore, you may not be anxious, saying, What may we eat? Or, What may we drink? Or, What may we put round? For all these do the nations seek for. Your heavenly Father does know that you have need of all these; but seek you first the reign of God and His righteousness, and all these shall be added to you.

Be not therefore anxious for tomorrow, for tomorrow shall be anxious for its own things. Sufficient for the day is the evil of it.

Chapter 7

Judge not, that you may not be judged; for in what judgment you judge, you shall be judged, and in what measure you measure, it shall be measured to you. And why do you behold the mote[3] that is in your brother's eye, and the beam that is in your own eye do not consider? Or, how will you say to

---

1 Commonly, this means money, material wealth, or anything that promises wealth.
2 I.e., an ancient unit based on the length of the forearm.
3 I.e., splinter, speck. A beam is a large piece of finished wood, used here figuratively in contrast to 'mote.'

your brother: Permit me that I may cast out the mote from your eye, and lo, the beam is in your own eye? Hypocrite, first cast out the beam out of your own eye, and then you shall see clearly to cast out the mote out of your brother's eye.

You may not give that which is holy to the dogs, nor cast your pearls before the swine, that they may not trample them under their feet, and having turned—may rend you.

Ask, and it shall be given to you; seek, and you shall find; knock, and it shall be opened to you; for everyone who is asking does receive, and he who is seeking does find, and to him who is knocking it shall be opened. Or who among you, of whom, if his son may ask a loaf—a stone will he present to him? And if a fish he may ask—a serpent will he present to him? If, therefore, you being evil, have known good gifts to give to your children, how much more shall your Father who is in the heavens give good things to those asking him?

In all things, therefore, whatever you may will that men do to you, so also do to them, for this is the law and the prophets.

Go you in through the strait[1] gate, because wide is the gate and broad the way that is leading to destruction, and many are those going in through it. How strait is the gate, and compressed the way that is leading to life, and few are those finding it!

But, take heed of the false prophets, who come unto you in sheep's clothing, and inwardly are ravening wolves. From their fruits you shall know them. Do men gather grapes from thorns? Or from thistles figs? So every good tree does yield good fruits, but the bad tree does yield evil fruits. A good tree is not able to yield evil fruits, nor a bad tree to yield good fruits. Every tree not yielding good fruit is cut down and is cast to fire; therefore, from their fruits you shall know them.

Not everyone who is saying to me Lord, lord, shall come into the reign of the heavens; but he who is doing the will of my Father who is in the heavens. Many will say to me in that day, Lord, lord, have we not in your name prophesied? And in your name cast out demons? And in your name done many mighty things? And then I will acknowledge to them that I never knew you, depart from me you who are working lawlessness.

Therefore, everyone who does hear of me these words and does do them, I will liken him to a wise man who built his house upon the rock; and the rain did descend, and the streams came, and the winds blew, and they beat on that house, and it fell not, for it had been founded on the rock. And everyone who is hearing of me these words, and is not doing them, shall be likened to a foolish man who built his house upon the sand; and the rain did descend, and the streams came, and the winds blew, and they beat on that house, and it fell, and its fall was great.

And it came to pass, when Jesus ended these words, the multitudes were astonished at his teaching, for he was teaching them as having authority, and not as the scribes.

Chapter 13[2]

Verses 18–23:

Jesus spoke to his disciples, saying: You, therefore, hear the parable of the sower:

> Every one hearing the word of the reign of God, and not understanding…this is the seed that falls by the way.

And that sown on the rocky places, this is he who hears the word and immediately with joy receives it, and he has not root in himself, but is temporary, and persecution or tribulation having happened because

---

1 I.e., cramped, constricted, or narrow.

2 Here are three examples of parables, stories or sayings using familiar images as analogies for less familiar, hidden, or deeper meanings. In other words, they act as similes. The verses just below contain Jesus's explanation of the parables' meaning.

of the word, immediately he is stumbled.

And that sown toward the thorns, this is he who hears the word, but is overwhelmed by the anxiety of this age, and the deceitfulness of the riches, chokes upon the word, and it becomes unfruitful.

And that sown on the good ground: this is he who is hearing the word, and is understanding, who indeed does bear fruit, and does make some indeed a hundredfold, and some sixty, and some thirty.

Verses 24–30:

Another parable he set before them, saying: The reign of the heavens was likened to a man sowing good seed in his field, and, while men are sleeping, his enemy came and sowed darnel[1] in the midst of the wheat, and went away, and when the herb sprang up, and yielded fruit, then appeared also the darnel.

And the servants of the householder, having come near, said to him: Sir, good seed did you not sow in your field? Why then has it the darnel? And he said to them: A man, an enemy, did this. And the servants said to him: Will you then allow us to gather it up?

And he said: No, for fear that—gathering up the darnel—you root up with it the wheat.

And he said: I will permit both to grow together till the harvest, and in the time of the harvest I will say to the reapers: Gather up first the darnel, and bind it in bundles, to burn it, and the wheat gather up into my storehouse.

Verses 31–32:

Another parable he set before them, saying: The reign of the heavens is like a grain of mustard, which a man having taken, did sow in his field. Though it is less than all the seeds, when it may be grown, it is greatest of the herbs and becomes a tree, so that the birds of the heaven do come and rest in its branches.

Jesus of Nazareth, "The Widow's Mite" from the Gospel of Mark[2]

Chapter 12

And [Jesus] was saying to them in his teaching, "Beware of the scribes,[3] who will to walk in long robes, and love salutations in the market-places, and first seats in the synagogues, and first couches in suppers, who are devouring the widows' houses, and for a pretense are making long prayers; these shall receive more abundant judgment."

And Jesus having sat down across from the treasury, was beholding how the multitude did put brass coins into the treasury, and many rich were putting in much. Having come there, a poor widow did put in two mites.[4]

---

1 I.e., ryegrass, a weed.

2 Mark 12:38–44 (56 CE). *Youngs-Literal-Translation.*

3 I.e., teachers of the religious laws.

4 Two pennies. The mite was the smallest and least valuable coin in circulation in Judaea. The brass coins represent large sums of money.

And having called near his disciples, he said to them, "Verily I say to you, that this poor widow has put in more than all those putting into the treasury; for all those, put in out of their abundance, but she put in out of her want, all that she had—all her livelihood."

Paul, "First Letter to the Corinthians"[1]

(56 CE)

Chapter 1

Now Christ [sent me] ... to proclaim good news; but not in wisdom of discourse[2] ... for it has been written, "I will destroy the wisdom of the wise, and the intelligence of the intelligent I will bring to nothing" ...

So to those called by Christ—both Jews and Greeks—we teach the power of God, and the wisdom of God ...

And you are in Christ Jesus, who came to us from God as wisdom, righteousness also, and sanctification, and redemption ...

Chapter 2

And I, having come unto you, brethren, came—not in superiority of discourse or wisdom—declaring to you the testimony of God, for I decided not to know anything among you, except Jesus Christ, and him crucified; and I, in weakness, and in fear, and in much trembling, was with you. And my word and my preaching was not in persuasive words of human wisdom, but in demonstration of the Spirit and of power—that your faith may not be in the wisdom of men, but in the power of God.

And wisdom we speak among the perfect, and wisdom not of this age, nor of the rulers of this age—of those becoming useless, but we speak the hidden wisdom of God in a secret, that God foreordained before the ages to our glory, which no one of the rulers of this age did know, for if they had known, the Lord of the glory they would not have crucified him.

But, according as it has been written, "What eye did not see, and ear did not hear, and upon the heart of man not came up, what God did prepare for those loving Him." But to us did God reveal this wisdom through His Spirit, for the Spirit does search all things, even the depths of God; for who have known the things of the man, except the spirit of the man that is in him? So also the things of God no one has known, except the Spirit of God.

Chapter 12

And concerning the spiritual things, brothers, I do not wish you to be ignorant ..., for which reason I

---

1 St. Paul, "First Letter to the Corinthians" 1:17, 19, 24, 30; 2:1–11; 12:1, 3, 7–12, 14, 16–17, 20, 23–27; 13: in toto (56 CE). *Youngs-Literal-Translation.*

2 I.e., the wisdom as exemplified in the Greek philosophical tradition.

give you to understand that no one speaking in the Spirit of God says Jesus is anathema,[1] and no one is able to say Jesus is Lord, except in the Holy Spirit....

And to each has been given the manifestation of the Spirit for their benefit; for to one through the Spirit has been given a word of wisdom, and to another a word of knowledge, according to the same Spirit; and to another faith in the same Spirit, and to another gifts of healings in the same Spirit; and to another in-workings of mighty deeds; and to another prophecy; and to another discernings of spirits; and to another various kinds of tongues; and to another interpretation of tongues. And all these does work the one and the same Spirit, dividing to each severally as he intends.

For, even as the body is one, and has many members, and all the members of the one body, being many, are one body, so also is the Christ...for also the body is not one member, but many...and if the ear may say, "Because I am not an eye, I am not of the body"; it is not, because of this, not of the body. And if the whole body were an eye, where the hearing? If the whole hearing, where the smelling?...indeed, there are many members, and one body...

And those members of the body that we think to be less honorable, around these we put more abundant honor, and our unseemly things have seemliness more abundant...and our seemly things have no need. But God did temper the body together, to the lacking part having given more abundant honor, that there may be no division in the body, but that the members may have the same anxiety for one another. And whether one member does suffer, suffer with it do all the members; or one member is glorified, rejoice with it do all the members; and

so, you are the body of Christ, and its members in particular....

Chapter 13

If with the tongues of men and of messengers I speak, and have not love, I have become brass sounding, or a cymbal tinkling. And if I have prophecy, and know all the secrets, and all the knowledge, and if I have all the faith, so as to remove mountains, and have not love, I am nothing. And if I give away to feed others all my goods, and if I give up my body that I may be burned, and have not love, I am profited nothing.

Love is long-suffering, it is kind, love does not envy, love does not vaunt itself, is not puffed up, does not act unseemly, does not seek its own things, is not provoked, does not impute evil, rejoices not over the unrighteousness, and rejoices with the truth.

All things it bears, all it believes, all it hopes, all it endures. Love does never fail; and whether there be prophecies, they shall become useless; whether tongues, they shall cease; whether knowledge, it shall become useless; for in part we know, and in part we prophecy; and when that which is perfect may come, then that which is in part shall become useless.

When I was a babe, as a babe I was speaking, as a babe I was thinking, as a babe I was reasoning; and when I have become a man, I have made useless the things of the babe.

For we see now through a mirror obscurely, and then face to face; now I know in part, and then I shall fully know, as also I was known; and now there does remain faith, hope, love—these three; and the greatest of these is love.

---

1   I.e., cursed, vehemently disliked, extremely incorrect.

Questions

1. Compare Jesus's parables with the stories and proverbs in the early tradition.
2. Compare the Christian concept of love with the Confucian concept of *ren*, which has been translated as "humaneness," "loving-kindness," or "benevolence."
3. Compare the general moral views of Jesus with a) the Buddha, b) Socrates, or c) Aristotle. Are there differences?
4. Like most Christian thinkers, St. Paul suggests that the principal moral virtue is love. This virtue seems to occupy the same place as justice in the Greek and Roman tradition. Discuss the differences.
5. What is the moral lesson behind the Beatitudes, which suggests that God blesses the poor and unfortunate? Is this a departure from earlier thinking?
6. What is the point about the story of the widow and the two mites? Explain in your own words. What are the repercussions for moral philosophy?
7. Jesus suggests that it is virtuous to keep our good actions to ourselves and the Father in heaven. Why? What would other philosophers say about this?
8. What kind of attitude does Christianity promote with regard to our worldly possessions? How can this attitude be reconciled with capitalism and post-industrial consumerism? Or can it?
9. What analogy does St. Paul use in his letter to the Corinthians to explain how Christians filled with the Holy Spirit should live? What does this analogy tell us about the life of the early Christians?

Suggested Readings

Like Socrates, Jesus wrote nothing; yet he inspired innumerable others, who wrote extensively about his life and thought. The unavoidable starting point in studying his ethical teaching is to read the *New Testament*, which was written in the decades following his death. The four gospels contain vivid accounts of his life; the *Acts of the Apostles* recount the rise of Christianity; the epistles written by St. Paul to the early Christian communities are letters of instruction, which provide advice and counsel. The role of faith in Christian ethics is important and the *Book of Revelation* was written to bolster the strength of believers suffering severe persecutions at the time.

Two free, excellent online sources for biblical scholarship are the biblegateway.com and the biblehub.com. Together they provide multilingual editions of Old and New Testaments, a keyword search, biblical dictionaries, a Greek lexicon, study tools, concordances, and scholarly and devotional commentary.

Most of the ethical discussion in the literature has a religious perspective and it is difficult to suggest further readings without entering into theological disputes. For historical sources, see George Wolfgang Forell, *History of Christian Ethics, Volume I: From the New Testament to Augustine* (1979), and J.W. van Henten and Jozef Verheyden, eds., *Early Christian Ethics* (2013).

Other sources include R. Newton Flew, *Jesus and His Way: A Study of the Ethics of the New Testament* (1963), and Wolfgang Schrage, *The Ethics of the New Testament* (1988). In *The Philosophy of Jesus* (2016), Peter Kreeft argues that Jesus should be seen as a philosopher. The literature on the *Sermon on the Mount* includes D. Clough, "On the Relevance of Jesus Christ for Christian Judgements about the Legitimacy of Violence" (2009).

Chapter 18

Desert Fathers and Mothers

After the death of Jesus, the Romans persecuted the Christians because they refused to profess allegiance to the state or take up their civic duties. As a result of these persecutions, Paulus of Thebes renounced his inheritance in the late third century CE and fled into the desert, where he became a hermit. He was followed by others.

There were pagan hermits and some kind of existing tradition. It was not until St. Anthony the Great (c. 251–356 CE) went into the Scetes desert of Egypt, however, that it attracted large numbers of Christian aspirants and gave rise to the monastic ideal that flowered in the middle ages. The migration continued after the Roman persecutions came to an end, with the conversion of the Emperor Constantine. There was a similar movement in Syria and elsewhere.

The moral idea was to withdraw into the "huge silence" of the desert, where they would be closer to God. The monks lived in cells, which were often dug into the desert, or crude stone huts, which were often built far enough apart that the inhabitant of the cell could not see or hear his neighbors. On Saturday and Sunday, they would meet in church and pray together. The place where the monasteries initially grew up was called Cellia, because there were many cells scattered about the desert.

The hermits wore rough sheepskin robes, lived on meager rations of dried beans, unleavened bread, and brackish water, and wove baskets to sell at distant markets. They slept on the bare ground and worked with their hands. They may have possessed a "codex" containing some Scripture but the emphasis was on prayer and fasting. Many of the hermits deliberately avoided discussing theological questions so as to eliminate disputes about the meaning of Scripture. They were not committed to a refined theology or philosophy, but to a certain way of life.

The larger tradition eventually separated into three narrower streams. The first was the anchoritic tradition. Although anchorites often lived in close proximity to each other, they refused to take up public duties, devoting themselves to solitary prayer and asceticism. (The term "anchorite" can be traced back through French and Latin to a Greek root, ἀναχωρητής [anachōrētēs], which means "hermit" or "recluse" and is derived from the Greek verb anachōreō, which means to "withdraw" or "retire.")

247

The second tradition was cenobitic—i.e., it emphasized community—and included monks who lived in groups with rules and established customs. The third way of life, begun by Saint Amun in Nitria and Scetis, was semi-hermetic. It consisted of groups of two to six monks and nuns, who lived together under a spiritual elder. These groups would meet together for weekend worship. It is the third form of life, which attracted more educated monks, such as Evagrius Ponticus (345–399), who left us a written record of their life in the desert.

The majority of the monks were Coptic (Christian Church of Egypt) and had little or no formal education. St. Anthony could not read or write. They were accordingly more familiar with the indigenous Egyptian tradition, which was an older, oral tradition, and like other early traditions, prized terse, aphoristic formulations of wisdom. It also had a strong cosmological component, which surfaces in many of the stories of the desert fathers. The holy man has powers over animals, and nature, and is naturally respected by those in the wider community.

Philosophically, there was a decisive turning away from the theoretical inquiries of the Greeks. The monks believed that, in matters of religion and morality, abstract reasoning and logical demonstrations are unnecessary, even dangerous. St. Anthony chides the Greek philosophers who visit him, and engage him in argument, for their reliance on syllogisms. What Christian believers possess "is not skill with words, but faith through love that works for Christ." The proof of Christ's teachings is found in faith rather than argument. This gives Anthony, like Jesus Christ, the power to heal.

The moral life of the desert fathers seems to represent a half-way point between older views and a modern view. Evil was an external force, which existed physically, in the form of the devil, who was locked in a struggle with God for the souls of humanity. He must nevertheless be resisted internally. The notion of original sin played a large part in this, and human nature was seen as fallen, and could only be redeemed with grace, through divine assistance.

There was therefore a major turning inward, which saw ethics primarily as a matter of overcoming our corrupted nature. The victory over sin was nevertheless personal and subjective. For the most part, the monks believed that the ultimate source of spiritual and moral wisdom can be found inside us. As scripture says, "The kingdom of God is within you" (Luke 17:20–21). There are many parallels, whether with the Indian and the Buddhist traditions, the stoic idea of the microcosm, or the Christian mystical tradition, which was prominent in medieval times.

There was a matching rejection of society. The monks were ascetics and followed the example of earlier moralists, like the Cynics, living in poverty and repudiating the ordinary comforts of life. They also believed in self-sacrifice, however, and saw their ascetic practices as a kind of discipline or "training." This reflects the original use of the term "ascetic" (askēsis), which was used by athletes to describe their physical exercises. The desert fathers literally thought of themselves as spiritual athletes and soldiers, who achieved heroic feats of fasting, silence, self-mortification, and sleeplessness.

The practical ethics that went along with this early monasticism were simple and altruistic. The monks placed a high value—as we might expect in the Christian tradition—on good works. Moral wisdom and virtue are found in humility, obedience, chastity, and charity (love). They also placed a high value on forgiveness and the refusal to judge. There was still a desire for a kind of *ataraxia*, a mind free from disturbance. One of the goals of this early monasticism, in spite of its vigorous self-denial, was the equanimity that holiness brings. Menial work, much like prayer, was seen as a virtuous means to quiet the restless mind.

Most of the literature associated with the desert tradition was written in response to the widespread interest in monasticism in the early middle ages. These literary efforts can be traced to Athanasius of Alexandria, who wrote a biography of St. Anthony the Great in Greek, which was translated into Latin as the *Vita Antonii* (*Life of St. Anthony*). The Latin version was popular and influential. The increasing interest in monastic life ultimately led to the compilation of the *Apophthegmata Patrum*, the *Sayings of the Desert Fathers*, which were first published in Greek and then made their way into Latin as the *Vitae Patrum* (*The Lives of the Fathers*).

The *Sayings of the Desert Fathers* contains a diversity of material, which includes memorable statements, exchanges, and anecdotes. The collection contains over a thousand sayings and anecdotes attributed to twenty-seven abbas and three ammas. These terms were supposedly established by Pachomius to refer to the abba (father) or amma (mother) in charge of the monks or nuns, and implied that those entering a monastery were joining a new family. They were also used by Pelagius and those who compiled the *Sayings* as terms of respect, however, for senior and more reverend individuals. Some of the notable figures in the sayings are Abba Arsenius, Abba Poemen, Abba Macarius, and Amma Syncletica.

The reading contains an excerpt from the *Life of St. Anthony* (spelled as "Antony" in this reading) and a sample collection of the sayings, arranged by topic. It will be evident that, in spite of differences, the overall tone of the sayings recalls earlier ethical work, such as the collections of proverbs in the Jewish tradition, the Greek collections of aphorisms, and the kind of compilations that we find in the *Lunyu* in the Chinese tradition. Just as for proverbs, the communal authorship of the sayings is seen in the fact that, in some cases, the same saying is sometimes attributed to different individuals, depending on the source consulted. In addition, despite the fact that the title of our source for the sayings refers to "Fathers" only, there are sayings by Mothers, too. In societies for which the community is primary, what is said is more important than who said it.

Athanasius, *Life of St. Anthony the Anchorite*[1]

(St. Anthony of the Desert and the "Father of all monks," c. 251–356 CE)

Antony you must know was by descent an Egyptian: his parents were of good family and possessed considerable wealth, and as they were Christians he also was reared in the same Faith....

After the death of his father and mother... [the blessed Antony] entered [a] church,... and he heard the Lord saying to the rich man... 'If you would be perfect, go and sell [all] that you have and give to the poor; and come follow Me and you shall have treasure in heaven.' Antony... went out immediately from the church, and... [gave his inheritance] to the poor, reserving a little however for his [only sister]....

[Then he] devoted himself... to discipline,... training himself with patience....

But the devil, who hates and envies what is good,... took upon him the shape of a woman [one night] and imitated all her acts simply to beguile Antony.... But [Antony]... turned his thoughts to the threatened fire and the gnawing worm, and... passed through the temptation unscathed....

... [Antony] kept vigil to such an extent that he often continued the whole night without sleep... He ate once a day, after sunset, sometimes once in two days... His food was bread and salt, his drink, water only.... [and] for the most part he lay upon the bare ground....

... [One night, when he was praying in the tombs,] the enemy... called together his hounds and burst forth... And the place was... filled with the forms of lions, bears, leopards, bulls, serpents, asps, scorpions, and wolves, and each of them was moving according to his nature. The lion was roaring, wishing to attack, the bull seeming to toss with its horns, the serpent writhing but unable to approach, and the wolf as it rushed on was restrained; altogether the noises of the apparitions, with their angry ragings, were dreadful....

[Antony lay in pain, but his soul unshaken, and suddenly he saw] a ray of light descending to him. The demons suddenly vanished... [a]nd a voice came to him, 'Antony, I was here, [watching, and] since you have endured,... I will ever be a succour to you, and will make your name known everywhere.'...

... [F]or nearly twenty years he continued training himself in solitude... [many learnt of his battles with the demons, and] were eager... to imitate his discipline... cells arose even in the mountains, and the desert was colonised by monks, who came forth... and enrolled themselves for the citizenship [of] the heavens....

[And Antony] spoke to [the monks] in the Egyptian tongue...:

'... That they may get knowledge, the Greeks live abroad and cross the sea, but we have no need to depart from home for the sake of the kingdom of heaven... For the Lord... has said, "The kingdom of heaven is within you..." For when the soul has its spiritual faculty in a natural state virtue is formed.... Thus the matter is not difficult....

'And let us strive that wrath rule us not nor lust overcome us... [and] let us keep guard carefully... For we have terrible and crafty foes—the evil spirits—and against them we wrestle, as the Apostle said, Not against flesh and blood, but against the

1 Athanasius, *Life of St. Anthony*, trans. by H. Ellershaw, in Philip Schaff and Henry Wace, eds., *From Nicene and Post-Nicene Fathers*, Second Series, Vol. 4. (Buffalo, NY: Christian Literature Publishing Co., 1892). Available at http://www.newadvent.org/fathers/2811. htm (revised and edited by Kevin Knight).

principalities and against the powers[1]...

'First, therefore, we must know this: that the demons have not been created [evil]... Having fallen, however, from the heavenly wisdom...they move all things in their desire to hinder us from entry into the heavens; in order that we should not ascend up there from [where] they fell....

'When, therefore, they come by night to you and wish to tell the future, or say, we are the angels,... have no dealings with them; but rather sign yourselves... [in] the Lord's Cross,... take courage, and pray, and you shall see them vanish.... Once they came threatening and surrounded me like soldiers in full armour....

'[And o]nce a demon exceeding high appeared with pomp, and dared to say, I am the power of God and I am Providence, what do you wish that I shall give you? But I then...breathed upon him, and spoke the name of Christ, and set about to smite him. And I seemed to have smitten him, and immediately he, big as he was, together with all his demons, disappeared at the name of Christ....'

[And the monks rejoiced to hear Antony's words, and the mountains were] filled with holy bands of men who sang psalms, loved reading, fasted, prayed, rejoiced in the hope of things to come, labored in almsgiving, and preserved love and harmony one with another....

But when Antony saw himself beset by [so] many, [he went into the inner desert, where he passed the rest of his life, wrestling with the demons]...

[And henceforth many sought him. There was a young man, for example,] possessed by a demon...so terrible that the man possessed did not know that he was coming to Antony. But he even ate the excreta from his body. And Antony...prayed...with him all the night [and at dawn, the demon departed].

And...the young man [became] whole, and [rejoiced]...and gave thanks to God....

[Greek philosophers came] to mock him because he had not learned letters. And Antony said to them, 'What do you say? Which is first, mind or letters? And which is the cause of which—mind of letters or letters of mind?' And when they answered that mind is first and is the inventor of letters, Antony said, 'Whoever, therefore, has a sound mind has not need of letters.' This answer amazed...the philosophers, and they departed marveling that they had seen so much understanding in an ignorant man....

[And other philosophers came, and Antony said: 'Since] you prefer to lean upon demonstrative arguments,...tell [me] first how things in general and specially the recognition of God are accurately known.... And which is better, faith which comes through the inworking (of God) or demonstration by arguments?' And when they answered that faith which comes through the inworking[2] was better and was accurate knowledge, Antony said, 'You have answered well, for faith arises from disposition of soul, but dialectic from the skill of its inventors.... So the inworking through faith is better and stronger than your professional arguments.'

...[And among the crowd, there were some of them] very disquieted by demons, and bringing them into the midst [Anthony] said—'Do you cleanse them either by arguments and by whatever art or magic you choose, calling upon your idols, or if you are unable, put away your strife with us and you shall see the power of the Cross of Christ.' And having said this he...signed the sufferers two or three times with the sign of the Cross. And immediately the men stood up whole, and in their right mind...

---

1 Principalities and Powers, in Christian lore, were particular classes of angels in the celestial hierarchy which also included Thrones, Dominions, Archangels, etc. Anthony here speaks of the fallen angels in the service of Satan.

2 Internal operations.

Apophthegmata[1] of the Desert Fathers and Mothers[2]

(fourth century)

Activities (spiritual)

A brother said to Abba Poemen, 'Give me a word,' and he said to him, 'As long as the pot is on the fire, no fly nor any other animal can get near it, but as soon as it is cold, these creatures get inside. So it is for the monk; as long as he lives in spiritual activities, the enemy cannot find a means of overthrowing him.'

Alms-giving

[Amma Sarah] said, 'It is good to give alms for [people's] sake. Even if it is only done to please [others], through it one can begin to seek to please God.'

Anger

A brother questioned Abba Poemen saying, 'What does it mean to be angry with your brother without a cause?' He said, '… If he plucks out your right eye and cuts off your right hand, and you get angry with him, you are angry without cause. But if he separates you from God, then be angry with him.'

Athletes (spiritual)

[Amma Syncletica] said, 'Those who are great athletes must contend against stronger enemies.'

Beasts

One day Abba Theodore went to draw water with a brother. The brother going ahead, saw a dragon in the lake. The old man said to him, 'Go, and walk on his head.' But he was afraid and did not go. So the old man went. The beast saw him and fled away into the desert, as if it was ashamed.

[Abba Xanthias] said, 'A dog is better than I am, for he has love and he does not judge.'

Beginning

[Abba Isaiah] said, 'A beginner who goes from one monastery to another is like an animal who jumps this way and that, for fear of the halter.'

Charity

Abba Agathon said, 'If I could meet a leper, give him my body and take his, I should be very happy.' That indeed is perfect charity.

Commitment

[Amma Syncletica] said, 'If you find yourself in a monastery do not go to another place, for that will harm you a great deal. Just as the bird who abandons the eggs she was sitting on prevents them from hatching, so the monk or the nun grows cold and their faith dies, when they go from one place to another.'

---

1 Apophthegmata: plural of apophthegma (also spelled apothegma), a pithy maxim.
2 *The Sayings of the Desert Fathers. The Alphabetical Collection.* Translated, with a foreword by Benedicta Ward, SLG. Preface by Metropolitan Anthony of Sourrozh. Trappist, KY: Cistercian Publications, 1975; revised edition, 1984.

Compassion

Some [monks] came to see Abba Poemen and said to him, 'When we see brothers who are dozing [in church], [should] we rouse them so that they will be watchful?' He said to them, 'For my part, when I see a brother who is dozing, I put his head on my knees and let him rest.'

Faith

Abba Doulas, the disciple of Abba Bessarion said, 'One day when we were walking beside the sea I was thirsty and I said to Abba Bessarion, "Father, I am very thirsty." He said a prayer and said to me, "Drink some of the sea water." The water proved sweet when I drank some. I even poured some into a leather bottle for fear of being thirsty later on. Seeing this, the old man asked me why I was taking some. I said to him, "Forgive me, it is for fear of being thirsty later on." Then the old man said, "God is here, God is everywhere."'

Fasting

Abba John the Dwarf said, 'If a king wanted to take possession of his enemy's city, he would begin by cutting off the water and the food and so his enemies, dying of hunger, would submit to him. It is the same with the passions of the flesh: if a man goes about fasting and hungry the enemies of his soul grow weak.'

Fear of God

A brother asked [Abba Euprepius], 'How does the fear of God dwell in the soul?' [He] said, 'If a man is possessed of humility and poverty, and if he does not judge others, the fear of God will come to him.'

Happiness

Amma Syncletica said, 'In the beginning there are a great many battles and a good deal of suffering for those who are advancing towards God and afterwards, ineffable joy. It is like those who wish to light a fire; at first they are choked by the smoke and cry, and by this means obtain what they seek (as it is said: "Our God is a consuming fire" [Heb. 12:24]): so we also must kindle the divine fire in ourselves through tears and hard work.'

There was...an old man called Apollo. If someone came to find him about doing a piece of work, he would set out joyfully, saying, 'I am going to work with Christ today, for the salvation of my soul, for that is the reward he gives.'

Heresy

It was said concerning Abba Agathon that some monks came to find him having heard tell of his great discernment. Wanting to see if he would lose his temper they said to him[,] 'Aren't you that Agathon who is said to be a fornicator and a proud man?' 'Yes, it is very true,' he answered. They resumed, 'Aren't you that Agathon who is always talking nonsense?' 'I am.' Again they said[,] 'Aren't you Agathon the heretic?' But at that he replied[,] 'I am not a heretic.' So they asked him, 'Tell us why you accepted everything we cast [at] you, but repudiated this last insult.' He replied[,] 'The first accusations I take to myself, for that is good for my soul. But heresy is separation from God. Now I have no wish to be separated from God.' [With this reply,] they were astonished at his discernment and returned, edified.

Humility

[Amma Theodora] said that neither asceticism, nor vigils nor any kind of suffering are able to save, only true humility can do that....

It was said of Abba John the Persian that when some evildoers came to him, he took a basin and wanted to wash their feet. But they were filled with confusion, and began to do penance.

Judgment

Abba Theodore also said, 'If you are temperate, do not judge the fornicator, for you would then [break] the law just as much [as they]. [Remember:] he who said, "Do not commit fornication," also said, "Do not judge."'

A brother at Scetis committed a fault. A council was called to which Abba Moses was invited, but he refused to go to it. Then the priest sent someone to say to him, 'Come, for everyone is waiting for you.'... [So Abba Moses] took a leaking jug, filled it with water and carried it with him. The others came out to meet him and said..., 'What is this, Father?' The old man said to them, 'My sins run out behind me, and I do not see them, and today I am coming to judge the errors of another.' When they heard that they said no more to the brother but forgave him.

A brother who had sinned was turned out of the church by the priest; Abba Bessarion got up and went [out] with him, saying, 'I, too, am a sinner.'

Love

Abba John the Dwarf said, 'A house is not built by beginning at the top and working down. You must begin with the foundations in order to reach the top.' They [asked] him, 'What does this saying mean?' He said, 'The foundation is our neighbor, whom we must win [over with brotherly love], and that is the place to begin. For all the commandments of Christ depend on this one.'

Abba Pambo said, 'If you have a heart, you can be saved.'

Abba Anthony said, 'I no longer fear God, but I love Him. For love casts out fear.' (John 4:18)

Mercy

Three old men came to see Abba Sisoes, having heard about him. The first said to him, 'Father, how shall I save myself from the river of fire?' He did not answer him. The second said to him, 'Father, how can I be saved from the gnashing of teeth and the worm which [does not die]?' The third said, 'Father, what shall I do, for the [thought] of the outer darkness is killing me?' By way of reply the old man said to them, 'For my part, I do not keep in mind the [thought] of any of these things, for God is compassionate and I hope that he will show me his mercy.'...

Modesty

It was said concerning [Amma Sarah] that for sixty years she lived beside a river and never lifted her eyes to look at it. [So as not to see her own reflection upon the water.]

Monastic Precepts

[Abba Poemen] said, 'Poverty, hardship, austerity and fasting, such are the instruments of the solitary life....'

Amma Theodora said, 'Let us strive to enter by the narrow gate. Just as the trees, if they have not stood before the winter's storms cannot bear fruit, so it is with us; this present age is a storm and it is only through many trials and temptations that we can obtain an inheritance in the kingdom of heaven.'

Abba Ammonas was asked, 'What is the "narrow and hard way?"' (Matthew 7:14) He replied, 'The "narrow and hard way" is this, to control your thoughts, and to strip yourself of your will, for the sake of God. This is also the meaning of the sentence, "Lo, we have left everything and followed you."' (Matthew 19:27)

[Amma Syncletica] said, 'We must arm ourselves in every way against the demons. For they attack us from outside, and they also stir us up from within;... we lose as much by the exterior faults we commit as by the thoughts inside us. So we must watch for the attacks of [people] that come from outside us, and also repel the interior onslaughts of our thoughts.'

Obedience

It was said of Abba John the Dwarf that he withdrew and lived in the desert at Scetis with an old man of Thebes. His abba, taking a piece of dry wood, planted it and said to him, 'Water it every day with a bottle of water, until it bears fruit.' Now the water was so far away that he had to leave in the evening and return the following morning. At the end of three years the wood came to life and bore fruit. Then the old man took some of the fruit and carried it to the church saying to the brethren, 'Take and eat the fruit of obedience.'

[Amma Syncletica] said, 'As long as we are in the monastery [i.e., living in community], obedience is preferable to asceticism. The one [i.e., asceticism] teaches pride, the other [i.e., obedience] humility.'

Poverty

[When Abba Macarius returned to his hut, he found] a man who owned a beast of burden engaged in plundering [his] goods. So he came up to the thief as if he was a stranger and he helped him to load the animal.

He saw him off in great peace of soul, saying, '"We have brought nothing into this world, and we cannot take anything out of the world."' (1 Timothy 6:7) '"The Lord gave and the Lord has taken away; blessed be the name of the Lord."' (Job 1:21)

Blessed Syncletica was asked if poverty is a perfect good. She said, 'For those who are capable of it, it is a perfect good. Those who can sustain it receive suffering in the body but rest in the soul, for just as one washes coarse clothes by trampling them underfoot and turning them about in all directions, even so the strong soul becomes much more stable thanks to voluntary poverty.'

Prayer

[Abba Nilus] said, 'Prayer is the seed of gentleness and the absence of anger.'

It was said of [Abba John the Dwarf] that one day he was weaving rope for two baskets, but he made it into one without noticing, until it had reached the wall, because his spirit was occupied in contemplation.

Abba Macarius was asked, 'How should one pray?' The old man said, 'There is no need at all to make long discourses; it is enough to stretch out one's hands and say, "Lord, as you will, and as you know, have mercy." And if the conflict [in your soul] grows fiercer say, "Lord, help!" He knows very well what we need and he [shows] us his mercy.'

[Amma Theodora] said, 'It is good to live in peace, for the wise [person] practises perpetual prayer.... However, you should realize that as soon as you intend to live in peace, at once evil comes and weighs down your soul... [and] also attacks your body... so that one believes one is ill and no longer able to pray. But if we are vigilant, all these temptations fall away....'

Pride

[Abba Isidore] said, '... [I] f you think highly of your-self because [you fast regularly], then you had better eat meat. It is better ... to eat meat than to be inflated with pride....'

Purity

Amma Sarah said, '... [I] pray that my heart may be pure towards all.'

Renunciation

[Amma Syncletica] said, 'Do not let yourself be seduced by the delights of the riches of the world, as though they contained something useful on account of vain pleasure....'

Repentance

A soldier asked Abba Mius if God accepted repen-tance.... [The old man] said, 'Tell me, my dear, if your cloak is torn, do you throw it away?' [The sol-dier] replied, 'No, I mend it and use it again.' The old man said to him, 'If you are so careful about your cloak, will not God be equally careful about his creature?'

Silence

A brother came to [ask for a word of advice from] Abba Moses... The old man said to him, 'Go, sit in your cell, and your cell [in silence] will teach you everything.'

The same Abba Theophilus, the archbishop, came to Scetis one day. The brethren who were assembled said to Abba Pambo, 'Say [a word or two] to the archbishop, so that he may be edified.' The old man [replied], 'If he is not edified by my silence, he will not be edified by my speech.'

Slander

[Abba Hyperechius] said, 'It is better to eat meat and drink wine [than] to eat the flesh of one's [brothers] through slander.'

Temptation

[Abba Anthony said], '... Without temptations no-one can be saved.'

Thankfulness

Abba Copres said, 'Blessed is he who bears affliction with thankfulness.'

Vigilance

Abba Poemen said, 'Vigilance, self-knowledge and discernment; these are the guides of the soul.'... He also said, 'The beginning of evil is [lack of vigilance].'

Vigils

Abba Theodore said, 'Privation of food mortifies the body of the monk.' Another old man said, 'Vigils mortify it still more.'

Virtue

Abba Moses asked Abba Sylvanus, 'Can a man lay a new foundation [for virtue] every day?' The [Abba] said, 'If he works hard, he can lay a new foundation at every moment.'

Work

It was said of Abba John the Dwarf, that one day he said to his elder brother, 'I should like to be free of all care, like the angels, who do not work, but ceaselessly offer worship to God.' So he took off his cloak and went away into the desert. After a week he came back to his brother. When he knocked on the door, he heard his brother say, ... 'Who are you?' He said, 'I am John, your brother.' But he replied, 'John has become an angel, and ... he is no longer among men.'

Then the other begged him ... However, his brother did not let him in, but left him there in distress until morning. Then, opening the door, he said to him, 'You are a man and you must once again work in order to eat.' Then John made a prostration before him, saying, 'Forgive me.'

Works

[Abba James] said, 'We do not need words only, for ... there are many words among men[.] [W]e need works, for this is what is required, not words which do not bear fruit.'

Questions

1. Compare the monastic tradition in Buddhism and Christianity. What place does each tradition make for women?
2. There are tribal and Hebrew elements in the thought of the desert fathers and mothers. St. Anthony rejects Greek philosophy as "rhetoric." Instead of clever arguments, he says, we need faith. Comment and discuss.
3. Comment on the role of humility in the desert tradition. Is it a "Christian" virtue, or do you find it in earlier thinkers? Cite an ancient philosopher, from a different tradition.
4. The desert tradition came out of the Stoic and the Roman traditions. The ascetics saw morality as a battle with the forces of evil, and themselves as soldiers of Christ. Comment and discuss.
5. The ascetics saw their ascetic practices as workouts, essentially, which kept them spiritually fit. What attitude towards the body does this view presuppose?
6. The desert mothers and fathers also saw "fornication" as a great temptation. How does sexuality and renunciation fit into morality, in your view? Why have our views changed?
7. The monastic tradition places enormous emphasis on prayer. What is prayer, in your estimation, and what role does it play in morality? In wisdom?

Suggested Readings

There are a number of translations of the *Apophthegmata*. Besides Benedicta Ward's translation of the *Alphabetical Collection* see John Wortley's translation of the *Systematic Collection* (*The Book of the Elders*, 2012). Laura Swan, *The Forgotten Desert Mothers* (2001), covers the lives and sayings of women ascetics, even though many of the sayings attributed to them are already found in Ward's collection. There are stories of the interactions between novitiates and their mentors in John Chryssavgis's *In the Heart of the Desert* (2008). The Coptic Church of Egypt has a collection of sayings and material on St. Anthony and other figures at coptic.net. Derwas Chitty has translated *Seven Letters of Saint Anthony* (1975).

The origins of the *Apophthegmata* lie in the proverb tradition. This is evident in the *Ad Monachos*, a collection of proverbs by Evagrius Ponticus (345–399), which has been translated by Jeremy Driscoll, with commentary (2003).

The academic accounts of the Egyptian tradition are historical rather than philosophical. These include James E. Goehring, *Ascetics, Society, and the Desert: Studies in Early Egyptian Monasticism* (1999); Peter Brown, "The Rise and Function of the Holy Man in Late Antiquity" (1971); Norman Russell and Benedicta Ward, *Lives of the Desert Fathers* (1981); and E.R. Hardy, *Christian Egypt* (1952). *The Christian History Magazine* dedicated an issue to the desert tradition in 1999.

For an account of the Syrian tradition, which included extreme privations, see A. Voobus, *A History of Asceticism in the Syrian Orient*, vol. 2 (1960). Students interested in the monastic tradition may read Sherri Olson, *Daily Life in a Medieval Monastery* (2013).

PART III
MEDIEVAL SOURCES

Anti-Materialism. A Synthesis of Practical and Theoretical Wisdom

The medieval period is usually associated, in the West, with the slow break-up of the Roman Empire, which ushered in an age of religious belief. The ethical inquiry, which began to focus more explicitly on the conduct of individuals, was carried on within the parameters of the different religious and cultural traditions. The wise person followed the will of God.

In Rome, Stoicism held official sway for about five hundred years (with Epicureanism in the background) until it was finally supplanted by a respectful Christianity. Most of the philosophical schools present during the Hellenistic period were, in fact, supplanted in the centuries that followed by being adopted by different Christian thinkers and given a Christian form. Ancient skepticism tended to be used by Christian thinkers who wished to attack reason "with reason" in order to make room for faith. Platonism, Aristotelianism, Stoicism, and even Cynicism to a small extent were each developed along Christian lines by those who saw no conflict between faith and reason. Epicureanism was the only exception and found few takers within Christianity until the modern period.

Canonical thinkers in the medieval period were well aware of the wisdom tradition, which was present in the different religious traditions. In the West, which we focus on here, Judaism, Christianity, and Islam come to the fore. Religious thinkers accepted the role of revelation and received wisdom in determining how we should act and live. They were also aware of the philosophical tradition and developed syncretic ethical systems, within the moral framework provided by their own religious doctrine. The obvious examples of this, featured in this section, are al-Ghazālī, Maimonides, and Thomas Aquinas, all of whom reconciled elements of the Aristotelian and Greek tradition with religious and theological sources.

Major medieval thinkers were responding to many of the same cross-currents that confront us in the contemporary era and accordingly provide us with a helpful synthesis of practical and theoretical wisdom. The medieval period includes, for example, a convincing account of the natural law. The spread of Christianity was also significant because—like Buddhism—it promoted a religious egalitarianism, which in turn promoted the idea of personal salvation. As we see in Abelard, this brought in a heightened individualism, which internalized the notions of good and evil, and replaced the fatalism of earlier views.

The strong drive towards spirituality and religion in the period found its most intense expression in the mystical tradition, which had been part of the earlier monastic tradition with thinkers like the early Desert Fathers and Mothers. Maimonides's negative theology, the distribution of Plato's *Timaeus*, and the graphic examples of saints such as Francis of Assisi and Catherine of Sienna all supported the idea that we can directly experience a higher spiritual order. There was a popular belief that the active renunciation of the things of this world provides us with an ethical mechanics that puts us in touch with, and even allows us to live within, a transcendent world.

There were similar developments in China, with the further spread of Buddhism, which incorporated elements of Daoism into its teaching. The success of Buddhism re-invigorated Confucianism, which borrowed from the new tradition, but also rejected it, primarily on ethical grounds.

Chapter 19

The Jewish Tradition

Moses ben Maimon, known in the West by the Greek version of his name, Maimonides, was a rabbi, physician, theologian, and philosopher who lived in Morocco and Egypt. He is also known by Hebrew scholars as "the Rambam," an acronym for "Rabbi Moshe ben Maimon."

Maimonides was born into an affluent family in Cordova, Spain, studied the Torah under his father, a rabbinic scholar and judge, and developed a keen interest in astronomy, medicine, mathematics, and philosophy at an early age. Moving in cosmopolitan Christian, Islamic, and Jewish circles, he read the Greek philosophers in Arabic translations and summaries. He also read Christian sources and was naturally familiar with the rabbinical sources of his time.

When the Almohads, who were fundamentalist Muslims, invaded Cordova in 1148, the Jews were faced with a choice between conversion to Islam, exile, or death. Maimonides's family fled, perhaps after going through an "external" Muslim conversion. During much of his life, Maimonides was forced to elude religious persecution, moving from southern Spain to Morocco and finally settling in Cairo, Egypt, where a more liberal Muslim regime permitted peaceful co-existence between different faiths.

Maimonides was active in the affairs of the Jewish community throughout his life. He played a prominent role in purchasing the freedom of Jews who had been taken captive during the Crusades and became the prince or leader (*Nagid*) of the Jewish community in Egypt around 1171. At fifty, Maimonides married into an influential family with connections to the government and had at least one son.

When Maimonides's brother David was drowned at sea on a business trip to India, with the loss of the family's fortune, he turned to the practice of medicine. He was eventually appointed physician to the Grand Vizier, then to the Sultan and the royal family. His medical practice was cosmopolitan and brought him into contact with the elites throughout society. In addition to his work in theology and philosophy, he wrote extensively on medical matters.

In spite of his busy public life, Maimonides was an industrious scholar. His major ethical work is the *Mishneh Torah* (1180), in fourteen volumes, which contains a systematic commentary on the 613 precepts of Jewish law believed to be divinely received by Moses and contained in the Torah (known to Christians as the first five books of the Old Testament: *Genesis, Exodus, Leviticus, Numbers,* and *Deuteronomy*). In comparison to other, more literary sources, the *Mishneh Torah* provides a highly logical synthesis of the law and the entire rabbinic tradition, organized thematically in a straightforward, user-friendly fashion. Maimonides also summarized the basic principles of Judaic belief in his "Thirteen Principles of Faith," which are still recited in synagogues today.

Maimonides saw the Torah as a scriptural indictment of idolatry. While this is a conventional interpretation, he extended the notion of idolatry to encompass any intermediary between ourselves and God. This includes the text of Scripture, which should not be set up as a likeness of God and worshipped in its own right. Those who adopt a literal interpretation of scripture have accordingly sinned against God. This was a controversial position, which led some rabbis to ban Maimonides's writing.

Although Maimonides acknowledged the mystical elements in the Torah, he also took issue with the kabbalists, who saw the Torah in highly abstract metaphysical terms, as an opus with a mystical origin in the name of God. At its most extreme, this led to the historical assertion that the *Torah* itself, in its undefined essence, is God. Maimonides was an advocate of "rational religion" and was opposed in principle to the idea that the collection had an esoteric meaning available only to the initiated.

Maimonides took a relatively simple position, which was that the Torah deals with the welfare of the body and the soul. In the first instance, it contains precepts that provide for the government of the state and the people. In the second, it contains an intellectual formula for the contemplation of the highest spiritual truths. The problem was that its teachings are disparate, and quite fragmented. By Maimonides's time, the religious law was seen by most believers as a complicated and confusing collection of relatively arbitrary practices, which had lost most of their meaning.

Some of the difficulty can be traced to the text of the *Talmud,* a compendium of centuries of rabbinic commentary on Jewish law. The *Talmud* is accessible only to someone who already knows the foundations of the rabbinical tradition and its technical complexities. Although it says that there are 613 commandments in the Torah, for example, 248 positive commandments and 365 negative commandments, it does not enumerate them. Maimonides's purpose in writing the *Mishneh Torah* was accordingly to set out and explain the law in a simple form that would be accessible to ordinary believers. The result was a codification listing the 613 commandments.

It is difficult to gauge Maimonides's intentions, but it may have been to set out Jewish law rather than comment on and clarify it. This may explain some of the discomfort with Maimonides's work in rabbinical thought, which tends to regard his Torah as a companion piece to the Talmud, a *hibbur,* an independent text, which may be studied on its own, independently of its sources. It has been described as a "textbook" and is not seen as a definitive statement of the law.

The striking feature of the *Mishneh Torah* is its comprehensiveness. It provides us with a synthesis of an entire body of law in a single, unified whole, based on clear theoretical principles, which exhibits the cohesiveness of a system of thought rather than being a collection of scattered observations. In reality, Maimonides reformulates the very early

Jewish tradition, which was oral, cosmological, open-ended, and situational—in other words, which was deduced from experience rather than ideas—and reconstructs it on a theoretical basis. This reconstruction is implicitly scientific and foreshadows the modern tradition in philosophy, which has similar concerns.

In *The Guide for the Perplexed* (1186), Maimonides turns his attention to an intellectual Jewish audience, who may be "perplexed and bewildered on account of the ambiguous and figurative expressions employed in the holy writings." Maimonides argues against literal interpretations of Scripture, viewing religion as a path to truths that can be discovered either through philosophy or the symbols, figures of speech, and stories of the religious tradition. There is a strong Aristotelian influence in *The Guide*, though Maimonides uses many Aristotelian concepts in a novel manner. This is apparent, for example, in his discussion of the "Laws Concerning Character Traits."

The countervailing forces in Maimonides's work find expression in his practical ethics, which veers between two opposing ideals. One is religious, but also Platonic, and holds that the moral life is best embodied in a life of contemplation. Maimonides sees the study of metaphysics as a holy endeavor and describes the philosophical life in religious terms as the perfect intellectual worship of God. There is a related discussion among scholars concerning the relation between philosophy and revealed religion in his work.

The other ideal sees the moral life as an active life of charitable service. In this context, Maimonides writes that we should cultivate dynamic moral virtues that imitate the benevolent actions of God. The fully moral person will have loving-kindness (*hesed*), righteousness (*zedakah*), and judgment (*mishpat*). These virtues are essentially selfless. Loving-kindness requires an "excessive"—i.e., a heroic degree—of charity. Righteousness consists of showing kindness to every created being. Judgment entails meting out punishment or mercy in accordance with the fundamental principles of justice. It is significant that, in his own life, Maimonides chose to spend less time in his preferred intellectual endeavors and took on an exhausting medical practice that focused on caring for others.

The reading is from *The Guide for the Perplexed*, in which Maimonides exhorts his reader to study and learn. Although he is clearly captivated by the rational and philosophical tradition, there are, however, limits to human knowledge and reasoning, and these too must be learned. The highest intellectual and spiritual experience is reserved for the prophet or sage, and can only be achieved within the framework of religion, which recognizes the ineffability of God.

Moses Maimonides, Part III of *The Guide for the Perplexed*[1]

(1186)

Chapter XI

EVIL COMES FROM THE ABSENCE OF WISDOM

All the great evils which men cause to each other because of certain intentions, desires, opinions, or religious principles, are likewise due to non-existence, because they originate in ignorance, which is absence of wisdom. A blind man, for example, who has no guide, stumbles constantly, because he cannot see, and causes injury and harm to himself and others.

In the same manner various classes of men, each man in proportion to his ignorance, bring great evils upon themselves and upon other individual members of the species. If men possessed wisdom, which stands in the same relation to the form of man as the sight to the eye, they would not cause any injury to themselves or to others; for the knowledge of truth removes hatred and quarrels, and prevents mutual injuries. This state of society is promised to us by the prophet in the words: "And the wolf shall dwell with the lamb," etc....

The prophet also points out what will be the cause of this change; for he says that hatred, quarrel, and fighting will come to an end, because men will then have a true knowledge of God....

Chapter XII

THE UNIVERSE IS FUNDAMENTALLY GOOD

Men frequently think that the evils in the world are more numerous than the good things; many sayings and songs of the nations dwell on this idea.... Al-Razi wrote a well-known book *On Metaphysics.*[2] Among other mad and foolish things, it contains also the idea, discovered by him, that there exists more evil than good.... This author commenced to verify his opinion by counting all the evils one by one; by this means he opposed those who hold the correct view of the benefits bestowed by God and His evident kindness, namely, that God is perfect goodness, and that all that comes from Him is absolutely good. The origin of the error is to be found in the circumstance that this ignorant man, and his party among the common people, judge the whole universe by examining one single person. For an ignorant man believes that the whole universe only exists for him...If, therefore, anything happens to him contrary to his expectation, he at once concludes that the whole universe is evil.... If, however, he would take into consideration the whole universe, form an idea of it, and comprehend what a small portion he is of the Universe, he will find the truth....

---

1 Moses Maimonides, PART III of *The Guide for the Perplexed* (c. 1190), trans. M. Friedlaender, 4th revised ed. (New York: E.P. Dutton, 1904). Available at http://oll.libertyfund.org/titles/1256.

2 Abū Bakr Muhammad ibn Zakariyyā al-Rāzī (854–925) was a Persian polymath and physician. He wrote numerous works in a number of fields and made a number of advances in medicine. His works and ideas, known through translation, greatly influenced medical education in the Latin West.

PHYSICAL, SOCIAL, AND PERSONAL EVILS

The evils that befall man are of three kinds:

(1) The first kind of evil is that which is caused to man by the circumstance that he is subject to genesis [birth] and destruction, or that he possesses a body. It is on account of the body that some persons happen to have great deformities or paralysis of some of the organs.... We have already shown, however, that this so-called form of evil is a necessary condition of existence, and does not contradict the true kindness, and beneficence, and goodness of God....

(2) The second class of evils comprises such evils as people cause to each other, when, e.g., some of them use their strength against others. These evils are more numerous than those of the first kind; their causes are numerous and known; they likewise originate in ourselves, though the sufferer himself cannot avert them. This kind of evil is nevertheless not widespread in any country of the whole world. It is of rare occurrence that a man plans to kill his neighbour or to rob him of his property by night....

(3) The third class of evils comprises those which every one causes to himself by his own action. This is the largest class, and is far more numerous than the second class. It is especially of these evils that all men complain—only few men are found that do not sin against themselves by this kind of evil....

The sufferings of the soul in this regard are two-fold: First, such evils of the soul as are the necessary consequence of changes in the body...Secondly, the soul, when accustomed to superfluous things, acquires a strong habit of desiring things which are neither necessary for the preservation of the individual nor for that of the species. This desire is without a limit...since what is superfluous is without end—e.g., you desire to have your vessels of silver, but golden vessels are still better: others have even vessels of sapphire, or perhaps they can be made of emerald or rubies, or any other substance that could be suggested. Those who are ignorant and perverse in their thought are constantly in trouble and pain, because they cannot get as much of superfluous things as a certain other person possesses....

Chapter XXVI

Theologians are...divided as regards the object of the commandments which God gave us.... But our Sages generally do not think that such precepts have no cause whatever, and serve no purpose; for this would lead us to assume that God's actions are purposeless....

I will now tell you what intelligent persons ought to believe in this respect; namely, that each commandment has necessarily a cause, as far as its general character is concerned, and serves a certain object; but as regards its details we hold that it has no ulterior object. Thus killing animals for the purpose of obtaining good food is certainly useful, as we intend to show; that, however, the killing should not be performed by *nehirah* (poleaxing the animal), but by *shehitah* (cutting the neck), and by dividing the esophagus and the windpipe in a certain place; these regulations and the like are nothing but tests for man's obedience....

I give this instance only because it has been mentioned by our Sages; but in reality there is a reason for these regulations. For as it has become necessary to eat the flesh of animals, it was intended by the above regulations to ensure an easy death and to effect it by suitable means; whilst decapitation requires a sword or a similar instrument, the *shehitah* can be performed with any instrument; and in order to ensure an easy death our Sages insisted that the knife should be well sharpened....

Chapter XXVIII

The reason of a commandment, whether positive or negative, is clear, and its usefulness evident, if it directly tends to remove injustice, or to teach good conduct that furthers the well-being of society, or to impart a truth which ought to be believed...on its own merit...

There is no occasion to ask for the object of such commandments; for no one can, e.g., be in doubt as to the reason why we have been commanded to believe that God is one; why we are forbidden to murder, to steal, and to take vengeance, or to retaliate, or why we are commanded to love one another....

Chapter XXXIII[1]

Politeness is another virtue promoted by the Law. Man shall listen to the words of his neighbor; he shall not be obstinate, but shall yield to the wish of his fellow-men, respond to their appeal, act according to their desire, and do what they like. Thus the Law commands, "Circumcise therefore the foreskin of your heart..." (Deut. x. 16)...

THE FOURTEEN CLASSES OF PRECEPTS[2]

Chapter XXXVI

The reason of all precepts of the first class, [which provide the foundation of the *Torah*, the teaching] is obvious.... It is evident that the precepts which exhort and command us to learn and to teach are useful; for without wisdom there cannot be any good act or any true knowledge. The law which prescribes to honor the teachers of the Law is likewise useful;

for if they were not considered by the people as great and honourable men, they would not be followed as guides in their principles and actions....

Chapter XXXVII

The precepts of the second class are those which we have enumerated in the section "On idolatry." It is doubtless that they all tend to save man from the error of idolatry and the evil practices connected with it; e.g., observing the times, enchantment, witchcraft, incantation, consulting with familiar spirits, and the like....

Thus it is stated by the idolators...that if four women lay on their back, with their feet spread and lifted up, said certain words and did certain things whilst in this disgraceful position, hail would discontinue coming down in that place. The number of these stupid and mad things is great; in all of them without exception women are required to be the agent...

Chapter XXXVIII

[The precepts of the third class are the laws of personal development, which contain precepts such as to love one's fellow Jews; to rebuke but not embarrass; not to gossip or bear a grudge.]...they are rules concerning moral conduct by which the social relations of men are regulated....

Chapter XXXIX

The precepts in the fourth class include the laws of charity...When you examine these precepts you will

---

1 Maimonides lists some of the objects of the "perfect Law," which include a reduction of the desire for food, drink, and sexual intercourse.

2 Maimonides then divides the precepts into fourteen classes, which deal either with the relation between man and God, or the relation between man and man.

clearly see the use of every one of them: they teach us to have sympathy with the poor and infirm, to assist the needy in various ways; not to hurt the feelings of those who are in want, and not to vex those who are in a helpless condition[1]....

Chapter XL

The precepts of the fifth class, enumerated in the Section "On Damages" (*Sepher nezikin*), aim at the removal of wrong and the prevention of injury.... We are, therefore, responsible for all damage caused by our cattle; we must guard them. The same is the case with the law regarding fire and pits; they are made by man, and he can be careful that they do not cause damage....

Chapter XLI

The precepts of the sixth class comprise the different ways of punishing the sinner. Their general usefulness is known and has also been mentioned by us....

The punishment of him who sins against his neighbor consists in the general rule that there shall be done unto him exactly as he has done: if he injured any one personally, he must suffer personally; if he damaged the property of his neighbor, he shall be punished by loss of property.... Only to the murderer we must not be lenient[2] because of the greatness of his crime; and no ransom must be accepted of him. "And the land cannot be cleansed of the blood that is shed therein but by the blood of him that shed it" (Num. xxxi. 33)....

He who sins 1) involuntarily is, according to the distinct declaration of the Law, exempt from punishment, and free from all blame... If a person sins in 2) ignorance, he is blamable; for if he had been more considerate and careful, he would not have erred. Although he is not punished, his sin must be atoned for, and for this reason he brings a sin-offering....

3) He who has sinned knowingly must pay the penalty prescribed in the Law; he is put to death or receives stripes,[3] or—for transgression of prohibitions not punishable by stripes—other corporal punishment, or pays a fine....

4) If a person sins presumptuously, so that in sinning he shows impudence and seeks publicity, if he does not sin only to satisfy his appetite, if he does what is prohibited by the Law, not only because of his evil inclinations, but in order to oppose and resist the Law, he "reproaches the Lord," and must undoubtedly be put to death. None will act in such a manner but such as have conceived the idea to act contrary to the Law...

Chapter XLII

The precepts of the seventh class deal with fairness in commercial and private transactions...

Chapter XLIII

The precepts of the eighth class are enumerated in the Jewish calendar... The object of Sabbath[4] is obvious, and requires no explanation. The rest it affords to man is known; one-seventh of the life of every man, whether small or great, passes thus in comfort,

---

1 Namely, the widow, the orphan, and the like.
2 Maimonides had allowed for "leniency" in other punishments examined just before noting this exception.
3 Beatings with a rod or lash.
4 The Sabbath is a day of religious observance and abstinence from work. It is kept by Jews from Friday sunset to Saturday sunset. Most Christians observe this on Sunday.

and in rest from trouble and exertion.... The object of the Fast of Atonement[1] is evident. The Fast creates the sense of repentance...

Other holy days are appointed for rejoicing and for such pleasant gathering as people generally need. They also promote the good feeling that men should have to each other in their social and political relations....[2]

Chapter XLVII

The precepts of the twelfth class are those which we have enumerated in the section on "Purity," which deal with the restrictions on those who are unclean....

The uncleanness through leprosy we have already explained.... All agree that leprosy is a punishment for slander. The disease begins in the walls of the houses. If the sinner repents, the object is attained; if he remains in his disobedience, the disease affects his bed and house furniture; if he still continues to sin, the leprosy attacks his own garments, and then his body.... The good effect of this belief is evident. Leprosy is besides a contagious disease, and people almost naturally abhor it, and keep away from it....

Chapter XLVIII

The precepts of the thirteenth class are those which we have enumerated in the "Laws concerning forbidden food"...

I maintain that the food which is forbidden by the Law is unwholesome. There is nothing among the forbidden kinds of food whose injurious character is doubted, except pork, and fat. But also in these cases the doubt is not justified. For pork contains more moisture than necessary, and too much of superfluous matter. The principal reason why the Law forbids swine's flesh is to be found in the circumstance that its habits and its food are very dirty and loathsome.... And if the law allowed us to eat swine's flesh, the streets and houses would be more dirty than any cesspool, as may be seen at present in the country of the Franks.[3] A saying of our Sages declares: "The mouth of a swine is as dirty as dung itself"...

Chapter XLIX

The precepts of the fourteenth class are those which we enumerated in the Section on Women, the Laws concerning forbidden sexual intercourse, and cross-breeding of cattle... The law concerning circumcision belongs also to this class....

The law about forbidden sexual intercourse seeks in all its parts to inculcate the lesson that we ought to limit sexual intercourse altogether, hold it in contempt, and only desire it very rarely. The prohibition of pederasty and carnal intercourse with beasts is very clear. If in the natural way the act is too base to be performed except when needed, how much more base is it if performed in an unnatural manner, and only for the sake of pleasure....

It is well known that we must not indulge in any sensual enjoyment whatever with a father's wife, a brother's wife, an aunt, etc.; we must not even look at them if we intend to derive pleasure therefrom. We have explained this in "the laws about forbidden sexual intercourse," and shown that according

---

1 This is the fast done on the Day of Atonement (Yom Kippur), which is the holiest day of the year in Judaism. The day is often spent in synagogue services with fasting and prayer intended to atone for sins and repent.

2 Maimonides continues his study of the next three classes of laws: the ninth class deals with the love of God; the tenth, the laws of the Temple; the eleventh, the Divine Service and Sacrifices, which Maimonides says that God permitted to accommodate the customs of the past.

3 Christian kingdom in early medieval Europe.

to the Law we must not even engage our thoughts with the act of cohabitation or irritate the organ of generation;[1] and when we find ourselves unintentionally in a state of irritation, we must turn our mind to other thoughts, and reflect on some other thing till we are relieved. Our Sages, in their moral lessons, which give perfection to the virtuous, say as follows: "My son, if that monster meets you, drag it to the house of study. It will melt if it is of iron; it will break in pieces if it is of stone: as is said in Scripture, 'Is not my word like a fire? says the Lord, and like a hammer that breaks the rock in pieces?'"…

As regards circumcision, I think that one of its objects is to limit sexual intercourse, and to weaken the organ of generation as far as possible, and thus cause man to be moderate…. This commandment has not been enjoined as a complement to a deficient physical creation, but as a means for perfecting man's moral shortcomings. The bodily injury caused to that organ is exactly that which is desired; it does not interrupt any vital function, nor does it destroy the power of generation. Circumcision simply counteracts excessive lust; for there is no doubt that circumcision weakens the power of sexual excitement, and sometimes lessens the natural enjoyment; the organ necessarily becomes weak when it loses blood and is deprived of its covering from the beginning. Our Sages say distinctly: It is hard for a woman, with whom an uncircumcised had sexual intercourse, to separate from him….

There is, however, another important object in this commandment. It gives to all members of the same faith, i.e., to all believers in the Unity of God, a common bodily sign, so that it is impossible for any one that is a stranger, to say that he belongs to them….

Chapter LIV

The term *ḥokmah* ("wisdom") in Hebrew is used, in its third sense,… of the acquisition of moral principles….

According to this explanation, a person that has a true knowledge of the whole Law is called wise in a double sense; he is wise because the Law instructs him in the highest truths, and secondly, because it teaches him good morals. But as the truths contained in the Law are taught by way of tradition, not by a philosophical method, the knowledge of the Law, and the acquisition of true wisdom, are… two different things; real wisdom demonstrates by proof[2] those truths which the Law teaches us by way of tradition….

Hear now what I have to say after having given the above explanation. The ancient and the modern philosophers have shown that man can acquire four kinds of perfection. The first kind, the lowest, in the acquisition of which people spend their days, is perfection as regards property; the possession of money, garments, furniture, servants, land, and the like; the possession of the title of a great king belongs to this class. There is no close connection between this possession and its possessor…

The philosophers have shown that he whose sole aim in all his exertions and endeavors is the possession of this kind of perfection, only seeks perfectly imaginary and transient things; and even if these remain his property all his lifetime, they do not give him any perfection.

The second kind is more closely related to man's body than the first. It includes the perfection of the shape, constitution, and form of man's body; the utmost evenness of temperaments, and the proper order and strength of his limbs. This kind of perfection must likewise be excluded from forming our chief aim; because it is a perfection of the body, and

---

1 Stimulate the penis.

2 I.e., philosophically.

man does not possess it as man, but as a living being; he has this property besides in common with the lowest animal... The soul derives no profit whatever from this kind of perfection.

The third kind of perfection is more closely connected with man himself than the second perfection. It includes moral perfection, the highest degree of excellency in man's character. Most of the precepts aim at producing this perfection; but even this kind is only a preparation for another perfection... For all moral principles concern the relation of man to his neighbor; the perfection of man's moral principles is, as it were, given to man for the benefit of mankind....

The fourth kind of perfection is the true perfection of the individual man; the possession of the highest intellectual faculties; the possession of such notions which lead to true metaphysical opinions as regards God. With this perfection the individual man has obtained his final object; it gives him true human perfection; it remains to him alone; it gives him immortality...

The prophets... have expressed the same opinion on these things as the philosophers. They say distinctly that perfection in property, in health, or in character, is not a perfection worthy to be sought as a cause of pride and glory for us; that the knowl-edge of God, i.e., true wisdom [hokmah], is the only perfection which we should seek, and in which we should glorify ourselves. Jeremiah, referring to these four kinds of perfection, says: "Thus says the Lord, Let not the wise man glory in his wisdom, neither let the mighty man glory in his might, let not the rich man glory in his riches; but let him that glories glory in this, that he understands and knows me" (Jeremiah. ix. 22–23)....

The prophet does not content himself, however, with explaining that the knowledge of God is the highest kind of perfection... Rather he says that man can only glory in the knowledge of God and in the knowledge of His ways and attributes, which are His actions... We have already shown that the Divine acts which ought to be known, and ought to serve as a guide for our actions, are, hesed, "loving-kindness," mishpat, "judgment," and zedakah, "righteousness".... The object of the above passage is therefore to declare that the perfection, in which man can truly glory, is attained by him when he has acquired... the knowledge of God...

Having acquired this knowledge he will then be determined always to seek loving-kindness, judgment, and righteousness, and thus to imitate the ways of God....

Questions

1. Maimonides describes evil as the absence of wisdom, which renders us blind. If we were wise, he says, there would be no conflict in the world. What do you think? What is wisdom? Include a second philosopher in your answer.

2. Maimonides is a rationalist and implicitly rejected the tribal origins of the *Torah*. Like his Christian contemporaries, he emphasizes sin and moral blame, rather than fate. Discuss.

3. Maimonides divides the 613 precepts of Jewish law into fourteen classes. List three classes of the precepts and the reasons that Maimonides gives for each. Are the reasons sound?

4. Maimonides says that we can sin in four ways. List them. Which is the worst sin? What is the punishment for this sin, and why?

5. The *Torah* requires that all Jewish males be circumcised. What is the purpose of circumcision in Maimonides's view? Respond to his views.

6. Maimonides was not satisfied with the idea that we should know God. Knowing God is not enough. Elaborate.

7. Do Jews, Muslims, Christians, and Buddhists have extra moral obligations to people of their own faith? How far does this go? Refer to at least two philosophers and two different traditions.

8. It is not possible to deal with the historical use of force in the three monotheistic traditions—using the word 'violence' instead of force is controversial. You may nevertheless wish to consider under what circumstances the use of force is morally permitted.

Suggested Readings

Maimonides's key commentaries on Jewish Scripture include his *Commentary on the Mishna*, the *Sefer Hamitzvot* (*The Book of Commandments*) and the *Mishneh Torah*. His most famous philosophical work is nevertheless his magisterial *Guide for the Perplexed*. There are shorter ethical works in *Crisis and Leadership: Epistles of Maimonides* (1985). Marc D. Angel, *Maimonides: Essential Teachings on Jewish Faith and Ethics* (2012), contains selections from Maimonides, with commentaries from the editor.

For a biographical source, see Joel Kraemer's *Maimonides* (2008). For academic sources, see Alexander Broadie, "The Moral Philosophy of Maimonides" (1988), and Hermann Cohen, Almut Sh. Bruckstein, trans., *Ethics of Maimonides* [1908] (2004). For a more recent re-statement of Jewish and Maimonidean ethics, see Ira Bedzow, *Maimonides for Moderns* (2017). On the *Torah*, see Ruth Link-Salinger, ed., *Torah and Wisdom* (1992), which covers Maimonides.

See also Menachem Kellner's *Maimonides on Human Perfection* (1990). Readers interested in the relation between philosophy and revealed religion in Maimonides's work may want to consult Leo Strauss, "The Literary Character of the Guide for the Perplexed" (1952). In a comparative vein, see Michael P. Levine, "Why Maimonides Could Have Had a Doctrine of Natural Law Even If He Did Not" (1986).

There is also discussion of Maimonides's views in the medical literature. The Maimonides Institute for Medicine, Ethics, and the Holocaust is at mimeh.org. And see Fred Rosner, "Sex Ethics in the Writings of Moses Maimonides" (1994).

Chapter 20

Christian Neo-Platonism

Saint Augustine (Aurelius Augustinus, 354–430) was born in Thagaste, a Roman city in North Africa (now Algeria), into a family of some substance. He was the son of a Pagan father, Patricius, and a fervent Christian mother, Monica, who eventually converted her husband and son to Christianity.

After his regular schooling Augustine left for Carthage, where he studied rhetoric, a prominent discipline in the Latin curriculum. He soon took up with a concubine, who bore him a son, and joined the Manicheans, a Gnostic group. The Manicheans were moral dualists, who saw reality as an ongoing struggle between the power of light, a positive good, and physical matter, a positive evil. He later renounced their ideas.

Augustine eventually became a teacher and moved to Rome in 383 to open a school of rhetoric. He was poorly received in academic circles and irritated by students ("cheaters") who took his courses without paying their fees. Within a year, however, he was awarded a position as a professor of rhetoric to the Imperial Court at Milan. There, at the height of his academic success, he found himself afflicted by spiritual restlessness and self-doubt. Augustine turned to philosophy for consolation and read a number of unnamed Platonic texts—probably the (Neo-)Platonists Porphyry and Plotinus—which left a deep impact on his thinking. He also investigated Christianity, listening to the sermons of St. Ambrose, then bishop of Milan, who was admired for his intellectual sophistication. In 387, after a dramatic conversion, Augustine returned to North Africa. When his mother died, and later his son, he gave his inheritance to the poor, converting the family house into a monastery. In 391, he became a priest in Hippo Regius (modern-day Annaba, Algeria). He later became the Bishop of Hippo, and died thirty-five years later, as the Vandals, invading German tribes, surrounded the city.

St. Isidore of Seville (c. 560–636) famously said that anyone who claimed to have read all of Augustine is a liar. He wrote sermons, letters, theological treatises, philosophical dialogues, and polemical pieces. His principal works include *The Confessions*, an autobiography; *The City of God* (*De Civitate Dei*), a long work defending Christianity and discussing its role in society; *The Teacher* (*De Magistro*), a short explanation of how we think; *The Enchiridion*, a discussion of the Christian virtues of faith, hope, and love; and many doctrinal works, such as *On Christian Doctrine*, *On the Trinity*, and *On Free Choice of the Will*.

Augustine wrote so prolifically, and in so many different styles and formats, that it is hard to keep track of his philosophical opinions. His ethics nevertheless has its sources in (Neo-)Platonism and Christianity. His best-known work, the *Confessions*, is an introspective chronicle of his own journey from debauchery to a religious life. His writing has a psychological edge, poetic flair, and unusual clarity; but the book is written in a "high" prose style that many readers find challenging. The plot of the book reaches its climax with Augustine's conversion to Christianity, after which the narrative subsides into theological reflection.

We have already seen that the Christian tradition comes out of a fusion of the biblical and philosophical traditions. The historical origins of the Judaeo-Christian concept of God are complex, but include anti-materialistic elements, and a biblical change, by which God has been taken out of the cosmos and placed above it. Augustine's ethical theory is accordingly theological and rests morality on the primacy of God and the doctrine of original sin (the sin of Adam), which leaves us fallen and imperfect, only to be redeemed by the grace of God. This explains why he sees asceticism, which renounces our imperfect nature, as a manifestation of our love for God.

Augustine applies these theological principles to our personal relationships. At one point in the *Confessions*, we find him grieving the death of an absent friend. Everything that he used to love has become hateful because it reminds him of his loss. This experience, he reasons, is an inevitable consequence of directing our love towards perishing, earthly things. Our attachments to fellow human beings and material objects can only bring us true happiness if they bring us closer to God.

The thinking behind Augustine's argument is philosophical, however. Augustine rests his argument on the idea that the sensuous world—like Plato's cave—is an unsatisfying material reflection of the true, immaterial beauty that we find in God. Like Plato, he believes that morality liberates us from our physical desires and attachments, and gives us access to an immaterial ideal that is universal and eternal. The psychology of this is compelling: if we choose to love God, he suggests, we can never lose what we love.

In the *City of God*, Augustine distinguishes between the earthly city and the Godly city. The earthly city—pagan Rome—lives in accordance with our fallen nature. It rejoices in power and domination; it loves itself in the flesh, to the contempt of God, and tries to establish moral peace through fallible political means. The "pilgrim" city of God glorifies God, to the contempt of the flesh. It does not aim at domination; it loves neighbor and enemy; it aims at good works and prayer, and relies on religion for its moral foundations. The earthly city may enforce a moral code but it is to no avail, and the theological point is that morality is the preserve of religion. Augustine is adamant that virtue without God is a manifestation of pride, the worst human sin, for it presupposes a rejection of God, on whom we are utterly dependent. This view gives us a good sense of the strength of the religious fervor that swept through Europe with the Christian conversions.

The importance of Augustine's work in practical ethics derives from the role he played in establishing the theoretical framework in which we now see ethical issues. Although faith is a requirement of being saved, it is only "a preliminary condition," and the eternal life promised by the Church is only awarded to those who have earned it through merit.

This merit is moral, and consists of works of love, such as almsgiving, and requires penance for our sins.

Augustine accordingly makes moral goodness the focus of human teleology—the purpose of human life—and focuses intensely on the internal and subjective aspects of our conduct. The individualism in this view sets the stage for the modern development of ethics. Many of the elements in his ethical scheme still inform our thinking. There is, for example, "a scale of sins." He also sees God as chiefly forgiving—if we repent, our sins can and will be forgiven, an idea that has naturally entered into popular thinking. Augustine also probes the nature of evil. Metaphysically, like Plotinus, he argues that evil is an absence of good and does not exist in its own right (the Manichean view). In the pear tree story in *Confessions*, he concludes that wrongful acts are intoxicating because they flatter our pride, implicitly putting ourselves above God. The major difference between Augustine's views and the modern view lies in the fact that he still sees evil as an external force, personified in the devil, which exists in his own right. As a result, sin results from our failure to seek divine assistance in resisting it—and implicitly from a lack of faith—rather than from evil intention.

In his later work, Augustine emphasizes the need for grace. Because we have been tainted by original sin, morality requires a movement of the will which is impossible without Divine help. This idea was influential during the Protestant reformation and had a major impact on philosophers like Immanuel Kant.

The first reading contains brief excerpts from the *Confessions*, which give the reader a good sense of the tone of the book. The second reading is from the *Enchiridion* and briefly discusses some of the more technical features of Augustine's moral theory.

READING 20A

Augustine, *The Confessions*[1]

(397–400)

Book Two

IV. [THE PEAR TREE]

Your law, O Lord, punishes theft; and this law is so written in the hearts of men that not even the breaking of it blots it out: for no thief bears calmly being stolen from—not even if he is rich and the other steals through want. Yet I chose to steal, and not because want drove me to it—unless the want was a want of justice . . . For I stole things which I already had in plenty and of better quality. Nor had

---

1 Augustine, *The Confessions* (397–400), from F.J. Sheed, trans., *The Confessions of St. Augustine* (New York: Sheed & Ward, 1942).

I any desire to enjoy the things I stole, [and simply enjoyed] the stealing of them and the sin. There was a pear tree near our vineyard, heavy with fruit, but fruit that was not particularly tempting either to look at or to taste. [I went out with a] group of young blackguards[1] . . . to knock down the pears and carry them off late one night. For it was our bad habit to carry on our games in the streets till very late. We carried off an immense load of pears, not to eat—for we barely tasted them before throwing them to the hogs. Our only pleasure in doing it was that it was forbidden. Such was my heart, O God, such was my heart; . . . Let that heart now tell You what it sought when I was thus evil for no [purpose], having no cause for wrongdoing save my wrongness. The malice of the act was base and [therefore] I loved it—that is to say I loved my own undoing, I loved the evil in me—not the thing for which I did the evil, [but the evil itself. Thus was] my soul . . . depraved . . .

Book Three

I. [CARTHAGE]

I came to Carthage, where a cauldron of illicit loves leapt and boiled about me. I was not yet in love, but I was in love with love, and . . . I sought some object to love, since I was thus in love with loving; . . . For within I was hungry, all for the want of that spiritual food which is Thyself, my God; . . . I had no desire whatever for incorruptible food, not because I had it in abundance but [because] the emptier I was, the more I hated the thought of it. Because of all this my soul was sick, and broke out in sores, whose itch I agonized to scratch with the rub of carnal things . . .

Thus I polluted the stream of friendship with the filth of unclean desire and sullied its limpidity with the hell of lust. . . . And I did fall in love [and

consummate my love,] simply from wanting to. . . . [and] was scourged with the red hot rods of jealousy, with suspicions and fears and tempers and quarrels.

II. [STAGE PLAYS]

I developed a passion for stage plays, with the mirror they held up to my own miseries and the fuel they poured on my flame. How is it that a man wants to be made sad by the sight of tragic sufferings that he could not bear in his own person? Yet the spectator does want to feel sorrow, and it is actually his feeling of sorrow that he enjoys. Surely this is the most wretched lunacy? For the more a man feels such sufferings in himself, the more he is moved by the sight of them on the stage. . . .

[In the days] when I went to the theatres I was glad with lovers when they sinfully enjoyed each other . . . and when they lost each other I was sad for them . . . But today I have more pity for the sinner getting enjoyment from his sin than when he suffers torment from the loss of pleasure which is ultimately destructive . . .

. . . In my wretchedness I loved to be made sad and sought for things to be sad about: and in the misery of others—though fictitious and only on the stage—the more my tears were set to flowing, the more pleasure did I get from the drama . . . There I was, a wretched sheep strayed from Your fold and impatient of the Shepherd: what wonder that I became infected with a foul [spiritual] disease? That is why I loved those sorrows—not that I wanted them to bite too deep (for I had no wish to suffer the sorrows I loved to look upon), but simply to scratch the surface of my heart as I saw them on the stage: yet, as if they had been fingernails, their scratching was followed by swelling and inflammation and sores with pus flowing. Such was my life; but was that a life, my God?

---

1 An old-fashioned term for scoundrels.

III. [THE OVERTURNERS[1]]

... I wasted myself in baseness, pursuing a sacrilegious curiosity which led me ... to the ... deceiving service of devils ... For I dared so far one day within the walls of Your church ... to desire and carry out an act worthy of the fruits of death....

Those of my occupations at that time which were held as reputable were directed towards the study of the law, in which I meant to excel—and the less honest I was, the more famous I should be. The very limit of human blindness is to glory in being blind. By this time I was a leader in the School of Rhetoric and I enjoyed this high station and was arrogant and swollen with importance: though You know, O Lord, that I ... had no share in the riotousness of [those students called] the *eversores*—the Overturners ... Yet I was much in their company and much ashamed of the sense of shame that kept me from being like them.... [T]hough I abominated the acts that were their specialty—as when they made a butt of some hapless newcomer, assailing him with really cruel mockery for no reason whatever, save the malicious pleasure they got from it.... They were rightly called Overturners, since they had themselves been first overturned and perverted, tricked by those same devils who were secretly mocking them ...

IV. [THE PHILOSOPHICAL PURSUIT OF WISDOM]

With these men as companions of my immaturity, I was studying the books of eloquence; for in eloquence it was my ambition to shine ... Following the normal order of study I had come to a book ... [which] contains an exhortation to philosophy.[2] Quite definitely it changed the direction of my mind, ... gave me a new purpose and ambition. Suddenly all the vanity I had hoped in I saw as worthless, and with an incredible intensity of desire I longed after immortal wisdom. [Thus,] I had begun that journey upwards by which I was to return to You....

For with You is wisdom. Now love of wisdom is what is meant by the Greek word philosophy, and it was to philosophy that that book set me so ardently. There are those who seduce men's minds by philosophy, colouring and covering their errors with its great and fine and honourable name ... *Beware*[3] *lest any man cheat you by philosophy, and vain deceits; according to the tradition of men, according to the elements of the world, and not according to Christ* ... But the one thing that delighted me in Cicero's exhortation was that I should love, and seek, and win, and hold, and embrace, not this or that philosophical school but Wisdom itself, whatever it might be. The book excited and inflamed me; in my ardour the only thing I found lacking was that the name of Christ was not there....

V. [THE NATURE OF SCRIPTURE]

So [then] I resolved to make some study of the Sacred Scriptures and find what kind of books they were. But what I came upon was something not grasped by the proud, ... something utterly humble in the hearing but sublime in the doing, and shrouded deep in mystery. And I was not of the nature to enter into it or bend my neck to follow it. When I first read those Scriptures, ... they seemed to me unworthy to be compared with the majesty of Cicero....

VI. [THE MANICHEANS]

... [Later I fell in with the Manicheans, who synthesized Christian teachings and classical wisdom, and taught that evil and good were rival principles.] They

---

1   I.e., those who overturn a boat, throwing its passengers into the sea.
2   The book is Cicero's *Hortensius*, or *On Philosophy*.
3   As Paul advises in Colossians 2:8.

cried out "Truth, truth"; they were forever uttering the word to me, but the thing was nowhere in them…

Book Six

VI. [THE BEGGAR]

I was all hot for honours, money, marriage: and…suffered most bitter disappointments…I was in utter misery and…one day…I was preparing an oration in praise of the Emperor in which I was to utter any number of lies to win the applause of people who knew they were lies. My heart was much wrought upon by the shame of this…when I noticed a beggar. He was jesting and laughing and I imagine more than a little drunk. I fell into gloom and spoke to the friends who were with me about the endless sorrows that our own insanity brings us: for here were we striving away…and with all our striving, our one aim was to arrive at some sort of happiness without care: the beggar had [already] reached the same goal, before us, and we might quite well never reach it at all.…

Let my soul pay no heed to those who would say: "It makes a difference what one is happy about. The beggar found joy in his drunkenness, you sought joy in glory." But what glory, Lord? A glory not in You. For my glory was no truer than his joy, and it turned my head even more.…

Book Eight

XII. [MY CONVERSION]

When my most searching scrutiny[1] had drawn up all my vileness…and heaped it in my heart's sight,…a mighty storm arose in me, bringing a mighty rain of tears.… [I left my friend Alypius and] I flung myself down somehow under a certain fig tree…

[I said much, and complained, asking for an end to my uncleanness.] And suddenly I heard a [child's] voice from some nearby house,…a sort of sing-song, repeated again and again, "Take and read, take and read." I ceased weeping and immediately began to search my mind most carefully as to whether children were accustomed to chant these words in any kind of game, and I could not remember that I had ever heard any such thing. Damming back the…tears, I arose, interpreting the incident as quite certainly a divine command to open my book of Scripture and read the passage at which I should open. For…I had been told [that Saint] Antony…[heard:] *Go, sell what [you have] and give to the poor and [you shall] have treasure in heaven; and come follow Me.*[2]…So I was moved to return to the place where Alypius was sitting,…[where I had left the Apostle's book.] I snatched it up, opened it and in silence read the passage upon which my eyes first fell: *Not in rioting and drunkenness, not in chambering and impurities, not in contention and envy, but put [yourself] on the Lord Jesus Christ and make not provision for the flesh in its concupiscences.*[3]…I had no wish to read further, and no need. For in that instant, with the very ending of the sentence, it was as though a light of utter confidence shone in all my heart, and all the darkness of uncertainty vanished away.…

---

1 Augustine is examining his conscience.
2 The italicized reference is to Matthew 19:21.
3 Sinful lusts. The passage is from Paul's Letter to the Romans 13:1.

Augustine of Hippo, *The Enchiridion on Faith, Hope and Love*[1]

(421)

XI. What Is Called Evil in the Universe Is but the Absence of Good

And in the universe, even that which is called evil,... enhances our admiration of the good... For what is that which we call evil but the absence of good? In the bodies of animals, disease and wounds mean nothing but the absence of health; for when a cure is effected, that does not mean that the evils which were present—namely, the diseases and wounds—go away from the body and dwell elsewhere: they altogether cease to exist; for the wound or disease is not a substance, but a defect in the fleshly substance... [an accident, a privation of the good called health.]... Just in the same way, what are called vices in the soul are nothing but privations of natural good. And... when they cease to exist in the healthy soul, they cannot exist anywhere else.

XII. All Beings Were Made Good, but... Are Liable to Corruption

All things that exist,... seeing that the Creator of them all is supremely good, are themselves good. But because they are not, like their Creator, supremely and unchangeably good, their good may be diminished and increased. [It follows that] for good to be diminished is an evil, although, however much it may be diminished, it is necessary, if the being is to continue, that some good should remain to constitute the being....[2] Therefore, so long as a being is in process of corruption, there is in it some good

of which it is being deprived... Wherefore corruption can consume the good only by consuming the being....

XIII.... an Evil Man Is an Evil Good

... From all this we arrive at the curious result:... [for] when we say that a faulty being is an evil being, we just seem to [be saying] that what is good is evil,... [which] seems to be a contradiction... [And to put it another way:] if a man is a good thing because he is a being, what is an evil man but an evil good? [Still], when we accurately distinguish these two things, we find that it is not because he is a man that he is an evil, or because he is wicked that he is a good; but that he is a good because he is a man, and an evil because he is wicked....

XVIII. It Is Never Allowable to Tell a Lie ...

... [We must now consider a more practical question:] whether at any time it can become the duty of a good man to tell a lie? For some go so far as to contend that there are occasions on which it is a good and pious work to commit perjury even... To me, however, it seems certain that every lie is a sin, though it makes a great difference with what intention and on what subject one lies. For the sin of the man who tells a lie to help another is not so heinous as that of the man who tells a lie to injure another... No one, of course, is to be condemned as a liar who says what is false, believing

---

1 Augustine, *The Enchiridion on Faith, Hope and Love*, from *A Select Library of the Nicene and Post-Nicene Fathers: Series I, Volume III*, ed. Philip Schaff, trans. Professor J.F. Shaw (Buffalo: The Christian Literature Company, 1887).

2 The "being" refers to the existence a thing has while it still exists or 'is.'

it to be true, because such a one does not consciously deceive, but rather is himself deceived. And, on the same principle, a man is not to be accused of lying, though he may sometimes be open to the charge of rashness, if through carelessness he takes up what is false and holds it as true; but, on the other hand, the man who says what is true, believing it to be false, is, so far as his own consciousness is concerned, a liar....

XXII. A Lie Is Not Allowable, Even to Save Another from Injury

... Now it is evident that speech was given to man, not that men might therewith deceive one another, but that one man might make known his thoughts to another. To use speech, then, for the purpose of deception, and not for its appointed end, is a sin. Nor are we to suppose that there is any lie that is not a sin, because it is sometimes possible, by telling a lie, to do service to another. For it is possible to do this by theft also, as when we steal from a rich man who never feels the loss, to give to a poor man who is sensibly benefited by what he gets.... It cannot be denied that they have attained a very high standard of goodness who never lie except to save a man from injury; but in the case of men who have reached this standard, it is not the deceit, but their good intention, that is justly praised, and sometimes even rewarded....

LXII. By the Sacrifice of Christ ... Peace Is Made between Earth and Heaven

And, of course, the holy angels, taught by God, ... know how great a number of the human race are to ... fill up the full count of their citizenship [because, literally, some of those who are saved will replace the fallen angels, who had—as St. Antony said—become devils, and prompted men to sin.] ... And thus, through that single sacrifice in which the Mediator[1] was offered up, ... heavenly things are brought into peace with earthly things, and earthly things with heavenly....

LXVII. Faith without Works ... Cannot Save a Man

[Now some have believed that those] who have been baptized in the Church..., though they should live in the grossest sin,... shall be saved by fire: that is, that although they shall suffer a punishment by fire, lasting for a time proportionate to the magnitude of their crimes and misdeeds, they shall not be punished with everlasting fire.... [But] Holy Scripture, when consulted, gives a very different answer.... [And the faith which saves us is that which the Apostle Paul] describes when he says: "For in Jesus Christ neither circumcision [avails] anything, nor uncircumcision, but faith which [works] by love."[2] But if [this so-called faith works] evil, and not good, then without doubt, as the Apostle James says, "it is dead in itself."[3] The same apostle says again, "What [does] it profit, my [brothers], though a man say he [has] faith, and have not works? Can faith save him?"[4] And [consider that] if a wicked man shall be saved by fire on account of his faith alone, ... that must be false which Paul ... says in another place: "Be not deceived: neither fornicators, nor idolaters, nor adulterers, nor effeminate, nor abusers of themselves with mankind,[5] nor thieves, nor covetous, nor drunkards, nor revil-

---

1 I.e., Christ Jesus.
2 Galatians 5:6.
3 James 2:17.
4 James 2:14.
5 This passage is often interpreted as including all male homosexuals among the condemned, but some commentators regard this as the result of a mistranslation.

ers, nor extortioners, shall inherit the kingdom of God."[1]...

LXIX. It Is Not Impossible That Some Believers May Pass through a Purgatorial Fire in the Future Life

... [It is nevertheless possible that] some believers shall pass through a kind of purgatorial fire, and in proportion as they have loved with more or less devotion the goods that perish, be less or more quickly delivered from it. This cannot, however, be the case of any of those of whom [Paul] said, that they "shall not inherit the kingdom of God," unless after suitable repentance their sins be forgiven them. When I say "suitable," I mean that they are not to be unfruitful in almsgiving; for Holy Scripture lays so much stress on this virtue, that our Lord tells us beforehand, that [it is almsgiving that will divide the saved and the damned, at the last judgement]..., when He shall say to the former, "Come, [you] blessed of my Father, inherit the kingdom," and to the latter, "Depart from me, [you] cursed, into everlasting fire."[2]

LXXIII. The Greatest of All Alms Is...to Love Our Enemies

[Now no alms are] greater than to forgive from the heart a sin that has been committed against us. For it is a comparatively small thing to wish well to, or even to do good to, a man who has done no evil to you. It is a much higher thing, and is the result of the most exalted goodness, to love your enemy,...and when you have the opportunity, to do good to, the man who wishes you ill, and, when he can, does you harm. This is to obey the command of God: "Love your enemies, do good to them that hate you, and pray for them which persecute you."[3] But seeing that this is a frame of mind only reached by the perfect sons of God,...[it is enough] if a man, though he has not yet attained to loving his enemy, yet, when asked by one who has sinned against him to forgive his sin, does forgive him from his heart....

LXXIV. God Does Not Pardon the Sins of Those Who Do Not from the Heart Forgive Others

Now,...the man who does not from his heart forgive him who repents of his sin, and asks forgiveness, need not suppose that his own sins are forgiven of God....

CV. Man Was So Created as to Be Able to Choose Either Good or Evil: In the Future Life, the Choice of Evil Will Be Impossible

Now it was expedient that man should be at first so created, as to have it in his power both to will what was right and to will what was wrong; [for he will be rewarded if he wills the former, and punished if he wills the latter.] But in the [life after death] it shall not be in his power to will evil; and yet this will constitute no restriction on the freedom of his will.... [This is because it was God's plan to show how good a rational being is] who is able even to refrain from sin, and yet how much better is one who cannot sin at all...

CXI. After the Resurrection There Shall Be Two Distinct Kingdoms...

After the resurrection,...when the final, universal judgment has been completed, two groups of citizens, one Christ's, the other the devil's, shall have

---

1 1 Corinthians 6:9–10.

2 A reference to Jesus's parable about the final judgment found in the gospel of Matthew 25:31–46.

3 Matthew 5:44.

fixed lots; one consisting of the good, the other of the bad—both, however, consisting of angels and men. The former shall have no [desire], the latter no power, to sin...; but the former shall live truly and happily in eternal life, the latter shall [have] a miserable existence in eternal death without the power of dying; for both shall be without end....

CXXI. Love Is the End of All the Commandments, and God Himself Is Love

All the commandments of God...are embraced in love, of which the apostle says: "Now the end of the commandment is charity, out of a pure heart, and of a good conscience, and of faith unfeigned."[1] Thus the end of every commandment is charity, that is, every commandment has love for its aim. But whatever is done either through fear of punishment or from some other carnal motive, and has not for its principle that love which the Spirit of God sheds abroad in the heart, is not done as it ought to be done, however it may appear to men. For this love embraces both the love of God and the love of our neighbor, and "on these two commandments hang all the law and the prophets,"...Wherefore, all God's commandments, one of which is, "[You shall] not commit adultery,"...are rightly carried out only when the motive principle of action is the love of God, and the love of our neighbor in God....

Questions

1. What is evil, in Augustine's view? Compare his view with that of another philosopher.
2. Discuss the role of original sin and grace in Augustine's work. Refer to the story of the pear tree, or other examples from the readings, or your own life.
3. Augustine rejected the idea that knowledge is sufficient to overcome our immoral desires. Compare his views with those of Plato, or another ancient philosopher.
4. Augustine believed that willing and intention determine the morality of our actions. It follows that we are just as guilty, even if we do not commit the evil act. Do you agree? Is this in keeping with earlier views?
5. In *De mendacio*, Augustine mentions a deceitful person who knows a third person will not believe him. He accordingly tells the third person the truth, but only because he knows that it will lead him to believe a falsehood. Has this person lied? Discuss.
6. Augustine thinks morality must be rooted in religion and faith in God. Do you agree with this view? Why, why not?
7. Like the desert fathers, Augustine believed that faith in God is not enough. We have to earn a place in heaven, morally, through meritorious acts. What do you think of this scheme? Is there something right in it, or not?

Suggested Readings

There is no collection of Augustine's complete works, and students should begin with individual translations, fully aware that Augustine's rhetorical Latin style may be an obstacle for contemporary readers. Maria Boulding has an elegant and readable translation of the

---

1 1 Timothy 1:5.

Confessions with Vintage Books (1998) and New City Press (2001). There are countless other translations. The *Enchiridion* provides the most convenient summary of his ethical and theological opinions, which cannot be separated. His longer work, the *City of God* (*De Civitate Dei*), is available online, along with the *Confessions* and other works, at the Liberty Fund and newadvent.org.

The basic sources on Augustine's ethics include James I. Conway, "Neoplatonism and the Ethics of St. Augustine" (1947), William Werpehowski, "The Ethics of St. Augustine" (1992), and Bonnie Kent, "Augustine's Ethics" (2001).

For historical and comparative sources, see the appendix by Adolph von Harnack in the *Enchiridion*, trans. J.B. Shaw (1961, 1996) and Ann A. Pang-White, "The Fall of Humanity: Weakness of the Will and Moral Responsibility in the Later Augustine" (2000). L.E. Bacigalupo has commented on Augustine's reaction to Skepticism; Sarah Catherine Byers has discussed his debt to Stoicism.

On other issues, see Tamer Nawar, "Augustine on the Dangers of Friendship" (2015), and David Decosimo, "Just Lies: Finding Augustine's Ethics of Public Lying in His Treatments of Lying and Killing" (2010).

Chapter 21

Abelard and Heloise

Peter Abelard (Abailard or Abaelard, 1079–1142) was born near Nantes, in France. A brilliant student, he gave up his inheritance and a knighthood in order to become a "wandering scholar" and study philosophy. One of the leading figures that he studied under was William of Champeaux, whom he later debated, arguing against the existence of universals. After some years of study, Abelard became a celebrated teacher in Paris and was instrumental in founding the University of Paris.

Most of our knowledge of Abelard's life comes from his *Historia Calamitatum* (history of calamity), a bitter autobiography, which recounts the story of Abelard and Héloïse d'Argenteuil (c. 1098–1164), the niece of Canon Fulbert, a clergyman in the cathedral of Paris. Having decided to seduce her, Abelard convinced her uncle to take him into their household as a tutor. The inevitable occurred, and when Heloise became pregnant and had a son, Astrolabe, the two were secretly married. This was not enough to appease her uncle and family, who hired thugs who broke into Abelard's room at night and savagely castrated him. Abelard and Heloise then separated—he to a monastery and she to a convent.

Although Heloise was never a professional philosopher, she was a well-educated, eloquent, and capable woman who became, eventually, the abbess of an important convent and oratory, originally founded by Abelard. The letters exchanged between Abelard and Heloise provide a more intimate view of their romantic attachment. Heloise's urgent, introspective, and cultivated contribution to the exchanges produced a remarkable literary monument. After Heloise died, her remains were interred with those of Abelard.

Following his disastrous love affair with Heloise, Abelard's life was marked by querulous relations with his colleagues and superiors. While residing in the Monastery of Saint Denis, he quarreled with his fellow monks but wrote an influential theological work, *Sic et non* (*Yes and No*), which contains a series of 158 theological questions, each followed by a list of quotations that favor a positive and then a negative answer to the question. This format proved influential and was used by, among others, Thomas Aquinas in writing his *Summa Theologiae*.

When Abelard's theological writings were condemned by the church, he sought a life of contemplation in the wilderness but was besieged with students who entreated him to return to teaching. He then became an abbot, but incurred the anger of the monks who, we are told, repeatedly tried to poison him. Finally, he took up residence in a monastery near

Paris and resumed teaching, with great success. His penchant for controversy reasserted itself, however, and in the course of a dispute with Bernard of Clairvaux, his theological work was condemned a second time.

Abelard wrote important works in metaphysics, logic, dialectic, theology, and ethics. He is considered a forerunner of the Scholastics. Ramsay McCallum has argued that his moral views are a product of his position on universals. Realists, like William of Champeaux, took the position that universals—the quality that makes every human being a human, or that makes every green thing green, as examples—actually exist. This goes back to Plato's view that there is a universal form of the human being, in which every particular human being participates.

Abelard was a nominalist, however, who held that the universal is merely an idea, and that nothing is real and existent except particulars. This, McCallum writes, has moral implications: "the view that man is a free individual, rationally and morally autonomous, untrammeled by an inherent relation to general humanity, is at the root of all his thinking. For him the particular thing is the reality, and the individual man is the human centre of moral being and activity."

Abelard's major work in moral philosophy is *Ethica*: *Scito te ipsum* or, in English, the *Ethics: Know Thyself*. The subtitle is significant, since Abelard redirects the ethical inquiry inwards and argues that it is our subjective state which determines the wrongfulness of our actions. Abelard concludes that God does not condemn sin because our actions are good or bad in themselves, but because we have willingly consented to temptation, instead of resisting it; then we are in contempt of God.

Abelard's position is a departure from Augustine, who believed that we share in the original sin (or guilt, *culpa*) of Adam, which renders us incapable of acting morally without divine grace. We sin because we have failed to ask for God's grace. Abelard rejected this view, arguing that we share in Adam's punishment (*poena*), but not his guilt. The problem with Augustine's view, on Abelard's account, is that it minimizes the exercise of free will and the role of reason, which informs us about what is good and controls the will. It is the internal nature of our actions that is fundamental in salvation, rather than grace. Abelard also distances the devil from our evil actions, arguing that the devil acts indirectly, by placing things which attract us in our way. This ultimately removes the devil from the theater in which we commit evil acts.

It is notable that Abelard's position stands in opposition to the much earlier and ancient views that were fundamentally concerned with the fact of the offence. Prior to Abelard, it was believed that the gravity of a sin was determined by its external nature. This changes after Abelard, who brings in a subjective standard. Sin is "criminous" if it is deliberate and committed in full knowledge of our contempt of God. Critics have argued that Abelard's intentionalism fails to account for the physical reality of immoral acts.

There are many other modern elements in Abelard's work, such as his insistence that pleasure is not in itself sinful. The earlier view was that an illicit desire for sexual gratification was sinful. Abelard rejected this: it was the consent to such a desire that is sinful. Theologically, this left him arguing that the desire to sleep with your neighbor's wife is not in itself sinful; what is sinful is that you yield to it.

Abelard's contemporaries were scandalized by his views, which undermined the authority of the Church to determine what was wrong and seemed to give individuals a radical degree of freedom subject only to the power of reason. Abelard also argued that penance was a personal matter between the individual and God. This "moral individualism" played a decisive philosophical role in the Protestant Revolution, and prefigures the liberal tradition in ethics, which emphasizes the role of choice in morality.

Abelard's account of intention misses many of the finer distinctions that were subsequently brought into the moral analysis. He deals deftly, however, with many of the issues that have made their way into the analysis of moral blameworthiness in the criminal courts. His work was also significant in the development of the medieval practice of casuistry, which focused the ethical inquiry on the distinctions between particular cases. This analysis has been neglected in philosophy, but foreshadows the development of the common law, which adopts a similar case-by-case approach to the analysis of culpability.

The Abelard reading is from the *Ethics*. The excerpts catch the personal tone of Abelard's writing, provide a synopsis of his theory, canvass a few technicalities, and include a few of the provocative examples he uses to advance the "intentionalist" thesis.

We cannot grasp the intensity of the historic romance between Abelard and Heloise without some knowledge of the letters between them. The second reading includes a brief excerpt from one of Heloise's later letters. In the course of this exchange, Heloise comes across as a deeply compelling and powerfully human figure, whereas Abelard seems cold by comparison. As the wit of one older critic (Henry Adams) has it: Heloise was "by French standards worth at least a dozen Abelards."

READING 21A

Abelard, *Ethica: Scito te ipsum* ("Ethics: Know Thyself")[1]

(1140)

What Is Mental Vice and What Is Properly Said to Be Sin

And so vice is that by which we are made prone to sin, that is, are inclined to consent to what is not fitting so that we either do it or forsake it. Now this consent we properly call sin...For what is that consent unless it is contempt of God and an offence against him? For God cannot be offended against through harm but through contempt. He indeed is that supreme power who is not impaired by any harm but who avenges contempt of himself. And so

---

1 Abelard, *Ethica: Scito te ipsum* ("Know Thyself," published sometime before 1140), from Peter Abelard's *Ethics*, an edition with Introduction, English translation, and Notes by D.E. Luscombe (Oxford: Clarendon Press, 1971).

our sin is contempt of the Creator and to sin is to hold the Creator in contempt, that is, to do by no means on his account what we believe we ought to do for him, or not to forsake on his account what we believe we ought to forsake. So, by defining sin negatively, that is to say, as not doing or not forsaking what is fitting, we plainly show there is no substance of sin; it subsists as not being rather than being, just as if in defining darkness we say it is the absence of light where light used to be.

But perhaps you will say that the will to do a bad deed is also sin and makes us guilty before God, even as the will to do a good deed makes us just…But I say that if we consider this more carefully, our conclusion should be very different from what it seems.… For consider: there is an innocent man whose cruel lord is so burning with rage against him that with a naked sword he chases him for his life. For long that man flees and as far as he can he avoids his own murder; in the end and unwillingly he is forced to kill him lest he be killed by him.[1] Tell me, whoever you are, what bad will be had in doing this. If he wanted to escape death, he wanted to save his own life. But surely this was not a bad will? You say: not this, I think, but the will he had to kill the lord who was chasing him. I reply: that is well and cleverly said if you can show a will in what you claim. But, as has already been said, he did this unwillingly and under compulsion…

… [A]s has already been said, that will is in no way to be derided as bad through which he, as you say, wanted to evade death, not to kill the lord. And yet although he was constrained by fear of death, he did do wrong in consenting to an unjust killing which he should have undergone rather than have inflicted.… And so he wanted, as has been said, to avoid death, not to kill the lord. But because he consented to a killing to which he ought not to have consented, this unjust consent of his which preceded the killing was a sin.…

At any rate such a will which consists in great grief of mind is not, I would say, to be called will but rather suffering. That he wills this on account of that is the equivalent of saying that he endures what he does not will on account of the other things which he desires. Thus the sick man is said to want a cauterization or an operation in order to be healed…So it is evident that sometimes sin is committed entirely without bad will; it is therefore clear from this that what is sin is not to be called will.

Certainly, you will say, that is so where we sin under constraint, but not where we do so willingly, as for instance if we want to commit something which we know should not be done by us at all. There indeed that bad will and the sin seem to be the same. For example, someone sees a woman…and his mind is affected by the pleasure of the flesh, so that he is incited to the baseness of sexual intercourse. Therefore, you say, what else is this will and base desire than sin?…

[But this is not sin.] For he who said:[2] 'Go not after [your] lusts: but turn away from [your] own will,' taught us not to fulfil our lusts, but not to be entirely without them. The former is vicious, but the latter is not possible for our weakness. So sin is not lusting for a woman but consenting to lust; the consent of the will is damnable, but not the will for intercourse.

What we have said with respect to [lechery], let us consider with respect also to gluttony. Someone passes through another man's garden and seeing delightful fruits he falls into longing for them; however, he does not consent to his longing so as to remove something from there by theft or robbery, even though his mind has been incited to great desire by the pleasure of food. But where desire is, there undoubtedly is will.… In fact by the very nature of his infirmity he is compelled to desire what he is not allowed to take without the knowledge or the

---

1 The example is that of a lord being killed by his servant. This was a provocative example since the view in Abelard's time was that the actions of the servant were inexcusable.

2 [Author's Note] *Ecclesiastes* 18:30.

permission of the lord. He represses his desire; he does not extinguish it, but because he is not drawn to consent, he does not incur sin....

It shows, in short, that in such things also the will itself or the desire to do what is unlawful is by no means to be called sin, but rather, as we have stated, the consent itself. The time when we consent to what is unlawful is in fact when we in no way draw back from its accomplishment...Anyone who is found in this disposition incurs the fullness of guilt;...before God the person who to the extent of his power endeavours to achieve this is as guilty as the person who as far as he is able does achieve it—just as if, so the blessed Augustine reminds us,[1] he too had also been caught in the act....

There are people who may be considerably disturbed when they hear us say that the doing of sin adds nothing to the guilt or to damnation before God. They object that in the action of sin a certain pleasure may follow which increases the sin, as in sexual intercourse, or in that eating which we mentioned. They would not in fact say this absurdly if they were to prove that carnal pleasure of this sort is sin and that such a thing cannot be committed except by sinning. If they really admit this, it is definitely not lawful for anyone to have this fleshly pleasure. Therefore, spouses are not immune from sin when they unite in this carnal pleasure allowed to them, nor is he who enjoys the pleasurable consumption of his own fruit....

Yet again they say that marital intercourse and the eating of delicious food are in fact conceded in such a way that the pleasure itself is not conceded; they should be performed wholly without pleasure. But assuredly if this is so, they are allowed to be done in a way in which they cannot be done at all and it was an unreasonable permission which allowed them to be done in a way in which it is certain that

they cannot be done.... It is clear, I think, from all this that no natural pleasure of the flesh should be imputed to sin nor should it be considered a fault for us to have pleasure in something in which when it has happened the feeling of pleasure is unavoidable. For example, if someone compels a religious[2] who is bound in chains to lie between women and if he is brought to pleasure, not to consent, by the softness of the bed and through the contact of the women beside him, who may presume to call this pleasure, made necessary by nature, a fault?...

Moreover, I think everyone knows how often things that should not be done are done without sin, when, that is, they are committed under coercion or through ignorance, as for example if a woman is [forced] to lie with another woman's husband or if a man [who] has been tricked in some way or other sleeps with a woman whom he thought to be his wife.... And so it is not a sin to lust after another's wife or to lie with her but rather to consent to this lust or action. This consent to covetousness the Law calls covetousness when it says:[3] '[You] shall not covet.'... What the Lord said has similarly to be understood:[4] 'Whosoever shall look on a woman to lust after her,' that is, whosoever shall look in such a way as to fall into consent to lust, '[has] already committed adultery in his heart,' although he has not committed the deed of adultery, that is, he is already guilty of sin although he is still without its outcome.

If we carefully consider also all the occasions where actions seem to come under a commandment or a prohibition, these must be taken to refer to the will or to consent to actions rather than to the actions themselves...The Law forbids us to [marry our sisters or to have sexual intercourse with them], but there is no one who can keep this ordinance, since one is often unable to recognize one's sisters—no one, I mean, if the prohibition

---

1 [Author's Note] In *De libero arbitrio* (*On Free Choice*), i.3, n.8.

2 I.e., a monk or other man who has decided to live a celibate life devoted to God.

3 [Author's Note] *Deuteronomy* 5:21.

4 [Author's Note] *Matthew* 5:28.

refers to the act rather than to consent.[1] And so when it happens that someone through ignorance marries his sister, he is not surely the transgressor of an ordinance because he does what the Law has forbidden him to do? He is not a transgressor, you will say, because in acting ignorantly he did not consent to transgression. Therefore, just as he is not to be called a transgressor who does what is forbidden, but he who consents to that which it is evident has been prohibited, so the prohibition is not to be applied to the deed but to the consent, so that when it is said 'do not do this or that' the meaning is 'do not consent to do this or that,' just as if it were said 'do not venture this knowingly.' The blessed Augustine carefully considered this and reduced every commandment or prohibition to charity or cupidity[2] rather than to deeds... It is indeed obvious that works which it is or is not at all fitting to do may be performed as much by good as by bad men who are separated by their intention alone.... For God thinks not of what is done but in what mind it may be done, and the merit or glory of the doer lies in the intention, not in the deed. In fact the same thing is often done by different people, justly by one and wickedly by another, as for example if two men hang a convict, that one out of zeal for justice, this one out of a hatred arising from an old enmity, and although it is the same act of hanging and although they certainly do what it is good to do and what justice requires, yet, through the diversity of their intention, the same thing is done by diverse men, by one badly, by the other well....

That a Work Is Good by Reason of a Good Intention

In fact we say that an intention is good, that is, right in itself, but that an action does not bear anything good in itself but proceeds from a good intention. Whence when the same thing is done by the same man at different times, by the diversity of his intention, however, his action is now said to be good, now bad...

What Is Mental Vice and What Is Properly Said to Be Sin

... Who lastly may not know that what God forbids to be done is sometimes rightly performed or should be done, just as conversely he sometimes ordains some things which, however, it is not at all fitting to do? For consider, we know of some miracles of his that when by them he healed illnesses, he forbade that they should be revealed, as an example, that is, of humility, lest someone who had a similar grace granted to him should perhaps seek prestige. None the less they who had received those benefits did not stop publicizing them in honour, of course, of him who had both worked them and had prohibited their revelation. Of such it was written:[3] 'The more he charged them that they should not tell, so much the more did they publish it,' etc. Surely you will not judge such men guilty of transgression for acting contrary to the command which they had received and for even doing this knowingly? What will excuse them from transgression if not the fact that they did nothing through contempt of him who commanded; they decided to do this in honour of him. Tell me, I ask you, if Christ ordained what should not have been ordained or if they repudiated what should have been kept? What was good to be commanded was

---

1 Abelard has in mind the provocative scenario where a man and sister were separated in childhood and therefore do not know that they are brother and sister when adults.

2 Charity or cupidity are to be understood as referring to intention.

3 [Author's Note] *Mark* 7:36.

not good to be done. You at any rate will reproach the Lord in the case of Abraham, whom at first he commanded to sacrifice his son and later checked from doing so.[1] Surely God did not command well a deed which it was not good to do? For if it was good, how was it later forbidden? If, moreover, the same thing was both good to be commanded and good to be prohibited... you see that the intention of the command alone, not the execution of the deed, excuses God, since he did well to command what is not a good thing to be done. For God did not urge or command this to be done in order that Abraham should sacrifice his son but in order that out of this his obedience and the constancy of his faith or love for him should be very greatly tested and remain to us as an example. And this indeed the Lord himself subsequently avowed openly when he said:[2] 'Now I know that [you fear] the Lord,' as if he were saying expressly: the reason why I instructed you to do what you showed you were ready to do was so that I should make known to others what I myself had known of you before the ages. This intention of God was right in an act which was not right...; and just as the intention excuses him in the one case, so too in this case it excuses those who have not fulfilled the command in practice.[3]...

If therefore we think of deeds rather than the intention, we shall not only see that sometimes there is a will to do something against God's commandment but also that it is done and knowingly so without any guilt of sin. So, when the intention of him to whom the command is made does not differ from the will of the commander, one should not speak of an evil will or an evil action simply because God's commandment is not kept in a deed. Just as intention excuses the commander who commands to be

done what is however not at all fitting to be done, so also the intention of charity excuses him to whom the command is made.

To bring the above together in a brief conclusion, there are four things which we have put forward in order carefully to distinguish them from each other, namely the vice of the mind which makes us prone to sinning and then the sin itself which we fixed in consent to evil or contempt of God, next the will for evil, and [finally] the doing of evil.... When we say that sin or temptation occurs in three ways,[4] namely in suggestion, pleasure, and consent, it should be understood in this sense, that we are often led through these three to the doing of sin. This was the case with our first parents.[5] Persuasion by the devil came first, when he promised immortality for tasting the forbidden tree. Pleasure followed, when the woman, seeing the beautiful fruit and understanding it to be sweet to eat, was seized with what she believed would be the pleasure of the food and kindled a longing for it. Since she ought to have checked her longing in order to keep the command, in consenting she was drawn into sin. And although she ought to have corrected the sin through repentance in order to deserve pardon, she finally completed it in deed. And so she proceeded to carry through the sin in three stages. Likewise we also frequently arrive by these same steps not at sinning but at the carrying through of sin, namely by suggestion, that is, by the encouragement of someone who incites us externally to do something which is not fitting. And if we know that doing this is pleasurable, even before the deed our mind is seized with the pleasure of the deed itself and in the very thought we are tempted through pleasure. When in fact we assent to this pleasure through consent, we

---

1 For this story, see *Genesis* 22:1–19.

2 [Author's Note] *1 Corinthians* 10:13 [Editor's Note: Sic—it should be *Genesis* 22:12.]

3 The two cases being compared are the healed person's disobeying Jesus's prohibition against publicizing their healing (*Mark* 7) and God's commanding Abraham to sacrifice his son (*Genesis* 22).

4 Having explained sin, Abelard turns to the role of temptation in sinning.

5 The reference is to Adam and Eve. For the story of how they were tempted to sin, see *Genesis* 3.

sin. By these three we come at last to the execution of the sin....

Indeed this pleasure, which has become almost necessary,... [is] called by the Apostle human temptation when he says:[1] 'Let no temptation take hold on you, but such as is human. And God is faithful, who will not suffer you to be tempted above that which you are able; but will also make issue with temptation, that you may be able to bear it.' Now, temptation is generally said to be any inclination of the mind, whether a will or consent, to do something which is not fitting. But human temptation, such as carnal concupiscence or the desire for delicious food, is said to be that without which human infirmity can now scarcely or can never survive....

Why Works of Sin Are Punished Rather than Sin Itself

There are also those who are considerably troubled, when they hear us say that a work of sin is not properly called sin or that it does not add anything to increase a sin, as to why a heavier satisfaction is imposed on penitents for doing a deed than for being guilty of a fault. To these I answer first: why do they not chiefly wonder about the fact that sometimes a large penalty of satisfaction is instituted where no fault has occurred? And why ought we sometimes to punish those whom we know to be innocent? For, consider, some poor woman has a suckling baby and lacks clothing adequate to provide for the little one in the cradle and for herself. And so, stirred by pity for the baby she takes him to herself to keep him warm with her own rags, and finally in her weakness overcome by the force of nature, she unavoidably smothers the one she clasps with the utmost love.[2]... [W]hen she comes before the bishop for satisfaction, a heavy punishment is imposed upon her, not for the fault which she committed but so that subsequently she or other women should be rendered more cautious in providing for such things.... Indeed God alone... considers not so much what is done as in what mind it may be done... For he particularly sees... where no man sees, because in punishing sin he considers not the deed but the mind, just as conversely we consider not the mind which we do not see but the deed which we know.[3]...

---

1 [Author's Note] *1 Corinthians* 10:13.

2 I.e., the woman falls asleep and accidentally smothers her child.

3 Abelard goes on to say that the "cure" for sin lies in penitence, which proceeds from "the love of God rather than from fear." We are therefore sorry that we have offended him. God accepts penitence "more because he is good than because he is just."

Heloise, *Letters from Heloise*[1]

Letter II

To her Lord, her Father, her Husband, her Brother; his Servant, his Child, his Wife, his Sister, and to express all that is humble, respectful and loving to her Abelard, Heloise writes this.

A CONSOLATORY letter of yours to a friend happened some days since to fall into my hands; my knowledge of the writing and my love of the hand gave me the curiosity to open it.... I flattered myself I might claim a sovereign privilege over everything which came from you. Nor was I scrupulous to break through the rules of good breeding.... But how dear did my curiosity cost me!.... Though length of time ought to have closed up my wounds, yet the seeing them described by your hand was sufficient to make them all open and bleed afresh....

Seneca (with whose writings you made me acquainted), though he was a Stoic, seemed to be so very sensible to this kind of pleasure, that upon opening any letters from Lucilius[2] he imagined he felt the same delight as when they conversed together. I have made it an observation since our absence, that we are much fonder of the pictures of those we love when they are at a great distance than when they are near us.... If a picture, which is but a mute representation of an object, can give such pleasure, what cannot letters inspire? They have souls; they can speak; they have in them all that force which expresses the transports of the heart; they have all the fire of our passions, they can raise them as much as if the persons themselves were present; they have all the tenderness and the delicacy of speech, and sometimes even a boldness of expression beyond it. We may write to each other; so innocent a pleasure is not denied us....

The St. Austins, Tertullians and Jeromes have written to the Eudoxias, Paulas and Melanias.[3]... Can it be criminal for you to imitate St. Jerome and discourse with me concerning the Scriptures; or Tertullian and preach mortification; or St. Austin and explain to me the nature of grace? Why should I alone not reap the advantage of your learning? When you write to me you will write to your wife; marriage has made such a correspondence lawful, and since you can without the least scandal satisfy me, why will you not?... You have been the occasion of all my misfortunes, you therefore must be the instrument of all my comfort....

I have hated myself that I might love you; I came hither[4] to ruin myself in a perpetual imprisonment that I might make you live quietly and at ease. Nothing but virtue, joined to a love perfectly disengaged from the senses, could have produced such effects. Vice never inspires anything like this, it is too much enslaved to the body.... This was my cruel Uncle's notion; he measured my virtue by the frailty of my sex, and thought it was the man and not the person

---

1 *The Love Letters of Abelard and Heloise* (London: J.M. Dent and Co., 1901). Available at http://www.sacred-texts.com/chr/aah/aah00.htm.

2 This is an allusion to Seneca's "Moral Letters to Lucilius." Lucilius was then a Roman official in Sicily. Scholars doubt that there was an actual correspondence between the two and consider the work a fiction.

3 "St. Austin" is St. Augustine. Tertullian (c. 155–c. 240 BCE) was a Church Father of Latin Christianity and Western theology. St. Jerome (347–420 BCE) was a theologian and historian, best known for his translation of the Bible into Latin (known as the Vulgate). Eudoxia, Paula, and Melania are the names of women with whom the three men corresponded, respectively.

4 I.e., to the convent.

I loved. But he has been guilty to no purpose. I love you more than ever; and so revenge myself on him. I will still love you with all the tenderness of my soul till the last moment of my life. If, formerly, my affection for you was not so pure, if in those days both mind and body loved you, I often told you even then that I was more pleased with possessing your heart than with any other happiness, and the man was the thing I least valued in you.

[Remember] the extreme unwillingness I showed to marry you, though I knew that the name of wife was honourable...yet the name of your mistress had greater charms because it was more free. The bonds of matrimony...still bear with them a necessary engagement, and I was very unwilling to be necessitated to love.... I despised the name of wife that I might live happy with that of mistress.... It was infinitely preferable to me to live with Abelard as his mistress than with any other as Empress of the World.... Riches and pomp are not the charm of love. True tenderness makes us separate the lover from all that is external to him, and setting aside his position, fortune or employments, consider him merely as himself....

If there is anything that may properly be called happiness here below, I am persuaded it is the union of two persons who love each other with perfect liberty, who are united by a secret inclination, and satisfied with each other's merits....

Irresolute as I am I still love you, and yet I must hope for nothing. I have renounced life, and stripped myself of everything, but I find I neither have nor can renounce my Abelard. Though I have lost my lover I still preserve my love. O vows! O convent! I have not lost my humanity under your inexorable discipline! You have not turned me to marble by changing my habit; my heart is not hardened by my imprisonment; I am still sensible to what has touched me, though, alas! I ought not to be!...

... Without changing the ardor of our affections let us change their objects; let us...sing hymns; let us lift up our hearts to God and have no transports but for His glory!...Till that moment of grace arrives,[1] O think of me—do not forget me—remember my love and fidelity and constancy: love me as your mistress, cherish me as your child, your sister, your wife! Remember I still love you, and yet strive to avoid loving you. What a terrible saying is this! I shake with horror, and my heart revolts against what I say. I shall blot all my paper with tears. I end my long letter wishing you, if you desire it (would to Heaven I could!), forever adieu!

Questions

1. There is a good argument that the focus of the tribal and ancient views of morality was on the evil act. How does Abelard's view of morality differ? Cite other philosophers or readings in your answer.

2. Compare Abelard, Augustine, Maimonides, and Al-Ghazālī on their respective conceptions of sin.

3. The idea of consent was important to the medievals because we frequently want to do things that we know are wrong. It is giving in to the temptation, therefore, that is crucial. Is this the proper way to look at it? Include at least one philosopher in your answer.

4. Abelard's understanding of morality and intention eventually made its way into the

---

1 I.e., death.

idea of a crime, which requires voluntariness, an evil act, and evil intention. So is drunkenness a defense, on Abelard's account? Use examples.

5. Evaluate Abelard's affair with Heloise according to his own theory of morality. Assume they both consented. How is his account different from modern liberalism?

6. Do you agree with Heloise's conception of love? Why or why not?

7. Is writing letters an aspect of the good life, of charity, or even of moral duty? Do you write letters? Should you? How do letters and text messaging compare? Phone calls? Skypes? Sending photos? Are these ways of communicating the same or different?

Suggested Readings

There is no satisfactory collection of Abelard's original writings, which are in Latin and extend over many areas outside ethics. There are a number of translations of the *Ethics*. We have used the D.E. Luscombe translation (1971) as found in *Basic Issues in Medieval Philosophy*, second edition (2006). James Ramsay McCallum (*Abailard's Ethics*, 1935) is the first translation in English. Paul Vincent Spade's translation (*Peter Abelard: Ethical Writings*, 1995) includes a translation of Abelard's *Dialogue of a Philosopher with a Jew and a Christian*. E.R. Fairweather's *A Scholastic Miscellany* (1995) includes Abelard's commentary on St. Paul's Epistles to the Romans.

For general sources on Abelard, see Michael Clanchy, *Abelard: A Medieval Life* (1997), and John Marenbon, *The Philosophy of Peter Abelard* (1997). There is also *The Cambridge Companion to Peter Abelard* (2004).

For more specific sources, see Jean Porter, "Responsibility, Passion, and Sin: A Reassessment of Abelard's Ethics" (2000); Ian Wilks, "The Role of Virtue Theory and Natural Law in Abelard's Ethical Writings" (1997); Jimmy José Washburn, "The Role of Reason in Morality: The Case of Abelard's Ethics" (2010); and Peter King, "Abelard's Intentionalist Ethics" (1995). Virpi Mäkinen and Heikki Pihlajamäki argue that Abelard's ethical individualism was fundamental to the development of criminal responsibility in "The Individualization of Crime in Medieval Canon Law" (2004).

The situation with respect to Abelard's and Heloise's letters is somewhat complicated. While almost every scholar accepts that the later letters are authentic, recent scholarship has uncovered a series of earlier letters, entitled *Epistolae duorum amantium* (*Letters of Two Lovers*) which have been identified with the couple. Penguin Classics has put out a compilation of the later correspondence: *The Letters of Abelard and Heloise* (2004), edited with an introduction by Michael Clanchy and translated by Betty Radice. More recently, Clarendon Press (Oxford) has published a revised translation in a bilingual edition with a long introduction by noted scholar David Luscombe: *The Letter Collection of Peter Abelard and Heloise* (2013). There are 1901 and 1785 translations available online at sacred-texts.com and Gutenberg.org. For a fresh translation of the more recently discovered collection of 116 letters, see *Making Love in the Twelfth Century, "Letters of Two Lovers" in Context* by Barbara Newman (Princeton, 2016).

Constant Mews has discussed the influence of Heloise on Abelard's ethics in *Abelard and Heloise* (2005). Margaret Cameron responds in "Abelard (and Heloise?) on Intention" (2007). See also Sandrine Berges, "Rethinking Twelfth Century Ethics: The Contribution of Heloise" (2013).

Chapter 22

Medieval Mysticism

There are probably mystics in every religious tradition. The mystic, as a prophet or seer, played a decisive role in tribal and earlier societies, which continued in ancient times. Rome did not make important decisions without consulting the augurs—religious fortune-tellers. At the end of the Hellenistic period, a strong anti-materialism arose, which reached its height in the mysticism in the medieval Christian tradition. The religious sources behind such a development came from the monastic tradition; the philosophical sources can be found primarily in Neo-Platonism.

The seminal figure in the written tradition is Dionysius the Areopagite (c. 500), whose writing was translated into Latin by John Scotus Erigena in the ninth century under the title *Mystica Theologia* ("Mystical Theology") and widely disseminated. There were also indigenous works, like *The Cloud of Unknowing* and Richard of St. Victor's *Benjamin Minor*. It is notable that by the fourteenth century there is a definite separation between the material and spiritual realms. Mystical experience has become "ghostly" and more abstract, and has lost its "bodily" guise.

Although the reasons for the rise in mysticism is a matter of speculation, it may be related to social and political unrest. The "high" Middle Ages in Europe (1100–1450) was a time of escalating change. The feudal system was replaced by early capitalism, urbanization, and a new bourgeoisie. It seems clear that one of the principal responses to these changes was an intensification of religious and spiritual belief, which found an outlet in mysticism.

The gender of medieval mysticism is also significant. Although many of the prominent mystics—Bernard of Clairvaux, Francis of Assisi, and even Thomas Aquinas—were men, it is notable that medieval mysticism was predominantly female. Some of the celebrated mystics were Saint Catherine of Siena, Hildegard of Bingen, Clare of Assisi, Beatrijs of Nazareth, Angela of Foligno, and Julian of Norwich. It is evident from the historical record that women had a particular spiritual role in the medieval Church.

There were also demographic factors, however, and women outnumbered men. As a result, they entered into religious life in large numbers, seeking a life outside marriage. This gave rise to lay religious communities, outside the institutional confines of monastic or convent life, which provided women with an independence that was not available to them in larger society. Mystics such as Hadewijch of Antwerp, Mechthild of Magdeburg, and Angela of Foligno were associated with these communities.

The ethics of Christian mysticism raises at least two fundamental issues. The first is metaphysical. The idea that human beings can become one with God is logically and theologically perilous. The exact nature of the mystic's consciousness of God raises religious and psychological questions.

The second issue arises in practical ethics. Mysticism is usually associated with asceticism and a general renunciation of the self and society. The ethics of such a retreat from ordinary life raises serious questions, which are the object of considerable discussion in both the Western and Oriental traditions. In spite of worries about a self-absorbed and self-serving quietism, it is evident that the surrender of the self in medieval mysticism was often associated with heroic acts of altruism, good works, and miraculous interventions. The mystics of the Middle Ages had a social role as savants, prophets, and healers, and were consulted in practical matters.

The first reading is from the letters of St. Catherine of Siena (c. 1347–80), who was born Catherine Benincasa in Siena. Catherine had visions at a young age and rebelled, refusing to speak to her family and conducting many penances. Against the wishes of her family, she became a "Dominican tertiary,"[1] and lived within the home under strict religious rules. At the age of 20, she devoted herself to the sick and needy. In 1370, she was said to have died, only to return to life, hearing the voice of God.

Catherine's reputation grew within the Church, and she attracted many followers. She corresponded with a wide range of people, becoming a confidante and advisor to two Popes. Later, she took up residence in Rome and worked tirelessly to heal the rifts within the Church, which was facing a revolt in the Italian cities. Under the strain of her political duties, and alarmed by the corruption in the Church, she mystically dedicated herself as a sacrifice for the sins of the Church and the Romans.

Many of Catherine's letters were dictated, which may help to account for their vitality. She speaks frequently of "holy desire" and begins letters by saying: "I, Catherine—write to you—with desire." This desire—for holiness and the experience of God—is central to her mystical experience. She also speaks of love: "For nails would not have held God-and-Man fast to the Cross, had love not held Him there."

The second reading is from *The Cloud of Unknowing* (1375), whose author is unknown. He was apparently a cloistered monk, who belonged to an order devoted to the contemplative life. The book is notable for its plain-speaking. Although the author quotes learned sources, like Augustine and Aquinas, he dismisses the idea that the mystical experience can be attained by reason and study.

The mechanism for achieving the mystical experience is the "cloud of forgetting" or unknowing, which leaves the mind of the aspirant empty, but for "a naked intent stretching to God." This is not a passive state but an active state, and requires constant striving,

---

1   A member of the Third Order of St. Dominic, i.e., a lay person living a Christian life with a Dominican spirituality in the secular world.

in which we determinedly empty ourselves of ordinary knowing. We must put everything aside except a certain transcendental consciousness, which, left to itself, will lead us to God without the aid of human thought.

The anonymous medieval author describes mystical experience as a kind of darkness because it cannot be penetrated by reason. It is not an ordinary darkness, however, and Dionysius had earlier described it as a light—but a light which is "dark with excess of light." It is not possible to grasp the conception of God—to capture God in thinking; therefore, the mystic must love what he cannot think.

The Cloud of Unknowing places the highest value on the virtues of humility and charity. Humility teaches us that we are lost and imperfect without God. This knowledge of ourselves has its counterpart, however, in the knowledge of God, which can only be comprehended by the virtue of charity or love. These two virtues combine with the "good will" that is necessary for mystical experience.

The third reading is from the most popular medieval mystical work, *The Imitation of Christ (De Imitatione Christi)*, which is essentially a manual for those seeking a religious life of contemplation. It is now agreed that the book was probably compiled by a monastic, Thomas Haemmerlein (c. 1380–1471), who was also known as Thomas van (or von) Kempen, i.e., Thomas from Kempen, his place of birth (traditionally referred to as "Thomas à Kempis").

Thomas joined the order of the Brothers of Common Life and became a canon (a priest). For most of his long life, he lived at Mount St. Agnes, an Augustinian monastery, near Utrecht. He entered the monastery in 1406 and eventually became the sub-prior, which gave him responsibility for instructing novices. As a result, he wrote a series of booklets, which were eventually collected and published as the *Imitatione*. The book was not intended as an original work and is a compilation from many sources.

Thomas was a member of a movement called the *Devotio Moderna*, started by Gerard Groote, which popularized the contemplation of the "sacred mysteries." His book counsels readers to imitate Christ in their inner lives by withdrawing from the world. This withdrawal was envisaged as an alternative to the active imitation of Christ. In the final part of the book, Thomas sees the "devotion" to Holy Communion as the central feature of the contemplative life.

The final mystical reading is a passage from the autobiography of Teresa of Avila (1515–82). St. Teresa is a Spanish Counter-Reformation figure who, in her own way, attempted to reform the Roman Catholic Church from the sorts of abuses that inspired the Protestant Reformation. She was a cloistered nun who undertook to reform her powerful order of Carmelite nuns from what she saw as lax observances and a tepid spirituality. Founding a new order that eventually became known as the Discalced Carmelites (i.e., barefooted Carmelites), she played a busy practical and political role in administrating and founding convents and monasteries across Spain, sometimes in the face of great opposition.

Canonized by the Roman Catholic Church in 1622 and declared in 1970 a "Doctor of the Church," Teresa of Avila is best described as a mystical theologian. A friend and associate of the Spanish poet St. John of the Cross, she is the author of three books, considered classics in the Spanish Renaissance tradition: *The Way of Perfection* (c. 1566), her autobiography *The Life of Teresa of Jesus* (1567), and a work on spiritual prayer, *The Interior Castle* (1577). Her writing focuses on methods of prayer and the various stages of spiritual development. Her vigorous insights are largely based on her own personal experiences.

St. Teresa experienced an assortment of visions and ecstasies. The passage reproduced here describes one remarkable encounter with an angel who pierces her heart with a golden arrow, sending her into bliss. The incident is referred to as the "Transverberation" of St. Teresa and is interpreted as symbolic of her entrance into the state of Spiritual Marriage with God as incarnate in Christ. Her vivid description, which has erotic overtones, became the subject of a famous sculptural ensemble by Italian Renaissance artist Gian Lorenzo Bernini, which aptly captures the spirit of the Baroque period and the Counter-Reformation.

READING 22A

Catherine of Siena, *Letters*[1]

To Pope Gregory XI[2] (1375)

In the Name of Jesus Christ crucified and of sweet Mary:

To you, most reverend and beloved father in Christ Jesus, your unworthy, poor, miserable daughter Catherine, servant and slave of the servants of Jesus Christ, writes in His precious Blood; with the desire to see you a fruitful tree, full of sweet and mellow fruits, and planted in fruitful earth... that is, in the earth of true knowledge of yourself....

For if a man loves himself, perverse pride, head and source of every ill, lives in him, whatever his rank may be, prelate[3] or subject.... I say, then: if he

is a prelate, he does ill, because to avoid falling into disfavor with his fellow-creatures—that is, through self-love—in which he is bound by self-indulgence—holy justice dies in him. For he sees his subjects commit faults and sins, and pretends not to see them and fails to correct them; or if he does correct them, he does it with such coldness and lukewarmness that he does not accomplish anything, but plasters vice over; and he is always afraid of giving displeasure or of getting into a quarrel.

All this is because he loves himself. Sometimes men like this want to get along with purely peaceful means. I say that this is the very worst cruelty which can be shown. If a wound when necessary

---

1 Excerpts from three letters of St. Catherine of Siena (c. 1347–80), from *Saint Catherine of Siena as Seen in Her Letters*, trans. and ed. with an introduction by Vida Dutton Scudder (London and New York: J.M. Dent and E.P. Dutton, [1905] 1927). Available at http://www.drawnbylove.com/Scudder%20letters.htm.

2 A weak Pope, 1370–78, he had failed to deal with the rampant corruption in the Church. Catherine is also concerned with the threat of political rebellion in Tuscany, a region in central Italy.

3 I.e., a bishop or other high ecclesiastical dignitary.

is not cauterized or cut out with steel, but simply covered with ointment, not only does it fail to heal, but it infects everything, and many a time death follows from it....

Truly, then...I hope by the goodness of God, venerable father mine, that you will quench this in yourself, and will not love yourself for yourself, nor your neighbor for yourself, nor God; but will love Him because He is highest and eternal Goodness, and worthy of being loved...

This is what I wish to see in you. And if up to this time, we have not stood very firm, I wish and pray in truth that the moment of time which remains be dealt with manfully, following Christ, whose vicar you are, like a strong man. And fear not, father, for anything that may result from those tempestuous winds that are now beating against you, those decaying members which have rebelled against you. Fear not; for divine aid is near....

Give us, then, a remedy; and comfort you in Christ Jesus, and fear not. Press on, and fulfil with true and holy zeal what you have begun with a holy resolve, concerning your return, and the holy and sweet crusade. And delay no longer, for many difficulties have occurred through delay, and the devil has risen up to prevent these things being done because he perceives his own loss. Up, then, father, and no more negligence! Raise the gonfalon[1] of the most holy Cross, for with the fragrance of the Cross you shall win peace. I beg you to summon those who have rebelled against you to a holy peace, so that all warfare may be turned against the infidels....

To Sister Bartolomea Della Seta[2] (c. 1376)

In the Name of Jesus Christ crucified and of sweet Mary:

Dearest daughter in Christ Jesus, I Catherine, ser-

vant and slave of the servants of Jesus Christ, write to you in His precious Blood: with desire to see you a true bride, consecrated to the eternal Bridegroom....

I remember that I heard this said once to a servant of God, and it was said to her by the Sweet Primal Truth, when she was abiding in very great pain and temptation, and among other things, felt the greatest confusion...

Then our Savior, in this sweet and true humility, scattered the shadows and torments of the devil, as it happens when the cloud passes that the sun remains; and suddenly came the Presence of Our Savior. Thence she melted into a river of tears, and said in a sweet glow of love: "O sweet and good Jesus, where were you when my soul was in such affliction?" Sweet Jesus, the Spotless Lamb, replied: "I was beside you. For I move not, and never leave My creature, unless the creature leave Me through mortal sin....

"Do you wish Me to show you, daughter mine, how in those conflicts you did not fall into mortal sin, and how I was beside you? Tell me, what is it that makes sin mortal? Only the will. For sin and virtue consist in the consent of the will; there is no sin nor virtue, unless voluntarily wrought. This will was not in you; for had it been, you would have taken joy and delight in the suggestions of the devil; but since the will was not there, you did grieve over them....

"So you see that sin and virtue consist in choice—which I tell you, so you should not, on account of these conflicts, fall into disordered confusion. But I will that from this darkness you derive the light of self-knowledge, in which you may gain the virtue of humility and joy, and exult in a good will, knowing that then I abide in you secretly. The will is a sign to you that I am there; for had you an evil will, I should not be in you by grace....

"But do you know why I do this? Only to make the soul reach true perfection. You know that the soul

---

1 I.e., a banner or pennant hung from a crossbar.

2 A nun in the convent of Santo Stefano. This letter deals with the internal struggles of religious life. All nuns were seen as brides of Christ. The reference to the "ring of His Flesh" is a mystic reference to a wedding ring made of the foreskin of Christ.

cannot be perfect unless borne on these two wings, humility and charity. Humility is won through the knowledge of itself, into which it enters in the time of darkness; and charity is won by seeing that I, through love, have kept its will holy and good....

"And reflect, that such experience is very necessary to your salvation; for if the soul were not sometimes pressed by many temptations, it would fall into very great negligence, and would lose the exercise of continual desire and prayer...."

Now thus I tell you, dearest my daughter, what I want you to do. And be for me a mirror of virtue, following the footsteps of Christ crucified. Bathe yourself in the Blood of Christ crucified, and so live, as is my will, that you nor seek nor will anything but the Crucified, like a true bride, bought with the Blood of Christ crucified. Well see to it that you are a bride, and that He has wedded you and every creature, not with a ring of silver, but with the ring of His Flesh.

O depth and height of Love unspeakable...You, oh God have plucked the human race from the hands of the devil...and have wedded it with Your flesh. You have given Your Blood for a pledge, and at the last, sacrificing Your body, you have made the payment....

I say no more. Remain in the holy and sweet grace of God. Sweet Jesus, Jesus Love.

To Master Raimondo of Capua[1] (c. 1380)

... I was breathless with grief from the crucified desire which had been newly conceived in the sight of God. For the light of the mind had mirrored itself in the Eternal Trinity;[2] and in that abyss was seen the dignity of rational being, and the misery into which man falls by fault of mortal sin...

And the pain and fire of her desire increasing, she cried in the sight of God, saying: "What can I do, O unsearchable Fire?" And His benignity replied: "Do offer your life anew. You can refrain from ever giving yourself repose.... Take heed then, never to relax, but always to increase in desires; for I, impelled by love, am taking good heed to aid you with My bodily and spiritual grace."...

And the day passing by, full of marvel, the evening came. And I, feeling that the heart was so drawn by the force of love that I could offer no resistance to going to the place of prayer...and prostrated myself with great compunction...

And rising with the impression of what I have said before the eye of my mind, God placed me before Himself...in a new way, as if memory, intellect, and will had nothing whatever to do with my body....

All which then vanished from me through the increase of the inward fire: and I paid heed only to what should be done, that I should make a sacrifice of myself to God for Holy Church and for the sake of removing ignorance and negligence from those whom God had put into my hands. Then the devils called out havoc upon me, seeking to hinder and slacken with their terrors my free and burning desire. So these beat upon the shell of the body; but desire became the more kindled, crying, "O Eternal God, receive the sacrifice of my life in this mystical body of Holy Church! I have nothing to give save what You have given to me. Take then my heart, and may Your Bride lean her face upon it!"

Then Eternal God, turning the eyes of His mercy, removed my heart and offered it to Holy Church. And He had drawn it to Himself with such force that had He not at once bound it about with His strength—not wishing that the vessel of my body should be broken—my life would have gone. Then the devils cried much more clamorously, as if they

---

1 Master General of the Dominican Order from 1380 until his death (1399). He served as St. Catherine's spiritual director. In the third letter, Catherine offers herself, in imitation of Christ, as a "sacrificial victim" to God for the reform of the Church.

2 I.e., the three persons of God: the Father, the Son (Jesus Christ), and the Holy Spirit.

had felt an intolerable pain; forcing themselves to leave terror with me, threatening me so to disport[1] them that such an act as this could not be wrought....

But because Hell cannot resist the virtue of humility with the light of most holy faith, the spirit became more single, and worked with tools of fire,

hearing in the sight of the Divine Majesty words most charming and promises to give gladness. And because in truth it was thus in so great a mystery, the tongue from now on can suffice to speak of it no more....

READING 22B

Anonymous, *A Book Of Contemplation The Which Is Called The Cloud Of Unknowing, In The Which a Soul Is Oned With God*[2]

(1375)

Here Begins the Prologue

I do not care if fleshly janglers,[3] open praisers and blamers of themselves or of any other, tellers of trifles, ronners[4] and tattlers of tales, and all manner of pinchers,[5] never see this book. For my intent was never to write such a thing for them.

But if it be those men who are graciously disposed, by inward stirring after the privy[6] spirit of God, not continually like contemplatives, but now and then to be perceivers of God, in the highest point of this contemplative act; if such men might see this book, I say that by the grace of God they will find great comfort in it.

Here Begins the Fourth Chapter: The Cloud of Unknowing

And think not, because I call the subject of this little book a darkness or a cloud, that it be any cloud congealed of the humors that flee in the air, nor yet any darkness such as is in your house on nights when the candle is out....

I do not mean this. For when I say darkness, I mean a lacking of knowing: and for this reason it is not called a cloud of the air, but a cloud of unknowing, that is between you and your God.

---

1 I.e., to enjoy without restraint; to frolic.

2 Digest of Anonymous, *A Book Of Contemplation The Which Is Called The Cloud Of Unknowing, In The Which a Soul Is Oned With God* (1375), from Evelyn Underhill, ed., *A Book of Contemplation, etc.* (2nd ed.) (London: John M. Watkins, 1922). Available at http://catholicspiritualdirection.org/cloudunknowing.pdf.

3 I.e., talkers, slanderers.

4 I.e., gossips.

5 I.e., covetous or lazy people.

6 I.e., sharing in the knowledge of (something secret or private).

Here Begins the Fifth Chapter: The Cloud of Forgetting

And if ever you shall come to this cloud and dwell and work therein as I bid you...then first put a cloud of forgetting beneath you; between you and all the creatures that ever be made.... and not only the creatures themselves, but also all the works and the conditions of the same creatures...

Yea! And though it be good to think upon the kindness of God, and to love Him and praise Him for it, yet in this work of forgetting it is far better to think upon the naked being of Him, and to love Him and praise Him for Himself.

Here Begins the Sixth Chapter: The Question

But now you ask me, "How shall I think on Himself, and what is He?" and to this I cannot answer you but thus: "I know not."

For you have brought me with your question into that same darkness, and into that same cloud of unknowing of which I speak...For of God Himself can no man think. And therefore I would leave aside all those things that you can think, and choose to love that thing that you cannot think.

For why: Because He may be loved, and loved well, but not thought. By love may He be gotten and held; but never by thought....

And you shall step above this cloud of forgetting stalwartly, but also mistily, with a devout and a pleasing stirring of love, and try to pierce that darkness above you. And smite upon that thick cloud of unknowing with a sharp dart of longing love.

Here Begins the Thirteenth Chapter: Meekness

Now let us first see the virtue of perfect meekness, which is caused by...the over-abundant love and the worthiness of God in Himself, in the beholding of which all nature quakes, and all saints and angels be blind...

Here Begins the Four and Twentieth Chapter: Charity

And as it is said of meekness, how that it is truly and perfectly comprehended in the blind love of God, when it is beating upon this dark cloud of unknowing...so the same is said of charity.

For charity is nothing else...but love of God by Himself...For as it was said before, that the substance of this work is nothing else but a naked intent directed toward God for Himself.

Here Begins the Four and Thirtieth Chapter: Grace

And if you ask me by what means you shall come to this work, I beseech Almighty God of His great grace...to teach you Himself.... For that is the work only of God, and specially wrought by him.

Here Begins the Three and Fortieth Chapter: One's Own Being

Look that nothing be in your wit[1] nor in your will but only God. And tread all down under the cloud of forgetting....

And no wonder that you hate for to think on yourself in this unknowing, when you shall always

---

1 I.e., basic human intelligence; but also mental sharpness, keen intelligence.

feel sin there, a foul stinking lump…between you and your God: the lump which is no other thing than yourself….

Here Begins the One and Fiftieth Chapter: Your Ghostly[1] Heart

And lean meekly to the blind stirring of love in your heart. I mean not in your bodily heart, but in your ghostly heart, which is your will. And be well wary that you not conceive bodily that which is said ghostly.

Here Begins the Nine and Fiftieth Chapter: Time, Place and Body Should Be Forgotten

And know well that all those that set them to be ghostly workers, and especially in the work of this book, that although…the work of this book be called a stirring, nevertheless this stirring stretch neither up bodily, nor in any bodily way…

And it should rather be called a sudden changing, than any stirring of place. For time, place, and body: these three should be forgotten in all this ghostly working.

Here Begins the Seventieth Chapter: The Failing of Our Wits

And therefore leave your outward bodily wits[2] and all that they work in: for I tell you truly, that this work may not be conceived by them.

For by your senses you may not conceive of anything, unless it be by shape and color; and sound; and stench or savor, sour or sweet or the qualities of touch…And truly, God has none of these qualities…

And therefore it was that Saint Denis said, the most goodly knowing of God is that, the which is known by unknowing….

Here Begins the One and Seventieth Chapter: The Time of Ravishing[3]

Some think this matter so hard and so fearful, that they say this unknowing may not come without much work…

And yet some there be that without much and long ghostly exercise shall feel the perfection of this work, which is called ravishing. And some there be that be so at home with God in this grace of contemplation, that they may have this ravishing when they will: as it is in sitting, going, standing, or kneeling.

And…in this little love put upon this cloud of unknowing be contained all the virtues of man's soul…

---

1 I.e., of or relating to the soul; spiritual.
2 I.e., memory, reason, will, imagination, and sensuality.
3 I.e., ecstasy.

Thomas Haemmerlein, *De Imitatione Christi* (*Of the Imitation of Christ*)[1]

(c. 1418–27)

The First Book: Admonitions Profitable for the Spiritual Life

CHAPTER I
OF THE IMITATION OF CHRIST, AND OF CONTEMPT OF THE WORLD AND ALL ITS VANITIES

1. He that follows me shall not walk in darkness, says the Lord. These are the words of Christ; and they teach us that we must imitate His life and character, if we seek true illumination, and deliverance from all blindness of heart.

CHAPTER II
OF THINKING HUMBLY OF ONESELF

2. Rest from inordinate desire of knowledge, for therein is found much distraction and deceit....

3. The greater and more complete your knowledge, the more severely shall you be judged...Therefore be not lifted up by any skill or knowledge that you have...If it seems to you that you know many things, and understand them well, know also that there are many more things which you know not....

CHAPTER XIII
OF RESISTING TEMPTATION

3. There is no man wholly free from temptations so long as he lives because we have the root of tempta-

tion within ourselves in that we are born in concupiscence.

4. Little by little, through patience and long-suffering, you shall conquer temptation by the help of God, rather than by violence and your strength of will. In the midst of temptation often seek counsel; and do not deal harshly with one who is tempted, but comfort and strengthen him as you would have done to yourself.

The Second Book: Admonitions Concerning the Inner Life

CHAPTER XII
OF THE ROYAL WAY OF THE HOLY CROSS

1. That seems a hard saying to many: 'If any man will come after Me, let him deny himself and take up his Cross and follow Me.' But you will find it much harder to hear the last judgement, if you are to be thrown wicked into eternal fire.

2. Why do you fear to take up the cross, which leads to a kingdom? In the Cross is health, in the Cross is life, in the Cross is protection from enemies, in the Cross is heavenly sweetness, in the Cross strength of mind...Take up, therefore, your cross and follow Jesus and you shall go into eternal life...

---

1 Thomas à Kempis [Thomas Haemmerlein], *De Imitatione Christi* (*Of the Imitation of Christ*, c. 1418–27), from William Benham, trans., *The Imitation of Christ* (New York: E.P. Dutton [1874] rev. 1905). Available at Project Gutenberg at http://www.gutenberg.org/ebooks/1653.

The Third Book: On Inward Consolation

CHAPTER V
OF THE WONDERFUL POWER OF THE
DIVINE LOVE

3. Love is a great thing, a good above all others, which alone makes every heavy burden light... For it bears the burden and makes it no burden; it makes every bitter thing to be sweet and of good taste....

6. Enlarge me in the surpassing love of Jesus, therefore, that I may learn to taste with the innermost mouth of my heart how sweet it is to love God, to be dissolved, and to swim in love.... Let me sing the song of love, let me follow You my Beloved on high... Let me love You more than myself, not loving myself except for Your sake...

CHAPTER XXXIV
THAT TO HIM WHO LOVES, GOD IS SWEET
ABOVE ALL THINGS AND IN ALL THINGS

2. To him who tastes God, what can be distasteful? And to him who does not taste God, what is there which can make him joyous? But the worldly wise, and they who enjoy the flesh, these fail in Your wisdom; for in the wisdom of the world is found utter vanity, and to be carnally minded is death. But they who follow after You through contempt of worldly things, and mortification of the flesh, are found to be truly wise because they are carried from vanity to verity, from the flesh to the spirit....

CHAPTER LIV
OF THE DIVERSE MOTIONS OF NATURE AND
OF GRACE

My Son, pay diligent heed to the motions of Nature and of Grace...

2. Nature is deceitful and draws away, ensnares, and deceives many, and always has self for her end; but Grace walks in simplicity and... does all for the sake of God, in whom also she finally rests.

3. Nature is very unwilling to die... and unwilling to bear the yoke readily; but Grace studies self-mortification... and longs to be conquered...

4. Nature... considers what profit she may gain from another; but Grace considers... what may be profitable to the many.

5. Nature willingly receives honor and reverence; but Grace faithfully ascribes all honor and glory to God....

9. Nature... rejoices in earthly lucre... and is vexed by any little injurious word; but Grace reaches after things eternal... and is not embittered by any hard words...

11. Nature inclines you to... your own flesh, to vanities and dissipation; but Grace draws to God and to the virtues...

12. Nature is glad to receive some outward solace in which the senses may have delight; but Grace seeks to be comforted in God alone...

18. This Grace is a supernatural light... and the proper mark of the elect, and the pledge of eternal salvation...

CHAPTER LV
OF THE CORRUPTION OF NATURE AND THE
EFFICACY OF DIVINE GRACE

2. There is need of Your grace, yes, and of a great measure of it, that my nature may be conquered, which has always been prone to evil... For being fallen through the first man Adam, and corrupted through original sin, the punishment of this stain

descended upon all men;[1] so that Nature itself, which was framed good and right by You, is now used to express the vice and infirmity of corrupted Nature...

4. How entirely necessary, then, is Your Grace to me...For the gifts of Nature belong to good and evil alike; but the proper gift of the elect is grace—that is, love—and they who bear its mark are held worthy of everlasting life....

Teresa of Avila, *The Life of Teresa of Jesus*[2]

(1567)

Chapter XXIX

Of Visions. The Graces Our Lord Bestowed on the Saint. The Answers Our Lord Gave Her for Those Who Tried Her.

As to the vision of which I am speaking, there are no means of bringing it about; only we must behold it when our Lord is pleased to present it before us, as He wills and what He wills; and there is no possibility of taking anything away from it, or of adding anything to it; nor is there any way of effecting it, whatever we may do....

This is true of all visions without exception: we can contribute nothing towards them—we cannot add to them, nor can we take from them.... Our Lord would have us see most clearly that it is no work of ours, but of His Divine Majesty....

Many reproaches and many vexations have I borne while telling [confessors about my visions]—

and many suspicions and much persecution also.... As my visions grew in frequency, one of those who used to help me before...began to say that I was certainly under the influence of Satan.... This was a great hardship for me.... However, I did at last as I was bidden. I prayed much to our Lord, that He would deliver me from delusions. I was always praying to that effect, and with many tears....

Not long afterwards His Majesty began, according to His promise, to make it clear that it was He Himself who appeared, by the growth in me of the love of God so strong, that I knew not who could have infused it; for it was most supernatural, and I had not attained to it by any efforts of my own. I saw myself dying with a desire to see God.... Certain great impetuosities of love...overwhelmed me....

Great discretion, therefore, is necessary at first, in order that everything may proceed gently, and that the operations of the spirit may be within; all outward manifestations should be carefully avoided....

---

1 The reference is to the story found in the book of Genesis in the Hebrew and Christian Scriptures. Adam was the first man created by God. He sinned by disobeying God's command not to eat of the fruit of the tree of knowledge located in the center of the Garden of Eden. This constitutes the original sin, which all human beings inherit by virtue of being born human.

2 *The Life of St. Teresa of Jesus, of the Order of Our Lady of Carmel*. Written by Herself. Translated from the Spanish by David Lewis. Third Edition Enlarged. With additional Notes and an Introduction by Rev. Fr. Benedict Zimmerman, O.C.D. (London: Thomas Baker; New York: Benziger Bros., 1904). Available at http://www.gutenberg.org/files/8120/8120-h/8120-h.htm.

Our Lord was pleased that I should have at times a vision of this kind: I saw an angel close by me,...in bodily form.... He was not large, but small of stature, and most beautiful—his face burning, as if he were one of the highest angels, who seem to be all of fire: they must be those whom we call cherubim.... I saw in his hand a long spear of gold, and at the iron's point there seemed to be a little fire. He appeared to me to be thrusting it at times into my heart, and to pierce my very entrails; when he drew it out, he seemed to draw them out also, and to leave me all on fire with a great love of God. The pain was so great, that it made me moan; and yet so surpassing was the sweetness of this excessive pain, that I could not wish to be rid of it.... The pain is not bodily, but spiritual; though the body has its share in it, even a large one. It is a caressing of love so sweet which now takes place between the soul and God....

During the days that this lasted,...I wished to see, or speak with, no one, but only to cherish my pain, which was to me a greater bliss than all created things could give me.

I was in this state from time to time, whenever it was our Lord's pleasure to throw me into those deep trances, which I could not prevent even when I was in the company of others, and which, to my deep vexation, came to be publicly known....

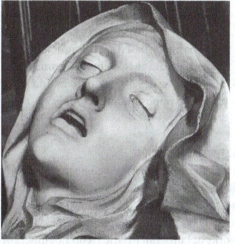

L'estasi di Santa Teresa (The Ecstasy of St. Theresa), Gian Lorenzo Bernini, 1647–54.

Questions

1. Compare the mystic tradition in Christianity with Buddhism. Comment on the notion of enlightenment.
2. Catherine of Siena attributes moral and immoral actions to a particular faculty. Which is it? Discuss her views and critique them, using examples.
3. As a young woman, Catherine of Siena went against the wishes of her father and refused to marry. She later became an independent voice for reform, urging Pope Gregory to deal "manfully" with corruption. St. Teresa reformed what she considered a decadent order of nuns in the face of enormous ecclesiastical and political opposition. Discuss the moral role of women mystics in the medieval and baroque Church.
4. The medievals associated the mystical experience—and morality, more generally—with sacrifice. What place, if any, do sacrifice and suffering have in personal morality?
5. The medievals believed that God's grace was necessary to overcome temptation. This suggests that something more than reason is needed to be moral. What do you think? Mention two philosophers.
6. The author of *The Cloud of Unknowing* says that we can only be "oned" with God in unknowing. Why? What moral lessons can we take from this?
7. As we saw with the desert fathers and mothers, the ascetic and mystic tradition in Christianity is based on a renunciation of ordinary physical and material desires. How do you explain this? Why was renunciation so important in the moral tradition?
8. St. Teresa writes of feeling pain and joy in her mystical embraces. Explain. How can these two opposite states co-exist at the same time?

Suggested Readings

The letters of Catherine of Siena, *The Cloud of Unknowing*, the *De Imitatione Christi*, and St. Teresa's autobiography are all available online. For other medieval sources, see two books: the treatises and poems of Teresa of Avila's spiritual director, John of the Cross, such as the *Ascent of Mount Carmel* (1578–79) and *Dark Night of the Soul* (1619), or the works of Lutheran mystic Jacob Boehme, such as *The Way to Christ* (1622). Modern mystics include Teilhard de Chardin, John Boruff (*How to Experience God*, 2009), James Goll (*Wasted on Jesus*, 2000), Richard Foster (*Celebration of Discipline*, 1978), and A.W. Tozer (*The Pursuit of God*, 1948).

For commentary on the medieval sources, see Ricardo Da Costa, "Transcendence above Immanence: The Soul in the Mysticism of Bernard of Clairvaux" (2009); Carmel Bendon Davis, *Mysticism and Space: Space and Spatiality in the Works of Richard Rolle, "The Cloud of Unknowing" Author, and Julian of Norwich* (2008); Elizabeth Alvilda Petroff, *Medieval Women's Visionary Literature* (1986); Michael Horst Zettel, "Female Mysticism in the Middle Ages" (1986); and Carol Mastrangelo Bové's discussion of Julia Kristeva's *Thérèse mon amour*: "Kristeva's *Thérèse*: Mysticism and Modernism" (2013). For more general sources, see Richard H. Jones, *Mysticism and Morality* (2004); Steven T. Katz's two articles: "Mysticism and Ethics in Western Mystical Traditions" and "Ethics and Mysticism in

Eastern Mystical Traditions" (1992); Joseph Dan, "Jewish Mysticism and Jewish Ethics" (1988); and Peter J. Awn, "The Ethical Concerns of Classical Sufism" (1982).

In an interesting twist, Christia Mercer has argued that the introspective turn in Descartes's *Meditations* derives from and parallels the introspective turn in St. Teresa of Avila. See "Descartes' Debt to Teresa of Ávila, or Why We Should Work on Women in the History of Philosophy" (2017).

Chapter 23

Thomas Aquinas

The name "Thomas Aquinas" (1225–74) means Thomas from Aquino, the town in central Italy where he was born. The son of a noble family, he was a thoughtful child and, from an early age, he set his mind on a religious vocation. As a pious teenager, he attempted to join a new religious order of teaching friars, the Dominicans, against the wishes of his family. This was such a radical and alarming choice that his mother responded by sending soldiers out to bring him back. He was then imprisoned in a tower for more than a year, until his family finally gave up their resistance and allegedly allowed him to escape in the night.

The Dominicans sent their new protégé to study theology at the University of Paris and the University of Cologne. Other students, noting that he was heavy-set, physically, and quiet, nicknamed him the "dumb ox." This had no effect on his reputation with his teachers, and it is said that his famous teacher, Albert the Great, retorted that the lowing of this dumb ox would be heard throughout the entire world. Thomas was accordingly marked out for an academic career early in his studies and went on to enjoy a successful university life.

The continuing tension between the religious and philosophical impulses in the medieval tradition is illustrated by Thomas's attitude towards philosophy, his chosen *métier*, at the end of his life. Near death and physically afflicted, he experienced, apparently, a mystical vision. Overwhelmed by the authority of this experience, which was beyond the reach of reason and argument, he reportedly dismissed his own writing, declaring: "All I have written is straw."

After his death, Thomas, commonly referred to as Aquinas, was declared a saint in the Catholic Church and became its most prominent philosopher. Some of his influence can be attributed to the central role played by the Catholic Church in medieval Europe. His work still forms an integral part of the active philosophical tradition and contains the basic teachings of the Catholic Church. The school of philosophy based on his work is called Thomism and its adherents are commonly called Thomists, as they expound a "Thomistic" philosophy.

From a philosophical perspective, Thomas was the pivotal figure in an Aristotelian revival. In the early Middle Ages, Christian philosophy was heavily influenced by Plato and his Academy. This exclusive emphasis changed in the twelfth century when Aristotle's works were re-introduced into Europe by Islamic thinkers and translated into Latin, the *lingua franca* of philosophy. In his work, Thomas synthesizes the two traditions, in most cases convincingly, with the intention of producing a Christian Aristotelianism.

Much of Thomas's work is a commentary on the arguments advanced by his predecessors, which were available in a large library of historical texts that had been collected by scholars. Thomas takes his own stand on individual issues but continually comments on the opinions of famous authorities such as Aristotle (he calls him simply "the philosopher"), the Islamic philosopher Ibn Rushd, or Averroes ("the commentator"), St. Augustine ("the theologian"), the Jewish philosopher Maimonides ("Rabbi Moses"), and others.

The systematic aspect of Thomas's work, which sets out a relatively complete theory of human conduct and humankind's place in the universe, foreshadows the modern era in philosophy. His work is still a compilation, however, like Maimonides's *Mishneh Torah*, which brings together the received teaching on specific issues in an organized, systematic whole. In both cases, however, the authors are synthesizing a tradition and an accumulation of wisdom, which gives primacy to the experience of the past rather than theory.

Thomas's major work is an encyclopedic treatise on theology called the *Summa Theologiae* (1265–74), which includes a detailed discussion of moral philosophy. The term '*Summa*' means 'summary,' but in an older sense: comprehensive treatise rather than an abbreviation of a longer work. He is also known for the *Summa contra Gentiles*, (*Against the Gentiles*),[1] where he elaborates upon the relationship between faith and reason and the function of reason within the larger scheme of providence.

There are two moral theories in Thomas's work. The first is the theory of the natural law, which was set out by the Greeks and developed by the Stoics and Roman philosophers. This theory—which has cosmological roots and still remains a living theory today—holds that morality is comprised of a law higher than human law, which is inherent within the universal order. In the Christian tradition, this morality can be traced to God, who has implanted something like a moral compass within our consciousness. We are obliged to follow its dictates.

In the *Summa Theologiae*, which contains the "classical" formulation of the natural law, Thomas holds that the natural moral order finds expression in our inalienable emotions, instincts, and desires. These are set out in the precepts of the natural law, which are based on natural inclinations for self-preservation, for reproduction, for marriage, family life, education, and peaceful co-operation with others. The more specific injunctions in the natural law are accessible to us through the exercise of the faculty of reason.

The second moral theory in Thomas's work, which comes directly from Aristotle, is virtue ethics. In the *Summa Theologiae*, he discusses the different virtues and vices, and their relation to each other, in considerable detail. He pays particular attention to the four "cardinal" virtues: fortitude (or courage), temperance, justice, and prudence, outlining and discussing the different ways in which they manifest themselves. He also covers a wide range of topics such as gratitude, friendliness, peace, joy, sloth, envy, folly, murder, backbiting, theft, and so on. In an innovation, he also adds a Christian element to Aristotle: the

---

1 'Gentiles' here means 'non-Christians.'

three "theological" virtues, faith, hope, and love (or charity), which complete and perfect what is naturally good about human beings.

Although Thomas was a working theologian, working within a religious tradition, it is notable that these theories are not particularly religious. In fact, his religious argument is that religion merely elaborates upon the natural morality that we are all obliged to follow. We are all obliged to keep our promises, be generous to other people, refrain from lies, refrain from murder, and so on. This gives rise, as in other traditions, to an ethics of reciprocity.

The reading is from the *Summa Theologiae*, which was written as a textbook in theology for the use of students. Sometimes referred to as the *Summa Theologica*, or simply the "*Summa*," the book was never quite finished. The final section is accordingly a supplement, made up of passages taken at a later date from Thomas's other works. The *Summa* is divided into four major parts: the First Part (*Prima Pars*) discusses God and the act of Creation; the "First Part of the Second Part" (*Prima Secundae*) discusses law and morality; the "Second Part of the Second Part" (*Secunda Secundae*) discusses the virtues and the vices; and, lastly, the Third Part (*Tertia Pars*), the supplement, discusses Christ, the sacraments, and the end of the world.

We have edited out most of the ancillary material in the excerpts in the reading, which focus on the natural law and the virtues. Readers may find the original text forbidding. The structure of the *Summa* comes from a form of debate, called *disputatio*, which was used in the universities of the time. The text is arranged systematically, by topic, under many headings and sub-headings. The discussion of these topics takes place in the form of questions and answers: Thomas begins by asking larger questions and responding to them. He then moves on to increasingly specific questions.

The answers to the questions follow a prescribed form. After each question, we find references to authors who have commented on the question. This is followed by Thomas's response to the question and comments—often in the form of a rebuttal—which may be followed by a second response, a surrebuttal, to further objections. This format provides a rigorous but supple framework for the discussion of philosophical questions.

Thomas Aquinas, *Summa Theologiae*[1]

First Part of the Second Part

QUESTION 61. THE CARDINAL VIRTUES

Article 2. Whether there are four cardinal virtues?

There are four cardinal virtues.

First, we have one principal virtue, which exists in the very act of reason, called 'Prudence.' Secondly, according to the manner in which the reason puts its order into... a) operations, we have 'Justice'; or b) into passions...

And in the case of the passions, we need two virtues. For the need of putting the order of reason into the passions is due to their thwarting reason: and this occurs in two ways. First, by the passions inciting to something against reason, and then the passions need a curb, which we call 'Temperance.' Secondly, by the passions withdrawing us from following the dictate of reason, e.g. through fear of danger or toil: and then man needs to be strengthened for that which reason dictates, lest[2] he turn back; and to this end there is 'Fortitude.'[3]

In like manner, we find that... there are four subjects of the virtues... namely 1) the power which is rational in its essence, and which is perfected by the virtue of 'Prudence'; and the power which is rational by participation, and is threefold: 2) the will, which is the subject of the virtue of 'Justice,' 3) the concupiscible faculty,[4] which is the subject of the virtue of 'Temperance,' and 4) the irascible faculty,[5] which is the subject of the virtue of 'Fortitude.'

QUESTION 62. THE THEOLOGICAL VIRTUES

Article 3. Whether faith, hope, and charity are fittingly reckoned as theological virtues?

The theological virtues direct man to supernatural happiness in the same way as by the natural inclination man is directed to his connatural end....

But since the natural order falls short of the supernatural order... man needed to receive in addition something supernatural to direct him to a supernatural end.[6] First, then, as regards the intellect, man receives certain supernatural principles, which are held by means of a Divine light: these are the articles of faith...

Secondly, the will is directed to this supernatural end... as something attainable—and this pertains to hope—and thirdly, the will is directed to a certain spiritual union... and this belongs to charity.[7]...

Article 4. Whether faith precedes hope and charity?

I answer that the order is twofold: by order of generation, and by order of perfection.

By order of generation,... faith precedes hope, and hope charity, as to their acts.... But in the order of perfection, charity precedes faith and hope:

---

1   Selections from Aquinas, *Summa Theologiae* (1265–74), from *The Summa Theologica of St. Thomas Aquinas*, second edition (Literally translated by Fathers of the English Dominican Province, 1920): First Part of the Second Part: Questions 61–62, Questions 90–91, 94, 96; Second Part of the Second Part: Question 27, Question 101, Question 120. Available at http://www.newadvent.org/summa/.

2   I.e., because of the possibility; in case.

3   I.e., courage.

4   I.e., the appetitive faculty (or capacity) to pursue what is agreeable to the senses and flee what is harmful.

5   I.e., the appetitive faculty to resist those forces that combat the agreeable and bring harm.

6   The supernatural end refers to the ultimate purpose of human life, which, for Aquinas, is union with God.

7   I.e., love.

because both faith and hope are quickened[1] by charity, and receive from charity their full complement as virtues. For thus charity is the mother and the root of all the virtues, inasmuch as it is the form of them all...

QUESTION 90. THE ESSENCE OF LAW

Article 1. Whether law is something pertaining to reason?

I answer that, Law is a rule and measure of acts, whereby man is induced to act or is restrained from acting: for 'lex' is derived from 'ligare,'[2] because it binds one to act. Now the rule and measure of human acts is reason... since it belongs to reason to direct to the goal, which is the first principle in all matters of action, according to Aristotle.... Consequently, it follows that law is something pertaining to reason.

Article 2. Whether the law is always something directed to the common good?

I answer that... the first principle in practical matters, which are the object of the practical reason, is the last end: and the last end of human life is bliss or happiness.... Consequently, the law must necessarily regard principally the relationship to happiness. Moreover, since every part is ordained to the whole... and since one man is a part of the perfect community, the law must necessarily regard properly the relationship to universal happiness.... A precept directed to a specific case is therefore devoid of the nature of a law, save in so far as it regards the common good. Therefore, every law is ordained to the common good.

Article 3. Whether the reason of any man is competent to make laws?[3]

I answer that... to order anything to the common good, belongs either to the whole people, or to someone who is the vice regent of the whole people. And therefore the making of a law belongs either to the whole people or to a public personage who has care of the whole people....

Article 4. Whether promulgation[4] is essential to a law?

I answer that... a law is imposed on others by way of a rule and measure.... In order that a law obtain the binding force which is proper to a law, it must necessarily be applied to the men who have to be ruled by it. Such application is made by its being notified to them by promulgation. Wherefore promulgation is necessary for the law to obtain its force.

Thus from the four preceding articles, the definition of law may be gathered; and it is nothing else than an ordinance of reason for the common good, made by him who has care of the community, and promulgated.

QUESTION 91. THE VARIOUS KINDS OF LAW

Article 1. Whether there is an eternal law?

A law is nothing else but a dictate of practical reason emanating from the ruler who governs a perfect community. Now it is evident... that the whole community of the universe is governed by Divine Reason. Wherefore the very Idea of the government of things in God the Ruler of the universe, has the nature of a law. And since the Divine Reason's conception of

---

1 I.e., made alive.

2 In Latin lex is 'law' and ligare is 'to bind.'

3 In other words: What is the source of law?

4 I.e., declaring publicly, thereby bringing the law into operation.

things is not subject to time but is eternal...this kind of law must be called eternal....

Article 2. Whether there is in us a natural law?

Since all things subject to Divine providence are ruled and measured by the eternal law, it is evident that all things partake somewhat of the eternal law; since, from its being imprinted on them, they derive their inclinations to their proper acts and ends. Now the rational creature, in particular, is subject to Divine providence in the most excellent way, since it partakes of a share of providence, by being provident both for itself and for others. Wherefore it has a share of the Eternal Reason, whereby it has a natural inclination to its proper act and end: and this participation of the eternal law in the rational creature is called the natural law...

The light of natural reason, whereby we discern what is good and what is evil, which is the function of the natural law, is nothing else than an imprint on us of the Divine light. It is therefore evident that the natural law is nothing else than the rational creature's participation of the eternal law.

Article 3. Whether there is a human law?

It is from the precepts of the natural law, as from general and indemonstrable principles, that the human reason needs to proceed to the more particular determination of certain matters. These particular determinations, devised by human reason, are called human laws...As a result of which Tully says in his Rhetoric[1] that "justice has its source in nature; as a consequence,.... those things which emanated from nature and were approved by custom, were sanctioned by fear and reverence for the law."

Article 4. Whether there was any need for a divine law?

I answer that, Besides the natural and the human law it was necessary for the directing of human conduct to have a Divine law. And this for four reasons. First...since man is ordained to an end of eternal happiness...therefore it was necessary that, besides the natural and the human law, man should be directed to his end by a law given by God.

Secondly, because, on account of the uncertainty of human judgment, especially on contingent and particular matters,...it was necessary for man to be directed...by a law given by God, for it is certain that such a law cannot err.

Thirdly...Man is not competent to judge of interior movements, that are hidden, but only of exterior acts...Consequently, human law could not sufficiently curb and direct interior acts; and it was necessary...a Divine law should supervene.

Fourthly, because, as Augustine says, human law cannot punish or forbid all evil deeds: since while aiming at doing away with all evils, it would...hinder the advance of the common good, which is necessary for human intercourse. In order, therefore, that no evil might remain unforbidden and unpunished, it was necessary to have a Divine law, which forbids all sins.

QUESTION 94. THE NATURAL LAW

Article 2. Whether the natural law contains several precepts, or only one?

The first principle of practical reason is one founded on the notion of good, namely that "good is that which all things seek after." Hence this is the first precept of law, that "good is to be done and pursued, and evil is to be avoided." All other precepts of the natural law are based upon this: so that whatever the

---

1 I.e., Cicero in *De Inventione Rhetorica ii.*

practical reason naturally apprehends as man's good (or evil) belongs to the precepts of the natural law as something to be done or avoided....

Because in man there is first of all an inclination to good in accordance with the nature which he has in common with all substances: inasmuch as every substance seeks the preservation of its own being, according to its nature: and by reason of this inclination, whatever is a means of preserving human life, and of warding off its obstacles, belongs to the natural law.

Secondly, there is in man an inclination to things that pertain to him more specially, according to that nature which he has in common with other animals: and in virtue of this inclination, those things are said to belong to the natural law, "which nature has taught to all animals" such as sexual intercourse, education of offspring and so forth.

Thirdly, there is in man an inclination to good, according to the nature of his reason, which nature is proper to him: thus man has a natural inclination to know the truth about God, and to live in society. And in this respect, whatever pertains to this inclination belongs to the natural law; for instance, to shun ignorance, to avoid offending those among whom one has to live, and other such things regarding the above inclination.

Article 4. Whether the natural law is the same in all men?

The practical reason, on the other hand, is busied with contingent matters[1] ... and consequently, although there is a principle of logical necessity in the general principles of the natural law, the more we descend into matters of detail and the facts of specific cases, the more frequently we encounter defects[2] ...

It is right and true for all to act according to reason: and from this principle it follows as a proper conclusion, for example, that goods entrusted to another should be restored to their owner. Now this is true for the majority of cases; but it may happen in a particular case that it would be injurious, and therefore unreasonable, to restore goods held in trust. For instance, if they are claimed for the purpose of fighting against one's country. And this principle will be found to fail the more, according as we descend further into detail, ... because the greater the number of conditions added, the greater the number of ways in which the principle may fail, so that it be not right to restore or not to restore.

Consequently, we must say that the general principles of the natural law are the same for all, both as to rectitude[3] and as to knowledge...And though the conclusions that we draw from those general principles...are the same for all in the majority of cases, both as to rectitude and as to knowledge; yet in some few cases it may fail, both as to rectitude...and as to knowledge...Thus, in some the reason is perverted by evil habit, or an evil disposition of nature; so that Julius Cesar tells us, for example, that theft, although it is expressly contrary to the natural law, was not considered wrong among the Germans...

Article 5. Whether the natural law can be changed?

A change in the natural law may be understood in two ways. First, by way of addition. In this sense nothing hinders the natural law from being changed: since many things for the benefit of human life have been added over time, which were not contemplated by the natural law...

Secondly, a change in the natural law may be understood by way of subtraction, so that something which was previously according to the natural law, ceases to be so. In this context, the natural law is nevertheless altogether unchangeable in its first principles: but in its secondary principles, which, as

---

1 I.e., those whose outcomes are not necessarily determined.
2 I.e., the more incomplete and unhelpful the natural law becomes.
3 I.e., morally correct behavior or thinking.

we have said, are certain detailed proximate conclusions drawn from the first principles, the natural law...may be changed in some particular cases of rare occurrence, through some special causes hindering the observance of such precepts...

The slaying of the innocent, adultery, and theft are against the natural law.[1] We can nevertheless find situations where these laws have been changed by God: as when God commanded Abraham to slay his innocent son (Genesis 22:2); and when he ordered the Jews to borrow and steal the vessels of the Egyptians (Exodus 12:35); and when He commanded Hosea to take to himself "a wife of fornications"[2] (Hosea 1:2).

In addition, death can be inflicted on any man, guilty or innocent, by the command of God, without any injustice whatever. In like manner adultery is intercourse with another's wife, who is allotted to him by the law emanating from God. Consequently, intercourse with any woman, by the command of God, is neither adultery nor fornication. The same applies to theft...since whatever is taken by the command of God, to Whom all things belong, is not taken against the will of its owner, whereas it is in this that theft consists.

Article 6. Whether the law of nature can be abolished from the heart of man?

There belong to the natural law, first, certain most general precepts, that are known to all; and secondly, certain secondary and more detailed precepts, which are, as it were, conclusions following closely from first principles. As to those general principles, the natural law, in the abstract, can nowise be blotted out from men's hearts. Although it can be blotted out in a specific case, insofar as

reason is hindered...on account of concupiscence or some other passion...

But as to the other, i.e., the secondary precept of the natural laws, the natural law can be blotted out from the human heart, either by evil persuasions...or by vicious customs and corrupt habits, as among some men, theft, and even unnatural vices,[3] as the Apostle Paul states were not esteemed sinful.

QUESTION 96. THE POWER OF HUMAN LAW

Article 2. Whether it belongs to the human law to repress all vices?

As Isidore[4] says, law should be "possible both according to nature, and according to the customs of the country."...Thus the same is not possible to a child as to a full-grown man: for which reason the law for children is not the same as for adults, since many things are permitted to children, which in an adult are punished by law or open to blame....

Now human law is framed for the general population, the majority of whom are not perfect in virtue. Wherefore human laws do not forbid all vices, from which the virtuous abstain, but only the more grievous vices, from which it is possible for the majority to abstain; and chiefly those that are to the hurt of others, without the prohibition of which human society could not be maintained: thus human law prohibits murder, theft and such like.

Article 4. Whether human law binds a man in conscience?[5]

On the other hand laws may be unjust in two ways: first, by being contrary to human good, through

---

1 Here Aquinas is replying to objections.
2 I.e., a promiscuous woman.
3 E.g., sexual vices, such as pederasty.
4 I.e., Saint Isidore of Seville (c. 560–636), a scholar and Archbishop of Seville.
5 Aquinas is really asking, Are we obliged to obey unjust human laws?

being opposed to the things mentioned above—either in respect of the end, as when an authority imposes on his subjects burdensome laws, conducive, not to the common good, but rather to his own cupidity[1] or vainglory—or in respect of the author, as when a man makes a law that goes beyond the power committed to him—or in respect of the form, as when burdens are imposed unequally on the community, although with a view to the common good. The like are acts of violence rather than laws; because, as Augustine says, "a law that is not just, seems to be no law at all."[2] As a result of which, such laws do not bind in conscience, except perhaps in order to avoid scandal or disturbance, for which cause a man should even yield his right...

Secondly, laws may be unjust through being opposed to the Divine good: such are the laws of tyrants inducing to idolatry, or to anything else contrary to the Divine law: and laws of this kind must nowise be observed, because, as stated in Acts 5:29, "we ought to obey God rather than man."

Second Part of the Second Part

QUESTION 27. THE PRINCIPLE ACT OF CHARITY, WHICH IS TO LOVE

Article 1. Whether to be loved is more proper to charity than to love?

To love belongs to charity...But to be loved is not an act of charity by the person loved...Hence it is clear that to love is more proper to charity than to be loved....

This can be exemplified in two ways. First, in the fact that friends are more commended for loving than for being loved, indeed, if they be loved and yet love not, they are blamed. Secondly, because a mother, whose love is the greatest, seeks rather to love than to be loved....

Article 7. Whether it is more meritorious to love an enemy than to love a friend?

When therefore it is asked which is better or more meritorious, to love one's friend or one's enemy, these two loves may be compared in two ways: first, on the part of our neighbor whom we love; secondly, on the part of the reason for which we love him.

In the first way, love of one's friend surpasses love of one's enemy, because a friend is both better and more closely united to us, so that he is a more suitable matter of love and consequently the act of love that passes over this matter, is better, and therefore its opposite is worse, for it is worse to hate a friend than an enemy.

In the second way, however, it is better to love one's enemy than one's friend, and this for two reasons. First, because it is possible to love one's friend for another reason than God, whereas God is the only reason for loving one's enemy. Secondly, because if we suppose that both are loved for God, our love for God is proved to be all the stronger through carrying a man's affections to things which are furthest from him, namely, to the love of his enemies, even as the power of a furnace is proved to be the stronger, according as it throws its heat to more distant objects. Hence our love for God is proved to be so much the stronger, as the more difficult are the things we accomplish for its sake, just as the power of fire is so much the stronger, as it is able to set fire to a less inflammable matter.

Yet just as the same fire acts with greater force on what is near than on what is distant, so too, charity loves with greater fervor those who are united to us than those who are far removed; and in this

---

1 I.e., inordinate desire.
2 *De Libero Arbitrio i*, 5.

respect the love of friends, considered in itself, is more ardent and better than the love of one's enemy.

Article 8. Whether it is more meritorious to love one's neighbor than to love God?

I answer that this comparison may be taken in two ways. First, by considering both loves separately: and then, without doubt, the love of God is the more meritorious... Secondly, the comparison may be understood to be between the love of God alone on the one side, and the love of one's neighbor for God's sake, on the other. In this way, love of our neighbor includes love of God, while love of God does not include love of our neighbor. Hence the comparison will be between perfect love of God, extending also to our neighbor, and inadequate and imperfect love of God, for "this commandment we have from God, that he, who loves God, love also his brother" (1 John 4:21).

QUESTION 101. PIETY

To whom does piety extend?

Man becomes a debtor to other men in various ways, according to their various excellences and the various benefits received from them. On both of these counts, however, God holds first place, for He is supremely excellent, and is for us the first principle of being and government. Firstly, then, we are debtors of God, and owe him worship and piety.

Secondly, the principles of our being and govern- ment are our parents and our country, which have given us birth and nourishment. Consequently, man is debtor chiefly to his parents and his country, after God....

So does it belong to piety... to give worship to one's parents and one's country. The worship due to our parents includes the worship given to all our kindred.... The worship given to our country includes homage to all our fellow-citizens and to all the friends of our country. Therefore, piety extends chiefly to these.

QUESTION 120. *EPIKEIA* OR EQUITY

Is *epikeia* a virtue?

When we were treating of laws, since human actions, with which laws are concerned, are com- posed of contingent singulars and are innumerable in their diversity, it was not possible to lay down rules of law that would apply to every single case....

Thus, the law, for example, requires deposits to be restored, because in the majority of cases this is just. Yet it happens sometimes to be injurious— for instance, if a madman were to put his sword in deposit, and demand its delivery while in a state of madness....

In these and like cases it is bad to follow the law, and it is good to set aside the letter of the law and to follow the dictates of justice and the common good. This is the object of *epikeia* which we call equity. Therefore, it is evident that *epikeia* is a virtue.

Questions

1. Aquinas's account of the cardinal virtues is very similar to Plato's account. List all four virtues and explain.
2. In question 90, Aquinas sets out four requirements of law. What are they?
3. Give an example of a moral act that violates each of the secondary precepts of natural law. The third secondary precept should be treated as two related precepts. So you need four examples. Note that an act may violate more than one precept.

4. Aquinas's view of unjust laws seems to lay the moral groundwork for the idea of civil disobedience. How does the natural law come into this? Use examples.

5. The concept of love is central in the Christian moral tradition. Compare Aquinas and one of the ancient philosophers—such as Aristotle—or philosophical schools—such as the Stoics—paying particular attention to his comments on friendship and charity.

6. Why does Aquinas say it is more meritorious to love one's enemy than one's friend? What if we take God out of it? Are we morally obliged to love our enemies? Why, why not?

7. What is *epikeia* and when does it come into play? Give examples.

Suggested Readings

Aquinas's most important work is the *Summa Theologiae* (or *Theologica*). The entire text is available online at newadvent.org, which uses the "literal translation" by the Fathers of the English Dominican Province. There are many other editions. The authoritative standard in scholarship is the Latin Leonine Edition of Aquinas's *Opera Omnia*. Aquinas composed many other theological and ethical works. For a more specific discussion, see his *Disputed Questions on the Virtues*, which includes five separate discussions: *On the Virtues in General*; *On Charity*; *On Brotherly Correction*; *On Hope*; and *On the Cardinal Virtues*. There is a recent translation by Ralph McInerny. For a comprehensive introduction to Thomistic ethics, see Rebecca Konyndyk DeYoung, Colleen McCluskey, and Christina Van Dyke, *Aquinas's Ethics: Metaphysical Foundations, Moral Theory, and Theological Context* (2009).

There are many sources and bibliographies. For a traditional perspective, see Peter Seipel, "Aquinas and the Natural Law" (2015), and J. Porter, "What the Wise Person Knows: Natural Law and Virtue in Aquinas's *Summa Theologiae*" (1999). On human rights, see Anthony J. Lisska, "Human Rights Theory Rooted in the Writings of Thomas Aquinas" (2013), and R. Mary Hayden Lemmons, "The Case for Aquinas's Personalist Natural Law" (2011).

In recent times, natural law ethics has seen something of a renaissance, particularly among Catholic and Christian thinkers. Jacques Maritain (*Natural Law: Reflections on Theory & Practice*, 2001, edited by William Sweet) and Ralph McInerny (*Ethica Thomistica*, 1997), provided an earlier impetus. Figures such as German Grisez, John Finnis, Robert George, Joseph Boyle, and William May represent a second wave of modern Thomism. Grisez (*Christian Moral Principles*, 1983) and Finnis (*Natural Law and Natural Rights*, 1980) played a particularly important role, reformulating natural law theory on the basis of a list of fundamental human goods. Ralph McInerny and Russell Hittinger (*A Critique of the New Natural Law Theory*, 1987) have offered critiques of this more recent approach. Robert George responds in *In Defence of Natural Law* (1999).

In philosophy of law, a natural law rationale provides the main contemporary opposition to legal positivism. For a procedural account of natural law in jurisprudence and the law, see Lon Fuller (*The Morality of Law*, 1964). Ronald Dworkin, though not a Thomist in the classical sense, also argues against legal positivism (*Laws Empire*, 1986). See also Grisez, Boyle, and Finnis, "Practical Principles, Moral Truth, and Ultimate Ends" (1987), and Finnis, "Natural Law Theory: Its Past and Present" (2012).

For the use of natural law concepts in applied ethics, see Eugene F. Rogers Jr., "Aquinas on Natural Law and the Virtues in Biblical Context: Homosexuality as a Test Case" (1999). See also Qi Zhao, "Relation-Centred Ethics in Confucius and Aquinas" (2013) for a comparative discussion.

Chapter 24

The Islamic Tradition

The Islamic tradition has its origins in the early seventh century, when God revealed Himself to Abū al-Qāsim Muḥammad ibn ʿAbd Allāh ibn ʿAbd al-Muṭṭalib ibn Hāshim (c. 570–632), who we know as Muhammad. Muslims, adherents of Islam, know him as the "Holy Prophet," and almost all Muslims consider him to be the last prophet sent by God to humankind.

Muhammad was orphaned at an early age and was raised under the care of an uncle. He lived as a merchant, but at forty years of age he reported that the angel Gabriel (*Jibril*) visited him in a mountain cave where he went to pray. This was the first of many revelations that he received throughout the rest of his life. He began preaching publicly three years after receiving his first revelation, proclaiming that "God (*Allāh*) is One," that complete surrender (which is the meaning of the word '*islam*') to Him is the only way acceptable to God, and that he was a prophet and messenger of God.

Muhammad was met with hostility from some of the tribes in Mecca, his birthplace. In 622, he went to Medina (then known as Yathrib) to escape persecution. He gained many converts, and in 629 marched on Mecca with an army of 10,000 converts and seized the city with little resistance. By the time of his death, most of the Arabian Peninsula had converted to Islam, and by the eighth century the Islamic empire stretched from modern-day Spain in the west to India in the east.

Muslims believe that Islam is a primordial faith—one that was revealed many times through human history. God first revealed Himself to Adam, and then through prophets such as Abraham, Moses, and Jesus, and finally Muhammad. As the last prophet, Muhammad's role was to restore the original, monotheistic faith announced by previous prophets. Muslims believe that the purpose of existence is to worship God. Life in this world is a preparation for the next world, with believers going to the Garden and the wicked to Gehenna.

The fundamental source of Islamic teaching is the holy *Qur'an*[1] (*lit.*, "*the recitation*"), which contains an account of Muhammad's revelations. His teachings and practices are also recorded in the Hadith and Sira literature. These writings provide the sources of Islamic law (*the sharî'a*), which touches on virtually every aspect of life and society. The practices

---

1 Scholars prefer the spelling *Qur'an*, though *Quran* and *Koran* are often seen.

of Islam include the five pillars of obligatory worship: faith, prayer, charity, fasting, and the *Hajj* (the pilgrimage to Mecca).

After Muhammad's death, Islam divided into rival camps, known as the Sunni and the Shia (or Shiite). It also has a mystical tradition, called Sufism, which recalls the desert fathers, and has much earlier origins. In spite of its divisions, Islam flowered after Muhammad's death, and the period from the eighth century to the thirteenth century is often called the Islamic Golden Age. The Islamic world flourished economically, culturally, and scientifically after Muhammad's death, and produced many distinguished scholars.

Abu Hamid Muhammad ibn Muhammad al-Ghazālī (c. 1058–1111), known as Al-Ghazālī in the West, was a theologian, jurist, and Sufi mystic, who wrote in the Arabic and Persian languages. He was broadly educated and familiar with the philosophical tradition. In his youth, he studied with a theologian at a nearby madrasa (a college associated with a mosque), which brought him into contact with the court of the Grand Sultan in the city of Nishapur. In 1091, the Sultan's grand-vizier (chief advisor) appointed him to a prestigious chair in Islamic jurisprudence at the Nizâmiyya Madrasa in Baghdad.

Al-Ghazālī quickly became an influential intellectual, attracting many students and speaking publicly on theological controversies. He was closely connected to the ruling elites, but soon became implicated in political intrigues. In the resulting crisis, he gave up his prestigious position, disposed of his wealth, and adopted the wandering, ascetic life of the Sufis, seeking God. After a pilgrimage to Mecca in 1096, Al-Ghazālī returned to his hometown, Tus, and devoted himself to teaching and further study.

Al-Ghazālī's work attests to the strength of the religious impulse that asserted itself after the Hellenistic decline. In an early work, *The Incoherence of the Philosophers* (*Tahâfut al-falâsifa*), he criticizes the Islamic philosophers (known as *falâsifa*) on the basis that the exclusive reliance on natural reason leads to skepticism. Like other thinkers of the time, he believes that religious experience gives us access to a higher and more certain form of knowledge. He accordingly places the highest value on the spiritual—and, seemingly, the intellectual—experience of the reality of God.

Towards the end of his life, Al-Ghazālī came to see himself as a *mujaddid*, someone divinely appointed to reinvigorate Muslim religious practice, and wrote an extensive ethical guide to everyday life. Islamic scholars consider this later work, entitled *The Revival of Religious Sciences* (*Iḥyāʾ ʿulūm al-dīn*), as his major achievement. In *The Revival*, he focuses on practical ethics. He also tempers his criticism of philosophy, and attempts, like al-Râghib al-Isfahânî (d. c. 1025), to reconcile the religious and philosophical traditions.

Al-Ghazālī's moral philosophy is remarkably realistic. Rather than give up human emotions and desires, which are an inherent part of human nature, we must learn to control hazardous traits like anger and sexual desire through the exercise of reason. The human soul, he says, is like a young horse, which needs discipline. This is a moral and religious imperative, for we will not be able to perform the good actions that warrant religious salvation unless we develop dependable character traits.

This approach is Aristotelian. He sets out a virtue ethics, which counterbalances the emphasis of Sunni scholars on the submission to religious law (*sharî'a*). In doing so, he recommends traditional virtues such as humility, patience, gratitude, wisdom, and charity, while disapproving of vices such as rancor, pride, conceit, and envy. We are morally deficient at birth and become morally imbalanced through the influence of other people. The solution in either case is constant discipline (*riyâda*) and training (*tarbiya*).

In his political writing, Al-Ghazālī exhorts rulers to adopt a principle of reciprocity, ruling over their subjects in the way that they would wish to be ruled. He identifies five earthly goods that rulers must maintain and protect: religion, life, intellect, offspring, and property. Whatever preserves these five goods is to be considered a public benefit (*maslaha*) and encouraged; whatever detracts from them is to be avoided. He also argues against rebellion, even against an evil tyrant, because he believes that the resulting public disorder will render a contemplative, virtuous life impossible.

There are two historical criticisms of Al-Ghazālī. Some critics have complained that his criticism of philosophy promoted dogmatism and an inward conservatism in Islam, which discouraged its intellectual development. Other critics, however, have complained that his work surreptitiously replaced the original understanding of the Muslim faith with a blend of Sufi mysticism and philosophy that is less authentic.

The first reading is from the *Qur'an*, which is considered the *verbatim* word of God, as revealed through the angel Gabriel. The verses are organized into 114 chapters (*suras*) and record Muhammad's revelations over a period of 23 years up until his death. Since many Islamic scholars have argued that the only authoritative text of the *Qur'an* is the original Arabic text, translations of the *Qur'an* are usually described as "interpretations" rather than "translations." The reading is based on *The Koran Interpreted* by Arthur Arberry (1905–69), which avoids sectarian interpretations of controversial passages. The excerpts address the mercy of God, the truth of Islam, and the character of virtue.

The second reading is from one of the later sections of *The Revival of Religious Sciences* entitled *The Book of Fear and Hope*. Al-Ghazālī—like the Skeptics—as a moral physician, describes therapies for the soul and demonstrates how fear and hope may motivate us to act ethically. The style recalls the Biblical tradition.

The *Qur'an*[1]

(644–656)

I. The Opening

In the Name of God, the Merciful, the Compassionate

Praise belongs to God, the Lord of all Being,
the All-merciful, the All-compassionate,
the Master of the Day of Doom.[2]

5 [You] only we serve; to [You] alone we pray for
    succour.
Guide us in the straight path,
the path of those whom [You have] blessed,
not of those against whom [You are] wrathful,
nor of those who are astray.

III. The House of Imran

In the Name of God, the Merciful, the Compassionate

...

God
there is no god but He, the
Living, the Everlasting.

He has sent down upon [you] the Book
with the truth, confirming what was before it,
and He sent down the Torah and the Gospel

[in an earlier time], as guidance to the people,
and He sent down the Salvation.

As for those who disbelieve in God's signs, for
them awaits a terrible chastisement; God is
All-mighty, Vengeful.

From God nothing whatever is hidden
in heaven and earth. It is He who forms you
in the womb as He will. There is no god but He,
the All-mighty, the All-wise....

As for the unbelievers, their riches
will not avail them, neither their children,
[anything at all] against God; those—they shall be
fuel for the Fire
like Pharaoh's folk,[3] and the people before them,
who cried lies to Our signs; God seized them
because of their sins; God is terrible
in retribution.

10 Say to the unbelievers: 'You shall be
overthrown, and mustered into Gehenna[4]—
an evil cradling!'...

IX. Repentance

... O believers, what is amiss with you, that when
it is said to you, 'Go forth in the way of God,'

---

1 Excerpt from the *Qur'an* (644–656), from A.J. Arberry, trans., *The Koran Interpreted*. Vols. 1 and 2 (London: George Allen & Unwin Ltd., and New York: The Macmillan Company, 1955 [2nd impression, 1963]).

2 I.e., the Day of Judgment.

3 "Pharaoh's folk" refers to the Egyptians who had enslaved the Israelites.

4 I.e., hell.

you sink down heavily to the ground? Are you so content with this present life, rather than the world to come? Yet the enjoyment of this present life, compared with the world to come, is a little thing.

If you go not forth, He will chastise you with a painful chastisement, and instead of you He will substitute another people; and you will not hurt Him anything, for God is powerful over everything....

XVII. The Night Journey

... [Your] Lord has decreed
you shall not serve
any but Him,
and to be good to parents,
whether one or both of them
attains old age with [you];
say not to them 'Fie'[1]
neither chide them, but
speak unto them words
respectful,
and lower to them the
wing of humbleness
out of mercy and say,
'My Lord,
have mercy upon them,
as they raised me up
when I was little.'...
And give the kinsman his right,
and the needy, and the traveler;
and never squander;...

35 And slay not the soul that God has forbidden, except by right. Whosoever is slain unjustly, We[2] have appointed to his next-of-kin authority; but let him not exceed in slaying[3]...

And do not approach the property of the orphan save in the fairest manner, until he is of age.
And fulfil the covenant...
And fill up the measure when you measure, and weigh with the straight balance;...
And pursue not [what you have] no knowledge of;
the hearing, the sight, the heart...

40 All of that—the wickedness of it is hateful in the sight of [your] Lord.

That is of the wisdom [your] Lord has revealed to
    [you]:
set not up with God
another god, or [you]
[will] be cast into
Gehenna, reproached
and rejected....

XXII. The Pilgrimage

40 Leave is given to those who fight because they were wronged[4]—surely God is able to help them—
who were expelled from their habitations without right, except that they say 'Our Lord is God.' Had God not driven back the people, some by the means of others,

---

1 'Fie' is a word used to express disgust or outrage.

2 I.e., God. Though God is one, He is sometimes referred to by the royal we, or majestic plural.

3 I.e., the person is not to exceed in exacting retribution for the unjust killing of one's kin.

4 This is a reference to a "minor jihad." In Arabic *jihad* literally means striving or struggling, especially with a praiseworthy aim. It can cover a range of struggles, from internal, spiritual battles within oneself to armed struggle or war against unbelievers.

there had been destroyed cloisters and churches,
oratories and mosques, wherein God's Name
is much mentioned. Assuredly God will
help him who helps Him…

XXV. Salvation

The servants of the All-merciful are
those who walk on the earth modestly
and who, when the ignorant address them,
say, 'Peace'…

XXXIII. The Confederates

35 Men and women who have surrendered,
believing men and believing women,
obedient men and obedient women,
truthful men and truthful women,
enduring men and enduring women,
humble men and humble women,
men and women who give in charity,
men who fast and women who fast,
men and women who guard their private parts,
men and women who remember God [often]—
for them God has prepared forgiveness
and a mighty wage.…

XLII. Counsel

… For the evildoers there awaits a
painful chastisement.
[You see] the evildoers going in fear
of [what] they have earned, [which] is about
to fall on them; but those who believe
and do righteous deeds are in Meadows
of the Gardens; whatsoever they will
they shall have with their Lord; that is

the great bounty.…

Say: 'I do not ask of you
a wage for this, except love for the
kinsfolk; and whosoever gains a good
deed, We shall give him increase of good
in respect of it. Surely God is
All-forgiving, All-thankful.…'

25 And He answers those who believe
and do righteous deeds, and He
gives them increase of His bounty.…

35 And those who avoid the heinous sins
and indecencies and when they are angry
forgive,
and those who answer their Lord, and
perform the prayer,…
and who, when insolence visits them,
do help themselves—
and the recompense of evil is evil
the like of it;[1] but whoso pardons
and puts things right, his wage [shall be paid by]
God…

XLIX. Apartments

… O believers, let not any people
scoff at another people who may be
better than they; neither let women
scoff at women who may be better
than themselves. And find not fault
with one another, neither revile one
another by nicknames. An evil name
is ungodliness after belief. And
whoso repents not, those—they are
the evildoers.…

---

1 I.e., an eye for an eye.

CIV. The Backbiter

...

Woe unto every backbiter, slanderer,
who has gathered riches and counted them over
thinking his riches have made him immortal!

No indeed; he shall be thrust into the Crusher;[1]
and what shall teach [you] what is the Crusher?
The Fire of God kindled
roaring over the hearts
covered down upon them,
in columns outstretched.

CVII. Charity

...

[Have you] seen him who [will tell] lies [on the day
    of judgment]?

That is he who repulses the orphan
and urges not the feeding of the needy.

So woe to those...
who make display
and refuse [to be charitable].

CXII. Sincere Religion

...

Say: 'He is God, One,
God, the Everlasting Refuge,
who has not begotten, and has not been begotten,
and equal to Him is not any one.'

READING 24B

Abū Ḥāmid Muḥammad ibn Muḥammad al-Ghazālī, *The Book of Fear and Hope*[2]

(c. 1096)

... In the name of God, the Merciful, the Compassionate.

Praise be to God whose loving kindness and reward are hoped for, whose stratagems and punishment are feared; who keeps alive the hearts of His saints with the breath of hope in Him, so that He may urge them on... [to] His courtyard...And with the lashes of threatening and His harsh upbraiding

---

1 Another reference to Gehenna, or hell.
2 Abū Ḥāmid Muḥammad ibn Muḥammad al-Ghazālī, *The Book of Fear and Hope* (c. 1096), adapted from William McKane, ed., trans., *Al-Ghazali's Book of Fear and Hope* (Leiden: E.J. Brill, 1965).

He has [also—in His mercy—driven those who shun Him] towards the house of His reward and preferment; and he has blocked them from…the butt of His wrath and vengeance by leading [them]…with chains of violence and coercion, and reins of compassion and graciousness, to His Garden….

Hope and fear are the two wings by means of which those who are brought near [to God] fly to every commendable station,[1] and two mounts on which every steep ascent of the paths of the next world is traversed. And nothing but the reins of hope will lead [the man who is heavy with burdens, and with the toils of members and limbs] to the vicinity of the Merciful and the joy of the Gardens…And nothing shall avert from the fire of Gehenna and the painful punishment the man who is [consumed by] the blandishments of lusts and the marvels of pleasures except the scourges of threatening and the assaults of violence. Consequently…[I propose to provide an exposition] of the essence and merits of them both,…[and join them together,] in spite of their polarity and mutual antipathy.[2]

Exposition of the Essence of Hope

… We are dealing at present with the essence of hope…. Its exposition is that everything that confronts you is either what is abhorred or what is desired, and is divided into what is existent at the moment, what has existed in the past, and what is expected in the future. When what has existed in the past occurs to your mind, it is called remembering and recollecting; if what occurs to your mind is existent at the moment, it is called finding and tasting and perceiving. It is called finding because it is a state which you find for yourself. And, if the existence of something in the future occurs to your mind and prevails over your heart, it is called expectation and anticipation. [Now i]f the thing expected

is abhorred, with pain in the heart resulting from it, it is called fear and distress. If it is something desired, with the pleasure and relief of heart resulting from the expectation of it and the attachment of the heart to it and the occurrence of its existence to your mind, that relief is hope.

Hence hope [looks to the future and] is the relief of the heart, because [it is] the expectation of what it esteems desirable. But the desirable thing which is anticipated must have a cause, so, if the expectation of it [arises from the fact that you have obtained] the majority of the means to it, the name of hope in relation to it is justified. If that expectation[, on the other hand,] is in spite of the defectiveness of the means to it and their disorder, the name of self-deceit and stupidity is more justified in relation to the expectation than that of hope. [And again, i]f the means are not specified either as existent or in mutual contradiction, the name of wishful thinking is more justified in relation to the expectation, because it is an expectation [that has no] cause….

[Now] the Spiritual Directors[3] teach that this present world [can be seen as a field to be tilled,] and the heart is as the earth, and faith is as the seed…, and obedience is…the turning over of the earth and the cleansing of it and the digging of channels to lead waters to [it]; and the heart which is infatuated with this present world and submerged in it is like swampy ground in which the seed does not [bear fruit]. And the Day of Resurrection is the day of reaping, and no one reaps except what he has sown…

For everyone who seeks good ground and casts into it seed of first quality which is neither moldy nor worm-eaten, who thereafter furnishes it with what is necessary to it, that is, the conducting of water to it at appropriate times; who then clears the ground of thorns and weeds and everything that obstructs the growth of the seed or makes it rot; who then sits down and expects from the bounty [or grace] of God

---

1 I.e., place of rest.

2 The first part of the book accordingly deals with hope and the therapy of hope; the second part with fear.

3 Literally, 'Spiritual Directors' is a translation of 'the masters of hearts.'

the warding off of thunderbolts and blights, until his crop is mature and he arrives at his goal—his expectation is called hope. [On the other hand], if he scatters his seed in ground which is baked hard or swampy, which is so elevated that the water does not flow into it, and does not labour one whit in the preparation of the [crop]—if he then expects a harvest from it, his expectation is called stupidity and self-deceit, not hope. And, if he scatters seed in ground which is good but without water, and proceeds to wait for the waters of the rains where they neither prevail nor are cut off, his expectation is called wishful thinking and not hope.

Therefore the name of hope is only used legitimately in relation to the expectation of a thing desired, [when all of those things, which come within the choice of the person, that would facilitate it have been done] and only what does not come within his choice remains, and this is the bounty of God in repelling birds and blights.

[And our hope for God's pardon can be compared to the hope of the owner of the crops for a good harvest, s]o when the [person] sows the seed of faith and irrigates it with the water of obedience and cleanses the heart from the thorns of vicious moral traits and [then relies upon] the bounty of God...[his] expectation [of pardon] is hope in its essence, and commendable in itself...

Exposition of the Therapy of Hope and the Way in which the State of Hope Is Obtained from It and Becomes Dominant

Know that two types of men have need of this therapy [of hope]; either the man over whom despair has become dominant, so that he has neglected worship; or the man over whom fear has become dominant, and who has been so extravagant in his perseverance

in worship, so that he has done injury to himself and his family.... [And therefore, in both cases] they have need of the treatment which will restore them to the equilibrium.

For the person who is disobedient and self-deceived, [on the other hand,] who has wishful thoughts of God in company with his evasion of worship and his blind plunging into deeds of disobedience—the therapeutic properties of hope are, in this case, turned into lethal poisons, just as is the case with honey which is a cure for the person who is overcome by cold and a lethal poison to the person who is overcome by heat. [Moreover], in the case of the self-deluded person, only the therapeutic properties of fear can be employed...and, for that reason,... [there must be someone] to preach to the people; one benevolently disposed who observes the incidence of diseases and treats every disease with its antidote and not with what it has excess of. For what is sought after is the equilibrium, and the goal with respect to all attributes and moral traits, and the optimum state of affairs, is their [true] mean. And [so, when an individual's personal] mean transgresses upon one of the two extremes, it must be treated with what returns it to the [true] mean, not with what would increase its tendency away from the mean....

The state of hope becomes dominant by means of two things; the one is reflection, and the other the reciting of the verses (... of the Qur'an) and traditions and reports [of the past]....

[In the case of reflection, a man must reflect on all the benefits that God has bestowed upon us.] And... included in reflection is the scrutiny of the wisdom of the Law and its Practice in respect of this-worldly benefits, and [the mercy of God which is in it.] ...

The second [form of therapy] is the reciting of the verses and the traditions, and the material which has to do with hope...

[So, for example,] Anas[1] reported in a tradition

---

1 This Anas likely refers to Mālik ibn Anas (711–795), an Arab Muslim jurist, theologian, and hadith traditionist. A hadith is one of various reports describing the words and actions of Muhammad.

that the Prophet said: When the creature commits a sin, it is recorded against him. [And]a nomadic Arab said: And, if he repents of it? He said: It is erased from him. He said: If he returns to sin? The Prophet said: It is recorded against him. The nomad said: And, if he repents? He said: It is blotted out from his page. He said: For how long? He said: For as long as he begs for pardon and repents towards God. Surely God does not grow weary in pardoning until the creature grows weary of begging for pardon. And, when the creature purposes a good deed, the Master of the right hand writes it down as a good deed before he performs it; and, if he performs it, he records ten good deeds. Then God multiplies it to seven hundred multiples....

[And when Muhammad, the Messenger of God, told the people that only nine hundred and ninety-nine out of every thousand are for the fire, the people despaired and became idle, ceasing to work. And when Muhammad attacked them,] [t]hey said: And who would occupy themselves with work after what you have related to us...?... [And he reassured them, saying:] Among the rest of the nations you are but as the white hair in the coat of the black bull...

So observe how he was driving the people with the whip of fear and leading them with the reins of hope to God. He drove them with the whip of fear at first, and, when that brought them beyond the point of equilibrium..., he cured them with the therapy of hope and returned them to the equilibrium....

The Exposition of the Essence of Fear

Know that fear [expresses] the suffering of the heart and its conflagration by means of the anticipation of what is abhorred as a future contingency. And this has been made clear in the exposition of the essence of hope....

The state of fear can [be explained] in terms of knowledge, state and action.... So that it is as if someone committed a crime against a king, then fell into his hands and feared that he would be put to death as an example... But the suffering of his heart through fear is in proportion to the strength of his knowledge of the means which would lead to his being put to death, such as the enormity of his crime and the fact that the king in himself is rancorous, wrathful and revengeful...

And [it is this] knowledge... which initiates and fans the conflagration and suffering of the heart, and that conflagration is [the 'state' of] fear. And, similarly, [in a theological context,]... the strength of [a man's] fear will be in proportion to his 'knowledge' of his defects and his 'knowledge' of the majesty [and power] of God...

Then, when 'knowledge' is perfected, the majesty of fear and the conflagration of the heart are produced. Then the trace of the conflagration flows from the heart into the body and the members and the attributes. In the body by means of emaciation and [paleness] and fainting and shrieking and weeping... In the members by restraining them from disobedience and binding them to deeds of obedience; by repairing what is defective and making ready for the future.... In the attributes by stifling the lusts and blackening the pleasures, so that the disobediences beloved by him become abhorrent, just as honey becomes abhorrent to the man who desires it, when he 'knows' that there is poison in it. So the lusts are burned up by fear and the members are trained, and [he obtains] self-abasement and humility and submissiveness and lowliness... in the heart...

Moreover he is absorbed with concern through his fear... And he has no preoccupation but vigilance and self-examination and spiritual combat and conserving breaths and glances and reprehending the soul for the suggestions and footsteps and words (sc. of Satan).... This is the state of the person over whom fear has prevailed and gained the mastery....

And the strength of vigilance and self-examination and spiritual combat[1] is in proportion to the strength of fear which is the suffering of the heart and its conflagration....

Therefore fear [becomes active] in the members through restraint and perseverance, and it is in virtue of restraint that it is given the new name of chastity which is refraining from the determinism of lusts. And abstinence is higher than it, since it is more universal, because it is refraining from everything forbidden. And higher than it is piety, since it is the name for refraining from the sum of things forbidden and dubious. And beyond it is the name [sincerity; for sincere piety may urge a man on to forsake what has no evil in it for fear of what has evil in it]...

Exposition that the Optimum Is the Dominance of Fear or the Dominance of Hope or the Two in Equilibrium

Know that the traditions concerning the merit of fear and hope are legion, and often the observer will inspect the two of them and doubt will overwhelm him as to which of the two is the higher good. The person who says: Is fear or hope the higher good?, asks a spurious question which resembles the question: Is bread or water the higher good? The answer to it is to say that bread is the higher good for the person who is hungry and water for the person who is thirsty. And, if both are present in union, one has regard to which is the more dominant; [so] if it is hunger, bread is the higher good and, if it is thirst, water is the higher good. If they are in balance, bread and water are on par. This is so because everything [that we want in order to reach] a goal has its merit

disclosed in relation to its goal, not to itself. And fear and hope are therapies by means of which hearts are cured and their respective merits are in proportion to the...disease [being cured]. For, if what has dominion over the heart is the disease of fancied security from the stratagems of God and being self-deceived thereby, fear is the higher good. And, if the most dominant factors are hopelessness and a despairing of the mercy of God, hope is the higher good. Similarly, if disobedience has mastery..., fear is the higher good.

And it [could be said] absolutely that fear is the higher good...because disobedience and self-deceit are...dominant [within us]. [But] if one looks at the source of fear and hope, hope is [absolutely] the higher good, because it is an outlet from the sea of mercy, and the outlet of fear is from the sea of wrath. And whoever is attentive to those attributes of God which decree kindness and mercy, love will dominate him and there is no station[2] beyond love. [And since the prop of fear] is a turning towards those attributes which decree severity[,...] love does not mingle with it as it does with hope....

[Now the] ultimate objective of the believer is that his hope and fear should be in equilibrium, and [since] the dominance of hope [would encourage]...self-deceit and a dearth of 'knowledge' [among our contemporaries,]...what is most salutary for...them, is the dominance of fear, with the proviso that it does not bring them to hopelessness and abandonment of action, and [sever the desire] for pardon...For that is despair and not fear, since fear is that which provides an incentive for action...and snatches the heart away from reliance on this world, and summons it to withdraw from the home of self-deceit. [And this is a] commendable fear...

---

1 I.e., the 'action' of fear.

2 I.e., no place of rest.

Questions

1. Do you agree with the idea of God in the Islamic tradition? What role does God have in morality?
2. Compare the *Torah* and the *Qur'an*. How does the tribal and customary law come into these texts?
3. What kind of life should a Muslim live in order to reach God's Garden in the next world? Does it differ from a Jewish, Christian, or Buddhist life?
4. Discuss the reference to "minor jihad" in the excerpts from the *Qur'an*. When can jihad in the form of an armed struggle be justified?
5. Al-Ghazālī argued that the path of "independent" reason—i.e., without religious revelation—is the path of Satan. What role, if any, does revealed wisdom have in moral theory? Mention a second philosopher in your answer.
6. Muslims believe that the revelations in the *Qur'an* come directly from God. Some Christians have a similar view of the Bible. What happens, then, if the two religions disagree? Mention two philosophers in your answer.
7. Discuss the use of parables or "similes" in Islam and another moral tradition. Do you find it helpful to think of your heart as a field in which the seed of faith is sown?
8. What is the role of fear, hope, and the mercy of God in morality?
9. Al-Ghazālī says that the "salutary" state for the people of his own era is fear. What about our era, then? What is the proper state: hope or fear? Why?

Suggested Readings

Although there are many English translations of the *Qur'an* online, most reflect the theological views of a particular branch of Islam. We have used a neutral translation. The introductory sources on Islam include Arthur Jeffery, *Islam: Muhammad and His Religion* (1958), and Charles Le Gai Eaton, *Islam and the Destiny of Man* (1994), which comments on the practice of Islam. For information and material on Sufism, see ias.org/sufism and Alan Godlas's site at the University of Georgia: islam.uga.edu.

Scholars agree that Al-Ghazālī is one of the major figures in the Islamic tradition. His *Revival of Religious Sciences* provides a comprehensive guide to ethical behavior in everyday life. An English translation is available at ghazali.org along with other sources.

The English sources on Al-Ghazālī include W. Montgomery Watt, *Muslim Intellectual: A Study of al-Ghazālī* (1963), and Margaret Smith, *al-Ghazālī the Mystic* (1944). For Al-Ghazālī's ethics, see Muhammad Abul Quasem, *The Ethics of Al-Ghazālī: A Composite Ethics in Islam* (1975), G.F. Hourani's "Ghazālī on the Ethics of Action" (1976) (reprinted in Hourani, *Reason and Tradition in Islamic Ethics* [1985]), and Hamid Reza Alavi, "Al-Ghazālī on Moral Education" (2007).

For the larger Islamic philosophical tradition, see Harry Austyn Wolfson, *The Philosophy of Kalam* (1976); Majid Fakhry, *A History of Islamic Philosophy*, 2nd ed. (1983); and Henry Corbin, *History of Islamic Philosophy*, trans. Liadain Sherrard (1993). For the ethical tradition, see Toshihiko Izutsu, *Ethico-Religious Concepts in the Quran* (1966), and Majid Fakhry, *Ethical Theories in Islam* (1991).

For current and applied work, see Al-Hasan Al-Aidaros et al., "Ethics and Ethical Theories from an Islamic Perspective" (2013), and J.E. Brockopp, *Islamic Ethics of Life: Abortion, War, and Euthanasia* (2003).

PART IV

MODERN SOURCES[1]

Sciences of Morality: The Rise of Liberalism and the Political, Psychological, and Religious Response

In the West, the Middle Ages were followed by the "Enlightenment," a term which implicitly discounts the value of the previous tradition. The return to non-Christian ancient sources, the successes of the scientific approach, the industrial revolution, and capitalism all favored materialism, which suggested that ethical principles could be rationally investigated. This tilted ethical inquiry back towards the pursuit of knowledge and theoretical wisdom, rather than practical wisdom.

The Protestant Reformation and the rejection of the centralized authority of the Roman Catholic Church gave individuals a right to answer religious and ethical questions for themselves. This change in perspective gave the moral conversation a subjective focus. Bishop Butler, for example, argues that it is in our rational self-interest to help other people. The echoes of his argument have continued down to the present.

The modern period also saw the beginnings of the contemporary political tradition,

---

1   Depending on the structure they find in the history of philosophy, scholars define its periods in different ways. The "modern" period is often counted as beginning with Descartes and ending with Kant—that is, roughly, from around 1630 to around 1800. For the purposes of our chapters, however, we have counted "modern" approaches as beginning during the sixteenth century (with the Renaissance) and ending when "contemporary" philosophy begins, at the end of the nineteenth century.

which is based on the idea that individuals have consented to a social contract. This idea, and the notion of moral choice behind it, later found expression in utilitarianism, deontology, and liberalism, which had a strong democratic element. Mainstream moral philosophy, which reflected these influences, was marked by rationalism and empiricism. The study of ethics was seen as a science, and even, in the case of Kant, an abstract science of human freedom. Many thinkers wanted to produce comprehensive moral systems with the same kind of explanatory power, for example, as the scientific theories of Isaac Newton. At times, scientifically-minded theoreticians appear to reduce good to the pleasure principle, something someone like Kant strongly reacts against. The sharp controversies that mark modern moral theory sometimes make it difficult to choose among conflicting views.

The response to liberalism—and to the inequality, oppression, and general loss of meaning that followed upon the industrial revolution—was varied. Utilitarians such as Bentham and Mill argued for legal and educational reform. A renegade like Mandeville argues that we should allow vice to freely flourish for the overall good of society. For authors such as Marx and Engels, the ethical course of action was to overthrow the existing political order. Kierkegaard took refuge in a radical faith. For Nietzsche and Schopenhauer, it is the task of philosophy to find the way forward in the midst of general nihilism and instill meaning into our despairing lives. There was also an attempt, in American pragmatism and British idealism, to develop ethical theories that reconcile the interests of the individual with the interests of the community in a larger whole. For some, this required an appeal to some outside source of wisdom, such as religion.

In the modern period, there is an increasing appreciation for diversity within the western tradition. One noticeable phenomenon is an increasing number of women thinkers and a rising opposition to inequalities between men and women. Authors such as Christina of Sweden, Wollstonecraft, and Harriet Mill Taylor engage in philosophical speculation, whereas politically militant figures such as Olympe de Gouges and Sojourner Truth take heroic stances against the unfair treatment of women and enslaved blacks.

Although space-constraints require a mainly western focus for the rest of the book, we have included one influential, modern Neo-Confucian, Wáng Yáng-míng. One can also detect important Buddhist themes in Schopenhauer.

Chapter 25

Neo-Confucianism

Wáng Yáng-míng, 王陽明 (1472–1529, whose "birth name" was Wang Shou-ren or Shou-jen), was a Neo-Confucian philosopher in the Ming Dynasty. His teaching was influential in China and Japan. Although he is usually described as an "idealist," the primary impetus in his teaching comes from his attempt to remove the hiatus between ethical ideas and actions.

Wang, born into the lesser nobility, was a precocious child, attracted to philosophy. Even at the age of ten, it is said that he had settled upon his chief purpose in life: to study to become a sage. He remained steadfast in this purpose throughout his life. Although he studied the Confucian classics, Wang was attracted to Daoism and Buddhism as a young man and apparently wasted time in "flowery composition." Later he wrote the civil service examinations, failing in his first attempts.

After ranking highly in the examinations in 1499, Wang was appointed to a position in government, which was extremely corrupt at the time. Early in his career, he was punished—beaten with forty strokes before the Emperor—for speaking out against the eunuch Liu Chin, who had usurped the Emperor's authority. As a result, he was given a minor post in a remote outpost, but was eventually promoted and took on a wide variety of duties. These duties included military service, in which he was remarkably successful, and led to his appointment as the Governor of Jiangxi province.

Wang was influenced by Mencius and by the twelfth-century Chinese scholar and philosopher Lu Jiuyuan (陸九淵) and is credited with reviving the decaying Neo-Confucian tradition. As a charismatic teacher, he attracted students and disciples from across China. His most famous philosophical work is a collection of exchanges and anecdotes compiled by his students, in the Chinese fashion, which has been admirably translated by Wing-tsit Chan under the title *Instructions for Practical Living*.

Wang's moral philosophy can be seen as a response to two facets of the Neo-Confucian tradition. The first was Buddhism, which he saw as a selfish attempt to leave the "sorrowful sea of life and death" and in fact rested on an attachment to phenomena. There are nevertheless elements of Buddhism in his philosophy, which probably explains his sudden epiphany (*wu*), in which he instantly realized that the focus of the investigation into things is inward and carried out in one's own mind.

The second facet of the prevailing Neo-Confucian tradition that Wang was responding to was the "rationalism" of the famous scholar Chu Hsi (1130–1200). Wang criticized Chu Hsi's edition of the *Great Learning*, one of the "Four Books" in the Confucian curriculum, which had changed the order of the traditional text and added an "amendment." These changes made "the investigation of things" the first step in a virtuous life, and the "sincerity of the will" second. This was a mistake, Wang argued, since it was not possible to investigate properly without a sincere will.

The differences between the two philosophers were metaphysical. Wang argued that the operation of the will was primary and that the "principles" that the mind investigated were internal rather than external. In a sense, at least, he argues that the mind and the world are one. There are complicated issues here, but the important thing is that Chu Hsi's position seemed to promote a "devotion to external things" and a "neglect of the internal." This had led to a general loss of moral authenticity, which explained the general social decline.

Wang's refusal to separate the internal and external aspects of experience reflects his Daoism. He responds to the rationalists, affirming—like many earlier Confucians—that we are one with stones, mountains, and all living things. "At bottom heaven and earth and all things are my body (*wushen*). Is there any suffering or bitterness of the great masses that is not disease or pain in my own body?" (*Instructions*, 179) It is the failure of the small-minded man to recognize this state of affairs that distinguishes him from the sage. But the reality is the same for both.

It is helpful, in working through these arguments, to understand that the Chinese historically located the mind in the heart, *xin* or *xing*, which was the seat of both our feelings and our intellectual understanding. Wang's teaching has been described as *xin-xue*, the teaching of the mind-heart and, in a very real sense, the argument is that we should follow our hearts. The *xin* is a natural faculty, which is "clear or shining" (*zhao*), i.e., illuminates the ethical and metaphysical reality of things. From a western perspective, this idea has affinities with the natural law.

The practical observation that arises out of Wang's metaphysical view—which also derives from Buddhism—is that we can investigate the moral and intellectual principles that give rise to reality through introspection. All human beings, as Mencius argued, have an innate, intuitive knowledge of morality. This knowledge or "good conscience" (*liangzhi*, 良知) is not a matter of learning but of sincerity. Thus, like Zhou Dunyi (1017–73) and Cheng Hao (1032–85), Wang argues that sincerity must be recovered.

Wang acknowledges that selfish desires and false learning can obscure the *xin*. We must therefore cultivate inner tranquility by means of the elimination of desire, regular self-examination, and "quiet sitting" (*jingzuo*, 靜坐). This is an active process, however. Since thinking and acting cannot be separated, it is not enough to disregard bad thoughts, which must be "rooted out." This is an arduous process, Wang says, which cost him "a hundred deaths and a thousand sufferings."

Wang saw the purpose of teaching as moral cultivation. Since the mind includes all principles, a student can, with proper effort and guidance, access the perfect moral knowledge that resides inside the original human mind. This is called the extension of the knowledge of the innate mind. The process of becoming a sage is a process of introspective self-realization, in which the individual merges with the larger world and becomes one with the *Dao*.

One of the most provocative aspects of Wang's metaphysics is the unity of knowledge and action, which openly rejects the distinction between theoretical and practical wisdom. Although the translation of the Chinese is problematic—because it is far less precise than English—there is a sense in which Wang argues that the separation that we make in English between moral knowledge and moral behavior is fallacious. A person who has moral knowledge will—by virtue of that fact—behave morally.

Moral knowledge is therefore associated with the will, which must be educated. As one of Wang's students wrote: "We dared not seek understanding through intellection but only tried to attain concrete, personal realization." This reflects the concerns in the classical Chinese tradition, which was interested in conduct rather than theory. Wang's ethics is inherently practical and calls for "direct" or "concrete" action, which requires participation in the ordinary affairs of life and society.

The first reading is from the *Ch'uan-hsi lu* (傳習錄), the *Instructions for Practical Living*. The translation of Chinese titles is hazardous but the Chinese may also be rendered, more simply, in explanatory terms as: transmit study practice records, i.e., *Records of what has been transmitted, studied [and] practiced*. This title is more accurate, since the book is essentially a memoir of Wang, which records conversations and teachings collected by his students, along with a few letters. The emphasis in the book is on his pedagogy rather than his thought.

The second reading is from Wang's exegesis on the *Great Learning*, one of the "Four Books," which sets out the eight steps in a life of perfect virtue. Like the *Great Learning*, Wang's essay draws our attention to the influence of Daoism on Confucian philosophy.

From the *Ch'uan-hsi lu*,[1] a Memoir of Wáng Yáng-míng[2]

(1572)

Part I

CONVERSATIONS RECORDED BY HSÜ AI

5. I did not understand the Teacher's doctrine of the unity of knowledge and action and debated it back and forth with Huang Tsung-hsien and Ku Wei-hsien without coming to any conclusion. Therefore I took the matter to the Teacher. The Teacher said, "Give an example and let me see." I said, "For example, there are people who know that parents should be served with filial piety and elder brothers with respect but cannot put these things into practice. This shows that knowledge and action are clearly two different things."

The Teacher said, "The knowledge and action you refer to are already separated by selfish desires and are no longer knowledge and action in their original substance. There have never been people who know but do not act. Those who are supposed to know but do not act simply do not yet know. When sages and worthies taught people about knowledge and action, it was precisely because…Suppose we say that so-and-so knows filial piety and so-and-so knows brotherly respect. They must have actually practiced filial piety and brotherly respect before they can be said to know them. It will not do to say that they know filial piety and brotherly respect simply because they show them in words…

"[Today, people] distinguish between knowledge and action and pursue them separately, believing that one must know before he can act. They will discuss and learn the business of knowledge first, they say, and wait till they truly know before they put their knowledge into practice. Consequently, to the last day of life, they will never act and also will never know. This doctrine of knowledge first and action later is not a minor disease and it did not come about only yesterday. My present advocacy of the unity of knowledge and action is precisely the medicine for that disease.…"

8. [The Teacher] further said, "Knowledge is the original substance of the mind. The mind is naturally able to know. When it perceives the parents, it naturally knows that one should be filial. When it perceives the elder brother, it naturally knows that one should be respectful. And when it perceives a child fall into a well, it naturally knows that one should be commiserative. This is innate knowledge of good…and need not be sought outside…However, the ordinary man is not free from the obstruction of selfish ideas. He therefore requires the effort of the extension of knowledge and the investigation of things in order to overcome selfish ideas and restore principle. Then the mind's faculty of innate knowledge will no longer be obstructed but will be able to penetrate and operate everywhere. One's knowledge will then be extended. With knowledge extended, one's will becomes sincere."…

[11.] [The Teacher said,] "The reason the world is not in order is because superficial writing is growing and

---

1 傳習錄, a phrase taken from Confucius's *Lunyu*, 1:4; literally translated as '[transmit] [study, put-into-practice] [record],' or: *Records of what has been transmitted studied [and] practiced*.

2 Heavily adapted from Wáng Yáng-míng, *Instructions for Practical Living*, from Wing-tsit Chan, trans., *Instructions for Practical Living and Other Neo-Confucian Writings by Wang Yang-ming*, Number LXVIII of the Records of Civilization: Sources and Studies, UNESCO Collection of Representative Works Chinese Series (New York and London: Columbia University Press, 1963).

concrete practice is declining. People advance their own opinions, valuing what is novel and strange, in order to mislead the common folks and gain fame. They merely confuse people's intelligence and dull people's senses, so that people devote much of their time and energy to competing in conventional writing and flowery compositions in order to achieve fame; they no longer remember that there are such deeds as honoring the fundamental, valuing truth, and returning to simplicity and purity. All this trouble was started by those who wrote {extensively and superficially}."...

CONVERSATIONS RECORDED BY LU CH'ENG

31. I asked, "I read books and do not understand. Why?"

{The Teacher said,} "This is because you only seek the meaning through words. This is why you do not understand...."

39.... The Teacher said, "In teaching people, don't insist on a particular, one-sided way. In the beginning, one's mind is like a restless monkey and his feelings are like a galloping horse. They cannot be tied down. His thoughts and deliberations mostly tend to the side of selfish human desires. At that point, teach him to sit in meditation and to stop those thoughts and deliberations. Wait a long time till his mind becomes somewhat settled. If, however, at this time he merely remains quiet in a vacuum, like dry wood and dead ashes, it is also useless. Rather, he must be taught self-examination and self-mastery. There is no letup in this work. It is like getting rid of robbers and thieves. There must be the determination to wipe them out thoroughly and completely. Before things happen, each and every selfish desire for sex, wealth, and fame must be discovered. The root of the trouble must be pulled up and thrown away so that it will never sprout again. Only then can

we feel fine. At all times be like a cat trying to catch a rat, with eyes single-mindedly watching and ears single-mindedly listening. As soon as an evil thought begins to arise, overcome it and cast it away...."

66.... The Teacher said, "The Way [Dao] has neither spatial restriction nor physical form, and it cannot be pinned down to any particular. To seek it by confining ourselves to literal meanings would be far off the mark. Take those people today who talk about Heaven. Do they actually understand it? It is incorrect to say that the sun, the moon, wind, and thunder constitute Heaven. It is also incorrect to say that man, animals, and plants do not constitute it. Heaven is the Way. If we realize this, where is the Way not to be found? People merely look at it from one corner and conclude that the Way is nothing but this or that. Consequently they disagree. If one knows how to search for the Way inside the mind and to see the substance of one's own mind, then there is no place nor time where the Way is not to be found. It pervades the past and present and is without beginning or end. Where do similarity and difference come in? The mind is the Way, and the Way is Heaven. If one knows the mind, he knows both the Way and Heaven."

[The Teacher then] said, "If you gentlemen want to understand the Way definitely, you must find it in your own minds, without depending on any search outside. Only then will it be all right."...

90. {The Teacher said,} "Merely to talk about manifesting the clear character[1] and not to talk about loving the people would be to behave like the Taoists and Buddhists."

91. {The Teacher said,} "The highest good is the nature. Originally the nature has not the least evil. Therefore it is called the highest good. To abide by it is simply to recover the nature's original state."...

---

1 See the next reading on this point.

94.... The Teacher said, "The mind is principle. To have no selfish mind is to be in accord with principle, and not to be in accord with principle is to have a selfish mind...."

CONVERSATIONS RECORDED BY HSUEH K'AN

99. Ts'ai Hsi-yüan asked, "Sagehood can be achieved through learning, but the abilities and efforts of sages Po-i and I-yin are after all different from those of Confucius. Why are they all called sages?"

The Teacher said, "The reason the sage has become a sage is that his mind has become completely identified with the Principle of Nature and is no longer mixed with any impurity of selfish human desires. It is comparable to pure gold, which attains its purity because its golden quality is perfect and is no longer mixed with copper or lead....

"However, the abilities of sages differ in degree, just as the several pieces of gold quantitatively differ in weight. The sage-emperors Yao and Shun may be compared to 10,000 pounds; King Wen and Confucius to 9,000 pounds; Kings Yu..., T'ang,... Wen, and Wu, 7 or 8,000 pounds; and Po-i and I-yin, 4 or 5,000 pounds. Their abilities and efforts differ, but in being completely identified with the Principle of Nature they were the same and may all be called sages. It is just like the several pieces of pure gold, which may be so called because they are qualitatively perfect although quantitatively different. Mix a 5,000 pound piece of gold with a 10,000 pound piece, and their quality remains the same.... Therefore even an ordinary person, if he is willing to learn so as to enable his mind to become completely identified with the Principle of Nature, can also become a sage, in the same way that although a one ounce piece, when compared with a 10,000 pound piece, is widely different in quantity, it is not deficient in perfection in quality. This is why it is said that 'every man can become Yao and Shun.'..."

[101.] I[1] asked, "The Buddhists also deny the distinction between good and evil. Are they different from you?"

The Teacher said, "Being attached to the non-distinction of good and evil, the Buddhists neglect everything and therefore are incapable of governing the world. The sage, on the other hand, in his non-distinction of good and evil, merely makes no special effort whatsoever to like or dislike, and is not perturbed in his vital force. As he pursues the kingly path and sees the perfect excellence, he of course completely follows the Principle of Nature and it becomes possible for him to assist in and complete the universal process of production and reproduction and apply it for the benefit of the people."...

[I said,] "In that case, good and evil are not present in things at all."

[The Teacher replied,] "They are only in your mind. Following the Principle of Nature is good, while perturbing the vital force is evil."...

109. I asked, "Why can't the most intelligent and the most stupid be changed?"

The Teacher said, "It is not that they cannot be changed. It is merely that they are unwilling to change."...

125.... Kuan-shih asked the Teacher to describe the condition of equilibrium somewhat. The Teacher said, "I cannot tell you any more than a dumb man can tell you about the bitterness of the bitter melon that he has just eaten. If you want to know the bitterness, you have to eat a bitter melon yourself."

At that time Hsu Ai was by the side of the Teacher. He said, "This is exactly a case where true knowledge and action are identical."

All the friends present attained a certain enlightenment all at once....

---

1 A person's name, pronounced 'E.'

Part II

LETTER IN REPLY TO LU YUAN-CHING

[162.]...To investigate things as things come is the task of the extension of knowledge. It is what the Buddhists called "Be always alert," that is, always preserve one's original state. In broad outline the two methods are about the same. However, the Buddhists are different from us because they have the mind that is motivated by selfishness. Now to wish to think of neither good nor evil and to want the mind of innate knowledge to be clear, tranquil, and at ease, means to have the mind of selfishness, leaning forward or backward, arbitrariness of opinion, and dogmatism....

[165.]...Innate knowledge is identical with the Way [Dao]. That it is present in the mind is true not only in the cases of the sages and worthies but even in that of the common man. When one is free from the driving force and obscurations of material desires, and just follows innate knowledge and leaves it to continue to function and operate, everything will be in accord with the Way.... To learn simply means to learn to follow innate knowledge....

167....The sage's effort at extending knowledge is characterized by his absolute sincerity which never ceases. The substance of his innate knowledge is as clear as a bright mirror without any slight obscuration. Whether a beautiful or an ugly object appears, it reflects the object as it comes, without anything being left behind on the bright mirror itself. This is what is meant by saying that the feelings of the sage are in accord with all things and yet of himself he has no feelings. The Buddhists have a saying, "One should have no attachment to anything and thus let the mind grow." This is not incorrect. In the bright mirror's response to things, what is beautiful appears beautiful and what is ugly appears ugly. In the same reflection all things are reflected and are true. This

is like the mind growing. What is beautiful appears beautiful and what is ugly appears ugly. The things pass on without remaining in the mirror. This is [why we say] the mirror has no attachment....

LETTER IN REPLY TO OU-YANG CH'UNG-I

[171.]...A superior man studies for his own sake. He does not worry about being deceived by others but will not deceive his own innate knowledge.... [Since he] does not deceive himself, his innate knowledge will have no falsehood and will be sincere. Given sincerity, there will be enlightenment. If one trusts himself, his innate knowledge will have no doubt and will be intelligent. Being intelligent, it will be sincere. Thus intelligence and sincerity produce each other. Consequently, innate knowledge always knows and always shines. Always knowing and shining, it is like a suspended brilliant mirror. As things appear before it, none can conceal its beauty or ugliness.... When we come to those with absolute sincerity, the wonderful operation of absolute sincerity itself is called spirit, not just *like* a spirit. Those with absolute sincerity have no knowledge and yet know all, and need not be described as being *able to* foreknow.

LETTER IN REPLY TO NIEH WEN-YU

179. Man is the mind of the universe. At bottom Heaven and Earth and all things are my body. Is there any suffering or bitterness of the great masses that is not disease or pain in my own body? Those who are not aware of this disease and pain in their own body are people without the sense of right and wrong. The sense of right and wrong is knowledge possessed by men without deliberation and ability possessed by them without their having acquired it by learning. It is what we call innate knowledge....

180. In later generations, the doctrine of innate knowledge has not clearly prevailed. People have used their selfishness and cunning to compete with

and rival one another.... Outwardly people make pretenses in the name of humanity and righteousness. At heart their real aim is to act for their own benefit. They lie in order to please the vulgar people and affect a certain conduct in order to obtain fame.... They are jealous of the worthy and envious of the talented, and yet consider themselves to have a universal sense of right and wrong....

Part III

CONVERSATIONS RECORDED BY CH'EN CHIU-CH'UAN

215. I was sick in bed in Ch'ien-chou. The Teacher said, "This thing, sickness, is also difficult to rectify...How do you feel?"

I replied, "The task is very difficult."

The Teacher said, "Always be cheerful. That is the task."...

CONVERSATIONS RECORDED BY HUANG I-FANG

226. I asked about the unity of knowledge and action. The Teacher said, "You need to understand the basic purpose of my doctrine.... I want people to understand that when a thought is aroused it is already action. If there is anything evil when the thought is aroused, one must overcome the evil thought. One must go to the root and the bottom and not allow that evil thought to lie latent in his mind. This is the basic purpose of my doctrine."...

CONVERSATIONS RECORDED BY HUANG MIEN-SHU

247. I asked, "Chu Hsi considers divination by means of tortoise shells and stalks of plants as fundamental,

while Ch'eng I, in his commentary, considers principle as fundamental. What do you think?"

The Teacher said, "...Because later generations regard divination as fundamentally fortune telling, they look upon it as a petty craft. They don't know that questions and answers between teachers and friends, such as we are engaging in today, and studying extensively, inquiring accurately, thinking carefully, sifting clearly, practicing earnestly, and the like are all forms of divination. Divination is no more than to remove doubt and to give the mind divine intelligence. The *Book of Changes* seeks answers from Heaven. Man has doubts and does not have sufficient self-confidence. He therefore seeks answers from Heaven by use of the *Book of Changes*.[1] The idea is that the human mind involves some [selfish desires]. Heaven alone leaves no room for falsehood."

CONVERSATIONS RECORDED BY HUANG MIEN-CHIH

269. The Teacher said, "Taoist seekers of immortality have reached the conclusion of the vacuity {of the mind}. Is the sage able to add an iota of reality to that vacuity? The Buddhists have reached the conclusion of non-being {of the mind}. Is the sage able to add an iota of being to that non-being? But the Taoist talk about vacuity is motivated by a desire for nourishing everlasting life, and the Buddhist talk about non-being is motivated by the desire to escape from the sorrowful sea of life and death. In both cases, certain selfish ideas have been added to the original substance {of the mind}, which thereby loses the true character of vacuity and is obstructed. The sage merely returns to the true condition of innate knowledge and does not attach to it any selfish idea..."

[290.] ... [I asked, "]Are desires also natural to the human mind?"

---

1 What is known as the *I Ching* or *Yi Jing* (易經), a classical Chinese source that provided a method for predicting the future.

The Teacher said, "Pleasure, anger, sorrow, fear, love, hate, and desire are the seven feelings. These seven are also natural to the mind.... When the seven feelings follow their natural courses of operation, they are all functions of innate knowledge, and cannot be distinguished as good or evil. However, we should not have any selfish attachment to them. When there is such an attachment, they become selfish desires and obscurations to innate knowledge....

292. I said, "You said that 'joy is characteristic of the original substance of the mind.' When one's parent dies and one cries sorrowfully, is this joy still present?"

The Teacher said, "There is real joy only if the son has cried bitterly. If not, there won't be any joy. Joy means that in spite of crying, one's mind is at peace. The original substance of the mind has not been perturbed."...

READING 25B

Wáng Yáng-míng, *Inquiry on the Great Learning*[1]

(1527)

Question: The Great Learning was considered by a former scholar as the learning of the great man. I venture to ask why the learning of the great man should consist in "manifesting the clear character."

Master Wang said: The great man regards Heaven, Earth, and the myriad things as one body. He regards the world as one family and the country as one person. As to those who make a cleavage between objects and distinguish between the self and others, they are small men.... Forming one body with Heaven, Earth, and the myriad things is not only true of the great man. Even the mind of the small[2] man is no different. Only he himself makes it small. Therefore when he sees a child about to fall into a

well, he cannot help a feeling of alarm and commiseration. This shows that his humanity forms one body with the child. It may be objected that the child belongs to the same species. Again, when he observes the pitiful cries and frightened appearance of birds and animals about to be slaughtered, he cannot help feeling an "inability to bear" their suffering. This shows that his humanity forms one body with birds and animals. It may be objected that birds and animals are sentient beings as he is. But when he sees plants broken and destroyed, he cannot help a feeling of pity. This shows that his humanity forms one body with plants. It may be said that plants are living things as he is. Yet, even when he sees tiles and stones shattered and crushed, he cannot help a feeling of regret. This shows that his humanity

---

1 Heavily adapted from a memoir of Wáng Yáng-míng, *Inquiry on the Great Learning*, adapted from *Wang Yang-ming, Instructions for Practical Living*, from Wing-tsit Chan, trans., *Instructions for Practical Living and Other Neo-Confucian Writings*, Number LXVIII of the Records of Civilization: Sources and Studies, UNESCO Collection of Representative Works Chinese series (New York and London: Columbia University Press, 1963). The original Chinese is 大學問, Daxue wen; literally '[Great learning/knowledge] [question].'

2 I.e., petty or petty-minded.

forms one body with tiles and stones. This means that even the mind of the small man necessarily has the humanity that forms one body with all. Such a mind is rooted in his Heaven-endowed nature, and is naturally intelligent, clear, and not beclouded. For this reason it is called the "clear character." Although the mind of the small man is divided and narrow, yet his humanity, which forms one body can remain free from darkness to this degree. This is due to the fact that his mind has not been aroused by desires and obscured by selfishness. When it is aroused by desires and obscured by selfishness, compelled by greed for gain and fear of harm, and stirred by anger, he will destroy things, kill members of his own species, and will do everything. In extreme cases he will even slaughter his own brothers, and the humanity that forms one body will disappear completely. Hence, if it is not obscured by selfish desires, even the mind of the small man has the humanity that forms one body with all as does the mind of the great man. As soon as it is obscured by selfish desires, even the mind of the great man will be divided and narrow like that of the small man. Thus the learning of the great man consists entirely in getting rid of the obscuration of selfish desires in order by his own efforts to make manifest his clear character, so as to restore the condition of forming one body with Heaven, Earth, and the myriad things, a condition that is originally so, that is all. It is not that outside of the original substance something can be added.

Question: Why, then, does the learning of the great man consist in loving the people?

Answer: To manifest the clear character is to bring about the substance of the state of forming one body with Heaven, Earth, and the myriad things, whereas loving the people is to put into universal operation the function of the state of forming one body. Hence manifesting the clear character consists in loving the people, and loving the people is the way to manifest

the clear character. Therefore, only when I love my father, the fathers of others, and the fathers of all men can my humanity really form one body with my father, the fathers of others, and the fathers of all men. When it truly forms one body with them, then the clear character of filial piety will be manifested. Only when I love my brother, the brother of others, and the brothers of all men can my humanity really form one body with my brother, the brother of others, and the brothers of all men. When it truly forms one body with them, then the clear character of brotherly respect will be manifested. Everything from ruler, minister, husband, wife, and friends to mountains, rivers, spiritual beings, birds, animals, and plants should be truly loved in order to realize my humanity that forms one body with them, and then my clear character will be completely manifested, and I will really form one body with Heaven, Earth, and the myriad things. This is what is meant by "manifesting the clear character throughout the world." This is what is meant by "regulation of the family," "ordering the state," and "bringing peace to the world." This is what is meant by "full development of one's nature."

Question: Then why does the learning of the great man consist in "abiding in the highest good"?

Answer: The highest good is the ultimate principle of manifesting character and loving people. The nature endowed in us by Heaven is pure and perfect. The fact that it is intelligent, clear, and not beclouded is evidence of the emanation and revelation of the highest good. It is the original substance of the clear character which is called innate knowledge of the good. As the highest good emanates and reveals itself, we will consider right as right and wrong as wrong. Things of greater or less importance and situations of grave or light character will be responded to as they act upon us. In all our changes and movements, we will stick to no particular point, but possess in ourselves the mean that is perfectly natural. This is the ultimate of the normal nature of man and the principle of things. There can be no consideration of adding or subtracting anything to or from it. Such a suggestion reveals selfish ideas and shallow cunning, and cannot be said to be the highest good. Naturally, how can anyone who does not watch over himself carefully, when alone, and who has no refinement and singleness of mind, attain to such a state of perfection? Later generations fail to realize that the highest good is inherent in their own minds, but exercise their selfish ideas and cunning and grope for it outside their minds, believing that every event and every object has its own peculiar definite principle. For this reason the law of right and wrong is obscured; the mind becomes concerned with fragmentary and isolated details and broken pieces; the selfish desires of man become rampant

and the Principle of Nature is at an end. And thus the learning of manifesting character and loving people is everywhere thrown into confusion. In the past there have, of course, been people who wanted to manifest the clear character. But simply because they did not know how to abide in the highest good, but instead drove their own minds toward something too lofty, they thereby lost them in illusions, emptiness, and quietness, having nothing to do with the work of the family, the state, and the world. Such are the followers of Buddhism and Taoism. There have, of course, been those who wanted to love their people. Yet simply because they did not know how to abide in the highest good, but instead sank their own minds in base and trifling things, they thereby lost them in scheming strategy and cunning techniques, having neither the sincerity of humanity nor that of commiseration. Such are the followers of the Five Despots[1] and the pursuers of success and profit....

Questions

1. There are elements of Daoism and Buddhism in neo-Confucian thought. Wang rejects both schools, however, and accuses them of self-interestedness. Why?

2. The Chinese view was that we are born good and then deviate. The Christian view is that we are born with original sin and must be redeemed. Whose side do you take? Refer to Wang and a Christian philosopher in your answer.

3. Is there room for the natural law in Wang's theory? Refer to the Stoics or Aquinas in your answer.

4. What is the basic problem in Wang's view when someone knows what to do, morally, but does not do it? Where does double-mindedness come from? Use examples.

5. Wang says that the mind and principle—and knowledge and action—are one. There is "no thing outside the mind." Discuss, with examples.

6. What is the "original state" and "innate knowledge" that corresponds to it? What is the most essential trait of the sage? How do these elements come together in Wang's moral and cosmological scheme?

7. How does the great man manifest a "clear character"? Why does he love the people?

---

1 In the latter half of the Chou (or Zhou) Dynasty (1045–221 BCE) the feudal rulers of different states, known as the five despots or dictators, successively took over real political control from the Emperor, who was too weak to be an effective ruler. These self-made dictators were known for their Machiavellian intrigue, shrewd cunning, and adroit scheming. They were sometimes given to luxurious excess.

Suggested Readings

The best source for Wáng Yáng-míng's work is Wing-tsit Chan's translation of the *Instructions for Practical Living and Other Neo-Confucian Writings* (1963), from which the readings have been taken. An electronic version can be found at archive.org. The same book contains Wang's *Inquiry on the Great Learning* and "Some Social and Political Measures," in which he applies his ethical views to official and political matters.

The name Yáng-míng is merely an honorific. There is accordingly a thorough discussion of Wang's thought under the name Wang Shou-jen (his formal name) in Volume 2 of Fung Yu-lan's *History of Chinese Philosophy* (1934, 1953), and a brief discussion (under the name Wang Shou-ren) in chapter 12.12 of Orient Lee's translation of Chi Yun Chang's *Confucianism: A Modern Interpretation* (2012).

The latter text also reviews the historical dissemination of the Confucian tradition in "Eastern Nations." This is worthy of investigation: Richard Kim reviews the development of a distinctive Neo-Confucian tradition in Korea in "Human Nature and Animal Nature: The Horak Debate" (2015).

The general sources include Philip Ivanhoe, *Ethics in the Confucian Tradition: The Thought of Mengzi and Wang Yangming* (1990); A.S. Cua, "Harmony and the Neo-Confucian Sage" (1983); and Stephen Angle, *Sagehood: The Contemporary Significance of Neo-Confucian Philosophy* (2009).

For specific and comparative sources, see Unsunn Lee, "A Comparative Study on Wang Yangming and Hannah Arendt" (2008), and Liseng Chen, "Research on the Issue of 'Evil' in Wáng Yángmíng's Thought" (2007).

Chapter 26

Social Contract Theory

Thomas Hobbes (1588–1679) and John Locke (1632–1704) were the most celebrated figures in the theory of the social contract, now called contractarianism. The introduction of such a theory marked a historical departure from the medieval political tradition, which was based primarily on divine authority. This departure was a response to the new individualism, which was reflected in both the Protestant Revolution and a move towards democracy. It was also a response to scientific thought, which promoted materialism and undermined the authority of the religious tradition.

Thomas Hobbes is known primarily as a political philosopher. It is said that he was born prematurely, when his mother took fright at the prospect of a Spanish invasion of England. Later he said that his mother simultaneously gave birth to twins: himself and fear. This is a salutary comment, which helps to explain his work. When Hobbes was fourteen, he entered Magdalen Hall at Oxford University, graduating with a Bachelor of Arts in 1608. He then became a tutor and companion to the young William Cavendish (later Earl of Devonshire), accompanying him to Europe. His relationship to the Earl and other pupils, such as the future King, Charles II, stood him in good stead during the rest of his life.

Hobbes's contemporaries found his political, ethical, and religious views disconcerting. In 1640, in the turmoil leading up to the civil war between the parliamentarians and royalists (1642–51), he was forced to flee England for Paris. There, his unorthodox religious views offended his fellow expatriates, and nine years later he was forced to flee back to England. After the Restoration of the monarchy in 1660, however, Charles II brought him into his court, with a yearly pension of £100. There, he protected Hobbes from his enemies, who constantly denounced his impiety. Although Hobbes's religious views are uncertain, he claimed to believe in God and accepted Christianity, receiving the sacraments when he died.

Hobbes did not turn to philosophy until he was over forty. He was interested in science and mathematics and spent much of his later life trying to square the circle. He was also a classical scholar, translating the *Iliad* and the *Odyssey*. His major philosophical aim was the elaboration of a comprehensive, materialistic explanation of the world, which he set out in his philosophical trilogy *De Cive* (*On Citizenship*, 1642), *De Corpore* (*On the Body*, 1655), and *De Homine* (*On Man*, 1658). This recalls the work of Lucretius and other Roman philosophers. As a materialist, he appears to have adopted the view that even God must have some form of physical being.

Hobbes is now remembered chiefly for his theory of the social contract, which was based on secular considerations that superseded the religious concerns of the medieval thinkers. He elaborates on his views in three influential books: *De Cive* (see above), *The Elements of Law* (published without his permission in 1650), and the widely-acknowledged masterpiece *Leviathan* (1651). The theory in *Leviathan* is based on the idea of a state of nature that existed—in theory—before government and organized society came into being. Since human beings, in Hobbes's view, are self-interested, life in the state of nature quickly descends into a "war" of everyone against everyone else, where life is "nasty, brutish, and short."

Hobbes argues that the way out of the state of nature is a social contract. To avoid the perils of a "war" against each other, rational individuals in the state of nature will agree to a covenant or contract to refrain from mutual violence and molestation. This means, however, that government is necessary, since such a contract cannot be enforced without a central authority, with sufficient power to punish those who violate it. There is no other way to secure peace and prosperity.

In point of fact, the state of nature that Hobbes posits is not in keeping with the historical facts, which reveal that tribes and early societies were based on moral customs that were respected by the people without government. The best that can be said is that Hobbes was responding to a relatively new individualism, which required management. The literature tends to take this development for granted and ignores the fact that the government requires power over the people in order to protect individuals from each other. The irony is that Hobbes protects personal freedoms by increasing the authority of government.

The mainstay of Hobbes's work is ethical realism, which can be seen in his frank avowal of self-interest. Although he believes in an authoritarian form of government—he is arguing for an absolute monarchy—he does not believe that we can ever be expected to act in ways that tend to our own destruction. Individuals have a legitimate self-interest and are entitled to protect themselves. As a result, in a state of nature where our lives are threatened, nothing seems to be immoral. The same principle also applies, however, if society turns against us.

John Locke was the most famous British philosopher of the seventeenth century. He was a trained physician with a keen interest in science. Locke served as physician, secretary, and tutor to the family of Anthony Ashley Cooper, the First Earl of Shaftesbury, a founder of the Whig political party. The Whigs were the voice of British liberalism. Shaftesbury also became a political ally. Locke left the country from 1683 to 1688 out of fear of political persecution. As a liberal, and in opposition to Hobbes, he favored a limited monarchy with parliamentary supremacy.

Locke was an industrious philosopher, whose work comments on epistemological issues, politics, morality, religious toleration, and even theology. He has a more positive conception of human nature than Hobbes. He sets out his religious views in a book entitled *The Reasonableness of Christianity*, where he aims to reconcile religious faith and reason. A defender of the truth of scripture, he nevertheless vigorously opposes the traditional religious notion of a divine right of kings and, like Hobbes, views political and legal issues in largely secular terms.

When it comes to politics and morality, Locke is remembered primarily for his *Two Treatises of Government*. His aim in these treatises is to set out a system of government that will ensure peaceful co-existence, the right to private property, and a sphere of private freedom. Locke has already moved on from Hobbes, and is more concerned about the potential for abuse in the wholesale transfer of power to government. He therefore insists, for example, that the people have a right to rebel if a tyrannical government no longer serves their needs. Locke's theory of the social contract promotes "constitutionalism," which limits the power of the political branch of government. His work was known to the American founding fathers and provided the philosophical inspiration for the Declaration of Independence.

The main contribution of Hobbes and Locke to moral philosophy was theoretical. Their work provided us with the general liberal framework within which most western philosophers have carried on the ethical inquiry ever since. The attempt to construct a model of government, based on rational inquiry, was a signal development in modern philosophy. In practical ethics, they generally accepted the views of their time. They nevertheless emphasized the sovereignty of the individual and the principles of freedom and equality, which have come to the fore in the subsequent discussions.

The first reading is from Hobbes's *Leviathan* and sketches out his basic moral and political theory. The second reading is from Locke's *Second Treatise on Government*, where he gives us a different view of the state of nature, which is regulated by the natural law. Like Aquinas, Locke believes that the natural law is accessible to everyone through the exercise of reason. The power of reason comes directly from God. Although the introduction of government provides a more efficient—and necessary—form of social regulation, Locke accordingly sees the state of nature as a moral realm.

Thomas Hobbes, *Leviathan*[1]

(1651)

Introduction

Nature…is imitated by the art of man…which can make an artificial animal. For seeing life is but a motion of limbs, the beginning whereof is in some principal part within, why may we not say that all automata (engines that move themselves by springs and wheels as does a watch) have an artificial life? For what is the heart, but a spring; and the nerves, but so many strings; and the joints, but so many

---

1 Thomas Hobbes, *Leviathan or The Matter, Forme, & Power of a Common-Wealth Ecclesiastical and Civill* (1651). Readily available online. The leviathan was a huge sea monster mentioned in the Old Testament; Hobbes uses the term figuratively to refer to the enormously powerful commonwealth—the political state created by humans for their common good.

wheels, giving motion to the whole body, such as was intended by the Artificer?[1]

Art goes yet further, imitating that rational and most excellent work of Nature, man. For by art is created that great Leviathan called a Commonwealth, or State (in Latin, *Civitas*), which is but an artificial man, though of greater stature and strength than the natural, for whose protection and defence it was intended; and in which sovereignty is an artificial soul, as giving life and motion to the whole body; the magistrates and other officers of the judiciary and the executive, artificial joints; reward and punishment (by which…every joint and member is moved to perform his duty) are the nerves;…the wealth and riches of all the particular members are the strength; *salus populi* (the people's safety) its business; counsellors, by whom all things necessary for it to know are suggested unto it, are the memory; equity and laws, an artificial reason and will; concord, health; sedition, sickness; and civil war, death.

Lastly, the pacts and covenants, by which the parts of this body politic were at first made, set together, and united, resemble that fiat, or the 'Let us make man,' pronounced by God in the Creation.

Part I: Of Man

VI: OF THE INTERIOR BEGINNINGS OF VOLUNTARY NOTIONS, COMMONLY CALLED THE PASSIONS; AND A DICTIONARY, CONTAINING THE WORDS BY WHICH THEY ARE EXPRESSED

This human endeavour, when it is toward something which causes it, is called appetite, or desire…. And when the endeavour is away from something, it is generally called aversion….

That which men desire they are said to love, and they are said to hate those things for which they have aversion. So that desire and love are the same thing; save that by desire, we signify the absence of the object; by love, most commonly the presence of the same. So also by aversion, we signify the absence; and by hate, the presence of the object….

But whatsoever is the object of any man's appetite or desire, that is it which he for his part calls good; and the object of his hate and aversion, evil…. For these words of good and evil…are used with relation to the person that uses them: there being nothing simply and absolutely so; nor any common rule of good and evil to be taken from the nature of the objects themselves; but from the person of the man;…or, in a Commonwealth, from the person that represents it….[2]

- For appetite with an opinion of attaining is called hope.
- The same, without such opinion, despair.
- Aversion, with opinion of hurt…, fear….
- Anger for great hurt done to another,…indignation.
- Desire of good to another, benevolence….
- Desire of riches, covetousness….
- Desire of office, or precedence, ambition….
- Love of persons for society, kindness.
- Love of persons for pleasing the sense only, natural lust….
- The same, with fear that the love is not mutual, jealousy….
- Desire to know why, and how, curiosity….
- Fear of power invisible, feigned by the mind, or imagined from tales publicly allowed, religion; not allowed, superstition. And when the power imagined is truly such as we imagine, true religion….
- Joy arising from imagination of a man's own power and ability…is called glorying: which,…

---

1 I.e., God, the Creator.
2 Hobbes then provides a moral dictionary.

if grounded on the flattery of others, or only supposed by himself...is called vainglory...

X: OF POWER, WORTH, DIGNITY, HONOUR AND WORTHINESS

The power of a man...is his present means to obtain some future apparent good, and is either original or instrumental. Natural power is the eminence of the faculties of body, or mind; as extraordinary strength, form, prudence, arts, eloquence, liberality, nobility.

Instrumental are those powers which, acquired by these, or by fortune, are means and instruments to acquire more; as riches, reputation, friends, and the secret working of God, which men call good luck....

The greatest of human powers is that which is compounded of the powers of most men, united by consent, in one person, natural or civil, that has the use of all their powers depending on his will; such as is the power of a Commonwealth....

XI: OF THE DIFFERENCE OF MANNERS

So that in the first place, I put for a general inclination of all mankind a perpetual and restless desire of power after power, that ceases only in death. And the cause of this is not always that a man hopes for a more intensive delight than he has already attained to, or that he cannot be content with a moderate power, but because he cannot assure the power and means to live well, which he has [at] present, without the acquisition of more....

Competition of riches, honour, command, or other power inclines to contention, enmity, and war, because the way of one competitor to the attaining of his desire is to kill, subdue, supplant, or repel the other....

Fear of oppression disposes a man to anticipate or to seek aid by society: for there is no other way by which a man can secure his life and liberty....

And they that make little or no inquiry into the natural causes of things, yet from the fear that proceeds from the ignorance itself of what it is that has the power to do them much good or harm are inclined to suppose, and invent for themselves, several kinds of powers invisible.... By which means it has come to pass that from the innumerable variety of imagination, men have created in the world innumerable sorts of gods. And this fear of things invisible is the natural seed of that which everyone in himself calls religion; and in them that worship or fear that power in another way than they do, superstition. And this seed of religion, having been observed by many, some...have been inclined thereby to nourish, dress, and form it into laws; and to add to it, of their own invention, any opinion...by which they thought they should best be able to govern others....

XIII: OF THE NATURAL CONDITION OF MANKIND AS CONCERNING THEIR FELICITY AND MISERY

Nature has made men so equal in the faculties of body and mind as that, though there be found one man sometimes manifestly stronger in body or of quicker mind than another, yet when all is calculated together the difference between man and man is not so considerable as that one man can thereupon claim to himself any benefit to which another may not pretend as well as he. For as to the strength of body, the weakest has strength enough to kill the strongest, either by secret machination or by union with others that are in the same danger with himself. And as to the faculties of the mind,...I find yet a greater equality among men than that of strength....

From this equality of ability arises equality of hope in the attaining of our ends. And therefore if any two men desire the same thing, which nevertheless they cannot both enjoy, they become enemies; and in the way to their end...endeavour to destroy or subdue one another....

Again, men have no pleasure (but on the contrary a great deal of grief) in keeping company where there is no power able to overawe them all.... So that in the nature of man, we find three principal causes of quarrel. First, competition; secondly, diffidence; thirdly, glory. The first makes men invade for gain; the second, for safety; and the third, for reputation. The first use violence, to make themselves masters of other men's persons, wives, children, and cattle; the second, to defend them; the third, for trifles....

Hereby it is manifest that during the time men live without a common power to keep them all in awe, they are in that condition which is called war; and such a war as is of every man against every man. For war consists not in battle only...but in a tract of time, wherein the will to contend by battle is known...

Whatsoever therefore is consequent to a time of war, where every man is enemy to every man, the same is consequent to the time wherein men live without other security than what their own strength and their own invention shall furnish them withal. In such condition there is no place for industry, because the fruit thereof is uncertain: and consequently no culture of the earth; no navigation, nor use of the commodities that may be imported by sea; no commodious building; no instruments of moving and removing such things as require much force; no knowledge of the face of the earth; no account of time; no arts; no letters; no society; and which is worst of all, continual fear, and danger of violent death; and the life of man, solitary, poor, nasty, brutish, and short....

To this war of every man against every man, this also is consequent; that nothing can be unjust. The notions of right and wrong, justice and injustice, have there no place. Where there is no common power, there is no law; where no law, no injustice. Force and fraud are in war the two cardinal virtues....

The passions that incline men to peace are: fear of death; desire of such things as are necessary to commodious living; and a hope by their industry to obtain them. And reason suggests convenient articles of peace upon which men may be drawn to agreement...which otherwise are called the laws of nature.

XIV: OF THE FIRST AND SECOND NATURAL LAWS, AND OF CONTRACTS

The right of nature, which writers commonly call *jus naturale*, is the liberty each man has to use his own power as he will himself for the preservation of his own nature; that is to say, of his own life; and consequently, of doing anything which, in his own judgement and reason, he shall conceive to be the most apt means to it....

A law of nature, *lex naturalis*, is a precept, or general rule, found out by reason, by which a man is forbidden to do that which is destructive of his life, or takes away the means of preserving the same, and to omit that by which he thinks it may be best preserved....

And consequently it is a precept, or general rule of reason: that every man ought to endeavour peace, as far as he has hope of obtaining it; and when he cannot obtain it, that he may seek and use all helps and advantages of war. The first branch of which rule contains the first and fundamental law of nature, which is: to seek peace and follow it. The second, the sum of the right of nature, which is: by all means we can to defend ourselves.

From this fundamental law of nature, by which men are commanded to endeavour peace, is derived this second law: that a man be willing, when others are so too, as far forth as for peace and defence of himself he shall think it necessary, to lay down this right to all things; and be contented with so much liberty against other men as he would allow other men against himself. For as long as every man holds this right—of doing anything he likes—so long are all men in the condition of war. But if other men will not lay down their right, as well as he, then there is no reason for anyone to divest himself of his: for that were to expose himself to prey...rather than to dispose himself to peace. This is that law of the gospel: Whatsoever you require that others should do to you, that do you to them....

The mutual transferring of right is that which men call contract....

If a covenant be made wherein neither of the parties perform presently, but trust one another, in the condition of mere nature...upon any reasonable suspicion, it is void: but if there be a common power set over them both, with right and force sufficient to compel performance, it is not void.

To make covenants with brute beasts is impossible.... To make covenant with God is impossible.... To promise that which is known to be impossible is no covenant....

Covenants entered into by fear...are obligatory. For example, if I covenant to pay a ransom...to an enemy, I am bound by it. For it is a contract, wherein one receives the benefit of life; the other is to receive money....

A covenant not to defend myself from force, by force, is always void. For...no man can transfer or lay down his right to save himself from death, wounds, and imprisonment, the avoiding whereof is the only end of laying down any right; and therefore the promise of not resisting force...is not obliging. For though a man may covenant thus, unless I do so, or so, kill me; he cannot covenant thus, unless I do so, or so, I will not resist you when you come to kill me....

XV: OF OTHER LAWS OF NATURE

From that law of nature by which we are obliged to transfer to another such rights as...hinder the peace of mankind, there follows a third; which is this: that men perform their covenants made; without which covenants are in vain, and but empty words; and...we are still in the condition of war. And in this law of nature consists the fountain and origin of justice....

But because covenants of mutual trust, where there is a fear of not performance...are invalid...while men are in the natural condition of war, this cannot be done. Therefore before the names of just and unjust can have place, there must be some coercive power to compel men equally to the performance of their covenants, by the terror of some punishment greater than the benefit they expect by the breach of their covenant,...and such power there is none before the erection of a Commonwealth.

... This is the fourth law of nature, which may be conceived in this form: that a man which receives benefit from another of mere grace endeavour that he which gives it have no reasonable cause to repent him of his good will....

A fifth law of nature is complaisance;...that every man strive to accommodate himself to the rest....[1]

The laws of nature are immutable and eternal; for injustice, ingratitude, arrogance, pride, iniquity, acception of persons,[2] and the rest can never be made lawful. For it can never be that war shall preserve life, and peace destroy it.... And the science of them is the true and only moral philosophy. For moral philosophy is nothing else but the science of what is good and evil in the conversation and society of mankind....

All men agree on this, that peace is good, and therefore also the ways or means of peace, which...are good; that is to say, moral virtues; and their contrary vices, evil. Now the science of virtue and vice is moral philosophy; and therefore the true doctrine of the laws of nature is the true moral philosophy....

The Second Part: Of Commonwealth

XVIII: OF THE RIGHTS OF SOVEREIGNS BY INSTITUTION

A commonwealth is said to be instituted when a multitude of men do agree, and covenant, everyone with every one, that to whatsoever man, or assembly of men, shall be given by the major part the right to present the person of them all, that is to say, to be

---

1 Hobbes goes on to describe a number of other laws of nature.
2 I.e., favoritism or partiality.

their representative; every one, as well he that voted for it as he that voted against it, shall authorize all the actions and judgements of that man, or assembly of men, in the same manner as if they were his own, to the end to live peaceably among themselves, and be protected against other men....

There can happen no breach of covenant on the part of the sovereign; and consequently none of his subjects, by any pretence of forfeiture, can be freed from his subjection.

XXI: OF THE LIBERTY OF SUBJECTS

Liberty, or freedom, signifies properly the absence of opposition (by opposition, I mean external impediments of motion).... For whatsoever is so tied, or environed, as it cannot move but within a certain space, which space is determined by the opposition of some external body, we say it has not liberty to go further. And so of all living creatures, while they are imprisoned, or restrained with walls or chains; and of the water while it is kept in by banks or vessels that otherwise would spread itself into a larger space; we use to say they are not at liberty to move in such manner as without those external impediments they would.... And according to this proper and generally received meaning of the word, a freeman is he that, in those things which by his strength and wit he is able to do, is not hindered to do what he has a will to.

XXX: OF THE OFFICE OF THE SOVEREIGN REPRESENTATIVE

The office of the sovereign, be it a monarch or an assembly, consists in the end for which he was trusted with the sovereign power, namely the procurement of the safety of the people, to which he is obliged by the law of nature, and to render an account thereof to God, the Author of that law, and to none but Him....

John Locke, *Second Treatise of Government*[1]

(1689)

An Essay Concerning the Original, Extent, and End, of Civil Government

Chapter II, Of the State of Nature

4. To understand political power aright, and derive it from its origin, we must consider what estate all men are naturally in, and that is, a state of perfect freedom to order their actions, and dispose of their possessions and persons as they think fit, within the bounds of the law of Nature, without asking leave or depending upon the will of any other man. A state also of equality, wherein all the power and jurisdiction is reciprocal, no one having more than another....

---

1 John Locke, *The Second Treatise of Government* (1689), later published as *The Second Treatise of Civil Government*. Readily available online.

6. But though this be a state of liberty, yet it is not a state of licence; though man in that state have an uncontrollable liberty to dispose of his person or possessions, yet he has not liberty to destroy himself, or so much as any creature in his possession, but where some nobler use than its bare preservation calls for it. The state of Nature has a law of Nature to govern it, which obliges every one, and reason, which comprises that law, teaches all mankind if they will but consult it; that being all equal and independent, no one ought to harm another in his life, health, liberty or possessions...

For men being all servants of one sovereign Master,[1] sent into the world by His order and about His business, they are His property...and made to last during His, not one another's pleasure.... Every one, as he is bound to preserve himself, and not to quit his station wilfully, so by the like reason...ought he as much as he can to preserve the rest of mankind, and not—unless it be to do justice on an offender—take away or impair the life, or what tends to the preservation of the life, the liberty, health, limb, or goods of another.

7. And that all men may be restrained from invading others' rights, and from doing hurt to one another, and that the law of Nature be observed, which wills the peace and preservation of all mankind, the execution of the law of Nature is in that original natural state put into every man's hands, whereby everyone has a right to punish the transgressors of that law to such a degree as may hinder its violation....

8. And thus, in the state of Nature, one man comes by a power over another, but yet no absolute or arbitrary power...according to the passionate heats or boundless extravagancy of his own will, but only to punish

him so far as calm reason and conscience dictate, what is proportionate to his transgression, which is so much as may serve for reparation and restraint. For these two are the only reasons why one man may lawfully do harm to another, which is that we call punishment.

Chapter VII, Of Political or Civil Society[2]

90. And hence it is evident that absolute monarchy, which by some men is counted for the only government in the world, is indeed inconsistent with civil society.... For the end of civil society is to avoid and remedy those inconveniences of the state of Nature which follow from every man's being judge in his own case, by setting up a known authority [i.e., a third-party referee][3] to which every one of that society may appeal...and which every one of the society ought to obey.

Now if people do not have not such a [neutral] authority to appeal to, and decide any difference between them, they are still in the state of Nature. And so is every absolute prince[4] in respect of those who are under his dominion.

91. For he being supposed to have all power, both legislative and executive, in himself alone, there is no judge to be found, no appeal lies open to anyone, who may fairly and indifferently, and with authority decide, whether the people are entitled to relief and redress for any injury or inconvenience that they may have suffered from the Prince, or by his order. So that such a ruler, however entitled, Czar, or Grand Signior, or how you please, is as much in the state of Nature, with all under his dominion, as he is with the rest of mankind. For wherever any two men are, who have no standing rule and common judge to

---

1 I.e., God.

2 Locke now describes civil society, which takes us out of the state of nature and replaces it with a political association. He rejects the idea of an absolute monarchy.

3 I.e., a duly appointed magistrate.

4 An absolute prince would be someone who is not subject to the rule of a magistrate.

appeal to on earth, for the determination of controversies of right between them, there they are still in the state of Nature, and under all the inconveniencies of it, with only this woeful difference, that they are the subject, or rather slave of an absolute prince.

Chapter XVI, Of Conquest

196. It is plain that shaking off a power which force, and not right, has set over any one, though it has the name of rebellion, yet is no offence before God, but that which He allows and countenances....

Chapter XIX, Of the Dissolution of Government

222. Whenever the legislators endeavour to take away and destroy the property of the people, or to reduce them to slavery under arbitrary power, they put themselves into a state of war with the people, who are thereupon absolved from any further obedience, and are left to the common refuge which God has provided for all men against force and violence.

Questions

1. The people who lived in tribes did not believe that they lived in a lawless world and the state of nature is mostly fiction. Why then, do Hobbes and Locke rely so heavily on the idea? How would you re-build their theories, if there were no state of nature?
2. What role does morality play in Hobbes's state of nature?
3. Hobbes does not separate law, politics, and morality. What is the principal role of the Sovereign Representative in his theory? How does morality come into this role? And how is the Sovereign governed?
4. Suppose you were fairly convicted of a particularly gruesome murder and are now in jail awaiting execution. Suddenly you realize that someone has left the door of your cell open. The medieval thinkers argued that you had a duty to escape. What is Hobbes's position? How has the moral discussion changed with Hobbes?
5. Both Hobbes and Locke think it is irrational to act immorally. Their reasoning nevertheless differs. Explain.
6. What would Hobbes and Locke think of civil disobedience? Is civil disobedience permitted?
7. It must always be remembered that Hobbes's views reflect the circumstances of the time in which he lived. What about times of peace and security? Do we need someone firmly in charge, to control self-interest and keep us out of the state of nature?
8. A feminist might argue that Hobbes's description of the state of nature reflects predominantly male/manly concerns and neglects female/womanly concerns. Discuss.

Suggested Readings

Hobbes wrote a wide variety of works. Broadview's revised edition of *The Leviathan*, his major work, includes a set of historical and contemporary appendices, an introduction, explanatory notes, and a chronology of Hobbes's life. Hobbes's view of the social contract can also be found in *De Cive* (*On Citizenship*, 1642) and *The Elements of Law* (1650). His materialistic explanation of the world is set out in the philosophical trilogy: *De Cive*, *De Corpore* (*On the Body*, 1655), and *De Homine* (*On Man*, 1658).

John Locke's political philosophy can be found in the *Two Treatises of Government*. The *First Treatise* is an argument against the divine right of kings; the *Second Treatise* explains his theory of government. Locke's major philosophical work is *An Essay on Human Understanding*. Broadview has republished an edition of Locke's *A Letter Concerning Toleration* (Kerry Walters, 2013), which argues for freedom of thought. The complete works of Hobbes and Locke can also be found at oll.libertyfund.org.

Terence Irwin's *The Development of Ethics* (Volume 2, 2008), devotes chapters 34–36 to Hobbes and chapter 41 to "Locke and the Natural Law." Other sources include John Deigh, "Reason and Ethics in Hobbes's *Leviathan*" (1996); John Colman, *John Locke's Moral Philosophy* (1983); and Nicholas Wolterstorff, *John Locke and the Ethics of Belief* (1996).

For contrasting views, see Derek Reiners, "Biological Correctness: Thomas Hobbes' Natural Ethics" (2008), and Ericka Tucker, "Diversity and Felicity: Hobbes's Science of Human Flourishing" (2016).

Chapter 27

Anti-Moralism

The work of Bernard de Mandeville (1670–1733), which contains a kind of anti-moralism or "anti-ethics," has largely been ignored in the contemporary philosophical commentary. It nevertheless provides considerable insight into the ethical undercurrents of the modern era and continues the tradition of ethical realism that can be found in proverbs and fables and the earlier Hobbes.

Mandeville was a satirist whose work was influential in the eighteenth century. He was born in Holland. His father was a physician in Rotterdam and the young Mandeville followed his example, graduating with a medical degree from Leiden University in 1691. After traveling, he settled down in London, learning English so well that many who heard him speak refused to believe that he was from outside the country.

It is now clear that there were family troubles behind Mandeville's move to England. This did not interfere with his success. He eventually married Ruth Elizabeth Laurence, had at least two children, and practiced medicine until his death from influenza in 1733. He also had literary aspirations, however, and wrote in poetry and prose, commenting on the economic, political, religious, moral, and social issues of the day.

England in the eighteenth century was increasingly urban, energetic, unruly, and politically tumultuous. There was rampant corruption, free-wheeling capitalism, and many forms of social evil. There were also many reformers. Mandeville first made his mark as a pamphleteer and a "Grub Street" writer, a pejorative term for the hacks that worked in the more desperate end of writing and journalism, peddling frankness and realism to the general public.

Mandeville published a number of popular books, including a translation of La Fontaine's fables, *Some Fables After the Easie and Familiar Method of Monsieur La Fontaine* (1703), which was then expanded in *Aesop Dress'd, or a Collection of Fables Writ in Familiar Verse* (1704). He followed these works with several editions of an attack on medical quackery, *A Treatise of the Hypochondriack and Hysterick Passions* (1711, 1715, 1730). In 1724, there appeared an anonymous satirical work, *A Modest Defence of Publick Stews* (brothels). Generally thought to be from Mandeville's pen, the book argues, in bawdy and ironic tones, that the best way to deal with the social evil of "whoring" is through legalization and public regulation.

Mandeville's reputation mostly rests on an anonymous poem of about four hundred lines that was first published in 1705 under the title *The Grumbling Hive, or Knaves Turned Honest*. It was republished as *The Fable of the Bees, or Private Vices, Publick Benefits* in 1714, along with "An Enquiry into the Origin of Moral Virtue" and twenty 'Remarks.' The poem became immensely popular and was re-published in 1724, 1725, 1728, 1729, and 1732, with an ever-increasing number of appendices that included remarks, essays, and responses to detractors. The popularity of the poem led Mandeville to publish a second part, *The Fable of the Bees: Part II*, in 1728, 1730, and 1733.

The poem is a satire, in doggerel, and in imitation of Aesop, which relates the parable of a grumbling hive of bees that—sanctimoniously—lament their vice-ridden ways. The hive is an obvious metaphor for England, a prosperous and powerful state, ruled by a limited monarchy. When Jove, the Roman god, grows tired of the complaints and transforms the bees into honest, virtuous individuals, the economic activity of the hive declines, leading to an economic and political collapse.

The moral of the tale is that the personal self-interest and even the greed of the individual best serve the interests of society as a whole. Private vices lead to public benefits. High standards of moral conduct, in contrast, in repressing and limiting our desires, lead to torpor and a kind of personal retrenchment, which stifle the entrepreneurial, scientific, and technological impulses that feed the prosperity of the country. Mandeville attributes the advances in science and technology to the unrestrained capitalism of his time, which provides the engine of progress.

Mandeville sees society in economic terms. He describes the system of justice, for example, as an industry that benefits the country, since it employs lawyers, judges, police officers, and prisoner-guards. He applauds moral faults such as vanity, since it is the people who are vain who buy expensive and frivolous clothes and fund the cosmetic industry. Even those who drink in excess contribute to the public good by providing a brisk business for the farmers who grow the grain, and for those who make and serve the alcohol.

As one might expect, these arguments offended those who saw themselves as the guardians of public decency. Although *The Fable of the Bees* was essentially a best-seller, it gave rise to a public outcry and was condemned in the pulpit as a libertine attack on all morality. In France, it was reputedly burned by the common hangman. Mandeville was denounced as a "Man-devil," an immoralist, and a scoffer. Dr. Samuel Johnson quipped that every up-to-date young man kept a copy in the sure belief that it was a thoroughly wicked book.

In 1723 and 1728, at the height of the outrage, a grand jury recommended that the book be declared a public nuisance, describing the poem and its attachments as "Works of Darkness," and charged that "studied artifices and invented colours have been made use of to run down religion and virtue as prejudicial to society, and detrimental to the state; and to recommend luxury, avarice, and pride, and all vices, as being necessary to public welfare." Although he was never prosecuted, Mandeville vigorously defended his position and responded to the bill of presentment—the formal accusation—as an "abusive letter" attacking his work in subsequent editions of *The Grumbling Hive*.

Mandeville is not a philosopher in the professional sense. Like most eighteenth-century thinkers, he prizes himself as an essayist, who deals adroitly with a wide variety of issues in an urbane, conversational style of prose, which appealed to the readers of the time. This is evident in the essays included in the later editions of *The Fable of the Bees*, "An Enquiry into the Origin of Moral Virtue" and "A Search into the Nature of Society," which deserve more attention.

Philosophically, Mandeville's thinking might be described as a kind of Neo-Epicureanism. The hedonism in his work is plain. Like the Epicureans and like Hobbes before him, his moral perspective is subjective. He rejects any account of morality that fails to acknowledge that the primary motivation in human actions is self-interest. His defense is that he is simply describing what he has observed in the moral life of society.

Most of Mandeville's critics misunderstood his position. He was not recommending that individual people act immorally—although it may be difficult to root out that implication from his work. Rather than counsel us to act unethically, he subscribes to a negative view of human nature, and rejects the optimism of the liberal view, which commonly holds out the possibility of moral improvement. The larger point in *The Fable of the Bees* is that a moral philosophy which fails to deal honestly with the realities of social life cannot possibly provide a viable account of politics or ethics.

Mandeville's position is staunchly conservative and recognizes the reality of evil. In practical ethics, these traits enter into his comments on the issues of his day, like the issue of prostitution and the case for public executions. Some of the uproar concerning *The Fable of the Bees* concerned his views on charity schools, which was a contentious issue at the time. Although his views are no longer acceptable, they need to be examined in their historical context.

The reading contains a selection of verses from the fable as well as excerpts from the essay on the nature of society and his response to the presentment of the jury. As he himself explains, the "main design of the fable" is to expose the hypocrisy of those who, "wonderfully greedy after all the benefits they can receive," yet spend their time denouncing the "vices and inconveniences" that provide them.

Bernard de Mandeville, *The Fable of the Bees*[1]

(1732)

Cover from the second printing of
The Fable of the Bees

The Grumbling Hive: or, Knaves turned Honest.

A SPACIOUS hive well stocked with Bees,
That lived in luxury and ease;
And yet as famed for laws and arms,
As yielding large and early Swarms;
Was counted the great Nursery
Of Sciences and Industry.
No Bees had better Government,
More Fickleness,[2] or less Content:
They were not Slaves to Tyranny,

Nor ruled by wild Democracy;
But Kings, that could not wrong, because
Their Power was circumscribed by Laws.

These Insects lived like Men, and all
Our Actions they performed in small...

Vast numbers thronged the fruitful Hive;
Yet those vast Numbers made them thrive;
Millions endeavouring to supply
Each other's Lust and Vanity...

The Lawyers, of whose Art the Basis
Was raising Feuds and splitting Cases,
Opposed all Registers,[3] that Cheats
Might make more Work...
And to defend a wicked Cause,
Examined and surveyed the Laws...
To find out where they would best break through.

Physicians valued Fame and Wealth
Above the drooping Patient's Health,
Or their own Skill: The greatest Part
Studied, instead of Rules of Art,
Grave pensive Looks and dull Behaviour...

Among the many Priests of Jove,[4]
Hired to draw Blessings from Above...
Some few were Learned and Eloquent,
But thousands hot and ignorant:
Yet all passed Muster that could hide
Their Sloth, Lust, Avarice and Pride;...

---

1 Bernard de Mandeville, *The Fable of the Bees*. From the 1806 edition. Variously available online.
2 I.e., deceit.
3 I.e., official lists or records.
4 I.e., the king of the gods in Ancient Roman religion and mythology, but in the poem, another name for God.

The soldiers, that were forced to fight,
If they survived, got honour by it;
Though some that shunned the bloody fray,
Had limbs shot off, that ran away;
Some valiant Generals fought the Foe;
Others took Bribes to let them go...
[Those soldiers] quite disabled, and put by,
They lived on half their Salary;
While others never came in Play,
And stayed at Home for double Pay.

Their Kings were served, but Knavishly,
Cheated by their own Ministry...
Many, that for their Welfare slaved,[1]
Robbing the very Crown they saved...
And when Folks understood their Cant,
They changed that for Emolument;[2]
Unwilling to be short or plain,
In anything concerning Gain...

Justice[3] herself, famed for fair Dealing,
By Blindness had not lost her Feeling;
Her Left Hand, which the Scales should hold,
Had often dropped them, bribed with Gold;
And, though she seemed Impartial,
Where Punishment was corporal...
Yet, it was thought, the Sword she bore
Checked but the Desperate and the Poor...

Thus every Part was full of Vice,
Yet the whole Mass a Paradise...
Such were the Blessings of that state;
Their Crimes conspired to make them Great:
And Virtue, who from Politics
Has learned a Thousand Cunning Tricks...
Was, by their happy influence,
Made Friends with Vice: And ever since,

The worst of all the Multitude
Did something for the Common Good....

The root of evil, avarice.
That damned and ill-natured baneful vice;
Was slave to Prodigality,
That noble Sin; while Luxury
Employed a Million of the Poor,
And odious Pride a Million more:
Envy itself, and Vanity,
Were Ministers of Industry;
Their darling Folly, Fickleness,
In Diet, Furniture and Dress,
That strange ridiculous Vice, was made
The very Wheel[4] that turned the Trade....

Thus Vice nursed Ingenuity,
Which joined with time and industry,
Had carried Life's Conveniences,
Its real Pleasures, Comforts, Ease,
To such a Height, the very Poor
Lived better than the Rich before...

[Had they but known] that Perfection here below
Is more than Gods can well bestow;
The Grumbling Brutes had been content
With Ministers and Government.
But they, at every ill Success,
Like Creatures lost without Redress,
Cursed Politicians, Armies, Fleets;
While everyone cried, Damn the Cheats...

[And] all the Rogues cried brazenly,
Good Gods, Had we but Honesty!
Mercy smiled at the Impudence,
And others called it want of Sense,
Always to rail at what they loved:

---

1 I.e., worked for the government.
2 I.e., payment.
3 Justice was often personified in art as a woman wearing a blindfold, holding scales and a sword.
4 Allusion here to a water-wheel providing the power for machinery.

But Jove with Indignation moved,
At last in Anger swore, He'd rid
The bawling Hive of Fraud; and did....

But, Oh ye Gods! What Consternation,
How vast and sudden was the Alteration!
In half an Hour, the Nation round,
Meat fell a Penny in the Pound.
The Mask [of] Hypocrisy's sitting down,
From the great Statesman to the Clown...
The Bar[1] was silent from that Day;
For now the willing Debtors pay...

Justice hanged some, set others free;
And after Jail delivery,
Her Presence being no more required,
With all her Train and Pomp retired....

Though Physick[2] lived, while Folks were ill,
None would prescribe, but Bees of skill...
Waved vain disputes, and strove to free
The Patients of their Misery...

Their Clergy roused from laziness,
Laid not their charge on journey-bees;
But served themselves, exempt from Vice,
The Gods with Prayer and Sacrifice...
[The High-Priest] chased no Starvling from his
        Door,
Nor pinched the Wages of the Poor;
But at his House the Hungry's fed...

Among the King's great Ministers,
And all the inferior Officers
The Change was great; for frugally
They now lived on their Salary...

Vain cost is shunned as much as fraud;
They have no forces kept abroad;
Laugh at the Esteem of Foreigners,
And empty Glory got by Wars;
They fight but for their country's sake,
When right or liberty's at stake....
Now mind the glorious hive, and see
How honesty and trade agree.
The Show is gone, it thins apace;
And looks with quite another Face.
For it was not only that they went,
By whom vast Sums were Yearly spent;
But Multitudes that lived on them,
Were daily forced to do the same.
In vain to other trades they would fly;
All were overstocked accordingly.

The Price of Land and Houses falls;
Miraculous Palaces, whose Walls,
Like those of Thebes, were raised by Play,
Are to be let,[3]
The building Trade is quite destroyed,
Artificers are not employed...

Those, that remained, grown temperate, strive,
Not how to spend, but how to live,
And, when they paid their Tavern Score,[4]
Resolved to enter it no more...

The slight and fickle Age is past;
And Clothes, as well as Fashions, last.
Weavers, that joined rich Silk with Plate,[5]
And all the Trades subordinate,
Are gone. Still Peace and Plenty reign,
And every Thing is cheap, though plain...

---

1 I.e., the law courts.
2 I.e., doctors.
3 I.e., the palaces are empty and need renters.
4 I.e., their account owed to the tavern.
5 I.e., decorative thread covered with gold or silver.

As Pride and Luxury decrease,
So by degrees [merchants] leave the Seas....
All Arts and Crafts neglected lie;
Content, the Bane of Industry,
Makes them admire their homely store,
And neither seek nor covet more....

THE MORAL.

THEN leave Complaints: Fools only strive
To make a Great and Honest Hive.
To enjoy the World's Conveniences,
Be famed in War, yet live in Ease,
Without great Vices, is a vain
Utopia seated in the Brain.
Fraud, Luxury and Pride must live,
While we the Benefits receive...
Do we not owe the Growth of Wine
To the dry shabby crooked Vine?
Which, while its Shoots neglected stood,
Choked other Plants, and ran to Wood;
But blest us with its noble Fruit,
As soon as it was tied and cut:

So Vice is beneficial found,
When it's by Justice lopped and bound...
Bare Virtue can't make Nations live
In Splendor; they, that would revive
A Golden Age, must be as free,[1]
For Acorns, as for Honesty.

A SEARCH into the Nature of Society.[2]

THE Generality of Moralists and Philosophers have hitherto agreed that there could be no virtue without self-denial; but a late author...imagines that men without any trouble or violence upon themselves may be naturally virtuous. He seems to require and expect goodness in his species, as we do a sweet taste in grapes and China oranges, of which, if any of them are sour, we boldly pronounce that they are not come to that perfection their nature is capable of. This noble writer (for it is the Lord Shaftesbury...) fancies, that as man is made for society, so he ought to be born with a kind affection to the whole, of which he is a part, and a propensity to seek the welfare of it. In pursuance of this supposition, he calls every action performed with regard to the public good, virtuous; and all selfishness, wholly excluding such a regard, vice.

In respect to our species this writer looks upon virtue and vice as permanent realties that must ever be the same in all countries and all ages, and imagines that a man of sound understanding, by following the rules of good sense, may not only find that *pulchrum & honestum*[3] both in morality and the works of art and nature, but likewise govern himself by his reason with as much ease and readiness as a good rider manages a well-taught horse by the bridle.

The attentive reader, who perused the foregoing part of this book, will soon perceive that two systems cannot be more opposite than his Lordship's and mine. His notions I confess are generous and refined: They are a high compliment to humankind, and capable by the help of a little enthusiasm of inspiring us with the most noble sentiments concerning the dignity of our exalted nature. What pity it is that they are not true. I would not advance thus much if I had not already demonstrated in almost every page of this treatise, that the solidity of them is inconsistent with our daily experience.

But to leave not the least shadow of an objection that might be made unanswered, I design to expand at length on some things which hitherto I have but slightly touched upon, in order to convince the reader...that it would be utterly impossible, either

---

1 I.e., care as little.

2 This commentary is from Mandeville, which was published with the later editions of the poem.

3 Latin for beautiful and true or beautiful and honorable. This Latin phrase was often used to refer to two (out of three or four) ways of being good; it is subject to a wide variety of translation.

to raise any multitudes into a populous, rich and flourishing nation, or when so raised, to keep and maintain them in that condition, without the assistance of what we call evil both natural and moral.

The better to perform what I have undertaken, I shall...examine into the reality of the *pulchrum & honestum*...that the ancients have talked of so much: The meaning of this is to discuss, whether there be a real worth and excellency in things...[on] which everybody will always agree....

[Now three] hundred years ago men were shaved as closely as they are now: since then they have worn beards, and cut them in vast a variety of forms, that were all as becoming when fashionable as now they would be ridiculous. How mean and comically a man looks, that is otherwise well dressed, in a narrow-brimmed hat when everybody wears broad ones; and again, how monstrous is a very great hat, when the other extreme has been in fashion for a considerable time? Experience has taught us, that these modes seldom last above ten or twelve years....

The many ways of laying out a garden judiciously are almost innumerable, and what is called beautiful in them varies according to the different tastes of nations and ages....

In morals there is no greater certainty. Plurality of wives is odious among Christians, and all the wit and learning of a great genius in defence of it has been rejected with contempt: But polygamy is not shocking to a Mahometan.[1] What Men have learned from their infancy enslaves them, and the force of custom warps nature, and at the same time imitates her in such a manner, that it is often difficult to know which of the two we are influenced by. In the East formerly sisters married brothers, and it was meritorious for a man to marry his mother. Such alliances are abominable; but it is certain that, whatever horror we conceive at the thoughts of

them, there is nothing in nature repugnant against them, but what is built upon mode and custom....

Which is the best religion? is a question that has caused more mischief than all other questions together. Ask it at Peking, at Constantinople,[2] and at Rome, and you'll receive three distinct answers extremely different from one another, yet all of them equally positive and peremptory. Christians are well assured of the falsity of the Pagan and Mahometan superstitions; as to this point there is a perfect union and concord among them; but enquire of the several sects they are divided into, which is the true Church of Christ? And all of them will tell you, it is theirs....

It is manifest then that the hunting after this *pulchrum & honestum* is not much better than a wild-goose chase that is but little to be depended upon. But this is not the greatest fault I find with it. The imaginary notion that men may be virtuous without self-denial is a vast inlet to hypocrisy, which hypocrisy being once made habitual, we must not only deceive others, but likewise become altogether unknown to ourselves....

It remains then that I should set forth the variety of obstacles[3] that hinder and perplex man in the labour he is constantly employed in, in the procuring of what he wants; and which in other words is called the business of self-preservation.... The obstacles I speak of relate either to our own frame,[4] or the globe we inhabit.... Water drowns and fire consumes those who unskillfully approach them.... It is impossible to repeat all the injuries we receive from plants, and creatures, and the wind and weather...

But consider the garden of Eden, before the Fall...when man was wholly rapt up in sublime meditations on the infinity of his Creator...

In such a Golden Age no reason or probability can be alleged why mankind ever should have raised themselves into such large societies as there

---

1 I.e., a Muslim.
2 Peking = Beijing; Constantinople = Istanbul.
3 I.e., evils.
4 I.e., our own individual fate.

have been in the world, as long as we can give any tolerable account of it. Where a man has everything he desires, and nothing to vex or disturb him, there is nothing can be added to his happiness; and it is impossible to name a trade, art, science, dignity or employment that would not be superfluous in such a blessed state. If we pursue this thought we shall easily perceive that no societies could have sprung from the amiable virtues and loving qualities of man, but on the contrary that all of them must have had their origin from his wants, his imperfections, and the variety of his Appetites....

In addition, be we savages or politicians, it is impossible that man, mere fallen man, should act with any other view but to please himself.... There is no difference between will and pleasure in one sense, and every motion made in spite of them must be unnatural and convulsive. Since then our action is so confined, and we are always forced to do what we please,...it is impossible we could be sociable creatures without hypocrisy. The proof of this is plain,...and if all we think was to be laid open to others in the same manner as it is to ourselves, it is impossible that endued with speech we could be sufferable to one another.

I am persuaded that every reader feels the truth of what I say; and I tell my antagonist that his conscience flies in his face, while his tongue is preparing to refute me. In all civil societies men are taught insensibly to be hypocrites from their cradle; nobody dares to own up to what he gets by public calamities.... The sexton[1] would be stoned should he wish openly for the death of the parishioners, though everybody knew that he had nothing else to live upon....

It is certain that the fewer desires a man has and the less he covets,...the more he will be beloved.... But let us be just.... What earthly good can this do, to promote the wealth, the glory and worldly greatness of nations? No, it is the sensual courtier that sets no

limits to his luxury; the fickle strumpet that invents new fashions every week; the haughty duchess that in equipage, entertainments, and all her behaviour would imitate a princess; the profuse rake and lavish heir:...it is these that are the prey and proper food of a full grown Leviathan;[2] or in other words, such is the calamitous condition of human affairs that we stand in need of the plagues and monsters I named,...to procure an honest livelihood for the vast multitudes of working poor.... And it is folly to imagine that great and wealthy Nations can subsist, and be at once powerful and polite without them....

What estates have been got by tea and coffee! What a vast traffic maintains thousands of families, simply to preserve two silly if not odious customs; the taking of snuff and smoking of tobacco; both which it is certain do infinitely more hurt than good to those that are addicted to them....

It is the necessities, the vices and imperfections of man, together with the various inclemencies of the air and other elements, that contain in them the seeds of all arts, industry and labour.... Hunger, thirst and nakedness are the first tyrants that force us to stir: afterwards, our pride, sloth, sensuality and fickleness are the great patrons that promote all arts and sciences, trades, handicrafts and callings; while the great taskmasters, necessity, avarice, envy, and ambition...keep the members of the society to their labour, and make them all submit, most of them cheerfully, to the drudgery of their station; kings and princes not excepted....

I therefore flatter myself to think that, neither the friendly qualities and kind affections that are natural to man, nor the real virtues he is capable of acquiring by reason and self-denial, are the foundation of society; but that what we call evil in this world, moral as well as natural, is the grand principle that makes us sociable creatures, the solid basis, the life and support of all trades and employments without exception:

---

1 The sexton is a gravedigger, and as such wants people to die because he gets paid for digging their graves.
2 I.e., (the) state, imagined (as by Hobbes) as a huge powerful sea-monster.

That there we must look for the true origin of all arts and sciences, and that the moment evil ceases, the society must be spoiled, if not totally dissolved....

A VINDICATION OF THE Book, from the Aspersions Contained in a Presentment of the Grand Jury of Middlesex, and from an Abusive Letter to Lord C.[1]

What I have to say in my behalf I shall address to all men of sense and sincerity, asking no other favour of them than their patience and attention....

But I will likewise own very freely, that, if I had written with a design to be understood by the meanest capacities...I would have bestowed a page or two on the meaning of the word 'evil'; after that I would have taught them, that every defect, every want was an evil; that on the multiplicity of those wants depended all those mutual services which the individual members of a society pay to each other; and that consequently, the greater variety there was of wants, the larger number of individuals might find their private interest in labouring for the good of others, and united together, compose one political or civic body.

Is there a trade or handicraft but what supplies us with something we wanted? This want certainly, before it was supplied, was an evil, which that trade or handicraft was to remedy, and without which it could never have been thought of. Is there an art or science that was not invented to mend some defect? Had this latter not existed, there could have been no occasion for the former to remove it....

Now I lay down as a first principle, that in all societies, great or small, it is the duty of every member of it to be good; that virtue ought to be encouraged; vice discountenanced; the Laws obeyed, and the transgressors punished. There is not a line in the book that contradicts this doctrine, and I defy my enemies to disprove what I have advanced;...that if I have shown the way to worldly greatness, I have always without hesitation preferred the road that leads to virtue.

No man ever took more pains not to be misconstrued than myself.... When I say that societies cannot be raised to wealth and power, and the top of earthly glory, without vices; I don't think that by so saying I bid men be vicious, any more than I bid them be quarrelsome or covetous, when I affirm, that the profession of the law could not be maintained in such numbers and splendor, if there was not abundance of too selfish and litigious people....

The first impression of the *Fable of the Bees*, which came out in 1714, was never carped at,[2] or publicly taken notice of; and all the reason I can think on why this second edition should be so unmercifully treated...is an essay on charity and charity-schools, which is added to what was printed before. I confess that it is my sentiment, that all hard and dirty work ought in a well-governed nation to be the lot and portion of the poor, and that to divert their children from useful labour till they are fourteen or fifteen years old, is a wrong method to qualify them for it when they are grown up....

If the arguments I have made use of are not convincing, I desire they may be refuted.... But vast sums are gathered for these charity-schools, and I understand human nature too well to imagine, that the sharers of the money should hear them spoke against with any patience....

For this reason, it cannot be thought, that it was

---

1 In his commentary, Mandeville also responds to a jury's charge that the book is a criminal nuisance. The Presentment (i.e., a formal accusation) of the Grand Jury complains that publications like *The Grumbling Hive* "have a direct tendency to propagate Infidelity, and consequently corruption of all morals" by 1) openly blaspheming, 2) denying the providence and government of God in the world, 3) subverting discipline in the Church and striving to bring contempt on all religion, 4) promoting a general libertinism, and 5) using "studied artifices and invented colours...to run down religion and virtue as prejudicial to Society...and to recommend luxury, avarice, pride, and all kind of vices, as being necessary to public welfare...with design, we conceive, to debauch the Nation." The letter, to the *British Journal*, attacked him for his criticism of charity-schools in one of the appendices.

2 I.e., complained about.

a great surprise to me, when in that extraordinary Letter to Lord C. I saw myself called profligate author,... and what I had done so stunning, so shocking, so frightful, so flagrant an enormity, that it cried for the vengeance of Heaven....

I am sorry if the words "private vices, public benefits," have ever given any offence to a well-meaning man... but no man of sincerity will question the innocence of them, that has read the last paragraph, where I conclude by repeating the seeming paradox... that private vices by the dexterous management of a skillful politician, may be turned into public benefits....

But I set aside all what I have said in this my vindication; and if in the whole Book... there is to be found the least title of blasphemy or profaneness, or anything tending to immorality or the corruption of manners, I desire that it may be published; and if this be done without invective, personal reflections, or setting the mob upon me,... I will not only recant, but likewise beg pardon of the offended public in the most solemn manner; and (if the hangman might be thought too good for the Office[1]) burn the book myself at any reasonable time and place my adversaries shall be pleased to appoint.

Questions

1. Mandeville's thought has been described as "neo-Epicureanism." Compare the two thinkers.

2. In "An Enquiry Into The Origin Of Moral Virtue," Mandeville suggests that the real source of our so-called morality is pride. This is promoted, socially, by the "cunning" use of flattery. Comment.

3. Mandeville seems to assign the chief role in his theory to self-interest. Is his position really that different from contemporary thinkers who argue that the profit motive is the engine of a sound economy? Explain your answer, with proper qualifications.

4. What is the purpose of society and government in the moral scheme set out in *The Fable of the Bees*? Are the actions of governments "moral" or "immoral"? How?

5. Mandeville's ethical realism is troubling because he simply accepts that society will always have classes and that the poor will—always—work for the rich. What is your response?

6. Mandeville adopts the kind of ethical relativism that we find in the ancient Sophists and Skeptics. Compare Mandeville's position with that of an earlier philosopher.

7. Suppose we put you on the Middlesex grand jury that found the publication of *The Fable of the Bees* a public nuisance in 1723. What would you say to your fellow jurors? Do you think the book undermined the public morality of the time?

Suggested Readings

Mandeville was a prolific writer and provocative wit who specialized in scandalous opinions. Although he is remembered for *The Fable of the Bees*, he published many "broad-

---

1 I.e., for this job.

sheets" on topical issues of the day. These include *Aesop Dress'd; or a Collection of Fables Writ in Familiar Verse* (1704); *The Virgin Unmask'd: or, Female Dialogues Betwixt an Elderly Maiden Lady, and Her Niece* (1709); and *A Modest Defence of Publick Stews* (1724). A facsimile edition of the *Collected Works of Bernard Mandeville* is available in eight volumes (Bernhard Fabian and Irwin Primer, 1981–99).

For Mandeville's philosophy, see Malcolm Jack, *The Social and Political Thought of Bernard Mandeville* (1987). Mandeville's argument regarding luxury formed part of a larger philosophical debate. See, for example, Lisa Broussois, "Francis Hutcheson on Luxury and Intemperance: The Mandeville Threat" (2015).

There are many historical sources. See, for example, Eugene Heath, "Private Vices, Publick Benefits? The Contemporary Reception of Bernard Mandeville" (1999). In "Du Châtelet, Voltaire, and the Transformation of Mandeville's Fable" (2012), Felicia Gottmann writes that the French translator of *The Fable of the Bees* modified the text along Epicurean lines to defend the idea of progress. Many of the historical sources discuss the responses of Rousseau, Adam Smith, and others to *The Fable of the Bees*. In business ethics, see George Bragues, "Business Is One Thing, Ethics Is Another: Revisiting Bernard Mandeville's *The Fable of the Bees*" (2005).

Chapter 28

The Anglican Tradition

Joseph Butler (1692–1752) sets out a theory of "rational altruism," which is philosophically informed but comes out of the Protestant tradition. The son of a prosperous, Presbyterian textile merchant, Joseph Butler was born in the town of Wantage, Berkshire, west of London. He was the youngest of eight children, and after regular grammar school, he attended a Dissenters' Academy for Protestants who had broken from the Church of England (the Anglican Church) in Tewkesbury. After leaving the Academy, and reconsidering his religious loyalties, Butler converted to the Church of England, with the idea of pursuing an ecclesiastical career. He enrolled in Oriel College at Oxford and, on graduation, was ordained as an Anglican deacon and then a priest (1718).

Butler never married and devoted his life to the church, filling multiple posts, which included: preacher at Rolls Court (1719–26), Rector of Stanhope (1725–40), Bishop of Bristol (1738–50), Dean of St. Paul's Cathedral (1740–50), and Bishop of Durham (1750–52). He was apparently a mild-mannered, self-effacing clergyman, who was well liked by parishioners. Towards the end of his career, he drew up a tentative plan for the establishment of the Anglican episcopacy in America.

Butler served as head chaplain to Queen Caroline (1736–37) and to King George II (1747–52). He seems to have been a particular favorite of the Queen, who required his presence from seven to nine every evening for theological discussion. While serving as the Bishop of Bristol, Butler demanded that Methodist reformer John Wesley leave his diocese because he disapproved of his excess "enthusiasm." He himself was accused of "Popish" sympathies by mud-racking pamphleteers at the end of his life. He is buried in Bristol Cathedral.

There are stories that Butler was generous to a fault. It was said that beggars harassed him so relentlessly that he had to hide in his rectory and that he was once forced to flee a large crowd of them, galloping away on his black pony. Hostile commentators have drawn attention to his complaints about his remuneration when he was appointed the Bishop of Bristol, but the evidence is unclear, and he may have seen this as a matter of principle. By all accounts, he seems to have spent most of his personal fortune on public causes, lavishing attention on church buildings and dividing his estate among his relatives, the Newcastle Infirmary, and the Society for the Propagation of the Gospel in Foreign Parts.

Butler had developed philosophical interests and ultimately obtained a Doctor of Laws degree at Oxford (1733). As a young man, he engaged in a philosophical dispute with Samuel Clark, a famous Divine, about the latter's proof for the existence and attributes of God. He was primarily interested in philosophy, however, as an aid to ethics and a proper understanding of the Christian religion. During his time at Oxford, he complained: "We are obliged to mis-spend so much time here in attending frivolous lectures and unintelligible disputations, that I am quite tired out with such a disagreeable way of trifling."

Butler accordingly bridges both sides of the history of moral philosophy. He was a philosopher in the modern sense, and interested in the theoretical side of ethics, but only because it has a concrete, practical effect on people's lives. He also took an interest in the moral and political issues of his day, publishing sermons on missionary work, poor relief, charity schools, and hospitals. It has been suggested that he published some of his writing in order to advance his career within the church and there may be some merit in such a criticism. It is tantalizing that he included a provision in his will that any remaining sermons, letters, and papers "be burnt without being read by anyone," a wish that was apparently respected.

Butler is mostly remembered in moral philosophy for the publication of two editions of *Fifteen Sermons Preached at the Rolls Chapel* (1726, 1729), and a short essay entitled "Dissertation on Virtue," which is appended at the end of his *Analogy of Religion, Natural and Revealed* (1736). The book of sermons won the praise of David Hume and is still studied by philosophers. From what we know, there is no record that the sermons were actually given, and it is far more likely that the idea of fifteen consecutive sermons was a literary device, which provided a convenient means of presenting his ideas.

The tone of the *Sermons* is nevertheless pastoral, rather than academic, and probably comes from Butler's preaching. In the preface, Butler distinguishes two ways of doing moral philosophy: we can derive specific moral principles from abstract, theoretical relations, or from the observed facts of human life. He himself takes the second approach, setting out a theory of human nature based on our common experience of life, which he then uses to answer the questions that arise in the moral inquiry.

It is evident that Butler's basic purpose is to mount a defense of morality in response to a libertine, skeptical challenge that is hostile, not only to religion, but to traditional values. His response to rival thinkers such as Thomas Hobbes and Anthony Ashley Cooper, the third Earl of Shaftesbury, is that they fail to distinguish between the different aspects of the human constitution. There are two forms of benevolence, for example, which must be distinguished. There is a higher-level inclination towards others, which provides the real source of human happiness, and a lower-level human passion.

This kind of linguistic argument is distinctly modern. Butler argues that there is no deep conflict between human tendencies towards self-love and benevolence. The real danger to morals is not self-love but an unreasoning pursuit of pleasure that pushes us to ruinous excess. Butler recognizes that self-interest plays a legitimate role in morality. He openly says that self-love counsels us to do whatever is necessary for our own happiness. Happiness depends on our good relations with others, however, and includes the kind of self-esteem that we derive from benevolent activity. It seems clear that a person who is properly ordered, internally, will also take a certain happiness in acting ethically.

For Butler, like the Stoics, virtue consists of following nature. His view of human nature is hierarchical, however. We find human appetites, passions, and affections at the lower levels of experience, which are subordinate to the general tendencies towards self-love and benevolence. These general tendencies are themselves subordinate, however, to the natural authority of the human conscience, which has an ingrained capacity for ethical reflection and evaluation. We can trust this "universal moral faculty" because it is "the guide assigned us by the Author of our nature." Those who oppose the voice of conscience ignore an important part of themselves; they betray who and what they truly are.

There seems to be a theory of the natural law under Butler's argument. The modern proposition in his work, however, is that the practice of virtue, which "consists in good actions, proceeding from a good principle, temper, or heart," serves our interests. A rational, self-interested person will accordingly be altruistic. This proposition has received enormous attention in the subsequent tradition and is still a fundamental focus of liberal ethics.

There is a practical side to the *Sermons*, which also discusses many practical matters, such as the vice of excess talkativeness, resentment, forgiveness, compassion, the love of our neighbors, the love of God, and human ignorance. Two criticisms might also be mentioned. The first is that morality sometimes requires a relatively high level of self-sacrifice—a heroic altruism—that cannot be reconciled so easily with the search for human happiness. The second is that the origins of conscience need further analysis in a contemporary context.

The reading is from the *Sermons* and provides a synopsis of Butler's views, with particular attention to the natural origins of virtue, his idea of conscience, and the principle of benevolence.

READING 28

Joseph Butler, *Fifteen Sermons Preached at the Rolls Chapel*[1]

(originally published in 1726, with six additional sermons in 1749)

Preface

There are two ways in which the subject of morals may be treated. One begins from inquiring into the abstract (i.e., theoretical) relations of things; the other, from a matter of fact, namely, what the particular nature of man is, its several parts, their economy or constitution; from whence it proceeds

---

1 Joseph Butler, *Fifteen Sermons Preached at the Rolls Chapel* (originally published in 1726, with six additional sermons in 1749) (Cambridge: Hilliard and Brown; Boston: Hilliard, Gray, Little, and Wilkins, 1827), online at http://anglicanhistory.org/butler/rolls/01.html. See also *Principles of Moral Science. Containing Bishop Butler's Three Sermons on Human Nature, and Dissertation on Virtue, with an introduction, analysis, vocabulary, etc. by the Rev. Henry Bower* (South India Christian School Book Society, 1857). There is another online version at Wikisource.

to determine what course of life it is, which is correspondent to this whole nature. In the former method the conclusion is expressed thus, that vice is contrary to the nature and reasons of things; in the latter, that it is a violation or breaking in upon our own nature. Thus they both lead us to the same thing, our obligations to the practice of virtue; and thus they exceedingly strengthen and enforce each other.

The first approach seems the most direct formal proof, and in some respects the least liable to cavil and dispute: the latter, which appears to correspond to practical wisdom, is in a peculiar manner adapted to satisfy a fair mind, and is more easily applicable to the several particular relations and circumstances in life.

The following discourses proceed chiefly in this latter method.... They were intended to explain what is meant by the nature of man, when it is said that virtue consists in following it, and vice in deviating from it...

Now the idea of a system, economy, or constitution, of any particular nature, or particular anything...is a one or a whole, made up of several parts; and yet that the several parts, even considered as a whole, do not complete the idea, unless, in the notion of a whole, you include the relations and respects which those parts have to each other.

Every work both of nature and of art is a system: and as every particular thing, both natural and artificial, is for some use or purpose out of and beyond itself, one may add, to the idea of what makes a system, its conduciveness to this one or more ends. Let us instance in a watch: Suppose the several parts of it taken to pieces, and placed apart from each other: let a man have ever so exact a notion of these several parts, unless he considers the respects and relations which they have to each other, he will not have anything like the idea of a watch. Suppose further these several parts be brought together and anyhow united: neither will he yet, be the union ever so close,

have an idea which will bear any resemblance to that of a watch. But let him view those several working parts put together...let him form a notion of the relations which those several parts have to each other—all conducive, in their respective ways, to this purpose, showing the hour of the day; and then he has the idea of a watch.

Thus it is with regard to the inward frame of man. Appetites, passions, affections, and the principle of reflection, considered merely as the several parts of our inward nature, do not at all give us an idea of the system or constitution of this nature: because the constitution is formed by somewhat not yet taken into consideration, namely, by the relations which these several parts have to each other; the chief of which is found in the authority of reflection or conscience. It is from considering the relations which the several appetites and passions in the inward frame have to each other, and, above all, the supremacy of reflection or conscience, that we get the idea of the system or constitution of human nature. And from this idea itself it will as fully appear, that this our nature, i.e., constitution, is adapted to virtue, as from the idea of a watch it appears, that its nature, i.e., constitution or system is adapted to measure time....

Like the brutes,[1] the generality of mankind also obey their instincts and principles, all of them; those inclinations we call good, as well as bad. Therefore, it is not a true representation of mankind, to affirm that they are wholly governed by self-love, the love of power and sensual appetites: since, as on the one hand, they are often actuated by these, without any regard to right or wrong; so on the other, it is manifest fact, that the same persons, the generality, are frequently influenced by friendship, compassion, gratitude, and even general abhorrence of what is base, and the linking of what is fair and just, takes its turn among the other motives of action.

But that is not a complete account of man's nature. Somewhat further must be brought in to

---

1 I.e., animals, thought of as lacking reason or intelligence.

give us an adequate notion of it; namely, that one of those principles of action, conscience, or reflection, compared with the rest, as they all stand together in the nature of man, plainly bears upon it marks of authority over all the rest, and claims the absolute direction of them all, to allow or forbid their gratification…

The practical reason of insisting so much upon this natural authority of the principle of reflection or conscience is that it seems in a great measure overlooked by many, who are by no means the worst sort of men.… Whereas, in reality, the very constitution of our nature requires that we bring our whole conduct before this superior faculty; wait its determination; enforce upon ourselves its authority; and make it the business of our lives, as it is absolutely the whole business of a moral agent, to conform ourselves to it. This is the true meaning of that ancient precept, reverence yourself.[1]

The not taking into consideration this authority, which is implied in the idea of reflex approbation or disapprobation, seems a material deficiency or omission in Lord Shaftesbury's *Inquiry concerning Virtue.* He has shown, beyond all contradiction, that virtue is naturally the interest of happiness, and vice the misery of such a creature as man, placed in the circumstances which we are in this world.…

But suppose there are particular exceptions.… Or suppose a case…of a sceptic not convinced of this happy tendency of virtue, or being of a contrary opinion:…leaving out the authority of reflex approbation or disapprobation, such a one would be under an obligation to act viciously; since interest, one's own happiness, is a manifest obligation, and there is not supposed to be any other obligation under Shaftesbury's system.

The observation that man is thus, by his very nature, a law to himself…is of the utmost importance; because from it will follow, that though men

reject the idea that God punishes those who violate the moral law; yet, they would still be under an obligation to act virtuously…

Sermon I. Upon the Social Nature of Man

Letter of Paul to the Romans; xii, 4–5: For as we have many members in one body, and all members have not the same office; so we being many, are one body in Christ, and every one members of each other…

The relation which the several parts or members of the natural body have to each other, and to the whole body, is here compared to the relation which each particular person in society has to other particular persons, and to the whole society; and the latter is intended to be illustrated by the former. And if there be a likeness between these two relations, the consequence is obvious: that the latter shows us we were intended to do good to others, as the former shows us, that the several members of the natural body were intended to be instruments of good to each other, and to the whole body.…

And since the apostle speaks of the several members as having distinct offices, which implies the mind, it cannot be thought an unallowable liberty, instead of the body and its members, to substitute the whole nature of man, and all the variety of internal principles which belong to it. And then the comparison will be between the nature of man as respecting himself, and tending to private good, his own preservation and happiness; and the nature of man as having respect to society, and tending to promote public good, the happiness of that society.…

From this review and comparison of the nature of man as respecting self, as respecting society, it will plainly appear, that there are as real and the same kind of indications in human nature, that we were made for society and to do good to our fellow creatures, as

---

1 Or, respect yourself, a saying attributed to Pythagoras of Samos (c. 570–c. 495 BCE), a Greek philosopher and mathematician who founded the philosophical/religious tradition of Pythagoreanism.

that we were intended to take care of our own life, and health, and private good; and that the same objections lie against one of these assertions as against the other.

For;

First, there is a natural principle of benevolence in man, which is in some degree to society, what self-love is to the individual. And if there be in mankind any disposition to friendship; if there be any such thing as compassion, for compassion is momentary love; if there be any such things as the paternal of filial affections; if there be any affection in human nature, the object and end of which is the good of another; this is itself benevolence, or the love of another....

I must however remind you, that though benevolence and self-love are different; though the former tends most directly to public good, and the latter private; yet they are so perfectly coincident, that the greatest satisfactions to ourselves depend upon our having benevolence in a due degree; and that self-love is the one chief security of our right behaviour towards society....

Secondly, this will further appear from observing, that our passions and affections...do in general contribute and lead us to public good...

It is enough to the present argument, that the desire of esteem from others...the love of society as distinct from affection to the good of it and indignation against successful vice...are public affections or passions...and naturally lead us to regulate our behaviour in such a manner as will be of service to our fellow creatures....

It may be added, that as persons...would preserve life merely from the appetite of hunger; so, by acting merely from regard to reputation, without any consideration of the good of others, men often contribute to public good. In both these instances they are plainly instruments in the hands of...Providence, to carry on ends, the preservation of the individual and good of society, which they themselves have not in their view or intention. The sum is, men have various appetites, passions, and particular affections, quite distinct both from self-love and from benevolence; all of these have a tendency to promote both public and private good, and may be considered as respecting others and ourselves equally and in common...

Thirdly, there is a principle of reflection in men, by which they distinguish between, approve, and disapprove their own actions.... This principle in man, by which he approves or disapproves his heart, temper, and action, is conscience; for this is the strict sense of the word, though sometimes it is used so as to take in more. And that this faculty tends to restrain men from doing mischief to each other, and leads them to do good, is too manifest to need being insisted upon. Thus, a parent has the affection of love to his children: this leads him to take care of, to educate, to make due provision for them.

The natural affection leads to this; but the reflection that it is his proper business...that it is right and commendable so to do...becomes a much more settled principle, and carries him on through more labour and difficulties for the sake of his children, than he would undergo from that affection alone...It cannot possibly be denied, that there is this principle of reflection or conscience in human nature.... It is needless to compare the respect it has to private good, with the respect it has to public; since it plainly tends as much to the latter as to the former...

Sermon II. Upon the Natural Supremacy of Conscience[1]

Romans; ii, 14: For when the Gentiles, which have not the law, do by nature the things contained in the law, these having not the law, are a law unto themselves.

To this someone may respond: "It may indeed be absurd and unnatural for men to act without any

---

1 In the following, Butler restates his thesis that conscience is natural to man and then sets out an objection.

reflection; or rather, without regard to that particular kind of reflection which you call conscience; because this does belong to our nature.... In spite of this, however, it is evident that interest and passion do come in, and are often too strong for, and prevail over reflection and conscience.... Now, as brutes have various instincts,... is not man in the same condition, with this difference only, that to man's instincts is added the principle of reflection or conscience? And as brutes act agreeably to their nature, in following that principle or particular instinct which for the present is strongest in them; does not man likewise act agreeably to his nature... by following that principle... which for the present happens to be strongest in him?

"Thus, different men are by their particular nature hurried on to pursue honor, or riches, or pleasure.... Let everyone then quietly follow his nature; as passion, reflection, appetite, the several parts of it, happen to be the strongest; but let not the man of virtue take upon him to blame the ambitious, the covetous, the dissolute; since these, equally with him, obey and follow their nature...."

Now all this licentious talk goes upon a supposition that men follow their nature in the same sense, in violating the known rules of justice and honesty for the sake of a present gratification.... And if this were true, that could not be so which St. Paul asserts, that men are "by nature a law to themselves."...

The objection will be fully answered, and the text before us explained, by observing, that nature is considered in different views, and the word used in different senses; and by showing in what view it is considered,... when intended to express and signify that which is the guide of life, that by which men are a law to themselves.

I. By nature is often meant no more than some principle in man.... Thus, the passion of anger, and the affection of parents to their children, would be called equally natural. And as the same person hath

often contrary principles, which at the same time draw contrary ways, he may by the same action both follow and contradict his nature in this sense of the word...

II. Nature is frequently spoken of as consisting in those passions which are strongest, and most influence the actions... Thus St. Paul says of the Gentiles, who were dead in trespasses and sins, and walked according to the spirit of disobedience, that they were by nature the children of Wrath.[1] They, therefore, could be no otherwise children of wrath by nature, than they were vicious by nature.

Here then are two different senses of the word nature, in neither of which men can at all be said to be a law to themselves. They are mentioned only... to prevent their being confounded... with another sense of it, which is now to be inquired after and explained.

III. The apostle asserts, that the Gentiles do by nature the things contained in the law.... It is plain the meaning of the word here is not the same in this passage as in the former, where it is spoken of as evil; for in this latter it is spoken of as good; as that by which they acted, or might have acted virtuously. What that is in man by which he is naturally a law to himself is explained in the following words: Which shows the work of the law, written in their hearts, their consciences also bearing witness...

If there be a distinction to be made between the works written in their hearts, and the witness of conscience; by the former must be meant, the natural disposition to kindness and compassion... and by means of which he naturally acts a just and good part in society, unless other passions or interest lead him astray.

Yet since other passions, and interest, which lead us astray, are themselves in a degree equally natural... it is plain the natural disposition to kindness and compassion can no more be a law to us than the latter.... unless there is a superior principle of

---

1 Ephesians 2:3.

reflection or conscience in every man which distinguishes between the internal principles of his heart, as well as his external actions; which passes judgment upon himself and them; pronounces determinately some actions to be in themselves just, right, good; others to be in themselves evil, wrong, unjust: and which... magisterially exerts itself, and approves or condemns him, the doer of them, accordingly...

It is by this faculty of conscience, natural to man, that he is a moral agent, that he is a law to himself. By this faculty, I say, not to be considered merely as a principle in his heart, which is to have some influence as well as others; but considered as a faculty, in kind and in nature, supreme over all others, and which bears its own authority of being so....

This is its right and office: thus sacred is its authority. And how ever often men violate and rebelliously refuse to submit to it, for supposed interest which they cannot otherwise obtain, or for the sake of passion which they cannot otherwise gratify; this makes no alteration as to the natural right, and office of conscience....

Sermon III. Continuing Sermon II, on the Natural Supremacy of Conscience

The natural supremacy of reflection or conscience being thus established; we may from it form a distinct notion of what is meant by human nature, when virtue is said to consist in following it, and vice in deviating from it.

As the idea of a civil constitution of a state implies in it united strength, various subordinations, under one direction, that of the supreme authority;... if you leave out the subordination, the union, and the one direction, you destroy and lose it. So reason, several appetites, passions, and affections, prevail in different degrees of strength in human nature;... human nature consists in these several principles considered as having a natural respect to each other, in the several passions being naturally subordinate to the one

superior principle of reflection or conscience. Every bias, instinct, inclination within, is a real part of our nature, but not the whole: add to these the superior faculty, whose office it is to adjust, manage, and preside over them, and take in this its natural superiority, and you complete the idea of human nature.

And as in civil government the constitution is broken in upon and violated, by power and strength prevailing over authority; so the constitution of man is broken in upon and violated by the lower faculties or principles within prevailing over that, which is in its nature supreme over them all...

Sermon XI. Upon the Love of Our Neighbor

Romans; xiii, 9: And if there be any other commandment, it is briefly comprehended in this saying, namely, You shall love your neighbor as yourself.

Self-love and interestedness was stated to consist in or be an affection to ourselves, a regard to our own private good: it is, therefore, distinct from benevolence, which is an affection to the good of our fellow creatures. But that benevolence is distinct from, that is, not the same thing with self-love, is no reason for its being looked upon with any peculiar suspicion, because every principle whatever, by means of which self-love is gratified, is distinct from it: and all things, which are distinct from each other, are equally so....

We use the word 'property' so as to exclude any other person's having an interest in that of which we say a particular man has the property: and we often use the word 'selfish' so as to exclude in the same manner all regards to the good of others. But the cases are not parallel: for though that exclusion is really part of the idea of property; yet such positive exclusion, or bringing this peculiar disregard to the good of others into the idea of self-love, is in reality adding to the idea, or changing it from what it was before stated to consist in, namely, in an affection to ourselves. This being the whole idea of self-love, it can no otherwise exclude good will or love of others…than it excludes love of arts, or reputation, or of anything else.

Thus it appears,[1] that there is no peculiar contrariety between self-love and benevolence; no greater competition between these, than between any other particular affections and self-love.…

That an affection tends to the happiness of another, does not hinder its tending to one's own happiness, too.… So a pursuit which tends to promote the good of another, yet may have as great tendency to promote private interest, as a pursuit which does not tend to the good of another at all, or which is mischievous to him. All particular affections whatever, resentment, benevolence, love of arts, equally lead to a course of action for their own gratification, i.e., the gratification of ourselves; and the gratification of each gives delight: so far, then, it is manifest, they have all the same respect to private interest.…

Now there have been persons in all ages, who have professed that they found satisfaction in the exercise of charity, in the love of their neighbor, in endeavoring to promote the happiness of all they had to do with, and in the pursuit of what is just, and right, and good…And will anyone take upon him to say…that such a person has…less satisfaction and peace of mind than the ambitious or dissolute man?…

The general mistake, that there is some greater inconsistency between endeavoring to promote the good of another and self-interest, than between self-interest and pursuing anything else, seems, as has already been hinted, to arise from our notions of property; and to be carried on by this property's being supposed to be itself our happiness or good.…

For, if property and happiness are one and the same thing, as by increasing the property of another, you lessen your own property, so by promoting the happiness of another, you must lessen your own happiness. But whatever occasioned the mistake…, I hope it has been fully proved…that every particular affection, benevolence among the rest, is subservient to self-love, by being the instrument of private enjoyment; and that in one respect benevolence contributes more to private interest, i.e., enjoyment or satisfaction, than any other of the particular common affections, as it is in a degree its own gratification.

And to all these things may be added, that religion, from whence arises our strongest obligation to benevolence, is so far from disowning the principle of self-love, that it often addresses itself to that very principle, and always to the mind in that state when reason presides;…by convincing men, that the course of life we would persuade them to is not contrary to their interest.…

Let it be allowed, though virtue or moral rectitude does indeed consist in affection to and pursuit of what is right and good, as such: yet that, when we sit down in a cool hour, we can neither justify to ourselves the pursuit of what is right and good, as such, or any other pursuit, till we are convinced that it will be for our happiness, or, at least, not contrary to it.…

Questions

1. Butler is a modern thinker. Compare his views with the Stoics, or a medieval philosopher such as Augustine or Aquinas. How did the Enlightenment change the focus of the moral conversation? How do individual choice and reason fit into this?

---

1 Butler regards benevolence as an affection, like any other.

2. How does Butler see the relationship between human nature and nature? What is the end of human life, in Butler's view? Do you agree with him?

3. Briefly describe the role of conscience in Butler's moral system. Do you agree with Butler? Where does an individual's conscience come from, in your view?

4. Butler suggests that the moral skeptic has a conscience—an intuitive reflex of approbation or disapprobation—and is therefore obliged to act virtuously. Discuss, with reference to one of the ancient Skeptics.

5. What role do God—and providence—play in Butler's moral theory?

6. The most significant moral argument in Butler is probably that benevolence and self-love are not inconsistent with each other. How does Butler explain their compatibility? Is he right?

7. Butler was primarily interested in practical ethics and saw philosophical thought as a means of helping us deal with the moral issues in our lives. How, then, would you apply Butler's theory to your own life? Use examples.

Suggested Readings

Butler did not leave a large philosophical *oeuvre*. Early in his career, he published a series of philosophical letters to Samuel Clark about proofs of God's existence (*Several Letters to the Reverend Dr. Clarke*, 1716). Much later, he published a defense of Christianity against the attacks of the Deists (*Analogy of Religion, Natural and Revealed, to the Constitution and Course of Nature*, 1736), which was influential in its time. His philosophical reputation nevertheless rests on his *Fifteen Sermons* (published with six additional sermons in 1749). The text is available at anglicanhistory.org, libertyfund.org, and wikisource.org.

David White has a good introduction to Butler in the *Internet Encyclopedia of Philosophy*. For a sympathetic discussion of Butler's moral philosophy by an influential contemporary philosopher, see Terence Penelhum, *Butler* (1985). Another source is Bob Tennant, *Conscience, Consciousness and Ethics in Joseph Butler's Philosophy and Ministry* (2011).

In "Keeping the Heart: Natural Affection in Joseph Butler's Approach to Virtue" (2009), Sarah Moses considers the role of the natural emotions in Butler's theory. The literature suggests that Butler's analysis is scientifically sound. See, for example, Arthur J. Dyck and Carlos Padilla, "The Empathic Emotions and Self-Love in Bishop Joseph Butler and the Neurosciences" (2009), and Nigel Biggar, "Evolutionary Biology, 'Enlightened' Anthropological Narratives, and Social Morality" (2013). For a comparison with David Hume, see John R. Bowlin, "Sieges, Shipwrecks, and Sensible Knaves: Justice and Utility in Butler and Hume" (2000).

Chapter 29

Emotivism

David Hume[1] (1711–76) was a Scottish philosopher and a British empiricist who is known for his emotive thesis in moral philosophy. This thesis holds that ethics are a product of sentiment and cannot be rationally established.

Hume was born in Edinburgh. A studious boy, he left for Edinburgh University with his brother before he was twelve. Unimpressed, he left the university a few years later, and after working as a clerk for a Bristol sugar importer, he moved to France. There he settled close to the Jesuit College of La Flèche, where he lived frugally, studying and writing. He returned to England in 1738 and published his *Treatise of Human Nature* but was disappointed in the book's reception, famously saying that it "fell dead-born from the press."

Hume never married. He pursued a university career but was turned down for the Chair of Ethics and Pneumatical ("Mental") Philosophy at Edinburgh in 1745 and the Chair of Logic at Glasgow in 1751. In spite of these disappointments, he continued his philosophical writing. In 1745, he was employed to tutor the Marquess of Annandale—who turned out to be insane—and then became the secretary to his cousin, the Lieutenant-General James St. Clair, in his military and diplomatic pursuits.

Hume was most successful as a historian. In 1752, he became the librarian for the Edinburgh Faculty of Advocates (i.e., lawyers) and, using the large library at his disposal, undertook the writing of English history "from the Invasion of Julius Caesar to the Revolution in 1688." Published in six volumes from 1754 to 1762, his *History of England* became a best-seller and secured his financial estate.

Later, Hume acted as the private secretary of the English Ambassador to France, where he enjoyed the company of eminent *philosophes*. He also served as an Under-Secretary of State in London, returning to Edinburgh in 1769. There he built a house and finished his life, studying, writing, and socializing with friends. In spite of a public row with Jean-Jacques Rousseau and fits of temper with James Beattie, a foe, he earned a reputation as witty and engaging company.

Hume has left us a text which clearly tells us how he wanted to be seen. In the last year of

---

1 His family name at birth was spelled 'Home.'

his life, beset with cancer, he wrote a "funeral oration of myself" called "My Own Life," in which he chronicles his rise from modest beginnings to literary fame and financial success through hard work, cheerfulness, frugality, and moderation. An avid reader of Cicero, he saw himself as a man of classical letters, lived moderately, and asked to be buried in a "simple Roman tomb."

The final episode in Hume's life seems significant. By the end of his life, Hume had become famous as an irreconcilable atheist, though the exact nature of his views are unknown. Many of his contemporaries did not believe that it was possible for someone who did not believe in an afterlife to die with equanimity. As a result, Adam Smith and other friends visited him on his deathbed, assuring the public that he had died peacefully and with great composure. This was nevertheless contradicted by his housekeeper, who said that Hume was putting on a show and that his mood changed drastically as soon as his visitors had left.

Hume saw himself as a skeptic. It follows that there is nothing entirely certain in moral matters. The motivations for human behavior, in his view, are the product of passions, non-rational impulses, training, and inculcation. These are subjective factors and do not arise from the existence of facts. This led Hume to suggest that the process of reasoning that derives moral conclusions from factual premises is fallacious. This logical jump has been called the "naturalistic fallacy" in the contemporary literature and has received considerable attention from liberal and analytical philosophers.

The problem identified by contemporary philosophers, also called the "is-ought problem," rests on Hume's observation that the moral discourse inevitably moves from descriptive statements—statements of fact that declare what *is* the case—to prescriptive statements which tell us what we *ought* to do. We may consider, he says, the facts of murder. However unpleasant they may be, the facts of murder do not in themselves disclose what we should or should not do. So how do we arrive at such conclusions? Hume's "law," sometimes called "Hume's guillotine," holds that we cannot make a jump from facts to value. So ethics has no logical foundation.

The source of such moral conclusions can only be found in our feelings, Hume says, and have no rational proof. "It is not against reason," he proclaims, "that I should prefer the destruction of half the world to the pricking of my little finger." It is our feelings that tell us that such a preference would be immoral. Reason is, in Hume's own terminology, the slave of feelings. Our ethical views, he says, can always be traced to an emotional attraction or repulsion to something. We can use reason to determine the best means for possessing or avoiding what we like, but we do not use reason to select our goals.

Hume believes that morality comes from benevolence or "sympathy." There is a seed of benevolence lodged in the human breast. We naturally care for other people. These feelings also motivate us to follow the formal rules of "justice" that regulate the division and distribution of property in the society in which we live. These rules are an artificial contrivance, however, and lose their moral authority when they fail to promote the good of human society. He also tells us that people have a right to break them in exigencies, such as war, famine, or family necessity. For the most part, these rules provide a useful means of avoiding human conflict.

Hume claims that virtues are social and universal. They represent "universal sentiments of censure or approbation, which arise from humanity [i.e., from human nature], or from views of general usefulness." He defines as virtue or personal merit "every quality of the mind, which is useful or agreeable to the person himself or to others." The notion of "usefulness" foreshadows the ethical concept of utility.

Hume sets up pride—a cardinal sin in Christianity—as the guardian and safeguard of the moral virtues. The unorthodox nature of such a view is easily exaggerated, however, since it is apparent that he was simply adopting the Roman view, which saw the love of fame and reputation as a moral trait, which promotes ethical behavior. He also denounced asceticism and self-denial as vices and attributed such practices to "the delusive glosses of superstition and false religion."

Hume's practical ethics were conventional, if decidedly liberal. He has been admired for his progressive views on the oppression of women and his implicit rejection of ethnocentrism and colonialism. These aspects of his views undoubtedly reflect the relativism inherent in his skepticism, which leaves considerable latitude for a divergence in individual opinions. On a negative note, a recent controversy has linked Hume to financial dealings that profited from the slave trade. Nonetheless, the deep influence of his theoretical thought on modern moral philosophy cannot be denied.

Hume's work is often seen as a turning point in modern philosophy. Along with his early *Treatise*, his works include *An Enquiry Concerning the Principles of Morals* (1751), which was a re-compilation of earlier material, *Essays, Moral, Political, and Literary* (1752), and *The Natural History of Religion* (1757). His *Dialogues Concerning Natural Religion* (1779) was published posthumously. The two readings are from the most important sources for Hume's moral philosophy, which are found in Book II and Book III of his *Treatise*, and the *Enquiry*, which Hume judged to be "of all my writings . . . incomparably the best." The first reading contains an excerpt from Book II of the *Treatise*, where Hume argues that "reason alone can never produce any action." It also contains Hume's remarks on the "is-ought" problem in Book III. The second reading, from the *Enquiry*, provides a sketch of some of the basic features of his moral theory.

David Hume, *A Treatise of Human Nature*[1]

(1739)

A

TREATISE

OF

Human Nature :

BEING

An ATTEMPT to introduce the experimental Method of Reasoning

INTO

MORAL SUBJECTS.

*Rara temporum felicitas, ubi sentire, quæ velis; & quæ
sentias, dicere licet.*   TACIT.

VOL. I.

OF THE

UNDERSTANDING.

LONDON:
Printed for JOHN NOON, at the *White-Hart*, near
Mercer's-Chapel, in *Cheapside*.
MDCCXXXIX.

Book II: Of the Passions

PART III. OF THE WILL AND DIRECT
PASSIONS

Section III. Of the Influencing Motives of the Will

Nothing is more usual in philosophy, and even in common life, than to talk of the combat of passion and reason, to give the preference to reason, and assert that men are only so far virtuous as they conform themselves to its dictates. Every rational creature, it is said, is obliged to regulate his actions by reason; and if any other motive or principle challenge the direction of his conduct, he ought to oppose it, 'till it be entirely subdued,' or at least brought to a conformity with that superior principle.

On this method of thinking the greatest part of moral philosophy, ancient and modern, seems to be founded; nor is there an ampler field, as well for metaphysical arguments, as popular declamations, than this supposed pre-eminence of reason above passion. The eternity, invariableness, and divine origin of the former have been displayed to the best advantage: The blindness, inconstancy, and deceitfulness of the latter have been as strongly insisted on. In order to show the fallacy of all this philosophy, I shall endeavour to prove first, that reason alone can never be a motive to any action of the will; and secondly, that it can never oppose passion in the direction of the will....

It is obvious that when we have the prospect of pain or pleasure from any object, we feel a consequent emotion of aversion or propensity,[2] and are carried to avoid or embrace what will give us this uneasiness or satisfaction.... And these emotions extend themselves to the causes and effects of that object, as they are pointed out to us by reason and experience....

Since reason alone can never produce any action, or give rise to volition, I infer that the same faculty is as incapable of preventing volition, or of disputing the preference with any passion or emotion.... Nothing can oppose or retard the impulse of pas-

---

1 David Hume, *A Treatise on Human Nature* (1739), ed. L.A. Selby-Bigge (Oxford: Clarendon Press, 1888).
2 I.e., an inclination towards something.

sion, but a contrary impulse.... Thus it appears that the principle which opposes our passion cannot be the same with reason, and is only called so in an improper sense. We speak not strictly and philosophically when we talk of the combat of passion and of reason. Reason is, and ought only to be the slave of the passions, and can never pretend to any other office than to serve and obey them....

Passions can be contrary to reason only so far as they are accompanied with some false judgment or false opinion. According to this principle,... it is only in two senses, that any affection can be called unreasonable. First, when a passion, such as hope or fear, grief or joy, despair or security, is founded on the supposition or the existence of objects, which really do not exist. Secondly, when in exerting any passion in action, we choose means insufficient for the designed end, and deceive ourselves in our judgment of causes and effects. Where a passion is neither founded on false suppositions, nor chooses means insufficient for the end, the understanding can neither justify nor condemn it. It is not contrary to reason to prefer the destruction of the whole world to the scratching of my finger. It is not contrary to reason for me to choose my total ruin, to prevent the least uneasiness of an Indian or person wholly unknown to me. It is as little contrary to reason to prefer even my own acknowledged lesser good to my greater, and have a more ardent affection for the former, than the latter....

Book III: Of Morals

PART I. OF VIRTUE AND VICE IN GENERAL

Section I. Moral Distinctions Not Derived from Reason

Can there be any difficulty in proving that vice and virtue are not matters of fact, whose existence we can infer by reason? Take any action allowed to be vicious: Wilful murder, for instance. Examine it in all lights, and see if you can find that matter of fact, or real existence, which you call vice. In whichever way you take it, you find only certain passions, motives, volitions and thoughts. There is no other matter of fact in the case. The vice entirely escapes you, as long as you consider the object. You never can find it, till you turn your reflection into your own breast, and find a sentiment of disapprobation, which arises in you, towards this action.

Here is a matter of fact; but it is the object of feeling, not of reason. It lies in yourself, not in the object. So that when you pronounce any action or character to be vicious, you mean nothing, but that from the constitution of your nature you have a feeling or sentiment of blame from the contemplation of it. Vice and virtue, therefore, may be compared to sounds, colours, heat and cold, which, according to modern philosophy,[1] are not qualities in objects, but perceptions in the mind: And this discovery in morals, like that other in physics, is to be regarded as a considerable advancement of the speculative sciences; though, like that too, it has little or no influence on practice. Nothing can be more real, or concern us more, than our own sentiments of pleasure and uneasiness; and if these be favourable to virtue, and unfavourable to vice, nothing more is needed to regulate our conduct and behaviour.

I cannot forbear adding[2] to these reasonings an observation, which may, perhaps, be found of some importance. In every system of morality, which I have hitherto met with, I have always remarked that the author proceeds for some time in the ordinary way of reasoning, and establishes the being of a God, or makes observations concerning human affairs; when of a sudden I am surprized to find that instead of the usual copulations[3] of propositions, is, and is

---

1 The natural sciences were in Hume's day called "natural philosophy."
2 Hume will now remark, famously, on the "is-ought" distinction.
3 I.e., connections.

not, I meet with no proposition that is not connected with an ought, or an ought not.

This change is imperceptible; but is, however, of the greatest consequence. For as this ought, or ought not, expresses some new relation or affirmation, it is necessary that it should be observed and explained; and at the same time that a reason should be given, for what seems altogether inconceivable, how this new relation can be a deduction from others, which are entirely different from it. But as authors do not commonly use this precaution, I shall presume to recommend it to the readers; and am persuaded, that this small attention would subvert all the vulgar systems of morality, and let us see, that the distinction of vice and virtue is not founded merely on the relations of objects, nor is perceived by reason.

READING 29B

David Hume, *Enquiry Concerning the Principles of Morals*[1]

(1748)

Section 3. Of Justice

PART 1

Let us suppose that nature has bestowed on the human race such profuse abundance of all external conveniences, that, without any uncertainty in the event, without any care or industry on our part, every individual finds himself fully provided with whatever his most voracious appetites can want, or luxurious imagination wish or desire.... The raw herbage affords him the most delicious fare; the clear fountain, the richest beverage. No laborious occupation is required.... Music, poetry, and contemplation form his sole business: Conversation, mirth, and friendship his sole amusement.

It seems evident that, in such a happy state, every other social virtue would flourish,...but the cautious, jealous virtue of justice would never once have been dreamed of. For what purpose make a partition of goods where everyone has already more than enough? Why give rise to property, where there cannot possibly be any injury? Why call this object mine, when, upon the seizing of it by another, I need but stretch out my hand to possess myself of what is equally valuable? Justice, in that case, being totally USELESS, would be an idle ceremonial, and could never possibly have place in the catalogue of virtues....

Again; suppose that, though the necessities of the human race continue the same as at present, yet the mind is so enlarged and so replete with friendship and generosity, that every man has the utmost tenderness for every man, and feels no more concern for his own interest than for that of his fellows: It seems evident, that the USE of justice would, in this case, be suspended by such an extensive benevolence, nor would the divisions and barriers of property and obligation have ever been thought of. Why should I bind another, by a deed or promise, to do me any good office, when I know that he is already

---

1 David Hume, *An Enquiry Concerning the Principles of Morals* (1751, 1772, 1777), ed. Tom L. Beauchamp (Oxford and New York: Oxford University Press, 1998): Section 3. Of Justice, Part 1, pp. 83–90; Section 9. Conclusion, Part 1. Widely available online.

prompted, by the strongest inclination, to seek my happiness....

Let us reverse the foregoing suppositions.... Suppose a society to fall into such want of all common necessaries, that the utmost frugality and industry cannot preserve the greater number from perishing and the whole from extreme misery: It will readily, I believe, be admitted, that the strict laws of justice are suspended in such a pressing emergency and give place to the stronger motives of necessity and self-preservation. Is it any crime, after a shipwreck, to seize whatever means or instrument of safety one can lay hold of, without regard to former limitations of property? Or if a city besieged were perishing with hunger; can we imagine that men will... lose their lives, from a scrupulous regard to... the rules of equity and justice? The USE and TENDENCY of that virtue[1] is to procure happiness and security by preserving order in society: But where the society is ready to perish from extreme necessity,... every man may now provide for himself by all the means which prudence can dictate or humanity permit. The public, even in less urgent necessities, opens granaries....

When any man, even in political society, renders himself, by his crimes, obnoxious to the public, he is punished by the laws in his goods and person; that is, the ordinary rules of justice are, with regard to him, suspended for a moment, and it becomes equitable to inflict on him, for the benefit of society, what, otherwise, he could not suffer without wrong or injury.... And were a civilized nation engaged in battle with barbarians, who observed no rules even of war; the former must also suspend their observance of them, where they no longer serve to any purpose; and must render every action or encounter as bloody and pernicious as possible to the first aggressors.

Thus, the rules of equity or justice depend entirely on the particular state and condition in which men are placed, and owe their origins and existence to that UTILITY which results to the public from their strict and regular observance. Reverse, in any considerable circumstance, the condition of men: Produce extreme abundance or extreme necessity: Implant in the human breast perfect moderation and humanity, or perfect rapaciousness and malice: By rendering justice totally useless, you thereby totally destroy its essence, and suspend its obligation upon mankind.

The common situation of society is a medium amid all these extremes. We are naturally partial to ourselves and to our friends.... Hence the ideas of property become necessary in all civil society: Hence justice derives its usefulness to the public: And hence alone arises its merit and moral obligation....

Were there a species of creatures, intermingled with men, which, though rational, were possessed of such inferior strength, both of body and mind, that they were incapable of all resistance, and could never, upon the highest provocation, make us feel the effects of their resentment; the necessary consequence, I think, is that we should be bound, by the laws of humanity, to give gentle usage to these creatures but should not, properly speaking, lie under any restraint of justice with regard to them.... This is plainly the situation of men with regard to animals....

The great superiority of civilized EUROPEANS above barbarous INDIANS, tempted us to imagine ourselves on the same footing with regard to them,[2] and allowed us throw off all restraints of justice, and even of humanity, in our treatment of them. In many nations, the female sex is reduced to like slavery and is rendered incapable of all property....

---

1 I.e., the respect for property.

2 Hume is saying that the situation of men with regard to animals puts Europeans on the same footing with regard to Indians, i.e., there can be no restraint of justice with regard to them. He is referring to the European encounter with the Indigenous peoples of the Americas.

Section 9. Conclusion

PART 1

It may justly appear surprising that any man in so late an age should find it requisite to prove by elaborate reasoning that PERSONAL MERIT consists altogether in the possession of mental qualities, useful or agreeable to the person himself or to others. It might be expected that this principle would have occurred even to the first rude, unpracticed enquirers concerning morals, and been received from its own evidence without any argument or disputation. Whatever is valuable in any kind, so naturally classes itself under the division of useful or agreeable, the *utile* or the *dulce*, that it is not easy to imagine why we should ever seek further, or consider the question as a matter of nice research or enquiry.

And as everything useful or agreeable must possess these qualities with regard either to the person himself or to others, the complete delineation or description of merit seems to be performed as naturally as a shadow is cast by the sun, or an image is reflected upon water. If the ground on which the shadow is cast be not broken and uneven; nor the surface from which the image is reflected, disturbed and confused; a just figure is immediately presented without any art or attention. And it seems a reasonable presumption that systems and hypotheses have perverted our natural understanding; when a theory so simple and obvious could so long have escaped the most elaborate examination.

But however the case may have fared with philosophy, in common life these principles are still implicitly maintained, nor is any other topic of praise or blame ever recurred to when we employ any panegyric or satire, any applause or censure of human action and behaviour. If we observe men in every intercourse of business or pleasure, in every discourse and conversation, we shall find them

nowhere, except in the schools, at any loss upon this subject....

As every quality, which is useful or agreeable to ourselves or others, is in common life allowed to be a part of personal merit, so no other will ever be received where men judge of things by their natural, unprejudiced reason, without the delusive glosses of superstition and false religion. Celibacy, fasting, penance, mortification, self-denial, humility, silence, solitude, and the whole train of monkish virtues; for what reason are they everywhere rejected by men of sense, but because they serve to no manner of purpose; neither advance a man's fortune in the world, nor render him a more valuable member of society; neither qualify him for the entertainment of company, nor increase his power of self-enjoyment?

We observe, on the contrary, that they cross all these desirable ends, stupefy the understanding and harden the heart, obscure the fancy and sour the temper. We justly, therefore, transfer them to the opposite column and place them in the catalogue of vices; nor has any superstition sufficient force among men of the world to pervert entirely these natural sentiments. A gloomy, hair-brained enthusiast, after his death, may have a place in the calendar,[1] but will scarcely ever be admitted, when alive, into intimacy and society, except by those who are as delirious and dismal as himself.

It seems a happiness in the present theory that it enters not into that vulgar dispute concerning the degrees of benevolence or self-love which prevail in human nature;.... It is sufficient for our present purpose, if it be allowed,...that there is some benevolence, however small, infused into our bosom; some spark of friendship for human kind; some particle of the dove kneaded into our frame, along with the elements of the wolf and serpent.

Let these generous sentiments be supposed ever so weak; let them be insufficient to move even a hand or finger of our body; they must still direct the deter-

---

1 I.e., have a place in the calendar as a saint with a feast day.

minations of our mind, and where everything else is equal, produce a cool preference of what is useful and serviceable to mankind above what is pernicious and dangerous. A moral distinction, therefore, immediately arises, a general sentiment of blame and approbation, a tendency, however faint, to the objects of the one, and a proportionate aversion to those of the other....

The notion of morals implies some sentiment common to all mankind, which recommends the same object to general approbation, and makes every man, or most men, agree in the same opinion or decision concerning it. It also implies some sentiment so universal and comprehensive as to extend to all mankind and render the actions and conduct, even of the persons the most remote, an object of applause or censure, according as they agree or disagree with that rule of right which is established. These two requisite circumstances belong alone to the sentiment of humanity here insisted on.[1]...

When a man denominates another his enemy, his rival, his antagonist, his adversary, he is understood to speak the language of self-love, and to express sentiments peculiar to himself and arising from his particular circumstances and situation. But when he bestows on any man the epithets of vicious or odious or depraved, he then speaks another language and expresses sentiments in which he expects all his audience are to concur with him. He must here, therefore, depart from his private and particular situation, and must choose a point of view common to him with others....

If he mean, therefore, to express that this man possesses qualities whose tendency is pernicious to society, he has chosen this common point of view and has touched the principle of humanity in which every man, in some degree, concurs. While the human heart is compounded of the same elements as at present, it will never be wholly indifferent to public good, nor entirely unaffected with the tendency of characters and manners.... This concern being common to all men, it can alone be the foundation of morals, or of any general system of blame or praise. One man's ambition is not another's ambition.... but the humanity of one man is the humanity of every one....

But the sentiments which arise from humanity are not only the same in all human creatures and produce the same approbation or censure, but they also comprehend all human creatures; nor is there any one whose conduct or character is not by their means an object, to everyone, of censure or approbation.... If you represent a tyrannical, insolent, or barbarous behaviour in any country or in any age of the world, I soon carry my eye to the pernicious tendency of such a conduct and feel the sentiments of repugnance and displeasure towards it. No character can be so remote as to be, in this light, wholly indifferent to me. What is beneficial to society or to the person himself must still be preferred. And every quality or action of every human being must, by this means, be ranked under some class or denomination expressive of general censure or applause....

Whatever conduct gains my approbation by touching my humanity procures also the applause of mankind by affecting the same principle in them: But what serves my avarice or ambition pleases these passions in me alone, and affects not the avarice and ambition of the rest of mankind. There is no circumstance of conduct in any man, provided it have a beneficial tendency that is not agreeable to my humanity, however remote the person. But every man, so far removed as neither to cross nor serve my avarice and ambition, is regarded as wholly indifferent by those passions.

The distinction, therefore, between these species of sentiment being so great and evident, language must soon be moulded upon it, and must invent a peculiar set of terms in order to express those universal sentiments of censure or approbation, which arise from humanity, or from views of general use-

---

1 I.e., benevolence.

fulness and its contrary. VIRTUE and VICE become then known. Morals are recognized. Certain general ideas are framed of human conduct and behaviour. Such measures are expected from men, in such situations. This action is determined to be conformable to our abstract rule; that other, contrary. And by such universal principles are the particular sentiments of self-love frequently controlled and limited....

What wonder then, that moral sentiments are found of such influence in life, though springing from principles which may appear, at first sight, somewhat small and delicate? But these principles, we must remark, are social and universal. They form, in a manner, the party of humankind against vice or disorder, its common enemy. And as the benevolent concern for others is diffused, in a greater or less degree, over all men and is the same in all, it occurs more frequently in discourse, is cherished by society and conversation, and the blame and approbation, consequent on it, are thereby routed from that lethargy into which they are probably lulled in solitary and uncultivated nature! Other passions, though perhaps originally stronger, yet being selfish and private, are often overpowered by its force and yield the dominion of our breasts to those social and public principles.

Another spring of our constitution that brings a great addition of force to moral sentiment is the love of fame, which rules with such uncontrolled authority in all generous minds and is often the grand object of all their designs and undertakings. By our continual and earnest pursuit of a character, a name, a reputation in the world, we bring our own deportment and conduct frequently in review and consider how they appear in the eyes of those who approach and regard us. This constant habit of surveying ourselves, as it were, in reflection keeps alive all the sentiments of right and wrong, and begets in noble natures a certain reverence for themselves as well as others; which is the surest guardian of every virtue....

I am sensible that nothing can be more unphilosophical than to be positive or dogmatic on any subject.... Yet, I must confess, that this enumeration puts the matter in so strong a light that I cannot...be more assured of any truth, which I learn from reasoning and argument, than that personal merit consists entirely in the usefulness or agreeableness of qualities to the person himself possessed of them, or to others....

Yet men still dispute concerning the foundation of their moral duties...When I reflect on this,...I fall back into diffidence and scepticism...and suspect that any convincing hypothesis, had it been a true one, would long before now have been received with the unanimous affirmation and consent of mankind....

Questions

1. Philosophers like Plato maintained that morality is a matter of siding with reason over our appetites. Hume thinks this is the wrong way to think of moral judgments. What role does reason play in Hume's morality?

2. Joseph Butler and Hume both place enormous importance on the feeling of approbation. Compare their views.

3. It has become common since Hume to distinguish "is" from "ought," facts from values, and descriptive from prescriptive statements. Explain the difference, with examples.

4. Hume imagines a state of nature where everything is plentiful and a state of nature where our survival is threatened by scarcity. He thinks there is no room for justice in either case. Why?

5. Hume enjoyed good times and denigrated "the whole train of monkish virtues": "celibacy, fasting, penance, mortification, self-denial, humility, silence, and solitude." Indeed, he goes so far as to call all these qualities vices. Do you agree with Hume? Or with the Desert Fathers? Why, why not?

6. Hume writes that calling "another his enemy" is not the same as calling him "odious or depraved." The "language of self-love" and the language of "morality" are different. Is he right? Discuss.

7. Does Hume have a negative or positive account of human beings? Even if human beings have selfish tendencies, what serves to reinforce our moral tendencies?

Suggested Readings

Hume's earliest work is the three-volume *A Treatise of Human Nature: Being an Attempt to Introduce the Experimental Method of Reasoning into Moral Subjects* (1739–40). The treatise was poorly received and Hume set out his views in more popular form in *Philosophical Essays Concerning Human Understanding* (1748) and *An Enquiry Concerning the Principles of Morals* (1751). Hume's ethical essays were collected in *Essays, Moral, Political and Literary* (1753). In his later career, Hume turned to history, producing a highly popular six-volume series on *The History of England* (1754–62). His *Dialogues Concerning Natural Religion* (1779), an attack on natural theology in the form of a Platonic dialogue, was published posthumously. His works are widely available.

The scholarship on Hume focuses on his epistemology and skepticism. See, for example, Kevin Meeker, "Ethics and Epistemology in Hume" (2013). For his emotivism, see Philip Mercer, *Study of the Relationship between Sympathy and Morality with Special Reference to Hume's Treatise* (1972).

Hume has been described as a utilitarian, a proponent of virtue ethics, and an Epicurean. See, for example, Daniel E. Flage, "Hume's Ethics" (1985); Marcia L. Homiak, "Does Hume Have an Ethics of Virtue?" (2000); and Annette Baier, "Hume's Place in the History of Ethics" (2013).

Xiusheng Liu, *Mencius, Hume and the Foundations of Ethics* (2003), compares the ethics of Hume and Mencius. In applied ethics, see William Kline, "Hume's Theory of Business Ethics Revisited" (2012).

Chapter 30

Kantian Deontology

Immanuel Kant (1724–1804) became the most celebrated German philosopher of the modern era. His work represents a high point in systematic ethics and illustrates the scope of modern philosophy, which attempts to provide a comprehensive theory that offers a rational model for the investigation of virtually all ethical questions. His emphasis on rationality, duty, and autonomy left an indelible mark on the liberal moral tradition.

Kant was born in Königsberg, then the capital of Prussia, now the city of Kaliningrad in Russia. He was born with a defect in his shoulder and was small, feeble, and stooped. His parents were Pietists, a Puritan-like Lutheran sect that believed in a literal interpretation of the Bible, rigid moral standards, and the private devotion to God. Kant was educated at home and began taking classes at the University of Königsberg when he was sixteen years old. He ultimately spent his entire academic career at the university, obtaining "Magister" (Master's) and doctoral degrees.

Kant never married; he kept aloof from his wider family and supposedly never traveled more than ten miles from his birthplace. It is said that he displayed no enthusiasm for the beauties of nature; he was largely averse to musical entertainment, theater, and the visual arts. When he found it difficult to concentrate on his philosophy because of the loudness of the hymns sung at a nearby prison, he wrote a letter to the prison-inspector, asking to be relieved "of the stentorian devotion of the hypocrites in prison."

Mostly, Kant worked on his lectures, read voluminously, and wrote prodigiously. It was said that he led such a regular existence that local housewives would set their clocks by the precise timing of his daily walk. He had little patience for frivolity or sentimentality, arguing, for example, that children should not be allowed to read novels because such sentimental amusements might be habit-forming. In spite of this, he enjoyed billiards as a young man, and was known, in later life, as the gracious host of regular dinner parties.

Kant was appointed Full Professor of Logic and Metaphysics in 1770. Along with trend-setting works in metaphysics and epistemology, he published three important works on moral philosophy: *The Groundwork for the Metaphysics of Morals* (1785), *The Critique of Practical Reason* (1788), and *The Metaphysics of Morals* (1797). In these three texts, Kant develops a coherent and influential moral theory based on notions of duty, moral law, dignity, and individual autonomy.

Although he distanced himself from his parents' religious views and the overt practice of religion in his philosophical work, Kant gives God a necessary place in his moral scheme. Although we cannot prove the existence of God using (theoretical) reason, neither can we account for the existence of morality (or freedom of the will) without positing the existence of God. He occasionally wrote on religious subjects and one of his last books, *Religion Within the Boundaries of Mere Reason* (1793), was censured by the Prussian Imperial Censor because he was critical of the way that insincere Christians practice their faith.

Kant's moral philosophy is usually called a "deontology" or a "deontological ethics." The word "deontology" derives from the Greek *deon*, meaning 'duty or obligation' and *logia* meaning 'study of, reasoning about.' Kant's philosophy, then, is based on the idea that one must act morally because it is one's duty and not for extraneous considerations, such as self-interest, because it makes us happy or wins the approval of others, or because we will be punished if we fail to do so. One does one's duty simply because it is one's duty.

Kant believes that our feelings, tastes, inclinations, and self-interest often push us in an immoral direction. The most fundamental requirement for moral behavior is a good will, which gives us the power to act properly, in accordance with our moral duties, in spite of our inclination to do otherwise. It follows that the morality of our actions is determined not by the consequences of those actions but by the goodness or badness of our intentions.

Kant conceives of the normative requirements of morality in terms of the moral law. He describes the rule at the basis of all moral requirements as a categorical imperative, a command that leaves no room for exceptions. Although Kant provides several different formulations of the categorical imperative, he suggests—rather unconvincingly—that they add up to the same basic principle.

Two formulations of the categorical imperative nevertheless stand out. In the first, Kant claims that we must always act so that the maxim of our acts—the axiom that provides the guiding principle behind our intention—can be construed as a universal law of nature. This brings a kind of reciprocity into his system and means, essentially, that we must always act in the way that we would want everyone else to act in the same circumstances.

In the second formulation, Kant argues that individual human beings must be treated as "ends-in-themselves"; i.e., we cannot use other human beings merely to obtain our own ends, without taking into consideration their own welfare and interests. Behind this is the idea that humans cannot be treated as mere objects. Human beings are "persons" with infinite or incalculable worth. They must be treated with dignity because they are moral beings, endowed with reason.

Kant distinguishes between moral laws that apply in every case and moral laws that only apply in some cases, which he describes as "perfect" and "imperfect" moral duties, respectively. So, for example, the moral law against murder rests on a perfect duty that applies in every case. We can never murder anyone, whatever the circumstances. The moral law that we should give money to charity is, in comparison, an imperfect moral duty, which does not apply in every case—if you are desperately poor, you are not required to give money to charity. The moral law "do not tell a lie" is a perfect moral duty.

These concepts are based on a distinction between autonomous and heteronomous agents. The word 'autonomy' derives from the Greek, *autos* meaning 'self' and *nomos* meaning 'law or custom,' and was used to describe Greek city-states that governed themselves without foreign interference. In Kantian ethics, it refers to an individual who is self-governed. For Kant, this is based on the idea that, at the deepest level, we are rational agents. We accordingly act autonomously only when we act rationally. Indeed, Kant goes so far as to argue that it is illogical to act immorally, which always involves some sort of contradiction.

This idea of autonomy also explains Kant's rather odd notion of freedom. According to Kant, freedom does not consist of doing whatever we feel like doing. Freedom is a matter of acting rationally, in accordance with the duties that we have imposed upon ourselves. Immoral agents are heteronomous (or non-autonomous) because they act according to a law that comes from outside their own rational natures. They are enslaved to something outside themselves.

The nature of Kant's moral philosophy tends to dissolve the distinction between theoretical and practical ethics. His personal views were an interesting mix of moderation and rigidity, which reflect his larger ethical scheme. He stressed equality, for example, both in contracts and in marriage. His view in favor of capital punishment was unforgiving and absolute. His view of international relations foreshadowed the idea of the United Nations and goes against the realism of earlier figures such as Hobbes.

The first reading is from *The Groundwork for the Metaphysics of Morals* and sets out the fundamentals of Kant's moral philosophy. It includes the most acclaimed formulation of the categorical imperative and his codicils on "personhood" and the metaphysical limits of the philosophical inquiry. The second and third readings summarize Kant's notion of autonomy and heteronomy and respond briefly to the criticism he faced for his position that we can never tell a lie, whatever the consequences.

Immanuel Kant, *The Groundwork for the Metaphysics of Morals*[1]

(1785)

First Section: Transition from the Common Rational Moral Cognition to the Philosophical Moral Cognition

[GOOD WILL]

Nothing can possibly be conceived in the world, or even out of it, which can be called good without qualification, except a *good will*. Intelligence, wit, judgment, and the other talents of the mind, however they may be named, or courage, resolution, perseverance, as qualities of *temperament*, are undoubtedly good and desirable in many respects; but these gifts of nature may also become extremely bad and mischievous if the will which is to make use of them ... is not good. It is the same with the *gifts of fortune* such as power, riches, honor, even health.... The sight of a being, therefore, who is not adorned with a single feature of a pure and good will ... can never give pleasure to an impartial spectator. Thus a good will appears to constitute the indispensable condition even of being worthy of happiness....

Moderation in the affections and passions, self-control, and calm deliberation are not only good in many respects, but even seem to constitute part of the *inner* worth of the person; but they are far from deserving to be called good without qualification.... For without the principles of a good will, they may become extremely evil; and the coldness[2] of a villain not only makes him far more dangerous, but also directly makes him more abominable in our eyes....

A good will is good not because of what it accomplishes or effects ... [but] is good in itself, and considered by itself is to be esteemed much higher than all that can be brought about by it.... Even if it should happen that, owing to a step-motherly nature, this will should wholly lack power to accomplish its purpose, if with its greatest efforts it should yet achieve nothing, and there should remain only the good will (not, to be sure, a mere wish, but the summoning of all means in our power), then, like a jewel, it would still shine by its own light, as a thing which has its whole value in itself. Its usefulness or fruitlessness can neither add to nor take away anything from this value....

[DUTY]

[W]e will [next consider] the concept of duty....

I omit here all actions which are already recognized as contrary to duty.... I also set aside those actions which really conform to duty, [which men perform] impelled thereto by some other inclination.... For example, it is always a matter of duty that a dealer should not overcharge an inexperienced purchaser; and wherever there is much commerce the prudent tradesman does not overcharge, but keeps a fixed price for everyone, so that a child buys from him as well as any other. People are thus *honestly* served; but this is not enough to make us believe that the tradesman has so acted from duty and from principles of honesty; his own advantage required

---

1   Kant, *Groundwork for the Metaphysic of Morals* (*Grundlegung zur Metaphysik der Sitten*, 1785) from Thomas Kingsmill Abbott, trans., *Kant's Critique of Practical Reason and Other Works on the Theory of Ethics* (London: Longmans, Green, 1873), updated and modified by Lara Denis, ed., *Groundwork for the Metaphysics of Morals* (Peterborough, ON: Broadview, 2005).

2   Or calmness.

it…Accordingly the action was done neither from duty nor from immediate inclination, but merely with a selfish purpose.

On the other hand, it is a duty to preserve one's life; and, in addition, everyone has also an immediate inclination to do so. But on this account the often anxious care which most people take for it has no intrinsic worth, and their maxim[1] has no moral content. They preserve their life *in conformity with duty*, no doubt, but not *from duty*. On the other hand, if adversity and hopeless sorrow have completely taken away the relish for life, if the unfortunate one, strong in mind…wishes for death, and yet preserves his life without loving it—not from inclination or fear, but from duty—then his maxim has moral content.

To be beneficent when one can is a duty; and besides this, there are many minds so sympathetically constituted that…they find a pleasure in spreading joy around them…. But I maintain that in such a case an action of this kind, however proper, however amiable it may be, has nevertheless no true moral worth, but is on a level with other inclinations, for example, the inclination to honor, which if it is happily directed to that which is in fact of public utility and accordant with duty…deserves praise and encouragement, but not [moral] esteem. For the maxim lacks the moral content, namely, that such actions be done from duty, not from inclination….

To secure one's own happiness is a duty…for discontent with one's condition, under a pressure of many anxieties and amidst unsatisfied needs, might easily become a great *temptation to transgression of duty*. But here again…all men have already the strongest and most intimate inclination to [their own] happiness…. [Y]et [there] remains in this, as in all other cases, this law—namely, that he should promote his happiness not from inclination but from duty, and by this would his conduct first acquire true moral worth.

It is in this manner, undoubtedly, that we are to understand those passages of Scripture in which we are commanded to love…our enemy…even [when we are] repelled by a natural and unconquerable aversion. This is *practical* love, and not *pathological*[2]—a love which is seated in the will, and not in the propensities of feeling—in principles of action and not of tender sympathy; and it is this love alone which can be commanded….

An action done from duty derives its moral worth, not from the purpose which is to be attained by it, but from the maxim by which it is determined, and therefore does not depend on the realization of the object of the action, but merely on the principle of volition by which the action has taken place….

Duty is the necessity of acting from respect for the law…[A]n action done from duty must wholly exclude the influence of inclination,…so that nothing remains which can determine the will except objectively the *law*, and subjectively *pure respect* for this practical law, and consequently the maxim that I should follow this law even to the thwarting of all my inclinations.

Thus the moral worth of an action does not lie in the effect expected from it…. For all these effects…could have been also brought about by other causes, so that for this there would have been no need of the will of a rational being…. The pre-eminent good which we call moral can therefore consist in nothing else than *the representation of the law* in itself,…insofar as this representation, and not the expected effect, determines the will….

Although, no doubt, common human reason does not conceive [of morality] in such an abstract and universal form, yet it really always has it before its eyes and uses [duty] as the standard of judgment…. Therefore, we do not need science and philosophy to know what we should do to be honest and good, yes, even to be wise and virtuous….

---

1 Kant uses the term 'maxim' to refer to a general rule of conduct.

2 Kant's translator here uses the word 'pathological' to mean 'relating to the feelings or emotions.' This archaic sense of that word is, however, true to what Kant intended.

Here we cannot withhold admiration when we see how great an advantage practical judgment has over the theoretical in the common human understanding.... [I]n the practical sphere...[an untutored power of judgment] may even have as good a hope of hitting the mark as any philosopher whatever can promise himself. Indeed it is almost more sure of doing so, because the philosopher...may easily perplex his judgment by a multitude of considerations foreign to the matter, and so turn aside from the right way. [We may ask then:] Would it not therefore be wiser in moral concerns to acquiesce in the judgment of common reason, or at most only to call in philosophy for the purpose of rendering the system of morals more complete and intelligible, and its rules more convenient for use (especially disputation), but not so as to draw off the common understanding from its happy simplicity, or bring it by means of philosophy into a new path of inquiry and instruction?

Innocence is indeed a glorious thing; but, on the other hand, it is very sad that it cannot well maintain itself, and is easily seduced.... [There is a powerful counterweight to all the commands of duty in a man's] needs and inclinations, the entire satisfaction of which he sums up under the name of happiness....

Thus is the *common human reason* compelled to go out of its sphere and to take a step into the field of *practical philosophy*...in order to attain information and clear instructions regarding [the source and formulation of rational principles,] in opposition to the maxims that are based on wants and inclinations...[This is necessary, so] that it may escape from the perplexity of opposite claims, and not run the risk of losing all genuine moral principles through the equivocation into which it easily falls. Thus, when practical reason cultivates itself, there insensibly arises in it a dialectic which forces it to seek aid in philosophy....

Second Section: Transition from Popular Moral Philosophy to the Metaphysics of Morals

[HYPOTHETICAL VERSUS CATEGORICAL IMPERATIVES]

The conception of an objective principle, in so far as it is obligatory for a will, is called a command (of reason), and the formula of the command is called an **imperative**....

Now all imperatives command either *hypothetically* or *categorically*. The former represent the practical necessity of a possible action as means to something else that is willed.... The categorical imperative would be that which represented an action as necessary of itself without reference to another end, that is, as objectively necessary....

If now the action is good only as a means *to something else*, then the imperative is *hypothetical*; if it is conceived as good *in itself* and consequently [belongs necessarily to] a will which of itself conforms to reason, then it is *categorical*....

There is *one* end, however, which...all rational beings...actually *do have* by a natural necessity, and this is *happiness*.... [Nevertheless, in spite of this] the imperative which refers to the choice of means to one's own happiness, that is, the precept of prudence, is still always *hypothetical*; the action is not commanded absolutely, but only as means to another purpose.

Finally, there is an imperative which commands a certain conduct immediately, without having as its condition any other purpose to be attained by it. This imperative is **categorical**. It concerns not the matter of the action, or its intended result, but its form and the principle of which it is itself a result; and what is essentially good in it consists in the mental disposition, let the consequence be what it may. This imperative may be called that of **morality**....

[UNIVERSAL FORMULATION OF THE CATEGORICAL IMPERATIVE]

There is therefore but one categorical imperative, namely, this: Act only on that maxim whereby you can at the same time will that it become a universal law....

[Or again] the imperative of duty may be expressed thus: Act as if the maxim of your action were to become by your will a **universal law of nature**.[1] ...

1. Someone reduced to despair by a series of misfortunes feels wearied of life, but is still so far in possession of his reason that he can ask himself whether it would not be contrary to his duty to himself to take his own life. Now he inquires whether the maxim of his action could become a universal law of nature. His maxim is: From self-love I adopt it as my principle to shorten my life when its longer duration is likely to bring more ill than satisfaction. It is asked then simply whether this principle founded on self-love can become a universal law of nature. Now we can see at once that a system of nature of which it should be a law to destroy life by means of the very feeling [of self-love] whose vocation it is to impel to the improvement of life would contradict itself, and therefore could not exist as a system of nature; hence that maxim cannot possibly exist as a universal law of nature, and consequently would be wholly inconsistent with the supreme principle of all duty.

2. Another finds himself forced by necessity to borrow money. He knows that he will not be able to repay it, but sees also that nothing will be lent to him unless he promises firmly to repay it within a determinate time. He wants to make this promise, but he has still so much conscience as to ask himself: Is it not unlawful and inconsistent with duty to get out of a difficulty this way? Suppose, however, that he resolves to do so, then the maxim of his action would be expressed thus: When I think myself in want of money, I will borrow money and promise to repay it, although I know that I never can do so. Now this principle of self-love ... may perhaps be consistent with my whole future welfare; but the question now is, Is it right? I change then the suggestion of self-love into a universal law, and state the question thus: How would it be if my maxim were a universal law? Then I see at once that it could never hold as a universal law of nature, but would necessarily contradict itself. For supposing it to be a universal law that everyone when he thinks himself in a difficulty should be able to promise whatever he pleases, with the purpose of not keeping his promise, the promise itself would become impossible, ... since no one would consider that anything was promised to him, but would ridicule all such statements as vain pretenses.

3. A third finds in himself a talent which with the help of some culture might make him a useful human being in many respects. But he finds himself in comfortable circumstances and prefers to indulge in pleasure rather than to take pain in enlarging and improving his fortunate natural predispositions. He asks, however, whether his maxim of neglect of his natural gifts, besides agreeing with his inclination to indulgence, agrees also with what is called duty. He sees then that a system of nature could indeed subsist with such a universal law, although human beings (like the South Sea islanders) should let their talents rust and resolve to devote their lives merely to idleness, amusement, and propagation of their species—in a word, to enjoyment; but he cannot possibly **will** that this should be a universal law of nature, or be implanted in us as such by a natural instinct. For as a rational being, he necessarily wills that his faculties be developed...

4. Yet a fourth, who is in prosperity, while he sees that others have to contend with great wretchedness and that he could help them, thinks: What concern is it of mine? ... I will take nothing from him nor even envy him, only I do not wish to contribute anything to his welfare or to his assistance in need! Now no doubt, if such a mode of thinking were a universal law, the

---

1 Kant follows with four examples of how to apply the categorical imperative.

human race might very well subsist.... But although it is possible that a universal law of nature might exist in accordance with that maxim, it is impossible to **will** that such a principle should have the universal validity of a law of nature. For a will which resolved this would contradict itself, inasmuch as many cases might occur in which one would have need of the love and sympathy of others, and in which, by such a law of nature, sprung from his own will, he would deprive himself of all hope of the aid he desires....

If now we attend to ourselves on occasion of any transgression of duty, we will find that we in fact do not will that our maxim should be a universal law,... only we assume the liberty of making an *exception* in our own favor or (just for this time only) in favor of our inclination....

[THE "PERSONHOOD FORMULATION" OF THE CATEGORICAL IMPERATIVE]

Now I say: the human being and in general every rational being exists as an end in itself, *not merely as a means* to be arbitrarily used by this or that will, but in all his actions, whether they concern himself or other rational beings, must be always regarded at the same time as an end.... [Beings] if they are non-rational beings, only [have] a relative value as means, and are therefore called *things*; rational beings, on the contrary, are called *persons*, because their very nature restricts all choice (and is an object of respect). These, therefore, are not merely subjective ends whose existence has a worth *for us* as an effect of our action, but *objective ends*, that is, things whose existence is an end in itself—an end, moreover, for which no other can be substituted, to which they should serve *merely* as means, for otherwise nothing whatever would possess absolute worth; but if all worth were conditioned and therefore contingent, then there would be no supreme practical principle of reason whatever.

[The] categorical imperative... [must be] as follows: So act as to treat humanity, whether in your own person or in that of any other, in every case at the same time as an end, never as a means only....[1]

First, under the head of necessary duty to oneself: Someone who contemplates suicide should ask himself whether his action can be consistent with the idea of humanity *as an end in itself*. If he destroys himself in order to escape from painful circumstances, he uses a person merely as a *means to* maintain a tolerable condition up to the end of life. But a human being is not a thing, that is to say, something which can be used merely as a means, but must in all his actions be always considered as an end in itself. I cannot, therefore, dispose in any way of a human being in my own person by mutilating, damaging, or killing him....

Second, as regards necessary duties... towards others: He who is thinking of making a lying promise to others will see at once that he would be using another human being *merely as a means*.... This violation of the principle of humanity in other human beings is more obvious if we take in examples of attacks on the freedom and property of others...

Third, as regards contingent (meritorious) duties to oneself.... [T]here are in humanity capacities of greater perfection;... to neglect these might perhaps be consistent with the *maintenance* of humanity as an end in itself, but not with the *advancement* of this end.

Fourth, as regards meritorious duties toward others: The natural end which all human beings have is their own happiness. Now humanity might indeed subsist although no one should contribute anything to the happiness of others... [but] this would only harmonize negatively, not positively, with *humanity as an end in itself*.... [And] the ends of any subject which is an end in itself ought as far as possible to be *my* ends also, if that conception is to have its *full* effect in me....

---

1 Kant then examines the previous examples to show that this personhood formulation of the categorical imperative is consistent with the universal formulation above.

Third Section: Transition from the Metaphysics of Morals to the Critique of Pure Practical Reason: On the Extreme Boundary of All Practical Philosophy

Hence it comes to pass that a human being claims the possession of a will which takes no account of anything that comes under the head of desires and inclinations, and on the contrary conceives actions…as necessary, which can only be done by disregarding all desires and sensible inclinations…. [H]e knows nothing more than that…pure reason alone, independent of sensibility, gives the law; moreover, since it is only…as an intelligence, that he is his proper self…those laws apply to him directly and categorically….

The question, then, how a categorical imperative is possible, can be answered to the extent that we can assign the only hypothesis on which it is possible, namely, the idea of freedom…but how this hypothesis itself is possible can never be discerned by any human reason….

Immanuel Kant, *The Critique of Practical Reason*[1]

(1788)

Book II. Inquiry into the a priori Operations of the Will

CHAPTER I. ANALYTIC OF PRINCIPLES

Section 8. Position IV. Autonomy and Heteronomy

Autonomy of will is the lone foundation of morality, and of the duties springing from it; and every other principle whatsoever…is in fact subversive of morality. In being independent of the matter of any law (a desired object), and being determinable by the legislative form of his own maxims, consists the ethical nature of man, and that which renders him a subject for morality; that independence [from objects of desire] is freedom negatively, while [moral] self-legislation is freedom positively.

The moral law expresses, therefore, nothing but the autonomy of reason…

When the subject matter of a volition (nothing else than the object of a desire) is made into the practical law [and we allow ourselves to be governed by our inclinations and desires]…then heteronomy, a false principle of morals, results; the will ceases to prescribe to itself its own law, and is left exposed to laws taken from pathological phenomena. In this case, the motivation adopted by the will is formally unfit for a universal law, and not only grounds no obligation, but subverts the principles of practical reason itself.

---

1   Excerpt from Kant, *Critique of Practical Reason* (1788), from "Book II: Inquiry into the a priori Operations of the Will," Sec. 8: Position IV, from *The Critique of Practical Reason*," in Immanuel Kant, *The Metaphysics of Ethics* by Immanuel Kant, trans. J.W. Semple, ed. with an Introduction by Rev. Henry Calderwood (Edinburgh: T. & T. Clark, 1886) (3rd ed.). Also available at http://oll.libertyfund.org/titles/kant-the-metaphysics-of-ethics.

Immanuel Kant, "On the Supposed Right to Lie from Benevolent Motives"[1]

(1799)

[Now Benjamin Constant[2] writes:] 'The moral principle that it is one's duty to speak the truth, if it were taken singly and unconditionally, would make all society impossible. We have the proof of this in the very direct consequences which have been drawn from this principle by a German philosopher,[3] who goes so far as to affirm that to tell a falsehood to a murderer who asked us whether our friend, of whom he was in pursuit, had not taken refuge in our house, would be a crime.'[4]

Truth in utterances that cannot be avoided is the formal duty of a man to everyone, however great the disadvantage that may arise from it to him or any other.... By making a false statement...I do wrong to men in general in the most essential point of duty...so far as by my lies I discredit human declarations in general, so that all rights founded on contract should lose their force; and this is a wrong which is done to mankind.

If, then, we define a lie merely as an intentionally false declaration towards another man, we need not add that it must injure another...for it always injures another; if not another individual, yet mankind generally, since it vitiates the source of justice.... The duty of truthfulness...is an unconditional duty which holds in all circumstances....

Questions

1. Kant's thought came out of the Enlightenment. Compare his general moral position with that of the Stoics or Aquinas, who relied heavily on the natural law. Is there any room for a natural law analysis in Kant? Why, why not?

2. Kant has usually been seen as an opponent to utilitarianism (the subject of the next chapter), which suggests that the moral course of action is the action that makes the most people happy. Discuss.

3. Why does Kant believe that intention—rather than consequences—is the most important part of a moral act? Do you agree with him?

4. Kant thinks that we should aim at duty instead of happiness. Why?

---

1   Immanuel Kant, "On the Supposed Right to Lie From Benevolent Motives," originally published in *Berlinische Blaetter by Biester* (1799). This translation is from an Appendix to Thomas Kingsmill Abbott, *Kant's Critique of Practical Reason and Other Works on the Theory of Ethics, trans. with prefaces and other material* (London: Longmans, Green, 1889), pp. 361–65, Available at https://archive.org/stream/critiquepractic00kantuoft#page/n7/mode/2up; Kant is here responding to criticism of his concept of the categorical imperative.

2   Henri-Benjamin Constant de Rebecque (1767–1830) was a Swiss-French political activist and writer on politics and religion.

3   I.e., Kant.

4   In the reply that follows, Kant reiterates his position.

5. In what sense is morality, in the first formulation of the categorical imperative, categorical as opposed to merely hypothetical?

6. Explain Kant's distinction between persons and objects or things. In which class would non-human animals fall? The environment? Discuss the moral implications of these results.

7. Use an example of someone using someone else as a means to an end. Why, according to Kant, is this immoral?

8. Kant believes that there are no exceptions to the moral law. The moral law must apply universally: it is therefore always wrong to tell a lie. Do you agree or disagree? Justify your position.

Suggested Readings

The most important ethical works of Kant are *The Groundwork for the Metaphysics of Morals* (1785), *The Critique of Practical Reason* (the "Second Critique," 1788), and the *Metaphysics of Morals* (1797). The best introduction to his system is the *Groundwork* (German: *Grundlegung zur Metaphysik der Sitten*; variously translated as *The Foundations* or *The Grounding of/for the Metaphysics of Morals*). There are many translations in print and online, including those by Thomas Abbott (from 1883), H. Paton (from 1948), Lewis Beck, James Ellington, Mary Gregor, and Allen W. Wood. Broadview Press has a revised translation of the Abbott edition, edited by Lara Denis. Students should not be discouraged if they find Kant's prose difficult. Modernized versions of his works can be found at earlymoderntexts.com.

See, generally, *The Blackwell Guide to Kant's Ethics* and the annotated bibliography on "Kant's ethics" at ethikseite.de. The philosophical literature includes Christine Korsgaard, *The Sources of Normativity* (1996), Barbara Herman, *Moral Literacy* (2007), and Christian Onof, "Reconstructing the Grounding of Kant's Ethics" (2009). The commentary includes Allen W. Wood, *Kant's Ethical Thought* (1999); Oliver Sensen, ed., *Kant on Moral Autonomy* (2013); Michael Cholbi, *Understanding Kant's Ethics* (2016); and Barbara Herman, *Morality as Rationality: A Study of Kant's Ethics* (2016).

For comparative studies, see S. Radhakrishnan ("Ethics of the Bhagavad Gita and Kant," 1911), Julia Ching ("Chinese Ethics and Kant," 1978), Godwin Azenabor ("African Ethics and Kant's Categorical Imperative," 2008), and Günter Wohlfart ("Kantianism versus Confucianism," 2015).

In applied ethics, see Matthew Altman, *Kant and Applied Ethics* (2011); F. Heubel and N. Biller-Andorno, "The Contribution of Kantian Moral Theory to Contemporary Medical Ethics" (2005); Sue Martinelli-Fernandez, "Kant, Lies, and Business Ethics" (2002); and G. Vong, "In Defence of Kant's Moral Prohibition on Suicide Solely to Avoid Suffering" (2008).

Chapter 31

Utilitarianism

The moral philosophy of utilitarianism began as an eighteenth-century English movement which evaluated the ethical worth of our actions on the basis of their contribution to the general happiness. In an age of prominent industrial advances, it is perhaps natural that utilitarian thinkers thought that morality—like other aspects of life—could be judged by its practical usefulness. This "utility" was to be measured in terms of the total amount of happiness or pleasure produced for society as a whole.

The two major historical figures associated with British utilitarianism are Jeremy Bentham and John Stuart Mill. There were a host of prominent but lesser known utilitarians, however, such as William Godwin (1756–1836), at the time a highly influential political theorist (and husband of Mary Wollstonecraft), and the famous Christian apologist and clergyman William Paley (1743–1805). The movement monopolized Anglo-American moral philosophy well into the twentieth century. The erudite Hendry Sidgwick (1838–1900) compared utilitarianism, "egoism," and "intuitionism" in *The Methods of Ethics* (1874) without coming to any decisive conclusions in favor of one school over the others. The movement is still viable, and there have been many contemporary utilitarians, such as J.J.C. Smart (1920–2012), who promoted an "extreme" form of act utilitarianism, David Braybrooke (1924–2013), who, perhaps surprisingly, undertook to reconcile natural law theory and utilitarianism, the prominent British analytic philosopher R.M. Hare (1919–2002), who devised a "two-level utilitarianism" (or Government House utilitarianism), and Peter Singer (b. 1946), the renowned Benthamite exponent of animal rights.

Jeremy Bentham (1748–1832) was a reformer associated with the liberal side of eighteenth-century British politics. A child prodigy, he attended Oxford at the age of 12 and graduated at the age of 15. He later studied law but turned against his professor, William Blackstone, the famous author of the *Commentaries*, and instinctively questioned the authority of the judiciary. Bentham showed little interest in a legal career, or any other recognized profession, and lived primarily off his inheritance. Most of his time was spent in study, writing, and cultivating the political associations necessary to advance his many causes.

Bentham saw himself as a practical, common sense thinker, whose platform of reform was based on a general critique of English society. He wrote voluminously, although much of his writing—amounting to tens of thousands of pages—was not published during his lifetime. His most important published work is the *Introduction to the Principles of Morals and Legislation* (1789). He also produced a number of highly polemical treatises: *Anarchical Fallacies* (against the French Revolution, 1796), *Defence of Usury* (1787), *Parliamentary Reform Catechism* (1817), *Church-of-Englandism* (1818), *Not Paul But Jesus* (1823), *A Treatise on Judicial Evidence* (1825), and *Constitutional Code* (1830).

In his lifetime, Bentham was principally known as a staunch advocate of the codification of the common law. Like other reformers, he believed that codification provided a more rational, systematic, and scientific means of tabulating the law. This reflects a modern preference for comprehensive theoretical models over the accumulation of practical wisdom. Bentham also wanted, however, to take the power of determining the law away from the judiciary and place it firmly within the control of the legislature. Although Bentham was a liberal, he rejected the idea of natural or inalienable rights, and appears to have placed his faith in the process of political reform and statutory social improvement, which later found expression in legal pragmatism.

Bentham's quixotic side found expression in the medical use of cadavers, which was a controversial issue at the time. In a symbolic but eccentric gesture, he accordingly left his body to medicine but made careful preparations for the public display of his remains—his skeleton and mummified head—in a wooden closet that he called his "auto-icon." The remains, dressed in his own clothes and stuffed with straw, can still be viewed at University College London.

John Stuart Mill popularized the idea of utilitarianism thirty years after Bentham's death when he published, in 1861, three articles in *Fraser's Magazine*, a literary periodical with a wide, middle-class readership. These articles were republished as a book in 1863, under the title *Utilitarianism*, which was intended to demonstrate that the idea of utility provided a plausible basis for a common-sense ethics. It has been suggested that the success of the book can be attributed to its failure to deal with the more troubling aspects of the theory.

Mill nevertheless identifies the greatest happiness principle as "the foundation of morals," which

> holds that actions are right in proportion as they tend to promote happiness, wrong as they tend to produce the reverse of happiness [and where] by happiness is intended pleasure, and the absence of pain; by unhappiness, pain, and the privation of pleasure.

The optimism of Mill's decidedly liberal utilitarianism can be seen in the assumption that pleasure is a positive value, rather than the absence of pain, as most ancients suggested.

Mill acknowledges that there is no way to prove the greatest happiness principle but insists that it accords with a deep human sentiment. He believes in a universal hedonism, which views the production of as much pleasure as possible as the ultimate human goal. Unlike Epicurus, whose hedonism was frankly egoistic, Mill argues that the moral individual should not prefer his or her own happiness over that of others. There are obvious questions regarding whether this is psychologically possible or even preferable.

According to Mill, it is the quality of pleasure, and not merely its quantity, that matters. It is morally better to be a discontented Socrates than a happy pig, since intellectual pleasures are worth more on the scale of happiness than sensual pleasures. Mill also argues, against Kant and the earlier tradition, that it is not the intention but the good consequences of an act—the happiness that it produces—that determine its moral worth. This is a problematic standard, which explains why utilitarianism has sometimes been dismissed as a kind of consequentialism.

William Godwin was a political thinker who took a relatively radical stance in favor of "universal benevolence," raising the ire of his critics when he suggested that emotions and our natural judgments, exercised without judgment, do not provide a satisfactory basis of moral judgment. He later tempered his views, allowing a greater role for our natural affections, but steadfastly maintained his basic premise, using the example of Brutus executing his two sons to preserve the Roman state, as a better example of the way in which the public good trumps our family interests.

Godwin's utilitarianism rests solidly on his view that the determination of what produces the maximum happiness lies within the private judgment of each individual. Although individuals should consult public opinion, they must decide for themselves what constitutes the right moral reaction to a particular situation. He therefore rejects the idea that a public body, like a legislature, has the final say in such matters.

The utilitarians were generally liberal in practical ethics. They believed in reason, progress, individual rights, and the democratic system. They questioned the authority of religious institutions, favored science and education, and supported legislation to regulate the work place. Bentham pushed for the equality of women, for the separation of church and state, for penal reform, for a liberalization of laws regulating sexual practices and homosexuality, and for laws protecting animal welfare.

There are nevertheless competing tendencies in utilitarianism, which has its "government" side. Bentham certainly saw legislation as the most effective means of introducing the greatest happiness principle into public policy, which could then be enforced with all the powers of the state. The intrusive side of utilitarianism comes to the fore in Bentham's model prison, the "Panopticon" (the "seeing-everywhere"), which was based on the idea that prisoners could be reformed by placing them in a situation where they believed that they were being watched by the wardens at all times. The level of social control and psychological coercion in such a policy has contributed to the idea of the surveillance state.

The first reading is from Bentham's *Introduction to the Principles of Morals and Legislation* (1780) and contains the original formulation of the utilitarian theory; it sketches out some of the factors that go into the determination of the greatest amount of happiness. The second reading, from Mill's *Utilitarianism* (1863), responds to some of the early objections to the theory and addresses a few of the problems of determining the value to be assigned to particular pleasures. The third reading is from William Godwin's *An Enquiry Concerning Political Justice* (1793). It presents a provocative argument for saving the life of an archbishop over that of his chambermaid because the former contributes more to the general good than does the latter.

Jeremy Bentham, *An Introduction to the Principles of Morals and Legislation*[1]

(1780, 1823)

Chapter I: Of the Principle of Utility

I. Nature has placed mankind under the governance of two sovereign masters, pain and pleasure. It is for them alone to point out what we ought to do, as well as to determine what we shall do. On the one hand the standard of right and wrong, on the other the chain of causes and effects, are fastened to their throne. They govern us in all we do, in all we say, in all we think: every effort we can make to throw off our subjection, will serve but to demonstrate and confirm it. In words a man may pretend to abjure their empire: but in reality he will remain subject to it all the while. The principle of utility recognizes this subjection, and assumes it for the foundation of that [utilitarian] system....

II. By the principle of utility is meant that principle which approves or disapproves of every action whatsoever according to the tendency it appears to have to augment or diminish the happiness of the party whose interest is in question....

III. By utility is meant that property in any object, whereby it tends to produce benefit, advantage, pleasure, good, or happiness, (all this in the present case comes to the same thing) or (what comes again to the same thing) to prevent the happening of mischief, pain, evil, or unhappiness to the party whose interest is considered: if that party be the community in general, then the happiness of the community: if a particular individual, then the happiness of that individual....

IV. The community is...composed of the individual persons who are considered as constituting as it were its members. The interest of the community then is, what is it?—the sum of the interests of the several members who compose it....

V. A thing is said to promote the interest, or to be for the interest, of an individual, when it tends to add to the sum total of his pleasures: or, what comes to the same thing, to diminish the sum total of his pains.

VI. An action then may be said to be conformable to the principle of utility, or, for shortness sake, to utility, (meaning with respect to the community at large) when the tendency it has to augment the happiness of the community is greater than any it has to diminish it....

IX. A man may be said to be a partisan of the principle of utility, when the approbation or disapprobation he annexes to any action, or to any measure, is determined by and proportioned to the tendency which he conceives it to have to augment or to diminish the happiness of the community....

X. Of an action that is conformable to the principle of utility one may always say either that it is one that ought to be done, or at least that it is not one that ought not to be done. One may say also,...that it is a right action; at least that it is not a wrong action. When thus interpreted, the words ought, and right and wrong and others of that stamp, have a meaning: when otherwise, they have none.

XI. Has the rectitude of this principle been ever

---

1   Jeremy Bentham, *An Introduction to the Principles of Morals and Legislation* (printed in 1780 but not published until 1789; republished in 1823); this excerpt from Jeremy Bentham, *An Introduction to the Principles of Morals and Legislation* (Oxford: Clarendon Press, 1907), is available at http://oll.libertyfund.org/titles/bentham-an-introduction-to-the-principles-of-morals-and-legislation.

formally contested? It should seem that it had by those who have not known what they have been meaning. Is it susceptible of any direct proof? It should seem not: for that which is used to prove everything else, cannot itself be proved: a chain of proofs must have their commencement somewhere. To give such proof is as impossible as it is needless....

XII. By the natural constitution of the human frame, on most occasions of their lives men in general embrace this principle, without thinking of it:...

XIII. When a man attempts to combat the principle of utility, it is with reasons drawn, without his being aware of it, from that very principle itself. His arguments, if they prove anything, prove not that the principle is wrong, but that, according to the applications he supposes to be made of it, it is misapplied....

Chapter II: Of Principles Adverse to that of Utility

II. A principle may be different from that of utility in two ways: 1. By being constantly opposed to it: this is the case with a principle which may be termed the principle of asceticism. 2. By being sometimes opposed to it, and... this is the case with another [principle], which may be termed the principle of sympathy and antipathy.

III. By the principle of asceticism I mean that principle, which, like the principle of utility, approves or disapproves of any action, according to the tendency which it appears to have to augment or diminish the happiness of the party whose interest is in question; but in an inverse manner: approving of actions in as far as they tend to diminish his happiness; disapproving of them in as far as they tend to augment it.

IV. It is evident that anyone who reprobates the least particle of pleasure, as such,... is a partisan of the principle of asceticism....

V. There are two classes of men... by whom the principle of asceticism appears to have been embraced; the one a set of moralists, the other a set of religionists.... Hope, that is the prospect of pleasure, seems to have animated the former class:... the hope of honor and reputation at the hands of men. Fear, that is the prospect of pain, motivated the latter class: fear, the offspring of superstitious fancy: the fear of future punishment at the hands of a spiteful and revengeful Deity....

VI. The philosophical party[1] have scarcely gone farther than to reprobate pleasure: the religious party have frequently gone so far as to make it a matter of merit and of duty to court pain....

VII. From these two sources[2] have flowed the doctrines... which have disposed humans to unite upon various occasions against the common enemy, the partisan of the principle of utility, whom they joined in branding with the odious name of Epicurean.

X. The principle of utility is capable of being consistently pursued; and it is but tautology to say that the more consistently it is pursued, the better it must ever be for humankind. The principle of asceticism never was, nor ever can be, consistently pursued by any living creature. Let but one tenth part of the inhabitants of this earth pursue it consistently, and in a day's time they will have turned it into a hell.

XI. Among principles adverse to that of utility, that which at this day seems to have most influence in matters of government, is what may be called the principle of sympathy and antipathy. By the principle of sympathy and antipathy, I mean that principle which approves or disapproves of certain actions,... merely because a man finds himself disposed to approve or disapprove of them: holding up

---

1 I.e., the moralists.

2 I.e., the philosophical moralist and the religious.

that approbation or disapprobation as a sufficient reason for itself, and disclaiming the necessity of looking out for any extrinsic ground....

XIII. In looking over the catalogue of human actions...in order to determine which of them are to be marked with the seal of disapprobation, an adherent of the principle of sympathy and antipathy believes you need but to take counsel of your own feelings: whatever you find in yourself a propensity to condemn, is wrong for that very reason.... For the same reason it is also meet for punishment:...The fine feelings of the soul are not to be overborne and tyrannized by the harsh and rugged dictates of political utility.

Chapter IV: Value of a Lot of Pleasure or Pain, How to Be Measured

I. Pleasures then, and the avoidance of pains, are the ends that the legislator has in view; it is incumbent on him therefore to understand their value....

II. To a person considered by himself, the value of a pleasure or pain considered by itself, will be greater or less, according to the four following circumstances:

　　1. Its intensity.
　　2. Its duration.
　　3. Its certainty or uncertainty.
　　4. Its proximity or remoteness....

III. But when the value of any pleasure or pain is considered...there are two other circumstances to be taken into the account. These are:

　　5. Its fecundity, or the chance it has of being followed by sensations of the same kind....

　　6. Its purity, or the chance it has of not being followed by sensations of the opposite kind....

IV. To a number of persons,...the value of a pleasure or a pain...will be greater or less, then, according to seven circumstances: to wit, the six preceding ones; namely,

　　1. Its intensity.
　　2. Its duration.
　　3. Its certainty or uncertainty.
　　4. Its proximity or remoteness.
　　5. Its fecundity.
　　6. Its purity.

And one other; to wit:

　　7. Its extent; that is, the number of persons to whom it extends....

V. To take an exact account then of the general tendency of any act...proceed as follows. Begin with any one person of those whose interests seem most immediately to be affected by it: and take an account,

　　1. Of the value of each distinguishable pleasure which appears to be produced by it in the first instance.

　　2. Of the value of each pain which appears to be produced by it in the first instance.

　　3. Of the value of each pleasure which appears to be produced by it after the first....

　　4. Of the value of each pain which appears to be produced by it after the first....

　　5. Sum up all the values of all the pleasures on the one side, and those of all the pains on the other. The balance, if it be on the side of pleasure, will give the good tendency of the act upon the whole, with respect to the interests of that

individual person; if on the side of pain, the bad tendency of it upon the whole.

6. Take an account of the number of persons whose interests appear to be concerned; and repeat the above process with respect to each. Sum up the numbers expressive of the degrees of good tendency, which the act has....

Do this again with respect to each individual, in regard to whom the tendency of it is bad upon the whole. Take the balance which if on the side of pleasure, will give the general good tendency of the act, with respect to the total number or community of individuals concerned; if on the side of pain, the general evil tendency, with respect to the same community.

VI. It is not to be expected that this process should be strictly pursued previously to every moral judgment, or to every legislative or judicial operation. It may, however, be always kept in view....

READING 31B

John Stuart Mill, *Utilitarianism*[1]

(1863)

Chapter 2: What Utilitarianism Is

The creed which accepts as the foundation of morals, Utility, or the Greatest Happiness Principle, holds that actions are right in proportion as they tend to promote happiness, wrong as they tend to produce the reverse of happiness. By happiness is intended pleasure, and the absence of pain; by unhappiness, pain, and the privation of pleasure.... The theory of life on which this theory of morality is grounded holds that pleasure, and freedom from pain, are the only things desirable as ends; and that all desirable things...are desirable...as means to the promotion of pleasure and the prevention of pain.

Now, such a theory of life excites in many minds, and among them in some of the most estimable in feeling and purpose, inveterate dislike. To suppose that life has no higher end than pleasure—no better and nobler object of desire and pursuit—they designate as utterly mean and groveling; as a doctrine worthy only of swine, to whom the followers of Epicurus were, at a very early period, contemptuously likened....

When thus attacked, the Epicureans have always answered, that it is not they, but their accusers, who represent human nature in a degrading light; since the accusation supposes human beings to be capable of no pleasures except those of which swine are capable.... Human beings, as they assert, have faculties more elevated than the animal appetites, and when once made conscious of them, do not regard anything as happiness which does not include their gratification....

---

1 John Stuart Mill, "Utilitarianism" (originally published in 1861 in *Fraser's Magazine*), from Colin Heydt, ed., *Utilitarianism* (Peterborough, ON: Broadview, [1863] 2011).

There is no known Epicurean theory of life which does not assign to the pleasures of the intellect, of the feelings and imagination, and of the moral sentiments, a much higher value as pleasures than to those of mere sensation.... and it is quite compatible with the principle of utility to recognize the fact that some kinds of pleasure are more desirable and more valuable than others. It would be absurd that while, in estimating all other things, quality is considered as well as quantity, the estimation of pleasures should be supposed to depend on quantity alone.

Now if I am asked, what I mean by difference of quality in pleasures...there is but one possible answer. Of two pleasures, if there be one to which all or almost all who have experience of both give a decided preference, irrespective of any feeling of moral obligation to prefer it, that is the more desirable pleasure. If one of the two is, by those who are competently acquainted with both, placed so far above the other that they prefer it, even though knowing it to be attended with a greater amount of discontent...we are justified in ascribing to the preferred enjoyment a superiority in quality, so far outweighing quantity as to render it, in comparison, of small account....

Few human creatures would consent to be changed into any of the lower animals, for a promise of the fullest allowance of a beast's pleasures; no intelligent human being would consent to be a fool, no instructed person would be an ignoramus, no person of feeling and conscience would be selfish and base, even though they should be persuaded that the fool, the dunce, or the rascal is better satisfied with his lot than they are with theirs.... A being of higher faculties requires more to make him happy, and is capable probably of more acute suffering...but in spite of these liabilities, he can never really wish to sink into what he feels to be a lower grade of existence. We may give what explanation we please of this unwillingness...but its most appropriate appellation[1]

is a sense of dignity,...and which is so essential a part of the happiness of those in whom it is strong, that nothing which conflicts with it could be, otherwise than momentarily, an object of desire to them.

Whoever supposes that this preference takes place at a sacrifice of happiness—that the superior being, in anything like equal circumstances, is not happier than the inferior—confounds the two very different ideas of happiness and content. It is indisputable that the being whose capacities of enjoyment are low, has the greatest chance of having them fully satisfied; and a highly endowed being will always feel that any happiness which he can look for...is imperfect.

A highly endowed being can nevertheless learn to bear its imperfections,...and they will not make him envy the being who is indeed unconscious of the imperfections.... It is better to be a human being dissatisfied than a pig satisfied; better to be Socrates dissatisfied than a fool satisfied. And if the fool, or the pig, are of a different opinion, it is because they only know their own side of the question. The other party to the comparison knows both sides.

It may be objected that many who are capable of the higher pleasures, occasionally, under the influence of temptation, postpone them to the lower. But this is quite compatible with a full appreciation of the intrinsic superiority of the higher. Men often, from infirmity of character, make their election for the nearer good, though they know it to be the less valuable; and this no less when the choice is between two bodily pleasures than when it is between bodily and mental. They pursue sensual indulgences to the injury of health, though perfectly aware that health is the greater good....

Men lose their high aspirations as they lose their intellectual tastes because they have not time or opportunity for indulging them; and they addict themselves to inferior pleasures, not because they deliberately prefer them, but because they are either

_____

1 I.e., name.

the only ones to which they have access, or the only ones which they are any longer capable of enjoying....

On a question which is the best worth having of two pleasures, or which of two modes of existence is the most grateful to the feelings, apart from its moral attributes and from its consequences, the judgment of those who are qualified by knowledge of both or, if they differ, that of the majority among them, must be admitted as final. What means are there of determining which is the acutest of two pains, or the most intense of two pleasurable sensations, except the general suffrage of those who are familiar with both?

We not uncommonly hear the doctrine of utility inveighed against as a godless doctrine. If it be necessary to say anything at all against so mere an assumption, we may say that the question depends upon what idea we have formed of the moral character of the Deity. If it be a true belief that God desires, above all things, the happiness of his creatures, and that this was his purpose in their creation, utility is not only not a godless doctrine, but more profoundly religious than any other.... A utilitarian who believes in the perfect goodness and wisdom of God, necessarily believes that whatever God has thought fit to reveal on the subject of morals, must fulfil the requirements of utility in a supreme degree.

Christian revelation was only intended to tell mankind, in a very general way, what is right, and to determine that more particularly, we need a doctrine of ethics, carefully followed out, to interpret to us the will of God. Whether this opinion is correct or not...whatever aid religion...can provide in the ethical investigation is as available to the utilitarian as any other moralist, who may regard it as the testimony of God to the usefulness or hurtfulness of any given course of action...

Again, defenders of utility often find themselves called upon to reply to such objections as this—that there is not time, previous to action, for calculating and weighing the effects of any line of conduct on the general happiness. This is exactly as if any one were to say that it is impossible to guide our conduct by Christianity, because there is not time, when there is something to be done, to read through the Old and New Testaments.... Mankind has by this time acquired positive beliefs as to the effects of some actions on their happiness; and...this will be sufficient for the philosopher until he has succeeded in finding better....

Mankind have still much to learn as to the effects of actions on the general happiness, I admit, or rather, earnestly maintain. The corollaries from the principle of utility...admit of indefinite improvement, and, in a progressive state of the human mind, their improvement is perpetually going on.

We are told that a utilitarian will be apt to make his own particular case an exception to moral rules, and, when under temptation, will see a utility in the breach of a rule greater than he will see in its observance.... It is not the fault of...utilitarianism, however, that rules of conduct cannot be so framed as to require no exceptions....

There is no ethical creed which does not temper the rigidity of its laws by giving a certain latitude...to accommodate the peculiarities of circumstances; and...at the opening thus made, self-deception and dishonest casuistry get in. There exists no moral system under which there do not arise unequivocal cases of conflicting obligation. These are the real difficulties, the knotty points both in the theory of ethics and in the conscientious guidance of personal conduct.

William Godwin, *An Enquiry Concerning Political Justice*[1]

(1793)

Book II. Principles of Society

CHAPTER II. OF JUSTICE

Justice, as it exists among individuals, is a rule of conduct originating in the connection of one percipient being with another. A comprehensive maxim which has been laid down upon the subject is, "that we should love our neighbor as ourselves." But this maxim, though possessing considerable merit as a popular principle, is not modelled with the strictness of philosophical accuracy.

In a loose and general view I and my neighbor are both of us men, and of consequence entitled to equal attention. But in reality it is probable that one of us is a being of more worth and importance than the other. A man is of more worth than a beast; because, being possessed of higher faculties, he is capable of a more refined and genuine happiness. In the same manner the illustrious archbishop of Cambray[2] was of more worth than his chambermaid, and there are few of us that would hesitate to pronounce, if his palace were in flames, and the life of only one of them could be preserved, which of the two ought to be preferred....

That life ought to be preferred which will be most conducive to the general good. In saving the life of Fenelon, suppose at the moment when he was conceiving the project of his immortal Telemachus, I should be promoting the benefit of thousands, who have been cured by the perusal of it of some error, vice and consequent unhappiness. Nay, my benefit would extend farther than this, for every individual thus cured has become a better member of society, and has contributed in his turn to the happiness, the information and improvement of others.

Supposing I had been myself the chambermaid, I ought to have chosen to die, rather than that Fenelon should have died. The life of Fenelon was really preferable to that of the chambermaid. But understanding is the faculty that perceives the truth of this and similar propositions; and justice is the principle that regulates my conduct accordingly. It would have been just in the chambermaid to have preferred the archbishop to herself. To have done otherwise would have been a breach of justice.

Supposing the chambermaid had been my wife, my mother or my benefactor. This would not alter the truth of the proposition. The life of Fenelon would still be more valuable than that of the chambermaid; and justice, pure, unadulterated justice, would still have preferred that which was most valuable. Justice would have taught me to save the life of Fenelon at the expense of the other. What magic is there in the pronoun "my," to overturn the decisions of everlasting truth? My wife or my mother may be a fool or a prostitute, malicious, lying or dishonest. If they be, of what consequence is it that they are mine?

---

1 William Godwin, Book II, Chapter II: Of Justice, from Godwin, *Enquiry Concerning Political Justice, and Its Influence on General Virtue and Happiness* (1793), vol. 1 (London: G.G.J. and J. Robinson, 1793). Available at http://oll.libertyfund.org/titles/godwin-an-enquiry-concerning-political-justice-vol-i.

2 I.e., François de Salignac de la Mothe-Fénelon, or François Fénelon (1651–1715), a French Roman Catholic archbishop, writer, and moralist. He is known mostly for his moralistic novel, *The Adventures of Telemachus*, which is referred to in the next paragraph. He was championed as a very influential moralist and a pillar of good social values.

Questions

1. Although Bentham and Mill think highly of the Epicureans, there is a fundamental way in which utilitarianism differs from Epicureanism. Discuss.
2. Bentham's caricature of asceticism misses the mark. Think of the Stoics. How would they respond to Bentham?
3. Utilitarianism was more than a philosophy. It was also a political reform movement, dedicated to the improvement of the conditions of the working classes during the Industrial Revolution. Bentham was a progressive and thought that utilitarianism provided the right machinery for formulating and implementing government policy and legislation. Explain.
4. How does John Stuart Mill modify Bentham's theory? Explain his motivations.
5. Do you think that Mill provides a satisfactory criterion for judging among the qualitative worth of various pleasures? Why, why not?
6. Many Christians were attracted to utilitarianism. How does Mill explain the link? Can you see a link between utilitarianism and other religions?
7. Godwin thought he was being a consistent utilitarian, dedicated to the common good. His piece caused great scandal at the time, however. If you were in a hotel on fire and had to choose between saving your mother or saving a famous scientist—or philosopher—who would you choose? Why?

Suggested Readings

Jeremy Bentham is usually considered the father of utilitarianism. His *Introduction to the Principles of Morals and Legislation* was certainly influential. But there are many precedents, including Francis Hutcheson, *An Inquiry into the Original of Our Ideas of Beauty and Virtue* (1725); John Gay, *Concerning the Fundamental Principle of Virtue or Morality* (1731); and William Paley, *The Principles of Moral and Political Philosophy* (1785).

Although there is a scholarly edition of *The Works of Jeremy Bentham* (edited by John Bowring in 1838), the Bentham Project at University College London, in collaboration with the university's Centre for Digital Humanities, is currently compiling a new and complete collection of his work, which will include his unpublished manuscripts. The most widely read account of the ethical theory is John Stuart Mill's *Utilitarianism*. Broadview has two editions available: the Heydt edition (2011) features appendices and associated historical materials; the Bailey edition (2016) may be more suitable for students.

Modern utilitarians include Henry Sidgwick, R.M. Hare, and Peter Singer. Sidgwick's *Methods of Ethics* (1907) contains a sophisticated analysis of the theory. A comprehensive set of resources can be found at utilitarianism.com. We should also note that Charles Dickens's novel *Hard Times* (1854) includes a harsh critique of utilitarianism.

More recent sources include William Shaw's *Contemporary Ethics: Taking Account of Utilitarianism* (1999); John Jamieson Carswell Smart and Bernard Williams, *Utilitarianism: For and Against* (1973); and Emilie Dardenne, "From Jeremy Bentham to Peter Singer" (2010).

For specific studies in applied ethics, see Matti Häyry, *Liberal Utilitarianism and Applied Ethics* (1994); William H. Shaw, *Utilitarianism and the Ethics of War* (2016); and Claus Strue Frederiksen, "The Presentation of Utilitarianism within the Field of Business Ethics" (2012). The relationship between utilitarianism and modern economics is also important. See, for example, Shiri Cohen Kaminitz, "Economics and Ethics under the Same Umbrella: Edgeworth's 'Exact Utilitarianism,' 1877–1881" (2013).

Chapter 32

Early Feminism

Feminism might be said to have its roots in the European Enlightenment, which brought in a rationalism and a new individualism, and which eventually gave rise to a liberalism that questioned received beliefs and the authority of the traditional social order. This movement led, in the view of many commentators, to an awakening of classes and groups that had been historically disadvantaged. This included women.

In this chapter, we consider three figures who can be seen, in various ways, as precursors of feminism: Kristina Wasa (1626–89), who reigned as Queen Christina Alexandra of Sweden and, after abdicating the throne, fashioned a public role for herself as a philanthropist and intellectual; Olympe de Gouges (1748–93), a playwright and author who died tragically in the French Revolution; and Sojourner Truth (c. 1797–1883), who began her life as a slave and gained notoriety as an anti-slavery, equal-rights activist. These three women all led remarkable lives given their circumstances. We can scarcely do justice to their many accomplishments here.

Kristina Wasa was the daughter and sole heir of Gustav Adolf, who died defending Protestantism in Germany during the Thirty Years' War. She became the "girl Queen" of Sweden in 1633 when she was only six years old. After a very rigorous education of the sort ordinarily reserved for boys, she was formally crowned as monarch of Sweden in 1644. She reigned until 1654, when she abdicated and, in a move that caused great scandal across much of Europe, converted to Roman Catholicism. She moved to Rome and, despite several attempts to re-enter political life, mostly spent her time as a frequent participant in the intellectual life of the *salons*, a patron of artists, scientists, philosophers, and musicians, and a flamboyant socialite. She is one of only three women to be buried in the Vatican grottoes.

Queen Christina played a crucial political role in promoting the Treaty of Westphalia, intended to put an end to the religious wars caused by the conflict between Protestants and Catholics in Europe. Although she was of a more scholarly bent, she was a devoted Queen, immersing herself in the political decision-making process with intense dedication. She was determined to make Sweden a cutting-edge center of learning—a new Athens of the North—actively supporting theater, dance, music, libraries, and museums, and inviting renowned intellectuals, scientists, poets, and artists to Sweden. Queen Christina's most famous philosophical guest in Sweden was René Descartes, who came on a mission to conduct private lessons for her. She founded the first Swedish newspaper in 1645.

Queen Christina was known for odd and even erratic behavior. Her unconventional lifestyle, and her signal disregard for courtly decorum, made her famous and the subject of gossip. In 1657, she had one of her servants executed in her presence for what she saw as treason, an act that could not be prosecuted (as she was royalty) but profoundly shocked the public and led to rumors about her state of mental health. She often dressed like a man and expressed "an insurmountable distaste for marriage." (This played a role in her abdication, since a queen was expected to provide future heirs to the throne.) Speculating about her sexual orientation, some surmise Christina had a lesbian relationship with Ebba Sparre, a close female confidante and friend. Others have suggested that she was trans-gendered or that she was autistic. We must be cautious when diagnosing historical figures.

Throughout her life, she carried on a vigorous correspondence with a wide variety of intellectuals, aristocrats, and politicians, among them Descartes, Pierre Gassendi, Blaise Pascal, and Hugo Grotius. As for her philosophy, Christina was well read in ancient classical authors and particularly impressed with the Stoics. She wrote essays on Caesar and Alexander the Great. She was, generally, an enlightened intellectual, defending in writing tolerance of the Huguenots and of Roman Jews. Christina left an unfinished autobiography, *The Life of Queen Kristina, Written by Herself, Dedicated to God*, and three collections of moral aphorisms written in the spirit of wisdom literature such as that of King Solomon.

Olympe de Gouges, born Marie Gouze, was a French playwright, pamphleteer, and political activist around the time of the French Revolution. Born in southwestern France, she was convinced that she was the illegitimate daughter of Jean-Jacques Lefranc, the Marquis de Pompignan. Much to her chagrin, she was never properly recognized as heir. After a brief and unhappy early marriage, in 1770 she changed her name to Olympe de Gouges, and moved to Paris with her son. Vowing never to marry again, she entered into a long, intimate relationship with a wealthy businessman, Jacques Biétrix de Rozières, which came to an end with the revolution.

In Paris, de Gouges mingled with writers and intellectuals and educated urban society, frequenting the intellectual *salons* that were fashionable at that time. Beginning in 1784, she launched her career as a public intellectual, writing many plays, essays, manifestos, literary treatises, and political pamphlets that argued for social and political reform. She took stands against slavery, against capital punishment, for equal rights for women, for relaxing the laws against divorce, for the rights of illegitimate children and unmarried mothers, and for more permissive sexual attitudes.

De Gouges wrote an abolitionist play protesting slavery entitled *The Slavery of the Negroes*, which had a brief performance in 1789. She wrote a manifesto demanding equal rights for women. In December 1792, she wrote to the National Assembly, offering to defend the king, whom, she believed, ought to be sent into exile rather than executed. In 1793, she was arrested after publishing a broadsheet, *Les trois urnes, ou le salut de la Patrie, par un voyageur aérien* (*The Three Voting Urns, or How to Save the Fatherland, by a Flying Traveler*), demanding that voters be allowed to choose among three forms of government: a republic, a federation, or a constitutional monarchy.

Refused an attorney, she spent three months in jail, on trumped-up charges, trying to defend herself against accusations that she had plotted to reinstate the monarchy and overthrow the Republic. She managed to publish two texts, *Olympe de Gouges before the Revolutionary Tribunal* and *A Woman Patriot Persecuted*, in which she condemned the Jacobin Reign of Terror. Associated with the more moderate Girondin faction, she was guillotined in Paris on November 3, 1793.

Sojourner Truth was an African-American abolitionist, religious enthusiast, social reformer, and women's rights activist. Born Isabella Baumfree into a family of thirteen children, her parents were enslaved Africans on a plantation located in a Dutch settlement in upstate New York. When she was nine years old, Isabella was sold to a farmer, along with a herd of sheep, for $100. Two years later, she was sold again, to a tavern keeper, for $105, and then again, a year-and-a-half later, to another farmer, for $175. She experienced cruel treatment and may have been sexually abused. In total she had five children: one from Robert, an enslaved man with whom she fell in love, and four from Thomas, an older enslaved man she was forced to marry.

The state of New York planned to outlaw slavery in 1827. Truth's owner promised to set her free a year early but reneged on his promise. In the meantime, her five-year-old son Peter had been illegally sold to an owner in Alabama. Aided by Quakers, Truth was able to secure her freedom from her owner and then regain her child through an official complaint in court. She was one of the first black women to win a court case against a white man.

It was a time of reform movements, Christian revivals, and social upheaval. Influenced, in part, by mystical experiences, Truth became a Christian and a Methodist, associating with various spiritualist, abolitionist, and utopian groups. In the 1830s, she worked for a religious commune headed by Robert Matthews ("the Prophet Mathias"). Then in 1843, Isabella felt a call to a new way of life. She changed her name to "Sojourner Truth," telling her friends, "The Spirit calls me, and I must go."

She spent the rest of her life as an itinerant social activist, at the forefront of various public causes, speaking and preaching extemporaneously in favor of abolitionism, prison reform, women's suffrage, temperance, an end to capital punishment, and for Christian conversion. She campaigned for the Union during the Civil War, encouraged the recruitment of black troops, worked at a government refugee camp for those who had been freed from slavery, and campaigned for Western land grants to former enslaved persons. She met Presidents Abraham Lincoln and Ulysses S. Grant and, after steadfast activism, hampered by intermittent illness, died at home with her two daughters when she was eighty-six years old. In October 2008, she became the first black woman honored with a bust in the US Capitol.

Sojourner Truth must have been an impressive figure, standing about six feet tall, talking in a strong Dutch accent about her own experiences as an enslaved person. Although she did meet with hostile audiences, she was said to have a "miraculous" effect on listeners. She reported that she had hated white people, but that once she found Jesus, she was filled with love for everyone. Once slavery was abolished, she argued for equal treatment of black women. Truth was never able to read or write. We only know her speeches through second-hand reports. Her most famous speech, retrospectively entitled "Ain't I a Woman," was a plea to the Ohio Women's Rights Convention (1851) to promote the rights of black as well as white women. Throughout her public life, she persistently and fearlessly bore witness to the basic moral principle of equality for all.

The readings included here begin with a letter vividly describing the habits and character of Queen Christina, followed by a selection of her maxims. This is followed by Olympe de Gouges's manifesto, *Declaration of the Rights of Woman and the Female Citizen*. The final reading is a newspaper description of Sojourner Truth's "Ain't I A Woman" speech.

READING 32A

Some Passages Concerning the Person, Character, Manner of Living and Government of Christina Queen of Sweden by Father Mannerschied SJ[1]

(December 10, 1653)

I am confident I shall do you an agreeable office, if I write you something concerning the Queen of Sweden, whom I daily see, and reverence as the singular miracle and prodigy of our age.... She is low in stature; her forehead is large; her eyes very full and bright, and withal very lovely. Her nose is aquiline; her mouth middling wide and handsome. She has nothing feminine about her but the sex. Her voice is masculine, and so is her manner of speaking, her movement and gesture. I see her on horseback almost every day; and though she sits in the saddle as ladies do, yet she shakes and bends her body in such a manner, as that one who is not very near her, would take her for a man. When she rides,...her skirts alone discover her to be a woman. She keeps but one foot in the stirrup, and yet she rides so hardily, that none are able to keep up with her. One would think her flying rather than running....

At court she wears clothes so very plain, that I never saw any gold or silver about her but a single ring. She takes no manner of care in decking her person; she adjusts her hair but once a week; and sometimes only once a fortnight.[2] On Sundays she spends half an hour in dressing, on week days scarcely a quarter. I have sometimes, when I was discoursing with her, seen her smock stained with many spots of ink, occasioned by her writing much; and sometimes torn. When she is advised to bestow

1 Father Mannerschied SJ, *Some Passages Concerning the Person, Character, Manner of Living and Government of Christina, Queen of Sweden*, in "Christina, Queen of Sweden, 1626–1689," *The Works of Christina Queen of Sweden: Containing Maxims and Sentences in Twelve Centuries, and Reflections on the Life and Actions of Alexander the Great* (London: Printed for D. Wilson and T. Durham..., 1753); there is an online 1776 facsimile version at https://catalog.hathitrust.org.

2 I.e., once every two weeks.

more pains in adorning her person, she says it is an idle employment.

She allots three or four hours to sleep, and never more. She goes to bed very late and rises early.... When she rises in the morning, she spends five hours reading various books. She thinks herself a martyr when she is obliged to eat in public. At other times, she never sits above half an hour at table; she drinks water only. She has never been heard to complain of her victuals,[1] whether they were well or ill cooked. I have seen her often at meals, and observed the dishes she eats; they were always plain; the rest were sent off untouched.

I have heard her say she was never disturbed by anything; that she knows nothing so important, so cross or so noxious, that could rob her of the tranquility of her mind. She says that she regards death no more than sleep. In the severest winter she goes out into the fields, in her coach, in the dead of night, sometimes four and sometimes six hours together. She allots her mornings to public affairs, and goes every day to the senate, or rather to her council. I have known her, immediately after being let blood,[2] go to the council, and there remain five hours. She was once in a severest disorder for twenty-eight days together; and yet never in all that time omitted the management of public affairs. She says that it is a duty required by her Maker, to take the best care she can of the concerns of the kingdom; that she will do what in her lies; that, if things succeed not as may be wished, she shall have this comfort, that nothing has been wanting on her part.

She administers and finishes all public business herself. The ambassadors of potentates transact everything with her in person, and are remitted to no minister or secretary. When she gives public audiences to ambassadors, she alone makes all the answers to them. It is scarcely to be believed, but 'tis what I see every day, that these very Swedish generals, whose name and arms have so long made Germany tremble, in her presence stand speechless, as if they were dumb, and seem to be in the greatest confusion. She was scarce seven years old when she lost her father: who could believe that the daughter, at the age of twenty-seven, could so establish her power....

She reads all treaties concerning state affairs, however tedious and prolix. I knew, upon a certain occasion, that when treaties were presented to her, containing twenty-eight sheets, she read them over, and rendered them in Latin, and explained them to an ambassador in a very short space of time. She loves all nations; she loves virtue in all, and nothing else. She says there are but two different nations in the world; the one of good men, the other of bad; that she hates the latter, and loves the former without regard to the names by which different countries are distinguished.

She cannot bear the mention of marriage; she says she was born free and will die free. In common conversation she is so familiar, that one who is present would think her, not a queen, but not even a lady of distinction; she touches those she talks to, prompts them to discourse, laughs and jokes freely, and yet to her own people she is so awful,[3] that they stand like infants in her presence. When she treats of serious affaires, when she gives audience to ambassadors, she assumes such state as strikes fear in the boldest persons. She hath noble ladies in her service at court, but...she seems to despise them, and trusts all affairs to men only. If she were at war with any

---

1 I.e., food prepared for consumption; meals.

2 The expression 'being let blood' refers to the practice of bloodletting, which was a medical treatment at the time. By letting out blood, the illness was thought to leave the body as well. The fact that Queen Christina went to work immediately after such a treatment is a testament to her sense of duty in performing her public functions as well as to her fortitude or strength since the treatment was thought to weaken the person.

3 I.e., awe-inspiring; inspiring reverential wonder or fear (the archaic meaning of awful).

nation, it is past doubt that she would march against the enemy in person.

She understands ten or eleven languages, to wit, Latin, Greek, French, Italian, Spanish, High-Dutch, both the Swedish tongues, Finnish, and, if I be not mistaken, the Danish. She can read likewise, and in some measure, understands Hebrew and Arabic. She has read and understands all the ancient poets. The modern poets, both Italian and French, she has almost by heart. She hath read many of the ancient Church fathers....

Her memory seems to be more than human. She seems to be ignorant of nothing, and to forget nothing. She tires out daily I know not how many secretaries, to whom she dictates; and corrects, turns over and finishes everything herself. She is so liberal, that if she exceeds the due bounds in anything, it is in making presents. She has called into Sweden the most learned men, and the most excellent artificers from Italy, France and Germany; and dismisses none without large gifts.

She is a most strict observer of justice; she says herself that she very seldom pardoned any criminal that deserved death: but none was executed by her orders for whom she did not shed tears. Her civility is so very extraordinary, that it must be owned not to fall short of her other virtues. All foreigners are witness of this, who come to see her court and are there received in the most obliging and polite manner.

READING 32B

Maxims and Sentences of Christina Queen of Sweden; Being the Employment of Her Leisure Hours[1]

(1753)

Century First

3. Merit is of greater worth than thrones and fortune.

4. Thrones are not worthy of being purchased at the price of crimes.

20. One cannot be happy without being wise, just, and brave.

21. One may render all misfortunes glorious, however great they are.

26. A husband or a wife is a good or an evil that few know how to do without.

37. The greatest pleasure that an elevated station[2] gives is to do good.

41. True opinions, just and magnanimous senti-

---

1 Modernized from Christina, Queen of Sweden, *The Works of Christina Queen of Sweden: Containing Maxims and Sentences in Twelve Centuries, and Reflections on the Life and Actions of Alexander the Great* (London: Printed for D. Wilson and T. Durham..., 1753); facsimile version at hathitrust.org.

2 I.e., one's social rank or position.

ments, and noble actions constitute the glory and happiness of men. All the rest is mere vanity.

43. Merit consists in thinking well, speaking well, and acting well.

46. The heart is made for loving; it must love.

49. People do not always love what they esteem; but they always esteem what they love.

53. Fools are more to be feared than the wicked.

55. There are occasions on which great men weep, without injuring themselves.

59. Fears and weakness are what makes liars.

71. Conscience is the only looking glass that neither flatters nor cheats.

77. Ingratitude ought not to hinder the doing of good.

78. With benefits as with feed-grains, we should throw them about with profusion and at a venture.[1]

82. The world seldom does justice to merit and always flatters good fortune.

83. We should be more parsimonious of our time than of our money.

85. Nourishment, rest, and amusements are equally necessary.

88. Those who amuse themselves too much weary themselves.

92. Reason affords not all the assistance it promises.

100. The body ought to submit. We should treat it like a slave; but like such a slave as deserves charity.

Century II

4. We ought to love elegant things; but we ought to love them reasonably.

5. Men learn at schools everything they ought to forget.

6. It is as shameful to know some things as it is to be ignorant of others.

7. Everything that does not render a man wiser, braver, and happier is useless to him.

8. The sciences are but the pompous titles of human ignorance; we are not more knowing for knowing them.

9. To live well and die well is the science of sciences.

13. To speak well one should speak little.

23. Stupid persons often pass for wise ones.

43. One must have merit and good fortune in order to be at once great and happy.

52. Men always disapprove of what they cannot do themselves.

56. Those that accuse Epicurus of being voluptuous, would be more chaste than they are, and die of hunger, if they lived as he did.

74. We ought to acquit ourselves of our duty, let it cost us ever so much.

---

1 I.e., at random, without a thought.

81. Reading is part of a good man's duty.

90. The knowledge of what is past is of great use with respect to what is to come.

99. We ought to be more satisfied with the merit of another, than with our own.

100. We ought to pardon everything in others, sooner than in ourselves.

Century III

6. We ought to fear more those we love, than those we hate.

17. In the very moment, while justice is being executed upon thieves and robbers, others are cutting the spectators' purses.

23. If kings abuse that right, which they have over their subjects, they are answerable to God only.

28. We ought to esteem and praise our enemies, when they deserve it.

29. We ought to pardon both in friends and enemies, whatever is pardonable.

55. Jealousy injures the person who is capable of it.

69. To avail oneself of the credulity[1] of people is a very useful art.

70. Men are never deceived but by themselves.

72. We should never give any person reason to repent his having obeyed the dictates of his own conscience.

75. We ought to hope least for that which we desire most.

77. Weakness is the greatest of all misfortunes and of all failings.

94. It belongs to the duty of princes to punish with regret and reward with joy.

95. A prince ought seldom to pardon those that deserve punishment.

100. Every man who confesses his fault, and asks forgiveness, deserves it.

Century V

33. We should not be afraid of offending anyone whatsoever. When it is necessary, we should offend.

Century VI

15. Those who are always in tears, are either weak, or wicked.

19. To believe everything is weakness; to believe nothing is folly.

Century X

7. If life is good, we ought to enjoy it with thankfulness; if it is an evil, we ought to suffer it with resignation.

13. Epictetus, who was born a slave and was contented and satisfied with his lot, made his chains more glorious, than many others have done their scepters.

---

1 I.e., to make use of the gullibility of the crowd.

29. Wicked men and tyrants are less to be feared than fools.

31. The hour of death is the hour of truth.

32. We should reckon all mankind as our relations, and the universe our country.

33. We should not think of our particular country, but when the business is to serve it.

35. To enjoy is of greater importance than to know.

36. God alone is the proper object of all the astonishment and all the admiration we are capable of.

38. Even if God had made us, on purpose to burn in hell eternally, he would not therefore less deserve our love and adoration.

40. We ought blindly to submit to the church of Rome; it is the only oracle by which God explains himself.

43. We ought to believe the mysteries of our religion, without delving into them.

47. We ought to humble ourselves before God; both upon the account of what we have done and what we have not done, good as well as evil.

49. To love our enemies is an heroic affection, worthy in some measure of God who commands it.

68. Despair is a kind of pride; it is a secret and criminal presumption.

76. Reason can with difficulty be convinced of the truths of Christianity; the will must subject it to obedience.

Century XII

6. All religions would be holy, if those that were dissatisfied with them were at liberty to leave them. No doubt few would remain; but these few would be holy according to their own rules.

24. Saints and heroes only made in the opinion of the world, are made at a cheap rate.

25. We ought to be saints after the manner of God.

26. God hates everything that is false.

41. The famous maxim, "Know thyself," which some would make the source of all human wisdom, is only the source of human misery.

42. That irrevocable decree imposed on mankind: the hard necessity of knowing their own worthlessness, and of not being able to disguise themselves to themselves.

47. The world ought to be considered as a kind of inn, in which we are to pass but a few moments.

50. It is of no importance how one is born; but of great importance how one dies.

65. To know that God is God, and will be so forever, is sufficient to live and die contented.

66. We can do nothing without God, whatever fine reasonings we use, whatever fine resolutions we put on.

READING 32C

Olympe de Gouges, *Declaration of the Rights of Woman and the Female Citizen*[1]

(1791)

To be decreed by the national assembly in its last meetings or in the next legislature.

Preamble

The mothers, daughters, sisters, and female representatives of the nation, demand to be constituted in a national assembly. Insomuch as ignorance, neglect, and the contempt of woman's rights, are the unique cause of public troubles and of the corruption of government, [they] have determined to expose, in a solemn declaration, the natural, inalienable, and sacred rights of women, so that…the claims of female citizens, based from this point forward on simple and incontestable principles, will promote, always,…the happiness of everyone. As a result, that sex which is superior in beauty and shows more courage in childbearing, acknowledges and declares, in the presence of and under the protection of the Supreme Being, the following rights of Woman and Female citizens.

Article One

Woman is born free and remains equal to man in her rights….

II

The goal of every political association is the safeguarding of the natural and inalienable rights of Women and Men: these rights are liberty, property, security, and resistance against oppression.

III

All sovereignty essentially resides in the Nation, which is only the union of Woman and Man; no body, no individual can exercise an authority other than that which emanates from it directly.

V

The laws of nature and of reason prohibit all behavior that is detrimental to society; anything else, which is not prohibited by these wise and divine laws must be allowed; no one can be constrained to do something other than what these laws require.

VI

Law must be the expression of the general will: all female and male citizens must personally participate, or by their representatives, in its formation; the law must be the same for everyone: all male and female citizens…should be equally admissible for every privilege, position, and public employment, according to their capacities and without any distinctions other than those that derive from their virtues and talents.

VII

No woman is an exception: she can be accused, arrested, incarcerated in those cases set out by the law. Women are to obey, like men, the rigors of the law.

IX

Every woman that has been declared guilty shall be held strictly accountable….

---

1 Original translation of the 1792 publication of the historical document by Louis Groarke. French version available at http://gallica.bnf.fr/ark:/12148/bpt6k426138/f9.image.

X

The law shall respect the opinions and the most basic beliefs of everyone; woman has the right to mount the gallows; she must have equal right to mount the speaker's rostrum....

XI

The free communication of thoughts and of opinions is one of woman's most precious rights; because this liberty can be used to verify and ensure the legitimacy between fathers and children. Every woman citizen should be able to freely proclaim: "I am the mother of your child, of which you are the father"...

XII

The guarantee of woman's rights and the rights of female Citizens... must be instituted for the advantage of everyone and not only for the good of women.

XIII

For the upkeep of public order... the contributions of men and women are equal; woman must take part in all public work and in all difficult tasks; she must, therefore, have an equal part in the distribution of positions, employments, responsibilities, honors, and work.

XVI

Property belongs to both sexes, united or separate; they each have an inviolable and sacred right to property; no one can be deprived of the property to which they have a natural right, unless public necessity, legally formulated, unequivocally requires it, along with the provision of a fair and prior indemnity.

Postamble

... It is necessary to say several words on the troubles that produced... the decree in favor of the colored races in our colonies. Here nature trembles with horror; here reason and humanity have yet to touch the hardest hearts.... The colonists claim to reign as despots on men of which they are the fathers and brothers; and misunderstanding the rights of nature, they trace the source of human rights to the most dilute shade of color in their blood. These inhuman colonists tell themselves: our blood circulates in their veins but we will spill it all, if it is necessary, to satisfy our greed and our blind ambition.... A divine hand seems to grant everywhere an inheritance of freedom: Law alone has the right to repress this liberty, if it degenerates into licence; but it must be equal for all; that is what must be affirmed by the National Assembly in a decree dictated by prudence and by justice.

Sojourner Truth, *Speech Delivered at the Akron, Ohio Convention on Women's Rights*[1]

(1851)

One of the most unique and interesting speeches of the Convention was made by Sojourner Truth, an emancipated slave. It is impossible to transfer it to paper, or convey any adequate idea of the effect it produced upon the audience. Those only can appreciate it who saw her powerful form, her whole-souled, earnest gestures, and listened to her strong and truthful tones. She came forward to the platform and addressing the President said with great simplicity:

May I say a few words? Receiving an affirmative answer, she proceeded; I want to say a few words about this matter. I am for a woman's rights. I have as much muscle as any man, and can do as much work as any man. I have plowed and reaped and husked and chopped and mowed, and can any man do more than that? I have heard much about the sexes being equal; I can carry as much as any man, and can eat as much too, if I can get it. I am as strong as any man that is now.

As for intellect, all I can say is, if woman have a pint and man a quart—why can't she have her little pint full? You need not be afraid to give us our rights for fear we will take too much—for we can't take more than our pint will hold. The poor men seem to be all in confusion, and don't know what to do. Why children, if you have woman's rights give it to her and you will feel better. You will have your own rights, and they won't be so much trouble.

I can't read, but I can hear. I have heard the bible and have learned that Eve caused man to sin. Well if woman upset the world, do give her a chance to set it right side up again. The Lady has spoken about Jesus, how he never spurned woman from him, and she was right. When Lazarus died, Mary and Martha came to him with faith and love and besought him to raise their brother. And Jesus wept—and Lazarus came forth.

And how came Jesus into the world? Through God who created him and woman who bore him. Man, where is your part? But the women are coming up blessed be to God and a few of the men are coming up with them. But man is in a tight place, the poor slave is on him, woman is coming on him, and he is surely between a hawk and a buzzard.

Questions

1. How does the life of Christina of Sweden explode many of the stereotypes that we have about women in the past?
2. Queen Christina was, in some sense, a skeptic and a religious believer. Explain. Do you agree with her attitude towards religious faith?

---

1   Sojourner Truth, *Speech Delivered at the Akron, Ohio Convention on Women's Rights*, as reported by the *Anti-Slavery Bugle* (Salem, Ohio) on June 21, 1851; widely available online.

3. Olympe de Gouges believes the right to free speech was important for improving the situation of women, unwed mothers, and illegitimate children. Explain. Relate this to her personal life-story.

4. Olympe de Gouges writes, "Law alone has the right to repress this liberty, if it degenerates into licence." What is the difference, in the tradition, between liberty and licence?

5. Olympe de Gouges was guillotined during the reign of terror. What lessons can we learn about the excesses of the French Revolution and the life of Olympe de Gouges?

6. Isabella Baumfree wrote under the pseudonym Sojourner Truth. Why do you think she changed her name? Would you ever change your name? If so, why?

7. Compare and contrast the views and lives of Queen Christina, Olympe de Gouges, and Sojourner Truth. How do they differ? How are they the same?

Suggested Readings

Much of the literature on Queen Christina focuses on her flamboyant life rather than her moral thought. The best scholarly material on her philosophy is in French, the language she herself used for her philosophical labors. Two French-language editions make her work available in a contemporary format: Jean-François de Raymond's *Apologies: Christine de Suède* [*In Defense of Christina of Sweden*] (1994), and Chantal Thomas's collection, *Maximes* (1996). A very old (1753) English translation entitled *Works of Christina, Queen of Sweden, Containing Maxims and Sentences, in Twelve Centuries: And Reflections on the Actions of Alexander the Great; First Translation from the French* is available online. Susanna Ackerman presents an up-to-date English discussion of Queen Christina's philosophy and its influences in *Queen Christina of Sweden and Her Circle: The Transformation of a Seventeenth-Century Philosophical Libertine* (1991).

The primary source material on Olympe de Gouges is, obviously, in French. Most of her writing would be classified as literature rather than philosophy. The Bibliothèque nationale de France (French National Library) has an extensive collection of her original writings available for free online at bnf.fr. The following site has several English translations and a generous amount of background material: www.olympedegouges.eu/departdenecker.php.

Sojourner Truth was not a writer but she dictated her memoirs to her friend Olive Gilbert and produced a book with added material, which she sold to support herself and her activism. Penguin Classics has published an enlarged contemporary reprint (1998) with a helpful introduction and notes by historian Nell Irvin Painter. The original title of the definitive 1884 edition is informative: *Narrative of Sojourner Truth; A Bondswoman of Olden Time, Emancipated by the New York Legislature in the Early Part of the Present Century; With a History of Her Labors and Correspondence Drawn from Her "Book of Life;" Also, a Memorial Chapter, Giving the Particulars of Her Last Illness and Death*. Dover Publications has also published a very inexpensive thrift edition (1997).

Chapter 33

Pessimism

Arthur Schopenhauer (1788–1860) was a German philosopher, a pessimist with an interest in Eastern philosophical sources, who brought European idealism and Eastern religious and philosophical thought together in a comprehensive metaphysical theory. Although he is usually described as an "idealist," it seems more accurate to simply say that he rejected the ultimate reality of material phenomena. Like Kant and Hegel, Schopenhauer wanted to provide a complete philosophical account of being.

Schopenhauer was born into a wealthy family. When he was still an adolescent, his father gave him a choice. He could enter a "gymnasium"[1] and prepare for university, or accompany his father and the family on a tour of Europe, and then enter business as a merchant. He chose the second option, but changed his mind at nineteen, after his father's apparent suicide. He then turned his attention to his studies with the idea of following an academic career. Schopenhauer was a brilliant student but his relationships with his professors and mentors, such as Johann Wolfgang von Goethe, were tainted by "attitude" issues.

Over time, Schopenhauer took a wide selection of courses at the University of Göttingen and the University of Berlin, eventually receiving a doctorate in philosophy *in absentia* from the University of Jena. He then embarked on a disappointing university career. Much of the failure seems to have been a product of his own vanity: when he first lectured at the University of Berlin, he scheduled his lectures so as to compete with the lectures of G.W.F. Hegel, who was exceedingly popular. As a result, he had almost no students. A second stint at the university was also a failure.

Schopenhauer never married and seems to have had strained relations with women. He frequently quarreled with his mother Johanna, who became a prolific author and presided over a celebrated Weimar literary salon. Schopenhauer felt that his mother was a social climber, who had neglected her marital and motherly duties, and accused her of being the cause of his father's apparent suicide. She finally severed their relationship. In Berlin, he was convicted of injuring a middle-aged seamstress, who lived in the same boarding house, because she was interrupting his academic work. Required to pay her a stipend, he wrote a Latin pun on her death certificate: *Obit anus, abit onus* ("Dead woman, lifts burden").

---

1 I.e., a strongly academic high school, preparatory for university.

In spite of the setbacks, Schopenhauer refused to give up his philosophical aspirations. Having carefully arranged his financial affairs, he moved to Frankfurt in 1833, where he lived a scholarly life until his death, twenty-seven years later. He lived quietly but followed a firm routine, studying in the morning and playing the flute, after which he went out for dinner, walked with his poodles, and attended cultural events. In his will, he donated his estate to charity, for the purpose of assisting disabled Prussian soldiers and the families of soldiers killed in the 1848 revolution.

Schopenhauer had already completed the first edition of his master-work *The World as Will and Representation* by the time he was thirty (1819). Two further editions appeared during his lifetime (1844, 1859). Although Schopenhauer's work was gaining in prominence when he died, he was largely ignored by the academic community, and it must be wondered if pessimism provided him with the emotional and psychological means to deal with the personal and professional disappointments in his life.

Schopenhauer's moral philosophy is nevertheless grounded in his metaphysics, which combines different strands of German philosophy with the anti-materialism in Indian philosophy and the Vedic tradition. In *The Basis of Morality* (1840), he rejects Kant's formulation of the categorical imperative as a theological holdover, and bases his own ethical system on a kind of intuitionism, which begins with our intuitive perception of goodness, rather than reason.

Metaphysically, Schopenhauer argues that individual human beings are only particular manifestations of a cosmological source of energy that he identifies as "the Will" or "the Will as thing-in-itself." Suffering arises out of the objectification and fragmentation of this all-inclusive energy, which can be seen in the pitting of each individual will against other wills in a restless struggle for domination. The solution is to break through the illusion of individuality, so that we feel empathy for other people and other sentient beings.

Schopenhauer's moral philosophy is informed by an unusual range of sources. Although he disdained "optimistic" religions such as Protestantism, Judaism, and Islam, he had a high opinion of Buddhism, of Vedanta Hinduism, and of the monastic strands of Roman Catholicism. His interest in Indian thought seems to unite with a natural skepticism of thought and a rejection of the materialism in the scientific and Enlightenment tradition.

The term "pessimism" is easily misunderstood and should be distinguished from "nihilism," which usually refers to the philosophical or psychological rejection of existence. Schopenhauer counsels resignation, rather than a rejection of life, and recognizes that we enjoy moments of happiness. The wisdom of pessimism is that it teaches us, he says, quoting Plato, that "nothing in human affairs is worth any great anxiety."

Like the Epicureans, he argued that happiness should be understood in a negative way, that is, as the avoidance and elimination of pain. In his *Aphorisms*, he quotes from Aristotle's *Nicomachean Ethics*: "not pleasure, but freedom from pain, is what the wise man will aim at" (VII.12). The pursuit of pleasure is illusory and runs us the risk of meeting pain, which is real. Instead of trying to impose our will on others, Schopenhauer claims that we should devote ourselves to the pursuit of wisdom, to the appreciation and contemplation of art, and to the practice of asceticism.

Like Jean Paul Sartre, Schopenhauer seems to locate unhappiness in other people. As a result, he advises us to be self-sufficient. "Hence Aristotle's remark—to be happy means to be self-sufficient—cannot be too often repeated." We must find our happiness in ourselves. Schopenhauer rejects public displays—"ships festooned and hung with pennants," "beating of drums and blowing of trumpets, shouting and applauding" as a show, designed to fool us into thinking there is "joy" where it does not exist.

The main argument against Schopenhauer's ethics is that it reduces us to inaction and removes us from any participation in the affairs of the world. The nature of Schopenhauer's views tended to remove him from the kinds of issues that normally arise in practical ethics. There is more than a little arrogance in his comments on ordinary people; he nevertheless embraced the liberal principle that we should refrain from harming others and was an early champion of the ethical treatment of animals. He also argued against suicide, which he saw as a violent attempt to impose one's own will on reality, and was interested in parapsychology.

Schopenhauer disparaged marriage and rejected the equality of the sexes. In a notorious essay, entitled "Of Women," he argues that women are the weaker sex and therefore have no choice but to defend themselves with all the "arts of dissimulation." He believes that women are more compassionate than men and should be consulted in the affairs of life, but have little interest in "abstract principles of thought" or "fixed rules of conduct."

In the first reading, from *The Basis of Morality* (*Über die Grundlage der Moral*, 1840), Schopenhauer argues that the moral value of our actions, like the virtues of justice and loving-kindness, have their roots in compassion. The second reading is from an essay entitled "On the Sufferings of the World" and sets out the basic outlines of pessimism. Life is suffering. The saving grace, ethically, is that this insight teaches us to be compassionate to others. The third reading contains a few examples of Schopenhauer's aphorisms, which recalls the early wisdom tradition. These aphorisms highlight the literary nature of Schopenhauer's work, which is much broader in its range than the philosophy of his academic contemporaries and displays his willingness to draw empirical inferences, like the ancients and earlier thinkers, from his own observations of the ordinary experiences of life.

READING 33A

Arthur Schopenhauer, *Über die Grundlage der Moral* (*The Basis of Morality*)[1]

(1840)

Part III. The Founding of Ethics

CHAPTER V. STATEMENT AND PROOF OF THE ONLY TRUE MORAL INCENTIVE

The preceding considerations, which were unavoidably necessary in order to clear the ground, now enable me to indicate the true incentive which underlies all acts of real moral worth. The seriousness, and indisputable genuineness, with which we shall find it is distinguished, removes it far indeed from the hair-splittings, subtleties, sophisms, assertions formulated out of airy nothings, and *a priori* soap-bubbles, which all systems up to the present have tried to make at once the source of moral conduct and the basis of Ethics.

This incentive I shall not put forward as an hypothesis to be accepted or rejected, as one pleases; I shall actually prove that it is the only possible one. But as this demonstration requires several fundamental truths to be borne in mind, the reader's attention is first called to certain propositions which... may properly be considered as axioms...

(1) No action can take place without a sufficient motive; as little as a stone can move without a sufficient push or pull...

(3) Whatever moves the Will,—this, and this alone, implies the sense of weal and woe,[2] in the widest sense of the term; and conversely, weal and woe signify "that which is in conformity with, or which is contrary to, a Will." Hence every motive must have a connection with weal and woe....

From these propositions the following conclusion is obvious: the weal and woe, which (according to our third axiom) must, as its ultimate object, lie at the root of everything done, or left undone, is either that of the doer himself, or that of some other person, whose role with reference to the action is passive. Conduct in the first case is necessarily egoistic, as it is impelled by an interested motive.

And this is not only true when men... plainly shape their acts for their own profit and advantage; it is equally true when from anything done we expect some benefit to ourselves, no matter how remote, whether in this or in another world. Nor is it less the fact when our honor, our good name, or the wish to win the respect of someone, the sympathy of the lookers on, etc., is the object we have in view; or when our intention is to uphold a rule of conduct, which, if generally followed, would occasionally be useful to ourselves, for instance, the principle of justice, of mutual succor and aid, and so forth.... In short, one may make the ultimate incentive to an action what one pleases; it will always turn out, no matter by how circuitous a path, that in the last resort what affects the actual weal and woe of the agent himself is the real motive; consequently, what he does is egoistic, and therefore without moral worth.

---

1 Arthur Schopenhauer, *The Basis of Morality* (*Über die Grundlage der Moral*, 1840) Prize Essay on the Basis of Morality for the Danish Royal Society of Sciences. From Arthur Schopenhauer, *The Basis of Morality*, translated with an Introduction and Notes by Arthur Brodrick Bullock (London: Swan Sonnenschein & Co., 1903). Available at Project Gutenberg at www.gutenberg.org.

2 Weal means well-being, prosperity, or happiness; and woe, troubles, great sorrow or distress.

There is only a single case in which this fails to happen: namely, when the ultimate incentive for doing something, or leaving it undone, is precisely and exclusively centered in the weal and woe of someone else, who plays a passive part; that is to say, when the person on the active side, by what he does, or omits to do, simply and solely regards the weal and woe of another and has absolutely no other object than to benefit him, by keeping harm from his door, or, it may be, even by affording help, assistance, and relief. It is this aim alone that gives to what is done, or left undone, the stamp of moral worth; which is thus seen to depend exclusively on the circumstance that the act is carried out, or omitted, purely for the benefit and advantage of another....

But if what I do is to take place solely on account of someone else, then it follows that his weal and woe must directly constitute my motive, just as, ordinarily, my own weal and woe form it. This narrows the limits of our problem, which may now be stated as follows: How is it possible that another's weal and woe should influence my will directly, that is, exactly in the same way as otherwise my own move it? How can that which affects another for good or bad become my immediate motive and actually sometimes assume such importance that it more or less supplants my own interests, which are, as a rule, the single source of the incentives that appeal to me? Obviously, only because that other person becomes the ultimate object of my will, precisely as usually I myself am that object; in other words, because I directly desire weal, and not woe, for him, just as habitually I do for myself.

This, however, necessarily implies that I suffer with him, and feel his woe, exactly as in most cases I feel only mine, and therefore desire his weal as immediately as at other times I desire only my own. But, for this to be possible, I must in some way or other be identified with him; that is, the difference between myself and him, which is the precise *raison d'être* of my Egoism, must be removed, at least to a certain extent. Now, since I do not live in his skin,

there remains only the knowledge, that is, the mental picture, I have of him, as the possible means whereby I can so far identify myself with him, that my action declares the difference to be practically effaced.

The process here analyzed is not a dream, a fancy floating in the air; it is perfectly real, and by no means infrequent. It is what we see every day—the phenomenon of Compassion; in other words, the direct participation, independent of all ulterior considerations, in the sufferings of another, leading to sympathetic assistance in the effort to prevent or remove them; whereon in the last resort all satisfaction and all well-being and happiness depend. It is this Compassion alone which is the real basis of the cardinal virtues of voluntary justice and all genuine loving-kindness. Only so far as an action springs therefrom, has it moral value; and all conduct that proceeds from any other motive whatever has none. When once compassion is stirred within me by another's pain, then his weal and woe go straight to my heart, exactly in the same way, if not always to the same degree, as otherwise I feel only my own. Consequently, the difference between myself and him is no longer an absolute one....

CHAPTER VI. THE VIRTUE OF JUSTICE

If we look more closely at this process called Compassion, which we have shown to be the primary ethical phenomenon, we remark at once that there are two distinct degrees in which another's suffering may become directly my motive, that is, may urge me to do something, or to leave it undone. The first degree of Compassion is seen when, by counteracting egoistic and malicious motives, it keeps me from bringing pain on another and from becoming myself the cause of trouble, which so far does not exist. The other higher degree is manifested, when it works positively and incites me to active help.

The distinction between the so-called duties of law and duties of virtue, better described as the duties arising from the cardinal virtues of justice and loving-kindness, which was effected by Kant in such a forced and artificial manner, here results entirely of itself; whence the correctness of the principle is attested. It is the natural, unmistakable, and sharp separation between negative and positive, between doing no harm, and helping....

It is hoped that these considerations have made it clear that, however contrary appearances may be at first sight, yet undoubtedly justice, as a genuine and voluntary virtue has its origin in Compassion....

It will now be seen that injustice or wrong always consists in working harm on another. Therefore, the conception of wrong is positive, and antecedent to the conception of right, which is negative, and simply denotes the actions performable without injury to others; in other words, without wrong being done. It is an easy inference that right also includes whatever is done for the purpose of warding off whatever works harm on ourselves or others...

The negative character of justice is...established...by the familiar formula: "Give to each one his own." Now, there is no need to give a man his own, if he has it. The real meaning is therefore: "Take from none his own." And since the requirements of justice are merely negative and merely protect us from wrong, they may be such as to justify the use of force, through the coercive apparatus of the state, whose sole *raison d'être* is to protect its subjects, individually from each other and collectively from external foes.

It is true that a few German would-be philosophers of this venal age[1] wish to distort the state into an institution for the spread of morality, education, and edifying instruction. But such a view contains, lurking in the background, the Jesuitical aim of doing away with personal freedom and individual development and of making men mere wheels in a huge Chinese governmental and religious machine.... Frederick the Great[2] showed that he at least never wished to tread it, when he said: "In my land every one shall care for his own salvation, as he himself thinks best...."

We have now seen that 'wrong' and 'right' are convertible synonyms of 'to do harm' and 'to refrain from doing it,' and that under 'right' is included the warding off of injury from oneself. It will be obvious that these conceptions are independent of, and antecedent to, all positive legislation. There is, therefore, a pure ethical right, or natural right, and a pure doctrine of right, detached from all positive statutes....

CHAPTER VII. THE VIRTUE OF LOVING-KINDNESS

It is true that loving-kindness has existed at all times in practice and in fact; but it was reserved for Christianity...to theoretically formulate and expressly advance it not only as a virtue, but as the queen of all; and to extend it even to enemies. We are thinking of course only of Europe. For in Asia, a thousand years before, the boundless love of one's neighbor had been prescribed and taught, as well as practiced: the Vedas are full of it; while in the Dharma-Śāstra, Itihāsa, and Purāna it constantly recurs, to say nothing of the preaching of Śakya-muni, the Buddha. And to be quite accurate we must admit that there are traces to be found among the Greeks and Romans of a recommendation to follow loving-kindness....

It has therefore been demonstrated that the sense of Compassion, however much its origin is shrouded in mystery, is the one and sole cause whereby the suffering I see in another, of itself and as such, becomes directly my motive; and we have seen that the first stage of this process is negative. The second degree is sharply distinguished from the first, through the positive character of the actions resulting therefrom; for at this point Compassion does more than keep

---

1 Schopenhauer is clearly referring to Georg Wilhelm Friedrich Hegel.

2 I.e., Frederick II (1712–86), King of Prussia from 1740 to 1786.

me back from injuring my neighbor; it impels me to help him....

So that in this direct suffering with another, which rests on no arguments and requires none, is found the one simple origin of the cardinal virtue of loving-kindness, *caritas*, *agapē* in other words, that virtue whose rule is: *Omnes, quantum potes, juva* (help all people, as far as lies in your power)....

Arthur Schopenhauer, "On the Sufferings of the World"[1]

(1893)

There is so much suffering in our lives that, if our life has any other purpose, it clearly fails to meet that purpose. It is absurd to look upon the enormous amount of pain that abounds everywhere in the world and originates in needs and necessities inseparable from life itself, and suggest that it serves no purpose at all and is the result of mere chance....

I know of no greater absurdity than that propounded by most systems of philosophy in declaring that evil is negative in its character.[2] Evil is in fact what is positive; it makes its own existence felt.... It is the good which is negative; in other words, happiness and satisfaction always imply some desire fulfilled, some state of pain brought to an end.

This explains the fact that we generally find pleasure to be not nearly so pleasant as we expected, and pain very much more painful. The pleasure in this world, it has been said, outweighs the pain; or, at any rate, there is an even balance between the two. If the reader wishes to see shortly whether this statement is true, let him compare the respective feelings of two animals, one of which is engaged in eating the other....

We are like lambs in a field, disporting themselves under the eye of the butcher, who chooses out first one and then another for his prey. So it is that in our good days we are all unconscious of the evil Fate may have presently in store for us—sickness, poverty, mutilation, loss of sight or reason....

Certain it is that work, worry, labor and trouble, form the lot of almost all men their whole life long. But if all wishes were fulfilled as soon as they arose, how would men occupy their lives? What would they do with their time? If the world were a paradise of luxury and ease, a land flowing with milk and honey, where every Jack obtained his Jill at once and without any difficulty, men would either die of boredom or hang themselves; or there would be wars, massacres, and murders; so that in the end mankind

---

1 Selections from Arthur Schopenhauer, "On the Sufferings of the World," from *Parerga und Paralipomena* ("Appendices and Omissions") in T. Bailey Saunders, trans., *The Essays of Arthur Schopenhauer: Studies in Pessimism* (London: Swan Sonnenschein & Co., 1893). Available online at Project Gutenberg at www.gutenberg.org. In this excerpt, Schopenhauer sets out his pessimism, which refers to his belief that life is inherently unhappy. This is a descriptive rather than a prescriptive belief, i.e., a belief about how things are, not about how we ought to live.

2 I.e., that evil is the privation of good.

would inflict more suffering on itself than it has now to accept at the hands of Nature.

In early youth, as we contemplate our coming life, we are like children in a theatre before the curtain is raised, sitting there in high spirits and eagerly waiting for the play to begin. It is a blessing that we do not know what is really going to happen. Could we foresee it, there are times when children might seem like innocent prisoners, condemned, not to death, but to life, and as yet all unconscious of what their sentence means....

I shall be told, I suppose, that my philosophy is comfortless—because I speak the truth; and people prefer to be assured that everything the Lord has made is good. Go to the priests, then, and leave philosophers in peace! At any rate, do not ask us to accommodate our doctrines to the lessons you have been taught. That is what those rascals of sham philosophers will do for you. Ask them for any doctrine you please, and you will get it. Your University professors are bound to preach optimism; and it is an easy and agreeable task to upset their theories.

I have reminded the reader that every state of welfare, every feeling of satisfaction, is negative in its character; that is to say, it consists in freedom from pain, which is the positive element of existence. It follows, therefore, that the happiness of any given life is to be measured, not by its joys and pleasures, but by the extent to which it has been free from suffering—from positive evil....

If you want a safe compass to guide you through life, and to banish all doubt as to the right way of looking at it, you cannot do better than accustom yourself to regard this world as a penitentiary, a sort of a penal colony....

Amongst the Christian Fathers, Origen,[1] with praiseworthy courage, took this view, which is further justified by certain objective theories of life. I refer not to my own philosophy alone, but to the wisdom of all ages, as expressed in Brahmanism and Buddhism, and in the sayings of Greek philosophers like Empedocles and Pythagoras; as also by Cicero, in his remark that the wise men of old used to teach that we come into this world to pay the penalty of crime committed in another state of existence—a doctrine which formed part of the initiation into the mysteries....

If you accustom yourself to this view of life you will regulate your expectations accordingly, and cease to look upon all its disagreeable incidents, great and small, its sufferings, its worries, its misery, as anything unusual or irregular; nay, you will find that everything is as it should be, in a world where each of us pays the penalty of existence in his own peculiar way....

Pardon's the word to all! Whatever folly men commit, be their shortcomings or their vices what they may, let us exercise forbearance; remembering that when these faults appear in others, it is our follies and vices that we behold. They are the shortcomings of humanity, to which we belong; whose faults, one and all, we share; yes, even those very faults at which we now wax so indignant, merely because they have not yet appeared in ourselves. They are faults that do not lie on the surface. But they exist down there in the depths of our nature; and should anything call them forth, they will come and show themselves, just as we now see them in others.

The advantage of this view is evident, since the conviction that the world and man is something that had better not have been, is of a kind to fill us with indulgence towards one another. Nay, from this point of view, we might well consider the proper form of address to be, not "Sir," but "my fellow-sufferer"! This may perhaps sound strange, but it is in keeping with the facts; it puts others in a right light; and it reminds us of that which is after all the most necessary thing in life—the tolerance, patience, regard, and love of neighbor, of which everyone stands in need, and which, therefore, every man owes to his fellow.

---

1 Influential third-century Christian theologian.

Arthur Schopenhauer, "Aphorismen zur Lebensweisheit" ("Aphorisms on the Wisdom of Life")[1]

(1896)

General Rules

SECTION 3

Men of any worth or value soon come to see that they are in the hands of Fate, and gratefully submit to be molded by its teachings. They recognize that the fruit of life is experience, and not happiness; they become accustomed and content to exchange hope for insight; and, in the end, they can say, with Petrarch,[2] that all they care for is to learn...

Our Relation to Ourselves

SECTION 9

It is really a very risky, nay, a fatal thing, to be sociable; because it means contact with natures, the great majority of which are bad morally, and dull or perverse, intellectually. To be unsociable is not to care about such people; and to have enough in oneself to dispense with the necessity of their company is a great piece of good fortune; because almost all our sufferings spring from having to do with other people; and that destroys the peace of mind, which, as I have said, comes next after health in the elements of happiness....

Society is in this respect like a fire—the wise man warming himself at a proper distance from it; not coming too close, like the fool, who, on getting scorched, runs away and shivers in solitude, loud in his complaint that the fire burns.

SECTION 13

If you hold small objects close to your eyes, you limit your field of vision and shut out the world. And, in the same way, the people or the things which stand nearest, even though they are of the very smallest consequence, are apt to claim an amount of attention much beyond their due, occupying us disagreeably and leaving no room for serious thoughts and affairs of importance. We ought to work against this tendency.

Our Relation to Others

SECTION 28

Men are like children in that, if you spoil them, they become naughty. Therefore, it is well not to be too indulgent or charitable with anyone. You may take it as a general rule that you will not lose a friend by refusing him a loan, but that you are very likely to do so by granting it; and, for similar reasons, you will not readily alienate people by being somewhat proud and careless in your behavior; but if you are very kind and complaisant towards them, you will

---

1 Arthur Schopenhauer, "Aphorismen zur Lebensweisheit" ("Aphorisms on the Wisdom of Life") from volume 1 of *Parerga und Paralipomena* ("Appendices and Omissions") (1851), in T. Bailey Saunders, trans. [and ed.], *Counsels and Maxims: Being the Second Part of Schopenhauer's Aphorismen zur Lebensweisheit*, 2nd. ed. (London: Swan Sonnenschein & Co., 1891). Available at Project Gutenberg at www.gutenberg.org.

2 Fourteenth-century Italian scholar and poet, an important influence on Renaissance humanistic thought.

often make them arrogant and intolerable, and so a breach will ensue....

And in this view it is advisable to let everyone of your acquaintance—whether man or woman—feel now and then that you could very well dispense with their company. This will consolidate friendship. Nay, with most people there will be no harm in occasionally mixing a grain of disdain with your treatment of them; that will make them value your friendship all the more.

SECTION 36

Politeness is a tacit agreement that people's miserable defects, whether moral or intellectual, shall on either side be ignored and not made the subject of reproach; and since these defects are thus rendered somewhat less obtrusive, the result is mutually advantageous....

Wax, a substance naturally hard and brittle, can be made soft by the application of a little warmth, so that it will take any shape you please. In the same way, by being polite and friendly, you can make people pliable and obliging, even though they are apt to be crabbed and malevolent. Hence politeness is to human nature what warmth is to wax.

SECTION 41

If you have reason to suspect that a person is telling you a lie, look as though you believed every word he said. This will give him courage to go on; he will become more vehement in his assertions, and in the end betray himself.

Worldly Fortune

SECTION 50

Do not omit to sacrifice to evil spirits. What I mean is that a man should not hesitate about spending time, trouble, and money, or giving up his comfort, or restricting his aims and denying himself, if he can thereby shut the door on the possibility of misfortune.... The rule I am giving is best exemplified in the practice of insurance—a public sacrifice made on the altar of anxiety. Therefore, take out your policy of insurance!

Questions

1. In *The Basis of Morality*, Schopenhauer argues that Kant's ethics "turns out to be nothing else than Egoism, the latter being the secret interpreter of the direction which it contains." Why does he say this? Where does moral worth come from, in Schopenhauer's view?

2. What is the relationship between compassion, justice, and loving-kindness?

3. What does Schopenhauer mean when he says that the requirements of justice are only negative?

4. How does Schopenhauer express the rule—i.e., the duty—of loving-kindness?

5. Do you agree with Schopenhauer's moral pessimism? Is suffering the major element in life? How should we respond morally, if he is right?

6. Compare Schopenhauer's idea of happiness with the idea of happiness in Aristotle or Epicurus.

7. In one passage, Schopenhauer tells us that human beings are like porcupines on a cold day, who try to huddle together for warmth. Eventually they discover that the best solution is to remain a little distance from one another, so that they do not prick each other with their quills. Do you think this is a good metaphor for human relations? How does morality come into it?

Suggested Readings

Schopenhauer was a vivid writer and a master of aphorisms. His magnum opus is *The World as Will and Representation* (*Die Welt als Wille und Vorstellung*, 1819, 1844, 1859). There is a readily available translation by E.F.J. Payne (1969) and scholarly editions from the *Longman Library of Primary Sources in Philosophy* and Cambridge University Press.

Schopenhauer published *The Two Fundamental Problems of Ethics* (*Die beiden Grundprobleme der Ethik*) in 1841, which contains "On Freedom of the Human Will" and "On the Basis of Morality." There is a recent translation by Christopher Janaway. At the end of his life, Schopenhauer also published a codicil to his work entitled *Parerga und Paralipomena* (*Appendices and Omissions*, 1851), which provides a convenient introduction to his work.

For general sources on Schopenhauer, see Julian Young, *Schopenhauer* (2005); Barbara Hannan, *The Riddle of the World: A Reconsideration of Schopenhauer's Philosophy* (2009); and Alex Neill and Christopher Janaway, eds., *Schopenhauer's Philosophy of Value* (2010).

The literature on Schopenhauer has focused on the role of metaphysics and compassion in his ethics, often comparing him to Kant and Ludwig Wittgenstein. Paul F.H. Lauxtermann (2000) brings in Kant and Goethe; Milan Vukomanovic (2004) brings in Wittgenstein and Buddhism. K. Hamburger (1985) has compared Rousseau and Schopenhauer.

On applied issues, see Dale Jacquette, "Schopenhauer on the Ethics of Suicide" (2000), and G.E. Varner, "The Schopenhauerian Challenge in Environmental Ethics" (1985).

Chapter 34

Theistic Existentialism

Søren Aabye Kierkegaard (1813–55) was a Danish writer who was originally trained as a theologian and philosopher. He is regarded as one of the great stylists in the Danish language. In his literary work, he developed a narrative form of moral inquiry, which uses a variety of literary techniques to raise searching questions about the meaning of modern life.

Kierkegaard was born and lived most of his life in Copenhagen. His father, Michael Pedersen Kierkegaard, was a wealthy cloth merchant who entered into a second marriage with the household maid, Ane Sørensdatter Lund. A sternly religious man, he believed that his children were cursed because he had sinned, both by cursing God as a young man and by having carried on a sexual relationship with his wife before their marriage. As a result, he persisted in the gloomy belief that his children were fated to die before they were thirty-three years old, Jesus's age when he was crucified.

These dark suggestions left their mark on Kierkegaard, who was known for his caustic wit and his introspective, overly-sensitive personality. He nevertheless received a good classical high-school education and went on to study theology, philosophy, and literature at the University of Copenhagen. Despite some youthful extravagances, he finished his undergraduate degree in 1838. His father died the same year. Kierkegaard seemed to be destined for a career and family life as a Lutheran pastor. In 1840, he entered the seminary and became engaged to a woman named Regina Olsen. The following year, to the surprise of his acquaintances, he suddenly broke off the engagement.

Kierkegaard never married and continued to harbor deep feelings for Regina throughout the rest of life. There is much speculation about the break with his former fiancée. It is nevertheless clear that he found the thought of the obligations of family life overwhelming, and realized that he could do what he wanted on his inheritance, as long as he did not marry. It has also been suggested that he felt he was too melancholy for married life and that he was haunted by some hidden sin, which he refused to communicate to others.

Kierkegaard defended his Master's dissertation at the University of Copenhagen the same year. The thesis demonstrates his interest in the dialectical method—which he seems to have internalized in his writing—and was entitled *On the Concept of Irony with Continual Reference to Socrates*. Kierkegaard was allowed to submit his dissertation in

Danish, but only on condition that he defend it in Latin, which was still the language of scholarship. It is said that the examination session lasted seven-and-a-half hours.

After he had obtained his Master's degree, Kierkegaard turned his attention to his literary career. Although he took several short trips to Berlin for further study, he spent almost all of his adult life in Copenhagen. Without regular employment or a family, he spent his days strolling the city streets, writing in the evening and at night. Although he developed a reputation as a noteworthy intellectual, he became embroiled in at least two controversies.

In 1846, Kierkegaard was offended by a perfunctory review of one of his books in a muck-raking society newspaper called *The Corsair*, and challenged it to cover his literary career. The paper responded by ridiculing Kierkegaard over a period of several months. It belittled his odd appearance and eccentric habits, and published caricatures, one of which depicted him sitting on the back of Regina Olsen with a cane in his hand. As a result, he became a laughing stock and was taunted by children in the streets, who gleefully chanted "either-or, either-or, either-or" (the title of his first book) when they saw him approaching.

There was a more principled contretemps in 1854, when one of Kierkegaard's former professors was appointed a bishop. Stung by the politics of the appointment, he attacked the official status of the Lutheran Church (the "Danish People's Church") in the Danish state. In a series of vitriolic newspaper editorials and pamphlets (now collected in a book, *Attack Upon Christendom*), he criticized the unchristian orientation of what he called "Official Christianity" or "Christendom." This reflects the intensity of Kierkegaard's own religious views, which were based on individual conversion and a sincere commitment to the divine.

Although Kierkegaard had some success, the reality is that he was forced to pay for the publication of most of his books. Some of his major works include *Either/Or* (1843), *Fear and Trembling* (1843), *Eighteen Upbuilding Discourses* (1843–45), *Concluding Unscientific Postscript* (1846), *The Sickness Unto Death* (1849), *The Lilies of the Field and the Birds of the Air: Three Devotional Discourses* (1849), *Training in Christianity* (1850), and *What Christ Judges of Official Christianity* (1855). The titles reflect the moral and religious orientation of his thought.

Kierkegaard's books do not fit into a standard format. They contain theological and philosophical speculation, side by side with narrative and fictional elements. Kierkegaard often strings together separate texts in one continuous narrative. His philosophical reflections take the form of aphorisms, diary entries, stories, sermons, essays, letters, and even newspaper articles. It is a provocative and fractured form of analysis, which nevertheless has many of the elements that recall the earlier wisdom tradition.

Kierkegaard is difficult to catalogue, philosophically, but is often thought of as the first existentialist. This probably reflects the intense sense of alienation in his work, which he seems to be struggling to repair. In his books, he is continually searching for meaning in the experience of ordinary existence, out of which he constructs a compelling intellectual narrative that defies any straightforward scientific or logical analysis.

The basic philosophical methodology in Kierkegaard's work is clearly a reaction against the academic conventions of his time. Kierkegaard rejected the Hegelianism then fashionable. Rather than provide a universal, overarching theory that contains a rational explanation of essentially everything in a single system, he turns to a kind of philosophical "impressionism," a chronicling of ordinary experience based on character types and an ironic, mordant analysis of modern culture. This has many elements of the practical ethics in the early and ancient tradition.

Kierkegaard is often seen as someone struggling to assert the viability of the religious impulse in the modern world, without regard to its logical, material, or scientific credibility. Although he did not use the phrase, he is famous for postulating a "leap of faith" in response to the stubborn rationalism that we find in Kant and Hegel. His work rejects the idea that logic and abstract reason are sufficient to grasp the kind of metaphysical or cosmological reality that we find in God.

In the two readings, Kierkegaard distinguishes between three levels of human achievement: the aesthetic, the ethical, and the religious. In *Either/Or*, the first reading, he explores life from the perspective of someone who sees life as a work of art. In doing so, he presents the papers of an alienated young man, dubbed "A," who tries to solve the problem of boredom by inventing a method of diversion that he calls the "rotation of crops."

The second excerpt, in the same reading, contains the letters from "B," a judge, to A, which take the form of a defense of conjugal love over romantic love. Although romantic love is intense, it is also ephemeral. The love between spouses has a continuity through time that provides a stable identity for the individual. In considering the nature of ethical commitment, Judge B insists on the universal character of the ethical and the inward origins of ethical duty.

In the second reading, from *Fear and Trembling*, Kierkegaard moves to the religious, through the vehicle of the Biblical story of Abraham, who was "tempted" by God to sacrifice his son. Kierkegaard points to an even higher level of religious existence, which paradoxically transcends our ordinary notions of morality in favor of a particular relationship with the absolute, which represents the divine.

Søren Kierkegaard, *Either/Or: A Fragment of Life*[1]

(*Enten – Eller*, originally published under the pseudonym Victor Eremita[2] in 1843)

Part I, Containing A's Papers

DIAPSALMATA (MUSICAL INTERLUDES) *AD SE IPSUM* (TO HIMSELF)

What is a poet? A poet is an unhappy being whose heart is torn by secret sufferings, but whose lips are so strangely formed that when the sighs and the cries escape them, they sound like beautiful music. His fate is like that of the unfortunate victims whom the tyrant Phalaris imprisoned in a brazen bull,[3] and slowly tortured over a steady fire; their cries could not reach the tyrant's ears so as to strike terror into his heart; when they reached his ears they sounded like sweet music. And men crowd about the poet and say to him: "Sing for us soon again"; that is as much as to say: "…the music is delicious."…

I do not care for anything. I do not care to ride, for the exercise is too violent. I do not care to walk, walking is too strenuous. I do not care to lie down, for I should either have to remain lying, and I do not care to do that, or I should have to get up again, and I do not care to do that either. *Summa summarum*:[4] I do not care at all….

In addition to the rest of the numerous circle of my acquaintances, I still have one intimate confi-dant—my melancholy. In the midst of my joy, in the midst of my work, he beckons to me and calls me aside…My melancholy is the most faithful mistress I have known; what wonder, then, that I love in return….

I say of my sorrow what the Englishman says of his house: my sorrow is my castle….

I feel as if I were a piece in a game of chess, when my opponent says of it: That piece cannot be moved….

I feel like a letter printed backward in the line…

THE ROTATION METHOD: AN ESSAY IN THE THEORY OF SOCIAL PRUDENCE

…Boredom is the root of all evil….

The history of this can be traced from the very beginning of the world. The gods were bored, and so they created man. Adam was bored because he was alone, and so Eve was created. Thus boredom entered the world, and increased in proportion to the increase of population. Adam was bored alone; then Adam and Eve were bored together; then Adam and Eve and Cain and Abel were bored *en famille*;[5] then the population of the world increased, and the peoples were bored *en masse*.[6] To divert themselves they conceived the idea of constructing a tower high

---

1 Søren Kierkegaard, *Either/Or* (*Enten – Eller*), originally published in two volumes in 1843, from Søren Kierkegaard, *Either/Or: A Fragment of Life*, in 2 vols.; vol. 1 trans. by David F. Swenson and Lillian Marvin Swenson; vol. 2 trans. by Walter Lowrie (Princeton, NJ: Princeton University Press, 1944).

2 Latin for 'Victorious Hermit.'

3 Phalaris was the tyrant of Akragas in Sicily from approximately 570 to 554 BCE. He was known for his excessive cruelty, including the practice of roasting his victims inside a hollow brass statue of a bull by a fire kindled beneath it.

4 Latin for 'all in all' or 'on the whole.'

5 French for 'in one's family'; 'at home.'

6 French for 'as a whole' or 'in a body.'

enough to reach the heavens.[1] This idea is itself as boring as the tower was high, and constitutes a terrible proof of how boredom gained the upper hand. The nations were scattered over the earth, just as people now travel abroad, but they continued to be bored....

[S]ince boredom as shown above is the root of all evil, what can be more natural than the effort to overcome it?...Everyone who feels bored cries out for change....

One tires of living in the country, and moves to the city; one tires of one's native land, and travels abroad;...finally one indulges in a sentimental hope of endless journeyings from star to star. Or...[o]ne tires of porcelain dishes and eats on silver; one tires of silver and turns to gold...This method defeats itself...

My method...resembles the true rotation method in changing the crop and the mode of cultivation. Here we have at once the principle of limitation...The more you limit yourself, the more fertile you become in invention. A prisoner in solitary confinement for life becomes very inventive, and a spider may furnish him with much entertainment. One need only hark back to one's schooldays, when...one's instructors...were...very tiresome; how fertile in invention did not one prove to be! How entertaining to catch a fly and hold it imprisoned under a nut shell, watching it run around the shell; what pleasure, from cutting a hole in the desk, putting a fly in it, and then peeping down at it through a piece of paper! How entertaining sometimes to listen to the monotonous drip of water from the roof!...Here we have...[a] method which seeks to achieve results intensively, not extensively.[2]

The more resourceful in changing the mode of cultivation one can be, the better; but every particular change will always come under the general categories of *remembering* and *forgetting*. Life in its entirety moves in these two currents, and hence it is essential to have them under control....

To forget—all men wish to forget, when something unpleasant happens...But forgetting is an art that must be practiced beforehand.... No moment must be permitted a greater significance than that it can be forgotten when convenient; each moment ought, however, to have so much significance that it can be recollected at will.... To remember in this manner, one must be careful how one lives...Enjoying an experience to its full intensity to the last minute, will make it impossible either to remember or to forget.... From the beginning one should keep the enjoyment under control....

[F]orgetting is really a tranquil and quiet occupation, and one which should be exercised quite as much in connection with the pleasant as with the unpleasant. A pleasant experience has[, once] past[,] something unpleasant about it, by which it stirs a sense of privation; this unpleasantness is taken away by an act of forgetfulness. The unpleasant has a sting, as all admit. This, too, can be removed by the art of forgetting....

Part Second (The 'Or'), Containing the Papers of B; Letters to A

AESTHETIC VALIDITY OF MARRIAGE

... [T]he aesthetic ideal becomes richer and fuller in proportion as the importance of time is duly emphasized. How, then, can the aesthetic be [best] represented...Answer: by living it.... It is in this way aesthetics is neutralized and reconciled with life...

Let us now glance at the relation between romantic and conjugal love...Conjugal love begins with possession and acquires inward history. It is faithful. So is romantic love—but now note the difference.

---

1 An allusion to the Tower of Babel, an origin myth intended to explain why people speak different languages, as told in Genesis 11:1–9.

2 I.e., in greater intensity (quality) rather than in greater number (quantity).

The faithful romantic lover waits, let us say, for fifteen years—then comes the instant which rewards him.... A married man is faithful for fifteen years, yet...[a]t the end of the fifteen years he has apparently got no further than he was at the beginning, but he has lived in a high degree aesthetically.... He has not fought with lions and ogres, but with the most dangerous enemy: with time.... The married man, being a true conqueror, has not killed time but has saved it and preserved it in eternity. The married man who does this, truly lives poetically.... And now even if this is something which cannot be represented in art, let it be your comfort...that the highest and most beautiful things in life are not to be heard about, nor read about, nor seen, but, if one will, may be lived. When, then, I willingly admit that romantic love lends itself more aptly to artistic representation than does conjugal love, this is not by any means to say that the latter is less aesthetic than the former; on the contrary, it is more aesthetic. In one of the tales of the Romantic School...there is one character who has no desire to write poetry like the others among whom he lives, because it is a waste of time and deprives him of the true enjoyment—he prefers to live.[1] Now if he had had the right conception of what it is to live, he would have been the man for me....

[Consider] the predicates commonly applied to conjugal love. It is faithful, constant, humble, patient, long-suffering, indulgent, sincere, contented, vigilant, willing, joyful. All these virtues have the characteristic that they are inward qualifications of the individual.... And by these virtues nothing else is acquired, only they themselves are acquired....

Here I would recall the definition I gave a while ago of the ethical, as that by which a man becomes what he becomes. The ethical then will not change

the individual into another man but makes him himself; it will not annihilate the aesthetical but transfigures it.... Commonly one regards the ethical quite abstractly and therefore has a secret horror of it.... The reason for such a fear is the reluctance of the individual to become transparent to himself...When a man is afraid of being transparent he always shuns the ethical, for precisely this is what the ethical wills....

In opposition to an aesthetical view which would enjoy life, one often hears of another view which finds the significance of life in living for the fulfillment of its duties.... The fault [here] is that the individual is placed in an outward relation to duty.... Such a life of duty is of course very uncomely and tiresome, and if the ethical had not a far deeper connection with personality, it would be very difficult to defend it against the aesthetical....

[T]he very derivation of the word [duty] indicates an inward relation; for what is incumbent upon me,...in accordance with my true nature, that surely stands in the most inward relation to myself. For duty is not an imposition.... When duty is viewed thus it is a sign that the individual is in himself correctly oriented.... He has clad himself in duty, for him it is the expression of his inmost nature. When he has thus oriented himself he has become absorbed in the ethical and will not chase breathlessly after the fulfillment of his duties. The genuine ethical individual therefore possesses calmness and assurance because he has not duties outside himself but in himself. The more profoundly a man has planned his life ethically, the less will he feel the need of talking every instant about duty, of being fearful every instant as to whether he has fulfilled it, of taking counsel every instant with others about what his duty is. When the ethical is rightly viewed

---

1   Kierkegaard is alluding to the character of Julius in Friedrich Schlegel's novel *Lucinde* (1799), a book that was considered an obscene venture in experimental literature at the time. The Romantic School refers to Romanticism, an artistic, literary, musical, and intellectual movement that originated in late eighteenth-century Europe and emphasized emotion, individualism, nature, and the past, partly as a revolt against the prescribed rules of classicism. Philosophically, it was a reaction to the Enlightenment's emphasis on rationality.

it makes the individual infinitely secure in himself, when it is not rightly viewed it makes the individual insecure...

If one views the ethical as outside the personality and in an external relation to it, then one has abandoned everything, then one has fallen into despair....

The ethical is the universal and so it is the abstract. In its complete abstraction the ethical is therefore always prohibitive. So it appears as law.... The Jews were the people of the Law. Hence they understood perfectly most of the commandments in the Laws of Moses... This is the secret of conscience... He who regards life ethically sees the universal, and he who lives ethically expresses the universal in his life, he makes himself the universal man... [E]very man as such is the universal man, that is to say, to every man the way is assigned by which he becomes the universal man. He who lives ethically labors to become the universal man. So for example when a man is aesthetically in love the adventitious plays a prodigious role, and it is a matter of importance to him that no one has loved as he does, with all the nuances. When he who loves ethically marries he realizes the universal....

Since, then, the ethical lies deepest in the soul it is not always visible to the eye, and the man who lives ethically may do exactly the same things as the man who lives aesthetically, so that for a time this may create a deception, but finally there comes an instant when it is evident that he who lives ethically has a limit which the other does not recognize. In this assurance that his life is ethically planned the individual reposes with secure confidence and therefore does not torment himself... The fact that the man who lives ethically leaves a large space for the indifferent I find quite natural, and it is indicative of veneration for the ethical that one will not press it into every insignificant affair....

Let us now for once compare an ethical and an aesthetical individual. The principal difference, and one on which everything hinges, is that the ethical individual is transparent to himself... The ethical individual knows himself, but this knowledge is not a mere contemplation..., it is a reflection upon himself which itself is an action, and therefore I have deliberately preferred to use the expression "choose oneself" instead of know oneself[1].... By the individual's intercourse with himself he impregnates himself and brings himself to birth. This self which the individual knows is at once the actual self and the ideal self which... he nevertheless has in him since it is the self. Only within him has the individual the goal after which he has to strive, and yet he has this goal outside him, inasmuch as he strives after it....

Hence, the ethical life has this duplex character, that the individual has his self outside himself and in himself.... With this picture it is as with man's shadow: in the morning man casts his shadow before him, at midday it goes almost unobserved beside him, in the evening it falls behind him....

---

1 "Know oneself" recalls the ancient Greek philosophy of "Know yourself." The motto (*gnōthi seauton*) was allegedly written over the courtyard of the Greek temple dedicated to Apollo at Delphi.

Søren Kierkegaard, *Fear and Trembling*[1]

(*Frygt og Bæven*, originally published under the pseudonym Johannes de silentio[2] in 1843)

A Panegyric[3] upon Abraham

By faith Abraham went out from the land of his fathers and became a sojourner in the land of promise. He left one thing behind, took one thing with him: he left his earthly understanding behind and took faith with him...By faith he was a stranger in the land of promise...

By faith Abraham received the promise that in his seed all races of the world would be blessed. Time passed, the possibility was there, Abraham believed; time passed, it became unreasonable, Abraham believed.... Abraham became old, Sarah became a laughingstock in the land, and yet...Abraham believed and held fast the expectation. If Abraham had wavered,...he would not be the father of faith....

Then came the fulness of time.... Praise therefore to that story! For Sarah, though stricken in years, was young enough to desire the pleasure of motherhood, and Abraham, though gray-haired, was young enough to wish to be a father.... [Abraham] accepted the fulfillment of the promise, he accepted it by faith, and it came to pass according to the promise and according to his faith...

Then there was joy in Abraham's house...

But it was not to remain thus. Still once more Abraham was to be tried.... Now all the terror of the strife was concentrated in one instant. "And God tempted Abraham and said unto him, Take Isaac, thine only son, whom thou lovest, and get thee into the land of Moriah, and offer him there for a burnt offering upon the mountain which I will show thee."

So all was lost—more dreadfully than if it had never come to pass! So the Lord was only making sport of Abraham! He made miraculously the preposterous actual, and now in turn He would annihilate it....

Yet Abraham believed and did not doubt, he believed the preposterous....

We read in those holy books:[4] "And God tempted Abraham, and said unto him, Abraham, Abraham, where art thou?"...Abraham: joyfully, buoyantly, confidently, with a loud voice, he answered, "Here am I." We read further: "And Abraham rose early in the morning"—as though it were to a festival, so he hastened, and early in the morning he had come to the place spoken of, to Mount Moriah. He said nothing to Sarah, nothing to Eleazar. Indeed who could understand him?...He cleft the wood, he bound Isaac, he lit the pyre, he drew the knife.... Isaac's fate was laid along with the knife in Abraham's hand. And there he stood, the old man, with his only hope! But he did not doubt, he did not look anxiously to the right or to the left, he did not challenge heaven with his prayers. He knew that it was God the Almighty who was trying him, he knew that it was the hardest sacrifice that could be required of him; but he knew also that no sacrifice was too hard when God required it—and he drew the knife....

Venerable Father Abraham! In marching home from Mount Moriah thou hadst no need of a pan-

---

1 Søren Kierkegaard, *Fear and Trembling* (*Frygt og Bæven*), from Walter Lowrie, *Fear and Trembling and The Sickness Unto Death* (Princeton, NJ: Princeton University Press [1941, 1954] third printing, 1970).

2 Latin for 'John of Silence.'

3 I.e., a public speech or published text in praise of someone or something.

4 I.e., Genesis 22:1–19.

egyric which might console thee for thy loss; for thou didst gain all and didst retain Isaac.... Thousands of years have run their course since those days, but...every language calls thee to remembrance...Venerable Father Abraham! Second Father of the human race!...[T]hou who first didst know that highest passion, the holy, pure and humble expression of the divine madness which the pagans admired—forgive him who would speak in praise of thee, if he does not do it fittingly....

Problemata

PROBLEM I: IS THERE SUCH A THING AS A TELEOLOGICAL SUSPENSION OF THE ETHICAL?

The ethical as such is the universal, and as the universal it applies to everyone...[I]t has nothing [outside] itself which is its *telos*,[1] but is itself *telos* for everything outside it, and when this has been incorporated by the ethical it can go no further.... [T]he particular individual is the individual who has his *telos* in the universal, and his ethical task is to express himself constantly in it, to abolish his particularity in order to become the universal. As soon as the individual would assert himself in his particularity over against the universal he sins...Whenever the individual after he has entered the universal feels an impulse to assert himself as the particular, he is in temptation..., and he can labor himself out of this only by penitently abandoning himself...in the universal. If this be the highest thing that can be said of man..., then the ethical has the same character as man's eternal blessedness, which to all eternity and at every instant is his *telos*...

[If morality is the highest category,] Hegel is...wrong in not protesting loudly and clearly against the fact that Abraham enjoys honor and glory as the father of faith, whereas he ought to be prosecuted and convicted of murder.

For faith is this paradox, that the particular is higher than the universal—yet in such a way...that consequently the individual...now as the particular isolates himself as higher than the universal. If this be not faith, then Abraham is lost, then faith has never existed in the world...

Faith is precisely this paradox, that the...particular is higher than the universal,...yet in such a way...that the individual as the particular stands in an absolute relation to the absolute. This position...remains to all eternity a paradox, inaccessible to thought. And yet faith is this paradox—or else...Abraham is lost....

Now the story of Abraham contains such a teleological suspension of the ethical. There have not been lacking clever pates[2] and profound investigators who have found analogies to it.... If one will look a little more closely, I have not much doubt that in the whole world one will not find a single analogy (except a later instance which proves nothing),...Abraham is the representative of faith, and that faith is...so paradoxical that it cannot be thought at all.... By virtue of the absurd he gets Isaac again. Abraham is therefore at no instant a tragic hero but something quite different, either a murderer or a believer.... Hence it is that I can understand the tragic hero but cannot understand Abraham, though in a certain crazy sense I admire him more than all other men....

The difference between the tragic hero and Abraham is clearly evident. The tragic hero still remains within the ethical....

With Abraham the situation was different. By his act he overstepped the ethical entirely and possessed a higher *telos* outside of it, in relation to which he suspended the former. For I should very much like to know how one would bring Abraham's act into relation with the universal,...except the fact that

---

1   Greek for 'end,' 'goal,' or 'aim.' In the Aristotelian tradition, it is often considered the final cause, that for the sake of which an action or activity is performed.

2   I.e., a person's head.

he transgressed it.... Abraham's whole action...is a purely private undertaking....

Why then did Abraham do it? For God's sake, and (in complete identity with this) for his own sake. He did it for God's sake because God required this proof of his faith; for his own sake he did it in order that he might furnish the proof. The unity of these two points of view is perfectly expressed by the word which has always been used to characterize this situation: it is a trial, a temptation...A temptation—but what does that mean? What ordinarily tempts a man is that which would keep him from doing his duty, but in this case the temptation itself is the ethical...which would keep him from doing God's will. But what then is duty? Duty is precisely the expression for God's will.

Here is evident the necessity of a new category if one would understand Abraham....

Therefore, though Abraham arouses my admiration, he at the same time appalls me.... One approaches [Abraham] with a *horror religiosus*,[1] as Israel approached Mount Sinai[2]....

How then did Abraham exist? He believed. This is the paradox...which he cannot make clear to any other man, for the paradox is that he as the individual puts himself in an absolute relation to the absolute.... [I]f he is justified, it is not by virtue of anything universal, but by virtue of being the particular individual....

The story of Abraham contains therefore a teleological suspension of the ethical. As the individual he became higher than the universal.... If such is not the position of Abraham, then he is not even a tragic hero but a murderer.... [T]o him who follows the narrow way of faith...no one can understand. Faith is a miracle, and yet no man is excluded from it...

Questions

1. Phalaris was an ancient tyrant of Sicily who, according to ancient sources, had a bronze bull made, with an open mouth, so that he could hear the shrieks of his victims while eating his dinner. Kierkegaard softens the image slightly; he has the mouth of the bull transform the victims' anguished shrieks into dinner music. The sense of abject suffering remains. Why, then, does "A," the young man in *Either/Or*, compare the poet to Phalaris's victims?

2. What does the judge, B, mean when he says that the ethical is the universal rather than the particular? Why does the Jewish model of the Ten Commandments fit into this model of morality? Use one of the Ten Commandments to explain your point.

3. Compare the judge's account of duty with Kant's account of duty or the account in the ancient Stoics.

4. In *Fear and Trembling*, Kierkegaard accepts that we cannot make sense of Abraham's readiness to sacrifice his own son from the perspective of morality. Why? How does Kierkegaard defend Abraham? Could you forgive Abraham, if you were Isaac?

5. What does Kierkegaard mean by the phrase "the teleological suspension of the ethical"? Can you think of other circumstances where it might apply?

---

1 Latin, for 'religious terror.'
2 This is where Moses received the Ten Commandments.

6. Explain Kierkegaard's distinction between the aesthetic, the ethical, and the religious. How does the individual at each stage act? What are the guiding principles he lives by? Refer to both readings.

Suggested Readings

Kierkegaard's work ranges from fiction to autobiography, and from editorial comments on the issues of the day to sermons, scriptural exegesis, and probing philosophical reflection. Many of Kierkegaard's books were self-published under pseudonyms. Although he wrote in Danish, multiple English translations are available. The standard scholarly edition of Kierkegaard's work in English is *Kierkegaard's Writings*, volumes I–XXVI, edited by H.V. Hong et al. (Princeton University Press, 1968–2000. His principle works include *Either/Or* (*Enten–Eller*, 2 vols., 1843), *Repetition* (*Gjentagelsen*, 1843), *Fear and Trembling* (*Frygt og Bæven*, 1843), *Philosophical Fragments* (1844), *Concluding Unscientific Postscript* (1846), and *The Sickness Unto Death* (1849). Penguin has a translation of his unpublished writing (Alastair Hannay, *Papers and Journals: A Selection*, 1996). Anthony Storm deserves credit for sorenkierkegaard.org, which has useful links and resources.

Some academic sources include Ralph McInerny, "Ethics and Persuasion: Kierkegaard's Existential Dialectic" (1955); James J. Valone, *The Ethics and Existentialism of Kierkegaard: Outlines for a Philosophy of Life* (1983); and George Pattison, "Fear and Trembling and the Paradox of Christian Existentialism" (2012).

On Kierkegaard's philosophy of religion, see Edward F. Mooney, ed., *Ethics, Love, and Faith in Kierkegaard: Philosophical Engagements* (2008), and W. Glenn Kirkconnell, *Kierkegaard on Ethics and Religion* (2008). Kierkegaard has been compared with Spinoza (Michael Strawser), Kant (Roi Benbassat), Ludwig Wittgenstein (Onno Zijlstra), Levinas (Robyn Brothers and Adam Wells), and Derrida (Mark Dooley).

For applied ethics, see Gordon Marino, "Commentary: An Ethics Consult with Kierkegaard" (2004).

Chapter 35

Marxism

Marxism is known primarily as a political and an economic theory. It nevertheless contains a moral philosophy and makes its own ethical claims. This has generally been minimized in Marxist circles—Marx supposedly laughed openly when his political opponents relied on moral arguments—but this is easily misconstrued and merely reflects his belief that moral arguments were generally used, rhetorically, to justify the existing social and political order.

The moral appeals in Marxism were also obscured by a new kind of fatalism—now described as "determinism"—which holds that history unfolds itself in a logical, pre-ordained pattern. This idea is a legacy of the theoretical exercise in modern philosophy and science, which assumes that there is a rational order that explains everything. Marx was interested in historical developments that rendered individuals relatively insignificant in his moral scheme.

It follows that Marx was not particularly interested in the subjective and personal side of morality. The important thing in his mind was to take the side of history. This should not be allowed to obscure the moral reality of the practical justification of revolution in the Marxist scheme, namely that the capitalist system and the industrial and political complex are fundamentally unfair. This is an ethical claim, which comes to the surface in the *Communist Manifesto*, and it is difficult to see how revolution can be justified without it.

Karl Marx (1818–83) was born in Germany. Although his father came from a long line of rabbis, he allowed himself to be baptized as a Protestant in order to maintain his legal practice. Marx received a classical education and then enrolled in the faculty of law, first at the University of Bonn and then at the University of Berlin. He quickly became interested in philosophical matters and participated in the affairs of the Young Hegelians society.

Marx eventually became a journalist. In 1842, he became the editor of the *Rheinische Zeitung (Rhenish Newspaper)* in Cologne, but aroused the ire of the Prussian censors, who closed the paper. He then married and went to France, where he met Engels, but was expelled. Re-locating in Brussels, he undertook his own course of studies, and wrote *The German Ideology* (which was only published posthumously). In it he argued that it is the material conditions of production that drive history relentlessly forward and determine the nature of individuals.

461

Marx and Engels became active in the German Communist League in 1845, a collaboration that led to the publication of the *Communist Manifesto* in 1848. Marx also returned to Cologne to edit the *Neue* (New) *Rheinische Zeitung*, but was again expelled. He then returned to England, where he spent the rest of his life working slowly and steadily on his study of political economy, which Marx saw as a "scientific" study of the evolution of the relations between capital and labor. The first volume, *Das Kapital* (*Capital: A Critique of Political Economy*), was published in 1867. The two remaining volumes of the opus were published by Engels after his death.

Friedrich Engels (1820–95) was born in Prussia. His father owned a textile factory and was a partner in a cotton mill in Manchester, England. Engels was "radicalized" while still in high school, and began writing for the radical press under the pseudonym Friedrich Oswald, but agreed to enter an export company to appease his father. He later settled in Berlin and joined the Young Hegelians, quickly becoming an atheist and rejecting Christianity.

Engels eventually convinced his father to send him to England, where he investigated the social conditions in Manchester and wrote articles on issues such as child labor. After meeting Marx in 1844, the two men wrote a critique of the Young Hegelians entitled *The Holy Family*. The following year, Engels published *The Conditions of the Working Class in England*, which was well-received. After joining the German Communist League, Engels took part in unsuccessful revolutionary activities in Germany. It is interesting to note that Schopenhauer's sympathies were on the other side.

Engels then returned to the cotton mill in Manchester, under constant surveillance, and became Marx's financial patron. The ethical issues raised by his life in business have never been properly addressed. Both men remained politically active and participated in the interminable squabbles of the communist movement. Although most of Engels's writing was polemical, his philosophical works include *The Origin of the Family, Private Property and the State*, and *Ludwig Feuerbach and the Outcome of Classical German Philosophy*. It is said that he was a *bon vivant*, in spite of his views, and an engaging conversationalist, who enjoyed the arts, fox hunting, and parties.

Marxism has roots in the thought of Jean-Jacques Rousseau (1712–78) and G.W.F. Hegel (1770–1831). If Rousseau's social-contract theory is a more distant influence, Marx's youthful education was dominated by a vigorous Hegelianism. Hegel was an idealist: he argued that history was based on a rational progression from thesis to antithesis, and then synthesis. His philosophy saw the world spirit (*Geist*) moving through levels of enlightenment, an argument that ultimately fed into a triumphant German nationalism. Marx dispensed with the nationalism, but held similar millenarian views.

Marx's work has been described as "Hegel materialized." As Vladimir Lenin put it, Marx and Engels "saw that it is not the development of mind that explains the development of nature but that, on the contrary, the explanation of mind must be derived from nature, from matter." Marx's "dialectical" materialism holds that history moves through a series of conflicts, between slave and master, peasant and noble, and proletariat and capitalist, which ultimately resolves itself in a classless utopia.

Marx saw his own historical work as scientific. In his view, the productive forces of the economy are sufficient in themselves to change the nature of the relations between individuals, abolish private property, and create a new human society based on socialism. Marx's later work also shows the influence of Adam Smith and the early science of economics, which aimed at general prosperity.

Marxism usually refers to the political idea that there is a struggle between classes in society, which gives rise to revolution. In his eulogy on Marx, Engels wrote that he was "before else a revolutionist." Marx's "real mission" in life was to contribute to "the overthrow of capitalist society and of the state institutions which it had brought into being." The moral imperative that surfaces in such a view is problematic because it subverts our usual understanding of ethics and forces us to engage in a relative calculus, which can be used to justify any conduct that serves the greater end. This kind of reasoning also lends itself to rhetorical manipulation.

There are difficult issues here. The ethical motivation behind the work of Marx and Engels is undeniable. The practical politics associated with Marxism are nevertheless full of treachery. Mikhail Bakunin, an adversary in the First International, who nevertheless admired *Das Kapital*, accused Marx and Engels of "political calumny, lying, and intrigue." These kinds of accusations point to the larger historical observation that Marxism has a totalitarian side and has been used to justify its own ethical brutalities.

In the first reading, which features two excerpts from essays written in 1844, Marx describes the social, psychological, and philosophical changes brought about by the industrial revolution and the emergence of capitalism. He maintains that the introduction of an economy based on money and the capitalist ownership of the means of production alienates—separates—workers, not merely from themselves and their own work, but also from their natural relations with other people. This produces a society that imposes a false notion of an individualized freedom while depriving our lives of meaning and purpose.

The second reading is from *The Communist Manifesto*, which was based, in part, on Engels's "Communist Confession of Faith" and was a response to current events in Germany. In spite of this, the *Manifesto* provides a good synopsis of the views of Marx and Engels, and speaks more broadly to the rampant poverty and oppression that accompanied the industrial revolution and the emergence of capitalism. All of the complexities aside, the moral imperative that arises out of such conditions is revolution.

Karl Marx, *Essays*[1]

(1844)

"Money and Alienated Man," from "Excerpts-Notes of 1844"[2]

... As an *equivalent* [private property] ... has become *value* and immediately *exchange value*. Its existence as *value* is a determination of *itself*, ... outside of its specific nature, and *externalized*—[it now has] only a *relative* existence. ...

[This] relationship of exchange being presupposed, *labor immediately* becomes *wage-labor*. This relationship of alienated labor reaches its apex only by the fact (1) that on the one side *wage-labor*, the product of the laborer, stands in no *immediate* relationship to his need ... (2) that the *buyer* of the product is not himself productive but exchanges what has been produced by others. ...

The more ... one-sided the producer's output becomes ... the more does his labor fall into the category of *wage-labor*, until it is eventually nothing but wage-labor and until it becomes entirely *incidental* and *unessential* whether the producer immediately enjoys and needs his product and whether the *activity*, the action of labor itself, is his self-satisfaction and the realization of his natural dispositions and spiritual aims.

The following elements are contained in *wage-labor*: (1) the chance relationship and alienation of labor from the laboring subject; (2) the chance relationship and alienation of labor from its object; (3) the determination of the laborer through social needs which are an alien compulsion to him, a compulsion to which he submits out of egoistic need and distress—[and to which he responds in providing his labor, which is] merely a source of providing the necessities of life for him, just as he is merely a slave for them; (4) the maintenance of the worker's individual existence appears to him as the *goal* of his activity and his real action is only a means; he lives to acquire the means of *living*.

The greater and the more articulated the social power is within the relationship of private property, the more *egoistic* and asocial man becomes, the more he becomes alienated from his own nature.

Just as the mutual exchange of products of *human activity* appears as *trading* and *bargaining*, so does the mutual reintegration and exchange of the activity itself appear as the *division of labor*, making man as far as possible an abstract being, an automaton, and transforming him into a spiritual and physical monster.

Precisely the unity of human labor is regarded as being its *division* because its social nature comes into being only as its opposite, in the form of alienation. The *division of labor* increases with civilization.

Within the presupposition of the division of labor, the product and material of private property gradually acquire for the individual the significance of an *equivalent*. ... He no longer immediately exchanges his product for the product he *needs*. The equivalent becomes an equivalent in *money* which is

---

1 Karl Marx, *Selected Writings*, edited by Lawrence H. Simon (Indianapolis/Cambridge: Hackett Publishing Company, Inc., 1994); the two excerpts come from "Money and Alienated Man" in "Excerpts-Notes of 1844" and "Alienated Labour" in "Economic and Philosophic Manuscripts" (1844).

2 Previous to this excerpt, Marx wrote that private property changes with the introduction of money. It becomes a medium of exchange, which has equivalence with other products. Marx now turns to a few implications of this point.

the immediate result of wage-labor and the *medium of exchange*....

What formerly was the domination of one person over another has now become the general domination of the *thing* over the *person*, the domination of the product over the producer. Just as the determination of the *externalization* of private property lay in the *equivalent* and in value, so is *money* the sensuous, self-objectified existence of this *externalization*....

"Alienated Labor,"[1] from "Economic and Philosophic Manuscripts" (1844)

We have proceeded from the presuppositions of political economy. We have accepted its language and its laws.... From political economy itself, in its own words, we have shown that the worker sinks to the level of a commodity, the most miserable commodity; that the misery of the worker is inversely proportional to the power and volume of his production; that the necessary result of competition is the accumulation of capital in a few hands and thus the revival of monopoly in a more frightful form; and finally that the distinction between capitalist and landowner, between agricultural laborer and industrial worker, disappears and the whole society must divide into the two classes of *proprietors* and propertyless *workers*....

All these consequences follow from the fact that the worker is related to the *product of his labor* as to an *alien* object. For it is clear according to this premise: The more the worker exerts himself, the more powerful becomes the alien objective world which he fashions against himself, the poorer he and his inner world become, the less there is that belongs to him.... The *externalization* of the worker in his product means not only that his work becomes an object, an *external* existence, but also that it exists

outside him independently, alien, an autonomous power, opposed to him. The life he has given to the object confronts him as hostile and alien....

[And this holds true, even as he] becomes a slave to his objects [because it is the objects which give him the means of his physical existence.]...

[And] [h]ow could the worker stand in an alien relationship to the product of his activity if he did not alienate himself from himself in the very act of production? After all, the product is only the résumé of activity, of production. If the product of work is externalization, production itself must be active externalization, externalization of activity, activity of externalization....

Finally, the external nature of work for the worker appears in the fact that it is not his own but another person's, that in work he does not belong to himself but to someone else....

The result, therefore, is that man (the worker) feels that he is acting freely only in his animal functions—eating, drinking, and procreating, or at most in his shelter and finery—while in his human functions he feels only like an animal. The animalistic becomes the human and the human the animalistic.

To be sure, eating, drinking, and procreation are genuine human functions. In abstraction, however, and separated from the remaining sphere of human activities and turned into final and sole ends, they are animal functions.

We have considered labor, the act of alienation of practical human activity, in two aspects: (1) the relationship of the worker to the *product of labor* as an alien object dominating him....; (2) the relationship of labor to the *act of production* in *labor*. This relationship is that of the worker to his own activity as alien and not belonging to him...

We have now to derive a third aspect of *alienated labor* from the two previous ones.

---

1 The term 'alienated labor' refers to the conceptual separation of the worker from his work and the resulting 'externalization' of work, the objects he produces, other workers, and even himself.

Man is a species-being[1]...not only in that he practically and theoretically makes his own species as well as that of other things his object, but also—and this is only another expression for the same thing—in that as present and living species he considers himself to be a *universal* and consequently free being....

Man [therefore] makes his life activity itself into an object of will and consciousness....

The consciousness which man has from his species is altered[,] [however,] through alienation, so that species-life becomes a means for him.

(3) Alienated labor hence turns the *species-existence of man*...into an existence *alien* to him, into the *means* of his *individual existence*. It alienates his spiritual nature, his *human essence*, from his own body and likewise from nature outside him.

(4) A direct consequence of man's alienation from the product of his work, from his life activity, and from his species-existence, is the *alienation of man* from [other men]....

Let us now see further how the concept of alienated, externalized labor must express and represent itself in actuality....

If my own activity does not belong to me, if it is an alien and forced activity, to whom then does it belong?

To a being *other* than myself.

Who is this being?

Gods? To be sure, in early times the main production, for example, the building of temples in Egypt, India, and Mexico, appears to be in the service of the gods, just as the product belongs to the gods. But gods alone were never workmasters....

So [t]he *alien* being who owns labor and the product of labor, whom labor serves and whom the product of labor satisfies can only be *man* himself.

That the product of labor does not belong to the worker...is possible only because this product belongs to *a man other than the worker*. If his activity is torment for him, it must be the *pleasure* and the life-enjoyment for another....

If man is related to the product of his labor, to his objectified labor, as to an *alien*, hostile, powerful object independent of him, he is so related that another alien, hostile, powerful man independent of him is the lord of this object. If he is unfree in relation to his own activity, he is related to it as bonded activity, activity under the domination, coercion and yoke of another man....

Thus through *alienated externalized labor* does the worker create the relation to this work of man alienated to labor and standing outside it. [This relation also] produces the relation of the capitalist to labor, or whatever one wishes to call the lord of labor....

---

1 The German is *Gattungswesen*. What Marx means by this claim is debated among scholars. But it seems to refer to the ability of individual human beings to become aware of themselves as members of a biological species living within specific social circumstances that influence how their biological needs can be met.

Karl Marx and Friedrich Engels, *Manifesto of the Communist Party*[1]

(1848; commonly known as *The Communist Manifesto*)

Cover of the first edition of the *Communist Manifesto*.

A spectre is stalking Europe—the spectre of Communism. All the Powers of Old Europe have bound themselves in a crusade against this spectre: the Pope and the Czar, Metternich and Guizot,[2] French Radicals and German police....

It is high time that the Communists openly set forth before the whole world their perspective, their aims, their tendencies, and meet this fairy tale about the Spectre of Communism with a Manifesto of the Party itself.

To this end, Communists of the most diverse nationalities have assembled in London, and devised the following Manifesto, that is to be published in the English, French, German, Italian, Flemish and Danish languages.

Bourgeois and Proletarians

The history of all society hitherto is the history of class struggles.

Freeman and slave, patrician and plebeian, lord and serf, guild-master and journeyman,[3] in short, oppressor and oppressed, situated in constant opposition to one another, carried on an uninterrupted, now hidden, now open conflict, a fight that each time ended in a revolutionary transformation

---

1 Karl Marx and Friedrich Engels, *The Communist Manifesto*, edited and translated by L.M. Findlay (Peterborough, ON: Broadview Press, 2004).

2 Klemens von Metternich (1773–1859) was a German diplomat and statesman who served as the Austrian Empire's Foreign Minister from 1809 until 1848, when the liberal revolutions forced his resignation. François Pierre Guillaume Guizot (1787–1874) was a French historian and statesman who supported limiting the political franchise to propertied men. The French Radicals refers to politicians that advocated for democratic reforms, particularly universal suffrage, to promote social progress during the nineteenth century.

3 'Freeman and slave' refers to Ancient Greece; 'patrician and plebeian' refers to Ancient Rome; 'lord and serf' refers to the feudal agricultural system of the European middle ages; 'guild-master and journeyman' refers to the tradesmen of the European middle ages; and 'bourgeoisie and proletariat' refers to the industrial capitalist class structure.

of the entire society or in the common ruin of the contending classes....

The modern bourgeois society that has sprouted from the ruins of feudal society has not done away with class antagonisms. It has but established new classes, new conditions of oppression, new forms of struggle in place of the old ones....

[O]ur epoch, the epoch of the bourgeoisie, possesses, however, this distinct feature: it has simplified class antagonisms. Society as a whole is more and more splitting up into two great hostile camps, into two great classes directly facing each other—Bourgeoisie and Proletariat....

We see, therefore, how the modern bourgeoisie is itself the product of a long course of development, of a series of revolutions in the modes of production and of exchange.

Each of these steps in the development of the bourgeoisie was accompanied by a corresponding political advance of that class. An oppressed cohort under the sway of the feudal nobility,...[the] bourgeoisie has at last, since the establishment of big industry and of the world market, acquired for itself, in the modern representative State, exclusive political sway. The executive of the modern State is but a committee for managing the common affairs of the whole bourgeoisie.

The bourgeoisie has played an intensely revolutionary part in history.

The bourgeoisie, wherever it has got the upper hand, has put an end to all feudal, patriarchal, idyllic relations. It has remorselessly torn asunder the motley feudal ties that bound people to their natural superiors, and has left remaining no other nexus between two people than naked self-interest, than callous "cash payment." It has drowned the heavenly ecstasies of religious fervour, of chivalrous enthusiasm, of philistine sentimentalism, in the ice-cold water of egotistical calculation. It has dispersed personal worth into exchange value, and in place of the numberless chartered, fully earned freedoms has set up a single, unconscionable freedom—Free Trade. In a word, in place of exploitation, veiled by religious and political illusions, it has substituted public, shameless, direct, blatant exploitation.

The bourgeoisie has stripped of its halo every occupation hitherto honoured and looked up to with reverent awe. It has converted the physician, the lawyer, the priest, the poet, the researcher, into its paid wage-labourers....

In a word, it creates a world after its own image.

The bourgeoisie...has created enormous cities...Just as it has made the country dependent on the town, so it has made barbarian and semi-barbarian countries dependent on the civilised ones, nations of peasants on nations of bourgeois, the East on the West.

The bourgeoisie keeps more and more doing away with the scattered state of the population, of the means of production, and of property. It has agglomerated the population, centralised means of production, and concentrated property in a few hands. The necessary consequence of this was political centralisation. Independent or but loosely connected provinces with separate interests, laws, governments and systems of taxation, were pressed together into one nation, one government, one code of laws, one national class-interest, one tariff-zone.

The bourgeoisie, during its rule of scarce one hundred years, has created more massive and more colossal productive forces than have all preceding generations together. Subjection of Nature's forces to man, machinery, application of chemistry to industry and agriculture, steam-navigation, railways, electric telegraphs, clearing of whole continents for cultivation, making river-traffic possible, whole populations conjured out of the ground—what earlier century had even a presentiment that such productive forces slumbered in the lap of social labour?

We have seen then, that the means of production and of exchange, on whose foundation the bourgeoisie built itself up, were generated in feudal society. At a certain stage in the development of these means of production and of exchange, the conditions under which feudal society produced and exchanged, the feudal organisation of agriculture and manufacturing industry, in a word, the feudal relations of property became no longer compatible with the already developed productive forces; they transformed themselves into so many fetters. They had to be burst asunder; they were burst asunder.

Into their place stepped free competition, accompanied by the social and political constitution adapted to it, and by the economical and political sway of the bourgeois class.

A similar movement is going on before our very eyes. Modern bourgeois society with its relations of production, of exchange and of property, a society that has conjured up such gigantic means of production and of exchange, is like the sorcerer who is no longer able to control the powers of the nether world whom he has summoned by his spells.... It is enough to mention the commercial crises that by their political return put on trial, ever more threateningly, the existence of the entire bourgeois society. In these commercial crises a great part not only of the products produced but also of the previously created productive forces, are regularly destroyed. In these crises there breaks out a social epidemic that in all earlier epochs would have seemed an absurdity— the epidemic of over-production. Society suddenly finds itself returned to a state of passing barbarism; it appears as if a famine, a universal war of devastation had cut off the supply of every means of subsistence; industry and commerce seem to be destroyed. And why? Because there is... too much industry, too much commerce. The productive forces at our disposal no longer tend to further the development of the relations of bourgeois civilisation; on the contrary, they have become too powerful for these relations by which they are encumbered, and so soon as they overcome these encumbrances, they bring into disorder the whole of bourgeois society...

But not only has the bourgeoisie forged the weapons that bring death to itself; it has also called into existence the people who are to wield those weapons—the modern workers, the proletarians.

To the same degree as the bourgeoisie, i.e., capital, is developed, so is the proletariat, the modern working class, developed—a class of labourers, who live only so long as they find work, and who find work only so long as their labour increases capital. These workers who must sell themselves piecemeal are a commodity, like every other article of commerce, and are consequently exposed equally to... all the fluctuations of the market.

Owing to the expanded use of machinery and to division of labour, the work of the proletarians has lost all individual character, and, consequently, all charm for the worker. He becomes a mere appendage of the machine, and it is only the most simple, most monotonous, and most easily acquired dexterity that is required of him. The cost of production of workers is restricted, almost entirely, to the means of subsistence that they require to maintain themselves and reproduce their [race]....

Modern industry has converted the little workshop of the patriarchal master into the great factory of the industrial capitalist. Masses of workers, pressed together in the factory, are organised like soldiers. As ordinary soldiers in the industrial army they are placed under the command of a comprehensive hierarchy of sub-officers and officers. Not only are they slaves of the bourgeois class, and of the bourgeois state; they are daily and hourly enslaved by the machine, by the overseer, and, above all, by the individual bourgeois manufacturer himself....

The lower strata of the middle class—the small tradespeople, shopkeepers, and retired tradesmen, the handicraftsmen and peasants—all these cohorts sink into the proletariat, partly because their meagre capital does not suffice for the scale on which big industry is carried on, and is swamped in the competition with the bigger capitalists, partly because their skill is rendered worthless by new methods of production. Thus the proletariat is recruited from all classes of the population.

The proletariat goes through various stages of development. With its birth begins its struggle with the bourgeoisie.

At first the contest is carried on by individual labourers, then by the workpeople of a factory, then by the operatives of one trade, in one locality.... They direct their attacks not only against the bourgeois conditions of production, but they direct them against the instruments of production themselves;...they smash machinery, they set factories ablaze, they seek to restore by force the vanished status of the worker in the Middle Ages.

At this stage the workers form a mass scattered over the whole country...

But with the development of industry the proletariat not only increases in number; it becomes concentrated into greater masses, its strength grows, and it feels its strength more.... Thereupon the workers begin to form combinations[1] against the bourgeois.... Here and there the struggle breaks out into riots.

From time to time the workers are victorious, but only for a time. The real fruit of their struggles lies, not in the immediate result, but in the ever more inclusive union of the workers. It is assisted by the enhanced means of communication that are created by big industry and that place the workers of different localities in contact with one another....

This organisation of the proletarians into a class, and consequently into a political party, is at every instant unsettled again by the competition between the workers themselves. But it always rises up again, stronger, firmer, mightier. It compels legislative recognition of particular interests of the workers by making use of the divisions within the bourgeoisie itself. And so the Ten Hours Bill in England.[2]...

Finally, in times when the class struggle nears decision, the process of dissolution inside the ruling class,...assumes such a violent, glaring character,

that...a portion of the bourgeoisie goes over to the proletariat, and in particular a portion of the bourgeois ideologists, who have raised themselves to a theoretical understanding of the historical in its entirety.

Of all the classes that stand face to face with the bourgeoisie today, the proletariat alone is a really revolutionary class. The other classes decay and go under in the presence of big industry....

All previous historical movements were movements of minorities, or in the interest of minorities. The proletarian movement is the independent movement of the immense majority in the interest of the immense majority....

The advance of industry, whose unwilling and unstoppable instrument is the bourgeoisie, replaces the isolation of the workers due to competition by their revolutionary combination due to association.... The bourgeoisie produces...above all, its own grave-diggers. Its fall and the victory of the proletariat are alike inevitable.

Proletarians and Communists

In what relation do the Communists stand to the proletarians in general?

The Communists do not constitute a party distinct from other workers' parties.

They have no interests separate from those of the proletariat as a whole.

They do not lay out any principles peculiar to themselves, through which they wish to mould the proletarian movement.

The Communists are distinguished from the other working-class parties by this only, that, in the various national struggles common to the proletarians, they point out and bring to prominence the shared interests of the entire proletariat, independent of nationality; and that, on the other hand, in the various stages of

---

1 I.e., unions.

2 The Ten Hours Bill, or the Factory Act of 1847, was a United Kingdom Act of Parliament which restricted the working hours of women and youth (13–18) in textile mills to ten hours per day.

development which the struggle of the working class against the bourgeoisie passes through, they always represent the interests of the movement as a whole.

The Communists, therefore, are in effect, the most resolute section of the workers' parties of every country, always pressing further; on the other hand, they have over the great mass of the proletariat the theorising edge in understanding the conditions, heading, and the general results of the proletarian movement.

The immediate aim of the Communists is the same as that of all the other proletarian parties: formation of the proletariat into a class, overthrow of the bourgeois rule, conquest of political power by the proletariat.

The theoretical conclusions of the Communists are in no way based on ideas or principles that have been invented, discovered by this or that global improver.

They are simply general versions of actual relations in an existing class struggle, in a historical movement going on before our eyes. The abolition of existing property relations is not an indicator exclusive to Communism....

Position of the Communists in Relation to the Various Existing Opposition Parties

From Section II the relation of the Communists to the already constituted workers' parties is plain, and accordingly their relation to the Chartists in England[1] and the agrarian reformers in North America....

In France the Communists ally themselves with the Social-Democrats, against the conservative and radical bourgeoisie....

In Switzerland they support the Radicals, without losing sight of the fact that this party consists of antagonistic elements, partly of democratic socialists in the French sense, partly of radical bourgeois....

In Germany, as soon as the bourgeoisie acts in a revolutionary fashion the Communist party battles along with them against the absolute monarchy, feudal land tenure, and the petty bourgeoisie....

In a word, the Communists everywhere support every revolutionary movement against the existing social and political order of things.

In all these movements they foreground the property question as the fundamental question for the movement, no matter its degree of development.

Finally, they labour everywhere for the union and agreement of the democratic parties of all countries.

The Communists disdain to conceal their views and aims. They openly declare that their objectives can be attained only by the forcible overthrow of all existing social orders. Let the ruling classes tremble at a communist revolution. In it proletarians have nothing to lose but their chains.

Proletarians of all lands unite![2]

Questions

1. Marx says that "wage-labor," like money, only has a relative value. Workers have been transformed into "abstract beings," who become the slaves—wage slaves, essentially—of the objects of production. Discuss the broader moral significance of such a development. How would it affect our moral attitude towards work?

---

1 The Chartists were a nineteenth-century reform movement (mostly peacefully) advocating democratic reforms to increase the political power of the working class.

2 This phrase later evolved into the phrase "Workers of the World, Unite!" which became the rallying-cry of the Communist Party.

2. Marx argues that capitalism has introduced a level of abstraction into work that separates us, conceptually, from the activity of work, its product, and even ourselves and other people. This "externalizes" these aspects of our lives. How would this externalization affect us morally?

3. Marx saw the efforts of the utilitarians and others to introduce legislative reforms as half-hearted attempts to fix the unfixable problems generated by industrial capitalism. Do you agree with Marx, or with the reformers? Why, why not?

4. Marx writes that one of the effects of alienated labor is to make our animal functions final and sole ends. How do we deal with this?

5. What is the Marxist response to the moral individualism in John Stuart Mill, Jeremy Bentham, or even Abelard, who all contributed to the liberal tradition?

6. Marx glorifies the industrial revolution and could be seen as a closet capitalist who merely preferred collective ownership over the means of production. If this is the case, what makes his position morally preferable to the private ownership of the capitalists?

7. What is right and wrong in an ethics of revolution? Why are there grounds for concern, theoretically and practically?

Suggested Readings

The largest collection of Karl Marx's work in English is the expansive *Marx/Engels Collected Works* (known by the acronym *MECW*), which contains 50 volumes published from 1975 to 2005 by Progress Publishers, Moscow. This massive reference work includes unpublished works, correspondence, and even Marx's early poetry. Three books by the younger Marx provide a window into his basic mindset: *On the Jewish Question* (1843), *Critique of Hegel's Philosophy of Right* (1843), and *Economic and Philosophic Manuscripts of 1844* (also known as *The Paris Manuscripts* and published posthumously). The latter includes the young Marx's famous theory of alienation.

The most famous of Marx's works is his collaborative effort with his patron, Friedrich Engels, which produced the *Communist Manifesto*, originally written in German (*Manifest der kommunistischen Partei*) and published in London in 1848, in the "Year of Revolutions." During Marx's later years, he focused on economics (then called "political economy") with his ponderous, three-volume *Das Kapital* (1867, 1885, 1894). A rich archive of public material is also available online at marxists.org.

George G. Brenkert (*Marx's Ethics of Freedom*, 1983) and Eugene Kamenka (*The Ethical Foundations of Marxism*, 2nd ed. [1972; rpt. 2015]) have argued, against the traditional position that Marx's "scientific views" contain a moral theory. Philip J. Kain (*Marx and Ethics*, 1988) and Steven Lukes (*Marxism and Morality*, 1985) trace Marx's personal evolution and the moral motivations behind his political position. See also A.M. Shandro, "Marx and Ethics" (1991).

Chapter 36

Liberalism

Historically, John Stuart Mill (1806–73) is, doubtless, the most influential English liberal thinker, but liberalism also gave rise to early movements dedicated to the emancipation of women, a political cause that Mill vigorously supported. Along with Mill, we include, then, selections from Mary Wollstonecraft (1759–97) and from Mill's wife, Harriet Taylor Mill (1807–58).

Mary Wollstonecraft was a journalist, writer, translator, political commentator, and educational reformer. Largely self-taught, she led a turbulent life. Her father squandered away most of his family's means. Leaving home, determined to make it on her own, she started a school with her sister, worked as a domestic, and, finally, dedicated herself to writing.

In 1792 Wollstonecraft went to Paris to observe and report on the French Revolution. She met an American, Captain Gilbert Imlay, with whom she had a daughter, but the relationship soon ended, leaving her so distraught that she attempted suicide. Returning to England, she entered into a more loving relationship with William Godwin, the noted utilitarian, whom she married after becoming pregnant with his child. She died ten days after giving birth to Mary Wollstonecraft Godwin, the author of *Frankenstein* and Percy Bysshe Shelley's second wife.

Wollstonecraft was a regular magazine contributor. She wrote a novel, a conservative critique of the French Revolution, and a popular travel journal as well as a number of books on the moral education of young girls and ladies. But her most famous work is the feminist classic, *A Vindication of the Rights of Woman* (1792). Wollstonecraft attacks romantic stereotypes of women as beautiful weak creatures of feeling totally lacking in reason.

John Stuart Mill became the preeminent public intellectual and "radical" (or liberal) voice in nineteenth-century British society. Mill's father, James Mill (1773–1836), a Scottish disciple of Jeremy Bentham, was intent on raising a child prodigy who would later champion the same radical political causes. He accordingly schooled his son at home, teaching him Greek when he was three years old, making him study Plato's dialogues (in Greek) and the proofs of Euclid at eight, and undertaking a comprehensive survey of Aristotelian and medieval logic by the time he was ten. Mill's severe home-schooling produced an accomplished young author who, however, suffered a nervous breakdown when he was twenty. He later attributed the breakdown to his strict utilitarian upbringing, and its emphasis on a cold, corrosive, analytic rationality. In his autobiography, he writes that he pulled himself out of his despondency by renewing his acquaintance with poetry, literature, and art.

Following the example of his father, Mill skipped university, and became a clerk for the East India Company, rising through the ranks to the position of Chief Examiner in charge of all correspondence. This was a very influential post, which provided him with a handsome income and left him time for intellectual and political activities. Mill retired on a comfortable pension in 1858 and was elected to the House of Commons in 1865. He also served as Lord Rector of the University of St. Andrews.

Mill had a scandalous private life, sharing a "chaste intimacy" with Harriet Taylor, a married woman who was separated from her husband, for many years. The two were married after her husband's death in 1851, causing a serious rupture in Mill's family. Harriet's contribution to Mill's writing has been the subject of much debate and speculation, though most scholars see Mill's recognition of her in *On Liberty* (1859) as an emotional testament to their relationship, rather than a statement of joint authorship.

Mill was well-published. Although his *System of Logic* (1843) became a standard textbook for many years, he is now remembered for *Utilitarianism* (1863) and for political works such as *The Principles of Political Economy* (1848), *On Liberty* (1859), and *The Subjection of Women* (1869), which argues for women's rights.

On Liberty, Mill's most famous work, has been described as "the bible of liberalism." The book was intended as a political essay, but has a moral underpinning that situates the ultimate source of human value in individual choice. Mill holds that individuals are autonomous and have a right to govern themselves. It follows—and this is the decisive step—that the legal limits on individual freedoms can only be justified when our actions harm other people. This principle, which has been called the "non-harm" principle, provides a basic constraint on democratic liberal government, which otherwise leads to "the tyranny of the majority."

The "non-harm" principle also finds a positive expression in the rule that actions which negatively affect other people may be regulated and curtailed by the state. The rule against "harm" and "negative effects" is deceptively simple, however, and notoriously difficult to apply in contentious moral cases. If someone buys pornography or rides a motorcycle without a helmet, have they negatively affected other people? There is no consensus about such questions.

Mill's focus is on freedom, however, rather than harm. As a general principle, even when we disagree vehemently with the behavior of other people, we have no right to interfere with their self-regarding actions. Nor do we have any right to step in when two participating parties consent to conduct that we feel negatively affects one of the participating parties. This is why consent has become a major issue in liberal literature.

Mill's overall position rests on an optimistic view of human nature. A moral theory that rests its authority on the sovereignty of the individual will run into serious difficulties if we cannot trust individuals to make sound or responsible decisions. Mill and other liberals, accordingly, put their faith in the moral judgment of the individual. This is, in part, a legacy of the Protestant Reformation, which allowed individuals to interpret scripture for themselves, but it stands in stark contrast to another Reformation conviction, the Augustinian view that humans are indelibly stained with original sin and utterly depraved.

Mill is wary of collective moral decisions. He believes that society inevitably errs when it censors our opinions—which leads to mistakes, like the condemnation of Socrates or the crucifixion of Jesus. Moreover, a liberal society must be supportive of the exercise of our individual freedoms by creating a social and psychological climate in which individuals can develop true character and proper judgment. Mill's main argument in *On Liberty* is simply that a certain kind of positive, energetic individualism should be fostered in society.

His view of utilitarianism, liberalism, and virtue ethics are all subordinated to this theme. Mill believes that a liberal society promotes a kind of virtue ethics, which displays itself in genius and energetic character. It also meets the goals of utilitarianism and promotes the happiness of the greatest number. The problem is naturally that these theories are often inconsistent and run counter to each other. The state and civil society frequently restrict our personal freedoms on utilitarian grounds, in order to protect the social welfare. Historically, *On Liberty* looks like a response to the increasing powers of the modern state, which began—under the influence of utilitarianism—to intervene more and more readily in the affairs of society. Mill's failure to address these tensions reflects the fact that he was writing for the general public. He has a journalistic, *belles lettres* style. The tone is distinctly rhetorical and, as a result, Mill's work has a discernible lack of philosophical rigor.

Mill's strong belief in individualism is important, not merely for its own sake, but also because it brings in the notion of equality, which has been the main engine of rights in the contemporary era. This dynamic is apparent in his discussion of women's rights.

Mill's future wife, Harriet Taylor Mill, was an invalid (suffering perhaps from tuberculosis) who had an estranged relationship with her husband, the father of her three children. While she was still married, Mill and Taylor frequented each other on a regular basis, enjoying an intimate relationship based on shared ideas and radical liberal causes. Taylor published little work under her name during her lifetime, but she commented on and perhaps helped edit Mill's voluminous output. In her writing, one discerns the same keen commitment to themes of progressive politics, the emancipation of women, and individual choice as a sovereign right for both men and women.

The readings for this chapter begin with selections from Wollstonecraft's *Vindication* that emphasize the importance of education in preparing young women for marriage, for employment, and for equal citizenship. They continue with a *précis* of the major elements in liberalism—still the dominant position in the ethical literature today—from Mill's *On Liberty*, and end with an excerpt from Taylor's journal article, "The Enfranchisement of Women" (1851).

Mary Wollstonecraft, *A Vindication of the Rights of Woman*[1]

(1792)

I do not believe that a private education can work the wonders which some sanguine writers have attributed to it.... Till society be differently constituted, much cannot be expected from education.... The most perfect education, in my opinion, is such an exercise of the understanding as is best calculated to strengthen the body and form the heart. Or, in other words, to enable the individual to attain such habits of virtue as will render it independent....

All the writers who have written on the subject of female education and manners...have contributed to render women more artificial, weak characters, than they would otherwise have been; and, consequently, more useless members of society.... My objection extends to the whole purport of [their] books, which tend, in my opinion, to...render women pleasing at the expense of every solid virtue.... I, therefore, will venture to assert, that till women are more rationally educated, the progress of human virtue and improvement in knowledge must receive continual checks....

The first care of those mothers or fathers, who really attend to the education of females, should be, if not to strengthen the body, at least, not to destroy the constitution by mistaken notions of beauty and female excellence.... The mother, who wishes to give true dignity of character to her daughter, must...proceed on a plan diametrically opposite to that which Rousseau[2] has recommended....

Throughout the whole animal kingdom every young creature requires almost continual exercise, [hence] the infancy of [girls]...should be passed in harmless gambols[3] that exercise the feet and hands without requiring...the constant attention of a nurse.... To preserve personal beauty, woman's glory! the limbs and faculties are cramped with worse than Chinese bands,[4] and the sedentary life which they are condemned to live, whilst boys frolic in the open air, weakens the muscles and relaxes the nerves....

It is time to effect a revolution in female manners...and make them...labor by reforming themselves to reform the world.... Women...act contrary to their real interest...when they cherish or affect weakness under the name of delicacy.... The poisoned source of female vices and follies...has been the sensual homage paid to beauty. Can it be expected that a woman will resolutely endeavor to strengthen her constitution and abstain from enervating indulgencies, if artificial notions of beauty...have been early entangled with her motives of action?...Genteel women are, literally speaking, slaves to their bodies, and glory in their subjection.... Taught from their infancy that beauty is woman's sceptre,[5] the mind shapes itself to the body, and, roaming round its gilt cage, only seeks to adorn its prison....

Girls...are often cruelly left by their parents without any provision; and, of course, are dependent on...the bounty of their brothers.... But, when

---

1 Mary Wollstonecraft, *A Vindication of the Rights of Woman*, 1792. A complete text is available at wikisource.org.

2 Jean-Jacques Rousseau (1712–78) was, in this day, considered the expert in matters of education. Wollstonecraft criticizes him severely for an overly sentimental romantic view of women's education that emphasizes how different they are from men.

3 I.e., running or jumping about playfully.

4 In tenth-century China, foot binding—wrapping feet in tight cloth to make them smaller and give them a more beautiful shape—began as a popular practice; it began to die out only in the early twentieth century. Wollstonecraft compares the restrictions on the physical activities of girls to this limiting practice.

5 A staff held in the hand as a symbol of royal authority; here, figuratively, a symbol of power.

the brother marries,... [his sister] is viewed...as an intruder, an unnecessary burden on the benevolence of the master of the house, and his new partner...is displeased at seeing the property of her children lavished on a helpless sister.... [She] has recourse to cunning...till the spy is worked out of her home, and thrown on the world, unprepared for its difficulties; or sent,...with a small stipend, and an uncultivated mind, into joyless solitude....

I am, indeed, persuaded that the heart, as well as the understanding, is opened by cultivation.... Women, whose minds are not enlarged by cultivation...are very unfit to manage a family.... If [women] be moral beings, let them have a chance to become intelligent; and let love to man be only a part of that glowing flame of universal love, which, after encircling humanity, mounts in grateful incense to God....

Whoever rationally means to be useful must have a plan of conduct; in the discharge of the simplest duty, we are often obliged to act contrary to the present impulse of tenderness or compassion. Severity is frequently the most certain, as well as the most sublime proof of affection; and the want of this power over the feelings, and of that lofty, dignified affection, which makes a person prefer the future good of the beloved object to a present gratification, is the reason why so many fond mothers spoil their children....

Mankind seem to agree that children should be left under the management of women during their childhood.... Women of sensibility are the most unfit for this task, because they will infallibly, carried away by their feelings, spoil a child's temper. The management of the temper, the first, and most important branch of education, requires the sober steady eye of reason....

A woman who has lost her honor imagines that,...as for recovering her former station, it is impossible.... Having no other means of support, prostitution becomes her only refuge, and [her] character is quickly depraved.... Necessity never makes prostitution the business of men's lives; though numberless are the women who are thus rendered systematically vicious. This, however, arises, in a great degree, from the state of idleness in which women are educated, who are always taught to look up to man for a maintenance....

Children...form a much more permanent connection between married people than love. Beauty, [Rousseau] declares, will not be valued, or even seen after a couple have lived six months together; artificial graces and coquetry will likewise pall on the senses.... The man who can be contented to live with a pretty, useful companion, without a mind...has never felt the calm satisfaction...of being beloved by one who could understand him.... But how could Rousseau expect [women] to be virtuous and constant when reason is neither allowed to be the foundation of their virtue, nor truth the object of their inquiries?... Were women more rationally educated,...they would be contented to love but once in their lives; and after marriage calmly let passion subside into friendship, into that tender intimacy, which is the best refuge from care....

Virtue will never prevail in society till the virtues of both sexes are founded on reason.... To render this practicable, day schools...should be established by government, in which boys and girls might be educated together. The school for the younger children, from five to nine years of age, ought to be absolutely free and open to all classes.... To render also the social compact truly equitable, and in order to spread those enlightening principles, which alone can meliorate the fate of man, women must be allowed to found their virtue on knowledge, which is scarcely possible unless they be educated by the same pursuits as men....

John Stuart Mill, *On Liberty*[1]

(1859)

Dedication to Harriet Taylor Mill

To the beloved and deplored memory of her who was the inspirer, and in part the author, of all that is best in my writings…I dedicate this volume. Like all that I have written for many years, it belongs as much to her as to me…. Were I but capable of interpreting to the world one-half the great thoughts and noble feelings which are buried in her grave, I should be the medium of a greater benefit to it than is ever likely to arise from anything that I can write, unprompted and unassisted by her all but unrivalled wisdom.

Chapter I: Introductory

5. Like other tyrannies, the tyranny of the majority was at first, and is still vulgarly, held in dread, chiefly as operating through the acts of the public authorities. But reflecting persons perceived that when society is itself the tyrant…it practises a social tyranny more formidable than many kinds of political oppression, since…it leaves fewer means of escape, penetrating much more deeply into the details of life, and enslaving the soul itself. Protection, therefore, against the tyranny of the magistrate is not enough: there needs protection also against the tyranny of the prevailing opinion and feeling; against the tendency of society to impose, by other means than civil penalties, its own ideas and practices as rules of conduct on those who dissent from them; to fetter the development, and, if possible, prevent the formation, of any individuality not in harmony with its ways, and compel all

characters to fashion themselves upon the model of its own.

There is a limit to the legitimate interference of collective opinion with individual independence: and to find that limit, and maintain it against encroachment, is as indispensable to a good condition of human affairs, as protection against political despotism….

9. The object of this Essay is to assert one very simple principle, as entitled to govern absolutely the dealings of society with the individual in the way of compulsion and control, whether the means used be physical force in the form of legal penalties, or the moral coercion of public opinion. That principle is, that the sole end for which mankind are warranted, individually or collectively, in interfering with the liberty of action of any of their number, is self-protection. That the only purpose for which power can be rightfully exercised over any member of a civilised community, against his will, is to prevent harm to others. His own good, either physical or moral, is not a sufficient warrant. He cannot rightfully be compelled to do or forbear because it will be better for him to do so, because it will make him happier, because, in the opinions of others, to do so would be wise, or even right. These are good reasons for remonstrating with him, or reasoning with him, or persuading him, or entreating him, but not for compelling him, or visiting him with any evil in case he do otherwise. To justify that, the conduct from which it is desired to deter him must be calculated to produce evil to someone else. The only part of the conduct of any one, for which he is amenable to

---

1   John Stuart Mill, *On Liberty* (London: John W. Parker and Son, 1859).

society, is that which concerns others. In the part which merely concerns himself, his independence is, of right, absolute. Over himself, over his own body and mind, the individual is sovereign.

10. We are not speaking [here] of children, or of young persons below the age which the law may fix as that of manhood or womanhood.... For the same reason, we may leave out of consideration those backward states of society in which the race itself may be considered as in its nonage.[1]...

Despotism is a legitimate mode of government in dealing with barbarians, provided the end be their improvement, and the means justified by actually effecting that end. Liberty, as a principle, has no application to any state of things anterior to the time when mankind have become capable of being improved by free and equal discussion. Until then, there is nothing for them but implicit obedience to an Akbar or a Charlemagne,[2] if they are so fortunate as to find one....

11. I regard utility as the ultimate appeal on all ethical questions; but it must be utility in the largest sense, grounded on the permanent interests of man as a progressive being. Those interests, I contend, authorise the subjection of individual spontaneity to external control, only in respect to those actions of each, which concern the interest of other people. If any one does an act hurtful to others, there is a prima facie case for punishing him, by law, or, where legal penalties are not safely applicable, by general disapprobation. There are also many positive acts for the benefit of others, which he may rightfully be compelled to perform; such as, to give evidence in a court of justice; to bear his fair share in the common defence, or in any other joint work necessary to the interest of the society of which he enjoys the protection; and to perform certain acts of individual beneficence, such as saving a fellow-creature's life, or interposing to protect the defenceless against ill-usage, things which whenever it is obviously a man's duty to do, he may rightfully be made responsible to society for not doing....

12. But there is a sphere of action in which society, as distinguished from the individual, has, if any, only an indirect interest; comprehending all that portion of a person's life and conduct which affects only himself, or if it also affects others, only with their free, voluntary, and undeceived consent and participation.... This, then, is the appropriate region of human liberty. It comprises, first, the inward domain of consciousness; demanding liberty of conscience, in the most comprehensive sense; liberty of thought and feeling; absolute freedom of opinion and sentiment on all subjects, practical or speculative, scientific, moral, or theological....

The liberty of expressing and publishing opinions may seem to fall under a different principle,... but, being almost of as much importance as the liberty of thought itself, and resting in great part on the same reasons, is practically inseparable from it. Secondly, the principle requires liberty of tastes and pursuits; of framing the plan of our life to suit our own character; of doing as we like, subject to such consequences as may follow: without impediment from our fellow-creatures, so long as what we do does not harm them, even though they should think our conduct foolish, perverse, or wrong.

Thirdly, from this liberty of each individual, follows the liberty, within the same limits, of combination among individuals; freedom to unite, for any purpose not involving harm to others: the persons combining being supposed to be of full age, and not forced or deceived.

---

1 I.e., the period of immaturity or youth.
2 Akbar I (1542–1605) was the third Mughal emperor in India, reigning from 1556 to 1605; Charlemagne or Charles the Great (742–814) was a King and, from 800, the Holy Roman Emperor, ruling much of western and central Europe.

Chapter II: Of the Liberty of Thought and Discussion[1]

11. The feeling sure of a doctrine... [is not that] which I call an assumption of infallibility. It is the undertaking to decide that question for others, without allowing them to hear what can be said on the contrary side.... However positive any one's persuasion may be... of the pernicious consequences... of an opinion; [if], in pursuance of that private judgment, though backed by the public judgment of his country or his contemporaries, [someone] prevents the opinion from being heard in its defence, he assumes infallibility....

12. Mankind can hardly be too often reminded that there was once a man named Socrates, between whom and the legal authorities and public opinion of his time, there took place a memorable collision....
  This acknowledged master of all the eminent thinkers who have since lived... was put to death by his countrymen, after a judicial conviction, for impiety and immorality.... Of these charges the tribunal, there is every ground for believing, honestly found him guilty, and condemned the man who probably of all then born had deserved best of mankind, to be put to death as a criminal.

13. To pass from this to the only other instance of judicial iniquity... would not be an anticlimax: the event which took place on Calvary[2] rather more than eighteen hundred years ago. The man... was ignominiously put to death, as what? As a blasphemer. Men did not merely mistake their benefactor; they mistook him for the exact contrary of what he was, and treated him as that prodigy of impiety, which they themselves are now held to be, for their treatment of him....

Chapter III: Of Individuality, as One of the Elements of Well-Being

3. No one's idea of excellence in conduct is that people should do absolutely nothing but copy one another.... It is the privilege and proper condition of a human being, arrived at the maturity of his faculties, to use and interpret experience in his own way.... The human faculties of perception, judgment, discriminative feeling, mental activity, and even moral preference, are exercised only in making a choice. He who does anything because it is the custom, makes no choice. He gains no practice either in discerning or in desiring what is best. The mental and moral, like the muscular powers, are improved only by being used....

4. He who lets the world, or his own portion of it, choose his plan of life for him, has no need of any other faculty than the ape-like one of imitation. He who chooses his plan for himself, employs all his faculties. He must use observation to see, reasoning and judgment to foresee, activity to gather materials for decision, discrimination to decide, and when he has decided, firmness and self-control to hold to his deliberate decision....
  It really is of importance, not only what men do, but also what manner of men they are that do it. Among the works of man, which human life is rightly employed in perfecting and beautifying, the first in importance surely is man himself....

9. It is not by wearing down into uniformity all that is individual in themselves, but by cultivating it and calling it forth, within the limits imposed by the rights and interests of others, that human beings become a noble and beautiful object of contemplation;... In proportion to the development of his

---

1 In this chapter, Mill argues against the censorship of moral, religious, or political beliefs.
2 I.e., the site where Jesus Christ was crucified.

individuality, each person becomes more valuable to himself, and is therefore capable of being more valuable to others....

11. It will not be denied by anybody, that originality is a valuable element in human affairs. There is always need of persons... to commence new practices, and set the example of more enlightened conduct, and better taste and sense in human life....

Precisely because the tyranny of opinion is such as to make eccentricity a reproach, it is desirable, in order to break through that tyranny, that people should be eccentric....

14. If a person possesses any tolerable amount of common-sense and experience, his own mode of laying out his existence is the best, not because it is the best in itself, but because it is his own mode. Human beings are not like sheep; and even sheep are not undistinguishably alike....

READING 36C

Harriet Taylor Mill, from "The Enfranchisement of Women"[1]

(1851)

Most of our readers will probably learn from these pages for the first time, that there has arisen in the United States... an organized agitation on a new question—new, not to thinkers,... but new, and even unheard-of, as a subject for public meetings and practical political action. This question is the enfranchisement[2] of women; their admission, in law and in fact, to equality in all rights, political, civil, and social, with the male citizens of the community....

[The] traditional maxims of political justice [are] impossible to reconcile [with] the exclusion of all women from the common rights of citizenship. It is an axiom of English freedom that taxation and representation should be co-extensive. Even under the laws which give the wife's property to the husband, there are many unmarried women who pay taxes. It is one of the fundamental doctrines of the British Constitution, that all persons should be tried by their peers: yet women, whenever tried, are by male judges and a male jury.... It is an acknowledged dictate of justice to make no degrading distinctions without necessity. In all things the presumption ought to be on the side of equality.... We are firmly convinced [then] that the division of mankind into two castes, one born to rule over the other, is... an unqualified mischief; a source of perversion and demoralization, both to the favored class and to those at whose expense they are favored; producing none of the good which it is the custom to ascribe to it, and forming a bar, almost insuperable while it lasts, to any really vital improvement, either in the character or in the social condition of the human race.

---

1 Harriet Taylor Mill, "The Enfranchisement of Women," *Westminster and Foreign Quarterly Review*, July 1851.

2 I.e., the giving of a right or privilege, especially the right to vote.

We would endeavor to dispel the preliminary objections.[1] The chief of these obstacles is … custom. Women never have had equal rights with men. The claim in their behalf, of the common rights of mankind, is looked upon as barred by universal practice. This strongest of prejudices, the prejudice against what is new and unknown, has … lost much of its force. [Still, to] over three-fourths of the habitable world, even at this day, the answer, "it has always been so," closes all discussion. But it is the boast of modern Europeans, and of their American kindred, that they know and do many things which their forefathers neither knew nor did; and it is perhaps the most unquestionable point of superiority in the present above former ages, that habit is not now the tyrant it formerly was … and that the worship of custom is a declining idolatry. An uncustomary thought … still startles when first presented; but if it can be kept before the mind until the impression of strangeness wears off, it obtains a hearing, and as rational a consideration as the intellect of the hearer is accustomed to bestow on any other subject. …

There has been no political community or nation in which … women have not been in a state of political and civil inferiority. … No other explanation is needed than physical force. That those who were physically weaker should have been made legally inferior, is quite conformable to the mode in which the world has been governed. Until very lately, the rule of physical strength was the general law of human affairs. Throughout history, the nations, races, classes, which found themselves the strongest, either in muscles, in riches, or in military discipline, have conquered and held in subjection the rest. …

Many persons … have said that the pursuits from which women are excluded are unfeminine, and that the proper sphere of women is not politics or publicity, but private and domestic life. We deny the right of any portion of the species to decide for another portion, or any individual for another individual, what is and what is not their "proper sphere." The proper sphere for all human beings is the largest and highest which they are able to attain to. What this is, cannot be ascertained, without complete liberty of choice. [Activists] have therefore done wisely and right, in refusing to entertain the question of the peculiar aptitudes either of women or of men, or the limits within this or that occupation that may be supposed to be more adapted to the one or to the other. … They justly maintain, that these questions can only be satisfactorily answered by perfect freedom. Let every occupation be open to all, without favor or discouragement to any, and employments will fall into the hands of those men or women who are found by experience to be most capable of worthily exercising them. There need be no fear that women will take out of the hands of men any occupation which men perform better than they. Each individual will prove his or her capacities, in the only way in which capacities can be proved—by trial; and the world will have the benefit of the best faculties of all its inhabitants. But to interfere beforehand by an arbitrary limit … is not only an injustice to the individual, and a detriment to society, … but is also the most effectual mode of providing that, in the sex or class so fettered, the qualities which are not permitted to be exercised shall not exist.

Questions

1. Explain how Mill, Wollstonecraft, and Taylor Mill all emphasize individual choice in their respective excerpts.

---

1 I.e., objections to equality between men and women.

2. Mill argues openly that it is morally acceptable to impose despotism on "barbarians." Why? Relate to Taylor Mill's comments.

3. Mill complained that his education was too logical, too cerebral. He looked to Romantic poetry as a cure for his nervous depression. Compare this to Wollstonecraft's emphasis on the rational nature of women. How do you explain the stark difference in their views on education?

4. Mill talks about the tyranny of the majority. This was not an issue in tribal societies, which were governed by a moral consensus, and seems to be the price we pay for democratic government. What is the solution?

5. What is Mill's position on censorship? Do you agree with his use of the historical examples of Socrates and Jesus?

6. Mill distinguishes between the application of the no-harm principle to private/self-regarding acts and public/other-regarding acts. Give an example of each, explaining how the no-harm principle applies.

7. The no-harm principle is like a legal test, which determines how far society can go in regulating our behavior. It is not always clear, however, how much harm is sufficient to justify restrictions on our behavior. Where do you draw the line? Why?

Suggested Readings

Mill wrote voluminously in defense of a progressive intellectual, moral, political, and social agenda. His commentary spans the gamut from an influential textbook in logic (*A System of Logic*, 1843) to comments on liberalizing marriage and letters to the editor on various public issues. Mill's probing and unsentimental *Autobiography* (1873) is of philosophical as well as historical interest.

The authoritative edition of Mill's writings is J. Robson, ed., *The Collected Works of John Stuart Mill*, in thirty-three volumes. Broadview's edition of *On Liberty*, edited by Edward Alexander (1999), includes the responses to Mill's work by his contemporaries. Students may find Mill's discursive prose difficult and adapted versions of *On Liberty* (1859), *Utilitarianism* (1863), and *The Subjection of Women* (1869) are available in a more contemporary idiom at earlymoderntexts.com.

For a collection of sympathetic essays, see Eldon J. Eisenach, ed., *Mill and the Moral Character of Liberalism* (1999). For a discussion of equality, which is central in the liberal tradition, see Matthew Clayton, "Liberal Equality and Ethics" (2002). For the liberal tradition in Europe, see R.G. Collingwood's translation of Guido De Ruggiero, *The History of European Liberalism* (1927). The religious response to the secular liberal tradition includes Wesley J. Wildman, *Theology and Ethics for Christians Who Are Both Liberal and Evangelical* (2009), and James F. Drane, *A Liberal Catholic Bioethics* (2010).

There is a substantive entry on Harriet Taylor Mill and the controversy surrounding her collaboration with her husband at the online *Stanford Encyclopedia of Philosophy*. For a largely skeptical view regarding the extent of her contribution, see H.O. Pappe, *John Stuart*

Mill and the Harriet Taylor Myth (1960). For a very different interpretation, see Jo Ellen Jacobs, *The Complete Works of Harriet Taylor Mill* (2000) and her chapter "Harriet Taylor Mill's Collaboration with John Stuart Mill," in *Presenting Women Philosophers* (2000).

Wollstonecraft's oeuvre is collected in a seven-volume edition by Janet Todd and Marilyn Butler, eds., *The Works of Mary Wollstonecraft* (1989). Godwin's loving but candid biography *Wollstonecraft, Memoirs of the Author of A Vindication of the Rights of Woman* (1798), was reissued in 2001 by editors Pamela Clemit and Gina Luria Walker. The early editions of *A Vindication of the Rights of Woman with Strictures on Political and Moral Subjects* were published by Joseph Johnson (London, 1792, 1796) and are available online. Cambridge University Press has put out a contemporary edition (ed. Sylvana Tomaselli, 1995), as has Oxford University Press (ed. Janet Todd, 1993–94). See also Janet Todd, *The Collected Letters of Mary Wollstonecraft* (2003).

Chapter 37

Beyond Morality

The German philosopher Friedrich Wilhelm Nietzsche (1844–1900) is widely regarded as a troubling figure. His moral philosophy is nevertheless a response to the same crisis of meaning that surfaces in the work of Schopenhauer, Kierkegaard, and many other modern philosophers. Nietzsche believed that history—and our very conception of morality—had unfolded in a manner that gave rise only to a defeating nihilism, which he wanted to overcome.

Nietzsche lost his father and his brother as a young boy. This left him in the care of his mother, his grandmother, his aunts, and his younger sister, Elisabeth. There were no men in the household. Some commentators have suggested that the resulting imbalance was responsible for his uneasy relationships with women later in life. There are salacious allegations—which have widely been rejected—that he had incestuous relations with his sister Elisabeth.

Nietzsche grew up in Naumburg, Saxony, where he was enrolled in a prestigious German boarding school (the *Schulpforta*) and received a formidable education in the humanities, theology, and classical languages. In 1864, he entered the University of Bonn, and quickly lost his religious faith, renouncing his theological studies for philology, a painstakingly rigorous discipline which focused on the scientific analysis of early Greek, Roman, and Hebraic texts. The following year, he followed one of his professors to the University of Leipzig.

In 1867, Nietzsche interrupted his studies to complete his compulsory military service and entered a Prussian artillery regiment, but suffered a serious chest injury while trying to leap into the saddle of a horse and was declared unfit to serve. He accordingly returned to his studies, publishing a number of academic papers, and was enrolled in the doctoral program. Already seen as a rising academic star, he was awarded the position of Professor of Greek Language and Literature at the University of Basel in 1869.

Nietzsche went back to the military briefly in 1870 and served as a medical orderly during the Franco-Prussian War, but contracted diphtheria, dysentery, and perhaps syphilis, only to be dismissed again. He accordingly returned to Basel, where he taught for the next ten years and met some of the leading intellectuals in European academic circles. An amateur composer of classical music, he notably befriended the famous German composer Richard Wagner, whom he showered with extravagant praise but later denounced.

After the publication of *The Birth of Tragedy* (1872), under the influence of Wagner, Nietzsche's academic reputation began to decline to such a point that he eventually had difficulty attracting students. In 1878, at thirty-four, he accordingly negotiated a settlement with the university, which awarded him a small pension, and turned to his own writing. Although the next decade was the most productive period in his life, he lived a solitary, nomadic life, traveling continually in search of inexpensive accommodations.

Nietzsche's internal life has been the subject of much speculation. Although he apparently proposed to two women, he was turned down and remained single. When he was thirty-seven, he fell madly in love with Lou von Salomé, a twenty-one-year-old Russian student, but the stormy affair was over within six months. At least one scholar has suggested that he struggled with homosexuality. Whatever the reason, he suffered increasingly from physical and psychological ailments that continued to worsen.

Nietzsche wrote steadily but suffered from migraine headaches, problems with his eyesight, and painful, recurrent indigestion problems. Over time, he began to make annual treks through the cities on the continent, stopping in resorts and spas, trying to recover his deteriorating health. The climax came in 1889, when he supposedly saw a coachman whipping a horse. He threw his arms around the animal's neck and suffered a complete mental collapse. He never recovered and was nursed by his mother and sister for the rest of his life, dying in Weimar in 1900. Various authorities have attributed his insanity to syphilis, brain disease, a brain tumor, and drug abuse.

Nietzsche's moral philosophy is primarily romantic but clouded by provocative elements. He was fiercely opposed to Christianity, attacked conventional morality, and wrote in an intense, aphoristic style that ignores the usual conventions of philosophical argument. Emotionally, at least, his work has affinities with the work of Kierkegaard and Schopenhauer, and implicitly raises questions about the narrow logical approach adopted by so many academic philosophers.

The difficulties of Nietzsche's prose are legion. His style is literary and revelatory; his prose is full of hyperbole. There are passages that disclose original and even trenchant philosophical insights, amidst pages of rambling, repetitive, melodramatic prose. Nietzsche's sister Elisabeth, who managed his literary estate after he slipped into dementia, had become a notorious Nazi sympathizer. She has been accused of tailoring his work editorially so that it fit easily into Nazi ideology.

Scholars have pointed out correctly that Nietzsche himself displayed an open disdain for German nationalists and anti-Semites. In spite of this, however, it is impossible to overlook other passages that seem virulently chauvinistic, anti-Semitic, and misogynistic. Some commentators have argued that these exaggerated remarks are literary means of conveying uncomfortable truths about society and the human condition.

Some of Nietzsche's more important works include *The Birth of Tragedy* (1872), *Thus Spoke Zarathustra* (1883–85), *Beyond Good and Evil* (1886), *On the Genealogy of Morals*

(1887), *Twilight of the Idols* (1888), *The Antichrist* (1888), and *The Will to Power* (1901), which was published posthumously and which shows the signs of his deteriorating mind. It is nevertheless seriously philosophical and discernibly follows the rational German ideal, trying to explain history and all of metaphysics in a single theory.

Like Marx's materialism, Nietzsche's romanticism is complicated by his rejection of our ordinary understanding of morality. His work nevertheless contains a system of values, an account of human achievement and failure, and both praises and condemns specific behaviors. Nietzsche's opposition to mainstream values originates in definite opinions about what is admirable, noble, and good.

Nietzsche's famous proclamation that "God is dead" is based on his belief that modern science has dismantled the previous accounts of reality, which can be found in religion and the earlier cosmological views. This process has left us abandoned in a Darwinian world inhabited by individuals, ethnic groups, and species that compete with one another for supremacy. There is a violent and interminable struggle of the "will to power" and an instinctive desire to dominate others. We do not have any higher, supernatural purpose.

Nietzsche's view is easily misunderstood. He rejects pessimism and nihilism and is looking for a heroic affirmation of life. He finds this affirmation in a naturalistic account of morality, which focuses on the will. The "Overman" or "Superman" (the *Übermensch*) is the pinnacle of evolutionary perfection. Faced with the loss of meaning that characterizes the modern era, he creates values for himself and overcomes and subjugates his enemies with ruthless abandon. His drive to conquer and impose his will on others is the embodiment of the will to power at the heart of nature.

The first reading is from *On the Genealogy of Morals* (1887), which sets out this dynamic. The book is an attack on conventional morality and, in many ways, harkens back to the early views of the warrior ethic. Nietzsche traces the concepts of good and evil to a master race of "blonde beasts" who rejoice in their physical power and beauty. Their values are subverted, however, through the historical machinations of priests and slaves, too weak to confront their masters, who invert the meaning of 'good' and 'bad' for their own benefit.

The second reading is from *The Will to Power*, which was an anthology of unfinished passages compiled and published by Nietzsche's sister after his death. The book is incomplete, even inchoate, but illuminates Nietzsche's view of nihilism, Christianity, the *Übermensch*, and the evolutionary process by which the *Übermensch* asserts his superiority and the will to power.

Friedrich Nietzsche, *On the Genealogy of Morals*[1]

(1887)

Prologue

Because of a doubt peculiar to my own nature, which I am reluctant to confess—for it concerns itself with *morality*, with everything which up to the present has been celebrated on earth as morality—a doubt which came into my life so early, so uninvited, so irresistibly, in such contradiction to my surroundings,... that I would almost have the right to call it my "*a priori*" [*before experience*]—because of this, my curiosity as well as my suspicion had to pause early on at the question of where our good and evil really *originated*. In fact, already as a thirteen-year-old lad, my mind was occupying itself with the problem of the origin of evil.... Luckily at an early stage I learned to separate theological prejudices from moral ones.... Some education in history and philology, along with an inherently refined sense concerning psychological questions in general, quickly changed my problem into something else: Under what conditions did people invent for themselves those value judgments good and evil?... Have [those value judgments] hindered or fostered human well-being up to now? Are they a sign of some emergency, of impoverishment, of an atrophying life? Or is it the other way around? Do they indicate fullness, power, a will for life, its courage, its confidence, its future? To these questions I came across and proposed all sorts of answers for myself....

For me the issue was the *value* of morality—and in that matter I had to take issue almost alone with my great teacher Schopenhauer.... The most specific issue was the worth of the "unegoistic," of the instincts for pity, for self-denial, and for self-sacrifice, of things which Schopenhauer himself had painted with gold [and] deified,... for so long that they finally remained for him "value as such" and the reason why he *said No* to life and even to himself, as well. But a constantly more fundamental suspicion of *these* very instincts voiced itself in me, a scepticism which always dug deeper! It was precisely here that I saw the *great* danger to humanity, its most sublime temptation and seduction.—But in what direction? To nothingness?—It was precisely here I saw the beginning of the end, the standing still, the backward-glancing exhaustion, the will turning itself *against* life, the final illness tenderly and sadly announcing itself. I understood the morality of pity, which was always seizing more and more around it and which gripped even the philosophers and made them sick, as the most sinister symptom of our European culture, which itself had become sinister, as its detour to a new Buddhism? to a European Buddhism? to—*nihilism?*...

This problem of the *value* of pity and of the morality of pity (—I'm an opponent of the disgraceful modern effeminacy of feeling—)...[results in] a new demand. Let's proclaim this *new demand*: we need a *critique* of moral values, *we must first question the very value of these values*—and for that we need a knowledge of the conditions and circumstances out of which these values grew,...a knowledge of a sort that has not been there up to this point, that has not even been wished for. We have taken the *worth* of these "values" as given, as self-evident, as beyond all dispute. Up until now people have not even had the

---

1 From *On the Genealogy of Morals: A Polemical Tract*, translated by Ian Johnston (Arlington, VA: Richer Resources Publications. Revised edition, 2014). Full text available at http://fs2.american.edu/dfagel/www/GeneologyOfMorals.html.

slightest doubts about or wavered in setting up "the good man" as more valuable than "the evil man," of higher worth in the sense of improvement, usefulness, and prosperity with respect to mankind in general (along with the future of humanity). What about this? What if the truth were the other way around? Well? What if in the "good man" there even lay a symptom of regression, like a danger, a seduction, a poison, a narcotic, something which, for example, made the present live *at the cost of the future*? Perhaps in greater comfort and less danger, but also on a smaller scale and in a more demeaning way?... So that morality itself would be guilty if the inherently possible *highest power and magnificence* of the human type were never attained? So that morality itself might be the danger of dangers?...

First Essay: 'Good and Evil,' 'Good and Bad'

—These English psychologists, whom we have to thank for the only attempts up to this point to produce a history of the origins of morality—...serve up to us no small riddle....

The incompetence of their genealogies of morals reveals itself at the very beginning, where the issue is to determine the origin of the idea and of the judgment "good." "People," so they proclaim, "originally praised unegoistic actions and called them good from the perspective of those for whom they were done, that is, those for whom such actions were *useful*. Later people *forgot* how this praise began, and simply because unegoistic actions had, *according to custom*, always been praised as good, people also felt them as good—as if they were something inherently good."... Now, first of all, it's obvious to me that from this theory the essential source for the origin of the idea "good" has been sought for and established in the wrong place: the judgment "good" does *not* originate from those to whom "goodness" was shown! On the contrary, it was the "good people" themselves, that is, the noble, powerful, high-

er-ranking, and higher-thinking people who felt and set themselves and their actions up as good, that is to say, of the first rank, in opposition to everything low, low-minded, common, and vulgar. From this *pathos of distance* they first arrogated to themselves the right to create values, to stamp out the names for values. What did they care about usefulness! Particularly in relation to such a hot pouring out of the highest rank-ordering, rank-setting judgments of value, the point of view which considers utility is as foreign and inappropriate as possible. Here the feeling has reached the very opposite of the low level of warmth which is a condition for that calculating shrewdness.... The pathos of nobility and distance,... the lasting and dominating feeling, something total and fundamental, of a higher ruling nature in relation to a lower type, to a "beneath"—*that* is the origin of the opposition between "good" and "bad."...

I was given a hint of the *right* direction by the following question: What, from an etymological perspective, do the meanings of "good," as manifested in different languages, really signify? There I found that all of them lead back to the *same transformation of ideas*—that everywhere "noble" and "aristocratic" in a social sense is the fundamental idea out of which "good" in the sense of "spiritually noble," "aristocratic," "spiritually high-minded," "spiritually privileged" necessarily develops, a process which always runs in parallel with that other one that finally transforms "common," "vulgar," and "low" into the concept "bad."...

[T]here is no little interest in establishing the point that often in those words and roots which designate "good" there still shines through the main nuance of what made the nobility feel they were men of higher rank. It's true that in most cases they perhaps name themselves simply after their superiority in strength (as "the powerful," "the masters," "those in command") or after the most visible sign of this superiority, for example, as "the rich" or "the owners."... But they also name themselves after a *typical characteristic*, and this is the case which is our concern here. For instance, they call themselves "the truthful"...to mark a distinction from the *lying* common man....

To this rule that the concept of political superiority always resolves itself into the concept of spiritual superiority, it is at first not an exception...when the highest caste is also the *priestly* caste.... Here, for example, the words "pure" and "impure" first appear as contrasting marks of one's social position, and here, too, a "good" and a "bad" also develop.... [T]hese ideas of "pure" and "impure,"...to a degree we can hardly imagine, are originally much more coarse, crude, superficial, narrow, blunt, and, in particular, *unsymbolic.* The "pure man" is initially simply a man who washes himself, who forbids himself certain foods that produce diseases of the skin, who doesn't sleep with the dirty women of the lower people, who has a horror of blood—no more, not much more!...

You will have already guessed how easily the priestly way of evaluating can split from the knightly-aristocratic and then continue to develop into its opposite. Such a development receives a special stimulus every time the priestly caste and the warrior caste confront each other jealously and are not willing to agree amongst themselves about the reward. The knightly-aristocratic judgments of value have as their basic assumption a powerful physicality, a blooming, rich, even overflowing health, together with those things required to maintain these qualities—war, adventure, hunting, dancing, war games, and, in general, everything which involves strong, free, and happy action. The priestly-noble method of evaluating has, as we saw, other preconditions: these make it difficult enough for them when it comes to war! As is well known, priests are the *most evil of enemies*—but why? Because they are the most powerless. From their powerlessness, their hate grows among them into something huge and terrifying, to the most spiritual and most poisonous manifes-

tations. The really great haters in world history and also the cleverest haters have always been priests.... Human history would be a really stupid affair without the spirit that entered it from the powerless. Let us quickly consider the greatest example. Nothing on earth which has been done against "the nobility," "the powerful," "the masters," and "the possessors of power" is worth mentioning in comparison with what *the Jews*[1] have done against them: the Jews, that priestly people, who knew how to get final satisfaction from their enemies and conquerors merely through a radical transformation of their values, that is, through an act of *the most spiritual revenge....* In opposition to the aristocratic value equation (*good = noble = powerful = beautiful = fortunate = loved by god*), the Jews, with a consistency inspiring fear, dared to reverse things and to hang on to that with the teeth of the most profound hatred (the hate of powerlessness), that is, to "only those who suffer are good; the poor, the powerless, the low are the only good people; the suffering, those in need, the sick, the ugly are also the only pious people; only they are blessed by God; for them alone there is salvation.—By contrast, you privileged and powerful people, you are for all eternity the evil, the cruel, the lecherous, the insatiable, the godless; you will also be the unblessed, the cursed, and the damned for all eternity!"...[W]ith the Jews *the slave rebellion in morality* begins: that rebellion which has a two-thousand-year-old history behind it and which we nowadays no longer even notice because it—has triumphed....

Let's follow the facts: the people have triumphed—or 'the slaves,' or 'the rabble,' or 'the herd,' or whatever you want to call them—if this has taken place because of the Jews, then good for them!...The 'salvation' of the human race (namely, from 'the masters') is well under way. Everything is visibly turning Jewish or Christian or plebeian (what do the words matter!). The progress of this

---

1 Nietzsche held the Jews responsible for Christianity and the slave morality of the common man, which he will describe shortly.

poison through the entire body of humanity seems irresistible...

The slave revolt in morality begins when the *ressentiment*[1] itself becomes creative and gives birth to values: the *ressentiment* of those beings who are prevented from a genuine reaction, that is, something active, and who compensate for that with a merely imaginary vengeance. Whereas all noble morality grows out of a triumphant affirmation of one's own self, slave morality from the start says "No" to what is "outside," "other," "not itself." And *this* "No" is its creative act.... A race of such men of *ressentiment* will inevitably end up *cleverer* than any noble race....

How much respect a noble man already has for his enemies!—and such a respect is already a bridge to love.... In fact,...he has no enemy other than one in whom there is nothing to despise and a *great deal* to respect! By contrast, imagine..."the enemy" as a man of *ressentiment* conceives him—and right here we have his action...he has conceptualized "the evil enemy," "*the evil one*," as, in fact, a fundamental idea from which he now also thinks his way to a complementary image and counterpart, a "good man"—himself!...

Friedrich Nietzsche, *The Will to Power: An Attempted Transvaluation of All Values*[2]

(published posthumously in 1901)

First Book. European Nihilism

A PLAN

1. Nihilism is at our door: whence comes this most gruesome of all guests to us?—To begin with, it is a mistake to point to "social evils," "physiological degeneration," or even to corruption as a cause of Nihilism.... Evil, whether spiritual, physical, or intellectual, is, in itself, quite unable to introduce Nihilism, *i.e.*, the absolute repudiation of worth, purpose, desirability. These evils allow of yet other and quite different explanations. But there is one *very definite explanation* of the phenomena: Nihilism harbours in the heart of Christian morals.

2.... [T]he sense of truth, highly developed through Christianity, ultimately revolts against the falsehood and fictitiousness of all Christian interpretations of the world and its history. The recoil-stroke of "God is Truth" in the fanatical Belief, is: "All is false."...

3. Doubt in morality is the decisive factor.... [T]he inconsistency of one explanation of the world, to

---

1 Blaming others for one's own inferiority and failures.
2 Friedrich Nietzsche, *The Will to Power. An Attempted Transvaluation of All Values*. (1887–1888), trans. by Anthony M. Ludovici, originally from Vols. 14 and 15 of Oscar Levy, ed., *The Complete Works of Friedrich Nietzsche* (London and Edinburgh: T.N. Foulis, 1914 [vol. 1 of *Will* in vol. 14 of *Works*], 1910 [vol. 2 of *Will* in vol. 15 of *Works*]).

which men have devoted untold energy,—gives rise to the suspicion that all explanations may perhaps be false...

I. NIHILISM

2. What does Nihilism mean?—*That the highest values are losing their value....*

3. Thorough Nihilism is the conviction that life is absurd, in the light of the highest values already discovered; it also includes the *view* that we have not the smallest right to assume the existence of transcendental objects or things in themselves,[1] which would be either divine or morality incarnate.

This view is a result of fully developed "truthfulness": therefore a consequence of the belief in morality.

4. What *advantages* did the Christian hypothesis of morality offer?

(1) It bestowed an intrinsic value upon men, which contrasted with their apparent insignificance and subordination to chance in the eternal flux of becoming and perishing.

(2) It served the purpose of God's advocates, inasmuch as it granted the world a certain *perfection* despite its sorrow and evil—it also granted the world that proverbial "freedom": evil seemed full of *meaning*.

(3) It assumed that man could have a *knowledge* of absolute values, and thus granted him *adequate perception* for the most important things.

(4) It prevented man from despising himself as man, from turning against life, and from being driven to despair by knowledge: it was a self-preservative measure.

In short: Morality was the great *antidote* against practical and theoretical Nihilism.

5. But among the forces reared by morality, there was *truthfulness*: this in the end turns against morality, and exposes the *teleology* of the latter, its interestedness...

6. This is the *antinomy*:[2] In so far as we believe in morality, we condemn existence....

13.... [Nihilism] finds that the value of things consists precisely in the fact that these values are *not* real... [but] are only a symptom of strength on the part of the *valuer*, a simplification serving the *purposes of existence....*

24. Nihilism is not only a meditating over the "in vain!"—not only the belief that everything deserves to perish; but one actually puts one's shoulder to the plough; *one destroys.* This, if you will, is illogical;... [but Nihilism] is the condition of strong minds and wills... [for which] it is impossible to be satisfied with the negation of judgment: the *negation by deeds* proceeds from their nature....

Second Book. A Criticism of the Highest Values that Have Prevailed Hitherto

I. CRITICISM OF RELIGION
2. Concerning the History of Christianity

---

1 Kant argued that even though the human mind is only able to know things as they appear to it, there is still an unknowable objective reality 'behind' the appearances. Hence he assumed "the existence of transcendental objects or things in themselves," which Nietzsche here denies.

2 A paradox: what seems to entail an internal contradiction.

158.... What did Christ *deny*?—Everything which today is called Christian.

160.... [Jesus] is concerned purely with the *inner man*....

He points out how man ought to live in order to feel himself "deified," and how futile it is on his part to hope to live properly by showing repentance and contrition for his sins. "Sin is of no account" is practically his chief standpoint....

169. A God who died for our sins, salvation through faith, resurrection after death—all these things are the counterfeit coins of real Christianity, for which that pernicious blockhead Paul must be held responsible....

200. I regard Christianity as the most fatal and seductive lie that has ever yet existed—as the greatest and most *impious lie*...

[It establishes] [t]he *morality of paltry people* as the measure of all things: this is the most repugnant kind of degeneracy that civilization has ever yet brought into existence....

Third Book. The Principles of a New Valuation

I. THE WILL TO POWER IN SCIENCE
(c) The Belief in the "Ego." Subject.

481. In opposition to Positivism, which halts at phenomena and says, "These are only *facts* and nothing more," I would say: No, facts are precisely what is lacking, all that exists consists of *interpretations*. We cannot establish any fact "in itself": it may even be nonsense to desire to do such a thing. "Everything is *subjective*," [you] say: but that in itself is *interpretation*....

To the extent to which knowledge has any sense at all, the world is knowable: but it may be interpreted *differently*, it has not one sense behind it, but hun-

dreds... [Everything is] "Perspectivity."

It is our needs that *interpret the world*; our instincts and their impulses for and against. Every instinct is a sort of thirst for power; each has its point of view, which it would fain impose upon all of the other instincts as their norm.

II. THE WILL TO POWER IN NATURE
2. The will to power as life
(a) The organic process

656. The will to power can manifest itself only against *obstacles*; it therefore goes in search of what resists it... The act of appropriation and assimilation is, above all, the result of a desire to overpower, a process of forming, of additional building and rebuilding, until at last the subjected creature has become completely a part of the superior creature's sphere of power, and has increased the latter.—If this process of incorporation does not succeed, then the whole organism falls to pieces; and the *separation* occurs as the result of the will to power...

658.

(1) The organic functions shown to be but forms of the fundamental will, the will to power,—and buds thereof.

(2) The will to power specializes itself as will to nutrition, to property, to *tools*, to servants (obedience), and to rulers: the body as an example.—The stronger will directs the weaker. There is no other form of causality than that of will to will. It is not to be explained mechanically.

(3) Thinking, feeling, willing, in all living organisms. What is a desire if it be not: a provocation of the feeling of power by an obstacle (... and resisting forces)—so that it surges through it? Thus in all pleasure pain

is understood.—If the pleasure is to be very great, the pains preceding it must have been very long, and the whole bow of life must have been strained to the utmost.

(4) Intellectual functions. The will to shaping, forming, and making like, etc.

675.... All "objects," "purposes," "meanings," are only manners of expression and metamorphoses of the one will inherent in all phenomena: of the will to power....

All valuations are only [points of view that serve] *this* one will: valuing *in itself* is nothing save this—*will to power*....

679. Judged from the standpoint of the theory of descent, *individuation* shows the... continuous annihilation of individuals *for the sake of a few* individuals, which evolution bears onwards....

The fundamental phenomena: *innumerable individuals are sacrificed for the sake of a few*, in order to make the few possible.—One must not allow one's self to be deceived; the case is the same with *peoples* and *races*: they produce the "body" for the generation of isolated and valuable *individuals*, who continue the great process.

Fourth Book. Discipline and Breeding

I. THE ORDER OF RANK
1. The Doctrine of the Order of Rank

854. In this age of universal suffrage,[1] in which everybody is allowed to sit in judgment upon everything and everybody, I feel compelled to re-establish the order of rank.

---

1 The right to vote is granted to everyone.

855. Quanta of power alone determine rank and distinguish rank: nothing else does.

856. *The will to power.*—How must those men be constituted who would undertake this transvaluation? The order of rank as the order of power: war and danger are the prerequisites which allow of a rank maintaining its conditions....

859. The advantages of standing detached from one's age. Detached from the two movements, that of individualism and that of collectivist morality; for even the first does not recognise the order of rank, and would give one individual the same freedom as another. My thoughts are not concerned with the degree of freedom which should be granted to the one or to the other... but with the degree of power which the one or the other should exercise over his neighbour or over all; and more especially with the question to what extent a sacrifice of freedom, or even enslavement, may afford the basis for the cultivation of a *superior* type. In plain words: *how could one sacrifice the development of mankind* in order to assist a higher species than man to come into being.

2. The strong and the weak

902. *Concerning the ruling types.*—The shepherd as opposed to the "lord" (the former is only a means to the maintenance of the herd; the latter, the purpose for which the herd exists).

933. *In short*, what we require is to dominate the passions and not to weaken or to extirpate them!...

The "great man" is so, owing to the free scope which he gives to his desires, and to the still greater power which knows how to enlist these magnificent monsters into its service....

4. The lords of the earth

958. I am writing for a race of men which does not yet exist: for "the lords of the earth."

In Plato's *Theages*[1] the following passage will be found: "Every one of us would like if possible to be master of mankind; if possible, a *God*." *This* attitude of mind must be reinstated in our midst.

Englishmen, Americans, and Russians.

6. The highest man as lawgiver of the future

982. From warriors we must learn: (1) to associate death with those interests for which we are fighting...; (2)...to *sacrifice* numbers, and to take our cause sufficiently seriously not to spare men; (3) [to] practise inexorable discipline, and allow ourselves violence and cunning in war.

997. I teach that there are higher and lower men, and that a single individual may under certain circumstances justify whole millenniums of existence— that is to say, a wealthier, more gifted, greater, and more complete man, as compared with innumerable imperfect and fragmentary men.

1001. Not "mankind," but *Superman*[2] is the goal!

II. DIONYSUS[3]

1034. We, many or few, who once more dare to live in a *world purged of morality, we pagans* in faith,—we are probably also the first who understand what a *pagan faith* is: to be obliged to imagine higher creatures than man, but to imagine them *beyond* good and evil; to be compelled to value all higher existence as *immoral* existence. We believe in Olympus, and *not* in the "man on the cross."

III. THE ETERNAL RECURRENCE

1067. And do you know what "the universe" is to my mind? Shall I show it to you in my mirror? This universe is a monster of energy, without beginning or end; a fixed and brazen quantity of energy... which does not consume itself, but only alters its face;... forever blessing itself as something which recurs for all eternity,—a becoming which knows no satiety, or disgust, or weariness:—this, my Dionysian world of eternal self-creation, of eternal self-destruction...; this, my "Beyond Good and Evil," without aim...—*This world is the Will to Power—and nothing else!* And even you yourselves are this will to power—and nothing besides!

Questions

1. How does Nietzsche say the word 'good' was first defined? What was its next definition? How does the meaning and value of the word change?
2. Do you think that the notions of 'good' and 'evil' have any inherent value?
3. Briefly describe the values of the aristocratic or master morality and the priestly or slave morality.

---

1 A dialogue now widely considered to have been written by someone else, in the style of Plato.

2 This is a translation of Nietzsche's term *Übermensch*, more often, perhaps, translated as 'overman' nowadays. (The German word is sometimes spelled in English as 'Uebermensch.')

3 A Greek god associated with sensuality, emotions and instincts, irrationality and chaos. Nietzsche contrasts the Dionysian with the Apollonian, named for Apollo, the god associated with logic, rationality, clarity, prudence.

4. How does Nietzsche think we should respond to nihilism?

5. What is the value or measure Nietzsche thinks we should use to rank people? Do you agree with this value? Why, why not?

6. How should the *Übermensch* act, according to Nietzsche? Is this an ethical way of living? Why, why not?

7. One of the disquieting aspects of *The Will to Power* is that it was held in high regard by the Nazis. Why, do you think? Do you agree that life and reality is nothing other than a will to power? Why, why not?

8. If you are familiar with Freud, consider why many commentators maintain that his thought was substantially influenced by Nietzsche. In addition, why is Nietzsche also often considered to have been the first post-modern thinker?

Suggested Readings

An urgent sense of moral questioning pervades Nietzsche's diverse and idiosyncratic writings. Although there is no authoritative edition in English, there are many scholarly and popular editions of his work. Two of his well-known translators are Walter Kaufmann and R.J. Hollingdale, who has published a biography, *Nietzsche, the Man and His Philosophy* (1965).

Nietzsche's more important works include his interpretation of Greek theater, *The Birth of Tragedy* (1872); the magisterial *Thus Spoke Zarathustra* (*Sprach Zarathustra*, 1885); the seminal *On the Genealogy of Morals* (*Zur Genealogie der Moral*, 1887); and his final, largely autobiographical, work *Ecce Homo* (1888). His other ethical works include *Beyond Good and Evil* (1886), *Human, All Too Human* (1878–80), and *Twilight of the Idols* (1889). Christopher Middleton has edited a collection of letters (*Selected Letters of Friedrich Nietzsche*, 1996).

A few ethical sources are Peter Berkowitz, *The Ethics of an Immoralist* (1995); Simon May, *Nietzsche's Ethics and His War on 'Morality'* (1999); and Gudrun von Tevenar, ed., *Nietzsche and Ethics* (2007). Thomas H. Brobjer, Christine Swanton, and others have argued that Nietzsche's work belongs in virtue ethics.

Nietzsche has been compared with Tolstoy, Kant, Schopenhauer, Mill (on marriage), Weber, Santayana, Shusterman, and others. For a cross-cultural source, see Eric S. Nelson, "The Question of Resentment in Nietzsche and Confucian Ethics" (2013). See also Charles E. Scott, *Nietzsche, Foucault, Heidegger* (1990).

In applied ethics, see Ralph R. Acampora, "Using and Abusing Nietzsche for Environmental Ethics" (1994).

PART V
CONTEMPORARY SOURCES

Searching for Wisdom in the Midst of Disagreement

There is a diverse range of views in the contemporary literature; perhaps times are ripe, then, for a return to a new wisdom tradition, on the basis of a dialectic between competing views. This holds the promise, at least, of a new synthesis of practical and theoretical wisdom, which includes multicultural and progressive elements.

In moral philosophy, the beginning of the contemporary period was marked by the rise of the analytical approach on one side and by existentialism on the other. The existentialists renewed the attempt to find meaning in sheer experience and placed a high value on authenticity. Academic authors also revisited the elements of the major historical theories, such as virtue theory. More recently, in response to liberal and contractarian views, some of the literature has emphasized community; and, in feminism, which has taken on prominence, there is a call for resistance to the idea of gender oppression. The ethical discussion and moral education is often submerged in the language of rights, however, which has become the lingua franca of the current social and political debate. A feminist ethics of care, some conservative communitarian thinkers, and proponents of a new, broader sociology of morality have critiqued the narrowness of this standard approach.

Liberalism has contributed to the belief that wisdom is to be found in some form of personal self-realization. This requires some form of philosophical scrutiny, which gives rise to authentic moral judgments. Some philosophers have taken a stance, however, which implicitly endows each individual with the right to reject the established moral order.

Contemporary life is beset by uncertainty and generalized *anomie*—a term used by social scientists to describe a state in which individuals do not internalize the social norms that find expression in established moral conventions. This has spread confusion and even rancor among the proponents of different schools.

There is little agreement as to the social, philosophical, and religious beliefs that have historically provided the foundations of our ethical beliefs. As a result, many philosophers have turned their attention to the search for a wide consensus. This can be seen in the return to the theory of the natural law and the attempt to find common values and principles in competing religious traditions. There has also been an attempt to ground ethics in science. If a unified theory emerges, which establishes a consensus on the deeper theoretical issues, it will have to accommodate a plurality of views.

The advances in science and technology have also generated an interest in applied ethics and practical wisdom. There is a specialized literature in bioethics, business ethics, and environmental ethics, though most of the work has been done within the framework of existing ethical theories.

Chapter 38

Non-Cognitivism

Early in the twentieth century, many philosophers in the Anglo-American tradition, accepting Hume's position that the only way that anything was knowable was if it was observable by the senses or a matter of logic, began to explore the consequences of this position for ethics. It appeared to many of them that ethical assertions could not be shown true or false by either method; what then?

One early, and for a while, influential response was G.E. Moore's position. Moore agreed with Hume (and most other historical philosophers) that ethical propositions were not shown true or false by mere logic. More importantly, he argued that attention to terms involved in ethical appraisal ('good,' 'wrong,' etc.) showed that they could not be analyzed—defined—in terms of ordinary observable "natural" properties. (So, for example, the utilitarians were mistaken in thinking that one could determine what was the right thing to do by observing the total amount of pleasure or pain that resulted from that action.) But Moore was not willing to accept the seeming consequence of these positions: "non-cognitivism," i.e., the view that the truth or falsity of ethical assertions was not something capable of being known. Instead he postulated that ethical properties were "non-natural," not observable to be present or absent by the normal senses. Instead, they were known through another route to knowledge which he called "intuition." Thus, his intuitionism is a kind of cognitivism.

But some other philosophers found this approach unsatisfactory, relying as it did on a mysterious realm of properties other than the natural ones, and on an equally mysterious and dubitable way of non-empirically determining their presence or absence. Instead, they accepted non-cognitivism about ethical assertions. If there were no way of knowing their truth or falsity, they further reasoned, it made no sense to think of them as true or false. Instead, ethical utterances were to be thought of as expressions of positive or negative attitudes or emotions. Thus, their view has been called "emotivism" or, later, "expressivism." A.J. Ayer, Moore's contemporary, did not invent this position, but was its most influential exponent.

Moore (1873–1958) is known as G.E. Moore because he disliked his given names George Edward. As a young man, he graduated with first-class honors in Classics and Moral Science at Cambridge and became a fellow of Trinity College. After a brief departure in 1904, he returned as a lecturer in Moral Science and eventually earned a LittD (a Doctor of Letters, a degree higher than a PhD). In 1925, he was appointed to the post of Professor of Mental Philosophy and Logic in the same college.

Moore accordingly spent most of his life as a professor of philosophy at Trinity College, Cambridge, teaching alongside such analytic philosophers as Bertrand Russell and Ludwig Wittgenstein. When he was 43 and firmly settled, he married Dorothy Ely, a former student. All of the accounts agree that he was a devoted husband and an exemplary father to their two sons. Much of his professional influence derives from his tenure (1921–47) as the editor of the prestigious British philosophy journal *Mind*.

Moore's writing was extensive. He adopted an empirical, common-sense realism in epistemology and metaphysics, and avoided systematization, which he considered speculative. Moore's first book, *Principia Ethica* (Cambridge University Press, 1903), generated decades of discussion. His later books include *Ethics* (1912), *Philosophical Studies* (1922), and *Some Main Problems of Philosophy* (1953). He also published many papers, such as "The Refutation of Idealism" (1903), "The Conception of Intrinsic Value" (1922), "A Defence of Common Sense" (1925), and "Proof of an External World" (1939).

Moore's work was logically demanding, in spite of its vindication of common-sense views. It was nevertheless well-received outside of philosophy. The members of the Bloomsbury Group, who had links to Cambridge, were inspired by his view that aesthetic experience is the most important of the human goods. Clive Bell drew on Moore's "non-naturalistic" account of the good to produce a theory of art based on a similar account of "significant form." Moore's ideal of contemplative friendship was also widely admired.

A.J. Ayer (1910–89), the other major figure in the movement, cut a more colorful figure. Most formally (but rarely) called Sir Alfred Jules Ayer, he was known as "Freddie" to his associates. He attended Oxford University, and also studied in Vienna, where he learned the logical positivism of the Vienna Circle first-hand. After graduating, he lectured at Oxford, and then served in the Special Operations and MI6 during the war. After the war, he taught at University College, London (1946–59), later returning to Oxford as the Wykeham Professor of Logic until his retirement in 1978. He was knighted in 1970.

Ayer does not fit the usual stereotype of an academic. He liked good food, attractive women, and dancing. He was an avid cricket and (European) football fan. He also sought celebrity and became a radio and television personality. He was married four times (twice to the same woman) and had a child outside his marriages. Although he was a confirmed atheist, he had a near-death experience of a God-like Being in the last year of his life. Although clinically dead for four minutes, he reported that he had seen "a red light, exceedingly bright,... [that] was responsible for the government of the universe." There are debates about whether the incident had any effect on Ayer's steadfast commitment to atheism, either at the time it happened or afterwards.

Ayer wrote his most famous book, *Language, Truth, and Logic* (1936), when he was only 24. The book contains an uncompromising restatement of logical positivism, which held—using the "verifiability principle of meaning"—that the meaning of propositions depends upon their empirical verification. If this was true, and the good cannot be empirically verified, it seems to follow that ethical propositions are meaningless. Ayer backed away from this abyss by saying that ethical propositions are meaningful, but only as expressions of emotion.

Language, Truth, and Logic quickly became a standard in the classroom. Ayer's other publications are wide-ranging and include several collections of essays. Five lectures that he gave at Harvard University in 1970 were published as *Russell and Moore: The Analytic Heritage* (1971). His Gifford Lectures (1972–73) were also published as *The Central Questions of Philosophy* (1973). At the end of his life, he wrote a two-volume autobiography.

Moore and Ayer were pioneers in analytic philosophy, which brought a mathematical and scientific style of reasoning into the philosophical inquiry. Their outlook is skeptical, logically severe, and highly scientific. Analytic thinkers often denigrated their rivals' appeals to ordinary language, metaphysics, religion, and tradition as imprecise and unempirical. The influence of Moore and Ayer on their contemporaries was, nonetheless, remarkable. In his obituary of Moore, C.D. Broad wrote: "It is doubtful whether any philosopher known to history has excelled or even equaled Moore in sheer power of analyzing problems, [and] detecting and exposing fallacies and ambiguities." The extravagance of the praise is representative.

The major criticism of the approach followed by the non-cognitivists is that it seems to place our moral views beyond the reach of analysis. This promotes a kind of ethical complacency and raises a serious question whether the analytical approach has the substantive resources to deal with graver moral issues. Historically, the analytic approach has favored liberalism, which often escapes difficult ethical issues by leaving them to individuals. In spite of these criticisms, Ayer took an interest in social and political issues, and was a progressive, left-wing voice in politics. He also served as president of the British Humanist Association and the Homosexual Law Reform Society.

The first reading is from *Principia Ethica*, where Moore 1) sets out "the open-question argument" in an effort to demonstrate that the good is indefinable, and 2) argues that it is a naturalistic fallacy to attempt to derive moral judgments from empirical data. The good, he argues, is a "primitive" concept: a simple, unanalyzable, non-natural (i.e., non-scientific) property that we intuit directly, and that cannot be defined in terms of physical attributes or other concepts. Just as we see that something is yellow, without argument or analysis, we "see" that something is good through the use of our moral faculties.

The second reading is from *Language, Truth, and Logic*. Although Ayer relies on Hume's account of morality as a matter of feeling, he went further and provided a more psychological explanation of the moral impetus. Since the content of moral propositions can be found in feelings, he argues that the ethical discussion should be seen as an emotion-laden discourse. It is not subject to rational proof. As a result, moral argument is ultimately a matter of making others feel what we feel, rather than about rationally convincing them of the truth of our position.

G.E. Moore, *Principia Ethica*[1]

(1903)

The Subject-Matter of Ethics

5. But our question 'What is good?' may have still another meaning. We may...mean to ask, not what thing or things are good, but how 'good' is to be defined. This is an enquiry which belongs only to ethics....

6. Now, it may be thought that this is a verbal question.... But this is not the sort of definition I am asking for.... If I wanted that kind of definition I should have to consider in the first place how people generally used the word 'good'; but my business is not with its proper usage, as established by custom.... My business is solely with that object or idea, which I hold, rightly or wrongly, that the word is generally used to stand for. What I want to discover is the nature of that object or idea, and about this I am extremely anxious to arrive at an agreement.

But, if we understand the question in this sense, my answer to it may seem a very disappointing one. If I am asked 'What is good?' my answer is that good is good, and that is the end of the matter. Or if I am asked 'How is good to be defined?' my answer is that it cannot be defined, and that is all I have to say about it....

7. My point is that 'good' is a simple notion. Just as 'yellow' is a simple notion; that just as you cannot, by any manner of means, explain to anyone who does not already know it, what yellow is, so you cannot explain what good is. Definitions of the kind that I was asking for, definitions which describe the real nature of the object or notion denoted by a word...are only possible when the object or notion in question is something complex.

You can give a definition of a horse, because a horse has many different properties and qualities, all of which you can enumerate. But when you have enumerated them all, when you have reduced a horse to his simplest terms, then you can no longer define those terms. They are simply something which you think of or perceive, and to anyone who cannot think of or perceive them, you can never, by any definition, make their nature known....

All objects, not previously known, which we are able to define...are all complex; all composed of parts, which may themselves, in the first instance, be capable of similar definition, but which must in the end be reducible to simplest parts, which can no longer be defined. But yellow and good, we say, are not complex: they are notions of that simple kind, out of which definitions are composed and with which the power of further defining ceases....

8. We may, when we define horse, mean something much more important. We may mean that a certain object which we all know is composed in a certain manner: that it has four legs, a head, a heart, a liver, etc., etc., all of them arranged in definite relations to one another. It is in this sense that I deny good to be definable. I say that it is not composed of any parts, which we can substitute for it in our minds when we are thinking of it....

10. Consider yellow, for example. We may try to define it by describing its physical equivalent; we may state what kind of light-vibrations must stimu-

---

1   G.E. Moore, *Principia Ethica* (Cambridge: Cambridge University Press, [1903] 1992).

late the normal eye, in order that we may perceive it. But a moment's reflection is sufficient to show that those light-vibrations are not themselves what we mean by yellow. They are not what we perceive. Indeed, we should never have been able to discover their existence, unless we had first been struck by the patent difference of quality between the different colors. The most we can be entitled to say of those vibrations is that they are what corresponds in space to the yellow which we actually perceive.

Yet a mistake of this simple kind has commonly been made about 'good.' It may be true that all things which are good are also something else, just as it is true that all things which are yellow produce a certain kind of vibration in the light. And it is a fact that ethics aims at discovering what are those other properties belonging to all things which are good. But far too many philosophers have thought that when they named those other properties they were actually defining good; that these properties, in fact, were simply not 'other,' but absolutely and entirely the same with goodness. This view I propose to call the 'naturalistic fallacy' and of it I shall now endeavor to dispose....

13. 1) Whatever definition of the good be offered, it may always be asked, with significance, of the complex so defined, whether it is itself good. To take, for instance, one of the more plausible, because one of the more complicated, of such proposed definitions, it may easily be thought, at first sight, that to be good may mean to be that which we desire to desire.

Thus if we apply this definition to a particular instance and say 'When we think that A is good, we are thinking that A is one of the things which we desire to desire,' our proposition may seem quite plausible. But, if we carry the investigation further and ask ourselves, 'Is it good to desire to desire A?' it is apparent, on a little reflection, that this question is itself as intelligible, as the original question 'Is A good?'—that we are, in fact, now asking for exactly the same information about the desire to desire A, for which we formerly asked with regard to A itself. But it is also apparent that the meaning of this second question cannot be correctly analyzed into 'Is the desire to desire A one of the things which we desire to desire A': we have not before our minds anything so complicated as the question 'Do we desire to desire to desire A?'

Moreover, anyone can easily convince himself by inspection that the predicate of this proposition— 'good'—is positively different from the notion of 'desiring to desire' which enters into its subject: 'That we should desire to desire A is good' is not merely equivalent to 'That A should be good is good.' It may indeed be true that what we desire to desire is always also good perhaps, even the converse may be true: but it is very doubtful whether this is the case, and the mere fact that we understand very well what is meant by doubting it, shows clearly that we have two different notions before our minds....

2) And if a man will try this experiment with each suggested definition in succession, he may become expert enough to recognize that when he tries to define good, in every case he has before his mind a unique object with regard to its connection... with any other object, and a distinct question may be asked. Everyone does in fact understand the question 'Is this good?' When he thinks of it, his state of mind is different from what it would be, were he asked 'Is this pleasant, or desired, or approved?' It has a distinct meaning for him, even though he may not recognize in what respect it is distinct. Whenever he thinks of 'intrinsic value,' or 'intrinsic worth,' or says that a thing 'ought to exist,' he has before his mind the unique object—the unique property of things—which I mean by 'good.'

Everybody is constantly aware of this notion, although he may never become aware at all that it is different from other notions of which he is also aware. But, for correct ethical reasoning, it is extremely important that he should become aware of this fact; and, as soon as the nature of the problem is clearly understood, there should be little difficulty in advancing so far in analysis.

A.J. Ayer, *Language, Truth, and Logic*[2]

(1936)

Critique of Ethics and Theology

[We have taken the] view that all synthetic propositions[3] are empirical hypotheses....

We shall [therefore] set ourselves to show that in so far as statements of value are significant, they are ordinary "scientific" statements; and that in so far as they are not scientific, they are not in the literal sense significant, but are simply expressions of emotion which can be neither true nor false....

[O]rdinary system[s] of ethics, as elaborated in the works of ethical philosophers, ... are themselves of very different kinds. We may divide them, indeed, into four main classes. There are, first of all, propositions which express definitions of ethical terms, or judgements about the legitimacy or possibility of certain definitions. Secondly, there are propositions describing the phenomena of moral experience, and their causes. Thirdly, there are exhortations to moral virtue. And, lastly, there are actual ethical judgements. It is unfortunately the case that the distinction between these four classes, plain as it is,

14. 'Good,' then, is indefinable; and yet, so far as I know, there is only one ethical writer, Prof. Henry Sidgwick, who has clearly recognized and stated this fact....[1]

is commonly ignored by ethical philosophers; with the result that it is often very difficult to tell from their works what it is that they are seeking to discover or prove....

[O]nly the first of our four classes, namely that which comprises the propositions relating to the definitions of ethical terms, can be said to constitute ethical philosophy. The propositions which describe the phenomena of moral experience ... must be assigned to the science of psychology, or sociology. The exhortations to moral virtue are not propositions at all, but ejaculations or commands which are designed to provoke the reader to action of a certain sort. Accordingly, they do not belong to any branch of philosophy or science. As for the expressions of ethical judgements ... inasmuch as they are certainly neither definitions nor comments upon definitions, nor quotations, we may say decisively that they do not belong to ethical philosophy. A strictly philosophical treatise on ethics should therefore make no ethical pronouncements. But it should, by giving an analysis of ethical terms, show what is the [lin-

---

1 Henry Sidgwick (1838–1900) was a highly influential Victorian moral philosopher, known for his sophisticated and moderate defense of utilitarianism.

2 A.J. Ayer, *Language, Truth, and Logic* (New York: Dover Publications, Inc., 2nd ed. [1946], 1952).

3 Synthetic propositions are statements based on sense perception and experience; e.g., to know whether all cats like cheese would require presenting cheese to all (or a sufficient number of) cats, and seeing what their reaction is.

guistic] category to which all such pronouncements belong. And this is what we are now about to do. . . .

In admitting that normative ethical concepts are irreducible to empirical concepts, we seem to be leaving the way clear for the "absolutist" view of ethics—that is, the view that statements of value are not controlled by observation, . . . but only by a mysterious "intellectual intuition." . . . [This] makes statements of value unverifiable. For it is notorious that what seems intuitively certain to one person may seem doubtful, or even false, to another. So that unless it is possible to provide some criterion by which one may decide between conflicting intuitions, a mere appeal to intuition is worthless as a test of a [normative] proposition's validity. . . . When such differences of opinion arise in connection with an ordinary empirical proposition, one may attempt to resolve them by referring to, or actually carrying out, some relevant empirical test. But with regard to ethical statements, there is, on the "absolutist" or "intuitionist" theory, no relevant empirical test. We are therefore justified in saying that on this theory ethical statements are held to be unverifiable. . . .

[W]e seem to have reached a difficult position. We shall meet the difficulty by showing that the correct treatment of ethical statements is afforded by a third theory,[1] which is wholly compatible with our radical empiricism.

We begin by admitting that the fundamental ethical concepts are unanalysable . . . We say that the reason why they are unanalysable is that they are mere pseudo-concepts. The presence of an ethical symbol in a proposition adds nothing to its factual content. Thus if I say to someone, "You acted wrongly in stealing that money," I am not stating anything more than if I had simply said, "You stole that money." In adding that this action is wrong I am not making any further statement about it. I am simply evincing my moral disapproval of it. It is as if

I had said, "You stole that money," in a peculiar tone of horror, or written it with the addition of some special exclamation marks. The tone, or the exclamation marks, adds nothing to the literal meaning of the sentence. It merely serves to show that the expression of it is attended by certain feelings in the speaker.

If now I generalise my previous statement and say, "Stealing money is wrong," I produce a sentence which has no factual meaning—that is, expresses no proposition which can be either true or false. It is as if I had written "Stealing money!!"—where the shape and thickness of the exclamation marks show, by a suitable convention, that a special sort of moral disapproval is the feeling which is being expressed. It is clear that there is nothing said here which can be true or false. Another man may disagree with me about the wrongness of stealing, in the sense that he may not have the same feelings about stealing as I have, and he may quarrel with me on account of my moral sentiments. But he cannot, strictly speaking, contradict me. For in saying that a certain type of action is right or wrong, I am not making any factual statement, not even a statement about my own state of mind. I am merely expressing certain moral sentiments. And the man who is ostensibly contradicting me is merely expressing his [own] moral sentiments. So that there is plainly no sense in asking which of us is in the right. For neither of us is asserting a genuine proposition.

What we have just been saying about the symbol "wrong" applies to all normative ethical symbols. Sometimes they occur in sentences which record ordinary empirical facts besides expressing ethical feeling about those facts: sometimes they occur in sentences which simply express ethical feeling about a certain type of action, or situation, without making any statement of fact. But in every case in which one would commonly be said to be making an ethical judgement, the function of the relevant ethical word is purely "emotive." It is used to express feeling

---

1 Here Ayer rejects Moore's intuitionism for something epistemologically weaker and more subjective which is based on an even stronger appeal to non-cognitivism.

about certain objects, but not to make any assertion about them.

It is worth mentioning that ethical terms do not serve only to express feeling. They are calculated also to arouse feeling, and so to stimulate action. Indeed some of them are used in such a way as to give the sentences in which they occur the effect of commands. Thus the sentence "It is your duty to tell the truth" may be regarded both as the expression of a certain sort of ethical feeling about truthfulness and as the expression of the command "Tell the truth." The sentence "You ought to tell the truth" also involves the command "Tell the truth," but here the tone of the command is less emphatic. In the sentence "It is good to tell the truth" the command has become little more than a suggestion....

We can now see why it is impossible to find a criterion for determining the validity of ethical judgements. It is... because they have no objective validity whatsoever. If a sentence makes no statement at all, there is obviously no sense in asking whether what it says is true or false. And we have seen that sentences which simply express moral judgements do not say anything. They are pure expressions of feeling and as such do not come under the category of truth and falsehood. They are unverifiable for the same reason as a cry of pain or a word of command is unverifiable—because they do not express genuine propositions....

[Our theory] does not imply that the existence of any feelings is a necessary and sufficient condition of the validity of an ethical judgement. It implies, on the contrary, that ethical judgements have no validity....

It is plain that the conclusion that it is impossible to dispute about questions of value follows from our theory also. For as we hold that such sentences as "Thrift is a virtue" and "Thrift is a vice" do not express propositions at all, we clearly cannot hold that they express incompatible propositions.... For we hold that one really never does dispute about questions of value.

... [W]e certainly... engage in disputes which are ordinarily regarded as disputes about questions of value. But, in all such cases, we find, if we consider the matter closely, that the dispute is not really about a question of value, but about a question of fact. When someone disagrees with us about the moral value of a certain action or type of action,... we do not attempt to show by our arguments that he has the "wrong" ethical feeling towards a situation whose nature he has correctly apprehended. What we attempt to show is that he is mistaken about the facts of the case. We argue that he has misconceived the agent's motive: or that he has misjudged the effects of the action, or its probable effects in view of the agent's knowledge... [If we] feel that our own system of values is superior,... we cannot bring forward any arguments to show that our system is superior. For our judgement that it is so is itself a judgement of value, and accordingly outside the scope of argument. It is because argument fails us when we come to deal with pure questions of value, as distinct from questions of fact, that we finally resort to mere abuse....

We find that [correct] ethical philosophy consists simply in saying that ethical concepts are pseudo-concepts and therefore unanalysable. The further task of describing the different feelings that the different ethical terms are used to express, and the different reactions that they customarily provoke, is a task for the psychologist. There cannot be such a thing as ethical science, if by ethical science one means the elaboration of a "true" system of morals....

It appears, then, that ethics, as a branch of knowledge, is nothing more than a department of psychology and sociology. And in case anyone thinks that we are overlooking the existence of casuistry,[1] we

---

1 Casuistry is the "science" which attempts to derive the moral status of particular acts or kinds of acts by seeing how the general rules of ethics (or religion) apply to it.

may remark that casuistry is not a science, but is a purely analytical investigation of the structure of a given moral system. In other words, it is an exercise in formal logic....

As we have already said, our conclusions about the nature of ethics apply to aesthetics also. Aesthetic terms are used in exactly the same way as ethical terms. Such aesthetic words as "beautiful" and "hideous" are employed...not to make statements of fact, but simply to express certain feelings and evoke a certain response. It follows, as in ethics, that there is no sense in attributing objective validity to aesthetic judgements, and no possibility of arguing about questions of value in aesthetics...A scientific treatment of aesthetics would show us what in general were the causes of aesthetic feeling, why various societies produced and admired the works of art they did, why taste varies as it does within a given society, and so forth. And these are ordinary psychological or sociological questions. They have, of course, little or nothing to do with aesthetic criticism as we understand it. But that is because the purpose of aesthetic criticism is not so much to give knowledge as to communicate emotion. The critic, by calling attention to certain features of the work under review, and expressing his own feelings about them, endeavours to make us share his attitude towards the work as a whole. The only [significant] propositions that he formulates are propositions describing the nature of the work. And these are plain records of fact. We conclude, therefore, that there is nothing in aesthetics, any more than there is in ethics, to justify the view that it embodies a unique type of knowledge.

... [T]he only information which we can legitimately derive from the study of our aesthetic and moral experiences is information about our own mental and physical make-up.... It follows that any attempt to make our use of ethical and aesthetic concepts the basis of a metaphysical theory concerning the existence of a world of values, as distinct from the world of facts, involves a false analysis of these concepts. Our own analysis has shown that the phenomena of moral experience cannot fairly be used to support any rationalist or metaphysical doctrine whatsoever. In particular, they cannot, as Kant hoped, be used to establish the existence of a transcendent god.

This mention of God brings us to the question of the possibility of religious knowledge. We shall see that this possibility has already been ruled out by our treatment of metaphysics....

It is now generally admitted...that the existence of a being having the attributes which define the god of any non-animistic religion cannot be demonstratively proved....

What is not so generally recognised is that there can be no way of proving that the existence of a god, such as the God of Christianity, is even probable. Yet this also is easily shown.... It is sometimes claimed, indeed, that the existence of a certain sort of regularity in nature constitutes sufficient evidence for the existence of a god. But if the sentence "God exists" entails no more than [this], then to assert the existence of a god will be simply equivalent to asserting that there is the requisite regularity in nature; and no religious man would admit that this was all he intended to assert in asserting the existence of a god. He would say that in talking about God, he was talking about a transcendent being who might be known through certain empirical manifestations, but certainly could not be defined in terms of those manifestations. But in that case the term "god" is a metaphysical term. And...to say that "God exists" is to make a metaphysical utterance which cannot be either true or false....

Questions

1. Moore says that we can define something like a horse—some philosophers might disagree—but we cannot define the 'good.' Is he right? Why, Why not? Suppose this is proposed as a definition of the 'good': 'what one morally ought to seek to produce or maintain.' What would Moore reply?
2. Moore believes that whenever we devise a naturalistic definition of 'good,' any such definition is invariably open-ended and fails to provide closure in our quest for an ultimate explanation of what the "good" represents. This has been described as the "open question" argument. Discuss and explain.
3. What is the "naturalistic fallacy"? How does the theory advanced by Moore and Ayer derive from the "is-ought problem" in Hume?
4. Ayer is a logical positivist. He believes that the only meaningful statements are 1) statements that can be empirically verified as true or false statements; and 2) statements that stipulate logical truths. Where does this take us when it comes to moral judgments?
5. Ayer argues that morality is like an exclamation mark. He also thinks that moral arguments are not based on logical principles or rational persuasion. Explain what is really going on, in Ayer's view. Include examples.
6. Ayer's moral position has been called "emotivism" and "non-cognitivism." Explain these labels.
7. What would the practical consequences of Moore's intuitionism and Ayer's emotivism be? In other words, how would you live a moral life in agreement with their theoretical views on ethics?
8. Imagine an argument between two people who disagree on the morality of increasing taxation of the rich. What would Ayer say about this "disagreement"? Is he right?

Suggested Readings

The work of the intuitionist and non-cognitivist philosophers in the analytic tradition is characterized by its rigorous approach. Moore's rather formidable *Principia Ethica* (1903), from which the first reading is taken, is usually seen as the *locus classicus* of the theory. The second reading, from A.J. Ayer's *Language, Truth, and Logic* (1936), discusses the emotive character of moral language.

For an early defense of the movement, see H.A. Pritchard, "Does Moral Philosophy Rest on a Mistake?," which appeared in *Mind* (1912). C.D. Broad also defends intuitionism in *Five Types of Ethical Theory* (1930), which has chapters on Spinoza, Butler, Hume, Kant, and Sidgwick. W.D. Ross provides an account of defeasible duties based on intuitions in *The Right and the Good* (1930) and *Foundations of Ethics* (1939). C.L. Stevenson (*Ethics and Language*, 1944) and R.M. Hare (*The Language of Morals*, 1952) see moral statements as universal prescriptions.

Philip Stratton-Lake has a good introduction to intuitionism in both the *Routledge Companion to Ethics* and the *Stanford Encyclopedia of Philosophy*. Students may find J.O.

Urmson, "A Defense of Intuitionism" (1974–75), and S. Kirchin, "Why Be an Intuitionist?" (2005), instructive.

In applied ethics, see "Intuitionism" in the *Encyclopedia of Business Ethics and Society*, D.G. Arnold, R. Audi, and M. Zwolinski, "Recent Work in Ethical Theory and Its Implications for Business Ethics" (2010), and Neil Vance et al., "An Interdisciplinary Approach" (2015). For a defense against an "intuitionist" critique, see Torbjörn Tännsjö, "Applied Ethics: A Defence" (2011).

Chapter 39

Rights-Based Liberalism

This chapter focuses on the historical origins and contemporary applications of the notions of rights. The implication in the popular use of the term 'rights' is that certain ethical claims are mandatory and accordingly give rise to legal remedies. This idea reflects changes, both in our ethical views and the role of the courts, which have increasingly become a forum in which controversial ethical issues are ultimately resolved. The prevailing litigiousness reflects an increase in the willingness of individuals to assert their rights in the face of increasing moral uncertainty.

Although standard usage of the term 'rights' derives from the liberal conviction that individual humans have rights, the notion has been extended to ethnic, cultural, and religious groups and even to non-rational animals. As many commentators have observed, it is the principle of equality that provided the "ratchet" which was used to extend rights to broader and broader communities of individuals. The underlying formula is simple enough: if different categories of things are the same in some fundamental sense, the principle of equality stipulates that they are entitled to the benefit of the same prerogatives. This formula seems to explain the slow historical process by which rights were slowly claimed, and extended, to a wide variety of disadvantaged groups.

It follows that it is the egalitarian dynamic that must be considered philosophically in order to determine whether rights have natural limits. As a result, many philosophers have looked for some kind of dividing line—a bright line of demarcation, legally—which might provide a reliable means of determining who and what has rights. This dividing line was believed to exist, historically, in the exercise of the faculty of reason, which was believed to distinguish human beings from animals. The historical argument has lost its force, however, as it has become apparent that animals like monkeys and dolphins have some capacities for intelligence and are, therefore, arguably entitled to the same basic rights as human beings.

The provenance of our heightened sense of individual rights can be traced to the beginnings of the liberal tradition. These beginnings lie in the contractarianism of such thinkers as Thomas Hobbes, John Locke, and Hugo Grotius, which began by dividing the world into individuals, who then enter into legal relations with the state and government. These individuals remain sovereign in their private capacity and are therefore autonomous. It follows that they have the moral right, on the liberal argument, to decide personal issues involving sexuality, narcotics, suicide, invasive medical treatment, and so on.

The liberal support for individual rights expressed itself historically in "liberal constitutionalism," which gave these rights constitutional status in an effort to place moral limits on the power of the state. The constitutional idea goes back further, however, before the emergence of centralized government, to a time when those in power had no authority to change the customary law. The historical point is that the current emphasis on individual rights is a response to the increasing levels of social control exercised by government and the state.

The idea of "natural" or "inalienable" rights, which was prominent in the French and American Revolutions, has been succeeded by the concept of "human rights," which emerged in the international response to the crimes against humanity committed during the Second World War. These crimes led thinkers like Jacques Maritain to argue for a return to the natural law, which places ethical limits on the powers of the state, as set out in the *Universal Declaration of Human Rights*. A lucid account of the grounding of human rights in the concept of 'human dignity' can be found in *Pacem in Terris* (1963), an encyclical from Pope John XXIII.

It is impossible to review the enormous proliferation of human rights instruments here. The readings in this chapter, consequently, aim at two modest goals: (1) to provide a brief history of the notion of rights, and (2) to offer contemporary examples of the application of the principle of equality to extend rights to nonhuman animals.

The first reading is from Gregory Walters's summary of the historical evolution of the notion of rights. Walters (b. 1956) is a philosophy professor at Saint Paul University in Canada. In the reading, he focuses specifically on the historical development of the contemporary notion of human rights. At the very beginnings of this, philosophers and jurists traced the concept of 'natural rights' back to a concept of natural law, a moral rule thought to be inherent in rational human nature. As Walters reports, early Greek philosophers such as Plato, Aristotle, and the Stoics, argued that human rights derive from *physis* (nature), not merely from *nomos* (custom, law). The idea that rights are somehow dependent upon or derive from our membership in a particular human society is, historically, a later development.

The next two readings offer philosophical arguments for extending rights to animals. There are other, often overlooked, arguments for animal rights, which deserve consideration. Some of these arguments are religious and cosmological, as we see in the Buddhist and Hindu traditions. As mentioned, the original view was that it is our membership in society that gives us rights. Historically the limits of such a society are unclear, but often extended beyond the human species and encompassed the natural world. For instance, swine had "the freedom of the city" in the Middle Ages, which meant that they had the right to forage anywhere. This also came with liabilities. A pig who killed a child might be tried and hanged. It is also evident that animals have moral prerogatives in tribal and early societies, which look, at least, like rights. The philosophical arguments tend, generally, to rely on the principle of equality.

The second reading is from Peter Singer's *Animal Liberation*. Singer (b. 1946) is a controversial bioethics professor at Princeton University and a prominent spokesperson for animal rights. A liberal and a utilitarian, Singer takes much of his argument from Jeremy Bentham. He roots the notion of moral status in the idea that sentient beings have an interest in not suffering. Morality means respecting the interests of all, including nonrational animals. Singer feels obliged, then, to demonstrate scientifically that animals feel pain. Historically, science has proven to be unreliable in determining moral rights, which is a normative issue—one that gives rise to obligations and responsibilities—rather than an issue of fact. Be that as it may, the real thrust of Singer's argument is to remove the superior status of human beings in moral philosophy. He believes that it is merely the discriminatory attitude of "speciesism" that prevents human beings from taking into equal consideration the pain and suffering of different animals in order to determine the nature and extent of the rights that the particular animal possesses.

The third reading is from Christine Korsgaard (b. 1952), a student of John Rawls and, presently, a philosophy professor at Harvard. Korsgaard argues that one can expand Kant's notion of human beings as moral ends-in-themselves to the entire animal kingdom. Insomuch as earlier views of rights were premised on the Enlightenment idea that the (natural) world belongs to human beings, Korsgaard argues that nature belongs as much to other animals as to humans. This is a controversial position to take on Kant's notion.

READING 39A

Gregory J. Walters, "Human Rights in Historical Overview"[1]

(1995)

... The origin of "natural right" may be traced to the Greeks' distinction between "nature" (*physis*) and "convention" (*nomos*).[2] The Greeks contrasted animals and humans insofar as the habits of animals were uniform, whereas the practices of humans differed according to convention. The Skeptic philosophers... [accordingly concluded that] there was no uniform force behind human conventions. The notion of natural right was a rebuttal to this ancient [argument and held, on the contrary, that there is a universal human nature.]...

The Stoic idea of [a universal] "natural law"... influenced the writings of the Roman philosophers Seneca, Cicero, and others, and the Roman jurists

---

1 "Human Rights In Historical Overview," from the Introduction to Gregory J. Walters, ed., *Human Rights in Theory and Practice: A Selected and Annotated Bibliography*, with a foreword by Rhoda E. Howard and a preface by Claude E. Welch Jr., Magill Bibliographies (Metuchen, NJ and London: The Scarecrow Press, Inc.; and Pasadena, CA and Englewood Cliffs, NJ: Salem Press, 1995).

2 [Author's Note] Leo Strauss, *Natural Right and History* (Chicago and London: University of Chicago Press, 1953 [1950]), p. 90.

Ulpian and Gaius.[1] To use Heinrich Rommen's metaphor, Stoic philosophy was the mother of Roman jurisprudence [which] "sucked in the doctrine of the *ius naturale*[2] with its mother's milk."[3] Ulpian's definition of the function of justice—"to render each his right" (*suum ius cuique tribuere*)—moved beyond the limited political standard of the Greeks....

In the [earlier] Socratic-Platonic tradition, natural right—as justice—is independent of law.... For Aristotle..., actions can be just by nature or legally just. Natural justice or right is unalterable and [does not obtain its force] from any positive law[4] that may embody it. That which is legally just originates in the will of the lawmaker or an act of the *polis*,[5] and varies in history and time.... [Much later, following Aristotle,] Aquinas...distinguishes the general and immutable axioms of natural [law] from which mutable, specific rules of natural right are derived....

Some human rights historians...have emphasized the moral import of the teachings of Judaism and Christianity in the historical evolution of natural right and human rights.... [Although] the idea of a natural right that the individual can demand of society or government is entirely absent from the Bible[,]...Yahweh[6] hears the cries of those whose justice has been denied, whose "rights" have been violated....

Early Christianity reinterpreted the natural, tribal bonds of blood, religion, language, caste, class, and religion...[with a more universal idea, based on] "the new humanity of those whose loving faith makes them one with God and their neighbors."[7]...

Late Scholastics such as Vittoria..., Suarez..., Vasquez..., and the Italian Saint Robert Bellarmine[8]...held to a pre-political right[9] to property inhering in the human person rather than in the civil order. [This] legitimated the slave trade on the grounds that rights inhered in the human person rather than the civil order; as such, the human person could [therefore] sell them, forfeit them, or give them away. The Dominicans, under the influence of a revived Thomism, argued that people were not free to enslave themselves and could not rightfully be traded as slaves....

The seventeenth century marks the watershed for modern natural rights theory. Thomas Hobbes...turned the premodern emphasis upon duty upside down by [disputing] the political or social nature of human beings and by viewing law as an *actus voluntatis* rather than an *actus intellectus*[10] in his *Leviathan*...Deduced from the desire for self-preservation, natural right [which is therefore based on free choice] is now opposed to the natural law of the Scholastics and the earlier natural right of the Roman jurists.[11]

John Locke's... *Two Treatises of Government*... legitimated the Glorious Revolution of 1688 and

---

1 Ulpian (*Gnaeus Domitius Annius Ulpianus*, c. 170–223) was considered one of the great legal authorities of his time. Gaius (c. 110–c. 180) was a celebrated Roman jurist whose full name is unknown.

2 Sometimes: *jus naturale*. Latin for 'natural law' (or right or justice).

3 Heinrich A. Rommen, *The Natural Law: A Study in Legal and Social History and Philosophy*, trans. Thomas R. Hanely (London: B. Herder Book Co., 1948), p. 27.

4 Law made by humans, as opposed to natural law, which arises from human nature, human rationality, or God.

5 Greek for 'city' or 'city-state,' the Greek form of society in existence in the sixth and fifth centuries BCE.

6 The Hebrew name for God.

7 [Author's Note] Leroy S. Rouner, *To Be at Home: Christianity, Civil Religion, and World Community* (Boston: Beacon Press, 1991), p. 35.

8 Francisco de Vitoria (c. 1483–56) was a Roman Catholic philosopher, theologian, and jurist of Renaissance Spain. Francisco Suarez (1548–1617) was a Spanish Jesuit priest, philosopher, and theologian. Gabriel Vasquez (1549/51–1604) was a Spanish Jesuit theologian. St. Robert Bellarmine (1542–1621) was an Italian Jesuit and a Cardinal of the Roman Catholic Church.

9 I.e., a natural right.

10 I.e., a voluntary act (of the will) rather than an intellectual act (of the intellect).

11 I.e., the natural law (*jus naturale*) in Roman law and during the Middle Ages and the natural right (*lex naturalis*) in classical Greek and Roman thought. Roman law also had the law of nations (*jus gentium*).

resulted in the English Bill of Rights [of 1689.[1]] Locke presupposes an objective natural law for his political theory. His state of nature is not a state of war, but a state of "Men living together according to reason, without a common Superior on Earth, with Authority to judge between them." The state of nature has a corresponding law of nature, reason, that is not superceded by the social contract....

[These philosophical developments contributed to the French and American revolutions.] The eighteenth-century conception of the "rights of man" as embodied in the French *Déclaration des droits de l'homme et du citoyen* [(1789)] and the 1789 American Bill of Rights[2]... [created] a new social myth in which functional power is the prerogative not of a sovereign but rather a citizenry of "equals," endowed with inalienable rights and liberty based on the "Laws of Nature and of Nature's God" (Declaration of Independence).[3]...

[In his *Reflections on the Revolution in France*, Edmund Burke[4] rejected these developments and] delivers a critique of the modern interpretation of natural right by seeking the foundation of government not in the "imaginary rights of men" but in the provision of wants, and in a conformity to duties and virtue....

[Thomas Paine responded in *Rights of Man* (1791),[5] arguing] that a hereditary monarchy was contrary to nature insofar as it denied the equality of "man"... According to Paine,... [the] origin of human beings and of rights is divine and grounded in creation. Natural rights are those rights which pertain to the individual by virtue of created existence, and include "intellectual rights" and all those rights to secure "comfort and happiness" that do not harm others. Civil rights are those which pertain to the individual by virtue of being a member of society, and require preexisting natural right.

John Stuart Mill... made the distinction between *duties of justice*, which correspond to rights, and *acts of beneficence*, or the doing of good that goes beyond what justice requires (i.e., supererogatory acts).... Mill claimed that "duties of perfect obligation are those duties in virtue of which a correlative *right* resides in some person or persons; duties of imperfect obligation are those moral obligations which do not give birth to any right."[6] When we call something a right, then this means that a person has a valid claim on society to protect that right, either by force of law or by education and opinion.

[Some modern thinkers nevertheless rejected these developments.] The most decisive turning away from the tradition of natural right and natural law came at the hands of skeptics like David Hume... [since] natural law or right is for Hume merely a convention of moral sentiments[.]... [Jeremy] Bentham also ridiculed what he called the "fictions" of natural law, the social contract, and,

---

1   The Glorious Revolution of 1688–89 replaced the reigning Catholic king, James II, with the joint monarchy of his Protestant daughter Mary and her Dutch husband, William of Orange. One reason for the revolution was religious, i.e., to avoid a Catholic succession. The other reason was political, and resulted in the English *Bill of Rights* of 1689, which set out limits on the powers of the monarchy and the rights of the Parliament of England so that crown and Parliament became joint sovereigns of England.

2   The *Declaration of the Rights of Man and of the Citizen* is an important document of the French Revolution passed by France's National Constituent Assembly. The *Bill of Rights*, ratified in 1791, is the first ten amendments to the United States Constitution. The main purpose was to place clear limitations on the power of the federal government and to reserve all unspecified powers for the states or the people.

3   The *Declaration of Independence* (1776) stated that the thirteen American colonies regarded themselves as thirteen independent sovereign states no longer under British rule.

4   Edmund Burke (1729–97) was an Irish statesman, author, orator, political theorist, and philosopher. He was known for his conservative views, claiming that the French Revolution was destroying traditional institutions and the fabric of good society.

5   Thomas Paine (1737–1809) was an English-born American political activist, philosopher, political theorist, revolutionary, and one of the founding fathers of the United States. He defended the French Revolution against its critics.

6   [Author's Note] John Stuart Mill, *Utilitarianism* [1861]. In *Collected Works*, vol. 10, pp. 203–59 (Toronto: University of Toronto Press, 1969), pp. 246–49.

especially, natural rights on utilitarian grounds. "*Natural rights* is simple nonsense: natural and imprescriptible rights, rhetorical nonsense, —nonsense upon stilts."[1] ...

[Karl Marx also rejected the idea of natural rights:]

None of the supposed rights of man ... go beyond the egoistic man, man as he is, as a member of civil society—that is, an individual separated from the community, withdrawn into himself, wholly preoccupied with his private interest and acting in accordance with his private caprice. Man is far from being considered, in the rights of man, as a species-being; on the contrary, species-life itself—society— appears as a system [which] is external to the individual and as a limitation of his original independence. The only bond between human beings is natural necessity, need and private interest.[2] ...

[The philosophical development of the concept of rights found expression, politically, in constitutionalism.] With the rise of the modern nation-state, the Constitution of the state took the place of divine or natural law, thus marking a shift from the earlier grounding of the *Magna Carta* (1215)[3] in divine authority. A law became illegitimate if unconstitutional, rather than unjust because it was in violation of natural or divine law....

In the twentieth century, ["natural rights" were replaced by the concept of "human rights," which became part of the international law. This is usually attributed to the rise and fall of Nazi Germany, the inauguration of the United Nations Charter in 1945, and the adoption of the *Universal Declaration of Human Rights* (*UDHR*) in 1948.] ...

Since the advent of the UDHR, human rights have been generally viewed as universal, international, and unconditioned by race, sex, religion, social position, and nationality. As Louis Henkin notes, human rights claim that "every human being, in every society, is entitled to have basic autonomy and freedoms respected and basic needs satisfied."[4] More precisely, "if one has a human right, one is entitled to make a fundamental claim that an authority, or some other part of society, do refrain from doing—something that affects significantly one's human dignity."[5] ...

During the drafting of the Charter of the United Nations in 1945, the question of individual versus groups rights polarized many members. Should economic, social, and cultural interests be accorded the status of rights on par with the traditional liberal[6] values of free speech, religion, press, ... association[, etc.]? The drafters decided to draw up two separate covenants, one dealing with political and civil rights and the other treating economic, social, and cultural rights.... The two main international human rights covenants—the United Nations' International Covenant on Civil and Political Rights (ICCPR) and the United Nations' International Covenant on Eco-

---

1 Jeremy Bentham, *Anarchical Fallacies*, in Jeremy Waldron, ed., *Nonsense Upon Stilts: Bentham, Burke and Marx on the Rights of Man* (London and New York: Methuen, 1987), p. 53.

2 [Author's Note] Karl Marx, "On the Jewish Question," in *The Marx-Engels Reader*, ed. Robert C. Tucker, second edition (New York: W.W. Norton, 1978), p. 43.

3 I.e., *Magna Carta Libertatum* ("the Great Charter of the Liberties"). A document agreed to by King John of England (reigned 1199–1216) that spelled out the medieval relationship between the monarch and his barons by defining the rights of barons against the crown. The document became part of English political life over time and was interpreted as one concerned with the rights of ordinary people.

4 [Author's Note] Louis Henkin, "Introduction," in *The International Bill of Rights*, ed. by Henkin (New York: Columbia University Press, 1981), p. 7.

5 [Author's Note] David P. Forsythe, *The Internationalization of Human Rights* (Lexington, Massachusetts: Lexington Books, 1991), p. 1. [Editors' Note] These obligations cross borders, so to speak; they have international content.

6 I.e., individual.

nomic, Social and Cultural Rights (ICESCR)—were eventually opened for signature in 1966. and came into force in 1976. Together with the UDHR and the Optional Protocol to the [ICCPR], these instruments constitute the so-called International Bill of Rights....

[There are also four human rights protected by customary international law: freedom from slavery, genocide, racial discrimination, and torture. In addition, there may be "collective rather than individual" rights, such as a right to a healthy environment.[1]]

READING 39B

Peter Singer, *Animal Liberation*[2]

(1990)

... There are obviously important differences between humans and other animals, and these differences must give rise to some differences in the rights that each have. Recognizing this evident fact, however, is no barrier to the case for extending the basic principle of equality to nonhuman animals.... The extension of the basic principle of equality from one group to another does not imply that we must treat both groups in exactly the same way, or grant exactly the same rights to both groups. Whether we should do so will depend on the nature of the members of the two groups. The basic principle of equality does not require equal or identical *treatment*; it requires equal consideration. Equal consideration for different beings may lead to different treatment and different rights....

Jeremy Bentham ... incorporated the essential basis of moral equality into his system of ethics by means of the formula: "Each to count for one and none for more than one." In other words, the interests of every being affected by an action are to be taken into account and given the same weight as the like interests of any other being....

It is an implication of this principle of equality that our concern for others and our readiness to consider their interests ought not to depend on what they are like or on what abilities they may possess. Precisely what our concern or consideration requires us to do may vary according to the characteristics of those affected by what we do: concern for the well-being of children growing up in America would require that we teach them to read; concern for the well-being of pigs may require no more than that we leave them with other pigs in a place where there is adequate food and room to run freely. But the basic element—the taking into account of the interests of the being, whatever those interests may be—must, according to the principle of equality, be extended to all beings, black or white, masculine or feminine, human or nonhuman....

Many philosophers and other writers have proposed the principle of equal consideration of

1 Walters concludes by acknowledging that the international human rights regime is very weak. He also acknowledges that human rights have been criticized as a form of cultural imperialism, which is "rampant" with Western (i.e., liberal) moralism. This does not, however, invalidate the claim that human rights are universal and have "analogues in other cultures and societies."

2 Peter Singer, *Animal Liberation*, 2nd ed. (New York: *The New York Review of Books*, [1975] 1990).

interests, in some form or other, as a basic moral principle; but not many of them have recognized that this principle applies to members of other species as well as to our own. Jeremy Bentham was one of the few who did realize this. In a forward-looking passage written at a time when black slaves had been freed by the French but in the British dominions were still being treated in the way we now treat animals, Bentham wrote:

> The day *may* come when the rest of the animal creation may acquire those rights which never could have been withholden from them but by the hand of tyranny. The French have already discovered that the blackness of the skin is no reason why a human being should be abandoned without redress to the caprice of a tormentor.... What else is it that should trace the insuperable line? Is it the faculty of reason, or perhaps the faculty of discourse? But a full-grown horse or dog is beyond comparison a more rational, as well as a more conversable animal, than an infant of a day or a week or even a month, old. But suppose they were otherwise, what would it avail? The question is not, Can they *reason*? nor Can they *talk*? but, Can they *suffer*?

In this passage Bentham points to the capacity for suffering as the vital characteristic that gives a being the right to equal consideration. The capacity for suffering—or more strictly, for suffering and/or enjoyment or happiness—is not just another characteristic like the capacity for language or higher mathematics.... By saying that we must consider the interests of all beings with the capacity for suffering or enjoyment. Bentham does not arbitrarily exclude from consideration any interests at all—as those who draw the line with reference to the possession of reason or language do. The capacity for suffering and enjoyment is *a prerequisite for having interests at all*, a condition that must be satisfied before we can speak of interests in a meaningful way. It would be nonsense to say that it was not in the interests of a stone to be kicked along the road by a schoolboy. A stone does not have interests because it cannot suffer.... The capacity for suffering and enjoyment is, however, not only necessary, but also sufficient for us to say that a being has interests—at an absolute minimum, an interest in not suffering. A mouse, for example, does have an interest in not being kicked along the road, because it will suffer if it is.

Although Bentham speaks of "rights" in the passage I have quoted, the argument is really about equality rather than about rights....

In misguided attempts to refute the arguments of this book, some philosophers have gone to much trouble developing arguments to show that animals do not have rights.... These claims are irrelevant to the case for Animal Liberation. The language of rights is a convenient political shorthand.... [B]ut in the argument for a radical change in our attitude to animals, it is in no way necessary.

If a being suffers there can be no moral justification for refusing to take that suffering into consideration. No matter what the nature of the being, the principle of equality requires that its suffering be counted equally with the like suffering—insofar as rough comparisons can be made—of any other being. If a being is not capable of suffering, or of experiencing enjoyment or happiness, there is nothing to be taken into account....

Most human beings are speciesists. The following chapters show that ordinary human beings—not a few exceptionally cruel or heartless humans, but the overwhelming majority of humans—take an active part in, acquiesce in, and allow their taxes to pay for practices that require the sacrifice of the most important interests of members of other species in order to promote the most trivial interests of our own species....

Just as most human beings are speciesists in their readiness to cause pain to animals when they would not cause a similar pain to humans for the same reason, so most human beings are speciesists in their readiness to kill other animals…We need to proceed more cautiously here, however, because people hold widely differing views about when it is legitimate to kill humans, as the continuing debates over abortion and euthanasia attest. Nor have moral philosophers been able to agree on exactly what it is that makes it wrong to kill human beings, and under what circumstances killing a human being may be justifiable.

Let us consider first the view that it is always wrong to take an innocent human life. We may call this the "sanctity of life" view. People who take this view oppose abortion and euthanasia. They do not usually, however, oppose the killing of nonhuman animals—so perhaps it would be more accurate to describe this view as the "sanctity of *human* life" view. The belief that human life, and only human life, is sacrosanct is [accordingly] a form of speciesism. To see this, consider the following example.

Assume that, as sometimes happens, an infant has been born with massive and irreparable brain damage. The damage is so severe that the infant can never be any more than a "human vegetable," unable to talk, recognize other people, act independently of others, or develop a sense of self-awareness. The parents of the infant, realizing that they cannot hope for any improvement in their child's condition and being in any case unwilling to spend, or ask the state to spend, the thousands of dollars that would be needed annually for proper care of the infant, ask the doctor to kill the infant painlessly.

Should the doctor do what the parents ask? Legally, the doctor should not, and in this respect the law reflects the sanctity of life view. The life of every human being is sacred. Yet people who would say this about the infant do not object to the killing of nonhuman animals. How can they justify their different judgments?…The only thing that distinguishes the infant from the animal, in the eyes of those who claim it has a "right to life," is that it is, biologically, a member of the species Homo sapiens, whereas chimpanzees, dogs, and pigs are not. But to use *this* difference as the basis for granting a right to life to the infant and not to the other animals is, of course, pure speciesism. It is exactly the kind of arbitrary difference that the most crude and overt kind of racist uses in attempting to justify racial discrimination.…

Christine Korsgaard, "A Kantian Case for Animal Rights"[1]

(2012)

Kantian moral philosophy is usually considered inimical both to the moral claims and to the legal rights of non-human animals. Kant himself asserts baldly that animals are "mere means" and "instruments" and as such may be used for human purposes.…

---

1   Christine M. Korsgaard, "A Kantian Case for Animal Rights," in Margot Michel, Daniela Kühne, and Julia Hänni, eds., *Animal Law: Developments and Perspectives in the 21st Century* (Zurich/St. Gallen: Dike, 2012).

Kant explicitly links the moment when human beings first realized that we must treat one another as ends in ourselves with the moment when we realized that we do not have to treat the other animals that way....

In his account of legal rights, Kant introduces a further difficulty... For Kant, the point of legal rights is... to define and uphold a maximal domain of individual freedom for each citizen...

But non-rational animals apparently do not have the kind of freedom that rights... are intended to protect.... Rationality, for Kant, is not the same thing as intelligence. It is a normative capacity, grounded in what Kant took to be the unique human ability to reflect on the reasons for our beliefs and actions, and decide whether they are good reasons or bad ones....

This seems to suggest that Kant's philosophy is not the place to look for a philosophical foundation for animal rights.

Nevertheless,... I will argue that a case for both the moral claims and the legal rights of non-human animals can be made on the basis of Kant's own moral and political arguments....

Kant envisions the act of making a choice as the adoption of a certain "maxim" or principle as a universal law, a law that governs both my own conduct and that of others. My choosing something... involves conferring a kind of objective—or more properly speaking intersubjective—value on some state of affairs, a value to which every rational being must then be responsive....

[W]e presuppose our [own] value as beings for whom things can be good or bad..., as beings who have interests....

We "represent" ourselves as ends in ourselves insofar as we take what is good for us to be good absolutely. It is as if whenever you make a choice, you said, "I take the things that are important to me to be important, *period*, important absolutely, because I take *myself* to be important." So in pursuing what you think is good for you as if it were good absolutely, you show that you regard yourself as an end in itself [;] ... you *claim*... [moral] standing....

[T]here are two slightly different senses of "end in itself" at work in Kant's argument, which we might think of as an active and a passive sense. I must regard you as an end in itself in the active sense if I regard you as capable of legislating [the moral law] for me... I must regard you as an end in itself in the passive sense if I am obligated to treat your ends, or at least the things that are *good for you*, as good absolutely. Kant evidently thought that these two senses come to the same thing....

[T]here is no reason to think that... the normative presupposition [that morality applies] is only *about* autonomous rational beings.... [M]any of the things that I take to be good for me are not good for me merely insofar as I am an autonomous rational being. Food, sex, comfort, freedom from pain and fear, are all things that are good for me insofar as I am an animate being.... But of course things can be good or bad, in the relevant way, for any sensate being, that is, for any being who can like and dislike things, be happy or suffer. That suggests that the presupposition behind rational choice is that animals, considered as beings for whom things can be good or bad—as beings with interests—are ends in themselves....

[E]ven if it were not the case that the other animals could have rights against us, how exactly is it supposed to follow that we have rights over them?... [W]hy is it supposed to follow... that we can claim anything we find in the world, even an animate being with a life of its own...?

In the traditional doctrines of rights developed in the 17th and 18th century, especially in the theories of Locke and Kant, it is perfectly clear why this is supposed to follow. It follows from two theses. The first is a view originally derived from Genesis... that God gave the world and everything in it to humanity to hold in common. The second is a picture of what a right in general is... To claim that I have a right is to make a relational claim; and the relation is not between me and the object to which I have a right—

it is between me and other people. When we put these two claims together, we get a certain picture of what the general problem of individual rights is...

[T]he claim that God gave us the world in common...can be formulated in secular terms. It is the idea that others have just as good a claim on the resources of the world as we do, and that it behooves us to limit our own claims with that in mind....

But we are not the only creatures thus thrown into the world...If this is the basis of the presumption of common possession or ownership, why not assume that the earth and its resources are possessed in common by all of the animals?...

[W]e could drop the presupposition of common possession or common ownership altogether. But if we drop the presupposition altogether, we must also drop the version of it that comes down to us from Genesis. In that case, the world was not given to human beings in common, because it was not given to anyone. That means that what human beings have over the other animals is not, in general, a form of rightful ownership. *It is simply power....*

You need only look at what goes on inside of our factory farms and experimental laboratories to see what the possibility of such domination—the ability to do whatever we like with another animal—can

lead to. So long as there are profits to be made, and the tantalizing prospect of expanding the human lifespan by experiments on the other animals, there will be people who will do *anything*, no matter how cruel it is, to a captive animal. And what makes this possible is the legal status of animals as property. It is not plausible to hope that the human race will someday have a collective humanitarian conversion and bring all such practices to an end, without any help from the law.... No matter how well-intentioned we are, we can only be rightly related to our fellow creatures if we offer them some legal protections.

If we must presuppose that the world and all that is in it is possessed by us in common,...then we should presuppose that it is possessed by all of its creatures on the same ground. The other animals...are among those to whom the world and its resources belong. If we reject the presupposition of common possession or ownership, then we cannot pretend that the way we treat the other animals is anything but an exercise of arbitrary power...over the weak.... The other animals are...beings with interests, beings for whom things can be good or bad, and as such they are ends in themselves.... [T]he only way we can be rightly related to them is to grant them some rights....

Questions

1. What is a right? Where did the idea of rights originate? What was the relationship between moral rights and duties, historically?
2. What changed with Hobbes and the Enlightenment with the advent of liberalism and the modern state?
3. Edmund Burke, Jeremy Bentham, and Karl Marx all rejected the idea of rights. Why?
4. There seems to be something missing in Singer's argument. If crabs and clams and insects do not experience pain, does this mean that they have no rights, or fewer rights? Do animals lose their rights, if we devise ways of killing them without causing pain and suffering?
5. Singer would suggest that some people who are severely disabled may have to be sacrificed so that highly functioning animals can live. Would you accept this consequence to avoid being speciesist? Discuss.

6. Korsgaard writes, "We represent ourselves as ends in ourselves insofar as we take what is good for us to be good absolutely." Explain how she uses this idea to expand Kant's notion of human rights to animals.

7. Korsgaard believes that the problem is that animals are treated as property. Why does she think it is presumptuous for humans to believe they can own animals? What do you think? Should human beings be allowed to own animals?

Suggested Readings

The most convenient collection of sources in the historical development of human rights is Micheline Ishay's *Human Rights Reader* (2nd ed., 2008). For a concise but illuminating record of the development of crimes against humanity, see Michael R. Marrus, *The Nuremberg War Crimes Trial 1945–46*. The best online research site for human rights is probably the "Topical Database" on the website of the Yale Law School.

The essays in D.D. Raphael, ed., *Political Theory and the Rights of Man* (1967), trace the idea of human rights back to Hobbes and Locke. Rhoda Howard and Jack Donnelly set out the conventional liberal position in "Liberalism and Human Rights: A Necessary Connection" (1996). The philosophical discussion inevitably goes back to the concept of natural law. See, for example, Andrew Woodcock's "Jacques Maritain, Natural Law and the Universal Declaration of Human Rights" (2006). There is a lucid discussion of the use of human rights, grounded in the concept of dignity, to impose ethical limits on the power of the state in the 1963 encyclical, *Pacem in Terris*.

It is impossible to review the enormous proliferation of national and international human rights instruments here. One fast-breaking development is the extension of legal rights to animals, which Shawn Thompson and Erin McKenna discuss briefly in *Philosophy Now* (2015/2016) and *The Philosophers' Magazine* (2016). See also the Nonhuman Rights Project, online. For a further extension of rights, see Michael Marder, "Should Plants Have Rights?" (2013), and *Plant-Thinking: A Philosophy of Vegetal Life* (2013).

Chapter 40

Contemporary Contractarianism

The roots of liberal contractarianism extend back to the social contract theories of early modern thinkers such as Thomas Hobbes, John Locke, Hugo Grotius, and Samuel von Pufendorf. John Rawls (1921–2002) is the most influential recent contractarian. In *A Theory of Justice* (1971), he provides a contractarian argument that is intended to champion individual liberty while, at the same time, providing adequate support for disadvantaged members of a social welfare state.

Rawls was brought up in a religious faith. His childhood was marred by the death of his two younger brothers from illnesses (diphtheria and pneumonia) that they had caught from him. He later followed an older brother to Princeton University, where he graduated *summa cum laude* with a degree in theology in 1942. His undergraduate thesis was entitled *A Brief Inquiry into the Meaning of Sin and Faith: An Interpretation Based on the Concept of Community*, which explored the thought of Protestant figures such as Emil Brunner in religious ethics.

Rawls considered entering the Episcopalian priesthood upon graduation. World War II intervened, however, and instead he joined the American army as an infantryman, serving in the Pacific and winning a Bronze Star for meritorious service in a battle zone. He was promoted to Sergeant, but later demoted when he refused an order to discipline a fellow soldier. In the course of the conflict, he experienced the trials of trench warfare and passed through an obliterated Hiroshima after the atomic blast. Rawls later said that he was unable to reconcile the suffering he had witnessed firsthand with the idea of divine providence.

In an essay written near the end of his life ("On My Religion," 1997), Rawls reveals that he was deeply troubled by the problem of evil, which does not rule out the existence of God, but raises enough doubts to rule out the possibility of relying upon God and the received religious tradition for our moral guidance in matters of the public interest. We therefore need some other rationale outside the religious tradition to justify the kinds of moral initiatives that are needed to guarantee social justice. Rawls finds this justification in a kind of rationality and an abstract appeal to our individual interests, which establishes that reasonable people will agree on a fair redistribution of wealth and opportunity.

After the war, Rawls earned a PhD in moral philosophy from Princeton University. He was also awarded a Fulbright Fellowship, which he spent at Oxford University, where he met a number of leading figures in philosophy, including Isaiah Berlin, H.L.A. Hart, Stuart Hampshire, and R.M. Hare. He then returned to America, teaching at Cornell University, MIT, and Harvard University, where he taught for almost forty years. By all accounts, Rawls was a shy, self-effacing man with a stutter who enjoyed a quiet family life and devoted most of his time to his teaching.

Although Rawls was a political philosopher, the goal of his theory is to secure moral freedom and autonomy for individuals. This is a liberal goal: in order to accomplish it, he constructs a kind of moral contract out of self-interest and the abstract exercise of reason. His argument is striking because it argues, on liberal premises, that it is necessary to re-distribute the social and economic opportunities that individuals need, if they are to live freely chosen lives. As a result, his theory seems to reconcile two competing goals: it maximizes the prerogatives of the individual, but promotes social justice and provides for those who suffer disadvantages.

Rawls's *Theory of Justice* was assembled in successive drafts through the 1960s in response to the unsettled political climate of the period, which featured activism and protest. The immediate target of the book was utilitarianism, which had taken over the field of ethics. Rawls responds by setting out a contractarian theory of justice based on agreement rather than utility. He settles on the use of reason without invoking substantive principles because he wants a means of determining and justifying public policy that would appeal to everyone in a pluralistic society, no matter what their personal religious or cultural views.

In some ways, Rawls's theory recalls the natural law, since the purpose of his theory is to referee disagreements between individuals with different moral and religious worldviews. This aspect of Rawls's work came to the fore in a later book, *Political Liberalism* (1993), which made the "overlapping consensus" between individual citizens with competing worldviews the ultimate test for justice in democratic societies. Rawls also published a book on the principles of international justice, *The Law of Peoples* (1999), and a response to earlier criticisms of *A Theory of Justice*, in *Justice as Fairness* (2001). His university lectures have been collected in two books, *Lectures on the History of Moral Philosophy* (2000) and *Lectures on the History of Political Philosophy* (2007), which discuss the work of a wide range of political philosophers.

Michael Sandel (b. 1953) did his undergraduate work at Brandeis University. He subsequently went to Oxford on a Rhodes Scholarship, where he studied under the communitarian Charles Taylor and earned a doctorate in philosophy in 1981. He is currently a professor of government theory at Harvard University, where he teaches political philosophy. Like Rawls, Sandel has devoted himself to his teaching. He has earned himself a reputation as a leading lecturer for an undergraduate course in political philosophy called "Justice." These lectures are easily available online and have added significantly to his academic reputation. Sandel has also served on the President's Council on Bioethics.

Sandel's publications include *Liberalism and the Limits of Justice* (1982), *Democracy's Discontent: America in Search of a Public Philosophy* (1996), *Public Philosophy: Essays on Morality in Politics* (2005), *The Case Against Perfection: Ethics in the Age of Genetic Engin-*

eering (2007), *Justice: What's the Right Thing to Do?* (2010), and *What Money Can't Buy: The Moral Limits of Markets* (2012). He has also written on prominent topical issues in the public press in publications such as *The New York Times*, *The Atlantic Monthly*, and *The New Republic*.

The first reading is from Rawls's *Theory of Justice*, which sets out a hypothetical situation called the "original position," in which people are placed behind "a veil of ignorance," where they cannot know their individual circumstances, so as to prevent any possibility of favoritism. Rawls argues that rational people, placed in such a situation, would agree to establishing a social contract based on two fundamental principles. The first is the principle that citizens should enjoy as much liberty as possible. The second is a principle of distributive justice, which raises the standard of living of the poorest in society and opens up positions of power and influence to everyone without discrimination.

The original idea of the social contract was based on consent and assumed that there was a natural law. Rawls's work is novel because he believes that the terms of such a contract can be agreed upon, directly, through a process of "wide reflective equilibrium." He believes that rational agents will agree upon a benevolent liberalism, which distributes goods and services fairly, while jealously protecting individual choice. He nevertheless maintains that the value of liberty is "lexically prior" to the value of welfare—that is, that the right to liberty be satisfied before the right to welfare. It follows that, in the case of conflict, liberty considerations trump welfare considerations.

The second reading is from Sandel's *Liberalism and the Limits of Justice*, which rejects the idea that we can derive a satisfactory account of justice from a hypothetical social contract. There are two principal reasons for this: in the first place, imaginary contracts have no moral authority and are not binding. In the second place, the fact that we have hypothetically agreed to the terms of a contract does not automatically make these terms just. Morality is not a matter of agreement, and if the social contract is ethically binding, it is because the terms agreed to by participating parties are in keeping with an external moral standard, which needs to be established by reference to independent criteria. Sandel also rejects the assumption that we will necessarily agree to Rawls's terms, which appeal primarily to those who share his liberal sympathies.

John Rawls, *A Theory of Justice*[1]

([1971; 1975] 1999)

Chapter I. Justice as Fairness

3. THE MAIN IDEA OF THE THEORY OF JUSTICE

My aim is to present a conception of justice which generalizes and carries to a higher level of abstraction the familiar theory of the social contract as found, say, in Locke, Rousseau, and Kant. In order to do this we are not to think of the original contract as one to enter a particular society or to set up a particular form of government. Rather, the guiding idea is that the principles of justice for the basic structure of society are the object of the original agreement. They are the principles that free and rational persons concerned to further their own interests would accept in an initial position of equality as defining the fundamental terms of their association. These principles are to regulate all further agreements; they specify the kinds of social cooperation that can be entered into and the forms of government that can be established. This way of regarding the principles of justice I shall call justice as fairness.

Thus we are to imagine that those who engage in social cooperation choose together, in one joint act, the principles which are to assign basic rights and duties and to determine the division of social benefits. Men are to decide in advance how they are to regulate their claims against one another and what is to be the foundation charter of their society. Just as each person must decide by rational reflection what constitutes his good, that is, the system of ends which it is rational for him to pursue, so a

group of persons must decide [rationally,] once and for all what is to count among them as just and unjust....

In justice as fairness the original position of equality corresponds to the state of nature in the traditional theory of the social contract. This original position is not, of course, thought of as an actual historical state of affairs, much less as a primitive condition of culture. It is understood as a purely hypothetical situation characterized so as to lead to a certain conception of justice. Among the essential features of this situation is that no one knows his place in society, his class position or social status, nor does anyone know his fortune in the distribution of natural assets and abilities, his intelligence, strength, and the like. I shall even assume that the parties do not know their conceptions of the good or their special psychological propensities. The principles of justice are chosen behind a veil of ignorance. This ensures that no one is advantaged or disadvantaged in the choice of principles by the outcome of natural chance or the contingency of social circumstances. Since all are similarly situated and no one is able to design principles to favor his particular condition, the principles of justice are the result of a fair agreement or bargain. For given the circumstances of the original position, the symmetry of everyone's relations to each other, this initial situation is fair between individuals as moral persons, that is, as rational beings with their own ends and capable, I shall assume, of a sense of justice. The original position is, one might say, the appropriate initial status quo, and thus the fundamental agreements reached in it are fair. This explains the propriety of the name

---

1 John Rawls, *A Theory of Justice*, revised edition (Cambridge, MA: The Belknap Press of Harvard University Press [1971], 1999).

"justice as fairness": it conveys the idea that the principles of justice are agreed to in an initial situation that is fair. The name does not mean that the concepts of justice and fairness are the same, any more than the phrase "poetry as metaphor" means that the concepts of poetry and metaphor are the same.

Justice as fairness begins, as I have said, with one of the most general of all choices which persons might make together, namely, with the choice of the first principles of a conception of justice which is to regulate all subsequent criticism and reform of institutions. Then, having chosen a conception of justice, we can suppose that they are to choose a constitution and a legislature to enact laws, and so on, all in accordance with the principles of justice initially agreed upon. Our social situation is just if it is such that by this sequence of hypothetical agreements we would have contracted into the general system of rules which defines it.... No society can, of course, be a scheme of cooperation which men enter voluntarily in a literal sense; each person finds himself placed at birth in some particular position in some particular society, and the nature of this position materially affects his life prospects. Yet a society satisfying the principles of justice as fairness comes as close as a society can to being a voluntary scheme, for it meets the principles which free and equal persons would assent to under circumstances that are fair. In this sense its members are autonomous and the obligations they recognize self-imposed.

One feature of justice as fairness is to think of the parties in the initial situation as rational and mutually disinterested. This does not mean that the parties are egoists, that is, individuals with only certain kinds of interests, say in wealth, prestige, and domination. But they are conceived as not taking an interest in one another's interests.... Moreover, the concept of rationality must be interpreted as far as possible in the narrow sense, standard in economic theory, of taking the most effective means to given ends.... The initial situation must be characterized by stipulations that are widely accepted.

In working out the conception of justice as fairness one main task clearly is to determine which principles of justice would be chosen in the original position.... [I]t is an open question whether the principle of utility would be acknowledged. Offhand it hardly seems likely that persons who view themselves as equals, entitled to press their claims upon one another, would agree to a principle which may require lesser life prospects for some simply for the sake of a greater sum of advantages enjoyed by others.... In the absence of strong and lasting benevolent impulses, a rational man would not accept a basic structure merely because it maximized the algebraic sum of advantages irrespective of its permanent effects on his own basic rights and interests. Thus it seems that the principle of utility is incompatible with the conception of social cooperation among equals for mutual advantage....

I shall maintain instead that the persons in the initial situation would choose two rather different principles: the first requires equality in the assignment of basic rights and duties, while the second holds that social and economic inequalities, for example inequalities of wealth and authority, are just only if they result in compensating benefits for everyone, and in particular for the least advantaged members of society.... It may be expedient but it is not just that some should have less in order that others may prosper. But there is no injustice in the greater benefits earned by a few provided that the situation of persons not so fortunate is thereby improved.... The two principles mentioned seem to be a fair basis on which those better endowed, or more fortunate in their social position, neither of which we can be said to deserve, could expect the willing cooperation of others when some workable scheme is a necessary condition of the welfare of all. Once we decide to look for a conception of justice that prevents the use of the accidents of natural endowment and the contingencies of social circumstance as counters in a quest for political and economic advantage, we are led to these principles.

They express the result of leaving aside those aspects of the social world that seem arbitrary from a moral point of view.…

Justice as fairness is an example of what I have called a contract theory.…

The merit of the contract terminology is that it conveys the idea that principles of justice may be conceived as principles that would be chosen by rational persons, and that in this way conceptions of justice may be explained and justified.… Furthermore, principles of justice deal with conflicting claims upon the advantages won by social cooperation; they apply to the relations among several persons or groups. The word "contract" suggests this plurality as well as the condition that the appropriate division of advantages must be in accordance with principles acceptable to all parties.…

Chapter II. The Principles of Justice

11. TWO PRINCIPLES OF JUSTICE

I shall now state in a provisional form the two principles of justice that I believe would be agreed to in the original position.…

The first statement of the two principles reads as follows.

First: each person is to have an equal right to the most extensive scheme of equal basic liberties compatible with a similar scheme of liberties for others.

Second: social and economic inequalities are to be arranged so that they are both (a) reasonably expected to be to everyone's advantage, and (b) attached to positions and offices open to all.…

Thus we distinguish between the aspects of the social system that define and secure the equal basic liberties and the aspects that specify and establish social and economic inequalities. Now it is essential to observe that the basic liberties are given by a list of such liberties. Important among these are political liberty (the right to vote and to hold public office) and freedom of speech and assembly; liberty of conscience and freedom of thought; freedom of the person, which includes freedom from psychological oppression and physical assault and dismemberment (integrity of the person); the right to hold personal property and freedom from arbitrary arrest and seizure as defined by the concept of the rule of law. These liberties are to be equal by the first principle.

The second principle applies, in the first approximation, to the distribution of income and wealth and to the design of organizations that make use of differences in authority and responsibility. While the distribution of wealth and income need not be equal, it must be to everyone's advantage, and at the same time, positions of authority and responsibility must be accessible to all. One applies the second principle by holding positions open, and then, subject to this constraint, arranges social and economic inequalities so that everyone benefits.

These principles are to be arranged in a serial order with the first principle prior to the second. This ordering means that infringements of the basic equal liberties protected by the first principle cannot be justified, or compensated for, by greater social and economic advantages. These liberties have a central range of application within which they can be limited and compromised only when they conflict with other basic liberties. Since they may be limited when they clash with one another, none of these liberties is absolute; but however they are adjusted to form one system, this system is to be the same for all.…

The two principles are rather specific in their content… [They] are a special case of a more general conception of justice that can be expressed as follows.

All social values—liberty and opportunity, income and wealth, and the social bases of self-respect—are to be distributed equally unless an unequal distribution of any, or all, of these values is to everyone's advantage.

Injustice, then, is simply inequalities that are not to the benefit of all.…

As a first step, suppose that the basic structure

of society distributes certain primary goods, that is, things that every rational man is presumed to want. These goods normally have a use whatever a person's rational plan of life. For simplicity, assume that the chief primary goods at the disposition of society are rights, liberties, and opportunities, and income and wealth.... Imagine, then, a hypothetical initial arrangement in which all the social primary goods are equally distributed: everyone has similar rights and duties, and income and wealth are evenly shared. This state of affairs provides a benchmark for judging improvements. If certain inequalities of wealth and differences in authority would make everyone better off than in this hypothetical starting situation, then they accord with the general conception....

The fact that the two principles apply to institutions has certain consequences.... The first principle simply requires that certain sorts of rules, those defining basic liberties, apply to everyone equally and that they allow the most extensive liberty compatible with a like liberty for all. The only reason for circumscribing basic liberties and making them less extensive is that otherwise they would interfere with one another....

Now the second principle insists that each person benefit from permissible inequalities in the basic structure. This means that it must be reasonable for each relevant representative man defined by this structure, when he views it as a going concern, to prefer his prospects with the inequality to his prospects without it....

Chapter VII. Goodness as Rationality

65. THE ARISTOTELIAN PRINCIPLE

... [T]he Aristotelian Principle runs as follows: other things equal, human beings enjoy the exercise of their realized capacities (their innate or trained abilities), and this enjoyment increases the more the capacity is realized, or the greater its complexity. The intuitive idea here is that human beings take more pleasure in doing something as they become more proficient at it, and of two activities they do equally well, they prefer the one calling on a larger repertoire of more intricate and subtle discriminations. For example, chess is a more complicated and subtle game than checkers, and algebra is more intricate than elementary arithmetic. Thus the principle says that someone who can do both generally prefers playing chess to playing checkers, and that he would rather study algebra than arithmetic....

[I]n the design of social institutions[,] a large place has to be made for [the Aristotelian Principle], otherwise human beings will find their culture and form of life dull and empty....

[T]he principle does not assert that any particular kind of activity will be preferred. It says only that we prefer, other things equal, activities that depend upon a larger repertoire of realized capacities and that are more complex.... The actual course that a person follows, the combination of activities that he finds most appealing, is decided by his inclinations and talents and by his social circumstances, by what his associates appreciate and are likely to encourage....

Thus imagine someone whose only pleasure is to count blades of grass in various geometrically shaped areas such as park squares and well-trimmed lawns. He is otherwise intelligent and actually possesses unusual skills, since he manages to survive by solving difficult mathematical problems for a fee. The definition of the good forces us to admit that the good for this man is indeed counting blades of grass, or more accurately, his good is determined by a plan that gives an especially prominent place to this activity. Naturally we would be surprised that such a person should exist.... But if we allow that his nature is to enjoy this activity and not to enjoy any other, and that there is no feasible way to alter his condition, then surely a rational plan for him will center around this activity. It will be for him the end that regulates the schedule of his actions, and this establishes that it is good for him....

Michael Sandel, *Liberalism and the Limits of Justice*[1]

(1982, 1998)

Chapter 3. Contract Theory and Justification

THE MORALITY OF CONTRACT

Rawls locates his theory of justice in the tradition of social contract theory going back to Locke, Rousseau, and Kant. The 'guiding idea' is that the principles of justice are the object of an original agreement. 'Thus we are to imagine that those who engage in social co-operation choose together, in one joint act, the principles which are to assign basic rights and duties·and to determine the division of social benefits'... In designing the social contract, 'a group of persons must decide once and for all what is to count among them as just and unjust,' and the principles they choose are 'to regulate all subsequent criticism and reform of institutions'... In this respect, the original contract would seem a kind of ordinary contract writ large.

But for Rawls...the original agreement is not an actual historical contract, only a hypothetical one...Its validity does not depend on its terms actually having been agreed to, but rather on the idea that they *would* have been agreed to under the requisite hypothetical conditions. In fact, Rawls's hypothetical social contract is even more imaginary than most. Not only did his contract never really happen; it is imagined to take place among the sorts of beings who never really existed, that is, beings struck with the kind of complicated amnesia necessary to the veil of ignorance. In this sense, Rawls's theory is doubly hypothetical. It imagines an event that never really happened, involving the sorts of beings who never really existed.

But this would seem to undermine the moral analogy that gives contract theory much of its intuitive appeal. Once the social contract turns hypothetical, the original agreement is no longer a contract writ large, only a contract that *might* have been writ large but never was. And as Ronald Dworkin has written, 'A hypothetical contract is not simply a pale form of an actual contract; it is no contract at all'[2]...

When two people make an agreement we may typically assess its justice from two points of view. We may ask about the conditions under which the agreement was made, whether the parties were free or coerced, or we may ask about the terms of the agreement, whether each party received a fair share. While these two considerations may well be related, they are by no means identical...

The distinction between these two sorts of questions suggests that we may think of the morality of contract as consisting of two related yet distinguishable ideals. One is the ideal of autonomy, which sees a contract as an act of will, whose morality consists in the voluntary character of the transaction. The other is the ideal of reciprocity, which sees a contract as an instrument of mutual benefit, whose morality depends on the underlying fairness of the exchange.

Each ideal suggests a different basis for contractual obligation. From the standpoint of autonomy, a contract's moral force derives from the fact of its vol-

---

1   Michael J. Sandel, *Liberalism and the Limits of Justice*, second edition (Cambridge: Cambridge University Press [1982], 1998).

2   Ronald Dworkin (1931–2013) was a well-known American legal analyst and professor of law, a leading liberal thinker who wrote an influential text, *Law's Empire*, which elaborates a moralistic (as opposed to positivist) interpretation of the law based on principles of justice, fairness, and integrity.

untary agreement; when I enter freely into an agreement, I am bound by its terms, whatever they may be. Whether its provisions are fair or inequitable, favorable or harsh, I have 'brought them on myself,' and the fact that they are self-imposed provides one reason at least why I am obligated to fulfill them.

The ideal of reciprocity, on the other hand, derives contractual obligation from the mutual benefits of co-operative arrangements. Where autonomy points to the contract itself as the source of obligation, reciprocity points *through* the contract to an antecedent moral requirement to abide by fair arrangements, and thus implies an independent moral principle by which the fairness of an exchange may be assessed. With reciprocity, the emphasis is less on the fact of my agreement than on the benefits I enjoy; contracts bind not because they are willingly incurred but because (or in so far as) they tend to produce results that are fair....

Common sense suggests various reasons why, in practice, actual contracts may turn out unfairly... [and] it cannot be assumed that what *makes* [an agreement] just is the fact that it was agreed to....

WHAT REALLY GOES ON BEHIND THE VEIL
OF IGNORANCE

Bargaining in *any* sense requires some difference in the interests or preferences or power or knowledge of the bargainers, but in the original position [as described by Rawls], there are none. Under such conditions, it is difficult to imagine how any bargain, in any sense, could ever get going....

At this point it is important to distinguish two different senses of 'agreement.' The first involves agreement with a person (or persons) with respect to a proposition, the second agreement to a proposition. The first sort of agreement is a kind of 'choosing together,' and requires a plurality of persons.... It is this sort of agreement that is typically engaged in making a contract, where part of the agreement involves forming an intention....

The second sort of agreement, an agreement to a proposition, does not require more than a single person, and does not involve an exercise of will. In this sense of agreement, to agree to a proposition amounts to acknowledging its validity, and this requires neither that others be involved nor that I take the validity of the proposition to be a matter of choice. It may be enough that I *see* it to be valid, as when I agree to (or accept, or acknowledge) the proposition that 2 + 2 = 4. To agree in this sense is to grasp something already there. Although I may say I have 'decided' that the answer to this difficult problem in mathematics is '*x*,' it is not a decision that *decides* anything except whether I have got it right....

Rawls's account of the original agreement [now] appears in a new light. Passages that first seemed to describe an agreement in the voluntarist sense can now be seen to admit a cognitive interpretation as well. Where at first Rawls writes as though 'the choice... *determines* the principles of justice'..., in other places he writes as though the parties have merely to *acknowledge* principles already there....

Ironically, the Kantian interpretation of justice as fairness highlights the shift from the voluntarist interpretation to the cognitive one. Although some reference to choice remains, the parties are described less as willing agents than as subjects who *perceive* the world in a certain way....

[S]ince the veil of ignorance has the effect of depriving the parties, *qua* parties, to the original position, of all distinguishing characteristics, it becomes difficult to see what their plurality could possibly consist in....

Contracts, like discussions, require a plurality of persons, and when the veil of ignorance descends, this plurality dissolves....

The philosophical considerations by which Rawls would persuade us set out from the contractarian tradition. The well-ordered society he recommends 'comes as close as a society can to being a voluntary scheme'... But what begins as an ethic of choice and consent ends, however unwittingly, as an ethic of insight and self-understanding. In the final passage of the book, the language of choosing and willing is displaced by the language of seeing and perceiving...

> Once we *grasp* this conception, we can at any time *look* at the social world from the required *point of view*... Thus to *see* our place in society from the *perspective* of this position is to see it *sub specie aeternitatis*: it is to *regard* the human situation not only from all social but also from all temporal *points of view*. The *perspective of eternity* is not a *perspective* from a certain place beyond the world, nor the point of view of a transcendent being; rather it is a certain *form of thought* and feeling that ratio-

nal persons can adopt within the world.... Purity of heart, if one could attain it, would be *to see clearly* and to act with grace and self-command from *this point of view* [emphasis added][1]...

The secret to the original position—and the key to its justificatory force—lies not in what [individuals behind the veil of ignorance] do there but rather in what they apprehend there. What matters is not what they choose but what they see, not what they decide but what they discover. What goes on in the original position is not a contract after all, but the coming to self-awareness of an intersubjective being.

Questions

1. What is the "original position" and "the veil of ignorance"? Is Rawls right in thinking that we can use a hypothetical agreement to establish moral principles and the criteria of justice? Explain Sandel's uneasiness with this mechanism.
2. Rawls is following a neoliberal economic view, which holds that rational agents will do what is in their self-interest. Why, in his view, would we all agree to his social contract?
3. What does it mean to say that Rawls's liberty principle is prior to his equality principle? Why do some commentators think that this renders Rawls's commitment to social justice ineffective?
4. Under what circumstances do you think that Rawls would embrace or reject affirmative action? Explain your position.
5. Sandel distinguishes between (1) an agreement *with respect to* a proposition, and (2) an agreement *to* a proposition. He then argues that Rawls believes his view of justice is based on (1), when it is really based on (2). So it is not really a contractarian theory, after all. Explain.
6. Sandel argues that we can use an "autonomy" or a "reciprocity" criterion to determine whether an agreement is fair. Explain these criteria. Can they conflict with one another? How?

---

1   John Rawls, *A Theory of Justice: Original Edition* (London: Belknap Press, 1971), p. 587.

Suggested Readings

John Rawls's *A Theory of Justice* (1971) has been remarkably influential. There is nevertheless a discernible shift in his later *Political Liberalism* (1993), which focuses on notions of overlapping consensus and public reason. Rawls's Harvard lectures have been published in *Lectures on the History of Political Philosophy* (2007), which is a challenging read. Although there have been many critiques of Rawls's contractarianism, Michael Sandel's first book, *Liberalism and the Limits of Justice* (1982), stands as a particularly powerful response.

For a brief resume of Rawls's mature position, see Jan Garrett's page at http://people. wku.edu. David Gauthier's *Morals by Agreement* (1986) provides a standard decision-theory account of modern contractarianism. Jean Hampton sets out a feminist contractarian view in *The Intrinsic Worth of Persons* (2007). See also Benjamin Sachs, "Contractarianism as a Political Morality" (2016).

On the comparative side, see P.J. Naude, "What Can African Business Ethics Learn from John Rawls?" (2005), and Paul D'Ambrosio, "Approaches to Global Ethics: Michael Sandel's Justice and Li Zehou's Harmony" (2016).

For applied ethics, see Paul Kelly, "Contractarian Ethics" (2011). See also Daniel Thero, "Rawls and Environmental Ethics" (1995); Russell DiSilvestro, "Human Embryos in the Original Position?" (2005); Neelke Doorn, "Applying Rawlsian Approaches to Resolve Ethical Issues" (2010); Thomas Dunfee and Thomas Donaldson, "Contractarian Business Ethics" (2015); and David M. Douglas, "Towards a Just and Fair Internet: Applying Rawls's Principles of Justice to Internet Regulation" (2015).

For a response to Sandel from a business perspective, see Tim Worstall, "Michael Sandel's Three Mistakes about the Morality of Markets" (2012).

Chapter 41

Libertarianism and Conservatism

In this chapter, we consider two approaches to morality that have gained traction in the present-day cultural wars. Libertarianism and conservatism (or conservativism) often overlap but are, in fact, distinct points of view. In this chapter we consider Jan Narveson as a representative of libertarianism and John Kekes as a leading conservative spokesperson. But first, consider the general positions.

Libertarianism is a political movement with moral overtones that has become prominent in the United States during the last fifty years. It regards liberty as the chief issue in the political discourse and attempts to place limits on the legitimate actions of government. But libertarianism is also a moral theory, which tends to restrict moral obligation to behavior that obstructs or interferes with the freedom of others. Of course, libertarians personally approve or disapprove of specific behaviors or character traits. They maintain, however, that private behavior is not, strictly speaking, a matter of moral obligation. What one does apart from participation with unwilling others is, at best, a matter of personal aspiration that escapes severe moral censure.

To be sure, popular attitudes often lack theoretical sophistication, but the general libertarian idea that the ultimate criterion of morality is non-interference with others abounds in popular culture. The familiar opinion that one cannot impose one's values on others, that we ought to refrain from judgment when it comes to choices we disagree with, that we must respect other people's right to do whatever they want with their own personal lives, or that the only thing that matters morally is consent: this is moral libertarianism. Whether such views can be applied coherently and consistently is a matter of keen debate.

As for conservatism, the *Stanford Encyclopedia of Philosophy* distinguishes between 'conservatism,' as a philosophical position, and 'neo-conservatism,' which it regards as a political movement. The term 'neo-conservatism' also has associations with a laissez-faire economic position, so much so that some conservatives have claimed that many 'neo-conservatives' are nothing more than (economic) 'classical liberals.' It is evident that the terminology in the area is inherently vague, and refers to thematic elements that occur in the work of certain moral and political philosophers, rather than a cleanly-defined theory. Having said this, one of the features of neo-conservatism is that it generally reflects the secular orientation of contemporary philosophy, which has forced theorists to separate ethical theory from its foundations in metaphysical, religious, or cultural views.

From an ethical perspective, the conservative position has at least three major elements. The first is political realism, which has its foundations in a pessimistic philosophy of human nature. The second is a belief that long-standing moral, social, and political traditions should generally be respected. The third element is the recognition that we need order and social stability to achieve human goods. This recognition is decisive, since it justifies the authority of legitimate legal and political institutions. There are many additional elements, such as a concern for the common and collective good. The neo-conservative literature focuses more specifically on a critique of (political) liberalism and rejects the progressive notion of equality at any cost.

When it comes to libertarianism, the theoretical literature needs to be separated from the popular discussion. Many of the most controversial issues in the contemporary political arena—such as the unrestricted use of drugs or the control of firearms—are often framed in libertarian terms. As a result, the literature includes an over-abundance of topical and polemical commentary, which has relatively little to contribute to the substantive philosophical discussion.

Ayn Rand's popular libertarian novel *Atlas Shrugged* (1957) and her collection of objectivist essays published as *The Virtue of Selfishness: A New Concept of Egoism* (1964) are still avidly cited in public debate. Academic philosophers associated with libertarianism include John Hospers (1918–2011), who authored a "libertarian manifesto" and ran as the presidential candidate for the newly-formed Libertarian Party in the 1972 American election. Murray Rothbard, Robert Nozick, David Gauthier, Milton Friedman, and Friedrich Hayek have adopted libertarian perspectives. There is a distinct "left-libertarianism," with its own set of debates and anthologies, which has been discussed by Tibor R. Machan (1997) and Steven R. Smith (2004), among others.

There has been a renewed interest in conservatism in both the popular and the academic literature. Although terms like 'liberal' and 'conservative' have been muddied by the ideological battles in the popular realm, it is commonly agreed that historical figures such as Confucius, Plato, Aristotle, the Stoics, and Edmund Burke, among many others, are conservatives. A few current thinkers who self-identify as conservatives are Michael Oakeshott, Roger Scruton, Anthony Quinton, and John Kekes.

Our first selection is from Narveson (b. 1936), now a professor emeritus at the University of Waterloo and the chairman of a non-profit Canadian think-tank, The Institute for Liberal Studies. He earned undergraduate degrees in political science and philosophy from the University of Chicago and, after a year at Oxford University, graduated with a PhD in philosophy from Harvard in 1961. Narveson spent most of his university career at the University of Waterloo. He has held visiting positions at a variety of institutions, including the Center for Philosophy and Public Affairs at Bowling Green State University. In his life outside philosophy, Narveson has dedicated himself to classical music, refitting his own house with a concert studio for the benefit of the Waterloo Chamber Music Society.

536

Narveson is known as a compelling if controversial teacher, who is looking for a frank exchange with his opponents. Although his first book, *Morality and Utility* (1968), was an extended defense of utilitarianism, he later rejected utilitarianism and adopted instead a contractarianism, based on the work of Thomas Hobbes, to supply a solid theoretical basis for libertarian rights. Narveson explains his philosophical conversion in *The Libertarian Idea* (1988, 2001), which is probably the best introduction to libertarian ethics. His other books include *Moral Matters* (1993, 1999), *Respecting Persons in Theory and Practice* (2002), *You and the State* (2008), and *This Is Ethical Theory* (2010).

The major obstacle to the use of Hobbes's social contract, from a libertarian perspective, is that his solution to the war of all against all in the state of nature is to appoint a sovereign—in effect, a dictator—who will force citizens to abide by rules. This naturally restricts our freedom. Narveson (following Gauthier) argues that society can do without a sovereign if it inculcates moral habits that teach citizens to cooperate with other people when it is in their mutual self-interest. These moral dispositions will make us cooperate— i.e., not interfere—with those agents who cooperate with us, while avoiding interactions with non-co-operating agents. Ultimately, morality, rationality, and self-interest all converge in a minimalist social contract that focuses on one thing: negative liberty, understood as the freedom to do what we will.

John Kekes is a prominent figure in the new conservatism. Born in 1936 in Budapest, Hungary, he did his undergraduate training at Queen's University and received a PhD from Australian National University in 1967. He has taught at California State University Northridge, the University of Saskatchewan, and the State University of New York, Albany, where he is now professor emeritus. He has held visiting appointments at a variety of institutions, including the United States Military Academy at West Point.

Kekes's work focuses on ethical and political issues. His works in moral philosophy include *The Examined Life* (1988), *The Morality of Pluralism* (1996), *Moral Wisdom and Good Lives* (1997) (on the idea of wisdom and its contemporary application), *The Roots of Evil* (2007), and *The Enlargement of Life: Moral Imagination at Work* (2010). He has also made a case for conservatism in a series of books: *Against Liberalism* (1988), *A Case for Conservatism* (1998), *The Illusions of Egalitarianism* (2007), and *The Art of Politics: The New Betrayal of America and How to Resist It* (2008).

As the titles suggest, Kekes's work sometimes presents conservative views in opposition to liberal views. The economic side of his argument appears to have its roots in the classical liberal tradition. He accordingly criticizes the work of influential "social-justice" or "compassionate" liberals like John Rawls and Ronald Dworkin, who have promoted an ideological egalitarianism. His frank recognition of the reality of evil and the focus on the human propensity to do wrong contrasts sharply with liberal views of the inherent goodness of people. Politically and socially, the conservative view is that we need a strong system of moral belief, and an effective social and political system, to curtail our natural proclivities. Kekes sees the liberal tendency to categorize individuals as innocent social victims as naïve and liberal attempts at social reform as incapable of changing human nature. Although social factors do enter into the assignment of guilt, conservatism maintains that people make free choices, with varying degrees of intention and knowledge, and should be held responsible for their moral decisions. The conservative position accordingly favors punishments and rewards.

In the first reading Narveson sets out a secular alternative that turns morality into a minimal restriction for everyone without exception. The metaphysical appeals to intrinsic values in the historical canon, for example, or to a uniform human nature, are replaced by a frank and common-sense kind of ethical calculation. Narveson argues that we will all be better off if we are moral. Morality should enable social interaction in a pluralistic society without friction between citizens with opposing points of view.

The second reading from Kekes discusses the commitment of conservatism to four basic beliefs: skepticism, pluralism, traditionalism, and pessimism. It also introduces several internal goods claimed to be logically connected with a moral tradition.

READING 41A

Jan Narveson, *The Libertarian Idea*[1]

(1988)

The theory we need is Contractarianism.[2] The general idea of this theory is that the principles of morality are (or should be) those principles for directing everyone's conduct which it is reasonable for everyone to accept. They are the rules that *everyone* has good reason for wanting everyone to act on, and thus to internalize in himself or herself, and thus to reinforce in the case of everyone....

What the philosopher would really like is a universal "contract" in the sense of an agreement that literally everyone would find it reasonable to accept. It is not clear that this can be done. Perhaps people are too different, or have interests that are fundamentally, irresolvably antagonistic....

[S]uppose that morality is a kind of club—the "morality club." Anyone can join—no problem. Those who join have certain responsibilities and certain rights, and we, the people who run this club, offer a package that we think no remotely reasonable person could really refuse; but nevertheless, some might. All we are saying is that *our* package is such that it must appeal to the widest set of people any set of principles *could* appeal to. Anyone who doesn't buy our package wouldn't buy any package compatible with living among his fellows on terms that they could possibly accept. If we can make good on this offer, then the objection that our morality is not, after all, truly universal is hollow.... It's universal in the sense of being as nearly universal as any set of restrictive rules could be. And that, we can argue, is universal *enough*....

One of the contractarians' favorite real-world types is the philosopher Thomas Hobbes. In the

---

1 Jan Narveson, *The Libertarian Idea* (Broadview Press, [1988] 2001).

2 I.e., contractarianism is needed to ground libertarianism.

Hobbesian picture…the place to begin is a wild and unruly place known as the "state of nature." In this state…there is no morality at all. Nobody acknowledges any restrictions whatever on his or her behavior vis-à-vis others, nobody blames or praises anyone else's conduct, and it is quite literally everyone for him- or her-self.…

What is important to the argument here is that the *cause* of this condition[1] is the absence of rules, rules having precisely the character we have attributed to morality: namely, rules that can override the individual inclinations of any person to the contrary, and rules that are the same for all. The same, because the danger is the same and the cure is the same. Left absolutely to their devices, so the argument goes, people will perform actions that lead to a condition that will make their lives immeasurably worse than if they were instead subject to restrictions…

The libertarian's, and in general the liberal's, case is simply that a clear-headed appraisal will confirm the wisdom of signing the social contract instead of bashing ahead as one will, and that this wisdom will be found to obtain in almost (if not quite) complete independence of what those values in particular are. For the totally imprudent or the totally fanatical, to be sure, the compellingness of politics or even of morality might be nil. For everyone else, though, the contractarian has a strong case.…

[I]t is not quite true, as many people seem inclined to think, that libertarianism is a creed whose principles are canonically engraved in marble somewhere for all to see, but still, it does seem to me—and this is one of its attractions, isn't it?—that its basic idea can be stated quite simply. A summary of the findings in Part One goes roughly as follows:

1) Each person, A, has a determinate set of fundamental personal resources such that

2) A has the [negative] right[2] to use those resources in whatever way A sees fit, provided that in doing so, A does not violate the similar right of any other person, B, over the use of B's resources.

Or, more briefly yet: our sole basic duty is to refrain from utilizing the fundamental resources of others without their consent; and those resources include, at a minimum, the bodies and minds of those others.

The implications I will suppose we can draw from this are these, at least: (1) We have no *fundamental* general duty to provide others with such goods as the necessities of life, let alone some particular proportion of all the socially distributable goods there are; (2) we have in general a duty not to interfere with the operations of the "market," so long as it is truly a free market and not something else masquerading as same; (3) we should always in general prefer voluntary social arrangements to involuntary ones whenever this is definable and feasible. (4) Governments, in particular, are severely restricted in what they may properly do, and the blessings of a majority vote in favor of a given government activity is not in general a sufficient license of that activity, morally speaking.…

A Tale of Three Rules about Mutual Aid

[Now o]nce upon a time there were three ordinary blokes. B1, the first of the three, had read the New Testament and went about endeavoring to do unto others as he would have had them do unto him. B1 had some hard times. For one thing, there were a fair number of others who didn't want to be done unto as B1 would like to have had done to him, and this caused a certain amount of embarrassment. And

---

1 I.e., the state of nature.
2 The "right" in question is a negative right, also described in the Introduction.

then there were annoying people who took B1 for a merry ride, for B1's beneficence was unconditional. He shelled out unto seventy times seven, and then, of course, he went broke. B1 died rather young in the poorhouse, and he did not enjoy eternal life, for it turns out that there was none.

B3, on the other hand, was a realist, which...meant that B3 was pretty much of a cynic. *His* rule was to do unto others as they do unto you. If they were nasty to B3, B3 was superb at being equally so right back at them. B3 had read his Axelrod[1] but had forgotten about the first part: start by being nice, and *then* do what they do.... Things didn't go very well for B3 either. He lived a bit longer than B1 but not much, for of course nobody would lend a helping hand to B3, knowing they could count on his non-assistance at all times. He died one nice day for lack of a ride to the hospital.

B2 lived by the silver rule, which says: "Go out of your way a bit to be helpful, and don't stop at just once or twice, because it might take a while for the others to get the idea—but don't make a fetish of it either. Eventually they'll come around, and when everybody is into the habit of helping when it'll do a lot of good for the other fellow and won't cost a lot, then we'll all be better off in the end." And they were, and he was. And B2 lived a long and useful life, died in pretty good financial condition, and was much admired and respected by his fellows....

The Silver Rule is where prudence crosses paths with Morality. B2 does good unto others but expects a return on his investment. Not that he has his eye always fixed on the dollar signs in the distance when he gives a dollar to a beggar or spends a bit of extra

time drawing a nice clear map to show a stranger how to get to the public library. But B2 has his limits. When the ne'er-do-well comes around for the sixth time with palm outstretched, B2 rises to a certain eloquence in telling him where to get off.

Is there a *positive right* to the assistance of one's fellows? A tricky question, and if regarded as a question about our *fundamental* rights, then best answered in the negative. On the other hand, though, the totally unhelpful person needs a couple of earfuls.... In the world we live in, no one can reasonably expect to get along totally without the assistance of others... To be generally disposed to assist one's fellows when they are in need is virtuous, not in a merely conventional sense but rationally: that is, it is a disposition that it is rational to positively reinforce in others and in oneself....

The probability that you will someday benefit from the assistance of the very person you have helped, if that person is a total stranger, is not high. But the probability that you could very well benefit from the assistance of *some* stranger in the not-too-distant future is very high indeed.... If people generally are like that, then the probability that the next stranger will be helpful rather than the reverse is high.... [And] you will have made a good investment. Rational people will live by the Silver Rule...[and therefore expect] everyone to be tolerably helpful. As rules go, this one can't easily be improved upon. The totally helpful person is virtually certain to turn into an intolerably meddlesome person, and the totally unhelpful person will richly deserve the cold shoulders of his fellows.

---

1 Robert Axelrod (b. 1943) is an American professor of political science, best known as a specialist on decision theory or game theory, through which he showed the evolution of cooperation.

READING 41B

John Kekes, *A Case for Conservatism*[1]

(1998)

[Our] aim...is to convince reasonable and morally committed people that good lives are more likely to be lived under conservative political arrangements than under any other alternatives currently available. Conservatism is a political morality. It is political because it concerns the political arrangements that make a society good; and it is moral because it holds that the goodness of a society depends on the goodness of the lives of the people who live in it.

Conservatism has different versions because its advocates disagree about what political arrangements would make a society good. There is, however, no disagreement about having to find the right political arrangements by means of reflection on the history of the society whose arrangements they are.... The conservative attitude, therefore, is not indiscriminate prejudice in favor of traditional arrangements, but a reasonable and reflective defense of traditional arrangements that have stood the test of time.

One distinctive feature of the conservatism defended here is its commitment to four basic beliefs: skepticism, pluralism, traditionalism, and pessimism. These beliefs are not theoretical constructs invented as external standards for evaluating political arrangements. They are...extracted from political arrangements rather than imposed on them as conclusions derived from some philosophical, political, or moral theory.

Another distinctive feature of conservatism is its insistence that any adequate political morality must have three levels: universal, social, and individual. A good society requires the protection of possibilities and limits on each of these levels.... Some of these possibilities and limits are universal, because there are some conditions all good lives require, no matter how they are conceived; others are social, because there are some conditions that all good lives require within the context of a particular society...; and yet others are individual because they are required only by particular conceptions of a good life...Each good life, therefore, has universal, social, and individual requirements, and conservatives believe that the aim of political morality is to make political arrangements that protect these requirements on all three levels.

Political moralities must be concerned both with approximating the good and with avoiding evil. The first involves stressing possibilities; the second limits.... [A] further distinctive feature of conservatism [is] that it attributes equal importance to avoiding evil by setting limits. A good society must prohibit certain ways of living and acting. What these ways are depends on the universal, social, and individual requirements of good lives as they are historically conceived...How reasonable these historical conceptions are partly depends on the extent to which they reflect the fundamental importance of the basic conservative beliefs of skepticism, pluralism, traditionalism, and pessimism....

Before reasonable policies [can] be proposed it is necessary to formulate and defend the basic beliefs from which they could follow....

It is a characteristically conservative belief that in moral and political thought there is not much scope for novelty and originality. The fundamental nature of good and evil is well known...Most personal and political experiments in living are rearrangements

---

1   John Kekes, *A Case for Conservatism* (Ithaca and London: Cornell University Press, 1998).

and re-adjustments of familiar elements. If political arrangements are detrimental to good lives, it is not because of ignorance of good and evil. It is because knowledge of them is obscured by other considerations, or because there is disagreement about how that knowledge bears on changing historical circumstances, or because people prefer evil to good.

The case to be made for conservatism does not therefore consist in proposing a new theory. It rather has the form of reminding readers of what they already know, but perhaps tend to forget under the endlessly repeated liberal and socialist rhetoric that echoes the prevailing political orthodoxy....

[A] difference between conservative politics and most current alternatives to it is the insistence of conservatives on the importance of political arrangements whose purpose is to hinder evil. This difference is a direct result of...the optimistic belief of [liberals] in human perfectibility.... [They assume] that the prevalence of evil is due to bad political arrangements. If people were not poor, oppressed, exploited, discriminated against, and so forth,...then they would be naturally inclined to live good lives. The prevalence of evil, they assume, is due to the political corruption of human nature.... What is needed, therefore, is to make political arrangements that foster the good. The arrangements that hinder evil are unfortunate and temporary measures needed only until the effects of the good arrangements are generally felt.

Conservatives reject this optimism. They do not think that evil is prevalent merely because of bad political arrangements. They think, to the contrary, that one reason why political arrangements are bad is that those who make them have evil propensities.... [T]here is no guarantee whatsoever that political arrangements can be made good. Nor that, if they were made good, they would be sufficient to hinder evil.

Conservatives will insist, therefore, on...the enforcement of morality, the treatment of people according to their moral merit or demerit, the importance of swift and severe punishment for serious crimes, and so on. They will oppose...the absurd fiction of a fundamental moral equality between habitual evil-doers and their victims[; they will oppose] guaranteeing the same freedom and welfare-rights to good and evil people, and so forth.

Political arrangements that are meant to hinder evil are liable to abuse. Conservatives know and care about the historical record that testifies to the dreadful things that have been done to people on the many occasions when such arrangements have gone wrong. The remedy, however, cannot be to refuse to make the arrangements; it must be to make them, learn from history, and try hard to avoid their abuse....

Human nature provides a universal and objective standard by which reasons for or against specific political arrangements, traditions, and conceptions of a good life can be evaluated. But the appeal to this standard yields only reasons that fall far short of determining the nature of good lives. For these reasons provide only their minimum requirements, and beyond this level good lives may take a plurality of forms. The minimum, however, is sufficient to justify skepticism regarding the absolutistic attempt to identify the one good form that all lives must strive to approximate and the relativistic attempt to leave good lives merely at the mercy of the conventions that happen to hold in particular societies....

The traditionalism of conservatives excludes both the view that...individual autonomy should take precedence over...social authority and the reverse view...Traditionalists acknowledge the importance of both autonomy and authority, but they regard them as inseparable, interdependent, and equally necessary. The legitimate claims of both may be satisfied...Good political arrangements...[limit] the government's authority to interfere with either....

Consider [next, the way] people in a moral tradition...rely on their moral intuitions. They are confronted with a situation...They interpret the facts immediately and spontaneously, and they are moved to respond to them. Their beliefs, feelings, and motives are focused on the situation, even if they may remain unarticulated and untranslated into action. Their [moral] interpretations are fallible, although they seem natural and obvious to them. Nevertheless, reasons may lead them to recognize that the situation is more complex than they have supposed, that their intuitions are unreliable in that context, and then they may attempt to correct them. Suppose, however, that no such [conflicting] reason is presented. The people then have no reason to doubt their shared intuitions of a particular situation. If they were asked to justify them, their understandable reaction would be incomprehension. For why should they need justification for the obvious? They bought the goods, and that is why they pay the bill; their friend asked and that is why they help. What more needs to be said? What more could be said?

Situations of course are not always simple; there may be hidden facts, unrecognized complexities, deeper conflicts. Reliance on intuition is then misplaced. When complications occur, reasonable people recognize the need for reflection. Intuition is appropriate only in routine situations. It is a logical point, however, that the routine is what occurs most of the time. In the morality of everyday life, therefore, intuition is an appropriate and reliable guide....

If one's intuitions are contrary to [the moral intuitions] of informed others, then,...there is ground for doubting them. But if what seems obvious to an agent is reinforced by the concurring intuitions of others, then there is no reason for the agent to doubt it....

Critics of the conservative thesis...want to know how moral education in that tradition is to be distinguished from indoctrination with a moral outlook whose variable conventions may seem quite arbitrary to outsiders. They point at the intuitions suggested by charismatic, fundamentalist, puritan, rigidly hierarchical, or guilt-ridden moral traditions. And they refuse to grant even a presumption in favor of...[a moral] consensus..., unless the moral standing of the tradition is first established.

This demand is reasonable, but...it is hard to understand why it is thought to be telling against reliance on intuitions. The justification of moral traditions [and their attendant intuitions] is that they enable people who participate in them to make good lives for themselves. If the moral traditions fail to do that, then they are indeed unjustified, the moral identity they foster is valueless or worse...

A moral tradition is logically connected with...the internal [or private] goods that are obtainable through participation in it.... Internal goods are to be found by continued engagement in activities which are constitutive of living according to a conception of a good life. If all goes well, these activities are enjoyable. Enjoyment however is not the end at which they aim, but a by-product of engagement in them.... Examples of internal goods are the enjoyment people take in the activities central to their way of life, musicians in making music, athletes in the disciplined use of their body, couples in loving and being loved by each other, or citizens in approving and being approved by their society....

The first of these internal goods is self-direction. This is the activity of individuals through which they construct for themselves a conception of a good life. The material for it is provided by...the moral tradition and the construction consists in individuals selecting and adapting those among the conventional possibilities which seem...to fit their character and circumstances. Self-direction involves some view of what they want to make of themselves...They must ask and answer such questions as...whether [their] way [of life] will be scholarly, artistic, commercial, or athletic;...whether they aim at wielding power, [or] enjoying the luxuries wealth can provide, [or] receiving the recognition [that] status and prestige bestow, [or] basking in the love of a few intimates, or devoting themselves to a cause....

Intimacy is a second kind of internal good.... [P]ersonal relationships based on love, friendship, or joint dedication to some shared project...will vary from life to life...[T]hese [personal] contacts

[may] be provided by marriage, parenthood, solidarity with comrades, shared admiration of some ideal, love affairs, discipleship to someone great, or by the affection and loyalty of one's students, family members, colleagues, or fellow inquirers....

A third kind of internal good is civility. This is a reciprocal relationship that exists among members of a good society who are not intimates and who may not even be personally acquainted with each other. Their contacts occur in the routine conduct of affairs. They meet each other in queues, audiences, airplanes, waiting rooms, and stores; they are connected as clerks and customers, nurses and patients, buyers and sellers, fellow drivers on the road,...homeowners and repairmen, officials and clients, and so on.... [T]he internal good that characterizes these impersonal encounters shows itself in the presence of casual friendliness, spontaneous good will, and courtesy, and the absence of hostility, distrust, surliness, and a litigious disposition...

[An unjustified] moral tradition...will disintegrate. The disintegration thesis...claims that a society has good reason to exclude conceptions of a good life which violate its required conventions.... [P]art of the justification of a moral tradition...consists in the defense of those specific values and goods...that define the tradition, and that distinguish it from other traditions....

A moral tradition is good if through moral education...it thereby creates a shared moral identity for the individuals who adhere to it....

Since reasonable people will recognize that a shared moral identity is necessary for living a good life, they will want to embrace the conservative thesis.

Questions

1. Narveson believes that morality is like a club that we should all want to belong to. Why? How do we join the club? How should we treat people outside the club?

2. What is the most essential principle in Narveson's libertarianism? How does such a principle compare with the so-called "Silver Rule" in Confucius: What you do not want done to you, do not do to others?

3. Explain the libertarian view of taxes, which are often seen—on Rawls's social contract—as a means of re-distributing wealth. Do you agree with Rawls, or the libertarians? Why, why not?

4. What is the relationship between politics and morality, according to conservatism? What are some examples of "conservative political arrangements" which serve a moral purpose? How does this differ from libertarianism?

5. Where, according to Kekes, do moral intuitions come from? Can they be trusted? When do they need to be put to the test? What would a libertarian think about Kekes's theory in this specific respect?

6. How does Kekes explain the liberal and conservative view of human nature? Which view is right, do you think? Why? How is this reflected in the conservative attitude to crime and punishment? Compare to liberal attitudes.

Suggested Readings

Libertarianism is probably best described as a political and economic viewpoint with important ethical implications. Its contemporary pedigree is often traced to John Hospers, *Libertarianism: A Political Philosophy for Tomorrow* (1971). Robert Nozick then provided a philosophical defense of small government in *Anarchy, State, and Utopia* (1974), although he later changed his mind. Students can also consult Ronald Hamowy, ed., *The Encyclopedia of Libertarianism*, and the website at libertarianism.org.

Although Gary Watson ("Soft Libertarianism and Hard Compatibilism," 1999), Ishtiyaque Haji ("Libertarianism and the Luck Objection," 2000), and David Sobel ("Backing Away from Libertarian Self-Ownership," 2012) have raised theoretical problems, the academic literature mostly focuses on applied issues. Lester H. Hunt argues "Against a Legal Duty to Rescue" (1995); Tal Scriven sets out a libertarian theory of environmental ethics in *Wrongness, Wisdom, and Wilderness: Toward a Libertarian Theory of Ethics and the Environment* (1997); and David Rönnegard and N. Craig Smith discuss libertarian business ethics in "Shareholders vs. Stakeholders: How Liberal and Libertarian Political Philosophy Frames the Basic Debate in Business Ethics" (2013).

For criticism of libertarianism, see R.H.J. Ter Meulen, "The Lost Voice: How Libertarianism and Consumerism Obliterate the Need for a Relational Ethics in the National Health Care Service" (2008). Those interested in the popular debate can easily find it online.

Alongside Kekes's many books, Roger Scruton has published prolifically on conservatism. See *The Meaning of Conservatism* (1980), *Arguments for Conservatism* (2007), and *The Uses of Pessimism* (2012). Other sources may be found in Andy Hamilton's entry on "Conservatism" in the *Stanford Encyclopedia of Philosophy*.

Social psychologist Jonathan Haidt has argued that liberals have an unduly narrow account of morality in *The Righteous Mind: Why Good People Are Divided by Politics and Religion* (2013). Some conservative voices have taken exception to various liberal causes. Describing herself as an "equity feminist" who rejects male-averse "gender feminism," Christina Hoff Sommers has criticized contemporary feminism in books such as *Who Stole Feminism?* (1994) and *The War against Boys* (2000).

For a conservative perspective on applied ethics, see Robert Solomon, *Ethics and Excellence: Cooperation and Integrity in Business* (1992), and John Bliese, "Traditionalist Conservatism and Environmental Ethics" (1997). In bioethics, see Leon Kass, *Life, Liberty and the Defense of Dignity* (2002), and Eric Cohen, "Conservative Bioethics and the Search for Wisdom" (2006). The tone of the opposing literature is hostile and occasionally inflammatory. See, for example, L.P. Gramzinski, "Leon Kass and the American Jeremiad against Human Genetic Enhancement" (2013).

Chapter 42

Communitarianism

The term 'communitarianism' has been used—originally by critics of the movement—to describe the views of a loose group of moral philosophers who have reasserted the importance of community when confronted with the contemporary emphasis on liberal individualism. Understood as a philosophical worldview, communitarianism can be traced back to the influence of historical authors such as Jean-Jacques Rousseau (1712–78) and Georg Wilhelm Friedrich Hegel (1770–1831) on British Idealists such as Thomas H. Green (1836–82), Francis H. Bradley (1846–1924), and Bernard Bosanquet (1848–1923). In the present era, thinkers as diverse as Michael Sandel, Alasdair MacIntyre, Michael Walzer, John Gray, William Galston, Judith Shklar, Joseph Raz, and Allan Buchanan, have all been identified as communitarian. In this chapter, we feature excerpts from Charles Taylor, Amitai Etzioni, and Ifeanyi Menkiti.

We can discern three basic motivations behind communitarianism. The first has a theoretical, even metaphysical basis, and recalls Hegel and the British Idealists, who expressed deep concerns about the narrowness of the liberal conception of the individual. This side of communitarianism can be seen in the historical and cultural interests of a contemporary philosopher like Charles Taylor.

Secondly, there is a concern that the liberal and analytical literature has neglected both the social nature of the person and the larger social good. The current focus on autonomy and freedom of the individual is not enough, in itself, to provide a satisfactory account either of the moral person or the community. Moral philosophy requires a positive account of the relations among individuals, some larger good, and a description of conditions in which individuals can flourish.

The third motivation is more practical and political. It has sometimes been said that there is a "new" or "second generation" communitarianism, which focuses specifically on the measures needed to strengthen the sense of community in society. This leads to a renewed emphasis on the need to balance the common good with individual rights when examining specific ethical issues. Sociologist Amitai Etzioni, who has become a leading voice in the communitarian movement, has made a career of positively promoting common moral values around which a social consensus can be built from many sides of the political spectrum.

Charles Margrave Taylor (b. 1931) is a graduate of McGill University and Oxford University, where he was a Rhodes Scholar. He has taught at McGill University and All Souls College, Oxford, and has vigorously participated in public and political life in Canada and Quebec. He ran unsuccessfully for a seat in the Canadian parliament on four occasions in the 1960s. In 1991, he was appointed to the Quebec *Conseil de la langue française*, despite his criticism of Quebec's French-first commercial sign laws. A well-known public commentator on religious, cultural, and political issues, he was chosen in 2007 to co-lead a controversial Commission of inquiry into "reasonable accommodation" for immigrants from non-Western cultures, which has exposed a clear rift in the views of different groups and classes within Quebec society.

Having worked closely with philosophers Isaiah Berlin and G.E.M. Anscombe, Taylor has many publications, including *Sources of the Self: The Making of the Modern Identity* (1989), *Reconciling the Solitudes: Essays on Canadian Federalism and Nationalism* (1993), *Multiculturalism: Examining the Politics of Recognition* (1994), and *A Secular Age* (2007). His 1991 CBC Massey Lectures were published as *The Malaise of Modernity* (titled *The Ethics of Authenticity* in the US). Much of his theoretical work aims to reconcile the conflicting demands of preserving our cultural identity and modern-day liberalism. Although he rejects the communitarian label, replacing it with the term 'substantive liberalism,' his argument is notable primarily for its communitarian emphasis on the broader social origins of personal identity.

Amitai Etzioni (b. 1929) was born Werner Falk in Cologne, Germany, to a Jewish family that, fleeing the Nazis, moved to Palestine prior to World War II. He was eventually sent to a boarding school and lived on a kibbutz, later referring to these formative experiences as a "school in communitarianism." As a Jewish commando, he participated in a bombing raid on a British radar station. He then changed his name to hide his identity. After the Israeli war, Etzioni studied to be an adult education instructor, working under philosopher Martin Buber, whose personalist philosophy of "I and Thou" influenced his later thought. He completed degrees at the Hebrew University of Jerusalem and then attended the University of California at Berkeley, where in 1958 he obtained his PhD in a record time of eighteen months. He was professor of sociology at Columbia University and The George Washington University for over twenty years.

Like Taylor, Etzioni has been involved in politics, serving as a Senior Advisor to the White House 1979–80, after which he became the director of the Institute for Communitarian Policy Studies at The George Washington University. He founded the Communitarian Network in 1990, a non-profit, non-partisan communitarian organization. Editor of *The Responsive Community: Rights and Responsibilities*, the organization's quarterly journal, 1991–2004, he has been a commentator on public policy and politics in the popular media for several decades.

Etzioni has published over thirty books, including *The Moral Dimension: Toward a New Economics* (1988), *The Spirit of Community* (1993), *The New Golden Rule* (1996), *My Brother's Keeper: A Memoir and a Message* (2003), *Freedom versus Security in the Age of Terrorism* (2004), and *Security First: For a Muscular, Moral Foreign Policy* (2007).

Etzioni's interest in moral formation is apparent in "The Fast-Food Factories: McJobs Are Bad for Kids," a 1986 column in the *Washington Post*, in which he criticizes successful franchises such as McDonald's, Baskin-Robbins, and Kentucky Fried Chicken. The jobs they offer "undermine school attendance and involvement, impart few skills that will be useful in later life, and simultaneously skew the values of teenagers—especially their ideas about the worth of a dollar." "Many teens find the instant reward of money, and the youth status symbols it buys, much more alluring than credits in calculus courses, European history, or foreign languages."

Communitarianism has found a prominent voice in the black community. W.E.B. Du Bois's *The Souls of Black Folks* (1903) is an early classic of the genre that discusses the dislocated experience of American blacks as a "double consciousness" caught between loyalties to American and black identities. We have included a more recent excerpt from Ifeanyi Menkiti (1940–2019), who was a poet and Professor Emeritus of philosophy at Wellesley College. Born in Nigeria, Menkiti came to the US in 1961 and later earned a PhD in philosophy from Harvard, studying under John Rawls. Menkiti provides an African perspective on the self, which views the self as rooted in a community and whose identity is defined in terms of social relationships.

The first reading contains excerpts from Taylor's *The Malaise of Modernity*, where the author chronicles the worrisome effects of a liberal emphasis on individual "authenticity." Taylor claims that the present emphasis on a search for the true inner self closes off contact with the wider community, obscuring a larger "horizon of significance" that endows life with objective meaning.

In the second reading, Etzioni presents several communitarian ideas and argues for a moderate communitarianism that balances social order and individual freedom through a "third sector" of society comprising unofficial relationships with our peers. He also acknowledges universal moral truths that prevail over the normative standards in any single society.

The third reading, from Menkiti, contrasts African concepts of "social self-hood" and Western individualism. Some commentators believe that the picture he sketches is too extreme, but it serves well as a foil to atomic liberal individualism.

READING 42A

Charles Taylor, *The Malaise of Modernity*[1]

(1991)

I. Three Malaises

The first source of worry is individualism. Of course, individualism also names what many people consider the finest achievement of modern civilization. We live in a world where people have a right to choose for themselves their own pattern of life, to decide in conscience what convictions to espouse, to determine the shape of their lives in a whole host of ways that their ancestors couldn't control. And these rights are generally defended by our legal systems....

Very few people want to go back on this achievement. Indeed, many think that it is still incomplete, that economic arrangements, or patterns of family life, or traditional notions of hierarchy still restrict too much our freedom to be ourselves. But many of us are also ambivalent. Modern freedom was won by our breaking loose from older moral horizons. People used to see themselves as part of a larger order. In some cases, this was a cosmic order, a "great chain of Being," in which humans figured in their proper place along with angels, heavenly bodies, and our fellow earthly creatures. This hierarchical order in the universe was reflected in the hierarchies of human society.... Modern freedom came about through the discrediting of such orders....

[T]hese orders gave meaning to the world and to the activities of social life. The things that surround us were not just potential raw materials or instruments for our projects, but they had the significance given them by their place in the chain of being. The eagle was not just another bird, but the king of a whole domain of animal life. By the same token, the rituals and norms of society had more than merely instrumental significance. The discrediting of these orders has been called the "disenchantment" of the world. With it, things lost some of their magic....

The worry has been repeatedly expressed that the individual lost something important along with the larger social and cosmic horizons of action. Some have written of this as the loss of a heroic dimension to life. People no longer have a sense of a higher purpose, of something worth dying for. Alexis de Tocqueville sometimes talked like this in the last century, referring to the "petits et vulgaires plaisirs"[2] that people tend to seek in the democratic age. In another articulation, we suffer from a lack of passion. Kierkegaard saw "the present age" in these terms. And Nietzsche's "last men" are at the final nadir of this decline; they have no aspiration left in life but to a "pitiable comfort."...

This worry has recently surfaced again in concern at the fruits of a "permissive society," the doings of the "me generation," or the prevalence of "narcissism," to take just three of the best-known contemporary formulations. The sense [is] that lives have been [morally] flattened and narrowed, and that this is connected to an abnormal and regrettable self-absorption...

III. The Sources of Authenticity

The ethic of authenticity is something relatively new and peculiar to modern culture. Born at the end of the eighteenth century, it...is a child of the

---

1 Charles Taylor, *The Malaise of Modernity*, CBC Massey lectures series, 1991 (Concord, ON: House of Anansi Press, 1991); also published as *The Ethics of Authenticity*, 1991 Massey Lectures (Cambridge, MA: Harvard University Press, 1995).

2 French for 'small and vulgar pleasures.'

Romantic period... [which embraced the] notion that human beings are endowed with a moral sense, an intuitive feeling for what is right and wrong....

[T]he most important philosophical writer who helped to bring about this change [was] Jean-Jacques Rousseau.[1]... Rousseau frequently presents the issue of morality as that of our following a voice of nature within us. This voice is most often drowned out by the passions induced by our dependence on others, of which the key one is "amour propre"[2] or pride. Our moral salvation comes from recovering authentic moral contact with ourselves. Rousseau even gives a name to the intimate contact with oneself... that is a source of joy and contentment: "le sentiment de l'existence."[3]

Rousseau also articulated a closely related idea... what I want to call self-determining freedom. [This] is the idea that I am free when I decide for myself what concerns me, rather than being shaped by external influences.... Self-determining freedom demands that I break the hold of all such external impositions, and decide for myself alone....

Herder[4] [in turn] put forward the idea that each of us has an original way of being human.... Before the late eighteenth century no one thought that the differences between human beings had this kind of moral significance. [Like Herder we believe] [t]here is a certain way of being human that is *my* way. I am called upon to live my life in this way, and not in imitation of anyone else's. But this gives a new importance to being true to myself. If I am not, I miss the point of my life, I miss what being human is for *me*.

This is the powerful moral ideal that has come down to us. It accords crucial moral importance to a kind of contact with myself, with my own inner nature, which it sees as in danger of being lost, partly through the pressures towards outward conformity, but also because... I may have lost the capacity to listen to this inner voice. And then it greatly increases the importance of this self-contact by introducing the principle of originality: each of our voices has something of its own to say.... I can't even find the model to live by outside myself. I can find it only within.

Being true to myself means being true to my own originality, and that is something only I can articulate and discover. In articulating it, I am also defining myself. I am realizing a potentiality that is properly my own.... This is the background that gives moral force to the culture of authenticity, including its most degraded, absurd, or trivialized forms. It is what gives sense to the idea of "doing your own thing" or "finding your own fulfilment."...

IV. Inescapable Horizons

The general feature of human life that I want to evoke is its fundamentally *dialogical* character. We become full human agents, capable of understanding ourselves, and hence of defining an identity, through our acquisition of rich human languages of expression.... No one acquires the languages needed for self-definition on their own.... The genesis of the human mind is in this sense not "monological," not something each accomplishes on his or her own, but dialogical.... We define [ourselves] in dialogue with, sometimes in struggle against, the identities our significant others want to recognize in us. And even when we outgrow some of the latter—our parents, for instance—and they disappear from our lives, the conversation with them continues within us as long as we live....

---

1 Jean-Jacques Rousseau (1712–78) was a Genevan philosopher, writer, and composer. His political philosophy influenced Enlightenment thinkers across Europe.

2 French for 'self-love,' by which Rousseau intends 'indulgent self-love.'

3 French for 'the feeling of existence.'

4 Johann Gottfried Herder (1744–1803) was a German philosopher, theologian, poet, and literary critic.

To some people this might seem a limitation... This is one way of understanding the impulse behind the life of the hermit, or... the solitary artist. But from another perspective, we might see even this as aspiring to a certain kind of dialogicality. In the case of the hermit, the interlocutor is God. In the case of the solitary artist, the work itself is addressed to a future audience...

When we come to understand what it is to define ourselves, to determine in what our originality consists, we see that we have to take as background some sense of what is significant. Defining myself means finding what is significant in my difference from others. I may be the only person with exactly 3,732 hairs on my head... but so what?...

Perhaps the number 3,732 is a sacred one in some society; then having this number of hairs can be significant. But we get to this by linking it to the sacred....

Things take on importance against a background of intelligibility. Let us call this a horizon. It follows that one of the things we can't do, if we are to define ourselves significantly, is suppress or deny the horizons against which things take on significance for us....

It may be important that my life be chosen, as John Stuart Mill asserts in *On Liberty*, but unless some options are more significant than others, the very idea of self-choice falls into triviality and hence incoherence....

Following Nietzsche, I am indeed a truly great philosopher if I remake the table of values. But this means redefining values concerning important questions, not redesigning the menu at McDonald's, or next year's casual fashion.

The agent seeking significance in life, trying to define him- or herself meaningfully, has to exist in a horizon of important questions. That is what is self-defeating in modes of contemporary culture that concentrate on self-fulfilment *in opposition* to the demands of society, or nature, which *shut out* history and the bonds of solidarity. These self-centred "narcissistic" forms are indeed shallow and trivialized; they are "flattened and narrowed," as Bloom[1] says.... To shut out demands emanating beyond the self is precisely to suppress the conditions of significance, and hence to court trivialization. To the extent that people are seeking a moral ideal here, this self-immuring is self-stultifying; it destroys the condition in which the ideal can be realized....

Amitai Etzioni, "Communitarianism Revisited"[2]

(2014)

The 1980s

The term 'communitarianism' was first used in 1841 by John Goodwyn Barmby, founder of the Univer-sal Communitarian Association, and referred to the public philosophy of those concerned with the development of intentional and experimental communities. After that it was rarely employed until

---

1 Allan Bloom (1930–92) was an American philosopher and classicist who became famous for his criticism of contemporary American higher education.

2 Amitai Etzioni, "Communitarianism Revisited," *Journal of Political Ideologies* 19, no. 3 (2014).

the 1980s when it was used to refer to the works of Michael Sandel, Charles Taylor and Michael Walzer. Michael Sandel, particularly, was associated with the communitarian criticism of liberalism, the main theme of which was that there must be common formulations of the good rather than leaving it to be determined by each individual by him or herself, for themselves. Communitarianism hence holds that the state cannot be neutral....

The 1990s

The Spirit of Community[1] seems to be the first communitarian book aimed at a non-academic readership. Its main thesis was the next correction ought to be not pulling society in the opposite direction to rampant individualism—but toward a middle ground of balance between individual and communal concerns, between rights and the common good....

One account of the common good is that it is some benefit done for the sake of helping others with no regard for who those people are in particular beyond their membership in some community, including future generations. That is, the person acting to further the common good is unable to determine who will be the beneficiary of their actions.... For example, basic research, protecting the environment, preventing climate change and developing sustainable energy sources are all costly projects that will only pay off over the longer run, and then only to unknown, unpredictable beneficiaries. The common good also includes developing and nurturing and preserving goods that belong to the community but no particular person including the archaeological and historical sites and documents (e.g. the text of the Constitution)...

BALANCING, WITHIN HISTORY

Communitarians note that societies constantly adjust the balance between rights and the common good as internal and environmental conditions change. Moreover, they often overcompensate by moving too far towards one value when another one was or seemed underserved.... [O]ne might imagine this movement...as akin to a marble moving in a bowl that is subject to outside forces. Though the marble will swing back and forth over the centre of the bowl (the metaphorical optimal balance point), there is a risk that [it] will shoot up over the lip of the bowl, making a return to the bowl's nadir impossible. This metaphorical event stands in for the society that dissolves into irreparable chaos (e.g. Syria in 2011–2013) or break-up (e.g. the former Yugoslavia).

Although critics have challenged the very concept of balance, and advocates often champion one core value over all others, the courts of democratic societies and their legislatures are clearly balancing, and very much in the communitarian way...

COMMUNITY, THE THIRD SECTOR AND 'SOFT' COMMUNITARIANISM

Much of the public debate about basic principles concerning societal design has focused for the last two centuries on the role of the coercive sources of societal organization (the state)—versus that of voluntary transactions and exchanges (the economy). In this realm as well, strong advocates struck positions that centred on one principle ('That government is best which governs least,' vs. encompassing nationalization and central planning) while in effect all societies draw on some kind of balancing of the two or become highly dysfunctional.

Communitarianism leapfrogged this debate by pointing out that it overlooks the importance of the

---

1　A book published by Etzioni in 1993.

third sector, composed of families, local communities, voluntary associations, religious organizations and numerous social groupings including racial, ethnic, professional/vocational and others....

Individuals are, as Aristotle put it, social animals. That meant that they have bonds with others (e.g. family and community members) which affect their preferences and choices in two major ways. First, in the original formation of these preferences.... Second, as a source of... approbation and social censure to enforce established preferences or reformulate them....

[S]ocial bonding provides a major and distinct source of social order: a 'soft' one.... When people abide by norms due to informal social controls, to gain approbation of others to whom they are bonded, or avoid their censure, these 'control' mechanisms leave the ultimate choice to the person in contrast to outright coercion....

[I]nformal social controls are essential because the volume of transactions in a modern society is so large that there never can be enough accountants, inspectors, border guards, custom officials and police to limit anti-social behaviour to a level a free society can tolerate....

[C]ontrary to a widely held belief that moral dialogues lead to prolonged confrontations without resolutions (e.g. about abortion), most moral dialogues do lead to new shared moral understandings, which in turn change behaviour, as they are undergirded by informal social controls. Examples include the changed attitudes toward minorities, women, people of different sexual orientations and attitudes to the environment.

UNIVERSALISM VERSUS RELATIVISM

Observations that moral dialogues take place within communities have led some to conclude that com-

munities are the ultimate arbiters of the good. Michael Walzer, for example,... concludes that notions of justice come down to the extent to which life in a particular community reflects the shared values and understandings of the members of that community....

However, this is a position difficult to maintain given that a community of Nazis or the KKK or Afrikaners can conclude that lynching people of different colour than that of the members is morally appropriate... A communitarian hence needs an Archimedean moral point above and beyond the consensus of a community, and a substantive one, albeit not necessarily as thick[1] as local ones....

[W]ithout recognizing universal principles,... [we] could not challenge other nations' practices of stoning adulterous women, chopping off limbs of thieves, jailing dissenters and trading sex slaves, not to mention child labour, forced marriages and female circumcision....

[H]ow can one justify [the most basic] moral judgements?...

[O]ne cannot reliably build cross-cultural moral judgements... on consensus.

An alternative proposition has been posited by ethicists who champion deontological ethics.... A deontologist 'contends that it is possible for an action or rule of action to be the morally right or obligatory one... simply because of some other fact about it or because of its own nature.'... For example, when one points out that people have greater obligation to their own children than to the children of others, this moral claim speaks for itself, effectively and directly. One does not sense that there is a need for some consequentialist explanation, a calculus of harm, or some other form of utilitarian analysis. Indeed, one is unlikely to find a single person who maintains, believes or argues that people have the same moral obligation to all children that they have to their own.

---

1 Etzioni is referring to Michael Walzer's view that normative values can be either thick/maximalist or thin/minimalist, i.e., either values specific to a given culture and context or values that are universally shared and which can, therefore, be invoked in cross-cultural moral debate, respectively.

Statements about moral causes that present themselves as compelling are similar to what religious authorities speak of as revelation. This does not mean that one cannot reason about these matters.... However, here reason follows, buttresses or challenges revelation, rather than being the source of judgement. When one senses that certain positions are self-evident, one asks if one can find a compelling counterargument. If not, the judgement stands. Thus, when one recites the dictum that 'it is better to let a thousand guilty people walk free than to hang one innocent person,' it may at first seem self-evident. However, when one then notes that these freed criminals are sure to kill at least several innocent people, one finds that the certitude of the initial statement is no longer nearly as strong as it seemed at first blush....

All systems of thought, whether mathematical, scientific, religious or moral, require at least one starting point, primary concept or assumption that we must take for granted—which is another term for self-evident....

In short, behind every sustainable moral construction is a self-evident foundation...

One might ask: where do these self-evident truths come from? Nature? God? Or are they built into our humanity? The answer is not clear, but this matters little for the purpose at hand. The analogue is to see an arch and understand what holds it together, without any cement or glue or wire. It stands because the way the bricks are laid out generates a formation that is self-sustaining. One can recognize this quality of the arch without having the faintest idea who put it together. Similarly, self-evident truths feel complete without one having to know how such [a] point has been reached....

Ifeanyi Menkiti, "Person and Community in African Traditional Thought"[1]

(1984)

My aim...is to articulate a certain conception of the person found in African traditional thought....

The first contrast[2] worth noting is that whereas most western views of man abstract this or that feature of the lone individual and then proceed to make it the defining or essential characteristic which entities aspiring to the description "man" must have, the African view of man denies that persons can be defined by focusing on this or that physical or psychological characteristic of the lone individual. Rather, man is defined by reference to the environing community. As John Mbiti[3] notes, the African view of the person can be summed up in this statement: "I am because we are, and since we are, therefore I am."...

---

1 Ifeanyi Menkiti, "Person and Community in African Traditional Thought," in Richard A. Wright, ed., *African Philosophy: An Introduction*, 3rd ed. (Lanham, MD: University Press of America, 1984).

2 I.e., the contrast between the "African conception of the person and various other conceptions found in Western thought."

3 John Mbiti (1931–2019) was a Kenyan-born Christian religious philosopher.

[A]s far as Africans are concerned, the reality of the communal world takes precedence over the reality of individual life histories... It is in rootedness in an ongoing human community that the individual comes to see himself as man, and it is by first knowing this community as a stubborn perduring fact of the psychophysical world that the individual also comes to know himself as a durable, more or less permanent, fact of this world.... [J]ust as the navel points men to umbilical linkage with generations preceding them, so also does language and its associated social rules point them to a mental commonwealth with others whose life histories encompass the past, present, and future....

[I]n the African view it is the community which defines the person as person, not some isolated static quality of rationality, will, or memory.

This brings us to the second point of contrast between the two views of man, namely, the *processual* nature of being in African thought—the fact that persons become persons only after a process of incorporation. Without incorporation into this or that community, individuals are considered to be mere danglers to whom the description 'person' does not fully apply. For personhood is something which has to be achieved, and is not given simply because one is born of human seed.... Thus, it is not enough to have before us the biological organism, with whatever rudimentary psychological characteristics are seen as attaching to it. We must also conceive of this organism as going through a long process of social and ritual transformation until it attains the full complement of excellencies seen as truly definitive of man. And during this long process of attainment, the community plays a vital role as catalyst and as prescriber of norms....

[W]hereas Western conceptions of man go for what might be described as a minimal definition of the person... the African view reaches instead for what might be described as a maximal definition of the person. As far as African societies are concerned, personhood is something at which individuals could fail, at which they could be competent or ineffective, better or worse. Hence, the African emphasized the rituals of incorporation and the overarching necessity of learning the social rules by which the community lives, so that what was initially biologically given can come to attain social self-hood, i.e., become a person with all the inbuilt excellencies implied by the term.

That full personhood is not perceived as simply given at the very beginning of one's life, but is attained after one is well along in society, indicates straight away that the older an individual gets the more of a person he becomes. As an Igbo[1] proverb has it, "What an old man sees sitting down, a young man cannot see standing up." The proverb applies, it must be added, not just to the incremental growth of wisdom as one ages; it also applies to the ingathering of the other excellencies considered to be definitive of full personhood. What we have here then is both a claim that a qualitative difference exists between old and young, and a claim that some sort of ontological progression exists between infancy and ripening old age. One does not just take on additional features, one also undergoes fundamental changes at the very core of one's being....

In the particular context of Africa, anthropologists have long noted the relative absence of ritualized grief when the death of a young child occurs, whereas with the death of an older person, the burial ceremony becomes more elaborate and the grief more ritualized—indicating a significant difference in the conferral of ontological status....

After birth the individual goes through the different rites of incorporation, including those of initiation at puberty time, before becoming a full person in the eyes of the community. And then, of course, there is procreation, old age, death, and entry into the community of departed ancestral spirits—a community viewed as continuous with the commu-

---

1 The Igbo people are an ethnic group native to present-day south-central and south-eastern Nigeria.

nity of living men and women, and with which it is conceived as being in constant interaction....

For the ancestral dead are not dead in the world of spirits, nor are they dead in the memory of living men and women who continue to remember them, and who incessantly ask their help through various acts of libation and sacrificial offering. At the stage of ancestral existence, the dead still retain their person-hood and are, as a matter of fact, addressed by their various names...Later, however, after several genera-tions, the ancestors cease to be remembered by their personal names; from this moment on they slide into personal non-existence, and lose all that they once possessed by way of personal identity. This, for the traditional African world-view, is the termination of personal existence, with entities that were once fully human agents...ending their worldly sojourn as they had started out—as un-incorporated non-persons....

Just as the child has no name when it tumbles out into the world to begin the journey towards self-hood, so likewise, at the very end, it will have no name again....

[T]his phenomenon of a depersonalized status at the two polarities of existence makes a great deal of sense given the absence of moral function. The child, we all know, is usually preoccupied with his physical needs; and younger persons, generally, are notori-ously lacking in moral perception. Most often they have a tendency towards self-centeredness in action, a tendency to see the world exclusively through their own vantage point. This absence of moral function cannot but have an effect on the view of them as per-sons. Likewise for the completely departed ancestral spirits...[whose] contact with the human commu-

nity [has been] completely severed. The various soci-eties found in traditional Africa routinely accept this fact that personhood...is attained in direct propor-tion as one participates in communal life through the discharge of the various obligations defined by one's stations. It is the carrying out of these obliga-tions that transforms one...into the person-status of later years, marked by a widened maturity of ethical sense...

Western writers have generally interpreted the term 'community' in such a way that it signifies nothing more than a mere collection of self-interested persons, each with his private set of preferences....

Now this understanding of human commu-nity...is something completely at odds with the African view of community...[which] is not an additive 'we' but a thoroughly fused collective 'we'....[In the African view] there is assumed to be an *organic* dimension to the relationship between the component individuals, whereas in the [Western] understanding of human society as something [arti-ficially] *constituted* what we have is a non-organic bringing together of atomic individuals into a unit more akin to an association than to a community.... Whereas the African view...moves from society to individuals, the Western view moves instead from individuals to society....

African societies tend to be organized around the requirements of duty while Western societies tend to be organized around the postulation of individ-ual rights. In the African understanding, priority is given to the duties which individuals owe to the collectivity, and their rights...are seen as secondary to their exercise of their duties....

Questions

1. Taylor argues that our contemporary emphasis on the individual over the community, in spite of its welcome aspects, is often experienced as a loss. Explain the positive and the negative aspects of this shift in emphasis.

2. Explain the historical origin of the modern concept of 'authenticity.' Taylor goes on to argue (after these excerpts) that the focus on authenticity in the modern world leads to an increased need for recognition. Can you figure out why?

3. Etzioni argues that the state cannot be neutral in deciding between competing visions of the good. Explain his position, using the example of recreational drugs or some other contentious issue.

4. In addition to the state and the market, Etzioni includes a "third sector," the social bonds formed within other forms of association. How would the recognition of these moral bonds influence our (political) discussions on the state-market relationship?

5. Compare the idea of the person in African society (as Menkiti describes it) to the liberal idea of the person in Western society. What are the advantages and disadvantages of each view?

6. Compare the African notion of community (as Menkiti describes it) to the Western liberal account of community found, for example, in authors such as Hobbes, Locke, and the libertarians.

Suggested Readings

Taylor's *Ethics of Authenticity* (originally entitled *The Malaise of Modernity*) provides a convenient introduction to the communitarian-liberal debate. Taylor's *Sources of the Self* (1992) and *A Secular Age* (2007) are more challenging reads.

Two influential books by Etzioni are *The New Golden Rule: Community and Morality* (1996) and *The New Normal: Finding a Balance between Individual Rights and the Common Good* (2014).

The Essential Communitarian Reader (1998, ed. Etzioni) is a collection of essays from diverse commentators. Daniel Bell's *Communitarianism and Its Critics* (2004) contains a lively, accessible defense of communitarianism in dialogue form. For a feminist critique of communitarianism, consult E. Frazer and N. Lacey, *The Politics of Community: A Feminist Analysis of the Liberal-Communitarian Debate* (1993), and Judith Garber, "Defining Feminist Community" (2007). For web resources, see the website of The Institute for Communitarian Policy Studies at icps.gwu.edu and Etzioni's "Communitarian Network" at communitariannetwork.org.

Kwame Gyekye has argued in opposition to Menkiti for a more moderate communitarian interpretation of the African experience in *Tradition and Modernity: Philosophical Reflections on the African Experience* (1997). For a more recent comment on African communitarianism, see Precious Uwaezuoke Obioha, "A Communitarian Understanding of the Human Person as a Philosophical Basis for Human Development" (2014).

In applied ethics, see Jay Black, *Mixed News: The Public/Civic/Communitarian Journalism Debate* (1997); M. Parker, ed., *Ethics and Community in the Health Care Professions* (2nd ed., 2002); Carla Treloar and Lisa Maher, "Ethical Challenges and Responses in Harm Reduction Research: Promoting Applied Communitarian Ethics" (2005); and Erik Christensen, "The Re-emergence of the Liberal-Communitarian Debate in Bioethics" (2012).

Chapter 43

Contemporary Virtue Ethics

G.E.M. Anscombe and Alasdair MacIntyre (b. 1929) are usually credited with bringing back virtue ethics. This is an exaggeration. Earlier thinkers, such as F.H. Bradley and John Dewey, were fully aware of virtue ethics and incorporated elements of the tradition into their own work. Still, MacIntrye's well-received volume *After Virtue* (1981) raised a serious challenge to the usual curriculum in university ethics and brought virtue ethics back to the forefront of the academic discussion. Many discussions have followed, including those led by women philosophers such as Philippa Foot, Martha Nussbaum, Christine Swanton, and Rosalind Hursthouse.

MacIntyre was born in Glasgow and has Presbyterian roots. He has a BA in Classics from the University of London, an MA in Philosophy from the University of Manchester (1951), and an MPhil from Oxford University (1961). Later he taught at a number of English universities before moving to the United States in 1970, where he taught at various institutions, including the University of Notre Dame and Princeton. MacIntyre retired in 2010 and now holds Fellowships from the Notre Dame Center for Ethics and Culture and from the Centre for Contemporary Aristotelian Studies in Ethics and Politics (CASEP) at London Metropolitan University. He has served as the president of the American Philosophical Association.

MacIntyre is a distinguished moral and political philosopher whose intellectual life has led him from early Marxism, to Aristotelianism, to the "Thomism" of Thomas Aquinas, and to Roman Catholicism. He has become the most prominent voice in the present resurgence in virtue ethics. He has always looked at philosophy through an ethical lens. As early as 1966, in *A Short History of Ethics*, he argued that the meaning of key ethical terms has changed significantly. This seems problematic, since the residual meaning of such terms is associated with particular customs and views, and the terms continue to be used, essentially out-of-context, long after the associations have been lost. One of the general arguments in his work is that ethical theories must be studied in their historical context.

MacIntyre's most widely-read works are four volumes on the subject of virtue ethics: *After Virtue* (1981, 2007), *Whose Justice? Which Rationality?* (1988), *Three Rival Versions of Moral Enquiry* (1990), and *Dependent Rational Animals: Why Human Beings Need the Virtues* (1999).

MacIntyre is particularly critical of the emotivists, who followed Hume in arguing that our ethical impulses are essentially irrational. He devises a new virtue ethics based, not on Aristotle's metaphysical biology, but on a sociological analysis of history. On his account, human beings are social beings engaged in various specialized practices—such as portrait painting, medicine, university teaching, farming, or experimental physics—which require various virtues for success. We cannot succeed at our self-chosen practices without perseverance, patience, honest self-criticism, respect for our teachers, reverence for past masters, and so on. Each practice is identified with particular institutions and a living tradition.

MacIntyre goes further, however, and argues that we derive our personal identity from a narrative sense of self. In becoming a portrait painter, for example, I share my avocation with the members of a wide variety of communities, which include my fellow painters, the wider art community, and society as a whole. I also have affiliations with a set of collective institutions such as art schools, museums, and galleries. My success as a painter and the fact that it brings me a good income, or makes me famous, is extraneous, however, to MacIntyre's conception of virtue, and may actually undermine the internal good enshrined within the practice.

Philippa Foot (1920–2010) was a British atheist philosopher schooled in the analytic tradition. She had a long, distinguished career in academe, defending virtue ethics as a viable alternative to deontology and consequentialism (utilitarianism). Her maternal grandfather was, interestingly, the 22nd and 24th President of the United States, Grover Cleveland. She was a close friend of noted British novelist and philosopher Iris Murdoch.

Foot was educated at Somerville College, Oxford (1939–42), where she engaged in lengthy debate with Anscombe and taught throughout her academic career. She also did teaching stints at Cornell, MIT, UCLA, and City University of New York. She was also Griffin Professor of Philosophy at the University of California, Los Angeles, from 1976 to 1991 (while retaining her position at Oxford). She is the author of several influential books, including *Virtues and Vices and Other Essays in Moral Philosophy* (1978), *Natural Goodness* (2001), and *Moral Dilemmas* (2002).

Most of Foot's published works are in the areas of normative ethics or metaethics. She argued, similarly to MacIntyre, against the non-cognitive approach followed in the works of analytic philosophers; instead, she defended the cognitive character of moral judgment and the possibility of evaluating the truth of such judgments. Foot thereby brought the question of the rationality of morality into the debate. She attempted to answer the question "Why be moral?" over the course of her life and explored several different lines of inquiry in response to it.

Foot was decisively influenced by Kant and Aristotle. She thought that the most systematic accounts of the virtues and vices are to be found in Aristotle and in the blending of Aristotelian and Christian philosophy found in St. Thomas. As for Kant's influence, she has argued both for and against some of the main features of his deontology. In her earlier career, she suggested—in opposition to Kant—that morality might be conceived as a system of hypothetical (as opposed to categorical) imperatives. This makes moral judgments more flexible when it comes to individual circumstances.

As a final note, Foot introduced into contemporary discussion the well-known "trolley problem," which has caught the imagination of a number of philosophers. If one is faced with a choice between leaving a train running straight ahead and killing five people or pulling a switch to move it to another track where one person will be killed, what should one do? The problem highlights the differences between deontology and consequentialism; Foot used the example to make a distinction between killing and letting die.

The first reading contains excerpts from MacIntyre's *After Virtue*. They discuss the relationship between virtues and "practices," the concept of "a tradition," and the narrative character of our lives.

In the second reading, Foot is more sympathetic to Kant, arguing that virtues always involve some aspect of right intention or good will and that they are essentially "corrective" in that they are intended to overcome inevitably negative aspects of human nature. Other questions raised by virtue ethics are also examined.

Alasdair MacIntyre, *After Virtue*[1]

(1981)

Internal goods[2] are indeed the outcome of a competition to excel, but it is characteristic of them that their achievement is a good for the whole community... So when Turner transformed the seascape in painting or W.G. Grace advanced the art of batting in cricket in a quite new way[3] their achievement enriched the whole relevant community....

[We can] formulate [then] a first, even if partial and tentative definition of a virtue: A virtue is an acquired human quality the possession and exercise of which tends to enable us to achieve those goods which are internal to practices...

It belongs to the concept of practice... whether we are painters or physicists or quarterbacks...—that its goods can only be achieved by subordinating ourselves to the best standard so far achieved,... [and therefore,] to other practitioners. We have to learn to recognise what is due to whom; we have to be prepared to take whatever self-endangering risks are demanded along the way; and we have to listen carefully to what we are told about our own inadequacies and to reply with the same carefulness for the facts. In other words we have to accept as necessary components of any practice... the virtues of justice,

---

1 Alasdair MacIntyre, *After Virtue: A Study in Moral Theory* (Notre Dame, IN: University of Notre Dame Press, 1981).

2 I.e., the goods at which particular practices aim.

3 Joseph M.W. Turner (1775–1851) was an English Romantic painter, known for his expressive colorization and often violent marine paintings. William Gilbert Grace (1848–1915) was an English amateur cricketer, who was important in the sport's development and widely considered one of its greatest players.

courage and honesty. For not to accept these...so far bars us from achieving the standards of excellence or the goods internal to the practice that it renders the practice pointless except as a device for achieving external goods.[1]...

[T]he virtues are those goods by reference to which, whether we like it or not, we define our relationships to those other people with whom we share the kind of purposes and standards which inform practices....

[S]o long as we share the standards and purposes characteristic of practices, we define our relationships to each other...by reference to standards of truthfulness and trust, so we define them too by reference to standards of justice and of courage.... Justice requires that we treat others in respect of merit or desert according to uniform and impersonal standards...

The case with courage is a little different. We hold courage to be a virtue because the care and concern for individuals, communities and causes which is so crucial to so much in practices requires [it]. If someone says that he cares for some individual, community or cause, but is unwilling to risk harm or danger on his, her or its own behalf, he puts in question the genuineness of his care and concern. Courage, the capacity to risk harm or danger to oneself, has its role in human life because of this connection with care and concern....

[F]rom the standpoint of those types of relationship without which practices cannot be sustained: truthfulness, justice and courage—and perhaps some others—are genuine excellences; [they] are virtues in the light of which we have to characterise ourselves and others... [T]his recognition that we cannot escape the definition of our relationships in terms of such goods is perfectly compatible with the acknowledgment that different societies have and have had different codes of truthfulness, justice and courage. Lutheran pietists[2] brought up their children to believe that one ought to tell the truth to everybody at all times, whatever the circumstances or consequences, and Kant was one of their children. Traditional Bantu parents[3] brought up their children not to tell the truth to unknown strangers, since they believed that this could render the family vulnerable to witchcraft. In our culture many of us have been brought up not to tell the truth to elderly great-aunts who invite us to admire their new hats. But each of these codes embodies an acknowledgment of the virtue of truthfulness. So it is also with varying codes of justice and of courage.

Practices then might flourish in societies with very different codes; what they could not do is flourish in societies in which the virtues were not valued... For the kind of cooperation, the kind of recognition of authority and of achievement, the kind of respect for standards and the kind of risk-taking which are characteristically involved in practices demand for example fairness in judging oneself and others..., a ruthless truthfulness without which fairness cannot find application...and a willingness to trust the judgments of those whose achievement in the practice give them an authority to judge which presupposes fairness and truthfulness in those judgments...It is no part of my thesis that great violinists cannot be vicious or great chess-players mean-spirited. Where the virtues are required, the vices also may flourish. It is just that the vicious and mean-spirited necessarily rely on the virtues of others...

[A] practice...is never just a set of technical skills, even when directed towards some unified purpose and even if the exercise of those skills can on occasion be valued or enjoyed for their own sake.... Practices never have a goal or goals fixed for all time—painting has no such goal nor has physics...It

---

1   I.e., goods such as money or fame.

2   Lutheran Pietism combined emphasis on Biblical doctrine with an emphasis on individual piety and living a vigorous Christian life.

3   Bantu refers to the hundreds of ethnic groups that speak the Bantu languages. The Bantu peoples inhabit the geographical area covering much of the central and southern parts of Africa.

therefore turns out...that every practice has its own history and a history which is more...than that of the improvement of the relevant technical skills....

To enter into a practice is [therefore] to enter into a relationship not only with its contemporary practitioners, but also with those who have preceded us in the practice, particularly those whose achievements extended the reach of the practice to its present point. It is thus the achievement, and *a fortiori* the authority, of a tradition which I then confront and from which I have to learn. And for this learning...the virtues of justice, courage and truthfulness are prerequisite in precisely the same way...as they are in sustaining present relationships within practices....

Practices must not be confused with institutions. Chess, physics and medicine are practices; chess clubs, laboratories, universities and hospitals are institutions. Institutions are characteristically and necessarily concerned with what I have called external goods. They are involved in acquiring money and other material goods; they are structured in terms of power and status, and they distribute money, power and status as rewards. Nor could they do otherwise...For no practices can survive for any length of time unsustained by institutions.... [But] without justice, courage and truthfulness, practices could not resist the corrupting power of institutions....

The virtues are of course themselves in turn fostered by certain types of social institution and endangered by others. Thomas Jefferson[1] thought that only in a society of small farmers could the virtues flourish; and Adam Ferguson[2] with a good deal more sophistication saw the institutions of modern commercial society as endangering at least some traditional virtues.... [I]n any society which recognised only external goods competitiveness would be the dominant and even exclusive feature. We have a brilliant portrait of such a society in Hobbes's account of the state of nature...

Virtues then stand in a different relationship to external and to internal goods. The possession of the virtues...is necessary to achieve the latter; yet the possession of the virtues may perfectly well hinder us in achieving external goods.... [N]otoriously the cultivation of truthfulness, justice and courage will often, the world being what it contingently is, bar us from being rich or famous or powerful.... We should therefore expect that, if in a particular society the pursuit of external goods were to become dominant, the concept of the virtues might suffer first attrition and then perhaps something near total effacement, although simulacra might abound.

The time has come to ask the question of how far this partial account of a core conception of the virtues...is faithful to the tradition...How far, for example, and in what ways is it Aristotelian? It is—happily—not Aristotelian in two ways in which a good deal of the rest of the tradition also dissents from Aristotle. First, although this account of the virtues is teleological,...it does not require any allegiance to Aristotle's metaphysical biology.[3] And secondly, just because of the multiplicity of human practices and the consequent multiplicity of goods...which will often be contingently incompatible and which will therefore make rival claims upon our allegiance—conflict will not spring solely from flaws in individual character.... [I]f it turns out to be the case that this socially teleological account can support Aristotle's general account of the virtues,...these differences from Aristotle himself may well be regarded as strengthening rather than weakening the case for a generally Aristotelian standpoint....

In what does the unity of an individual life consist? The answer is that its unity is the unity of a

---

1 Thomas Jefferson (1743–1826) was an American Founding Father who was the principal author of the *Declaration of Independence*. He later served as the third President of the United States (1801–09).

2 Adam Ferguson (1723–1816) was a Scottish philosopher and historian of the Scottish Enlightenment.

3 Aristotle's metaphysical biology saw human beings, basically, as composites of a body and a soul (understood as a source of life-activities).

narrative embodied in a single life.... The unity of a human life is the unity of a narrative quest. Quests sometimes fail, are frustrated, abandoned or dissipated into distractions; and human lives may in all these ways also fail. But the only criteria for success or failure in a human life as a whole are the criteria of success or failure in a narrated or to-be-narrated quest. A quest for what?...

[W]ithout some at least partly determinate conception of the final *telos*[1] there could not be any beginning to a quest. Some conception of the good for man is required. Whence is such a conception to be drawn? Precisely from those questions which... transcend that limited conception of the virtues which is available in and through practices. It is in looking... for a conception of *the* good which will enable us to extend our understanding of the purpose and content of the virtues,... that we initially define the kind of life which is a quest for the good. But secondly it is clear the medieval conception of a quest is not at all that of a search for something..., as miners search for gold or geologists for oil. It is in the course of the quest and only through encountering and coping with the various particular harms, dangers, temptations and distractions which provide any quest with its episodes and incidents that the goal of the quest is finally to be understood. A quest is always an education both as to the character of that which is sought and in self-knowledge.

The virtues therefore are to be understood as those dispositions which... will also sustain us in the relevant kind of quest for the good,... and which will furnish us with increasing self-knowledge and increasing knowledge of the good. The catalogue of the virtues will therefore include... the virtues necessary for philosophical enquiry about the character of the good. We have then arrived at a provisional conclusion about the good life for man: the good life for man is the life spent in seeking for the good life for man... We have also completed the second stage in our account of the virtues, by situating them in relation to the good life for man and not only in relation to practices. But our enquiry requires a third stage.

For I am never able to seek for the good or exercise the virtues only *qua* individual.... [I]t is not just that different individuals live in different social circumstances; it is also that we all approach our own circumstances as bearers of a particular social identity. I am someone's son or daughter, someone else's cousin or uncle; I am a citizen of this or that city, a member of this or that guild or profession; I belong to this clan, that tribe, this nation.

Hence what is good for me has to be the good for one who inhabits these roles. As such, I inherit from the past of my family, my city, my tribe, my nation, a variety of debts, inheritances, rightful expectations and obligations. These constitute the given of my life, my moral starting point. This is in part what gives my life its own moral particularity....

I find myself part of a history and... one of the bearers of a tradition....

Traditions, when vital, embody continuities of conflict....

A living tradition then is a historically extended, socially embodied argument, and an argument precisely in part about the goods which constitute that tradition. Within a tradition the pursuit of goods extends through generations, sometimes through many generations. Hence the individual's search for his or her good is generally and characteristically conducted within a context defined by those traditions of which the individual's life is a part... Traditions decay, disintegrate and disappear. What then sustains and strengthens traditions? What weakens and destroys them?

The answer in key part is: the exercise or the lack of exercise of the relevant virtues.... Lack of justice, lack of truthfulness, lack of courage... corrupt traditions... Living traditions [constitute] a not-yet-completed narrative...

---

1   *Telos* is Greek for goal or end.

Philippa Foot, "Virtues and Vices"[1]

(2002)

[Let us start by making some remarks, admittedly fragmentary, about the concept of a moral virtue as we understand the idea.]

[First of all] [i]t seems clear that virtues are, in some general way, beneficial.... Nobody can get on well if he lacks courage, and does not have some measure of temperance and wisdom, while communities where justice and charity are lacking are apt to be wretched places to live...

Let us say then,... that virtues are in general beneficial characteristics, and indeed ones that a human being needs to have, for his own sake and that of his fellows.... [T]here are[, however,] many other qualities of a man that may be similarly beneficial, as for instance bodily characteristics such as health and physical strength, and mental powers such as those of memory and concentration. What is it, we must ask, that differentiates virtues from such things?

As a first approximation to an answer we might say... that virtue belongs to the will[.]...

[I]t is primarily by his intentions that a man's moral dispositions are judged. If he does something unintentionally this is usually irrelevant to our estimate of his virtue.... [Some] failures in performance rather than intention may show a lack of virtue. This will be so when, for instance, one man brings harm to another without realising he is doing it, but where his ignorance is itself culpable.[2]... [S]ometimes one man succeeds where another fails... because his heart lies in a different place; and the disposition of the heart is part of virtue....

What this suggests is that a man's virtue may be judged by his innermost desires as well as by his intentions and this fits with our idea that a virtue such as generosity lies as much in someone's attitudes as in his actions. Pleasure in the good fortune of others is... the sign of a generous spirit; and small reactions of pleasure and displeasure often the surest signs of a man's moral disposition.

None of this shows that it is wrong to think of virtues as belonging to the will; what it does show is that "will" must here be understood in its widest sense...

[W]isdom has special connexions with the will...

Wisdom, as I see it, has two parts. In the first place the wise man knows the means to certain good ends; and secondly he knows how much particular ends are worth. Wisdom in its first part is relatively easy to understand. It seems that there are some ends belonging to human life in general rather than to particular skills such as medicine or boatbuilding, ends having to do with such matters as friendship, marriage, the bringing up of children, or the choice of ways of life; and it seems that knowledge of how to act well in these matters belongs to some people but not to others. We call those who have this knowledge wise, while those who do not have it are seen as lacking wisdom. So, as both Aristotle and Aquinas insisted, wisdom is to be contrasted with cleverness because cleverness is the ability to take the right steps to any end, whereas wisdom is related only to good ends, and to human life in general rather than to the ends of particular arts.

Moreover,... there belongs to wisdom only that part of knowledge which is within the reach of any ordinary adult human being: knowledge that can

---

1 Philippa Foot, *Virtues and Vices and Other Essays in Moral Philosophy* (Oxford: Clarendon Press, 2002).

2 E.g., as in the case of negligence.

be acquired only by someone who is clever or who has access to special training is not counted as part of wisdom, and would not be so counted even if it could serve the ends that wisdom serves....

In short wisdom, in what we called its first part, is connected with the will in the following ways. To begin with it presupposes good ends: the man who is wise does not merely know *how* to do good things such as looking after his children well, or strengthening someone in trouble, but must also want to do them. And then wisdom, in so far as it consists of knowledge which anyone can gain in the course of an ordinary life, is available to anyone who really wants it....

The second part of wisdom, which has to do with values, is much harder to describe, because here we meet...the thought that some pursuits are more worthwhile than others, and some matters trivial and some important in human life. Since it makes good sense to say that most men waste a lot of their lives in ardent pursuit of what is trivial and unimportant it is not possible to explain the important and the trivial in terms of the amount of attention given to different subjects by the average man. But I have never seen, or been able to think out, a true account of this matter, and I believe that a complete account of wisdom...must wait until this gap can be filled. What we can see is that one of the things a wise man knows and a foolish man does not is that such things as social position, and wealth, and the good opinion of the world, are too dearly bought at the cost of health or friendship or family ties. So we may say that a man who lacks wisdom "has false values," and that vices such as vanity and worldliness and avarice are contrary to wisdom in a special way....

The idea that virtues belong to the will...helps to distinguish them from such things as bodily strength or intellectual ability...[But what about the distinction] between virtues and other practical excellences such as arts and skills....

In the matter of arts and skills,...voluntary error is preferable to involuntary error, while in the matter of virtues...it is the reverse.... If we think, for instance, of someone who deliberately makes a spelling mistake (perhaps when writing on the blackboard in order to explain this particular point) we see that this does not in any way count against his skill as a speller: "I did it deliberately" rebuts an accusation of this kind.... There is no comparable rebuttal in the case of an accusation relating to lack of virtue. If a man acts unjustly or uncharitably, or in a cowardly or intemperate manner, "I did it deliberately" cannot on any interpretation lead to exculpation. So, we may say, a virtue is not, like a skill or an art, a mere capacity: it must actually engage the will.[1]

... [The virtues] are *corrective*, each one standing at a point at which there is some temptation to be resisted or deficiency of motivation to be made good....

Let us first think about courage and temperance.... [I]t is only because fear and the desire for pleasure often operate as temptations that courage and temperance exist as virtues at all.... [W]e often want to run away...where we should stand firm; and we want pleasure not only where we should seek pleasure but also where we should not. If human nature had been different there would have been no need of a corrective disposition in either place, as fear and pleasure would have been good guides to conduct throughout life. So Aquinas says, about the passions,

[that] [t]hey may incite us to something against reason, and so we need a curb, which we name *temperance*. Or they may make us shirk a course of action dictated by reason, through fear of dangers or hardships.... For this *courage* is named....

---

1 I.e., engage the will in a good direction.

With virtues such as justice and charity it is a little different, because they correspond ... rather to a deficiency of motivation ... If people were as much attached to the good of others as they are to their own good there would no more be a general virtue of benevolence than there is a general virtue of self-love. And if people cared about the rights of others as they care about their own rights no virtue of justice would be needed to look after the matter, and rules about such things as contracts and promises would only need to be made public, like the rules of a game that everyone was eager to play....

[Now] the following difficulty presents itself: that we both are and are not inclined to think that the harder a man finds it to act virtuously the more virtue [he shows if he does act well. For on the one hand great virtue] is needed where it is particularly hard to act virtuously; yet on the other it could be argued that difficulty in acting virtuously shows that the agent is imperfect in virtue ... Who shows most courage, the one who wants to run away but does not, or the one who does not even want to run away? Who shows most charity, the one who finds it easy to make the good of others his object, or the one who finds it hard? ...

[W]e may count as courageous those few who without blindness or indifference are nevertheless fearless even in terrible circumstances. And when someone has a natural charity or generosity it is at least part of the virtue that he has[.] ... [Although we must keep in mind that] a kindly or fearless disposition could be disastrous without justice and wisdom, ... I have argued that the virtues can be seen as correctives in relation to human nature in general but not that each virtue must present a difficulty to each and every man.

Nevertheless many people feel strongly inclined to say that it is for moral effort that moral praise is to be bestowed, and that in proportion as a man finds it easy to be virtuous so much the less is he to be morally admired for his good actions. The dilemma can be resolved only when we stop talking about difficulties standing in the way of virtuous action as if they were of only one kind. The fact is that some kinds of difficulties do indeed provide an occasion for much virtue, but that others rather show that virtue is incomplete....

[C]onsider an example of honest action. We may suppose for instance that a man has an opportunity to steal, ... but that he refrains. And now let us ask our old question. For one man it is hard to refrain from stealing and for another man it is not: which shows the greater virtue in acting as he should? ... [I]t makes all the difference whether the difficulty comes from circumstances, as that a man is poor, or that his theft is unlikely to be detected, or whether it comes from something [bad] that belongs to his own character. The fact that a man is *tempted* to steal is something about him that shows a certain lack of honesty: of the thoroughly honest man we say that it "never entered his head," meaning that it was never a real possibility for him. But the fact that he is poor is something that makes the occasion more *tempting*, and difficulties of this kind make honest action all the more virtuous....

[S]ome actions are in accordance with virtue without requiring virtue for their performance ... Kant's trader was dealing honestly ... [because he was hoping for a profit],[1] and it is for this reason that his action did not have "positive moral worth." Similarly, the care that one ordinarily takes for one's life ... is something for which no virtue is required.... [T]here is no general virtue of self-love as there is a virtue of benevolence or charity, because men are generally attached sufficiently to their own good. Nevertheless in special circumstances virtues such as temperance, courage, fortitude, and hope may be needed if someone is to preserve his life.... [I]t is this

---

1 In Chapter 1 of *The Groundwork for the Metaphysics of Morals*, Kant produces the example of a shopkeeper who charges the same price to inexperienced customers as to everyone else, not out of a duty to be honest, but rather because the trust this inspires in customers will make him the most money in the long run.

that explains why...suicide is *sometimes* contrary to virtues such as courage and hope....

Aquinas, in his definition of virtue, said that virtues can produce only good actions...The common opinion nowadays is, however, quite different.... [H]ardly anyone sees any difficulty in the thought that virtues may sometimes be displayed in bad actions.... [M]ost people take it for granted that the virtues of courage and temperance may aid a bad man in his evil work....

What are we to say about this difficult matter? There is no doubt that the murderer who murdered for gain was *not a coward*...It does not follow, however, that an act of villainy can be courageous; we are inclined to say that it "took courage," and yet it seems wrong to think of courage as equally connected with good actions and bad....

[C]ourage is not operating as a virtue when the murderer turns his courage...to bad ends....

Someone reading the foregoing pages might... think that the author of this paper always admired most those people who had all the virtues, being wise and temperate as well as courageous, charitable, and just. And indeed it is sometimes so.... Yet the fact is that many of us look up to some people whose chaotic lives contain rather little of wisdom or temperance...And while it may be that this is just romantic nonsense I suspect that it is not. For while wisdom always operates as a virtue, its close relation prudence does not, and it is prudence rather than wisdom that inspires many a careful life. Prudence is not a virtue in everyone, any more than industriousness is, for in some it is rather an overanxious concern for safety and propriety, and a determination to keep away from people or situations which are apt to bring trouble with them; and by such defensiveness much good is lost....

Questions

1. Explain MacIntyre's account of the relationship between a virtue, a practice, an institution, and a tradition.
2. Consider your favorite sports team. A particular sport is a practice. How are the three main virtues that MacIntyre lists essential to the team's success?
3. A stockbroker once told one of the editors of this book that the most important thing needed for success on the stock market floor was morality. Use MacIntyre's theory to explain his point.
4. MacIntyre believes that we define ourselves in terms of narratives or stories such as a medieval "quest." Describe a story that defines the life, success or failure, happiness or unhappiness, of someone you know.
5. Foot thinks that virtues are "corrective." Compare her account of human nature with that of Kant. How are their views similar?
6. Can a murderer be courageous? Can an evil politician be industrious? What does Foot think? What do you think?
7. Do we deserve more moral credit when we have to fight temptation? Foot claims that it depends on the circumstance. Explain.
8. Describe what Foot means by wisdom.

Suggested Readings

For a general anthology, see Roger Crisp and Michael Slote, eds., *Virtue Ethics* (1997). For an Aristotelian approach, see Rosalind Hursthouse, *On Virtue Ethics* (1999). Christine McKinnon provides a naturalistic account in *Character, Virtue Theories, and the Vices* (1999). For a more recent account, see Stephen D. Carden, *Virtue Ethics: Dewey and MacIntyre* (2006). The literature also discusses individual virtues. For a discussion of the larger place of personality and character in ethics, see Joel Kupperman, *Character* (1991), and John Deigh's *Ethics and Personality* (1992).

For applied ethics, see Sandra L. Borden, *MacIntyre, Virtue Ethics and the Press* (2007); Alan E. Armstrong, *Nursing Ethics. A Virtue-Based Approach* (2007); Daniel Goldberg, "Pragmatism and Virtue Ethics in Clinical Research" (2008); Geoff Moore, "Virtue in Business" (2012); Mark C. Modak-Truran, "Corrective Justice and the Revival of Judicial Virtue" (2013); and Part III of Stan van Hooft, ed., *The Handbook of Virtue Ethics* (2014).

For bibliographies, see the Internet Encyclopedia of Philosophy, The Stanford Encyclopedia of Philosophy, ethikseite.de, and the sources under "Contemporary Virtue Theory" in Ethics Updates at ethics.sandiego.edu.

Chapter 44

Atheistic Existentialism

Jean-Paul Sartre (1905–80) was born in Paris, the only son of a military officer. He graduated with a doctorate in philosophy from the prestigious *École Normale Supérieure* in 1929. During his time as a student, he met his lifetime companion and occasional lover, Simone de Beauvoir. Sartre adopted the lifestyle of a bohemian intellectual and was openly promiscuous, but had no children. He frequented cafés and clubs, experimented readily with drugs, while pursuing his intellectual and journalistic ambitions. Drafted into the French army, he played a minor role as a weatherman, but was captured by German troops and spent nine tedious months as a prisoner of war. He was released from the army in 1941 because of bad health and returned to academic life, teaching philosophy.

Sartre's philosophical career can be divided into an existentialist phase and a Marxist phase. Deeply impressed by the analysis of being in *Being and Time* (1927) by the German philosopher Martin Heidegger, Sartre published an existentialist response entitled *L'Être et le néant* (*Being and Nothingness*) in 1943. He also published *Existentialism Is a Humanism* (1946), which was seen as an existential manifesto. Sartre was also the celebrated author of literary essays, novels, short stories, and plays.

During the second phase of his philosophical career, Sartre shifted his focus from philosophy to the struggle for social justice. He embraced Marxism and took on the role of a public intellectual, giving his support to a wide range of "left-wing" causes. He also traveled to Cuba to meet with Fidel Castro and Che Guevara, describing Guevara as the "era's most perfect man." In *The Critique of Dialectical Reason* (1960), he tried to reconcile Marxism with his earlier views, describing his new position as an "existential Marxism."

Albert Camus (1913–60) is a literary rather than a philosophical figure. He was born in Algeria, of European settlers, and grew up in extreme poverty. One of his early teachers noticed his literary talent and helped him win a scholarship to attend high school. He later graduated from the University of Algiers, having written a Master's thesis on the influence of Plotinus and Neoplatonism on Augustine's Christian metaphysics. An avid soccer player as a young man, he hoped to play professionally but fell ill with tuberculosis. He later confided to an interviewer, "what I know most surely about morality and the duty of man I owe to sport and learned it in the [soccer league]."

Camus was a political activist. He joined the Communist Party in his younger years but was quickly expelled. Later in life, he criticized the Soviet Union for its repressive policies, and had a falling out with Jean-Paul Sartre over the latter's commitment to Marxism. Although Camus was sympathetic to revolutionary movements, he was deeply suspicious of the authoritarianism in the resulting regimes. In spite of his atheism, he believed in the value of the religious search for transcendental meaning.

Camus began his career as a journalist. In 1943, he became the editor of *Combat*, the underground newspaper of the French resistance. He increasingly turned his attention to theater and literature, writing such notable works as *Caligula* (1938), *The Myth of Sisyphus* (1942), *L'Étranger* (*The Stranger* or *The Outsider*, 1942), *La Peste* (*The Plague*, 1947), and *L'Homme révolté* (*The Rebel*, 1951), a critique of political revolution that calls for ethical rebellion. In 1957, Camus was awarded the Nobel Prize for Literature. In its decision, the awarding committee cited his work for human rights and his essay against capital punishment, *Réflexions sur la guillotine* (*Thoughts on the Guillotine*).

He was married twice: first to Simone Hie, and secondly to Francine Faure, a musician and mathematician, and the mother of his twin children. He died in an automobile accident two years after receiving the Nobel Prize. He had originally planned to travel by train but accepted an invitation to travel by car at the last minute.

Existentialism was a response to the atrocities of World War II. Those responsible for the atrocities often excused themselves by relying on the defense of obedience to higher orders. Sartre and Camus reject such a defense. In his work, Sartre turns again and again to the idea that human beings bear complete responsibility for their choices. Even those who refuse to make a choice are choosing not to choose. In Sartre's memorable phrase, we are "condemned to be free."

Sartre's existentialism focuses on questions of freedom and individual responsibility in a world without God and which has been emptied of meaning. His philosophical arguments are based on phenomenology, a branch of European philosophy that focused on the internal structure of experience and consciousness. Ethical action consists of acting in a way that one grasps oneself "as freedom and facticity." The latter sees the physical, psychological, and social facts about one's self; the former goes beyond those facts to the realm of choices and values. Although this is an artistic act, and requires—to use a word from contractarianism—a maximizing of freedom, the substantive constraints on such an act are unclear.

Sartre says that we "will" our freedom. We are whatever we make ourselves to be. Nevertheless, Sartre believed that most people practice bad faith (*mauvaise foi*) in a vain attempt to evade moral responsibility. As a result, the ethical nature of an act is determined by its authenticity. There is an aesthetic dimension to this, and the artist is exercising a similar kind of freedom. Sartre nevertheless has difficulty explaining in definite terms what makes an act authentic. Everyone has a fundamental "project" and must act in accordance with that project—in good faith, as opposed to bad faith.

Although Camus disavowed the suggestion that he was an existentialist, his work begins explicitly with the experience of existing and the absurdity of the human condition. Like

Søren Kierkegaard and Friedrich Nietzsche, he sees the absurd as a direct consequence of the absence of God. Without God, we are left with the probability of suffering and the certainty of an empty death—a fate which human reason cannot accept. In the face of this absurdity, Camus argues, the universal reason championed by the thinkers of the Enlightenment has nothing to say.

Camus considers this issue in *The Plague*, where the arbitrariness of existence in a plague-struck town raises the question of suicide. In these circumstances, the experience of being is itself a moral act. Even though suffering surrounds us and injustice prevails, Camus's concept of the absurd is carefully qualified and does not justify giving in to nihilism and despair.

Both Camus and Sartre were involved in the social and political issues of their time. Camus became openly hostile to communism, rejecting the idea that ends can justify the means, and the arrogance of philosophies of history which claim to know the end in advance. In his later years, Sartre also renounced literature, declaring it a bourgeois distraction from social and political engagement, a point he makes in his autobiographical work *Les mots* (*Words*). In 1964, he was awarded but declined the Nobel Prize for Literature.

The first reading is from Sartre's *Existentialism Is a Humanism*, which was initially presented as a lecture. Although Sartre expressed misgivings about the text, it still stands as the philosophical *locus classicus* of existentialism.

The second reading is from *The Myth of Sisyphus*, which Camus described as an exercise in "methodical doubt," in an effort to determine what remains if "nothing has meaning." The original myth of Sisyphus is a metaphor of futility. Camus's response is that the "lucid" recognition of the absurdity of existence liberates us from belief in another life and permits us to live for the instant, in the beauty, pleasure, and "implacable grandeur" of existence. Lucidity refuses all comforting illusions and self-deception, but in the end Camus is more positive than either Sartre or earlier figures, such as Kierkegaard. He concludes: "One must imagine Sisyphus happy."

Jean-Paul Sartre, "Existentialism Is a Humanism"[1]

(1946)

My purpose here is to defend existentialism against some charges that have been brought against it.... [L]et us begin by saying that what we mean by "existentialism" is a doctrine that makes human life possible and also affirms that every truth and every action imply an environment and a human subjectivity. It is public knowledge that the fundamental reproach brought against us is that we stress the dark side of human life. Recently someone told me about a lady who, whenever she inadvertently utters some vulgar expression in a moment of anger, excuses herself by saying: "I think I'm becoming an existentialist." So it would appear that existentialism is associated with something ugly, which is why some people call us naturalists.... Those who find solace in the wisdom of the people—which is a sad, depressing thing—find us even sadder. Yet, what could be more disillusioning than such sayings as "Charity begins at home," or even "Appoint a rogue and he'll do you damage, knock him down and he'll do you homage." We all know countless such popular sayings, all of which always point to the same thing: one should not try to fight against the establishment; one should not be more royalist than the king, or meddle in matters that exceed one's station in life; any action not in keeping with tradition is mere romanticism; any effort not based on proven experience is doomed; since experience shows that men are invariably inclined to do evil, there must be strict rules to restrain them, otherwise anarchy ensues. However, since it is the very same people who are forever spouting these dreary old proverbs—the ones who say "It is so human!" whenever some repugnant act is pointed out to them, the ones who are always harping on realistic litanies—who also accuse existentialism of being too gloomy, it makes me wonder if what they are really annoyed about is not its pessimism, but rather its optimism. For when all is said and done, could it be that what frightens them about the doctrine that I shall try to present to you here is that it offers man the possibility of individual choice? To verify this, we need to reconsider the whole issue on a strictly philosophical plane. What, then, is "existentialism"?

Most people who use this word would be at a loss to explain what it means.... Yet it can be easily defined. What complicates the matter is that there are two kinds of existentialists: on one hand, the Christians, among whom I would include Karl Jaspers and Gabriel Marcel, both professed Catholics;[2] and, on the other, the atheistic existentialists, among whom we should place Heidegger, as well as the French existentialists and myself.[3] What they have in common is simply their belief that existence precedes essence; or, if you prefer, that subjectivity must be our point of departure. What exactly do we mean by that? If we consider a manufactured object, such as a book or a paper knife, we note that this object

---

1 Published as a pamphlet in 1946, this is based on a public lecture by the same name Sartre gave at the Club Maintenant in Paris in October 1945. This translation is by Carol Macomber (Yale University Press, 2007).

2 Karl Jaspers (1883–1969) was a German-Swiss psychiatrist and philosopher. Gabriel Marcel (1889–1973) was a French philosopher, playwright, and leading Christian existentialist.

3 Martin Heidegger (1889–1976) was a German philosopher. His first and best-known book, *Being and Time* (1927), is considered one of the central philosophical works of the twentieth century. The French existentialists likely include Camus, Simone de Beauvoir, and Maurice Merleau-Ponty, among others.

was produced by a craftsman who drew his inspiration from a concept: he referred both to the concept of what a paper knife is, and to a known production technique that is a part of that concept and is, by and large, a formula. The paper knife is thus both an object produced in a certain way and one that, on the other hand, serves a definite purpose. We cannot suppose that a man would produce a paper knife without knowing what purpose it would serve. Let us say, therefore, that the essence of the paper knife—that is, the sum of formulae and properties that enable it to be produced and defined—precedes its existence. Thus the presence before my eyes of that paper knife or book is determined. Here, then, we are viewing the world from a technical standpoint, whereby we can say "production precedes essence."

When we think of God the Creator, we usually conceive of him as a superlative artisan. Whatever doctrine we may be considering, say Descartes's or Leibniz's,[1] we always agree that the will more or less follows understanding, or at the very least accompanies it, so that when God creates he knows exactly what he is creating. Thus the concept of man, in the mind of God, is comparable to the concept of the paper knife in the mind of the manufacturer: God produces man following certain techniques and a conception, just as the craftsman, following a definition and a technique, produces a paper knife. Thus each individual man is the realization of a certain concept within the divine intelligence. Eighteenth-century atheistic philosophers suppressed the idea of God, but not, for all that, the idea that essence precedes existence. We encounter this idea nearly everywhere: in the works of Diderot, Voltaire, and even Kant.[2] Man possesses a human nature; this "human nature," which is the concept of that which

is human, is found in all men, which means that each man is a particular example of a universal concept—man. In Kant's works, this universality extends so far as to encompass forest dwellers—man in a state of nature—and the bourgeois, meaning that they all possess the same basic qualities. Here again, the essence of man precedes his historically primitive existence in nature.

Atheistic existentialism, which I represent, is more consistent. It states that if God does not exist, there is at least one being in whom existence precedes essence—a being whose existence comes before its essence, a being who exists before he can be defined by any concept of it. That being is man, or, as Heidegger put it, the human reality. What do we mean here by "existence precedes essence"? We mean that man first exists: he materializes in the world, encounters himself, and only afterward defines himself. If man as existentialists conceive of him cannot be defined, it is because to begin with he is nothing. He will not be anything until later, and then he will be what he makes of himself. Thus, there is no human nature since there is no God to conceive of it. Man is not only that which he conceives himself to be, but that which he wills himself to be, and since he conceives of himself only after he exists, just as he wills himself to be after being thrown into existence, man is nothing other than what he makes of himself. This is the first principle of existentialism.

It is also what is referred to as "subjectivity," the very word used as a reproach against us. But what do we mean by that, if not that man has more dignity than a stone or a table? What we mean to say is that man first exists; that is, that man primarily exists— that man is, before all else, something that projects itself into a future, and is conscious of doing so. Man

---

1 René Descartes (1596–1650) is often considered the father of modern philosophy. German philosopher Gottfried Wilhelm Leibniz (1646–1716) was one of the co-inventors of calculus.

2 Denis Diderot (1713–84), a French *philosophe*, edited a famous Enlightenment encyclopedia. François-Marie Arouet (1694–1778), known by his pen-name as Voltaire, was a highly-influential French writer and pamphleteer. German philosopher Immanuel Kant (1724–1804) was discussed in chapter 30.

is indeed a project that has a subjective existence, rather unlike that of a patch of moss, a spreading fungus, or a cauliflower. Prior to that projection of the self, nothing exists, not even in divine intelligence, and man shall attain existence only when he is what he projects himself to be—not what he would like to be. What we usually understand by "will" is a conscious decision that most of us take after we have made ourselves what we are. I may want to join a party, write a book, or get married—but all of that is only a manifestation of an earlier and more spontaneous choice than what is known as "will." If, however, existence truly does precede essence, man is responsible for what he is. Thus, the first effect of existentialism is to make every man conscious of what he is, and to make him solely responsible for his own existence. And when we say that man is responsible for himself, we do not mean that he is responsible only for his own individuality, but that he is responsible for all men....

The anguish we are concerned with is not the kind that could lead to quietism or inaction. It is anguish pure and simple, of the kind experienced by all who have borne responsibilities. For example, when a military leader takes it upon himself to launch an attack and sends a number of men to their deaths, he chooses to do so, and, ultimately, makes that choice alone. Some orders may come from his superiors, but their scope is so broad that he is obliged to interpret them, and it is on his interpretation that the lives of ten, fourteen, or twenty men depend. In making such a decision, he is bound to feel some anguish. All leaders have experienced that anguish, but it does not prevent them from acting. To the contrary, it is the very condition of their action, for they first contemplate several options, and, in choosing one of them, realize that its only value lies in the fact that it was chosen. It is this kind of anguish that existentialism describes, and as we

shall see it can be made explicit through a sense of direct responsibility toward the other men who will be affected by it. It is not a screen that separates us from action, but a condition of action itself....

I will mention the case of one of my students, who sought me out under the following circumstances: his father had broken off with his mother and, moreover, was inclined to be a "collaborator." His older brother had been killed in the German offensive of 1940, and this young man, with primitive but noble feelings, wanted to avenge him. His mother, living alone with him and deeply hurt by the partial betrayal of his father and the death of her oldest son, found her only comfort in him. At the time, the young man had the choice of going to England to join the Free French Forces[1]—which would mean abandoning his mother—or remaining by her side to help her go on with her life. He realized that his mother lived only for him and that his absence—perhaps his death—would plunge her into utter despair. He also realized that, ultimately, any action he might take on her behalf would provide the concrete benefit of helping her to live, while any action he might take to leave and fight would be of uncertain outcome and could disappear pointlessly like water in sand. For instance, in trying to reach England, he might pass through Spain and be detained there indefinitely in a camp; or after arriving in England or Algiers, he might be assigned to an office to do paperwork. He was therefore confronted by two totally different modes of action: one concrete and immediate, but directed toward only one individual; the other involving an infinitely vaster group—a national corps—yet more ambiguous for that very reason and which could be interrupted before being carried out. And, at the same time, he was vacillating between two kinds of morality: a morality motivated by sympathy and individual devotion, and another morality with a broader scope, but less likely to be fruitful. He had to choose between the two.

---

1 I.e., the World War II organization of French exiles in England that organized and supported the Resistance to the Nazis in occupied France.

What could help him make that choice? The Christian doctrine? No. The Christian doctrine tells us we must be charitable, love our neighbor, sacrifice ourselves for others, choose the "narrow way," et cetera. But what is the narrow way? Whom should we love like a brother—the soldier or the mother? Which is the more useful aim—the vague one of fighting as part of a group, or the more concrete one of helping one particular person keep on living? Who can decide that *a priori*? No one. No code of ethics on record answers that question. Kantian morality instructs us to never treat another as a means, but always as an end. Very well; therefore, if I stay with my mother, I will treat her as an end, not as a means. But by the same token, I will be treating those who are fighting on my behalf as a means. Conversely, if I join those who are fighting, I will treat them as an end, and, in so doing, risk treating my mother as a means.

If values are vague and if they are always too broad in scope to apply to the specific and concrete case under consideration, we have no choice but to rely on our instincts. That is what this young man tried to do, and when I last saw him, he was saying: "All things considered, it is feelings that matter; I should choose what truly compels me to follow a certain path. If I feel that I love my mother enough to sacrifice everything else for her—my desire for vengeance, my desire for action, my desire for adventure—then I should stay by her side. If, to the contrary, I feel that my love for my mother is not strong enough, I should go." But how can we measure the strength of a feeling? What gave any value to the young man's feelings for his mother? Precisely the fact that he chose to stay with her. I may say that I love a friend well enough to sacrifice a certain sum of money for his sake, but can claim that only if I have done so. I can say that I love my mother enough to stay by her side only if I actually stayed with her. The only way I can measure the strength of this affection is precisely by performing an action that confirms and defines it. However, since I am depending on this affection to justify my action, I find myself caught in a vicious circle....

You may say, "Well, he went to see a professor for advice." But if you consult a priest, for instance, it's you who has chosen to consult him, and you already know in your heart, more or less, what advice he is likely to give. In other words, to choose one's adviser is only another way to commit oneself. This is demonstrated by the fact that, if you are Christian, you will say "consult a priest." But there are collaborating priests, temporizing priests, and priests connected to the Resistance: which do you choose? Had this young man chosen to consult a priest connected to the Resistance, or a collaborating priest, he would have decided beforehand what kind of advice he was to receive. Therefore, in seeking me out, he knew what my answer would be, and there was only one answer I could give him: "You are free, so choose; in other words, invent. No general code of ethics can tell you what you ought to do; there are no signs in this world."...

Albert Camus, *The Myth of Sisyphus*[1]

(1942)

The gods had condemned Sisyphus to ceaselessly rolling a rock to the top of a mountain, whence the stone would fall back of its own weight. They had thought with some reason that there is no more dreadful punishment than futile and hopeless labor.

If one believes Homer, Sisyphus was the wisest and most prudent of mortals. According to another tradition, however, he was disposed to practice the profession of highwayman.[2] I see no contradiction in this. Opinions differ as to the reasons why he became the futile laborer of the underworld.[3] To begin with, he is accused of a certain levity in regard to the gods. He stole their secrets. Aegina, the daughter of Aesopus, was carried off by Jupiter.[4] The father was shocked by that disappearance and complained to Sisyphus. He, who knew of the abduction, offered to tell about it on condition that Aesopus would give water to the citadel of Corinth. To the celestial thunderbolts he preferred the benediction of water. He was punished for this in the underworld. Homer tells us also that Sisyphus had put Death in chains. Pluto[5] could not endure the sight of his deserted, silent empire. He dispatched the god of war, who liberated Death from the hands of her conqueror.

It is said that Sisyphus, being near to death, rashly wanted to test his wife's love. He ordered her to cast his unburied body into the middle of the public square.[6] Sisyphus woke up in the underworld. And there, annoyed by an obedience so contrary to human love, he obtained from Pluto permission to return to earth in order to chastise his wife. But when he had seen again the face of this world, enjoyed water and sun, warm stones and the sea, he no longer wanted to go back to the infernal darkness. Recalls, signs of anger, warnings were of no avail. Many years more he lived facing the curve of the gulf, the sparkling sea, and the smiles of earth. A decree of the gods was necessary. Mercury[7] came and seized the impudent man by the collar and, snatching him from his joys, led him forcibly back to the underworld, where his rock was ready for him.

You have already grasped that Sisyphus is the absurd hero. He *is*, as much through his passions as through his torture. His scorn of the gods, his hatred of death, and his passion for life won him that unspeakable penalty in which the whole being is exerted toward accomplishing nothing. This is the price that must be paid for the passions of this earth. Nothing is told us about Sisyphus in the underworld. Myths are made for the imagination to breathe life into them. As for this myth, one sees merely the whole effort of a body straining to raise the huge stone, to roll it, and push it up a slope a hundred

---

1 From *The Myth of Sisyphus* by Albert Camus, published in 1942 and translated from the French by Justin O'Brien, 96–99. Copyright 1955, Alfred A. Knopf.

2 The profession of a highwayman is that of a robber who steals from travelers.

3 In Greek mythology, the underworld is the world of the dead.

4 In Roman mythology, Aesopus is a river god and Jupiter is the king of the gods, the supreme god, the god of the sky, and associated with thunder and lightning.

5 I.e., the god of the underworld.

6 The rashness of Sisyphus's request lies in the fact that it would require his wife to show her love for him by not following Ancient Greek customs regarding appropriate rites required for a respectful burial.

7 I.e., the messenger of the gods.

times over; one sees the face screwed up, the cheek tight against the stone, the shoulder bracing the clay-covered mass, the foot wedging it, the fresh start with arms outstretched, the wholly human security of two earth-clotted hands. At the very end of his long effort measured by skyless space and time without depth, the purpose is achieved. Then Sisyphus watches the stone rush down in a few moments toward that lower world whence he will have to push it up again toward the summit. He goes back down to the plain.

It is during that return, that pause, that Sisyphus interests me. A face that toils so close to stones is already stone itself! I see that man going back down with a heavy yet measured step toward the torment of which he will never know the end. That hour like a breathing-space which returns as surely as his suffering, that is the hour of consciousness. At each of those moments when he leaves the heights and gradually sinks toward the lairs of the gods, he is superior to his fate. He is stronger than his rock.

If this myth is tragic, that is because its hero is conscious. Where would his torture be, indeed, if at every step the hope of succeeding upheld him? The workman of today works every day in his life at the same tasks, and his fate is no less absurd. But it is tragic only at the rare moments when it becomes conscious. Sisyphus, proletarian of the gods, powerless and rebellious, knows the whole extent of his wretched condition: it is what he thinks of during his descent. The lucidity that was to constitute his

torture at the same time crowns his victory. There is no fate that cannot be surmounted by scorn.

If the descent is thus sometimes performed in sorrow, it can also take place in joy. This word is not too much. Again I fancy Sisyphus returning toward his rock, and the sorrow was in the beginning. When the images of earth cling too tightly to memory, when the call of happiness becomes too insistent, it happens that melancholy arises in man's heart: this is the rock's victory, this is the rock itself. The boundless grief is too heavy to bear. These are our nights of Gethsemane.[1] But crushing truths perish from being acknowledged. Thus, Oedipus[2] at the outset obeys fate without knowing it. But from the moment he knows, his tragedy begins. Yet at the same moment, blind and desperate, he realizes that the only bond linking him to the world is the cool hand of a girl.[3] Then a tremendous remark rings out: "Despite so many ordeals, my advanced age and the nobility of my soul make me conclude that all is well." Sophocles' Oedipus, like Dostoevsky's Kirilov,[4] thus gives the recipe for the absurd victory. Ancient wisdom confirms modern heroism.

One does not discover the absurd without being tempted to write a manual of happiness. "What! by such narrow ways—?"[5] There is but one world, however. Happiness and the absurd are two sons of the same earth. They are inseparable. It would be a mistake to say that happiness necessarily springs from the absurd discovery. It happens as well that the feeling of the absurd springs from happiness.

---

1 Gethsemane is the garden where Jesus prayed, asking that God take away the cup of suffering he foresaw the night before his crucifixion. This event, during which his disciples fell asleep while Jesus was praying, is commonly called the agony in the garden.

2 Oedipus is a character in Greek mythology, described in the plays of Sophocles (c. 497–406 BCE). He is bound by fate to fulfill the prophecy that he will kill his father and sleep with his mother. When he unwittingly commits these crimes, bringing about disaster in the process, he blinds himself in despair.

3 I.e., Oedipus's daughters, Antigone and Ismene.

4 Kirilov is a character in *Demons*, by Fyodor Dostoevsky (c. 1821–81). Upon coming to believe that God does not exist, Kirilov commits suicide as a demonstration of his free will.

5 See Matthew 7:13–14 in the Christian bible: "Enter by the narrow gate; for wide is the gate and broad is the [way?] leads to destruction, and there are many who go in by it. How narrow is the gate and confined is the way which leads to [life? the] few who find it."

"I conclude that all is well," says Oedipus, and that remark is sacred. It echoes in the wild and limited universe of man. It teaches that all is not, has not been, exhausted. It drives out of this world a god who had come into it with dissatisfaction and a preference for futile suffering. It makes of fate a human matter, which must be settled among men.

All Sisyphus' silent joy is contained therein. His fate belongs to him. His rock is his thing. Likewise, the absurd man, when he contemplates his torment, silences all the idols. In the universe suddenly restored to its silence, the myriad wondering little voices of the earth rise up. Unconscious, secret calls, invitations from all the faces, they are the necessary reverse and price of victory. There is no sun without shadow, and it is essential to know the night. The absurd man says yes and his efforts will henceforth be unceasing. If there is a personal fate, there is no higher destiny, or at least there is but one which he concludes is inevitable and despicable. For the rest, he knows himself to be the master of his days. At that subtle moment when man glances backward over his life, Sisyphus returning toward his rock, in that slight pivoting he contemplates that series of unrelated actions which becomes his fate, created by him, combined under his memory's eye and soon sealed by his death. Thus, convinced of the wholly human origin of all that is human, a blind man eager to see who knows that the night has no end, he is still on the go. The rock is still rolling.

I leave Sisyphus at the foot of the mountain! One always finds one's burden again. But Sisyphus teaches the higher fidelity that negates the gods and raises rocks. He too concludes that all is well. This universe henceforth without a master seems to him neither sterile nor futile. Each atom of that stone, each mineral flake of that night-filled mountain, in itself forms a world. The struggle itself toward the heights is enough to fill a man's heart. One must imagine Sisyphus happy.

Questions

1. Sartre says that "existence comes before essence." We must therefore begin from "the subjective" (i.e., the fact of consciousness in a thinking subject). But this fact of consciousness does not seem to be enough to produce an adequate ethics, if morality is intended to regulate our relations with other people. Discuss.

2. Sartre sounds like Kant when he says that we are making ethical choices, not simply for ourselves, but as "a legislator deciding for the whole of mankind." He later called this the "singular universal." Is this the way to live an authentic life? Is this how we get past selfishness? Discuss.

3. Do you find Sartre's advice to his student helpful? Or an evasion? Why, why not?

4. Sartre later became a Marxist and participated actively in social and political causes. Is social action the real moral lesson in existentialism? What do you think? Refer to both readings in your answer.

5. The absurd occupies a central place in Camus's thought and is related to suicide, which he called the central philosophical question. Sisyphus is unable to commit suicide. But suppose he was? Should he continue to roll the stone uphill? Or kill himself? Why, why not?

6. Camus calls Sisyphus the "proletarian of the gods." How would you interpret the myth of Sisyphus, morally, from a Marxist perspective?

7. Although Camus did not consider himself an existentialist, his reduction of life to the mere fact of existing—and spontaneous "selfness"—firmly established his place within the movement. Comment.

8. What dual role does "the hour of consciousness" play in the life of Sisyphus? How does it relate happiness and the absurd? Do you find any comfort in this view?

Suggested Readings

Translations of Jean-Paul Sartre's *Existentialism Is a Humanism* (also, *Existentialism and Humanism*) are widely available. *Philosophy Now* has published "A Student's Guide" to the piece by Nigel Warburton (1996), which is available online.

Although Sartre's *Being and Nothingness* (1943) is often seen as the key existentialist text, its prose is demanding. Joseph Catalono's commentary (1974) provides a helpful guide. Sartre expressed his moral philosophy in his literary work, which includes the novel *Nausea* (1938) and a collection of short stories *The Wall* (*Le Mur*, 1939) and a series of plays: *No Exit* (*Huis clos*, 1944) and *Dirty Hands* (*Les Mains sales*, 1948).

Albert Camus became a bitter rival of Sartre. A prominent journalist, he was known for his novels *The Stranger* (*L'Étranger*, 1942) and *The Plague* (*La Peste*, 1947); for plays such as *Caligula* (1938); and for philosophical essays such as *The Myth of Sisyphus* (*Le Mythe de Sisyphe*, 1942) and *The Rebel* (*L'Homme révolté*, 1951).

The academic sources include Alvin Plantinga, "An Existentialist's Ethics" (1958); Christine Daigle, ed., *Existentialist Thinkers and Ethics* (2006); and Andre Benoit, "Rethinking Ethics in Existentialism" (2010). Simone de Beauvoir's work has also received considerable attention.

The applied literature brings existentialism into business ethics (Kevin T. Jackson, 2005; Kit Barton, 2010), design theory (Philippe D'Anjou, 2010), neuroscience (Christopher J. Frost and Augustus R. Lumia, 2012), and social media (Michael Stephen Lopato, 2016).

Valerie Pierce and Jamie Carnie's interview in "Existentialism, Education and Ethics— An Interview with Dame Mary Warnock" (1987) may also be of interest.

Chapter 45

Contemporary Feminism

The eighteenth-century writers the Marquis de Condorcet and Mary Wollstonecraft were among the first to argue that women must be accepted as full and unqualified citizens. John Stuart Mill makes a similar argument in *The Subjection of Women* (1869). The late nineteenth and early twentieth century saw a struggle for the extension of the suffrage to women and reforms to laws regarding property, marriage, and family. This has been called "first wave" feminism, and includes these and other figures such as Olympe de Gouges and Sojourner Truth, discussed earlier.

Contemporary feminism, or "second wave" feminism, has no precise dates, but can be conveniently traced to Simone de Beauvoir's *The Second Sex* (1949) and the response to her work. The social changes that took place in Western society beginning with the 1960s lead to an emphasis on activism, rather than theory, and the beginnings of feminist philosophy.

Although what demarcates "second-wave feminism" is vague, it is evident that a distinct branch of feminist philosophy emerged in North America in the 1970s, after the rise of a women's movement in the previous decade. In its early stages, at least, the argument in this literature was based on the thesis that men and women were the same. There was a general argument, which had some support in the statistical sciences, that the demographic differences between the sexes are a product of external social, cultural, and historical factors.

The argument shifted, however, after psychologist Carol Gilligan drew attention to differences between male and female moral approaches (see chapter 47). The idea that men and women are fundamentally different, psychologically, intellectually, and morally, has been called "essentialism." Gilligan's view provoked contentious debates between "equality feminists" and "difference feminists," or more generally, on the role of nature versus nurture, biology versus social environment, in the formation of gender and sexual identity.

These discussions seem to have been decisive in the emergence of a "third wave" of feminism, which can be traced to the early 1990s and is, again, difficult to summarize. Some of the momentum that went into third-wave feminism was based on the feeling that the feminist movement had so far privileged certain women and neglected the oppression of minorities and social outsiders. Feminists widened their perspective to speak out against the social and psychological oppression, not merely of women, but of marginalized groups in general. There is, as a consequence, a greater awareness of the hidden factors of oppression in much of the feminist literature.

It is a matter of debate whether there is a distinct "fourth-wave feminism," and whether it can be categorized as "post-feminist." The lack of agreement on a common terminology has made the discussion within the literature difficult to follow. Perhaps the most important development in late feminism is the emergence of a number of critical voices, which have adopted a less ideological tone than many of their peers, and insisted on the importance of a kind of ethical introspection within the movement.

The reality is that feminism has become fragmented. This is partly a product of a more general fragmentation within the recent academic literature with authors articulating feminist positions within existing philosophical theories, such as liberal feminism, Marxist feminism, eco-feminism, and so on. There is, however, a significant literature in "feminist ethics," which has reformulated traditional ethics, in an effort to include the moral experience of women within the historical account. Virtually all of the feminist literature contains a commitment to practical ethics, as opposed to theory. In this chapter, we include excerpts from Simone de Beauvoir (1908–86), Virginia Held (b. 1929), and Tram Nguyen (b. 1976).

Simone de Beauvoir was born in Paris to Georges Bertrand de Beauvoir and Françoise Brasseur. Her father, of minor nobility, was an atheist; her mother, a devout Catholic. The eldest of two daughters, Simone was an excellent student and was sent to a prestigious convent school. At fourteen, she suffered a crisis of faith and became an atheist. After further studies, she attended the Sorbonne, writing a thesis on Leibniz.

De Beauvoir placed second, behind Jean-Paul Sartre, in the highly-competitive French national exam in philosophy called the *agrégation*. At twenty-one, she was the youngest person to pass the test. She went on to teach in the French *lycée* system, and became a prominent social critic and existentialist also known for her unorthodox relationship with Sartre. She made a conscious decision to remain single in order to avoid the distractions of married life. Some commentators have criticized her sexual explorations, which mirrored Sartre's, and which included sexual relationships with underage female students. Having lost her teaching post as a result, she later argued for the decriminalization of consensual sexual relations, in certain cases, between adults and minors. De Beauvoir always remained close to Jean-Paul Sartre and was interred next to his tomb in the Cimetière du Montparnasse in Paris.

De Beauvoir was a public intellectual and a prolific writer. She worked in a wide variety of genres, publishing essays, journal articles, letters, diaries, short stories, novels, and an autobiography. Much of her work is a comment on her personal life and the activities of those within her intellectual circle. In *The Ethics of Ambiguity* (1947), she turns her hand to systematic moral philosophy, constructing an ethics based on existentialism. She criticizes moral systems based on external sources of authority such as religion, the state, or even reason. The terms that she uses—such as immanence and transcendence—derive from phenomenology. On her account, morality means being true to the choices that one makes. The spontaneous, subjective emphasis in her moral philosophy arguably makes it difficult to reconcile the exercise of personal freedom with our moral obligations to other people.

Virginia Held received her PhD in philosophy from Columbia University in 1968 and has worked at Hunter College as a philosophy professor throughout her career. She was named Distinguished Professor at the City University of New York's Graduate Center and Hunter College in 1996 and served as president of the Eastern Division of the American Philosophical Association in 2001–02. She has several books to her credit, including *Feminist Morality: Transforming Culture, Society, and Politics* (1993), and *The Ethics of Care: Personal, Political, and Global* (2006).

Tram Nguyen is an Assistant Professor at Hostos Community College, CUNY, whose research brokers connections between ethics, modernist literature, and feminist philosophy.

The first reading here is from the introduction to de Beauvoir's *The Second Sex*. De Beauvoir diagnoses the problem with gender relations as the dismissal and denigration of woman by men as the "Other." Her existential perspective emphasizes freedom rather than happiness. She urges women to liberate themselves from Otherness and forge a transcendent identity of their own.

The second reading is an excerpt from Held's paper "Feminist Transformations of Moral Theory," which succinctly summarizes three major feminist themes in moral philosophy.

The third reading is from Nguyen's "From SlutWalks to SuicideGirls," which acknowledges the moral narrative in the current feminist literature, but criticizes current feminism for having depoliticized feminism and failing to engage with other oppressed groups.

READING 45A

Simone de Beauvoir, *Le Deuxième Sexe* (*The Second Sex*)[1]

(1949)

I hesitated a long time before writing a book on woman. The subject is irritating, especially for women; and it is not new. Enough ink has flowed over the quarrel about feminism; it is now almost over: let's not talk about it anymore. Yet it is still being talked about. And the volumes of idiocies churned out over this past century do not seem to have clarified the problem. Besides, is there a problem? And what is it? Are there even women? True, the theory of the eternal feminine[2] still has its followers; they whisper, "Even in Russia, *women* are still very much women"; but other well-informed

---

1 "Introduction," from Simone de Beauvoir, *The Second Sex*, trans. Constance Borde and Sheila Malovany-Chevallier (New York: Alfred A. Knopf, 2010).

2 The "eternal feminine," for de Beauvoir, refers to a patriarchal myth or an archetype that gives a single definition of woman, a changeless essence, especially one that constructs woman as a passive "erotic, birthing, or nurturing body" or as simply a derivation of man.

people—and also at times those same ones—lament, "Woman is losing herself, woman is lost." It is hard to know any longer if women still exist, if they will always exist, if there should be women at all, what place they hold in this world, what place they should hold. "Where are the women?" asked a short-lived magazine recently.[1] But first, what is a woman? "*Tota mulier in utero*: she is a womb," some say. Yet speaking of certain women, the experts proclaim, "They are not women," even though they have a uterus like the others. Everyone agrees there are females in the human species; today, as in the past, they make up about half of humanity; and yet we are told that "femininity is in jeopardy"; we are urged, "Be women, stay women, become women." So not every female human being is necessarily a woman; she must take part in this mysterious and endangered reality known as femininity. Is femininity secreted by the ovaries? Is it enshrined in a Platonic heaven? Is a frilly petticoat enough to bring it down to earth? Although some women zealously strive to embody it, the model has never been patented. It is typically described in vague and shimmering terms borrowed from a clairvoyant's vocabulary. In Saint Thomas's time it was an essence defined with as much certainty as the sedative quality of a poppy. But conceptualism has lost ground: biological and social sciences no longer believe there are immutably determined entities that define given characteristics like those of the woman, the Jew, or the black; science considers characteristics as secondary reactions to a *situation*. If there is no such thing today as femininity, it is because there never was. Does the word "woman," then, have no content? It is what advocates of Enlightenment philosophy, rationalism, or nominalism vigorously assert: women are, among human beings, merely those who are arbitrarily designated by the word "woman"; American women in particular are inclined to think that woman as such no longer exists. If some backward

individual still takes herself for a woman, her friends advise her to undergo psychoanalysis to get rid of this obsession. Referring to a book—a very irritating one at that—*Modern Woman: The Lost Sex*, Dorothy Parker wrote: "I cannot be fair about books that treat women as women. My idea is that all of us, men as well as women, whoever we are, should be considered as human beings." But nominalism is a doctrine that falls a bit short; and it is easy for antifeminists to show that women *are* not men. Certainly woman like man is a human being; but such an assertion is abstract; the fact is that every concrete human being is always uniquely situated. To reject the notions of the eternal feminine, the black soul, or the Jewish character is not to deny that there are today Jews, blacks, or women: this denial is not a liberation for those concerned but an inauthentic flight. Clearly, no woman can claim without bad faith to be situated beyond her sex. A few years ago, a well-known woman writer refused to have her portrait appear in a series of photographs devoted specifically to women writers. She wanted to be included in the men's category; but to get this privilege, she used her husband's influence. Women who assert they are men still claim masculine consideration and respect. I also remember a young Trotskyite standing on a platform during a stormy meeting, about to come to blows in spite of her obvious fragility. She was denying her feminine frailty; but it was for the love of a militant man she wanted to be equal to. The defiant position that American women occupy proves they are haunted by the feeling of their own femininity. And the truth is that anyone can clearly see that humanity is split into two categories of individuals with manifestly different clothes, faces, bodies, smiles, movements, interests, and occupations; these differences are perhaps superficial; perhaps they are destined to disappear. What is certain is that for the moment they exist in a strikingly obvious way.

If the female function is not enough to define

---

1   [Author's Note] Out of print today, titled *Franchise*.

woman, and if we also reject the explanation of the "eternal feminine," but if we accept, even temporarily, that there are women on the earth, we then have to ask: What is a woman?

Merely stating the problem suggests an immediate answer to me. It is significant that I pose it. It would never occur to a man to write a book on the singular situation of males in humanity.[1] If I want to define myself, I first have to say, "I am a woman"; all other assertions will arise from this basic truth. A man never begins by positing himself as an individual of a certain sex: that he is a man is obvious. The categories masculine and feminine appear as symmetrical in a formal way on town hall records or identification papers. The relation of the two sexes is not that of two electrical poles: the man represents both the positive and the neuter to such an extent that in French *hommes* designates human beings, the particular meaning of the word *vir* being assimilated into the general meaning of the word "homo."[2] Woman is the negative, to such a point that any determination is imputed to her as a limitation, without reciprocity. I used to get annoyed in abstract discussions to hear men tell me: "You think such and such a thing because you're a woman." But I know my only defense is to answer, "I think it because it is true," thereby eliminating my subjectivity; it was out of the question to answer, "And you think the contrary because you are a man," because it is understood that being a man is not a particularity; a man is in his right by virtue of being man; it is the woman who is in the wrong. In fact, just as for the ancients there was an absolute vertical that defined the oblique, there is an absolute human type that is masculine. Woman has ovaries and a uterus; such are the particular conditions that lock her in her subjectivity; some even say she thinks with her hormones. Man vainly forgets that his anatomy also includes hormones and testicles. He grasps his body as a direct and normal link with the world that he believes he apprehends in all objectivity, whereas he considers woman's body an obstacle, a prison, burdened by everything that particularizes it. "The female is female by virtue of a certain *lack* of qualities," Aristotle said. "We should regard women's nature as suffering from natural defectiveness." And Saint Thomas in his turn decreed that woman was an "incomplete man," an "incidental" being. This is what the Genesis story symbolizes, where Eve appears as if drawn from Adam's "supernumerary" bone, in Bossuet's words. Humanity is male, and man defines woman, not in herself, but in relation to himself; she is not considered an autonomous being. "Woman, the relative being," writes Michelet. Thus Monsieur Benda declares in *Le rapport d'Uriel* (Uriel's Report): "A man's body has meaning by itself, disregarding the body of the woman, whereas the woman's body seems devoid of meaning without reference to the male. Man thinks himself without woman. Woman does not think herself without man." And she is nothing other than what man decides; she is thus called "the sex," meaning that the male sees her essentially as a sexed being; for him she is sex, so she is it in the absolute. She is determined and differentiated in relation to man, while he is not in relation to her; she is the inessential in front of the essential. He is the Subject; he is the Absolute. She is the Other.[3]

---

1 [Author's Note] The Kinsey Report, for example, confines itself to defining the sexual characteristics of the American man, which is completely different.

2 Like 'man' in English, '*homme*' in French was traditionally used to refer to male adults specifically, or to humankind in general. The same is true for the word that is its Latin origin, '*homo*.' '*Vir*' in Latin, however, usually meant male adult, never humankind.

3 [Author's Note] This idea has been expressed in its most explicit form by E. Levinas in his essay *Le temps et l'autre* (*Time and the Other*). He expresses it like this: "Is there not a situation where alterity would be borne by a being in a positive sense, as essence? What is the alterity that does not purely and simply enter into the opposition of two species of the same genus? I think that the absolutely contrary contrary, whose contrariety is in no way affected by the relationship that can be established between it and its correlative, the contrariety that permits its terms to remain absolutely other, is the feminine. Sex is not some specific difference... (continued)

The category of *Other* is as original as consciousness itself. The duality between Self and Other can be found in the most primitive societies, in the most ancient mythologies; this division did not always fall into the category of the division of the sexes, it was not based on any empirical given: this comes out in works like Granet's on Chinese thought, and Dumézil's on India and Rome. In couples such as Varuna–Mitra, Uranus–Zeus, Sun–Moon, Day–Night, no feminine element is involved at the outset; neither in Good–Evil, auspicious and inauspicious, left and right, God and Lucifer; alterity[1] is the fundamental category of human thought. No group ever defines itself as One without immediately setting up the Other opposite itself. It only takes three travelers brought together by chance in the same train compartment for the rest of the travelers to become vaguely hostile "others." Village people view anyone not belonging to the village as suspicious "others." For the native of a country inhabitants of other countries are viewed as "foreigners"; Jews are the "others" for anti-Semites, blacks for racist Americans, indigenous people for colonists, proletarians for the propertied classes. After studying the diverse forms of primitive society in depth, Lévi-Strauss could conclude: "The passage from the state of Nature to the state of Culture is defined by man's ability to think biological relations as systems of oppositions; duality, alternation, opposition, and symmetry, whether occurring in defined or less clear form, are not so much phenomena to explain as fundamental and immediate givens of social reality."[2] These phenomena could not be understood if human reality were solely a *Mitsein* based on solidarity and friendship. On the contrary, they become clear if, following Hegel, a fundamental hostility to any other consciousness is found in consciousness itself; the subject posits itself only in opposition; it asserts itself as the essential and sets up the other as inessential, as the object.

But the other consciousness has an opposing reciprocal claim: traveling, a local is shocked to realize that in neighboring countries locals view him as a foreigner; between villages, clans, nations, and classes there are wars, potlatches, agreements, treaties, and struggles that remove the absolute meaning from the idea of the *Other* and bring out its relativity; whether one likes it or not, individuals and groups have no choice but to recognize the reciprocity of their relation. How is it, then, that between the sexes this reciprocity has not been put forward, that one of the terms has been asserted as the only essential one, denying any relativity in regard to its correlative, defining the latter as pure alterity? Why do women not contest male sovereignty? No subject posits itself spontaneously and at once as the inessential from the outset; it is not the Other who, defining itself as Other, defines the One; the Other is posited as Other by the One positing itself as One. But in order for the Other not to turn into the One, the Other has to submit to this foreign point of view. Where does this submission in woman come from?

There are other cases where, for a shorter or longer time, one category has managed to dominate another absolutely. It is often numerical inequality that confers this privilege: the majority imposes its law on or persecutes the minority. But women are not a minority like American blacks, or like Jews: there are as many women as men on the earth. Often, the two opposing groups concerned were once inde-

---

Neither is the difference between the sexes a contradiction…Neither is the difference between the sexes the duality of two complementary terms, for two complementary terms presuppose a preexisting whole…[A]lterity is accomplished in the feminine. The term is on the same level as, but in meaning opposed to, consciousness." I suppose Mr. Levinas is not forgetting that woman also is consciousness for herself. But it is striking that he deliberately adopts a man's point of view, disregarding the reciprocity of the subject and the object. When he writes that woman is mystery, he assumes that she is mystery for man. So this apparently objective description is in fact an affirmation of masculine privilege.

1   Alterity means otherness here.

2   [Author's Note] See Claude Lévi-Strauss, *Les structures élémentaires de la parenté* (*The Elementary Structures of Kinship*). I thank Claude Lévi-Strauss for sharing the proofs of his thesis, which I drew on heavily, particularly in the second part, pp. 76–89.

pendent of each other; either they were not aware of each other in the past, or they accepted each other's autonomy; and some historical event subordinated the weaker to the stronger: the Jewish Diaspora, slavery in America, and the colonial conquests are facts with dates. In these cases, for the oppressed there was a *before*: they share a past, a tradition, sometimes a religion, or a culture. In this sense, the parallel Bebel draws between women and the proletariat would be the best founded: proletarians are not a numerical minority either, and yet they have never formed a separate group. However, not *one* event but a whole historical development explains their existence as a class and accounts for the distribution of *these* individuals in this class. There have not always been proletarians: there have always been women; they are women by their physiological structure; as far back as history can be traced, they have always been subordinate to men; their dependence is not the consequence of an event or a becoming, it did not *happen*. Alterity here appears to be an absolute, partly because it falls outside the accidental nature of historical fact. A situation created over time can come undone at another time—blacks in Haiti for one are a good example; on the contrary, a natural condition seems to defy change. In truth, nature is no more an immutable given than is historical reality. If woman discovers herself as the inessential and never turns into the essential, it is because she does not bring about this transformation herself. Proletarians say "we." So do blacks. Positing themselves as subjects, they thus transform the bourgeois or whites into "others." Women—except in certain abstract gatherings such as conferences—do not use "we"; men say "women," and women adopt this word to refer to themselves; but they do not posit themselves authentically as Subjects. The proletarians made the revolution in Russia, the blacks in Haiti, the Indo-Chinese are fighting in Indochina. Women's actions

have never been more than symbolic agitation; they have won only what men have been willing to concede to them; they have taken nothing; they have received.[1] It is that they lack the concrete means to organize themselves into a unit that could posit itself in opposition. They have no past, no history, no religion of their own; and unlike the proletariat, they have no solidarity of labor or interests; they even lack their own space that makes communities of American blacks, the Jews in ghettos, or the workers in Saint-Denis or Renault factories. They live dispersed among men, tied by homes, work, economic interests, and social conditions to certain men—fathers or husbands—more closely than to other women. As bourgeois women, they are in solidarity with bourgeois men and not with women proletarians; as white women, they are in solidarity with white men and not with black women. The proletariat could plan to massacre the whole ruling class; a fanatic Jew or black could dream of seizing the secret of the atomic bomb and turning all of humanity entirely Jewish or entirely black: but a woman could not even dream of exterminating males. The tie that binds her to her oppressors is unlike any other. The division of the sexes is a biological given, not a moment in human history. Their opposition took shape within an original *Mitsein*,[2] and she has not broken it. The couple is a fundamental unit with the two halves riveted to each other: cleavage of society by sex is not possible. This is the fundamental characteristic of woman: she is the Other at the heart of a whole whose two components are necessary to each other....

It is difficult for men to measure the enormous extent of social discrimination that seems insignificant from the outside and whose moral and intellectual repercussions are so deep in woman that

---

1 [Author's Note] See second part, page 126.
2 *Mitsein* means "being-with" or living with others.

they appear to spring from an original nature.[1] The man most sympathetic to women never knows her concrete situation fully. So there is no good reason to believe men when they try to defend privileges whose scope they cannot even fathom. We will not let ourselves be intimidated by the number and violence of attacks against women; nor be fooled by the self-serving praise showered on the "real woman"; nor be won over by men's enthusiasm for her destiny, a destiny they would not for the world want to share.

We must not, however, be any less mistrustful of feminists' arguments: very often their attempt to polemicize robs them of all value. If the "question of women" is so trivial, it is because masculine arrogance turned it into a "quarrel"; when people quarrel, they no longer reason well. What people have endlessly sought to prove is that woman is superior, inferior, or equal to man: created after Adam, she is obviously a secondary being, some say; on the contrary, say others, Adam was only a rough draft, and God perfected the human being when he created Eve; her brain is smaller, but relatively bigger; Christ was made man, but perhaps out of humility. Every argument has its opposite, and both are often misleading. To see clearly, one needs to get out of these ruts; these vague notions of superiority, inferiority, and equality that have distorted all discussions must be discarded in order to start anew.

But how, then, will we ask the question? And in the first place, who are we to ask it? Men are judge and party: so are women. Can an angel be found? In fact, an angel would be ill qualified to speak, would not understand all the givens of the problem; as for the hermaphrodite, it is a case of its own: it is not both a man and a woman, but neither man nor woman. I think certain women are still best suited to elucidate the situation of women. It is a sophism to claim that Epimenides should be enclosed within the concept of Cretan and all Cretans within the concept of liar:[2] it is not a mysterious essence that dictates good or bad faith to men and women; it is their situation that disposes them to seek the truth to a greater or lesser extent. Many women today, fortunate to have had all the privileges of the human being restored to them, can afford the luxury of impartiality: we even feel the necessity of it. We are no longer like our militant predecessors; we have more or less won the game; in the latest discussions on women's status, the UN has not ceased to imperiously demand equality of the sexes, and indeed many of us have never felt our femaleness to be a difficulty or an obstacle; many other problems seem more essential than those that concern us uniquely: this very detachment makes it possible to hope our attitude will be objective. Yet we know the feminine world more intimately than men do because our roots are in it; we grasp more immediately what the fact of being female means for a human being, and we care more about knowing it. I said that there are more essential problems; but this one still has a certain importance from our point of view: How will the fact of being women have affected our lives? What precise opportunities have been given us, and which ones have been denied? What destiny awaits our younger sisters, and in which direction should we point them? It is striking that most feminine literature is driven today by an attempt at lucidity more than by a will to make demands; coming out of an era of muddled controversy, this book is one attempt among others to take stock of the current state.

But it is no doubt impossible to approach any human problem without partiality: even the way of asking the questions, of adopting perspectives, presupposes hierarchies of interests; all characteristics comprise values; every so-called objective description is set against an ethical background. Instead of trying to conceal those principles that are

---

1 [Author's Note] Describing this very process will be the object of Volume II of this study.

2 The Creatan philosopher Epimenides (c. 600 BCE) was credited with the paradoxical statement: "All Cretans are liars."

more or less explicitly implied, we would be better off stating them from the start; then it would not be necessary to specify on each page the meaning given to the words "superior," "inferior," "better," "worse," "progress," "regression," and so on. If we examine some of the books on women, we see that one of the most frequently held points of view is that of public good or general interest: in reality, this is taken to mean the interest of society as each one wishes to maintain or establish it. In our opinion, there is no public good other than one that assures the citizens' private good; we judge institutions from the point of view of the concrete opportunities they give to individuals. But neither do we confuse the idea of private interest with happiness: that is another frequently encountered point of view; are women in a harem not happier than a woman voter? Is a housewife not happier than a woman worker? We cannot really know what the word "happiness" means, and still less what authentic values it covers; there is no way to measure the happiness of others, and it is always easy to call a situation that one would like to impose on others happy: in particular, we declare happy those condemned to stagnation, under the pretext that happiness is immobility. This is a notion, then, we will not refer to. The perspective we have adopted is one of existentialist morality. Every subject posits itself as a transcendence concretely, through projects; it accomplishes its freedom only by perpetual surpassing toward other freedoms; there is no other justification for present existence than its expansion toward an indefinitely open future. Every time transcendence lapses into immanence, there is degradation of existence into "in-itself,"[1] of freedom into facticity; this fall

is a moral fault if the subject consents to it; if this fall is inflicted on the subject, it takes the form of frustration and oppression; in both cases it is an absolute evil. Every individual concerned with justifying his existence experiences his existence as an indefinite need to transcend himself. But what singularly defines the situation of woman is that being, like all humans, an autonomous freedom, she discovers and chooses herself in a world where men force her to assume herself as Other: an attempt is made to freeze her as an object and doom her to immanence,[2] since her transcendence will be forever transcended by another essential and sovereign consciousness. Woman's drama lies in this conflict between the fundamental claim of every subject, which always posits itself as essential, and the demands of a situation that constitutes her as inessential. How, in the feminine condition, can a human being accomplish herself? What paths are open to her? Which ones lead to dead ends? How can she find independence within dependence? What circumstances limit women's freedom and can she overcome them? These are the fundamental questions we would like to elucidate. This means that in focusing on the individual's possibilities, we will define these possibilities not in terms of happiness but in terms of freedom.

Clearly this problem would have no meaning if we thought that a physiological, psychological, or economic destiny weighed on woman. So we will begin by discussing woman from a biological, psychoanalytical, and historical materialist point of view. We will then attempt to positively demonstrate how "feminine reality" has been constituted, why woman has been defined as Other, and what the

---

1 De Beauvoir is employing Sartre's concept of 'en-soi,' 'being-in-itself.' It refers to one of two types or ways of being he recognized. The other is 'pour-soi,' 'being-for-itself.' The en-soi is the way of being of things that have a complete and definable essence but are not conscious of it; e.g., rocks, birds, and trees. Human beings are described as pour-soi since they are defined by the possession of consciousness, specifically, by their consciousness of their own existence, which is a consciousness of lacking the complete, definable essence of the en-soi. De Beauvoir is (implicitly) associating (1) immanence with existing as en-soi and being an object and (2) transcendence with existing as pour-soi and being a subject.

2 I.e., rather than being a subject with the possibility for transcendence.

consequences have been from men's point of view. Then we will describe the world from the woman's point of view such as it is offered to her,[1] and we will

see the difficulties women are up against just when, trying to escape the sphere they have been assigned until now, they seek to be part of the human *Mitsein*.

Virginia Held, "Feminist Transformations of Moral Theory"[2]

(1990)

The history of philosophy...has been constructed from male points of view, and has been built on assumptions and concepts that are by no means gender-neutral. Feminists characteristically begin with different concerns and give different emphases...Far from providing mere additional insights which can be incorporated into traditional theory, feminist explorations often require radical transformations of existing fields of inquiry and theory....

[I]n [discussing] the history of ethics, I [have] focused on what, from a feminist point of view, are three of its most questionable aspects: 1) the split between reason and emotion and the devaluation of emotion; 2) the public/private distinction and the relegation of the private to the natural; and 3) the concept of the self as constructed from a male point of view....

In the area of moral theory in the modern era, the priority accorded to reason has taken two major forms. A) On the one hand has been the Kantian...search for very general, abstract, deontological, universal moral principles by which rational beings should be guided. Kant's Categorical Imperative is a foremost example: it suggests that all moral problems can be handled by applying an impartial,

pure, rational principle to particular cases....

B) On the other hand, the priority accorded to reason...has taken a Utilitarian form.... The Utilitarian approach...recognizes that persons have desires and interests, and suggests rules of rational choice for maximizing [their] satisfaction... [T]he Utilitarian approach relies on abstract general principles or rules to be applied to particular cases. And it holds that although emotion is, in fact, the source of our desires for certain objectives, the task of morality should be to instruct us on how to pursue those objectives most rationally. Emotional attitudes toward moral issues themselves interfere with rationality and should be disregarded....

Many feminist philosophers have questioned whether the reliance on abstract rules, rather than the adoption of more context-respectful approaches, can possibly be adequate for dealing with moral problems, especially as women experience them....

The work of psychologists such as Carol Gilligan and others has led to a clarification of what may be thought of as tendencies among women to approach moral issues differently. Rather than interpreting moral problems in terms of what could be handled by applying abstract rules of justice to particular

---

1 [Author's Note] This will be the subject of a second volume.

2 Virginia Held, "Feminist Transformations of Moral Theory," *Philosophy and Phenomenological Research*, Vol. 50, Supplement (Autumn 1990). Also available at jstor.org.

cases, many of the women studied by Gilligan tended to be more concerned with preserving actual human relationships, and with expressing care for those for whom they felt responsible. Their moral reasoning was typically more embedded in a context of particular others than was the reasoning of a comparable group of men.... [M]any feminists see our own consciously considered experience as lending confirmation to the view that what has come to be called "an ethic of care" needs to be developed. Some think it should supersede "the ethic of justice" of traditional or standard moral theory. Others think it should be integrated with the ethic of justice and rules....

The caring relationships important to feminist morality cannot be understood in terms of abstract rules or moral reasoning. And the "weighing" so often needed between the conflicting claims of some relationships and others cannot be settled by deduction or rational calculation. A feminist ethic will not just acknowledge emotion... It will embrace emotion as providing at least a partial basis for morality itself, and for moral understanding....

Caring, empathy, feeling with others, being sensitive to each other's feelings, all may be better guides to what morality requires in actual contexts than may abstract rules of reason, or rational calculation, or at least they may be necessary components of an adequate morality....

The second questionable aspect of the history of ethics... [is] the distinction between the public and the private.... [F]eminists are showing how gender-bias has distorted previous conceptions of the spheres, and we are trying to offer more appropriate understandings of "private" morality and "public" life....

[T]he [traditional] distinction has been accompanied by a supposition that what occurs in the household occurs as if on an island beyond politics, whereas [feminists believe that] the personal is highly affected by the political power beyond, from legislation about abortion to the greater earning power of men, to the interconnected division of labor by gender both within and beyond the household, to the lack of adequate social protection for women against domestic violence....

[T]raditionally... the public realm is seen as the distinctively human realm in which man transcends his animal nature, while the private realm of the household is seen as the natural region in which women merely reproduce the species....

Dominant patterns of thought have seen women as primarily mothers, and mothering as the performance of a primarily biological function. Then it has been supposed that while engaging in political life is a specifically human activity, women are engaged in an activity which is not specifically human. Women accordingly have been thought to be closer to nature than men, to be enmeshed in a biological function involving processes more like those in which other animals are involved than like the rational discussion of the citizen in the polis, or the glorious battles of noble soldiers, or the trading and rational contracting of "economic man."...

Human mothering is an extremely different activity from the mothering engaged in by other animals. The work and speech of men is recognized as very different from what might be thought of as the "work" and "speech" of other animals. Human mothering is fully as different from animal mothering. Of course all human beings are animal as well as human. But to whatever extent it is appropriate to recognize a difference between "man" and other animals, so would it be appropriate to recognize a comparable difference between "woman" and other animals, and between the activities—including mothering—engaged in by women and the behavior of other animals....

Consider nursing an infant, often thought of as the epitome of a biological process... There is no reason to think of human nursing as any more simply biological than there is to think of, say, a businessmen's lunch this way.... If men transcend the natural by... making deals over lunch to do so, women can transcend the natural by choosing not to nurse their children when they could,... or nursing in restaurants to overcome the prejudices against doing so, or thinking human thoughts as they nurse, and so forth. Human culture surrounds and characterizes the activity of nursing as it does the activities of eating, or governing, or writing, or thinking....

The very term 'reproduction' suggests mere repetition, the "natural" bringing into existence of repeated instances of the same human animal. But human reproduction is not repetition.... [T]he activity of creating new social persons and new kinds of persons is potentially the most transformative human activity of all. And it suggests that morality should concern itself first of all with this activity, with what its norms and practices ought to be, and with how the institutions and arrangements throughout society and the world ought to be structured to facilitate the right kinds of development of the best kinds of new persons. The flourishing of children ought to be at the very center of moral and social and political and economic and legal thought, rather than, as at present, at the periphery, if attended to at all....

Let me turn now to the third aspect of the history of ethics:... the concept of self. One of the most important emphases in a feminist approach to morality is the recognition that more attention must be paid to the domain between, on the one hand, the self as ego, as self-interested individual, and, on the other hand, the universal, everyone, others in general. Traditionally, ethics has dealt with these poles of individual self and universal all. Usually, it has called for impartiality against the partiality of the egoistic self; sometimes it has defended egoism against claims for a universal perspective. But most standard moral theory has hardly noticed as morally significant the intermediate realm of family relations and relations of friendship, of group ties and neighborhood concerns, especially from the point of view of women.... [S]tandard ethics has neglected the moral aspects of the concern and sympathy which people actually feel for particular others, and what moral experience in this intermediate realm suggests for an adequate morality.

The region of "particular others" is a distinct domain, where what can be seen to be artificial and problematic are the very egoistic "self" and the universal "all others" of standard moral theory. In the domain of particular others, the self is already constituted to an important degree by relations with others, and these relations may be much more salient and significant than the interests of any individual self in isolation. The "others" in the picture, however, are not the "all others," or "everyone," of traditional moral theory ... They are, characteristically, actual flesh and blood other human beings for whom we have actual feelings and with whom we have real ties.

From the point of view of much feminist theory, the individualistic assumptions of liberal theory and of most standard moral theory are suspect. Even if we would be freed from the debilitating aspects of dominating male power to "be ourselves" and to pursue our own interests, we would, as persons, still have ties to other persons, and we would at least in part be constituted by such ties.... We are, for instance, the daughter or son of given parents, or the mother or father of given children, and we carry with us at least some ties to the racial or ethnic or national group within which we developed into the persons we are.

If we look, for instance, at the realities of the relation between mothering person (who can be female or male) and child, we can see that what we value in the relation cannot be broken down into individual gains and losses for the individual members in the relation.... Self-development apart from the relation may be much less important than the satisfactory development of the relation. What matters may often be the health and growth of and the development of the relation-and-its-members in ways that cannot be understood in the individualistic terms of standard moral theories designed to maximize the satisfaction of self-interest....

READING 45C

Tram Nguyen, "From SlutWalks to SuicideGirls: Feminist Resistance in the Third Wave and Postfeminist Era"[1]

(2013)

... [I]n the January 1992 issue of *Ms.* magazine, Rebecca Walker called for a Third Wave of feminist consciousness. Walker was incensed by a collocation of events hinging on race, gender, and class ideologies. With Shannon Liss, she mobilized a collective and foundation to promote voting rights, education, wage, and prison reform. They provided those in need with emergency funding for abortions, women-led projects, and reproductive rights activism... Although she coined the term,[2] Walker is less interested in developing a coherent, new feminist theory than in building coalitions with other social justice leagues through the Third Wave Foundation. Hers is a feminism of intersectionality, but one that also proffers self-empowerment, lived experience, and the plurality of pleasure. *To Be Real*, an anthology of stories and testimonials from women and men, reflects the confessional and individualist drive of the Third Wave.

The work of conceptualizing this new feminism continues to be negotiated by feminist academics and practitioners for whom the core of Third Wave feminism is its rejection of Second Wave's seeming essentialist and rigid positioning of women's politics and lives.

But Third Wave feminism is troubled by divisions within its still-forming body of activism and theories, as well as by postfeminist seductions.... The term "postfeminism" first appears in Susan Bolotin's 1982 article "Voices from the Postfeminism Generation,"[3] in which the author contends that the battle for equality has been won, and it is time to stop "harping" on women's oppression. Naomi Wolf would go so far as to assert that Second Wave feminism victimizes women and exaggerates claims of women's suffering and gender inequalities. For Wolf, who is situated in both Third Wave and postfeminist camps, the alternative is "power feminism," which "believes women deserve to feel that the qualities of starlets and queens, of sensuality and beauty, can be theirs... [and which] knows that making social change does not contradict the principle that girls just want to have fun."[4]...

Heather Jarvis and Sonya Barnett co-founded SlutWalk Toronto[5] in April 2011 as a reaction to Toronto police constable Michael Sanguinetti's comment that "women should avoid dressing like sluts in order not to be victimized," a statement in which women are forced to inherit the blame of two social judgments: one, that it is socially permissible to judge, objectify, and morally categorize women based on their appearances and, two, that women,

---

1 Tram Nguyen, "From SlutWalks to SuicideGirls: Feminist Resistance in the Third Wave and Postfeminist Era," *Women's Studies Quarterly* 41:3/4 (Fall/Winter 2013).

2 I.e., 'Third Wave.'

3 *New York Times Magazine*, October 17, 1982, p. 29.

4 Nguyen then writes that the Third Wave must struggle to clarify its core feminist values so that women's sexual pleasures are not co-opted and commodified. She then examines SlutWalks and SuicideGirls, two products of the Third Wave and postfeminist era.

5 Although the SlutWalk movement began in Toronto, it became a transnational movement with protest marches being held in many other cities throughout the world. Its main message was to call for an end to "rape culture," which includes victim blaming and slut shaming of sexual assault victims.

rather than the rapists, attackers, assailants, bullies, and aggressors, are responsible for sexual violence committed against them....

By marching under the banner of "slut," the protesters take the poison out of the word, to change social attitudes about women's bodies and to empower women with the potential of their own sexualities. Women wrote messages on their arms, legs, chests, and faces. Others carrying placards [reading]: "Stop Slut Shaming," "Don't Tell Us How to Dress," [and] "This Is What a Slut Looks Like"...

SlutWalk Toronto's official T-shirt proclaims, "My body is not an insult," thus underscoring the movement's support of choice to express personal sexual freedom over gendered politics of sexual violence. Many of the participants appeared to work within the postfeminist and Third Wave model insofar as they performed fierceness by reveling in female sexual power as end games....

These performances do little[, however,] to disturb social understanding of a "slut"—instead, they reify and concretize the concept of "slut" as scantily clad, sexually immoral women. Moreover, these actions ultimately displace the somber and deadly issues of rape, domestic violence, sexual abuse, and street harassment....

I do not want to negate...the enormously important work done by SlutWalk activists;...however, these Walks yield three issues that shed light on this moment in feminist activism: first, the problem of inversion or reclamation promoted by the Walks; second, the media and general public's reception and perception of these protests; and third, the reaction from women of color.

T-shirts, buttons, and posters proclaiming, "This is what a slut looks like" seek to reclaim the insult "slut" through inversion, but, I argue, they leave in place the structure of subjugation. Although "queer"

has been successfully reclaimed and is dominant in academia, "[n*****]," "bitch," and "slut" still trigger deep historical wounds.... In essence, inversion leads not only to reaffirmation but also to normalization.

The primary images of SlutWalk perpetuated by mainstream news media are of young women scantily dressed.... Left in the hands of photographers, editors, and news agencies, publicized images of the SlutWalks reinstall the very objectification the movements are invested in challenging....

[The Crunk Feminist Collective[1]] makes the important point that "white women and liberal feminist women of color who argue that 'slut' is a universal category of female experience, irrespective of race," effectively ignore the brutal history and realities with which many Black women live.... For Crunk Feminists..., the sexualization of Black women is deeply connected to the history of American slavery, and reclamation of the word "slut," "ho," or "bitch" does not serve the interest of emancipation and equality....

Begun in 2001 as a woman-friendly, "indie" community of sexually empowered women (never mind that the models are referred to as "girls"), SuicideGirls sells access to nude images of "alternative" beauty on its website, Facebook, Twitter, and Tumblr pages...Co-founders Melissa Mooney ("Missy Suicide") and Sean Suhl ("Spooky Suicide") employ the language of sexual liberation on their website to describe the organization as "a vibrant, sex positive community of women (and men)...founded on the belief that creativity, personality and intelligence are not incompatible with sexy, compelling entertainment."...

The SuicideGirls corporation posits itself in opposition to mainstream pornography and in doing so situates itself as "nonconformist and...hand-

---

1 This collective aims to articulate a feminist consciousness for women and men of color who came of age in the hip hop generation. It supports the use of crunk music, a blend of Hip Hop Culture and Southern Black Culture, to express their form of consciousness and resistance to the oppression they experience "in the South."

crafted" real instead of the mass-cultural production of professionally produced pornography that is inorganic...

The many images of tattooed and nubile women, meanwhile, reproduce the very performativity of mainstream pornography: large, sultry eyes, pouty lips, thrusting breasts,...and lush bums.... [A]nd despite their electric colored hair, nipple piercings, and states of undress, their photographs are rather conventional....

I do not claim that SuicideGirls assumes the mantle of feminism. The company in fact rejects the "feminist" label...But it successfully co-opts cultural codes of feminism because postfeminism and Third Wave feminism depoliticize women's sexuality by extolling the virtues of individual self-expression through consumerism. Culturally conversant with the seductive lures of empowerment and free choice, SuicideGirls takes advantage of this depoliticization of women's sexuality for corporate gain....

The denial of exploitation and continuing emphasis on positive, empowered, grassroots porn perpetuates the myth that the employees of SuicideGirls are sexually liberated women, unfettered by the strictures of social codes, conservative sexual mores, and feminist problems. In truth, they are young women working at minimum-wage jobs...or students.... Hence,...they find themselves in a situation in which they are exploited by a company that turns their pleasure against them. SuicideGirls reveals the limits of Wolf's proposition "Good pleasures make good politics"[1]...Pleasure divorced from politics or at the expense of one group's political fight, I argue, does not yield equality, social transformation, or political advancement....

Taking stock of feminist goals and strategies is especially critical in this "intermezzo" period of feminist activism...In light of this, let us imagine discursive and political engagements that reach beyond inversion or subversion of preexisting terms.... Let us reassess feminist goals and tenets in order to enrich our understanding of women's roles in society. And finally, let us refuse the depoliticization of feminism and, instead, find new coalitions for creating social justice and transformation.

Questions

1. Briefly summarize Simone de Beauvoir's argument that woman is the "Other." How does "liberty" come into her analysis, and how should women claim it?

2. Held proposes child-rearing and parenting as a moral ideal. Could this morality of "particular others" be applied to other kinds of relationships and our behavior towards all different kinds of people? What do you think? Why or why not?

3. Held reports that feminists are leery of abstract general principles or moral rules. Is it possible to have a morality without general rules? What do you think?

4. What is your view of SlutWalk? Refer to the readings.

5. One of the themes in the feminist literature is that the exercise of power creates conditions in which oppression is hidden from view. This has led, for example, to a discussion of the "privileging" of white middle-class women within the feminist movement. Discuss these issues from a third-wave feminist perspective.

6. Feminists often attack Enlightenment values of reason and individual rights while

---

1 Naomi Wolf, *Fire with Fire, The New Female Power and How It Will Change the 21st Century*, 1993, p. 149.

focusing on autonomy as a key demand of contemporary women. Is there a contradiction here?

7. One of the pressing questions that has recently arisen in gender and queer studies—in the wake of feminism—is whether gender is a choice. What do you think? Discuss the ethical implications of such a question.

Suggested Readings

De Beauvoir's *The Second Sex* (1949) is the foundational text in "second wave" feminism. Her *Philosophical Writings* (2004) have also been published. Carol Gilligan's seminal *In a Different Voice* (1982) is excerpted in chapter 47. The work of Gilligan and Nel Noddings, who specializes in philosophy of education, led to the formulation of an ethic of care. See Noddings's *Caring: A Feminine Approach to Ethics and Moral Education* (1984). This was further developed by feminists such as Held, Annette Baier, and Sara Ruddick. Together with other members of the Hunter College Women's Studies Collective, Held has published a well-received textbook: *Women's Realities, Women's Choices: An Introduction to Women's Studies* (3rd ed., 2005).

There are many cross-currents in present-day feminism, some of which harken back to earlier work. Contractarian Jean Hampton has presented the social and political "case for feminism" in *The Liberation Debate* (1996). Students can find an interview with her in *Cogito* (1996). For an unusual Asian perspective, see Chenyang Li, "Revisiting Confucian Jen Ethics and Feminist Care Ethics" (2002).

For "third wave" feminism, consult the essays in Leslie Heywood and Jennifer Drake, *Third Wave Agenda* (1997), which discuss black feminism, "womanism," working-class feminism, interracial coalitions, and the tensions between the individual and collective interests. See also Dana Heller, ed., *Cross-Purposes: Lesbians, Feminists, and the Limits of Alliance* (1997), which explores the possibility of a "Butch-Feminist Retro-Future." For the "Crunk feminism" Nguyen references, see http://www.crunkfeministcollective.com/about/.

In applied ethics, see Christine James, "Feminist Ethics, Mothering, and Caring" (1995); Heather E. Keith, "Pornography Contextualized: A Test Case for a Feminist-Pragmatist Ethics" (2001); Ariel Sallah, "The Ecofeminism/Deep Ecology Debate" (1992); Susanne Claxton, *Heidegger's Gods: An Ecofeminist Perspective* (2017); and Simon Căbulea, "Liberal Feminism and the Ethics of Polygamy" (2012).

Chapter 46

Contemporary Religious Alternatives

There are contemporary philosophers who continue to highlight the link between religion and morality. In some cases, these associations are kept in the background or integrated into a more naturalistic perspective; in other cases, the religious connection is placed front-and-center in ethical discussion. One such alternative is called "divine command morality" and is chiefly championed by a new movement of philosophers in the Evangelical Protestant tradition. A second alternative promotes a worldwide ecumenism that attempts to synthesize moral views from all the world religions: Christianity, Hinduism, Buddhism, Islam, and so on.

The idea that morality is a matter of obeying a divine command has long historical roots. Although there are many examples, the Ten Commandments is an obvious case of moral legislation which is thought to derive its authority from God. The cosmological views of the early tribal and ancient peoples can be traced to a conception of divine authority as the source of the natural law and our moral obligations. This development can be seen in the much-misunderstood medieval notion of the divine right of kings, which placed ethical limits on the power and authority of rulers. Medieval philosophers and theologians from the Christian, Judaic, and Islamic traditions—such as Augustine, Peter Abelard, Moses Maimonides, Al-Ghazālī, and Thomas Aquinas—all had rigorous philosophical reasons for believing that morality was a matter of obeying God's laws. Kierkegaard went further by positing a higher religious level of existence.

Even today, much of the academic discussion of divine command theory revolves around Plato's dialogue the *Euthyphro*, which is often seen as an attack on the rationale behind divine command moralities. Socrates argues that something cannot be good merely because the gods will it. What the gods will, they will because it is, in some prior sense, good. These arguments may be over-stated, however. Plato consistently portrays Socrates as someone who adopts an attitude of pious submission to the divine and places the law of god over the law of Athens.

The origins of contemporary divine command morality can be found in the frustration that some commentators have felt with contemporary analytic ethics, which, they believe, has repeatedly failed to deal with substantive moral issues and to provide us with a workable ethics. This frustration is a prominent part of G.E.M. Anscombe's motivation in her well-known essay "Modern Moral Philosophy" (1958), where she writes that modern ethics has missed the entire point of the moral exercise. Although Anscombe, a student of Ludwig Wittgenstein and a convert to Catholicism, finds virtue ethics more convincing than the mechanical "consequentialism" of her contemporaries, her principal argument is that we cannot distinguish between the moral and non-moral senses of the "good" without positing the existence of a good God as ultimate judge and legislator. Like MacIntyre, she argues that the failure to capture the larger historical significance of moral terms has stunted contemporary moral philosophy.

Divine command morality is also a direct response to the increasingly skeptical orientation of academic philosophy. It returns us to earlier historical premises—the idea that religious faith, along with the received religious tradition, provides a better and more compelling basis for ethics than philosophical argument and speculation. Much recent work in divine command theory has, in spite of this, adopted the analytical standards and logical techniques that have become prominent in the secular academic literature. In this chapter, we have included excerpts from two contemporary philosophers working in the divine command theory, Robert Merrihew Adams and Carlton Fisher.

Adams (b. 1937) obtained a PhD in philosophy from Cornell University and theological degrees from Oxford University and the Princeton Theological Seminary. He is a past president of the American Society of Christian Philosophers. His publications include *The Virtue of Faith and Other Essays in Philosophical Theology* (1987), *Finite and Infinite Goods: A Framework for Ethics* (1999), and *A Theory of Virtue: Excellence in Being for the Good* (2006).

Fisher has a PhD in philosophy from the University of Notre Dame. He teaches at Houghton College in New York State and has edited, along with Michael Beaty and Mark Nelson, an influential study of Christian moral philosophy, *Christian Theism and Moral Philosophy* (1998).

In the face of historical conflicts, the second alternative embodied in the new ecumenical movement has not directed its efforts at any kind of doctrinal or liturgical conformity—which at this point, at least, seems impossible. It strives, instead, to facilitate a civil and open moral and religious dialogue between competing faiths. Religious leaders have accordingly taken a common stand on pressing global issues, without the divisions that set different religious groups at odds with one another. The term 'ecumenism' (from the Greek, meaning 'household') was originally used to refer to Christians the world over when thought of as members of a single family. The Christian ecumenical tradition has now been extended, however, to interreligious and intercultural activities that aim to unite diverse religions on a worldwide scale.

The first meeting of a Parliament of the World's Religions was held at the 1893 Chicago World Fair and included representatives from Christianity, Jainism, Buddhism, Hinduism, Islam, and the Bahá'í Faith. At the 1993 Parliament of Religions, held to commemorate the original 1893 meeting, participants discussed a resolution entitled "Towards a Global Ethic: An Initial Declaration." The resulting document, *Declaration Toward a Global Ethic*, was the initiative of, among many others, Hans Küng, who was a professor of "ecumenical theology" and the director of the Institute for Ecumenical Research at the University of Tübingen in

Germany. More than two hundred religious leaders from more than forty faiths signed the original draft. It has since been signed by many other leading religious figures.

Küng (1928–2021) was a Roman Catholic priest, and was a theological consultant for the Second Vatican Council in the 1960s. He was President of the German Foundation for a Global Ethic (*Weltethos*). His books include *Christianity and the World Religions: Paths of Dialogue with Islam, Hinduism, and Buddhism* (1986), *Christianity and Chinese Religions* (with Julia Ching, 1988), and *A Global Ethic for Global Politics and Economics* (1997). A controversial figure in Catholic circles, Küng questioned some elements of church doctrine.

Although the *Declaration* has been criticized for ignoring major points of religious contention, it represents a serious step towards the formulation of a moral consensus among religious groups. One of its central themes is that those individuals in positions of wealth and political power have routinely failed to meet their moral responsibilities to other people and the natural world. It identifies the "Golden Rule"—that we must treat others as we wish to be treated—as the basis for a shared set of common moral values. Despite calling for the protection of individual rights, gender equality, religious tolerance, and the redistribution of economic resources, it is far less clear on collective issues and intercultural differences.

The religious impulse behind such ecumenical initiatives has been questioned, since the salvation promised by most religions is based on an adherent's loyalty to a particular belief system and rituals. Although all religious traditions make reference to the wisdom tradition in ethics, the intensely personal experience provided by the visions, stories, and supernatural beliefs at the origin of most religions is singular and cannot be translated ecumenically. The idea that one can replace religious beliefs with an ambiguous amalgam of inter-denominational ethical beliefs seems naïve.

In the first reading, Adams makes a more technical argument, arguing for a modified divine command theory, which logically identifies the ethical property of moral wrongness with the property of being contrary to the commands of a loving God. He maintains that divine command moralities are in the best position to account for the existence of moral norms as objective, non-naturalistic facts that exist independently of human opinions and physical science.

In the second reading, Fisher sets out a propositional argument that there cannot be value in the world without the creative power of a good God. If we all discern value in things in the world, it is because God endowed these things with valuable natures. Although atheists have the in-born capacity to recognize moral goodness, this does not alter the proposition that the ultimate source of value remains in God.

The third reading contains excerpts from the *Declaration Toward a Global Ethic*. This ecumenical manifesto calls for a transformative global awakening that will embrace shared religious ideals including the protection of human rights, respect for life, equal treatment of men and women, community values, economic justice, and the cultivation of peace, tolerance, and truthfulness. The co-signatories maintain that these universal ethical norms, central to most religious teaching, can provide a hopeful basis for renewing a world in crisis.

Robert M. Adams, "Moral Arguments for Theistic Belief"[1]

(1987)

The divine command theory of the nature of right and wrong combines two advantages not jointly possessed by any of its nontheological competitors.... The first advantage of divine command metaethics[2] is that it presents facts of moral rightness and wrongness as objective, nonnatural facts—objective in the sense that whether they obtain or not does not depend on whether any human being thinks they do, and nonnatural in the sense that they cannot be stated entirely in the language of physics, chemistry, biology, and human or animal psychology. For it is an objective but not a natural fact that God commands, permits, or forbids something. Intuitively this is an advantage. If we are tempted to say that there are only natural facts of right and wrong, or that there are no objective facts of right and wrong at all, it is chiefly because we have found so much obscurity in theories about objective, nonnatural ethical facts.... The second advantage of divine command metaethics is that it is relatively intelligible. There are certainly difficulties in the notion of a divine command, but at least it provides us more clearly with matter for thought than the intuitionist and Platonic conceptions do....

[W]e cannot avoid discussing...the alleged disadvantages of divine command metaethics.... Here let us concentrate on three objections that are particularly important for the present argument.

(1)...[A] divine command theory is often construed as claiming that 'right' *means* commanded (or permitted) by God, and that 'wrong' *means* for-

bidden by God. This gives rise to the objection that people who do not believe that there exists a God to command or forbid still use the terms 'right' and 'wrong,' and are said (even by theists) to believe that certain actions are right and others wrong. Surely those atheists do not mean by 'right' and 'wrong' what the divine command theory seems to say they must mean....

One might reply that it is not obviously impossible for someone to disbelieve something that is analytically[3] implied by something else that he asserts....

The ordinary meanings of many terms that signify properties, such as 'hot' and 'electrically charged,' do not contain enough information to answer all questions about the nature (or even in some cases the identity) of the properties signified. Analysis of the meaning of 'wrong' might show, for example, that 'Nuclear deterrence is wrong' ascribes to nuclear deterrence a property about which the speaker may be certain of very little except that it belongs, independently of his views, to many actions that he opposes, such as torturing people just for fun. The analysis of meaning need not completely determine the identity of this property, but it may still be argued that a divine command theory identifies it most adequately.

(2) The gravest objection to the more extreme forms of divine command theory is that they imply that if God commanded us, for example, to make it our chief end in life to inflict suffering on other human

---

1 Robert M. Adams, "Moral Arguments for Theistic Belief," in Robert Merrihew Adams, *The Virtue of Faith and Other Essays in Philosophical Theology* (New York and Oxford: Oxford University Press, 1987).

2 Metaethics focuses on what morality itself is, examining the status and foundations of moral values, properties, and words.

3 I.e., because of the meanings of the words.

beings, for no other reason than that he commanded it, it would be *wrong* not to obey. Finding this conclusion unacceptable, I prefer a less extreme, or modified, divine command theory, which identifies the ethical property of wrongness with the property of being contrary to the commands of a *loving* God. Since a God who commanded us to practice cruelty for its own sake would not be a loving God, this modified divine command theory does not imply that it would be wrong to disobey such a command.

But the objector may continue his attack: "Suppose that God did not exist, or that he existed but did not love us. Even the modified divine command theory implies that in that case it would not be wrong to be cruel to other people. But surely it would be wrong."...

[But divine command moralists] can say that although wrongness is not a property that would be possessed by cruelty in a world without God, the possibility or idea of cruelty-in-a-world-without-God *does* possess, in the actual world (with God), a property that is close kin to wrongness: the property of being frowned on, or viewed with disfavor, by God. The experience of responding emotionally to fiction should convince us that it is possible to view with the strongest favor or disfavor events regarded as taking place in a world that would not, or might not, include one's own existence—and if [that is] possible for us, why not for God? If we are inclined to say that cruelty in a world without God would be wrong, that is surely because of an attitude of disfavor that we have in the actual world toward such a possibility. And if our attitude corresponds to an objective, nonnatural moral fact, why cannot that fact be one that obtains in the actual world, rather than in the supposed world without God?

(3) It may be objected that the advantages of the divine command theory can be obtained without an entailment of God's existence. For the rightness of an action might be said to consist in the fact that the action *would* agree with the commands of a loving God if one existed...This modification transforms the divine command theory into a nonnaturalistic form of the ideal observer theory of the nature of right and wrong.[1] It has the advantage of identifying rightness and wrongness with properties that actions could have even if God does not exist....

The flaw in this theory is that it is difficult to see what is supposed to be the force of the counterfactual conditional...If there is no loving God, what makes it the case if there were one, he would command this rather than that?...

No doubt some conclusions about what he would not command follow *logically* or analytically from the concept of a loving God. He would not command us to practice cruelty for its own sake, for example. But...it seems only contingent[2] that a loving God...would frown on increasing the happiness of other people by the painless and undetected killing of a person who wants to live but will almost certainly not live happily. Very diverse preferences...seem compatible with love and certainly with deity. Of course, you could explicitly build all your moral principles into the definition of the kind of hypothetical divine commands that you take to make facts of right and wrong. But then the fact that your principles *would* be endorsed by the commands of such a God adds nothing to the principles themselves; whereas, endorsement by an *actual* divine command would add something, which is one of the advantages of divine command metaethics....

---

1 The ideal observer theory (of the nature of right and wrong) holds that the truth of propositions expressing ethical judgments is determined with reference to an abstract ideal unbiased observer or a hypothetical universal cognitive subject.

2 I.e., not logically necessary or uncertain.

Carlton Fisher, "Because God Says So"[1]

(1990)

> ... And God saw that it was good ... and behold,
> it was very good.
> —Gen. 1:10, 12, 18, 21, 25, 31

It might be objected that to locate value in other characteristics ... is to cut value loose from its source in God and thus to propose a view which is unacceptable within a Christian context. After all, if object X is valuable because it has certain other properties a, b, and c (none of which is the property of being created or the property of being valued by God), then X would be valuable even if it were not created, even if there were no God. Also, if moral obligation stems from the value of things (and what is good or harmful to valuable things), then morality is possible without God; without God, some things *still* would be prohibited. A gulf is opened between God and morality which Christians are want to loathe. And down into that chasm falls all attempts to provide arguments for the existence of God on the basis of morality.

To illustrate, consider a divine command theory. If a moral obligation to refrain from doing X is the result of a divine command not to do X, then one could argue as follows:

(1) There is some action, X, the performance of which would be morally wrong.

Therefore,

(2) God exists.

However, if a moral obligation is not the result of

divine activity or volition, but the result of what will benefit or harm a valuable thing, then (1) implies only

(3) There is some thing which is valuable and which would be harmed if X were performed.

And from (3) one can hardly derive (2)....

Now I would suggest that the connection between God and morality which is part of a typical Christian view of things is [best] ... expressed ... by:

(5) Valuable things (other than God himself) cannot exist except for the creative activity of God.

[This premise] rests easily on the belief that things which existed merely as a result of the chance meandering of atomic particles could not be valuable in the way necessary to make certain kinds of behavior toward them morally obligatory or forbidden and that such is the remaining option once one denies an intelligent and purposive creator.

And now we can exhibit the connection between God and morality in this argument:

(1) There is some action, X, the performance of which would be morally wrong.

Therefore,

(3) There is some thing which is valuable and which would be harmed if X were performed.

---

1   Carlton D. Fisher, "Because God Says So," in Michael D. Beaty, ed., *Christian Theism and the Problems of Philosophy* (Notre Dame, IN: University of Notre Dame Press, 1990).

(5) Valuable things (other than God himself) cannot exist except for the creative activity of God.

Therefore,

(2) God exists.

The nonbeliever, as always when facing such argumentation...can simply deny the claim that valuable things must necessarily depend upon God for their existence (premise 5). He might offer this argument in return:

(1) There is some action, X, the performance of which would be morally wrong.

Therefore,

(3) There is some thing which is valuable and which would be harmed if X were performed.

(6) We do not know whether or not God exists and created us.

Therefore,

(7) God's existence and creative action is not necessary as a ground of moral obligation.

There is an error in this response which we must note. But first we might as well admit that the moral argument for God's existence has little polemic value when addressed to a nonbeliever who affirms the reality of moral obligation but sees no need for a creator God to help make sense of it. Nonetheless, it may be a sound argument. It may indeed be true that only creation, not random collections of atomic material, can produce valuable entities.

Well then, where is the error in the nonbeliever's counterargument? It is in the confusion of epistemic abilities with metaphysical realities. The fact that one who does not affirm the existence and creative activity of God can correctly perceive and affirm both the high value of human persons and the obligation-producing effects of such high value supports a conclusion about one's own epistemic state—valuable things do not require creation *for all I know*—but it does not support a claim that God's existence is not required in order for things to be valuable. The fact is that even the nonbeliever can recognize that human beings are valuable. This is an epistemological point. But the fact that he can recognize the value of humans and at the same time deny their createdness is *not* evidence that human beings *would be* valuable if they were *not* created.

But that is not his most crucial error.... I believe that the crucial error of the nonbeliever is in thinking that beings such as we are, complete with all the marvelous characteristics and abilities which make us valuable, could be the product of purely naturalistic nonintelligent forces at all—[his] rejection of premise 5. He correctly judges us to be valuable, and, in a sense, correctly says that we would be valuable no matter what our origin were, but errs in supposing that beings as valuable as we are could have the origins he suggests we have. *Believing* in God's existence and creative activity is not a necessary condition for recognizing the value of human beings and that is simply because human beings *are* valuable and we—believer and nonbeliever alike—have the God-given ability to recognize that. However, it might nonetheless be the case that God's existence is necessary for such valuable beings even to exist and have such value-recognizing abilities. And this the believer claims.

Thus we can affirm that God is the source of all value without affirming that *what* is valuable about valuable things is simply that they have God as their source. *If* valuable things came from other sources, then, trivially, they would have other sources and other sources would be the sources of valuable things. If there were some other way for me to come to be and to be as I am—namely in the image of God—I would in that case still be valuable and due moral consideration. But the antecedent[1] is false; God is the source of all things.

But still this last assertion, that on which the believer and nonbeliever strongly disagree, is not required as a point of agreement in order for normative moral discourse to continue. Believer and nonbeliever alike recognize the extreme value of human beings and that value results in moral obligations.

So, if God's creation is not valuable simply because it is his creation, if it is not valuable simply because he values it, in what does its value lie?...I think the final answer is found in a description of the creation and the affirmation of certain of the qualities found there that they are the qualities which make things valuable. If we think about the highest qualities of God's creation, it is our ability to love, to think, to act, to value, to plan, to enjoy, to thank, to forgive, to understand, etc. which makes us valuable. As the Genesis account puts it, God, having created, examined his handiwork and *saw* that that which he had created was good. This world and its inhabitants have been created by God and are valuable because of the way that God designed and created them. If we need assurance of that value beyond our own capacities to judge it, we can perhaps find some in "Because God says so." He has made it and it is good because he has made it so. Further, he knows and can testify to its goodness.[2] But it is not good simply because he says so.[3]...

Parliament of the World's Religions, *Declaration Toward a Global Ethic*[4]

(2018)

Introduction

...

The world is in agony....
     Peace eludes us...the planet is being destroyed... neighbors live in fear...women and men are estranged from each other...children die!

But this agony need not be.
...

---

1 I.e., the prior premise that there is some way for me to come to be valuable without God.

2 I.e., in Scripture.

3 I.e., in Scripture.

4 *Towards a Global Ethic* (Parliament of the World's Religions; 1993, revised 2018). Available online at parliamentofreligions.org. The document was drafted largely by Professor Hans Küng, in consultation with several hundred leaders and scholars representing numerous religious faiths and traditions.

The Principles of a Global Ethic

...

We are persons who have committed ourselves to the precepts and practices of the world's religions. We confirm that there is already a consensus among the religions which can be the basis for a global ethic—a minimal *fundamental consensus* concerning binding *values*, irrevocable *standards*, and *fundamental moral attitudes*.

PRINCIPLE I: NO NEW GLOBAL ORDER
WITHOUT A NEW GLOBAL ETHIC!

We women and men of various religions and regions of Earth therefore address all people, religious and non-religious. We wish to express the following convictions which we hold in common:

- We all have a responsibility for a better global order....

- The principles expressed in this Global Ethic can be affirmed by all persons with ethical convictions, whether religiously grounded or not.

- As religious and spiritual persons we base our lives on an Ultimate Reality, and draw spiritual power and hope therefrom, in trust, in prayer or meditation, in word or silence. We have a special responsibility for the welfare of all humanity and care for the planet Earth... [and] trust that the ancient wisdom of our religions can point the way for the future....

[W]e are convinced that, despite their frequent abuses and failures, it is the communities of faith who bear a responsibility to demonstrate that [our] hopes, ideals, and standards can be guarded, grounded, and lived. This is especially true in the modern state. Guarantees of freedom of conscience and religion are necessary, but they do not substitute for binding values, convictions, and norms which are valid for all humans regardless of their social origin, sex, skin color, language, or religion.

We are convinced of the fundamental unity of the human family on Earth. We recall the 1948 Universal Declaration of Human Rights of the United Nations. What it formally proclaimed on the level of rights we wish to confirm and deepen here from the perspective of an ethic: the full realization of the intrinsic dignity of the human person, the inalienable freedom and equality in principle of all humans, and the necessary solidarity and interdependence of all humans with each other....

By a global ethic we mean a fundamental consensus on binding values, irrevocable standards, and personal attitudes. Without such a fundamental consensus on an ethic, sooner or later every community will be threatened by chaos or dictatorship, and individuals will despair.

PRINCIPLE II. WE EXPRESS A
FUNDAMENTAL DEMAND: EVERY HUMAN
BEING MUST BE TREATED HUMANELY.

...We trust that our often millennia-old religious and ethical traditions provide an ethic which is convincing and practical for all women and men of good will, religious and non-religious.

At the same time, we know that our various religious and ethical traditions often offer very different bases for what is helpful and what is unhelpful for men and women, what is right and what is wrong, what is good and what is evil. We do not wish to gloss over or ignore the serious differences among the individual religions. However, they should not hinder us from proclaiming publicly those things which we already hold in common and which we jointly affirm, each on the basis of our own religious or ethical grounds.

We know that religions cannot solve the environmental, economic, political, and social problems of Earth. However, they can provide what obviously cannot be attained by economic plans, political programs, or legal regulations alone: a change in the inner orientation, the whole mentality, the "hearts" of people, and a conversion from a false path to a new orientation for life....

Now as before, women and men are treated inhumanely all over the world.... In the face of all inhumanity our religious and ethical convictions demand that every human being must be treated humanely!

This means that every human being without distinction of age, sex, race, skin color, physical or mental ability, language, religion, political view, or national or social origin possesses an inalienable and untouchable dignity. And everyone, the individual as well as the state, is therefore obliged to honor this dignity and protect it. Humans must always be the subjects of rights, must be ends, never mere means, never objects of commercialization and industrialization in economics, politics, and media, in research institutions, and industrial corporations....

There is a principle which is found and has persisted in many religious and ethical traditions of humankind for thousands of years: What you do not wish done to yourself, do not do to others. Or in positive terms: What you wish done to yourself, do to others! This should be the irrevocable, unconditional norm for all areas of life, for families and communities, for races, nations and religions....

This principle implies very concrete standards to which we humans should hold firm. From it arise four broad, ancient guidelines for human behavior which are found in most of the religions of the world.

PRINCIPLE III. WE COMMIT TO A SET OF IRREVOCABLE DIRECTIVES.

1. Commitment to a Culture of Non-violence and Respect for Life

...

a) In the great ancient religious and ethical

traditions of humankind we find the directive: You shall not kill! Or in positive terms: Have respect for life! Let us reflect anew on the consequences of this ancient directive: All people have a right to life, safety, and the free development of personality insofar as they do not injure the rights of others....

b) Of course, wherever there are humans, there will be conflicts. Such conflicts, however, should be resolved without violence within a framework of justice. This is true for states as well as for individuals. Persons who hold political power must work within the framework of a just order and commit themselves to the most non-violent, peaceful solutions possible.... Armament is a mistaken path; disarmament is the commandment of the times....

c) Young people must learn at home and in school that violence may not be a means of settling differences with others....

d) A human person is infinitely precious and must be unconditionally protected. But likewise the lives of animals and plants which inhabit this planet with us deserve protection, preservation, and care.... As human beings we have a special responsibility—especially with a view to future generations—for Earth and the cosmos, for the air, water, and soil. We are all intertwined together in this cosmos and we are all dependent on each other....

2. Commitment to a Culture of Solidarity and a Just Economic Order

...

a) In the great ancient religious and ethical traditions of humankind we find the directive:

You shall not steal! Or in positive terms: *Deal honestly and fairly!*...

c) Young people must learn at home and in school that property... carries with it an obligation, and that its uses should at the same time serve the common good....

e) To be authentically human in the spirit of our great religious and ethical traditions means the following:

• We must utilize economic and political power for service to humanity instead of misusing it in ruthless battles for domination....

3. Commitment to a Culture of Tolerance and a Life of Truthfulness

...

a) In the great ancient religious and ethical traditions of humankind we find the directive: *You shall not lie!* Or in positive terms: *Speak and act truthfully!*...

c) Young people must learn at home and in school to think, speak, and act truthfully. They have a right to information and education to be able to make the decisions that will form their lives....

4. Commitment to a Culture of Equal Rights and Partnership between Men and Women

...

a) In the great ancient religious and ethical traditions of humankind we find the directive: *You shall not commit sexual immorality!* Or in positive terms: *Respect and love one another!*...

b) We condemn sexual exploitation and sexual discrimination as one of the worst forms of human degradation....

c) Young people must learn at home and in school that sexuality is not a negative, destructive, or exploitative force, but creative and affirmative. Sexuality... [includes the responsibility] of caring for one another's happiness.

d) The relationship between women and men should be characterized not by patronizing behavior or exploitation, but by love, partnership, and trustworthiness. Human fulfillment is not identical with sexual pleasure. Sexuality should express and reinforce a loving relationship lived by equal partners.

Some religious traditions know the ideal of a voluntary renunciation of the full use of sexuality. Voluntary renunciation also can be an expression of identity and meaningful fulfillment.

e) The social institution of marriage, despite all its cultural and religious variety, is characterized by love, loyalty, and permanence. It aims at and should guarantee security and mutual support to husband, wife, and child. It should secure the rights of all family members....

5. Commitment to a Culture of Sustainability and Care for the Earth

Numberless men and women of all regions and religions strive to lead lives in a spirit of mutual harmony, interdependence, and respect for the Earth, its living beings and ecosystems. Nevertheless, in most parts of the world, pollution contaminates the soil, air and water; deforestation and over-reliance on fossil fuels contribute to climate change; habitats are destroyed and species are fished or hunted to extinction.... Too often, the poorest populations, though they have the smallest impact, bear the brunt of the damage done to the planet's atmosphere, land and oceans.

a) In the religious, spiritual, and cultural traditions of humankind we find the directive: You shall not be greedy! Or in positive terms: Remember the good of all!... We should help provide... [for] today's and tomorrow's children. The Earth, with its finite resources, is shared by our one human family.... Many religious, spiritual, and cultural traditions place us within the interdependent web of life;... they accord us a distinctive role and affirm that our gifts of knowledge and of craft place upon us the obligation to use these gifts wisely to foster the common good.

b) All of us have the responsibility to minimize... our impact on the Earth.... Caring and prudent use of resources... takes into account limits on what ecosystems can bear.... [W]e have the duty to speak up, to change our practices, and to moderate our lifestyles.

c)...Education about the environment and sustainable living should become part of the school curricula in every country of the world.

d)...Our relationship with each other and with the larger living world should be based on respect, care and gratitude. All traditions teach that the Earth is a source of wonder and wisdom. Its vitality, diversity, and beauty are held in trust for everyone including those who will come after us. The global environmental crisis is urgent and is deepening. The planet and its countless forms of life are in danger. Time is running out....

PRINCIPLE IV. WE WORK TOWARDS A TRANSFORMATION OF CONSCIOUSNESS!

Historical experience demonstrates the following: Earth cannot be changed for the better unless we achieve a transformation in the consciousness of individuals and in public life.... This transformation must also be achieved in the area of ethics and values!...

Keeping this sense of responsibility alive, deepening it and passing it on to future generations, is the special task of religions....

In conclusion, we appeal to all the inhabitants of this planet. Earth cannot be changed for the better unless the consciousness of individuals is changed. We pledge to work for such transformation in individual and collective consciousness, for the awakening of our spiritual powers through reflection, meditation, prayer, or positive thinking, for a conversion of the heart....

We invite all men and women,
whether religious or not,
to do the same.

Questions

1. What does Adams mean when he says that, according to a divine command theory, the "facts of moral rightness and wrongness" are objective, non-natural facts like science? How is this a response to emotivism? To MacIntyre's sociological virtue ethics?

2. How does Adams modify "extreme divine command theory"? Use the story of Abraham and Isaac to explain his concern. How do you think Kierkegaard would respond to his suggestion?

3. Fisher writes, "things which existed merely as a result of the chance meandering of atomic particles could not be valuable in the way necessary to make certain kinds of behavior toward them morally obligatory or forbidden." Explain his point.

4. Fisher believes that the creative designing power of God is the ultimate source of value. At the same time, he does not think that objects and behaviors are good simply because God says so in Scripture. He thinks it is a matter of moral metaphysics. Explain his point.

5. Do you think the idea of establishing a global ethic that all people would be willing to accept and live by is a realistic possibility? Or is the *Declaration* empty rhetoric? Discuss using specific examples.

6. Find places in the *Declaration* which refer, implicitly, to Kant, to Mill, to Jesus, and to the Ten Commandments of ancient Jewish law.

7. Which of the "irrevocable directives" in the *Declaration* do you find most compelling? Why? Provide examples.

Suggested Readings

G.E.M. Anscombe's ground-breaking essay "Modern Moral Philosophy," which appeared in the reputed journal *Philosophy*, is widely available. Anscombe's ethical work can be found in the third volume of her *Collected Philosophical Papers*, which is entitled *Ethics, Religion and Politics* (1981).

The reading from Robert Adams is from Adams's *The Virtue of Faith and Other Essays in Philosophical Theology* (1987). The analytical flavor of the current conversation can be traced to William Alston, whose work is included in Michael Beaty, ed., *Christian Theism and the Problems of Philosophy* (1990), which also features the reading from Carlton Fisher.

For general sources, see Philip Quinn's entry on "Divine Command Theory" in *The Blackwell Guide to Ethical Theory* (2000), Michael Austin's entry in the *Internet Encyclopedia of Philosophy*, and Mark Murphy's entry on "Theological Voluntarism" in the *Stanford Encyclopedia of Philosophy*.

The practical ethics associated with moral theology and divine command theory can be found in religious and conservative commentary in areas like bioethics. This literature focuses on the concept of human dignity. One of the influential figures in this area is Stanley Hauerwas; see his *Sanctify Them in the Truth: Holiness Exemplified* (2016). In a comparative vein, see Thaddeus Metz, "Dignity in the Ubuntu Tradition," which appears in Marcus Düwell, ed., *Cambridge Handbook on Human Dignity* (2014). In moral theology, see Edmund Pellegrino, "The Irreducibly Religious Character of Human Dignity" (2008, 2009).

The pedigree of the current ecumenical movement goes back to Simone Weil, who wrote a "Draft for a Statement of Human Obligation" in 1943 on the basis of a non-denominational profession of faith in the transcendent. Her draft can be found in Ronald Hathaway, ed., *Two Moral Essays* (Pendle Hill Pamphlet #240).

Hans Küng's "Explanatory Remarks Concerning A 'Declaration of the Religions for A

Global Ethic'" is available online. Also see Küng's *Yes to a Global Ethic* (1996) and Küng and Kuschel, eds., *A Global Ethic. The Declaration of the Parliament of the World's Religions* (1993).

There are many ecumenical resources online. The website globethics.ne maintains a searchable library that strives to be "fully ecumenical, global and sustainable," with links to many resources. The website religioustolerance.org may be of interest. See also the "learning platform" at global-ethic-now.de.

Chapter 47

Psychological Theories of Morality

In this chapter, we consider a debate in contemporary ethics that arose in the field of moral education. Lawrence "Larry" Kohlberg (1927–87), a distinguished American psychologist, had advanced a theory about the development of moral reasoning based on liberal and Kantian principles. It became a very influential model used in the American school system for teaching moral principles to children. Carol Gilligan (b. 1936), one of Kohlberg's students, objected to the theory, arguing that it had an overly masculine bias and did not give fair shrift to the way women come to moral judgments.

Kohlberg had an eventful life. Born in New York, he attended an elite private school and served with the merchant marines during the Second World War. Working on a ship hired by *Hanah*, a Zionist organization, to smuggle Jewish war refugees past a British blockade into Palestine, he was captured and imprisoned in Cyprus. Upon escaping, he moved on to the University of Chicago where he completed undergraduate and graduate studies. He went on to teach social psychology and education at Yale, Chicago, and Harvard.

Married, with two sons, Kohlberg was known to be sociable and engaging, and apparently opened his home to everyone. He suffered, however, from a parasitic infection, contracted in Belize, which undermined his health. He appears to have been deeply troubled with the problem of evil and had bouts of depression. In his later life, he posed questions such as "Why live?" and "Why be just in a universe that is largely unjust?" In 1987, while undergoing medical treatment, he drove to Boston Harbor and walked into the frigidly cold water, apparently committing suicide.

Kohlberg became interested in the moral reasoning of children through reading the work of Jean Piaget, who believed that children progress through different stages of moral reasoning. For his PhD dissertation, he interviewed seventy-two boys, asking them whether it would be ethical for a poor man, Heinz, to steal medicine for his dying wife. The results provided the initial basis for his theory of moral development.

Kohlberg was also impressed with the kibbutz settlements in Israel, which he visited. With the kibbutz model in mind, he participated in the formation of a "just community" school in Massachusetts in 1974, run on a democratic basis. This provided the model for other "just community" schools, which was also used in a women's prison. Similar schools were later established in Europe. He discussed his theory of "just communities," which could be seen as a kind of practical ethics, in *The Just Community School: The Theory and the Cambridge Cluster School Experiment* (1975).

Kohlberg's major work was the three-volume *Essays on Moral Development: Volume I, The Philosophy of Moral Development: Moral Stages and the Idea of Justice* (1981); *Volume II, The Psychology of Moral Development: Moral Stages and the Life Cycle* (1984); and *Volume III, Education and Moral Development: Moral Stages and Practice*. The last volume was never finished.

Kohlberg's work was unorthodox for his time. Mainstream psychology had generally followed the behaviorist model of conditioning, which focused on external factors of reward and punishment. His focus on cognitive development and the central role of reason in moral judgment reflects his interest in philosophers such as John Rawls, John Dewey, and Immanuel Kant. Kohlberg accepts Rawls's explanation that "justice is fairness"—a Rawls slogan—and emphasizes equality. He embraces Kant's single-minded focus on personal autonomy and human dignity as the mark of self-legislating, moral agents.

Kohlberg divides moral development into three levels: pre-conventional morality, conventional morality, and post-conventional morality. Each of these levels includes two stages of development: in the pre-conventional phase, "obedience and punishment," followed by "individualism and exchange"; in the conventional phase, "maintaining interpersonal relationships," followed by "law and order"; in the post-conventional phase, "social contract," and finally, in the highest phase, "universal principles."

Kohlberg believed that a majority of individuals today are grounded in stage four moralities, with some elements of stage five moralities. From a philosophical perspective, his deeper view is that Kant's deontological ethics is grounded upon stage six moralities and therefore beyond the morality of the majority of modern individuals. Before he died, he postulated that there might be a seventh stage of moral reasoning, perhaps religious, in which we attain a Buddhist-like calm, loving "Life, the Universe, God, or Nature."

In actual practice, Kohlberg says, we can reach just decisions by looking at a situation through one another's eyes. In the Heinz dilemma, the scenario he used in his PhD dissertation, this would mean that all parties—the druggist, Heinz, and his wife—take the roles of the others. To do this in an impartial manner, people can assume Rawls's "veil of ignorance," thinking as if they did not know which role they would eventually occupy. If the druggist did this, he would presumably recognize that he is compelled to provide the drug.

Kohlberg's research on the construction of gender and the development of "sex-roles" among children provided the background to the work of Carol Gilligan, who became his friend and research assistant. Gilligan later severely criticized his work on feminist grounds, arguing that he had focused on a male morality, which ignored the moral development of girls. Kohlberg responds to Gilligan's criticism in the second volume of *Essays on Moral Development*, where he raises questions about her empirical research.

Gilligan received a BA in English literature from Swarthmore College, a master's degree in clinical psychology from Radcliffe College, and a PhD in social psychology from Harvard University. In the course of a teaching career at Harvard, she was appointed Patricia Albjerg Graham Chair in Gender Studies. She went to New York University in 2002, where she is currently teaching in the School of Education and the School of Law. Gilligan is also a visiting professor at the University of Cambridge in the Centre for Gender Studies.

The specific focus of Gilligan's research in psychology was the moral development of girls. Among the number of works published in this field, she has authored (sometimes with her students) *Mapping the Moral Domain: A Contribution of Women's Thinking to Psychological Theory and Education* (1989), *Making Connections: The Relational Worlds of Adolescent Girls at Emma Willard School* (1990), and *Meeting at the Crossroads: Women's Psychology and Girls' Development* (1992). She has also published a novel, *Kyra* (2008), and co-written (with her son) a play, *The Scarlet Letter* (2011), based on the novel by Nathaniel Hawthorne.

Gilligan is best known for her 1982 book *In a Different Voice: Psychological Theory and Women's Development*, which broke with the reigning orthodoxy in moral psychology and philosophy of education. While working with Kohlberg in the 1970s, Gilligan ultimately grew dissatisfied with his justice-oriented, duty-bound interpretation of morality. Rejecting his moral ideal of a Kantian kingdom of ends regulated by categorical imperatives, which Gilligan labeled an "ethics of justice," she proposed instead an "ethics of care" that emphasizes welfare and implicitly adopts utilitarian values.

In presenting her findings, she claimed that there are differences in the moral development of young women and young men. Women tend to focus on relationships with others, and especially on maintaining caring relationships. As a consequence, Gilligan rejected Kohlberg's six stages of moral development because they do not capture the ethic of care that she attributed to women.

The first reading is from the introduction to the first volume of Kohlberg's *Essays on Moral Development*, which sketches out the plan of the work. The brief excerpt basically contains a digest of the first volume and reviews the philosophy behind his theory. The reading also includes an excerpt from an Appendix to the volume and contains a convenient summary of the six stages of moral development.

The second reading contains excerpts from Gilligan's *In a Different Voice* and considers the failure to include women's voices in the moral discussion as well as the importance of relationships in the female view.

Lawrence Kohlberg, *The Philosophy of Moral Development*[1]

(1981)

Preface to Essays on Moral Development

[These] volumes... [are directed to those who are] potentially interested in a theory of moral education that combines (1) a philosophical theory of justice with (2) a psychological theory of the process of moral development to produce (3) an educational theory prescribing a reasonable practice of moral education in the schools....

The basic conception of six psychological stages of moral development goes back to my 1958 doctoral dissertation. It took, however, twenty years of longitudinal study to validate empirically the conception of the stages....

In 1969, I was galvanized into deeper reflection when... a graduate student, Moshe Blatt, engaged intermediate and high school students in a semester of Socratic classroom dilemma discussions and found that a third of the students moved up a stage, in contrast to control students, who remained unchanged....

[The first volume here] presents essays written after my initial psychological and educational writing. The prod to writing was primarily educational. If an aim of education is stage growth, as I believe, then one must give a philosophic rationale for why a higher stage is a better stage....

For this reason, I have placed Volume I, on moral, political, and educational philosophy, before the volume on moral psychology[2] and its applica-

tions to education.[3] The reader is likely to start with Meno's psychological question... (in Plato's *Meno*[4]): "Can you tell me, Socrates, is virtue something that can be taught? Or does it come by practice? Or is it neither teaching or practice but natural aptitude or instinct?" For the psychologist, it is wiser... to reply, like Socrates, "You must think I am singularly fortunate to know whether virtue can be taught or how it is acquired. The fact is that far from knowing whether it can be taught, I have no idea what virtue itself is."

[It follows, for the psychologist, as for Socrates, that] the psychology of moral development and learning cannot be discussed without addressing the philosophic questions "What is virtue?" and "What is justice?"....

Volume I addresses the question posed by Socrates: "What is a virtuous man, and what is a virtuous school and society which educates virtuous men?" The answers given are not new. They are the answers given by Socrates...; next by Kant, as interpreted by John Rawls's *A Theory of Justice*...; then by John Dewey, in *Democracy and Education*...; and most recently by Piaget, in *The Moral Judgment of the Child*... Following Socrates, Kant, and Piaget, the answer I and my colleagues offer says that the first virtue of a person, school, or society is justice—interpreted in a democratic way as equity or equal respect for all people.

Democratic justice is an answer to the deontological question, "What are the rights of people, and what

---

1   Lawrence Kohlberg, "Preface to Essays on Moral Development" and "Appendix. The Six Stages of Moral Judgment," in Kohlberg, *The Philosophy of Moral Development: Moral Stages and the Idea of Justice* (Essays on Moral Development, vol. I) (San Francisco: Harper & Row, 1981), Preface, pp. ix–xiv; Appendix.

2   I.e., volume 2.

3   I.e., volume 3.

4   A dialogue written by Plato that examines whether virtue can be taught.

duties do these rights entail?"...[This still leaves] the teleological question "What is the purpose of a person's life or of a school or society's existence?" Our answer is John Dewey's answer (and, in a sense, Aristotle's): the aim of education and of civic life is intellectual, moral, and personal development...

What is new in our answers to these questions is the systematic stage framework with which we approach them.... [This is based on] the framework of *structuralism* (the analysis of invariant systems of relations among ideas), which underlies any attempt to define stages. On the philosophic side, this framework of structuralism gives rise to a theory of virtue as *justice*. Although Plato, Dewey, and Piaget each meant different things by *justice*, each recognized justice as the first virtue of a person because it is the first virtue of a society. Each recognized justice has a *structure*, a pattern of equilibrium or harmony in a group or society....

Volume I is divided into four parts. Part One uses the moral stages to approach the problems of educational philosophy. Like Socrates and Dewey, I and my colleagues feel that the question of moral philosophy (the question "What is virtue?"), is both first and finally a question of education, which is the practice of philosophy.

Part II focuses directly on issues of moral philosophy. Thus, the heart of Volume I is this part, containing two chapters, "From *Is* to *Ought*" (Chapter 4[, which discusses the uses of moral stage psychology in answering philosophic questions while avoiding David Hume's 'naturalistic fallacy']) and "Justice as Reversibility" (Chapter 5). These chapters argue that there are stages of moral reasoning and judgment, that the core of each stage is an underlying conception of justice, and that each higher stage is better for resolving justice problems....

Part Three applies the moral stages and the ideal of justice they imply to questions of political philosophy and the philosophy of law. It focuses on two U.S. Supreme Court decisions.

The first Supreme Court decision...is the *Fur-*

man decision, prohibiting many uses of capital punishment as a violation of the Eighth Amendment prohibiting "cruel and unusual punishment." Chapter 7 supports this decision on the grounds (1) that, very slowly, public and individual sentiment is moving toward viewing capital punishment as cruel and unusual, and (2) that capital punishment violates Rawlsian justice and other Stage 6 justice principles.

In Chapter 8, I consider a second decision, the *Schempp* decision, making religious observation and teaching in the school a violation of the First Amendment and of the separation of church and state. This decision has been interpreted as prohibiting moral education in the schools on the grounds that such education is the propagation of a creed of secular humanism. In the chapter, I argue that the teaching of justice in the schools...is, in fact, a part of the Founding Fathers' vision of the mission of the public schools....

Part Four reaches [beyond justice, into the humanities, and considers issues in literature and theology]...

Appendix. The Six Stages of Moral Judgment

LEVEL A. PRECONVENTIONAL LEVEL

Stage 1. The Stage of Punishment and Obedience

Content

Right is literal obedience to rules and authority, avoiding punishment, and not doing physical harm.

1. What is right is to avoid breaking rules, to obey for obedience's sake, and to avoid doing physical damage to people and property.

2. The reasons for doing right are avoidance of punishment and the superior power of authorities.

Social Perspective

This stage takes an egocentric point of view. A person at this stage doesn't consider the interests of others…, and doesn't relate two points of view. Actions are judged in terms of physical consequences rather than in terms of psychological interests of others. Authority's perspective is confused with one's own.

Stage 2. The Stage of Individual Instrumental Purpose and Exchange

Content

Right is serving one's own or other's needs and making fair deals in terms of concrete exchange.

> 1. What is right…is acting to meet one's own interests and needs and letting others do the same. Right is also what is fair; that is, what is an equal exchange, a deal, an agreement.

> 2. The reason for doing right is to serve one's own needs or interests in a world where one must recognize that other people have their interests, too.

Social Perspective

… A person at this stage separates [his or her] own interests and points of view from those of authorities and others. He or she is aware everybody has individual interests to pursue and these conflict…The person integrates or relates conflicting individual interests to one another through instrumental exchange of services, through instrumental need for the other and the other's goodwill, or through fairness giving each person the same amount.

LEVEL B. CONVENTIONAL LEVEL

Stage 3. The Stage of Mutual Interpersonal Expectations, Relationships, and Conformity

Content

The right is playing a good (nice) role, being concerned about the other people and their feelings, keeping loyalty and trust with partners, and being motivated to follow rules and expectations.

> 1. What is right is living up to what is expected by people close to one or what people generally expect of people in one's role as son, sister, friend, and so on. "Being good" is important and means having good motives, showing concern about others. It also means keeping mutual relationships, maintaining trust, loyalty, respect, and gratitude.

> 2. The reasons for doing right are needing to be good in one's own eyes and those of others… [I]f one puts oneself in the other person's place one would want good behavior from the self (Golden Rule).

Social Perspective

… A person at this stage is aware of shared feelings, agreements, and expectations, which take primacy over individual interests. The person relates points of view through the "concrete Golden Rule," putting oneself in the other person's shoes. He or she does not consider [a] generalized "system" perspective.

Stage 4. The Stage of Social System and Conscience Maintenance

Content

The right is doing one's duty in society, upholding the social order, and maintaining the welfare of society or the group.

1. What is right is fulfilling the actual duties to which one has agreed. Laws are to be upheld except in extreme cases where they conflict with other fixed social duties and rights. Right is also contributing to society, the group, or institution.

2. The reasons for doing right are to keep the institution going as a whole, self-respect... or the consequences: "What if everyone did it?"

Social Perspective

This stage differentiates [a] societal point of view from interpersonal agreement or motives. A person at this stage takes the viewpoint of the system, which defines roles and rules....

LEVEL B/C. TRANSITIONAL LEVEL

This level is postconventional but not yet principled.

Content of Transition

At Stage 4½, choice is personal and subjective. It is based on emotions, conscience is seen as arbitrary and relative, as are ideas such as "duty" and "morally right."

Transitional Social Perspective

At this stage, the perspective is that of an individual standing outside of his own society and considering himself as an individual making decisions without a generalized commitment or contract with society. One can pick and choose obligations,... but one has no principles for such choice.

LEVEL C. POSTCONVENTIONAL AND PRINCIPLED LEVEL

Moral decisions are generated from rights, values, or principles that are (or could be) agreeable to all individuals composing or creating a society designed to have fair and beneficial practices.

Stage 5. The Stage of Prior Rights and Social Contract or Utility

Content

The right is upholding the basic rights, values, and legal contracts of a society, even when they conflict with the concrete rules and laws of the group.

1. What is right is being aware... that most values and rules are relative to one's group. These "relative" rules should usually be upheld, however, in the interest of impartiality and because they are the social contract. Some nonrelative values and rights such as life, and liberty, however, must be upheld in any society and regardless of majority opinion.

2. Reasons for doing right are, in general, feeling obligated to obey the law because one has made a social contract to make and abide by laws for the good of all... Family, friendship, trust, and work obligations are also commitments or contracts freely entered into and entail respect for the rights of others. One is concerned that laws and duties be based on rational calculation of overall utility: "the greatest good for the greatest number."

Social Perspective

This stage takes a prior-to-society perspective—that of a rational individual aware of values and rights prior to social attachments and contracts. The person integrates perspectives by formal mechanisms of agreement, contract, objective impartiality, and due process. He or she considers the moral point of view and the legal point of view, recognizes they conflict, and finds it difficult to integrate them.

Stage 6. The Stage of Universal Ethical Principles

Content

This stage assumes guidance by universal ethical principles that all humanity should follow.

1. Regarding what is right, Stage 6 is guided by universal ethical principles. Particular laws or social agreements are usually valid because they rest on such principles. When laws violate these principles, one acts in accordance with the principle. Principles are universal principles of justice: the equality of human rights and respect for the dignity of human beings as individuals. These are not merely values that are recognized, but are also principles used to generate particular decisions.

2. The reason for doing right is that, as a rational person, one has seen the validity of principles and has become committed to them.

Social Perspective

This stage takes the perspective of a moral point of view from which social arrangements derive...The perspective is that of any rational individual recognizing the nature of morality or the basic moral premise of respect for other persons as ends, not means.

Carol Gilligan, *In a Different Voice: Psychological Theory and Women's Development*[1]

(1982)

The dilemma that these eleven-year-olds were asked to resolve was one in the series devised by Kohlberg to measure moral development...In this particular dilemma, a man named Heinz considered whether or not to steal a drug which he cannot afford to buy in order to save the life of his wife. In the standard format of Kohlberg's interviewing procedure, the description of the dilemma itself—Heinz's predica-

---

1 Carol Gilligan, *In a Different Voice: Psychological Theory and Women's Development* (Cambridge, MA and London: Harvard University Press, 1982).

ment, the wife's disease, the druggist's refusal to lower his price—is followed by the question, "Should Heinz steal the drug?"...

Jake, at eleven, is clear from the outset, that Heinz should steal the drug.... [H]e discerns the logical priority of life and uses logic to justify his choice...Asked about the fact that, in stealing, Heinz would be breaking the law, he says that "the laws have mistakes, and you can't go writing up a law for everything that you can imagine."...

Fascinated by the power of logic, this eleven-year-old boy locates the truth in math, which he says, is "the only thing that is totally logical." Concerning the moral dilemma to be "sort of like a math problem with humans," he sets it up as an equation and proceeds to work out the solution. Since his solution is rationally devised, he assumes that anyone following reason would arrive at the same conclusion and thus that a judge would also consider stealing the right thing for Heinz to do. Yet he is also aware of the limits of logic....

In contrast, Amy's response to the dilemma conveys a very different impression, an image of development stunted by a failure of logic, an inability to think for herself. Asked if Heinz should steal the drug, she replies in a way that seems evasive and unsure...Asked why he should not steal the drug, she considers neither property nor law but rather the effect that theft could have on the relationship between Heinz and his wife...

Seeing in the dilemma not a math problem with humans but a narrative of relationships that extends over time, Amy envisions the wife's continuing need for her husband and the husband's continuing concern for this wife and seeks to respond to the druggist's need in a way that would sustain rather than sever connection. Just as she ties the wife's survival to the preservation of relationships, so she considers the value of the wife's life in a context of relationships, saying that it would be wrong to let her die because, "if she died, it hurts a lot of people and it hurts her."...[S]he considers the problem in the dilemma to arise not from the druggist's assertion of rights but from his failure of response.

As the interviewer proceeds with the series of questions..., Amy's answers remain essentially unchanged, the various probes serving neither to elucidate or modify her initial response....

Norma Haan's (1975) research on college students[1] and Constance Holstein's (1976) three-year study of adolescents and their parents[2] indicate that the moral judgments of women differ from those of men in the greater extent to which women's judgments are tied to feelings of empathy and compassion and are concerned with the resolution of real as opposed to hypothetical dilemmas. However, as long as the categories by which development is assessed are derived from research on men, divergence from the masculine standard can be seen only as a failure of development. As a result, the thinking of women is often classified with that of children. The absence of alternative criteria that might better encompass the development of women, however, points not only to the limitations of theories framed by men and validated by research samples disproportionately male and adolescent, but also to the diffidence prevalent among women, their reluctance to speak publicly in their own voice, given the constraints imposed on them by their lack of power and the politics of relations between the sexes.

In order to go beyond the question, "How much like men do women think, how capable are they of engaging in the abstract and hypothetical construction of reality?" it is necessary to identify and define developmental criteria that encompass the categories of women's thought. Haan points out the necessity

---

1 "Hypothetical and Actual Moral Reasoning in a Situation of Civil Disobedience."

2 "Development of Moral Judgment: A Longitudinal Study of Males and Females."

to derive such criteria from the resolution of the "more frequently occurring, real-life moral dilemmas of interpersonal, empathic, fellow-feeling concerns" ... which have long been the center of women's moral concern. But to derive developmental criteria from the language of women's moral discourse, it is necessary first to see whether women's construction of the moral domain relies on a language different from that of men and one that deserves equal credence in the definition of development....

... When women construct the adult domain, the world of relationships emerges and becomes the focus of attention and concern. [David C.] McClelland (1975), noting this shift in women's fantasies of power, observes that "women are more concerned than men with both sides of an interdependent relationship" and are "quicker to recognize their own interdependence"[1] ... This focus on interdependence is manifest in fantasies that equate power with giving and care. McClelland reports that while men represent powerful activity as assertion and aggression, women in contrast portray acts of nurturance as acts of strength. Considering his research on power to deal "in particular with the characteristics of maturity," he suggests that mature women and men may relate to the world in a different style.

That women differ in their orientation to power is also the theme of Jean Baker Miller's analysis (1976).[2] Focusing on relationships of dominance and subordination, she finds women's situation in these relationships to provide "a crucial key to understanding the psychological order." This order arises from the relationships of difference, between man and woman and parent and child ... Because these relationships of difference contain, in most instances, a factor of inequality, they assume a moral dimension pertaining to the way in which power is used. On this basis, Miller distinguishes between relationships of temporary and permanent inequality, the former representing the context of human development, the latter, the condition of oppression. In relationships of temporary inequality, such as parent and child or teacher and student, power ideally is used to foster the development that removes the initial disparity. In relationships of permanent inequality, power cements dominance and subordination, and oppression is rationalized by theories that "explain" the need for its continuation.

Miller, focusing in this way on the dimension of inequality in human life, identifies the distinctive psychology of women as arising from the combination of their positions in relationships of temporary and permanent inequality. Dominant in temporary relationships of nurturance that dissolve with the dissolution of inequality, women are subservient in relationships of permanently unequal social status and power. In addition, though subordinate in social position to men, women are at the same time centrally entwined with them in the intimate and intense relationships of adult sexuality and family life. Thus women's psychology reflects both sides of relationships of interdependence and the range of moral possibilities to which such relationships give rise. Women, therefore, are ideally situated to observe the potential in human connection both for care and for oppression....

Like the stories that delineate women's fantasies of power, women's descriptions of adulthood convey a different sense of its social reality. In their portrayal of relationships, women replace the bias of men toward separation with a representation of the interdependence of self and other, both in love and in work. By changing the lens of developmental observation from individual achievement to relationships of care, women depict ongoing attachment as the path that leads to maturity....

Among the most pressing items on the agenda for research ... is the need to delineate *in women's*

---

1 *Power: The Inner Experience.*
2 *Toward a New Psychology of Women.*

own terms the experience of their adult life.... [T]he inclusion of women's experience brings to developmental understanding a new perspective on relationships that changes the basic constructs of interpretation. The concept of identity expands to include the experience of interconnection. The moral domain is similarly enlarged by the inclusion of responsibility and care in relationships....

Given the evidence of different perspectives in the representation of adulthood by women and men, there is a need for research that elucidates the effects of these differences in marriage, family, and work relationships. My research suggests that men and women may speak different languages that they assume are the same, using similar words to encode disparate experiences of self and social relationships. Because these languages share an overlapping moral vocabulary, they... [tend to create] misunderstandings which impede communication and limit the potential for cooperation and care in relationships....

As we have listened for centuries to the voices of men, so we have come more recently to notice not only the silence of women but the difficulty in hearing what they say when they speak. Yet in the different voice of women lies the truth of an ethic of care, the tie between relationship and responsibility, and

the origins of aggression in the failure of connection. The failure to see the different reality of women's lives and to hear the differences in their voices stems in part from the assumption that there is a single mode of social experience and interpretation. By positing instead two different modes, we arrive at a more complex rendition of human experience which sees the truth of separation and attachment in the lives of women and men and recognizes how these truths are carried by different modes of language and thought.

To understand how the tension between responsibilities and rights sustains the dialectic of human development is to see the integrity of two disparate modes of experience that are in the end connected. While an ethic of justice[1] proceeds from the premise of equality—that everyone should be treated the same—an ethic of care rests on the premise of nonviolence—that no one should be hurt. In the representation of maturity, both perspectives converge in the realization that just as inequality adversely affects both parties in an unequal relationship, so too violence is destructive for everyone involved. This dialogue between fairness and care not only provides a better understanding of relations between the sexes but also gives rise to a more comprehensive portrayal of adult work and family relationships....

Questions

1. Kohlberg's primary interest was in moral education. What, in your view, is the best way of teaching morality? Refer to Kohlberg and one of the philosophers in the earlier chapters in your answer.
2. Kohlberg lists six stages of moral development. Describe two consecutive stages from stages 1–4, explaining how an individual moves from the earlier to the later stage.
3. Think of Socrates's behavior in court at the end of his life. Where would you locate Socrates in Kohlberg's six-stage schema? Why?
4. Gilligan describes Jake's and Amy's responses to Kohlberg's Heinz dilemma. Explain, in your own words, the larger point they are intended to illustrate.

---

1 I.e., an ethic of (equal) rights.

5. Are men and women the same morally? Or, as Gilligan maintains, are we fundamentally different? Relate to second- and third-wave feminism (see chapter 45).

6. Relate Gilligan's division between an ethics of care and an ethics of justice to traditional gender roles. Does her theory support or detract from traditional categories?

7. Gilligan describes a male bias towards "separation" and a female bias towards "interdependence." Explain. How do these perspectives lead to different moralities?

8. At the end of her book, Gilligan suggests that the two ethics can be synthesized in a single standard. Do you agree? Relationships tend to be partisan: we favor our friends, children, parents, in specific ways. Justice requires impartiality: we are supposed to treat everyone the same. Can these two perspectives be reconciled? How?

Suggested Readings

Kohlberg's work has found its way into most of the textbooks in social and developmental psychology. Three examples of his earlier work are "Education for Justice: A Modern Statement of the Platonic View" (1970), "From *Is* to *Ought*: How to Commit the Naturalist Fallacy and Get Away with It in the Study of Moral Development" (1971), and "A Cognitive-Developmental Approach to Moral Education" (1972). His primary philosophical account, however, is in the first volume of *The Philosophy of Moral Development* (1981). For a more recent reconsideration of Kohlberg, see James R. Rest et al., "A Neo-Kohlbergian Approach to Morality Research" (2010). Kohlberg's work was instrumental in promoting the scientific study of moral character. Consult the suggested readings on virtue ethics (chapter 43).

Gilligan's subsequent work after *In a Different Voice* treats similar themes. She edited a number of collections with other scholars. See, for example, *Making Connections: The Relational Worlds of Adolescent Girls at Emma Willard School* (1990), *Between Voice and Silence: Women and Girls, Race and Relationships* (1997), and her own *The Birth of Pleasure* (2002). For more on Gilligan's influence, see also the suggested readings on the feminist ethics of care (chapter 45).

It must be said that significant numbers of social science commentators have severely criticized Gilligan's research methodology as anecdotal, agenda-driven, and statistically opaque. Cf., for example, Zella Luria, "A Methodological Critique" (1986), and conservative Christina Hoff Sommers, "The War against Boys," in *Atlantic Monthly* (May 2000).

Chapter 48

Contemporary Science and Morality

The readings in the present sourcebook cover the last 5,000 years of human existence. This is only a short space of time in the evolutionary record, which suggests that *homo sapiens* appeared at least 300,000 years ago. Up to this point in our history, the major sources of moral philosophy have been cosmological, religious, and philosophical. There may be a new source of moral philosophy, however, in science, which has begun to investigate the origins of ethics.

The dramatic increase in the authority of science can be traced to the work of thinkers such as Galileo Galilei and Isaac Newton in the seventeenth century. Newton's discovery of three universal laws of motion demonstrated the scope and power of the new physics. Charles Darwin's theory of evolution in the nineteenth century further eroded the traditional understanding. Proponents of science rejected past metaphysics, religion, and a familiar reliance on historical sources of wisdom.

In this chapter, then, we consider three different approaches to the challenges to traditional thought and moral philosophy posed by contemporary science. We begin with post-modernist philosopher Richard Rorty, who gives up on the project of erecting any objective scientific answer to deeper human aspirations, arguing instead for a pragmatic, largely practical response to moral problems. We next consider social psychologist Jonathan David Haidt, who articulates an up-to-date, social science answer to moral theory largely in line with traditional wisdom. Lastly, we consider transhumanist philosopher Nick Bostrom's optimistic account of a scientific future that provides successful technological solutions to human suffering.

Richard Rorty (1931–2007) was a philosophy professor who taught at a number of prestigious American universities. He is known for his "neo-pragmatism," which he saw as the next step in the scientific and Enlightenment project. This project, in his view, was to finally rid us of the dogmatic and implicitly authoritarian "onto-theological" accounts of truth and goodness in the historical record. Following the lead of John Dewey, he gave up on traditional moral philosophy, metaphysics, religion, and even science—his post-modern stance is sometimes described as "anti-theory"—and turned instead to literature as a better source of "narratives of social hope" that can push public policy in a progressive secular direction. The vagueness of such suggestions is perhaps unsettling; it is evident, moreover, that conservatives feel nothing but alarm at the loss of the traditional foundations of moral philosophy.

In *Philosophy and the Mirror of Nature* (1979) and *Consequences of Pragmatism* (1982), Rorty argues against "representationalism," and questions the idea that there is a reality independent of cognition to which scientists can objectively appeal to prove the truth and validity of their views. His essays, which often address political and moral issues, have been collected in four volumes of philosophical papers, including *Objectivity, Relativism, and Truth* (1991) and *Philosophy as Cultural Politics* (2007).

Jonathan Haidt (b. 1963) is a social psychologist who has focused on the psychology of morality and the moral emotions. His approach combines the findings of neuropsychology and an understanding of evolutionary processes to produce a broad but systematic account of the way the mind works. It incorporates elements of cultural psychology and anthropology, and chronicles how morality and emotion vary across cultures. Haidt works primarily in the academic field of "positive psychology," which is the scientific study of human flourishing and of positive emotions such as admiration and awe.

Haidt has developed a "social intuitionist" model of moral judgment. He uses a striking metaphor to explain the human condition: rational consciousness is like a small rider sitting on a very large elephant composed of automatic and intuitive physiological processes developed in the course of our evolutionary history. Moral judgments are mostly based on these automatic processes, on moral intuitions, rather than on conscious reasoning. Reasoning is usually done in support of the initial intuitive judgment.

Haidt's book, *The Happiness Hypothesis: Finding Modern Truth in Ancient Wisdom* (2006), looks at ten "Great Ideas" about happiness, fulfilment, and meaning discovered by a number of thinkers—some of the same ones covered in this anthology. He examines their ideas in the light of contemporary psychological research, attempting to reformulate in a scientific spirit those elements that still apply. Much of his recent research examines how moral judgments are made in the areas of business, politics, and other social systems.

The Swedish-born philosopher Nick Bostrom (b. 1973) is currently a professor at Oxford University and director of the Future of Humanity Institute and the Strategic Artificial Intelligence Research Center. He is a prolific author, whose many publications include works in the philosophy of science, principally *Anthropic Bias: Observation Selection Effects in Science and Philosophy* (2002), and in the ethics of biological enhancement.

Bostrom's research interests cover Artificial Intelligence (AI) and its implications for humanity, including the existential risk that AI poses to humanity over the coming century. His recent book, *Superintelligence: Paths, Dangers, Strategies* (2014), argues that smart machines—machines that are capable of improving themselves—will appear, and that the fate of the human species will come to depend on the actions of these superintelligent machines, much as the fate of gorillas depends more on human beings than on themselves.

Our first reading is from Giancarlo Marcetti's interview with Richard Rorty in the magazine *Philosophy Now*. Rorty explains his neo-pragmatist stance and shares his thoughts on the future of philosophy.

The second reading contains an excerpt from Haidt's research in moral psychology, which is based on surveys that are designed to determine the moral intuitions of individuals. The phrase "new synthesis" found in the title of the article is an expression coined by the American biologist E.O. Wilson, whose work *Sociobiology: The New Synthesis* (1975) was the first influential attempt at a synthesis of the natural and social sciences to form a new scientific field he called "sociobiology." Haidt is, therefore, following Wilson's basic project of taking an approach that is firmly rooted in evolutionary principles in order to explain human morality in both biological and cultural terms within the science of psychology. He proposes a much wider vision of morality than Kohlberg.

The last reading in the chapter is from Bostrom and sets out transhumanist values that are intended to guide human beings as we transition from the biological animals that we currently are, through a transhumanist phase, to finally arrive at the post-humanist phase of evolution. The post-humanist will be a technologically-enhanced human being. The major criticism of such over-arching moral work is that it glosses over the details that need to be negotiated assuming that such a transformation is possible.

READING 48A

Interview with Richard Rorty[1]

(2003)

GIANCARLO MARCHETTI: Let's turn to philosophy. Could you say what characterizes your own version of pragmatism?

RICHARD RORTY: I think that what I get out of reading the classical pragmatists is just the idea that there are no privileged descriptions and that therefore there is not much point in asking, "Is our way of talking about things objective or subjective?" I

think of pragmatists as the people who did the best job of getting rid of the subject/object distinction.[2]

MARCHETTI: In what way does your pragmatism differ from that of Hilary Putnam?[3]

RORTY: I'm not sure. Putnam wants something he has called substantive truth. And I'm not sure what 'substantive' means in that phrase. He wants some

---

1 "Interview with Richard Rorty," in *Philosophy Now* 43 (October/November 2003). Available at philosophynow.org.

2 The subject/object distinction refers to the subject that knows or experiences, while the object is that which is known or experienced by the subject and is often said to be 'other than' it or 'outside' it.

3 Hilary Putnam (1926–2016) was an American philosopher, mathematician, and computer scientist. He was a major figure in analytic philosophy.

kind of correspondence[1] that I don't see any need for, but I've never been quite clear what sort of correspondence it is....

MARCHETTI: If you had to draw a genealogy of pragmatism and the new pragmatism where would you place Davidson,[2] Putnam, and yourself?

RORTY: I think Putnam and I both have the same reaction to positivism.[3] We were persuaded by people like WVO Quine and Morton White[4] that it wasn't worthwhile making a big distinction between the analytic and the synthetic, between the observational and the theoretical, between fact and value, and that Dewey[5] was right in trying to get rid of these distinctions. I think Davidson is much more original than either Putnam or I. That is, I think his work in the philosophy of language... has given us a genuinely new conception of the relationship between language and the world....

MARCHETTI: What is special about pragmatist ethics?

RORTY: I don't think pragmatists have a special ethics. They have, if you like, a special meta-ethics. That is, they're dubious about the distinction between morality and prudence. Immanuel Kant is still the greatest influence on academic moral philosophy. If you read Kant, you think of morality as a very special, distinct phenomenon having little in common with anything else in culture. Dewey wrote book after book saying we don't need a great big distinction between morality and everything else, we don't even need a great big distinction between morality and prudence. It's all a matter of solving the problems that arise in relations between human beings. When these problems become acute we call them moral problems, when they don't become acute we call them prudential problems. It's a matter of importance rather than, as Kant thought, a difference between reason and emotion, or reason and sentiment, or the *a priori* and the *a posteriori*, or the philosophical and the empirical, and so on. Basically what Dewey did for moral philosophy was just to help get rid of Kant. I don't think the pragmatists have any further contribution to make to ethics.

MARCHETTI: What could pragmatism offer to the inhabitants of the global village?

RORTY: It gives us a philosophical apologia[6] for a thoroughly secularized culture, a culture in which what Nietzsche called "all the surrogates for God" have disappeared and human beings are on their own. I think of it as a version of humanism.

MARCHETTI: Pragmatism was of course launched as a philosophical movement in the 1870's at a time when Darwin's *Origin of Species* was having a huge

---

1 I.e., correspondence with an objective reality. Rorty is expressing his rejection of representationalism, i.e., the view that mental states, such as thoughts, beliefs, and perceptions, are about or refer to things (external to the mind).

2 Donald Davidson (1917–2003) was an American analytic philosopher, making influential contributions in areas such as semantic theory, epistemology, and ethics.

3 Positivism is the philosophical position that holds that all authentic knowledge can be scientifically (empirically) verified or is capable of logical or mathematical proof. It rejects, as a result, metaphysics, theology, and any assertions that cannot be so verified or proven.

4 Willard van Orman Quine (1908–2000) was an influential American philosopher best known for his arguments against Logical Empiricism. Morton White (1917–2016) was an American philosopher, historian of ideas, and a proponent of "Holistic Pragmatism." Both rejected the analytic-synthetic distinction, i.e., the sharp dichotomy between logical truths based on meanings of terms knowable by reason alone and empirical statements of fact knowable through sense perception.

5 John Dewey (1859–1952) was an American philosopher, psychologist, and educational reformer. He is one of the primary figures associated with the philosophy of pragmatism.

6 I.e., a defense.

impact everywhere. What do you think was Darwin's contribution to pragmatism?

RORTY: I think he provided the stimulus for pragmatism by saying…you don't need a supernatural explanation of the human mind or distinctively human abilities. Instead, you can think of human beings as clever animals. He gave philosophers a new task and the pragmatists were among the people who tried to rise to the challenge that Darwin presented. I think Darwin was the most important stimulus for the development of pragmatism, but that's different from making a contribution to it.…

MARCHETTI: Some critics, misunderstanding your work, have accused you of being a postmodern relativist. What do you answer to this charge? [I'm just giving you the chance to have the last word on why you are not a postmodern relativist.]

RORTY:…Well, I'm not sure that any clear meaning has ever been given to the term 'postmodern relativism.' I think that if it means anything, it means that postmodern relativists don't believe that there is one true description of the way the world really is, and in that sense I am indeed a postmodern relativist. I suppose the reason that position is called relativism is that people who believe there's no such thing as the way the world is in itself think that all descriptions of everything are the product of attempts to gratify human needs and interests. Those needs and interests change, so our sense of what's important will, in many areas, keep changing. 'Relativism' doesn't strike me as the right word. Maybe 'fallibilist' would be better. I don't think the word 'postmodern' has any clear meaning, so I try to avoid it.…

MARCHETTI: In many essays, you argue for a classless, casteless, egalitarian society. In what ways could we cooperate to realize such a social democracy?

RORTY: I don't think it's a matter of cooperation so much as of breaking the power of the rich and strong. In my country we need to arrange things so that the rich can't bribe the legislators and can't put on media blitzes in favor of candidates. There are all kinds of particular, practical, detailed things that have to be done. But again, I don't have anything new to say. Social democracy in America faces the same problems that any leftist movement has always faced in any other country.…

MARCHETTI: What is your general appreciation of the contribution of feminist thinkers?

RORTY: I think that feminism has been an extraordinarily successful social movement, one of the best things that has ever happened to the West.… But I don't think that the feminist philosophers have done anything special in the way of a feminist epistemology or a feminist metaphysics or a feminist ethics. They have just pointed out the role of what Derrida[1] called 'phallogocentrism'[2] in traditional philosophical thought. This is a genuine contribution, but it isn't the basis for a new philosophical outlook.…

MARCHETTI: How do you see your first book, *The Linguistic Turn*, 35 years after?

RORTY: I think that one of the things that the founders of analytic philosophy did was to persuade philosophers that, as Dummett[3] put it, philosophy of language is first philosophy. He concluded that if we don't have a systematic theory of meaning we

---

1   Jacques Derrida (1930–2004) was a French philosopher best known for developing a form of semiotic analysis known as deconstruction. He was a major figure of post-structuralism and postmodern philosophy.
2   The expression of male dominance in culture, writing, and thought.
3   Sir Michael Dummett (1925–2011) was a British philosopher who wrote on the history of analytic philosophy and made contributions to the philosophies of mathematics, logic, language, and metaphysics.

can't do philosophy. That line of thought seems to be a mistake. On the other hand, the replacement of experience by language in the work of people like Sellars[1] did help convince people that if you could talk about linguistic behavior then you didn't really have to talk about experience or consciousness. That was a step forward....

MARCHETTI: Which philosophical issues or views do you think are definitely obsolete?

RORTY: Well, I hope that the attempt to say the language of natural science is privileged because it tells you how things really are, like the attempt to say that the language of religion is privileged because it tells you how things really are, is on its last legs. I would hope that the kind of philosophy which says "this is the ultimate context in which everything else has to be placed," will come to seem ludicrous.

MARCHETTI: Which philosophical view would you like to deliver to the third millennium?

RORTY: I think that the linguistic turn is probably permanent. That is, I think that philosophers in the future will talk less and less about mind or experience and consciousness and more and more about descriptive vocabularies. At least I hope that's the case.

Jonathan Haidt, "The New Synthesis in Moral Psychology"[2]

(2007)

Principle 4: Morality Is about More Than Harm and Fairness

If I asked you to define morality, you'd probably say it has something to do with how people ought to treat each other. Nearly every research program in moral psychology has focused on one of two aspects of interpersonal treatment: (i) harm, care, and altruism (people are vulnerable and often need protection) or (ii) fairness, reciprocity, and justice (people have rights to certain resources or kinds of treatment). These two topics bear a striking match to the two evolutionary mechanisms of kin selection (which presumably made us sensitive to the suffering and needs of close kin) and reciprocal altruism (which presumably made us exquisitely sensitive to who deserves what). However, if group selection did reshape human morality, then there might be a kind of tribal overlay...—a coevolved set of cultural practices and moral intuitions that are not about how to treat other individuals but about how to be a part of a group, especially a group that is competing with other groups.

---

1 Wilfrid Sellars (1912–89) was an American philosopher and a prominent developer of critical realism, a philosophy of perception.
2 Jonathan Haidt et al., "The New Synthesis in Moral Psychology," *Science* 316 (2007). DOI: 10.1126/science.1137651.

In my cross-cultural research, I have found that the moral domain of educated Westerners is narrower—more focused on harm and fairness—than it is elsewhere. Extending a theory from cultural psychologist Richard Shweder…, Jesse Graham, Craig Joseph, and I have suggested that there are five psychological foundations, each with a separate evolutionary origin, upon which human cultures construct their moral communities…In addition to the harm and fairness foundations, there are also widespread intuitions about ingroup-outgroup dynamics and the importance of loyalty; there are intuitions about authority and the importance of respect and obedience; and there are intuitions about bodily and spiritual purity and the importance of living in a sanctified rather than a carnal way. And it's not just members of traditional societies who draw on all five foundations; even within Western societies, we consistently find an ideological effect in which religious and cultural conservatives value and rely upon all five foundations, whereas liberals value and rely upon the harm and fairness foundations primarily (Fig. 1 and Table 1).

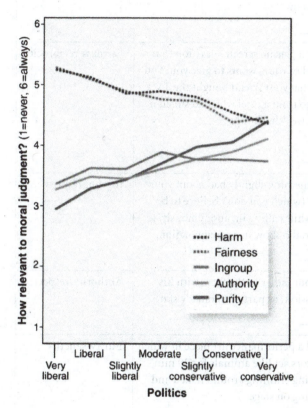

Fig. 1 Liberal versus conservative moral foundations. Responses to 15 questions about which considerations are relevant to deciding "whether something is right or wrong." Those who described themselves as "very liberal" gave the highest relevance ratings to questions related to the Harm/Care and Fairness/Reciprocity foundations and gave the lowest ratings to questions about the Ingroup/Loyalty, Authority/Respect, and Purity/Sanctity foundations. The more conservative the participant, the more the first two foundations decrease in relevance and the last three increase…All respondents were citizens of the United States. Data for 476 citizens of the United Kingdom show a similar pattern. The survey can be taken at www.yourmorals.org.

Table 1:

What's your price? Write in the minimum amount that someone would have to pay you (anonymously and secretly) to convince you to do these 10 actions. For each one, assume there will be no social, legal, or material consequences to you afterward. *Homo economicus* would prefer the option in column B to the option in column A for action 1 and would be more or less indifferent to the other four pairs. In contrast, a person with moral motives would (on average) require a larger payment to engage in the actions in column B and would feel dirty or degraded for engaging in some of these actions for personal enrichment. These particular actions were generated to dramatize moral motives, but they also illustrate the five-foundations theory of intuitive ethics…

	Column A	Column B	Moral Category
How much money would it take to get you to…			
1)	Stick a pin into your palm. $_____	Stick a pin into the palm of a child you don't know. $_____	Harm/care
2)	Accept a plasma screen television that a friend of yours wants to give you. You know that your friend got the television a year ago when the company that made it sent it, by mistake at no charge, to your friend. $_____	Accept a plasma screen television that a friend of yours wants to give you. You know that your friend bought the TV a year ago from a thief who had stolen it from a wealthy family. $_____	Fairness/reciprocity
3)	Say something slightly bad about your nation (which you don't believe to be true) while calling in, anonymously, to a talk-radio show in your nation. $_____	Say something slightly bad about your nation (which you don't believe to be true) while calling in, anonymously, to a talk-radio show in a foreign nation. $_____	Ingroup/loyalty
4)	Slap a friend in the face (with his/her permission) as part of a comedy skit. $_____	Slap your father in the face (with his permission) as part of a comedy skit. $_____	Authority/respect
5)	Attend a performance art piece in which the actors act like idiots for 30 min, including failing to solve simple problems and falling down repeatedly on stage. $_____	Attend a performance art piece in which the actors act like animals for 30 min, including crawling around naked and urinating on stage. $_____	Purity/sanctity
	Total for column A: $_____	Total for column B: $_____	

Research on morality beyond harm and fairness is in its infancy; there is much to be learned. We know what parts of the brain are active when people judge stories about runaway trolleys and unfair divisions of money. But what happens when people judge stories about treason, disrespect, or gluttony? We know how children develop an ethos of caring and of justice. But what about the development of patriotism, respect for tradition, and a sense of sacredness? There is some research on these questions, but it is not yet part of the new synthesis, which has focused on issues related to harm and fairness.

In conclusion, if the host of that erudite quiz show were to allow you 60 seconds to explain human behavior, you might consider saying the following: People are self-interested, but they also care about how they (and others) treat people, and how they (and others) participate in groups. These moral motives are implemented in large part by a variety of affect-laden intuitions that arise quickly and automatically and then influence controlled processes such as moral reasoning. Moral reasoning can correct and override moral intuition, though it is more commonly performed in the service of social goals as people navigate their gossipy worlds. Yet even though morality is partly a game of self-promotion, people do sincerely want peace, decency, and cooperation to prevail within their groups. And because morality may be as much a product of cultural evolution as genetic evolution, it can change substantially in a generation or two. For example, as technological advances make us more aware of the fate of people in faraway lands, our concerns expand and we increasingly want peace, decency, and cooperation to prevail in other groups, and in the human group as well.

READING 48C:

Nick Bostrom, "Transhumanist Values"[1]

(2003)

1. What Is Transhumanism?

Transhumanism is a loosely defined movement that has developed gradually over the past two decades. It promotes an interdisciplinary approach to understanding and evaluating the opportunities for enhancing the human condition and the human organism opened up by the advancement of technology. Attention is given to both present technologies, like genetic engineering and information technology, and anticipated future ones, such as molecular nanotechnology and artificial intelligence.

The enhancement options being discussed include radical extension of human health-span, eradication of disease, elimination of unnecessary suffering, and augmentation of human intellectual, physical, and emotional capacities. Other transhumanist themes include space colonization and the possibility of creating superintelligent machines,

---

1 Nick Bostrom, "Transhumanist Values," in Frederick Adams, ed., *Ethical Issues for the 21st Century* (Philosophical Documentation Center Press, 2003); reprinted in *Review of Contemporary Philosophy* vol. 4 (May 2005).

along with other potential developments that could profoundly alter the human condition. The ambit is not limited to gadgets and medicine, but encompasses also economic, social and institutional designs, cultural development, and psychological skills and techniques.

Transhumanists view human nature as a work-in-progress, a half-baked beginning that we can learn to remold in desirable ways. Current humanity need not be the endpoint of evolution. Transhumanists hope that by responsible use of science, technology, and other rational means we shall eventually manage to become posthuman, beings with vastly greater capacities than present human beings have....

In contrast to many other ethical outlooks, which in practice often reflect a reactionary attitude to new technologies, the transhumanist view...take[s] a more proactive approach to technology policy. This vision, in broad strokes, is to create the opportunity to live much longer and healthier lives, to enhance our memory and other intellectual faculties, to refine our emotional experiences and increase our subjective sense of well-being, and generally to achieve a greater degree of control over our own lives. This affirmation of human potential is offered as an alternative to customary injunctions against playing God, messing with nature, tampering with our human essence, or displaying punishable hubris.

Transhumanism does not entail technological optimism. While future technological capabilities carry immense potential for beneficial deployments, they also could be misused to cause enormous harm, ranging all the way to the extreme possibility of intelligent life becoming extinct. Other potential negative outcomes include widening social inequalities or a gradual erosion of the hard-to-quantify assets,...such as meaningful human relationships and ecological diversity. Such risks must be taken very seriously, as thoughtful transhumanists fully acknowledge.

Transhumanism has roots in secular humanist thinking, yet is more radical in that it promotes not only traditional means of improving human nature, such as education and cultural refinement, but also direct application of medicine and technology to overcome some of our basic biological limits.

2. Human Limitations

The range of thoughts, feelings, experiences, and activities accessible to human organisms presumably constitute only a tiny part of what is possible. There is no reason to think that the human mode of being is any more free of limitations imposed by our biological nature than are those of other animals.... [W]e humans may lack the capacity to form a realistic intuitive understanding of what it would be like to be a radically enhanced human (a "posthuman") and of the thoughts, concerns, aspirations, and social relations that such humans may have.

Our own current mode of being, therefore, spans but a minute subspace of what is possible or permitted by the physical constraints of the universe (see Figure 1). It is not farfetched to suppose that there

Figure 1

We ain't seen nothin' yet (not drawn to scale). The term "transhuman" denotes transitional beings, or moderately enhanced humans, whose capacities would be somewhere between those of unaugmented humans and full-blown posthumans. (A transhumanist, by contrast, is simply somebody who accepts transhumanism.)

The Space of Possible Modes of Being

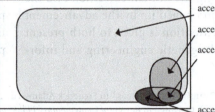

accessible by posthumans

accessible by transhumans

accessible by humans

accessible by animals

are parts of this larger space that represent extremely valuable ways of living, relating, feeling, and thinking.

...

BODY FUNCTIONALITY

We enhance our natural immune systems by getting vaccinations, and we can imagine further enhancements to our bodies that would protect us from disease or help us shape our bodies according to our desires....

A more radical kind of upgrade might be possible if we suppose a computational view of the mind.[1] It may then be possible to upload a human mind to a computer, by replicating *in silico*[2] the detailed computational processes that would normally take place in a particular human brain. Being an upload would have many potential advantages, such as the ability to make back-up copies of oneself (favorably impacting on one's life-expectancy) and the ability to transmit oneself as information at the speed of light. Uploads might live either in virtual reality or directly in physical reality by controlling a robot proxy....

3. The Core Transhumanist Value: Exploring the Posthuman Realm

... [T]he transhumanist view that we ought to explore the realm of posthuman values does not entail that we should forego our current values. The posthuman values can be our current values, albeit ones that we have not yet clearly comprehended.

Transhumanism does not require us to say that we should favor posthuman beings over human beings, but that the right way of favoring human beings is by enabling us to realize our ideals better and that some of our ideals may well be located outside the space of modes of being that are accessible to us with our current biological constitution....

Depending on what our views are about what constitutes personal identity, it could be that certain modes of being, while possible, are not possible for us, because any being of such a kind would be so different from us that they could not be us. Concerns of this kind are familiar from theological discussions of the afterlife. In Christian theology, some souls will be allowed by God to go to heaven after their time as corporal creatures is over. Before being admitted to heaven, the souls would undergo a purification process in which they would lose many of their previous bodily attributes. Skeptics may doubt that the resulting minds would be sufficiently similar to our current minds for it to be possible for them to be the same person. A similar predicament arises within transhumanism: if the mode of being of a posthuman being is radically different from that of a human being, then we may doubt whether a posthuman being could be the same person as a human being, even if the posthuman being originated from a human being.

We can, however, envision many enhancements that would not make it impossible for the post-transformation someone to be the same person as the pre-transformation person. A person could obtain quite a bit of increased life expectancy, intelligence, health, memory, and emotional sensitivity, without ceasing to exist in the process....

---

1 A computational view of the mind, called the computational theory of mind (CTM) in philosophy of mind, holds that certain mental processes are computational processes, i.e., they are the same processes as those of a computer or any thinking machine.

2 Latin for 'in silicon.' It refers to the main material used to make semiconductor computer chips, and the expression usually means 'performed on computer or via computer simulation.' In philosophy of mind, silicon is often contrasted with carbon since carbon is the main material of organic compounds and a common element of all known life forms, including human beings and their brains. The functionalist view of the mind holds that the same mental states, which are identified in terms of their functions, can be found in different material structures or substrates.

Preservation of personal identity, especially if this notion is given a narrow construal, is not everything. We can value other things than ourselves, or we might regard it as satisfactory if some parts or aspects of ourselves survive and flourish, even if that entails giving up some parts of ourselves such that we no longer count as being the same person....

Transhumanism promotes the quest to develop further so that we can explore hitherto inaccessible realms of value. Technological enhancement of human organisms is a means that we ought to pursue to this end....

5. Derivative Values

From these specific requirements flow a number of derivative transhumanist values that translate the transhumanist vision into practice....

To start with, transhumanists typically place emphasis on individual freedom and individual choice in the area of enhancement technologies. Humans differ widely in their conceptions of what their own perfection or improvement would consist in....

Another transhumanist priority is to put ourselves in a better position to make wise choices about where we are going. We will need all the wisdom we can get when negotiating the posthuman transition. Transhumanists place a high value on improvements in our individual and collective powers of understanding and in our ability to implement responsible decisions....

[A] certain epistemic tentativeness is appropriate, along with a readiness to continually reassess our assumptions as more information becomes available....

Since technological development is necessary to realize the transhumanist vision, entrepreneurship, science, and the engineering spirit are to be promoted....

Transhumanism advocates the well-being of all sentience, whether in artificial intellects, humans, and non-human animals (including extraterrestrial species, if there are any). Racism, sexism, speciesism, belligerent nationalism, and religious intolerance are unacceptable....

Finally, transhumanism stresses the moral urgency of saving lives, or, more precisely, of preventing involuntary deaths among people whose lives are worth living. In the developed world, aging is currently the number one killer. Aging is also the biggest cause of illness, disability and dementia.... Anti-aging medicine is, therefore, a key transhumanist priority. The goal, of course, is to radically extend people's active health-spans, not to add a few extra years on a ventilator at the end of life.

Since we are still far from being able to halt or reverse aging, cryonic suspension of the dead should be made available as an option for those who desire it. It is possible that future technologies will make it possible to reanimate people who have [been] cryonically suspended. While cryonics might be a long shot, it definitely carries better odds than cremation or burial.

Questions

1. Rorty suggests that one of pragmatism's biggest contributions to ethics is the way it definitively undermined Kantian morality. Explain the difference between Rorty's pragmatism and Kantian ethics.
2. Rorty both believes in modern science and does not believe in modern science. Explain. Do you agree with him, or not? Why?
3. Haidt's approach to morality is scientific and seeks to understand morality through

the genetic and cultural evolution of the human species. Do you think this is a valid way of understanding morality? Or is there something missing in this approach? Why, why not?

4. Try filling in the blanks for two of the scenarios in Table 1 in the Haidt reading, and explain what the results say about your moral philosophy.

5. Do you find the "transhumanist" idea of uploading your mind to a computer a worthwhile way of having an extended life? Why, why not? Would a drive on a computer qualify as a human being and enjoy rights?

6. Briefly describe the core transhumanist values as described by Bostrum. Do you disagree with any of these values? If so, which ones and why?

7. Do you agree with Bostrom regarding his posthuman prediction for the future of humanity? Is this the future or is this just science fiction?

8. Would a technologically-enhanced human being have to confront the same or different moral challenges than ordinary "biological" human beings? Explain with examples.

Suggested Readings

For Rorty's political views, see David McClean, *Richard Rorty, Liberalism, and Cosmopolitanism* (2014).

Other sources on postmodernism include Michael Williams, "Jesus, Pioneer of Post-Modern Ethics" (1999); Frederick Ferré, *Toward a Constructive Postmodern Ethics* (2001); and E. Jeffrey Popke, "Poststructuralist Ethics" (2016). Or see the bibliography on "anti-theory ethics" in Lawrence Hinman's *Ethics Updates* at ethics.sandiego.edu.

For comparative sources, see Jin Y. Park, *Buddhism and Postmodernity* (2010), and Jae-Seong Lee, *Postmodern Ethics, Emptiness, and Literature* (2015). In applied ethics, see Andrew Gustafson, "Making Sense of Postmodern Business Ethics" (2000), and A.T. Nuyen, "Lyotard's Postmodern Ethics and Information Technology" (2004).

Haidt has published two much-discussed books: *The Happiness Hypothesis* (2006) and *The Righteous Mind* (2012). There is a related philosophical literature. See, for example, Heidi Maibom, ed., *The Routledge Handbook of Philosophy of Empathy* (2017).

There is a growing social science literature on morality. In "Lean Not on Your Own Understanding" (2013), for example, Jared Piazza and Justin Landy provide data that measures the attitudes of those who subscribe to divine command theory. There are also evolutionary studies, such as Leonard D. Katz, ed., *Evolutionary Origins of Morality* (2000), and N. Hauser, *How Nature Designed Our Universal Sense of Right and Wrong* (2006).

Daniel Berthold-Bond implicitly questions the viability of transhumanist ethical theories in "A Debate between Hegel and Heidegger on the Meaning of Ecological Thinking" (1994). See also Andrew Bloodworth, "Enhancing Human Abilities and Characteristics Beyond Normality" (2015); William D. Casebeer, "Ethics and the Biologized Battlefield" (2010); and Dave Shunk, "Ethics and the Enhanced Soldier of the Near Future" (2015).

Three popular magazines discuss timely philosophical issues and can be found online: *Philosophy Now, The New Philosopher,* and *The Philosopher's Magazine.*

Epilogue

The New Cosmopolitanism: Why the History of Moral Philosophy Needs to Be Taught in Our Universities

Louis Groarke, Paul Groarke, and Paolo Biondi

As is evident in this text, we have proposed a broad historical approach to the teaching of undergraduate ethics, which we have dubbed "the new cosmopolitanism." This inclusive approach is based on a chronological, multicultural investigation of the historical ethical tradition that considers social, political, religious, and even psychological factors that gave rise to different theories without, however, reducing ethics to a sociological or merely historical analysis. We argue that the main business of moral philosophy is the achievement of wisdom understood as an innovative sort of judgment that is able to use big-picture knowledge to make sense of human aspiration in complicated contexts. The wisdom aspiration cannot be reduced to any recipe or formula; it is an ability, a sense of discernment that improves with exercise, something that is built up through repeated and sincere reflection on diverse viewpoints.

In our view, this wisdom-centered approach returns ethical inquiry to its roots and focuses on the real goal of moral philosophy by engaging with substantive everyday concerns that confront people who aim to live fulfilling lives of practical rectitude. We recommend going back to the beginning of human history, following along with primary source material from historical authors who do not separate applied ethics from theoretical ethics. We need to acknowledge that any discussion of practical issues depends ultimately on broad principles that reflect our understanding of reality and human nature. It is best to keep the connections between metaphysical, epistemological, and moral commitments front-and-center where they can be reviewed and inspected in an ongoing critical light. We also leave a larger place for religious traditions both East and West and for minority voices. This opens up the canon to a wider range of authorities, without omitting, of course, cornerstone philosophers such as Aristotle, Kant, and Mill.

The perspective we want to present here reflects the combined experience of the three authors teaching undergraduate university ethics over the years. The approach we recommend is intended as a challenge to the conventional curriculum, which can be traced to a number of factors, including an Enlightenment disparagement of history, an analytic suspicion about the epistemological rigor of moral judgements, liberal worries about conformity to a tradition, and even a post-modernist disenchantment with Western philosophy. The present curriculum is liable to reduce morality to matters of liberal justice; it may overemphasize specialized issues of moral epistemology and focus single-mindedly on intractable matters of moral disagreement (for example, between deontology and consequentialism); it often ignores the religious aspirations of students and avoids discussion of the larger metaphysical issues. Such overly narrow treatments leave students with few ethical principles to fall back on when dealing with everyday moral questions.

The term 'cosmopolitan' is associated with the ancient Stoics and derives from the Greek words for world or universe (*kosmos*) and citizen (*politēs*). These philosophers strove to develop a "cosmopolitan" ethics insofar as they saw themselves, not as members of a particular society, but as citizens of the universe (and sons and daughters of Zeus). The Roman Stoic Cicero, in *De Officiis* (*On Duty*), traces "the [moral] principles of fellowship and society that Nature has established among humans" back to an ultimate "first principle" that is to be found "in the connection subsisting between all the members of the human race, and that bond of connection is reason and speech, which by the processes of teaching and learning, of communicating, discussing, and reasoning, associate men together and unite them in a sort of natural fraternity."[1]

Although we are not arguing here for an exclusively Stoic approach to moral pedagogy, the basic Stoic idea that human beings are united by reason and language in a common bond of fraternity provides the background for a pedagogical approach to undergraduate ethics that is sensitive to all the major ethical traditions. The new cosmopolitanism we wish to promote recognizes that there are elements in every tradition that contribute to our moral understanding of the human condition and the world. Wide-ranging discussion based on a history of ideas approach puts us in the best position to deal with the moral issues that confront us in a pluralistic age faced with a multitude of complex issues. This new approach includes the analytical, epistemological, deontological, utilitarian, and liberal approaches within the parameters of a much broader historical account.

1. The New Cosmopolitanism

So, what do we mean by the "new cosmopolitanism"? First and foremost, we mean taking the history of ethics seriously. In the classroom, this means:

---

1 Cicero, *De Officiis*, trans. Walter Miller (London: William Heinemann; New York: The Macmillan Co, 1913), Book I, Chapter 16, 50.

- studying primary sources from the history and tradition of moral philosophy in a chronological order to learn from the accumulated experience of human beings who lived and live in different times and places;
- examining a variety of higher human aspirations and notions of the good life and good character as proposed by people past and present;
- understanding that despite many differences in time and place, human beings have reached a general agreement on a number of points regarding ethics over the course of time; and
- teaching people how to make wiser choices, according to their own consciences, within the broader context of living a moral life.

In the rest of this epilogue, we will argue that the implicit opposition to the historical approach to teaching ethics depends on an uncritical mythology, that cross-cultural views can be and are often compatible with each other, that the diversity of moral views one does encounter in the tradition teaches tolerance and sparks deeper reflection, that historical theories provide a more diverse and comprehensive selection of case-studies (which helps students develop their own ethical skills and moral judgment), that studying the historical origins of our modern-day moral vocabulary is an important step in moral understanding, that the ancients were correct in thinking of ethics primarily as a practical tool, and, lastly, that wisdom, properly understood, still ranks as the primary goal of moral theory.

2. A Prevalent Mythology

Let us begin by dispensing with three widespread notions, often taken for granted in public discussion, that hinder any prospect of serious change in moral pedagogy:

i) The idea that progress has made the moral philosophy of the past irrelevant and even dangerous.

Modern philosophy often seems to operate on the premise that historical advances have made the work of previous philosophers irrelevant. Such a trope often takes two forms. According to one view, earlier thinkers were at the mercy of superstition and unscientific religious views. According to another, historical moral views contain a wide array of racist, sexist, imperialist, hegemonic, colonialist, authoritarian attitudes, which may harm students. Such attitudes are based on exaggerations but they are, nonetheless, a potent cultural force.

It is not as if the past has nothing to teach us. Moral philosophy is not science, where inevitable progress often turns old theories into outdated curiosities. We share a common humanity with the ethical thinkers of the past, who thought their way through many of the everyday problems that we face and came up with time-tested responses to the human condition. Humanity has a story, which we have to learn, again and again, to fully understand what makes us human.

In *A Short History of Ethics*, Alasdair MacIntyre argues that different historical periods produce different moralities, focusing on different aspects of our ethical life.[1] We may take issue with some aspects of MacIntyre's argument, but his position helps to explain why the moral views of other periods provide such a useful corrective to our own narrow cultural concerns and ethnocentrism.[2] The history of humanity is diverse and pluralistic. Our approach to ethics needs to reflect this.

The reality is that the students in moral philosophy courses are already aware, however imperfectly, of teachings from figures as varied as Laozi, the Buddha, Plato, Jesus, Kant, Nietzsche, Marx, and Ayn Rand. If we are going to satisfy their needs and adequately answer their questions, we accordingly need a comprehensive approach that critically examines the loose compilation of ideas that floats through their world. We need to replace desultory acquaintance with serious analysis. This means going back to original sources.

Moreover, the original sources are not quite the racist, misogynist, sexually repressed, imperialist tirades we have been led to suspect. There are objectionable passages, of course, but the tradition is very wide, with ample space for contrary views. Plato believes that men and women are intellectually equal; Aristotle condemns tyranny; Epictetus was a slave; Thomas Aquinas thought that sexuality was a human good, and so on.

ii) A value-neutral (liberal) approach is open to *more* diversity and leaves *more* room for personal choice.

A second myth that still flourishes in the public sphere is that an epistemologically reticent, value-neutral, liberal approach is somehow more open to diversity and, implicitly, that by refusing to investigate the substantive content of different worldviews we somehow leave more room for personal choice. But a liberalism that closes down the discussion of past authors is contradictory and self-defeating. We want to make good choices for ourselves; that is the moral goal. We hardly aid this endeavor by shutting down any real discussion of the most fundamental issues in ethics.

It is important to emphasize that the claim from certain philosophers that their theories are value-neutral must itself be acknowledged as a partisan ethical position that rests on particular values and beliefs. Once we dig beneath the surface, we discover that many of those philosophers who propose value-neutrality in fact hold quite definite positions on a wide array of moral issues. They may be right or wrong, but they affirm and maintain specific positions just like other philosophers.

In Western culture, at least, the traditional subject of ethics is "the idea of the good." This is a substantive inquiry. Any overly narrowly approach that claims, in effect, that morality is either a matter of feelings, of self-interest, of personal preference, of private opinion prevents us from rationally discussing those questions that have historically been the subject of the ethical inquiry. This is unhealthy, since it implies that one idea of the good

---

1 Alasdair MacIntyre, *A Short History of Ethics: A History of Moral Philosophy from the Homeric Age to the Twentieth Century* (Notre Dame, IN: Notre Dame University Press, 1966, 1998).

2 Different moral traditions are not as incommensurable as MacIntyre suggests.

is as justified as any other, which no one really believes and which does little to advance the cause of moral reflection.

Michael Sandel argues that a "just society involves reasoning together about the good life." He comments:

> Rather than avoid the moral and religious convictions that our fellow citizens bring to public life, we should attend to them more directly—sometimes by challenging and contesting them, sometimes by listening to and learning from them. There is no guarantee that public deliberation about hard moral questions will lead in any given situation to agreement—or even to appreciation for the moral and religious views of others. It's always possible that learning more about a moral or religious doctrine will lead us to like it less. But we cannot know until we try.[1]

We agree with Sandel, especially when it comes to the undergraduate ethics curriculum, that a "politics of moral engagement" is a more inspiring ideal than a politics of avoidance. It is also a more promising basis for a just society and offers a better learning experience in the classroom.

One may, of course, take whatever attitude one wants towards particular religious or cultural beliefs, but the idea that one can teach ethics responsibly to university students without examining the foundations of our ethical views is short-sighted. Many influential positions in moral philosophy are linked inextricably to religious, metaphysical, or even political views of one sort or another; they cannot be understood outside their extra-philosophical foundations. It behooves us explore those foundations, at least to the extent that time permits.

iii) Philosophers always disagree with one another.

A third myth that has undermined the teaching of ethical history is the idea that philosophers always disagree with one another. The reality is that there is a wide degree of consensus on many ethical issues. Authors generally agree, for example, that the taking of innocent human life is a very serious matter, that the punishment should fit the crime, that promise-keeping is a good thing to do, that cruelty is vile and base, that telling the truth is admirable, that friendship carries special responsibilities, that we should protect the vulnerable, that we should give thanks, that generosity is noble, that courage is onerous and praiseworthy, and so on. Of course, there are strange, complicated, highly unusual circumstances in which moral reasoning has to bend to fit the circumstances. Even Kant, for example, makes a distinction between perfect and imperfect duties. In addition to heated disagreements, one, occasionally, encounters opinions that seem monstrous. But there is more agreement than most contemporary commentators are willing to admit. And even in the face of inevitable disagreement, there are many good reasons for discussing controversial moral issues.

---

1 Michael Sandel, *Justice: What's the Right Thing to Do?* (New York: Farrar, Straus and Giroux, 2009), pp. 268–69.

To begin with, this sort of exercise forces us to explore and examine our own views, which contributes to the Socratic project of knowing oneself or gaining self-understanding.

Secondly, it is good to investigate moral disagreement, for people (ourselves included) do sometimes change their moral views, and for the better. This is often because something they have read or heard strikes a chord that subsequently enlarges their understanding of a problem or a situation. In dealing directly with a variety of (sometimes discordant) values, we sometimes discover truths that we would not have discovered otherwise.

Thirdly, even when agreement is not possible, we may gain a better understanding of others and the reasons behind their beliefs through frank debate. Even when agreement does not result, increased mutual understanding may, and with this, mutual recognition and respect becomes more likely.

The cosmopolitan approach is not designed to protect worrisome views in the tradition from criticism. Indeed, students will better develop their rational skills when forced to respond to obviously dangerous views in the contemporary and the historical literature. The cosmopolitan approach to the ethical tradition qualifies, in fact, as a more robust form of liberalism than a pervasive soft relativism that seems to uncritically approve of a plurality of personal choices made by individuals without any serious testing of beliefs.

3. Positive Features of a New Cosmopolitan Approach

In this section, we review good reasons for turning to the history of ideas as a *modus operandi* for teaching moral philosophy.

3A. COMPATIBILITY

It is sometimes assumed that there is no adequate way to translate moral assertions from one culture into another. Such claims are exaggerated, however; this is not what we discover when we study primary sources in the historical record. Instead of differences, we continually find connections, resemblances, repeated tropes and themes. Even ethical disagreements between traditions and authors generally revolve around commonly accepted points of contention.

The ethical views of the ancient Greeks still resonate today. Stoics, Epicureans, Cynics, Skeptics, Aristotelians, Platonists—even Sophists—made major contributions to moral theory. That would not be possible if traditions were wholly incommensurable. But why should they be? We humans share a core set of human experiences: e.g., birth, death, childhood, parenthood, success, failure, illness, suffering, exclusion, loneliness, mistreatment, betrayal, social membership, and exile. These are circumstances faced by people in all traditions. The best moral thinking, in all traditions, converges around these very ordinary themes and realities.

Ancient Roman legal theorists spoke of *jus gentium*, the law of peoples. They used the term to refer to a sense of justice, based on reason, shared by Romans and all other peoples.

The history of ethics repeatedly makes reference to a body of values and principles much like *jus gentium*. Disagreement arises within the context of a larger human conversation with shared assumptions based on common experiences, that moves back and forth between participants. We cannot open students' minds through a narrow repetition of familiar views; a truly liberal education requires a wider knowledge of perspectives from many cultures and traditions.

3B. DIVERSITY

Making choices, whether collectively or individually, is an inevitable part of life. As Jean-Paul Sartre insisted, in presenting his doctrine of radical choice, everyone has to make a choice, for someone who refuses to choose has already made a choice. But making one's own choices is not enough. To responsibly choose one has to consider substantive issues in the light of reasonable belief and available evidence. This is what great thinkers in the moral philosophy tradition attempt to do. The history of ethics serves then as a diverse fund of moral ideas that can serve as the starting point for students embarking on the voyage of mature moral reflection. Familiarity with these texts provides students with the intellectual skills and abilities to make their own choices about how they are going to live out their lives.

Especially in a pluralistic, liberal society, students have to learn how to decide between competing ethical views. The historical record is particularly instructive in this context, since it forces students to consider a much wider range of beliefs. This has political as well as moral implications. In wide-ranging classroom discussion, students learn that reason and civil debate must prevail over social conformity, peer group pressure, cultural hegemony, or compulsion.

3C. CASUISTRY: PARTICULAR CASES

Contemporary anti-theorists such as Bernard Williams (and several others) argue that any theory with a limited number of principles lacks the resources it would need to fully capture individual cases precisely and definitively. They then reject theory in favor of a case-by-case analysis of ethical issues.

We believe that the anti-theorists make an important point but that they go too far. It is true that we normally acquire moral judgment by working our way through many examples. It does not follow, however, that there is nothing systematic about the moral enterprise. We all rely on theory, unwittingly or otherwise. It is in the background, providing an overall orientation to moral thoughts and attitudes.

As Aristotle maintains, moral theory has an inductive and a deductive phase: sometimes key moral concepts and principles have to be pointed out to us through examples, illustrations, stories, and anecdotes. Once we have induced these moral ideas, we have to apply them deductively to particular situations, reconsidering all the time, to make sure that we are reasoning correctly. As we have already suggested, theory needs to be supplemented by casuistry: the fitting of theories to particular circumstances, an overlooked element of the ethics tradition.

A cosmopolitan approach ties theoretical and applied ethics together. Theory pushes moral thought further, to foundational issues. But historical texts also supply a wide array of distinctive, multicultural examples. Having students apply theory to cases that are often different than the raging issues of the day can help them acquire the skills of casuistry without the interference of strong emotions associated with current partisan convictions on either side of the political spectrum. The recourse to historical examples provides more opportunities for students to practice such moral skills.

3D. A GENEALOGY OF MORAL LANGUAGE

There is an important place for a genealogy of moral terms in a course on moral philosophy. The hallmark of many of the most important philosophical thinkers is that they illuminate the meaning of ethical terms or introduce new terms, which capture something about the ethical dimension of our lives that other thinkers in the tradition have missed or misrepresented. We learn the meaning of key moral concepts by going back to their origins and tracing their historical development.

Any field of inquiry requires an adequate nomenclature. We have lost touch with much of the traditional language of ethical inquiry, which we often misunderstand. Consider, for example, what Aristotle means by the technical term *eudaimonia*. This Greek term is usually translated as 'happiness.' But this is not quite correct. For students today, 'happiness' usually connotes a transitory sense of pleasurable emotion. One can be happy one moment, then angry, then sad, and so on. *Eudaimonia* is nothing like that. It is better conveyed by words such as 'well-being,' 'flourishing,' and 'self-realization.' It is an abiding healthy state of mind and character that produces admirable acts over the entire length of a life. This well-being is not measured with reference to the individual's own desires but with respect to what is suitable for human beings objectively speaking. So 'happiness' meant something different to the ancient Greeks than it means to us.

And that is not all. In the history of western philosophy, this Greek notion was next given a Christian meaning by medieval thinkers such as Thomas Aquinas. Aquinas's term for human well-being and fulfilment was '*beatitudo.*' This, too, is sometimes translated into English by 'happiness,' although the terms 'beatitude,' 'blessedness,' or 'bliss' would be better and are sometimes employed. Aquinas chose this word because of his Christian belief in God and that human life continues after death, which enables human beings to be united with God and achieve this state of blessedness which is much greater than the state of *eudaimonia* achievable by human beings without the grace of God on Earth.

With the coming of the Enlightenment and Bentham's utilitarianism, the Greek notion of *eudaimonia* and the Christian notion of *beatitudo* eventually gave way to the secular meaning of happiness as pleasure prominent in present-day English. But happiness in this sense of "pleasant feeling" no longer conveys the same moral meaning.

Even within utilitarian moral thinking, this has led to serious problems of inconsistency. Hence Mill's strenuous (and contrived) attempt to distinguish between qualities as well as quantities of pleasure. Knowledge of this evolution in the meaning of human happiness (which has now come to mean, in contemporary utilitarianism, little more than preference-satisfaction) suggests a steady impoverishment of moral language. These are issues worth considering. They cannot be properly broached without some adequate chronological treatment.

Or to cite only one other brief example, consider the liberal concept of "rights," which can be traced all the way back to the Middle Ages (around the end of the twelfth century). Various moralists and theologians began to discuss whether a starving man is allowed to steal a loaf of bread.[1] Thomas Aquinas, for one, argues that the starving man has a right to the food because the baker has a duty to provide anyone starving with food.[2] Note the basic connection here between rights and duties. Aquinas thinks that rights begin in duties (that derive, ultimately, from God). One could at least argue that contemporary liberalism tends to emphasize rights and ignore duties. But rights do not just exist in a vacuum. It would be worthwhile to consider what reverse duties they presuppose and where we think they come from, whether that authority be God, reason, human nature, enlightened compassion, *jus gentium*, natural law, the happiness of the greatest number, or some other source.

There are many older terms dating all the way back to tribal times that have been overlooked, ignored, misunderstood. Think of concepts such as (in no particular order): *lex talionis*, *Dao*, *ren*, the Silver Rule, rectification of names, *shalom*, *ataraxia*, *phronēsis*, *physis*, *akrasia*, incontinence, "indifferents," invincible ignorance, the doctrine of double effect, cardinal/theological virtues, magnanimity, the seven deadly sins, *amour propre*, connaturality, proportionalism, Nietzschean resentment, the last man, Kierkegaardian despair, and so on. It is evident that a review of the moral terms and concepts used by earlier thinkers will challenge modern simplifications and stereotypes, and force students to develop their own moral vocabularies. This sort of inquiry should, at least, make students pause and reflect on their own understanding of morality.

A final point seems worth making. The contemporary approach to teaching moral philosophy has also been shaped (like everything else) by peer-reviewed academic journals. But the standards, appropriate for scientific or specialized technical disciplines, are largely out of place in the undergraduate ethics curriculum. Although many of the ethical thinkers of the past were writing in an academic setting, they often focused on fundamental moral questions rather than technical issues and tended to write in an accessible, even literary style. Even thinkers like Aristotle and Kant—both known for obscure prose—express moral ideas in a language that, with patience, opens itself up to ordinary logic and a non-technical understanding.

---

1 Peter Biller, "Intellectuals and the Masses: Oxen and She-Asses in the Medieval Church," in John Arnold, ed., *The Oxford Handbook of Medieval Christianity* (Oxford: Oxford University Press, 2014), p. 335.

2 Thomas Aquinas, *Summa Theologiae*, Fathers of the English Dominican Province, trans. (London: Burns Oates and Washbourne, second and revised edition, 1920), II.II.7. Question 66: "Whether it is lawful to steal through stress of need?"

3E. PRACTICAL ETHICS

John Sellars, in a discussion of the Roman Emperor Marcus Aurelius (121–180 CE), comments:

> From a modern perspective Marcus Aurelius is certainly not in the first rank of
> ancient philosophers. He is no Plato or Aristotle, nor even a Sextus Empiricus or
> Alexander of Aphrodisias. To a certain extent this judgment is perfectly fair and
> reasonable. However, in order to assess the philosophical qualities that Marcus
> does have and that are displayed in the *Meditations*, it is necessary to emphasize
> that in antiquity philosophy was not conceived merely as a matter of theoretical
> arguments. Such arguments existed and were important, but they were framed
> within a broader conception of philosophy as a way of life. The aim was not merely
> to gain a rational understanding of the world but to allow that rational under-
> standing to inform the way in which one lived. If one keeps this understanding
> of 'philosophy' in mind, then one becomes able to appreciate the function and
> the philosophical value of Marcus' *Meditations*.[1]

The *Meditations* became influential in the philosophical canon because it vividly expressed
how Stoicism is put into practice, and numerous people read it in order to find some guidance in their daily actions.

Epictetus, another Stoic, suggests that a philosophy which is solely theoretical is a waste
of time. It is not our ideas and abstract theories but the way we live our lives that matters at the end of the day. So ethics is not merely an interesting intellectual distraction;
it is something to be implemented in everyday living. It is necessary to examine whether
individual actions are right or wrong; but ethics is, more fundamentally, about choosing
a way of life. The study of ethics should, accordingly, include consideration of all sorts of
foundational issues.

Morality is sometimes presented in such a way that it gives students the impression that
morality is a marginal occupation that gets in the way of personal success and enjoyment.
This happens when morality is elaborated, mostly, in terms of rules about what we are
not supposed to do. But prohibitive rules, which have their place in ethics, form, at best,
the bare bones of morality. It is only when morality arises out of a broader conception of
human life that it compels conscientious compliance. To make sense of rules and norms,
we must place them within the larger context of a meaningful way of life. Rules offer a
means of achieving the purpose of life as we envision it, according to larger considerations.

3F. A RETURN TO WISDOM

The cosmopolitanism that we are advocating is a wisdom approach. One of the primary
goals of teaching ethics is to pass on the moral wisdom of the past so that we may learn

---

1 John Sellars, s.v. Marcus Aurelius, *Internet Encyclopedia of Philosophy*.

from it. If it is our ethical abilities that distinguish us as humans, it is even more important to cultivate the habits in our students that will teach them how to find satisfactory answers to difficult moral questions.

Whatever wisdom is, we all recognize it in certain people: perhaps a family member, an elder, an adept teacher, or a religious figure. We are drawn to these people because they have an active capacity, a power of discrimination, which gives them the ability to work through all sorts of moral considerations, when the need arises, sometimes with relative ease and proficiency, in order to find the appropriate moral response to a set of circumstances. Socrates, held up as the best example of wisdom in the ancient world, taught that wisdom is not a matter of accumulating more and more data. Using his method of *elenchus*, Socrates led interlocutors through a series of flawed arguments. It was not learning this or that argument by heart but the proficiency gained through such an exercise that mattered most of all. It follows that the natural way to teach wisdom lies in dialectical activity and is acquired by practice.

Students need to practice their broader dialectical skills in unexpected circumstances. Neglecting the larger tradition has removed the material that is needed for such an exercise, a material that already exists in the record left by the wise people who came before us when they confronted a wide diversity of moral questions and issues. We are not the first to think deeply about the right and the good. The natural way to teach ethics is to let students explore and discuss the historical record, taking what they need and discarding what they find of no use.

4. Concluding Remarks

The rigorous historical approach to teaching ethics that we propose is synoptic, implicitly cumulative, and recognizes the legitimacy of a multitude of views. Hopefully it provides students with a much broader understanding of ethical theory and leaves them informed, tolerant, and sophisticated enough to see through the moral, political, and religious simplifications we often meet with in popular debate. Students need a relatively deep foundation in ethical theory, if they are going to find sufficient motivation to make their own moral decisions, in the face of enormous social pressures to conform.

In our proposed curriculum, the primary concern is practical wisdom. Narrower approaches to moral philosophy do not equip students with a sufficient complement of arguments, principles, and values required to grapple adequately with the complex ethical issues that confront all of us in a pluralistic society. The new cosmopolitan approach we propose recognizes the connections between very different theories that nevertheless overlap. We might think of the genealogy of ethical theories like a family tree, in which many individual theories share in the same family heritage. Familiarizing oneself with the broad outlines of that tree is an integral part of any truly liberal education.

We need to return to the fund of moral wisdom that has been bequeathed to humanity by past thinkers the world over. The major thinkers in the different moral traditions—Eastern, Western, religious, secular, academic, or literary—took a much larger view of things. Ignoring this heritage oversimplifies our treatment of contemporary issues and narrows down our understanding of the human condition. It seems odd that university courses, however inadvertently, should contribute to the project of forgetting our moral past. This has occurred at the worst of times, when we face a wide array of contentious political and environmental issues that threaten to overwhelm us. Studying the history of moral philosophy can help us all, students and teachers and professors alike, by keeping us vigilant in a time of crisis.

Dictionary of Technical Terms

act utilitarianism: the type of utilitarianism that strives to maximize the pleasure (or preference-satisfaction) produced by each individual act (as opposed to rule utilitarianism)

ad hominem: Latin, 'against the man'; the argument (not always a fallacy) that one should
not accept what someone says because they have a bad or untrustworthy character

(the) aesthetic: *SEE* **(the) religious**

agapē: an entirely selfless love of the kind attributed to a benevolent God who loves others
for their own sakes without needing anything in return

agent, agency: a reference to someone who is capable of self-initiated, freely-willed behavior

agnosticism: the philosophical conviction that the existence or non-existence of God is
unknowable; in another version, a refusal to take a position on the question whether
God exists, or on any questions of principle

akrasia: Greek for 'weakness'; Aristotle's term for weakness of will

alienation: a condition in which one is estranged—separated—from oneself; Marx uses
the term to describe the moral experience of workers who find themselves used as mere
machines

altruism: putting the interests of others ahead of your own—usually selfish—interests

analytical (analytic) philosophy: the term describes the dominant approach in contemporary philosophy, which focuses on science, philosophy of language, and logic

anomie: Emile Durkheim's term for a condition in which an individual has not internalized the prevailing social norms and therefore lacks normal moral values; some

651

ethical theorists have argued that it is a product of a society without robust standards or punishments

anti-morality: the contemporary idea that we should give up trying to devise (complete) theories of morality, since they fail to capture the moral complexities that arise in concrete cases

apátheia: stoic apathy; the condition of being able to resist emotion as it clouds clear thinking about ourselves and the world

Apophthegmata Patrum: Latin, 'Sayings of the [Desert] Fathers'

applied ethics: that part of moral philosophy which focuses on 'application' of moral theory to concrete normative problems

aretē: a Greek and Aristotelian term for virtue, better translated as "human excellence"

asceticism: the practice of self-control or self-denial, often as a means of accepting the human condition, or for the sake of higher religious or supernatural goods

ataraxia: Greek, 'unperturbedness'; a conscious peace of mind or equanimity, related to the suspension of belief by the Skeptics, who saw it as the highest good

autonomy: self-rule; in Kant the ability to make moral, rational decisions

axiology: the study of the values that are at the origin of ethics and aesthetics

beatitudes: the eight blessings in Jesus's Sermon on the Mount, which declare that those who are unfortunate in this world will enjoy blessings in the next

begging the question: a move in argument, often unintended, which implicitly assumes (rather than argues for) the truth of the conclusion; which often includes the conclusion in its premises

bhikkhu: a Buddhist monk

bioethics: the specialized branch of moral philosophy that focuses on the ethical practice of medicine, the use of medical technologies, and related issues

calumny: a false, defamatory attack on someone designed to ruin their reputation; in Christianity, a serious sin

cardinal virtues: cardinal, from the Latin *cardo*, which means 'door hinge'; the four central virtues around which the rest of moral life was classically thought to revolve: temperance, courage, justice, prudence; central to Plato's *Republic*

(an ethics of) care: a feminist account of ethics that emphasizes compassionate relationships over liberal notions of justice; associated with Carol Gilligan and Nel Noddings

casuistry: the art of applying general ethical principles to complicated, specific circumstances

categorical imperative: Kant's term for the generalized form of the moral law, which is binding on all rational beings; a form of words that tells one what to do because that act is good in itself, not because it has good effects

charity: (from the Latin *caritas*); in Aquinas the most important virtue, understood as selfless love for God and (therefore) others; which connotes giving

civil disobedience: a deliberate, public violation of the law based on conscientious moral or political motives

common good: the good of the whole community, together

communitarianism: a moral or political view that emphasizes the importance of community over individual interests; the view, shared with many feminists, that individuals are always defined by their relationships to other people; a predominant view in the tribal, ancient, and medieval eras, usually discussed in opposition to the narrower forms of liberalism

Confucianism: the general approach to ethics associated with Kongzi (Confucius), his disciples and their students, known in China as 'the school of scholars' because of its emphasis on learning in the humanities, which was seen as an integral aspect of morality; Confucianism provided the basis for the introduction of civil service examinations, which were based on the idea that the advisors of a King or Emperor should be moral scholars

connatural knowledge: intuitive knowledge that comes through direct lived experience of moral virtues rather than through discursive reasoning; discussed by Maritain

conscience: a universal moral faculty that distinguishes between right and wrong, as discussed by Butler; in Aquinas, it operates through the application of moral knowledge to specific actions

consent: when agents freely agree to participate in an activity; a basic requirement for moral behavior in liberal thought

consequentialism: the idea that the moral status of an act depends on an evaluation of its consequences rather than on an evaluation of the actor's specific intentions; usually contrasted with deontology; discussed by Anscombe and Mill

continental philosophy: a philosophical approach that has dominated continental Europe, which embraces a rich historical analysis, with a focus on phenomenology and the interior of mental experience

corporal works of mercy: in Christian theology, seven acts of physical charity providing succor to the hungry, thirsty, unclothed, homeless, sick, imprisoned, and dead. *SEE* **spiritual works of mercy**

cosmology: from the Greek *cosmos*; in ethics, a moral view predominant in tribal pre-ancient and classical Chinese ethics, that evaluates right, wrong, and proper conduct from the perspective of the universe as a whole; conduct which is wrong upsets the cosmological balance and has repercussions which find expression, e.g., in fate

cosmopolitanism: the general idea that one is, morally (and now perhaps legally), a citizen of the world; a term originally coined and used by the Stoics

(moral) courage: one of the virtues, which in Aristotle and Aquinas includes rational control of the irascible passions

dao: in Chinese philosophy, the way (originally a path or road); a term that slowly acquired overwhelming cosmological and moral significance; the moral person follows the *dao* (the 'little' *dao* is the *dao* of a particular person); when the sage or the Emperor follows the *Dao*, the moral order is restored and the state and society flourish

Daoism: the older moral tradition in China, based on the *Dao*, which later found expression as an organized religion; associated with Laozi and the *Dao de jing*

dark night of the soul: a period of emotional and spiritual darkness in mystical practice that tests the mystic seeker's commitment; a state of purification

decalogue: the Ten Commandments (given to Moses)

deep ecology: the view that nature has intrinsic worth, not simply instrumental value as a means to human ends

defense of necessity: in Hobbes's moral philosophy, the idea that one is morally justified in doing whatever is necessary to preserve one's life; also a legal defense

deism: a belief in God that rejects supernatural intervention in the world and therefore emphasizes rational morality

deontological code: a list of specific duties that a professional (e.g., in medicine, law, or accounting) is obliged to uphold

deontology: any morality based primarily on the notion of duty

despair: lacking all hope; an emotional state of utter anguish and helplessness; in Kierkegaard, hating oneself; in Christianity, a very serious sin

deus caritas est: Latin from the vulgate, 'God is love' (1 John 4:8); the original *koinē* (Greek) has it that god is *agapē*

dharma (or *dhamma*): in Hinduism and Buddhism, virtue understood as behavior that is in keeping with the cosmic principles inherent in nature, in religious law, in social customs, in oneself

dignity: originally the idea that the members of society are entitled to a degree of deference from other members of society, the term is now sometimes associated with Kant, who held that rational individuals have intrinsic worth and cannot be used merely as means to some end

distributive justice: that aspect of justice that regulates the way in which goods, services, and political power are distributed in a society

divine command morality: the idea that morality coincides with or can be best defined as obeying the commands of God

'do no harm': usually considered the first principle of medical ethics; if one cannot help the patient, one should, at the very least, not harm them, or make their condition worse

(the doctrine of) double-effect: the view that there are moral actions which produce good and bad effects simultaneously, and that the bad effects are morally permissible if the good effect is the one intended and other conditions are met

ecumenism (and therefore **ecumenical**): the attempt to find common values and principles in different religious denominations and overcome denominational differences

(ethical) egoism: in moral philosophy, the belief that morality coincides with enlightened self-interest

elenchus: from the Greek, meaning 'cross-examination'; Socrates's favorite method

emotivism: the idea that morality is a matter of feelings, not reason, and that ethical statements are expressive, not propositional; an ethical view associated with Hume

Epicureanism: the hedonistic school founded by Epicurus, which placed a high value on private friendships and therapeutic philosophy; the word was used derogatorily by competing schools, such as the Stoics, who maintained that hedonism inevitably degenerated into the pursuit of baser pleasures over virtue; accordingly usually used nowadays to mean devotion to a life of pleasure, especially of good food

epochê: suspension of belief; which in ancient skepticism leads to peace of mind. *SEE ataraxia*

equality principle: in Rawls's contractarianism, the second, subordinate principle of justice divided into a fair equality of opportunity principle and a difference principle, that only allows differences in distributive justice that improve the lot of the worst-off

equipollence: in ancient skepticism, the balancing of arguments of equal weight on both sides of an issue to stop further craving for investigation

equity (*epikeia*): the virtue of sound judgment, which consists of applying the law correctly in circumstances that call conventional standards into question (in Aristotle, Roman law, and Aquinas); in an informal contemporary context the term refers, ambiguously, to fair and impartial treatment. *SEE* **casuistry**

Eros: the Greek god of love; hence erotic love is love that is prompted by or associated with desire for the loved object. *SEE agapē*

eudaimonia: literally, to have a 'good guiding demon' (or guardian angel); Aristotle's term for happiness understood not as a mere feeling but as human flourishing; to achieve an admirable destiny that fulfills all of one's promise and potential

euthanasia: from the Greek, meaning 'good death'; the practice of deliberately ending a life by active intervention or withholding medical treatment to relieve suffering; usually divided into 'active euthanasia,' actively ending someone's life, and 'passive euthanasia,' the practice of withholding medical treatment to hasten death; now often called 'assisted dying'

existentialism: a twentieth-century European philosophy that emphasized absolute freedom and responsibility of the individual; associated with Sartre, de Beauvoir, Camus

external goods: goods that depend on factors outside our control (e.g., money, health); deemed by Aristotle to be necessary for complete happiness

fable: a short tale intended to convey some often moral message or to display some example of wisdom and wit; as, famously, with Aesop

facts versus values: the emotivist claim that the descriptive claims of science and the prescriptive claims of ethics are independent of one another

fairness: a correctly measured or properly proportional judgment or act (usually, with respect to other people)

falasifa: from the Islamic term *falsafa* (literally, 'philosophy'); hence, the Islamic philosophers (largely inspired by Aristotle) with whom the more theological al-Ghazālī disputed

felicific calculus: Bentham's attempt to base the evaluation of moral acts on the precise measurement of the amount of happiness (or suffering) produced. *SEE* **utilitarianism**

feminism: used to describe a variety of sometimes conflicting political, social, and moral views that emphasize the rights and welfare of women; more broadly concerned with oppression; often accompanied by serious criticisms of historically antecedent values and practices

fideism: a philosophical position that encourages belief in God based wholly on faith rather than philosophical arguments

fidelity: the moral obligation of keeping one's promises

filial piety: the duty of respect, obedience, and honor one owes to one's parents, older family members, and ancestors; a fundamental moral duty in tribal and ancient cultures, and also in Chinese and other Asian cultures

first principle: a basic moral truth that depends on insight or intuition and is prior to argument

first, second, third, and possibly fourth wave: terms which have commonly been used to describe different generations of feminism, which moved from the struggle for rights to 'essentialism' to direct action and re-calibration; fourth-wave feminism has been called 'postfeminism'

five precepts: in Buddhism, basic training principles for lay devotees: do not harm other living beings; do not steal; do not lie; do not indulge in sexual misconduct or intoxication. Training rules for advanced spiritual practice include the eight precepts and the ten precepts

form of the good: in Plato, the highest immaterial idea and the source of all value

freethinker: generally, a nonconformist who rejects religious belief

free-rider problem: when an individual benefits from a good produced by a community without contributing his or her fair share of labor or effort to the cause

gehenna: essentially, hell; the Greek transliteration of the Hebrew *Ge Hinnom*, literally "Valley of Hinnom," a place outside the gates of Jerusalem historically linked to the practice of child-sacrifice and converted into something of a city-dump, where sewage, garbage, and corpses were continually being burned (for sanitation purposes)

golden rule: do unto others as you would have them do unto you; a central practical principle given a particularly salient emphasis by Jesus but implicit in most moral traditions. *SEE* **silver rule**

grace: the unearned help by God that facilitates moral or religious behavior

greatest happiness principle: the idea, adopted by Bentham and Mill, that the happiness of the greatest number is the proper criterion for moral evaluation

guilt by association: the argument (not always a fallacy) that we should not accept claims by someone who is part of an untrustworthy group

Hammurabi, law of: Hammurabi, King of Babylonia, was famous for his legal decisions, which were reproduced on a stele and exhibited in public

hedonic calculus: synonym for **felicific calculus**

hedonism: the moral philosophy that considers pleasure as the highest value and ultimate goal of human behavior

heteronomy: in Kant's scheme, moral failure understood as a lack of autonomy or successful self-government

Hippocratic oath: the formal vow taken by members of the ancient Greek school of medicine founded in Hippocrates's name, and still taken by some physicians; one of the earliest deontological codes

honor: a sense of dignity, self-respect, or noble worth that may be violated by oneself or others by wrong, disrespectful behavior; reputation that must be protected and defended, in some cases, by courageous behavior or even violence

hospitality: welcoming others, particularly strangers; a key tribal virtue

hubris: from the Greek, pride; overestimation of one's talents, power, or importance; mistaking oneself for a god; in ancient Greece, the worst fault

human law: *SEE* **positive law**

ideal observer theory: the view that moral knowledge consists of true propositions that describe the attitudes or judgments of a hypothetical ideal observer

idealism: a school of philosophy and metaphysics, which tends to adopt a communitarian point of view in politics and morality

induction: in moral reasoning, moving from examples or instances to the general principles on which morality is based

informed consent: consent that is accompanied by adequate information concerning relevant issues and consequences

inner citadel: a Stoic name for that internal domain of feelings, attitudes, and decision-making that we can control regardless of what happens outside us in the world

instrumental value: when something is not valued for its own sake, but is valued as a means of achieving something else. *SEE* **intrinsic value**

integrity: strength of character; undeviating adherence to one's principles regardless of appetites, obstacles, and opposition

intention: the interior motivation behind an act, what the individual is attempting to do; particularly important in deontology; key to Abelard's and Kant's concept of wrong

intrinsic value: when something is valued for its own sake; value inherent in the nature of something. *SEE* **instrumental value**

intuition: in modern usage, beliefs based on feeling; in an older tradition, knowledge of first principles derived from an immediate act of discernment without argument; hence ethical intuitionism, the view that feeling is at the root of moral knowledge

invincible ignorance: ignorance that is so ingrained (psychologically, culturally) that it can never be overcome; such ignorance may, to whatever extent, mitigate the responsibility of the ignorant agent

invisible hand doctrine: the economic and political doctrine associated with Adam Smith that, left to their own devices, agents will make the best individual decisions for the common good as if guided by an invisible hand; fundamental to liberalism

involuntary act: an act for which one is not held responsible because it was beyond one's control, either because of non-culpable ignorance or because it was a matter of compulsion

(ethical) irony: in Rorty and post-modernism, the notion that we should hold our foundational beliefs at arm's length, in the awareness that there are alternatives and that the deepest questions do not admit of proof

islam: an Arabic word meaning 'submission' or 'surrender,' a reference to the individual's submission to God; with an upper-case 'I,' the name of the religion of the Muslims. *SEE* **Muslim**

is-ought: often considered the critical problem in modern ethics; it arises from Hume's remark on the logical impossibility of deriving an ought-statement (with normative implications) from an is-statement, which merely describes the world; related to the naturalistic fallacy

jihad: an Arabic word meaning 'struggle'; there is a 'minor' and a 'major' jihad; only the major jihad contemplates war or force, which is only justified in defense of the faith

junzi: in Confucius, the son of a noble, a gentleman, 'superior person,' or the 'person with authoritative conduct'; ethically, the person with *ren*

jus ad bellum: Latin for 'right to war' or 'law of war'; the initial conditions under which a just (or lawful) war can be conducted

jus gentium: Latin for 'law of peoples'; beginning in Roman times, the international law understood as a consensus on points that different nations or groups could agree; more generally, the broad consensus about morality that develops through international discussion over time

jus in bello: Latin for 'the law in waging war'; the moral and legal conditions that must be met in conducting a just war

jus naturale: Latin for 'natural law'

just war theory: the doctrine, associated with Cicero, Augustine, and Aquinas in the western tradition, that lawful wars must fulfill certain conditions, usually justified as a defense to aggression

justice: the cardinal virtue that regulates our relationships with other people; often associated with the idea that we cannot harm others, but also including more positive demands such as our duty to care for our children or the requirement that we must treat other people fairly; law is the institution that enforces justice; hence, in Latin, *jus* (or *ius*) means both law and justice (and includes 'right')

karma: a term from the Sanskrit, meaning 'acting or doing'; most importantly, the general idea that good acts and intentions produce good effects on the doer and bad acts and intentions produce bad effects on the doer; a prominent idea in Indian religion and culture

'know thyself': from the Greek *gnōthi seauton*; the motto inscribed over the temple of Delphi; believed to be a key to a successful life and an effective cure for hubris

law: a compulsory prescription, which must be obeyed; in Aquinas, an ordinance of reason directed towards the common good promulgated by he or she who has care of the community

law [and therefore **right**] **of nature**: in Hobbes, the first principle of rational morality that one should attempt to cooperate with others but revert to hostilities if necessary; not to be confused with **natural law**

leap of faith: the idea, proposed by Kierkegaard, that the highest level of human achievement, the religious level, includes an element of paradox that requires an epistemological leap beyond logical argument

lex talionis: Latin, literally, the 'law of the sanction,' which is often mistakenly described as solely the law of retaliation; in fact it was a limiting principle, from pre-ancient times, which prevented the family of a victim from demanding more than an eye for an eye, a tooth for a tooth

li: the rites, a classical Chinese term, central in Confucianism, which is sometimes translated as 'propriety'; the term indicates that actions have been performed in accordance with the proper social and religious rituals, and is therefore in keeping with the moral and cosmological order

liberalism: a political or moral worldview, now associated with Kant and Mill, which generally argues for wider individual choice; used in many different (and sometimes conflicting) senses in non-technical discourse

liberation theology: a religious view developed by Latin American Catholics, under the influence of Marxism, which interprets the gospel message in a way that advocates a liberation from social, political, and economic oppression

libertarianism: an extreme form of liberalism that emphasizes individual freedom of choice as the most important principle or value

liberty principle: in Rawls's contractarianism, the first principle of justice that ensures the most extensive liberty of choice for all individuals (compatible with other requirements). *SEE* **equality principle**

maxim: in Kant's ethics, the rational principle that motivates an act: generally, in order to accomplish the purpose x, I do y

mean (or **golden mean**): in Aristotle (and elsewhere), the idea that moral virtue depends on having the right amount—not too much and not too little—of a specified character trait

mens rea: Latin for 'guilty mind'; now commonly called 'intention' and one of the necessary components of a crime; what Aquinas associates with the interior (invisible) mental act; as opposed to the *actus reus*, the external physical, visible act. *SEE* **intention**

mental reservation: a procedure associated with casuistry (and the Jesuits) whereby someone misleads by telling a literal truth in such a way that some greater evil is prevented; sometimes called mental equivocation; also, the practice of expressing the truth partly in speech and partly in the mind to conceal from humans what only god can know: called 'strict mental reservation'

meta-ethics: the study of the prior ideas and principles that give rise to normative conclusions (from 'meta,' beyond)

mixed act: in Aristotle, an act that is willful but also forced upon someone by the circumstances; e.g., a ship captain throwing goods overboard in a storm. Aristotle believes that such acts deserve forgiveness

(the) moral: *SEE* **(the) religious**

moral foundations theory: the contemporary sociological theory (developed by Haidt) that posits six basic dichotomies as the divergent foundations for multicultural moral views: care vs. harm, fairness vs. cheating, liberty vs. oppression, loyalty vs. betrayal, authority vs. subversion, and sanctity vs. degradation

moral luck: the idea that moral success may be hindered or frustrated by factors beyond our control (e.g., being raised by bad parents); most familiar contemporary consideration by Bernard Williams

morality: any system of principles, rules, or values that sets out standards for required conduct that typically apply universally; sometimes used in contrast to 'ethics,' which some thinkers view as a matter of more personal aspirations; but often these terms are used synonymously

mortal sin: in Christian theology, a very serious sin that severs an individual's positive relationship with God; a subject of interest in Augustine and Abelard; a sin which generally declares an open contempt of God. *SEE* **venial sin**

Muslim (or [now considered incorrect] **Moslem**): literally, one who submits or surrenders; an adherent of Islam. *SEE* **islam**

mysticism: the idea that there is a higher category of reality or human experience that exceeds logic and language but which can be accessed affectively and cognitively and which produces positive moral effects

natural law: the view that there is a moral law which is accessible to all through the faculty of reason; associated with the Stoics and Aquinas, but also with much earlier and later sources

naturalism: in contemporary technical discourse, usually the attempt to arrive at a purely natural (i.e., non-religious) explanation of things

naturalistic fallacy: for Moore, the mistake of identifying the non-natural property of the good with some natural feature of the world

negative freedom (and therefore **negative right**): the concept of freedom understood as (a right to) an absence of restrictions, found in a historical author such as Hobbes. *SEE* **positive freedom**

nihilism: literally, a belief in nothing; a rejection of all moral and metaphysical principles; the doctrine that there is no higher meaning in life; associated with Nietzsche

no-harm principle: the central doctrine of Mill's liberalism that we are free to act as we will as long as we do not harm (i.e., interfere with) others; earlier versions found in Hobbes and Epicurus

nomos: custom, convention; a term which suggests philosophically that moral customs and values are variable, relative, and artificial, and often a product of culture; the Greek philosophers debated whether morality was a matter of *nomos* or *physis* (nature)

non-cognitivism: the view that moral judgments merely report our feelings; associated with Hume and analytic philosophy; also called 'expressivism' or 'emotivism'

non-maleficence: the condition or requirement that one must not harm another

normative ethics: a subfield of ethics that studies how one ought to act, morally speaking; the standards for what makes an action right or wrong

noūs: (or noos) Greek term for 'mind, intellect, thought'; Aristotle's name for intuition as sense of an immediate intelligence that captures the first principles of knowledge

objectivism: the philosophical movement started by Ayn Rand that emphasizes radical egoism, scientific reason, heroic individual achievement, and free-market capitalism

open question test: the argument in Moore that any definition of the good in terms of natural properties can be questioned in turn and, consequently, there is no satisfactory natural explanation of the good. *SEE* **naturalistic fallacy**

original sin: in the Judeo-Christian tradition, the disobedience of Adam and Eve in the garden of Eden, which consisted of eating the fruit of the tree of the knowledge of good and evil; often construed as the original source of the tendency towards evil in humans

overman: *SEE übermensch*

paremiology: from the Greek *paroimía*, meaning 'proverb, maxim, saw'; hence, the study of proverbs

paternalism: intentionally benevolent decision-making that does not respect individual autonomy; treating someone as if one were their parent

perfectionism: the idea that humans can be morally improved and are capable of perhaps perfect rehabilitation; the view that morality is about perfecting, as much as possible, human character

person: a term originally attached to one's rank or role in society; legally a holder of rights; in Kant, a status or condition belonging to (and therefore synonymous with) an individual human being, who possesses infinite moral worth or dignity; an agent that possesses rights

personalism: the moral philosophy that maintains that all moral worth derives from the moral worth of persons; that personhood is the key metaphysical reality

pessimism: the view that suffering is inevitable and that immorality has a large role in the world; associated with Schopenhauer

phronêsis: Aristotle's term for the practical wisdom that guides competent decision-making; also translated, less rigorously, as 'prudence'

physis: objective moral nature understood as inherent in reality as opposed to artificial custom; the ancient Greek Sophists and the philosophers debated whether morality was a matter of *nomos* or *physis*

positive freedom (and therefore right): freedom understood as (a right to) well-being or welfare that may require contributions of goods or services from others. *SEE* **negative freedom**

positive or **human law**: statute law; human-made law that has been posited—written down or recorded by some legislative authority to regulate conduct within a particular society; in Aquinas, human law results from the application of natural law to specific circumstances

practical ethics: that field of moral philosophy that analyzes concrete normative issues by relying, primarily, on an immediate investigation of particular details rather than on a study of broad, abstract theories

pragmatism: a modern, American school of philosophy (associated with Dewey, James, and Charles Sanders Pierce) that, in ethics, recommended practical thinking based on what succeeds in ordinary experience

prescriptivism: the non-cognitivist theory that moral statements do not merely describe an opinion but are universal prescriptions (imperatives) that require compliance; coined by R.M. Hare

pride: the worst fault, in the Judeo-Christian tradition; the fault of Satan. *SEE* **hubris**

principle of charity: in philosophical discourse, the basic rule that we should interpret arguments, theories, and texts (e.g., from other schools, periods, and cultures) in a manner that is as convincing as possible

prisoner's dilemma: a moral puzzle in which self-interested agents (prisoners) appear to be worse off than co-operating agents

proportionalism: the idea that moral laws can be set aside if there is a proportionate reason for doing so (e.g., breaking a promise); usually with certain restrictions; used particularly in Roman Catholic theology

proverb: usually a short, pithy saying that encapsulates a moral truth, practical instruction, or wise teaching in a memorable way, frequently by parallelism; in early use, proverbs often provided an abbreviated means of repeating the point or 'moral' of a fable or traditional story

psychological hedonism: the idea (rejected by most ethicists) that moral behavior is always (or mostly) motivated by a self-interested psychology that seeks self-esteem or personal advantage

realism: (1) a perspective in politics or practical morality that steadfastly refuses to idealize the darker aspects of human life and aspiration; (2) in meta-ethics, the idea that the good is a real, objective, non-physical property of the world

reciprocal altruism: in evolutionary biology, the idea that an organism may benefit another organism to its own detriment in return for some future benefit; most moralists would argue that such behavior is too self-interested to be genuine altruism

rectification of names: the doctrine, prominent in the classical Chinese tradition, that moral behavior consists of acting in accordance with the name or title of the agent; e.g., a good doctor is a doctor who truly acts like a doctor

reductio ad absurdum: Latin for 'reducing to absurdity'; an argument strategy that reduces an opponent's position to a logical contradiction, i.e., an absurdity; a way of defeating opposing arguments

(ethical) relativism: in a moderate sense, the belief that morality changes according to the context; in an extreme form, the idea that there is no objective morality (most ethics accept moderate but not extreme relativism)

(the) religious: Kierkegaard sets out three stages of human accomplishment: 'the aesthetic,' which comprises diversion and immediate enjoyment; 'the moral,' which focuses on a loyal commitment to some aspiration (e.g., marriage); and 'the religious,' which requires religious faith. *SEE* **leap of faith**

ren (sometimes *jen*): a term in Confucianism and the classical Chinese tradition, usually translated as 'benevolence,' 'reciprocity,' or 'human-heartedness' (because it is what makes us human); the character, 仁, depicts the relationship between a person and someone else

resentment: in Nietzsche, "*ressentiment*," the worst fault; jealousy or spite in the weak man who lacks agency and plots a devious revenge

retribution: suffering of an equivalent wrong thought to be deserved by a wrong-doer

rhetoric: the art of persuasion, which in Plato is opposed to philosophy. *SEE* **Sophists**

right: to be entitled to something that should be provided by others; the corollary of a duty, being the recipient of benefits others have a duty to provide

rule utilitarianism: the type of utilitarianism that strives to maximize the pleasure (or preference-satisfaction) produced by conformity to the best set of rules for actions (as opposed to **act utilitarianism**)

sage: a wise person, particularly in the ancient world; someone who has attained the highest moral enlightenment; in Chinese philosophy, someone who brings the world into alignment with the *Dao* and therefore the moral and cosmological order

schadenfreude: from the German *Schaden*, harm, and *Freude*, joy, taking pleasure in someone else's misfortune; a moral fault (in English, epicaricacy)

scholasticism: a general term for later medieval philosophy known for its respect of tradition and very careful distinctions

seven deadly sins: medieval Christian catalogue of the worst vices: pride, greed, lust, envy, gluttony, wrath, and sloth

silver rule: do not do unto others what you would not want done to you; the negative formulation of the golden rule; given special emphasis in Confucianism but implicit in most moral traditions

sin: a religious conception of wrong as something that separates one from God

situation ethics (or **situationalism**): the doctrine that there is no hard-and-fast moral code but that moral requirements change according to each situation; popularized by Joseph Fletcher

skepticism: in ancient philosophy, the view championed by Pyrrho and later by Sextus that one should cultivate doubt (which they saw, in medical terms, as a purgative) in order to achieve peace of mind; in contemporary philosophy, the idea that knowledge claims or religious claims are inherently uncertain

slippery slope: in ethics, the idea that allowing minor instances of immoral behavior will lead, in time, to greater, even seriously evil, instances of immorality

social contract: in moral philosophy, the view that morality is based on an agreement with other members of society that we all promise to adhere to for the sake of our own safety and prosperity; or the hypothetical agreement that rational agents *would* make

social Darwinism: the belief that the order of human society is determined by natural selection (survival of the fittest)

sophia: a Greek word, used generally for 'wisdom'; but in Aristotle it refers to theoretical rather than practical wisdom; hence 'philosophy': *philia sophia* or love of wisdom

Sophists: a school of Greek rhetoricians famous for their moral relativism; notably, Protagoras

speciesism: a negative term used by animal rights activists to denounce what they see as human discrimination against other species; the favoritism practiced by humans towards other members of the same species

spiritual works of mercy: seven acts of intellectual charity in Christian theology: instruct the ignorant; counsel those in doubt; admonish sinners; bear wrongs patiently; forgive offenses; console the afflicted; pray for others. *SEE* **corporal works of mercy**

state of nature: the human way of living before (or without) government rule; in Hobbes, violent anarchy reigns; in Locke and Rousseau, things are not so dire

Stoicism: the moral school, started by Zeno of Citium, which focused on inner composure and social duty

subjectivism (moral): a denial of the objectivity of moral judgment; the belief that morality is a matter of private personal belief or choice

supererogatory act: an act of moral heroism; doing something that goes beyond the moral obligations required by duty

synderesis: or *synteresis*, a term of obscure origins, originally used by the Stoics, that came to mean the God-given spark of judgment (*scintilla conscientiae*) that, in Jerome and scholastic philosophy, recognizes the difference between right and wrong; root source of conscience

tathägata: Buddhist term for someone who has transcended the human condition and the cycle of birth and death

theological virtues: the religious virtues of faith, hope, and love (charity)

theoretical ethics: that branch of moral philosophy that focuses on general theories of ethics, as opposed to specific cases or specific normative judgments

three treasures: chief virtues in Daoism: compassion, frugality, and humility

tripartite soul: Plato's (or perhaps Socrates's) conception of the soul as comprising appetites, spirit (or will power), and mind (or reason)

two wrongs reasoning: the argument that one wrong should be permitted because another was or is already permitted; usually considered a fallacy

tyranny of the majority: the idea, in liberalism, that minorities are prey to moral authoritarianism and unfairly made to conform to the moral opinions of the majority

übermensch: Nietzsche's term for the greatest man who transcends societal restrictions and invents values for himself; translated as 'over-man' or 'superman'

utile: a measure of pleasure or preference satisfaction used in utilitarian calculations

utilitarianism: the view that morality can be seen as a universalistic hedonism, such that moral behavior ought to produce the greatest amount of happiness possible

veil of ignorance: in Rawls, ignorance of one's personal identity or situation that characterizes the hypothetical agents choosing the most just social contract

venial sin: a minor sin, which does not end one's positive relationship to God. *SEE* **mortal sin**

virtue: in classical thought, excellent character; a habitual inclination that serves morality

virtue ethics: a moral view that sees the development of good character traits as the foundation of morality and the criterion of moral success; associated with diverse thinkers, e.g., Aristotle, Confucius, MacIntyre

vita activa: Latin for 'active life'; a life devoted to serving the community; sometimes called the 'political life'

vita contemplativa: Latin for 'contemplative life'; a life devoted to thought, study, or prayer

weakness of will: the inability to withstand temptation, having a weak character. *SEE akrasia*

will to power: in Nietzsche, the evolutionary drive towards domination of others that is at the center of all forms of life and all human striving

wuwei: literally 'not doing,' the Daoist practice of following the *Dao* by inaction

xīnxué: the school of heart-mind, associated with Wáng Yáng-míng; a reaction to the school of principle

Permissions Acknowledgments

Anonymous. *A Book Of Contemplation The Which Is Called The Cloud Of Unknowing, In The Which a Soul Is Oned With God*, ed. Evelyn Underhill. 2nd edition. London: John M. Watkins, 1922. http://catholicspiritualdirection.org/cloudunknowing.pdf

Anonymous. Excerpts of "Dissoi Logoi: Two-Fold or Contrasting Arguments" adapted from *Contrasting Arguments: An Edition of the Dissoi Logoi*, trans. T.M. Robinson. Ayer Company, 1984. Copyright © 1979 by T.M. Robinson. Adapted by permission of the translator.

Anonymous. "The Greed of the Old Man and His Wife." *African Folktales*, ed. Paul Radin. Princeton University Press, 2015. Republished with permission of Princeton University Press conveyed through Copyright Clearance Center, Inc.

Anonymous. Excerpts from *The Life of Aesop, from Roger L'Estrange, Fables of Æsop and Other Eminent Mythologists*. London: A. & J. Churchill, and J. Hindmarsh, 1692. https://en.wikisource.org/wiki/Fables_of_%C3%86sop_and_Other_Eminent_Mythologists

Anonymous. "Little Rabbit Fights the Sun." *American Indian Trickster Tales*, ed. Richard Erdoes and Alfonso Ortiz. Penguin Books, 1998. Copyright © 1998 by Richard Erdoes and the Estate of Alfonso Oritz. Used by permission of Viking Books, an imprint of Penguin Publishing Group, a division of Penguin Random House LLC. All rights reserved.

Anonymous. "Warrior Maiden" from *American Indian Myths and Legends*, ed. Richard Erdoes and Alfonso Ortiz. New York: Pantheon Books, 1984. Copyright © 1984 by Richard Erdoes and Alfonso Ortiz. Used by permission of Pantheon Books, an imprint of the Knopf Doubleday Publishing Group, a division of Penguin Random House LLC. All rights reserved.

Abelard, Peter. Excerpts adapted from *Ethics*, trans. D.E. Luscombe. Oxford: The Clarendon Press, London: Oxford University Press, 1971. Copyright © Oxford University Press

1971. Adapted with the permission of Oxford Publishing Limited (Academic) through PLSclear.

Adams, Robert M. Excerpts from "Moral Arguments for Theistic Belief." *Rationality and Religious Belief*, ed. C.F. Delaney. University of Notre Dame Studies in the Philosophy of Religion, No. 1. Notre Dame: University of Notre Dame Press, 1979. Reprinted and adapted by permission of the University of Notre Dame Press.

Aesop. "The Wolf and the Shepherd," "The Fox and the Raven," "The Monkeys and the Two Men," "The Ant and the Cricket," "The Wolf and the Lamb," "The Boy Who Cried 'Wolf.'" "The Fox and the Stork," "The Wolf and the Lion," "The Dog, the Meat, and the Reflection," "The War between the Beasts and the Birds," "The Dog and the Hare," from *Aesop's Fables*, trans. Laura Gibbs. Oxford UK: Oxford University Press. Copyright © Laura Gibbs, 2002. Reproduced with the permission of Oxford Publishing Limited (Academic) through PLSclear.

Al-Ghazālī, Abū Ḥāmid Muḥammad ibn Muḥammad. Excerpts from *The Book of Fear and Hope*, trans. William McKane. Leiden: E.J. Brill, 1965.

Antiphon. "Truth," *Ancilla to the Pre-Socratic Philosophers: A Complete Translation of the Fragment in Diels, Fragmente der Vorsokratiker*, trans. Kathleen Freeman. Oxford: Basil Blackwell, 1948. pp 147–48.

Aquinas, St. Thomas. Selections from *Aquinas, Summa Theologiae, The Summa Theologica of St. Thomas Aquinas*, trans. Fathers of the English Dominican Province. 2nd revised edition, 1920. First Part of the Second Part: Questions 61–62, Questions 90–91, 94, 96; Second Part of the Second Part: Question 27, Question 101, Question 120. New Advent. http://www.newadvent.org/summa/

Aristocles of Messene. Excerpts adapted from *Testimonia and Fragments*, trans. Maria Lorenza Chiesara. Oxford: Oxford University Press, 2001. Reproduced with the permission of Oxford Publishing Limited (Academic) through PLSclear.

Aristotle. *Nicomachean Ethics*, from *The Nicomachean Ethics of Aristotle*, trans. F.H. Peters. 5th edition. London: Kegan Paul, Trench, Truebner & Co., 1893. The Online Library of Liberty. <http://oll.libertyfund.org/titles/903>

Athanasius. Excerpts of *The Life of St. Anthony*, ed. Philip Schaff and Henry Wace, trans. H. Ellershaw, from Nicene and Post-Nicene Fathers. 2nd Series. Vol. 4. Buffalo, NY: Christian Literature Publishing Co., 1892. Revised and edited for New Advent by Kevin Knight. Adapted by permission of Kevin Knight. http://www.newadvent.org/fathers/2811.htm

Augustine, Saint, Bishop of Hippo. Excerpts from *The Confessions of St. Augustine, Books I–X*, trans. F.J. Sheed. New York: Sheed & Ward, 1942. Copyright © 1942 by Sheed & Ward, Inc. *The Enchiridion on Faith, Hope and Love, A Select Library of the Nicene and Post-Nicene Fathers: Series I, Volume III*, ed. Philip Schaff, trans. Professor J.F. Shaw. Buffalo: The Christian Literature Company, 1887.

Aurelius, Marcus. "Meditations," *The Thoughts of the Emperor Marcus Aurelius Antoninus*, trans. George Long. London: Bell & Daldy, 1862. The Internet Classics Archive. http://classics.mit.edu/Antoninus/meditations.html

Ayer, A.J. Excerpts from *Language, Truth and Logic*. New York, NY: Dover Publications, Inc., 1946, 1952.

Barlow, Frances. Illustrations. "The Shepherd's Boy," "The Fox and Stork," "The Wolf and Lamb," "The Ant and Grasshopper," and "The Birds and Beasts," *Aesop's Fables with His Life: in English, French, and Latin*. London: H. Hills, 1687. LUNA: Folger British Book Illustrations Collection. https://luna.folger.edu/luna/servlet/view/search?q=call_number=%22A703%22

Beauvoir, Simone de. Excerpts from *The Second Sex*, trans. Constance Borde and Sheila Malovany-Chevallier. Translation copyright © 2009 by Constance Borde and Sheila Malovany-Chevallier. Used by permission of Alfred A. Knopf, an imprint of the Knopf Doubleday Publishing Group, a division of Penguin Random House LLC. All rights reserved.

Bentham, Jeremy. *An Introduction to the Principles of Morals and Legislation* (1789, 1823). Oxford: Clarendon Press, 1907. The Online Library of Liberty. http://oll.libertyfund.org/titles/bentham-an-introduction-to-the-principles-of-morals-and-legislation

Berndt, Ronald M., and Catherine H. Berndt. Excerpt from "Incestuous Dangidjara." *The Speaking Land: Myth and Story in Aboriginal Australia*. Rochester, VT: Inner Traditions International and Bear & Company. Copyright © 1994. All rights reserved. http://www.Innertraditions.com. Reprinted with permission of the publisher.

Bostrom, Nick. Excerpts from "Transhumanist Values." *Ethical Issues for the Twenty-First Century*, ed. Frederick Adams. *Journal of Philosophical Research* 30, Special Supplement (2005): 3–14. Excerpted and adapted from original source by permission of the Philosophy Documentation Center. https://doi.org/10.5840/jpr_2005_26

Butler, Joseph. *Fifteen Sermons Preached at the Rolls Chapel* (1726, rev. 1749) Cambridge: Hilliard and Brown; Boston: Hilliard, Gray, Little, and Wilkins, 1827. http://anglicanhistory.org/butler/rolls/01.html

Camus, Albert. Excerpts from *The Myth of Sisyphus*, trans. Justin O'Brien, translation copyright © 1955, copyright renewed 1983 by Penguin Random House LLC. Copyright © Alfred A. Knopf, an imprint of the Knopf Doubleday Publishing Group, a division of Penguin Random House LLC. All rights reserved. *Le Mythe de Sisyphe.* Copyright © Editions Gallimard, Paris, 1942. All rights reserved. Copyright © The Wylie Agency on behalf of Editions Gallimard and the Heirs of Albert Camus.

Carus, Titus Lucretius. Excerpts from *On the Nature of Things*, trans. Cyril Bailey. Oxford: Clarendon Press, 1910. The Online Library of Liberty. http://oll.libertyfund.org/titles/carus-on-the-nature-of-things

Catherine of Siena, Saint. Excerpts from *Saint Catherine of Siena as Seen in Her Letters*, ed./trans. with introduction by Vida Dutton Scudder. London, New York: J.M. Dent and E.P. Dutton, 1905, 1927. The letters to Gregory XI pp. 117–23; to Sister Bartolomea della Seta pp. 159–64; and to Master Raimondo of Capua pp. 342–45.

Christian, John. Adapted from *Behar Proverbs: Classified and Arranged According to Their Subject-Matter, etc., With Notes, Appendix and Two Indexes*. London: K. Paul, Trench, Trübner; 1891. Archive.org

Christina, Queen of Sweden. *Maxims and Sentences of Christina Queen of Sweden; Being the Employment of Her Leisure Hours. The Works of Christina Queen of Sweden: Containing Maxims and Sentences in Twelve Centuries, and Reflections on the Life and Actions of Alexander the Great.* London: Printed for D. Wilson and T. Durham, 1753. Hathi Trust Digital Library. https://catalog.hathitrust.org/Record/012502772

Cohen, Rev. Abraham. Adapted from *Ancient Jewish Proverbs*. London: John Murray, 1911. Archive.org

Empiricus, Sextus. Excerpts from *Outlines of Pyrrhonism (Pyrrhoniae Hypotyposes)*, trans. by R.G. Bury. Amhurst NY: Prometheus Books, 1990. pp. 17–27; 59; 74; 78; 256; 258–59; 261–65; 267.

Epictetus. "The Enchiridion," *The Moral Discourses of Epictetus*, trans. Elizabeth Carter. London and New York: J.M. Dent, E.P. Dutton, 1910. The Internet Classics Archive. http://classics.mit.edu/Epictetus/epicench.html

Etzioni, Amitai. Excerpts from "Communitarianism Revisited." *Journal of Political Ideologies* 19.3 (2014): 241–60. Copyright © 2014 Taylor & Francis. Reprinted by permission of Taylor & Francis Ltd, http://www.tandfonline.com. Adapted by permission of the author.

Fisher, Carlton D. Excerpts from "Because God Says So." *Christian Theism and the Prob-*

lems of Philosophy, ed. Michael D. Beaty. Copyright © 1990 University of Notre Dame Press. Notre Dame, IN: University of Notre Dame Press, 1990. Reprinted and adapted by permission of the University of Notre Dame Press.

Foot, Philippa. Excerpts adapted from "Virtues and Vices." *Virtues and Vices: And Other Essays in Moral Philosophy.* Oxford: Clarendon Press, 2002. Copyright © Philippa Foot 2002. Adapted with the permission of Oxford Publishing Limited (Academic) through PLSclear.

Gilligan, Carol. Excerpts from *In a Different Voice: Psychological Theory and Women's Development.* Cambridge, MA: Harvard University Press, 1982. Copyright © 1982, 1993 by Carol Gilligan. Adapted by permission of Harvard University Press.

Godwin, William. Book II, Chapter II: "Of Justice," *An Enquiry Concerning Political Justice, and Its Influence on General Virtue and Happiness* (1793). Vol. 1. London: G.G.J. and J. Robinson, 1793. pp. 81–83. The Online Library of Liberty: http://oll.libertyfund.org/titles/godwin-an-enquiry-concerning-political-justice-vol-i

Gouges, Olympe de. *Declaration of the Rights of Woman and the Female Citizen* [*Les Droits de la Femme*, 1791], trans. Louis Groarke. Original French version: http://gallica.bnf.fr/ark:/12148/bpt6k426138/f9.image

Haidt, Jonathan, et al. Excerpts from "The New Synthesis in Moral Psychology." *Science* 316 (2007): 998–1001. Copyright © 2007 by the American Association for the Advancement of Science. All rights reserved. Adapted with permission from AAAS.

Held, Virginia. Excerpts from "Feminist Transformations of Moral Theory." *Philosophy and Phenomenological Research* 50 Supplement (Autumn 1990): 321–44. Adapted with the permission of John Wiley & Sons—Books, conveyed through Copyright Clearance Center, Inc.

Hobbes, Thomas. *Leviathan or The Matter, Forme, & Power of a Common-Wealth Ecclesiastical and Civill* (1651).

Homer. Book XXII of the *Iliad*, from *The Illiad of Homer*, trans. Samuel Butler. London: Longmans, Green, & Co., 1898. http://classics.mit.edu/Homer/iliad.22.xxii.html

Hume, David. *An Enquiry Concerning the Principles of Morals* (1751, 1772, 1777), ed. Tom L. Beauchamp. Oxford and New York: Oxford University, 1998. Section 2. Of benevolence, Parts 1 & 2, pp. 78–82; Section 3. Of justice, Part 1, pp. 83–90; Section 9. Conclusion, Part 1, pp. 145–52. *A Treatise of Human Nature* (1739). Book II: Of the Passions, Part III. Of the will and direct passions, Section III. Of the influencing motives of the will, pp. 460–65; and Book III: Of Morals, Part I. Of virtue and vice in general, Section I. Moral distinctions not deriv'd from reason, p. 521.

Kant, Immanuel. Excerpt from *Critique of Practical Reason* (1788), *The Metaphysics of Ethics*, trans. J.W. Semple, ed. with Introduction by Rev. Henry Calderwood. 3rd edition. Edinburgh: T. & T. Clark, 1886. The Online Library of Liberty: http://oll.libertyfund.org/ titles/kant-the-metaphysics-of-ethics. *Groundwork for the Metaphysic of Morals* [*Grundlegung zur Metaphysik der Sitten*, 1785], *Kant's Critique of Practical Reason and Other Works on the Theory of Ethics*, trans. Thomas Kingsmill Abbott. London: Longmans, Green, 1873. Updated and modified in *Groundwork for the Metaphysics of Morals*, ed. Lara Denis. Peterborough, ON: Broadview, 2005. pp. 55–56, 58–62, 65–66, 73–76, 81–83, 87–89, 113–16. "On the Supposed Right to Lie from Benevolent Motives," originally published in *Berlinische Blaetter by Biester* (1799). Appendix, *Kant's Critique of Practical Reason and Other Works on the Theory of Ethics*, trans. with prefaces and other material by Thomas Kingsmill Abbott. 4th edition, revised. London: Longmans, Green, & Co., 1889), pp. 361–65. The Internet Archive. https://archive.org/stream/critiquepractic00kantuoft#page/n7/mode/2up

Kekes, John. Excerpts from *A Case for Conservatism*. Cornell University Press. Copyright © 1998 by Cornell University. Adapted by permission of the author and publisher.

Kempis, Thomas à. *De Imitatione Christi* [*Of the Imitation of Christ*], *The Imitation of Christ*, trans. William Benham. New York: E.P. Dutton, 1874, revised 1905. Project Gutenberg. http://www.gutenberg.org/ebooks/1653

Kierkegaard, Søren. Excerpts from *Either/Or: A Fragment of Life*. Volume One, trans. David F. Swenson and Lillian Marvin Swenson. Volume 2, trans. Walter Lowrie. Princeton, NJ: Princeton University Press, 1944. Copyright © 1944 by Princeton University Press. Abridged from the original by permission of the publisher. Excerpts from *Fear and Trembling and the Sickness Unto Death*, trans. Walter Lowrie. Princeton, NJ: Princeton University Press. Copyright © 1941, 1954, by Princeton University Press. All rights reserved. Abridged from the original by permission of the publisher.

Kohlberg, Lawrence. Excerpts from *The Philosophy of Moral Development: Moral Stages and the Idea of Justice. Essays on Moral Development, Volume I*. San Francisco, CA: Harper & Row, Publishers, 1981. Copyright © 1981 by Lawrence Kohlberg. All rights reserved. Adapted by permission of David Kohlberg.

Kongzi, Kŏngzǐ Jiāyǔ. "Teachings," excerpts adapted from *K'ung Tzŭ Chia Yü: The School Sayings of Confucius: Introduction, Translation of Sections 1–10 with Critical Notes*, by Dr. R.P. Kramers. Leiden: E.J. Brill, 1950. Excerpts from Kongzi, the *Lunyu* (the *Analects*) "Sayings and Conversations." Translation by Paul Groarke.

Excerpts from *The Koran Interpreted*, Volumes 1 and 2, trans. A.J. Arberry. London: George Allen & Unwin, 1955; New York: The Macmillan Company. Volume 1: pp. 29; 73–74; 211; 304–06. Volume 2: pp. 32; 62; 125; 194–97; 231; 353; 356; 361.

Korsgaard, Christine M. Excerpts from "A Kantian Case for Animal Rights." *Animal Law: Developments and Perspectives in the 21st Century*, ed. Margot Michel, Daniela Kühne, and Julia Hänni. Zurich/St. Gallen: Dike, 2012. Copyright © Christine M. Korsgaard/Dike Verlag AG, CH-Zurich. Adapted from the original with permission of the author and publisher.

Laertius, Diogenes. "Epicurus," *Book X of Diogenes Laertius, Lives of Eminent Philosophers*, trans. Robert Drew Hicks. Loeb Classical Library No. 184. Cambridge: Harvard University Press, 1925, 1972. Wikisource. https://en.wikisource.org/wiki/Lives_of_the_Eminent_Philosophers. Chapter 8. "Protagoras," *Book IX, Lives of Eminent Philosophers*, trans. Robert Drew Hicks. Loeb Classical Library No. 184. Cambridge: Harvard University Press, 1925. Wikisource. https://en.wikisource.org/wiki/Lives_of_the_Eminent_Philosophers. Chapter 11. "Pyrrho," *Book IX, Lives of Eminent Philosophers*, trans. Robert Drew Hicks. Loeb Classical Library No. 184. Cambridge: Harvard University Press, 1925. Wikisource. https://en.wikisource.org/wiki/Lives_of_the_Eminent_Philosophers. Chapter 1. "Zeno of Citium," *Book VII, Lives of Eminent Philosophers*, trans. Robert Drew Hicks. Loeb Classical Library No. 184. Cambridge: Harvard University Press, 1925, 1972. Wikisource. https://en.wikisource.org/wiki/Lives_of_the_Eminent_Philosophers

Excerpts from *Lǎozǐ* (*Dào dé jīng*). Translation by Paul Groarke.

Adapted from "Laws of Hammurabi," from *The Code of Hammurabi*, trans. L[eonard].W. King, introduction by Charles F. Horne, dated 1915. The Avalon Project, Yale Law School. http://avalon.law.yale.edu/ancient/hamframe.asp

Locke, John. *The Second Treatise of Government* (1690), later published as *The Second Treatise of Civil Government*.

Excerpts adapted from the *Long Discourses of the Buddha: A Translation of the Digha Nikaya by Maurice Walshe*. Somerville MA: Wisdom Publications. Copyright © Maurice Walshe, 1987, 1995, 2012. Adapted with the permission of Wisdom Publications and the English Sangha Trust on behalf of Maurice Walshe.

The Love Letters of Abelard and Heloise. The Temple Classics, ed. Israel Gollancz. London: J.M. Dent and Co., 1901. http://www.sacred-texts.com/chr/aah/aah00.htm

MacIntyre, Alasdair. Excerpts from *After Virtue: A Study in Moral Theory*. Notre Dame, IN: University of Notre Dame Press, 1981. Copyright © 1981 by Alasdair MacIntyre. Reprinted and adapted by permission of Alasdair MacIntyre and the University of Notre Dame Press.

Maimonides, Moses. Part III, *The Guide for the Perplexed*, trans. Michael Friedlaender. 4th revised edition. New York: E.P. Dutton, 1904. The Online Library of Liberty. http://oll.libertyfund.org/titles/1256

Mandeville, Bernard. *The Fable of the Bees*. London: T. Ostell; Edinburgh: Mundell and Son, 1806. Hathi Trust Digital Library. https://babel.hathitrust.org/cgi/pt?id=nyp.33433 061707588;view=1up;seq=15

Mannerschied SJ, Father. *Some Passages Concerning the Person, Character, Manner of Living and Government of Christina Queen of Sweden, "Christina, Queen of Sweden, 1626–1689," The Works of Christina Queen of Sweden: Containing Maxims and Sentences in Twelve Centuries, and Reflections on the Life and Actions of Alexander the Great*. London: Printed for D. Wilson and T. Durham, 1753. Hathi Trust Digital Library. https://catalog.hathitrust.org/Record/012502772

Marchetti, Giancarlo. Excerpts from "Interview with Richard Rorty." *Philosophy Now* 43 (Oct/Nov 2003). Adapted with the permission of Giancarlo Marchetti and Philosophy Now.

Marx, Karl. Excerpts from *Writings of the Young Marx on Philosophy and Society*, ed./trans. Loyd D. Easton and Kurt H. Guddat. Indianapolis, IN: Hackett Publishing Company, Inc., 1997. Copyright © 1994 by Hackett Publishing Company, Inc. Adapted by permission of Hackett Publishing Company, Inc. All rights reserved.

Marx, Karl, and Friedrich Engels. Excerpts from *The Communist Manifesto*, ed./trans. L.M. Findlay. Peterborough, ON: Broadview Editions, 2004.

Excerpts from Mencius, *The Mengzi*. Translation by Paul Groarke.

Menkiti, Ifeanyi. Excerpts from "Person and Community in African Traditional Thought." *African Philosophy: An Introduction*, 3rd edition, ed. Richard A. Wright. Lanham, MD: University Press of America, 1984. Copyright © 1984 University Press of America. Reproduced by arrangement with University Press of America. Adapted by permission of the Menkiti family.

Excerpts adapted from *The Middle Length Discourses of the Buddha: A New Translation of the Majjhima Nikāya*. Original translation by Bhikkhu Nāṇamoli; translation edited and revised by Bhikkhu Bodhi. Somerville MA: Wisdom Publications. Copyright © 1995, 2015 Bhikkhu Bodhi. Adapted with the permission of Bhikkhu Bodhi and Wisdom Publications.

Mill, Harriet Taylor. *The Enfranchisement of Women* (1851). Reprinted from the Westminster and Foreign Quarterly Review, July, 1851.

Mill, John Stuart. Excerpts from *On Liberty* (1859), Vol. XVIII of *The Collected Works of John Stuart Mill—Essays on Politics and Society*, ed. John M. Robson. Toronto: University of Toronto Press, 1977. pp. 213–310. *Utilitarianism*. Originally published in *Fraser's Magazine*, 1861. From Chapter 2: "What Utilitarianism Is," *Utilitarianism*, ed. Colin Heydt. Peterborough, ON: Broadview, [1871] 2010. pp. 41–63.

Moore, G.E. *Principia Ethica* (1903). Cambridge: Cambridge University, [1903] 1922. pp. 1–18

Narveson, Jan. *The Libertarian Idea*. Peterborough, ON: Broadview Press, [1988] 2001.

The New Testament. "The Sermon on the Mount" and other excerpts from the Gospel of Matthew, and "The Widow's Mite," the Gospel of Mark 12:38–44. Young's Literal Translation, Robert Young, 1898. Originally published by Baker Book House, Grand Rapids, Michigan, 1898. https://www.biblegateway.com/versions/Youngs-Literal-Translation-YLT-Bible/

Nguyen, Tram. Excerpts from "From SlutWalks to SuicideGirls: Feminist Resistance in the Third Wave and Postfeminist Era." *WSQ: Women's Studies Quarterly* 41, 3/4 (Fall/Winter 2013): 157–68. Copyright © 2013 by the Feminist Press at the City University of New York. Adapted by permission of the author and The Permissions Company, LLC on behalf of the publisher, www.feministpress.org.

Nietzsche, Friedrich. *On the Genealogy of Morals: A Polemical Tract* [*Zur Genealogie der Moral*, 1887], trans. Ian Johnston (last revised Dec. 21, 2001). http://fs2.american.edu/dfagel/www/GeneologyOfMorals.html. Excerpts from *The Will to Power: An Attempted Transvaluation of All Values*, trans. Anthony M. Ludovici. Volume I, Books I and II, London and Edinburgh: T.N. Foulis, 1914; pp. 5–6, 8–10, 16, 22, 132–34, 138, 163–64. Volume II, Books III and IV, London and Edinburgh: T.N. Foulis, 1910; pp. 12–13, 130, 132, 146, 152–53, 295–96, 330, 348, 365, 379, 386–87, 407, 431–32. Originally from *The Complete Works of Friedrich Nietzsche*, Vol. 14, 15, ed. Oscar Levy. London and Edinburgh: T.N. Foulis, 1910, 1914. The Internet Archive. Volume I. https://archive.org/details/NIETZSCHETHE WILLTOPOWER12/page/n8. The Internet Archive. Volume II. https://archive.org/details/completeworksoff00niet/page/n5

Paul, St. "First Letter to the Corinthians," *The New Testament*. Young's Literal Translation, Robert Young, 1898. Originally published by Baker Book House, Grand Rapids, Michigan, 1898. https://www.biblegateway.com/versions/Youngs-Literal-Translation-YLT-Bible/

Plato. "The Allegory of the Cave," from *The Republic*, Book VII, *The Dialogues of Plato*, trans. Benjamin Jowett. 2nd edition. Vol. 3. Oxford: Clarendon Press, 1875. http://classics.mit.edu/Plato/republic.html. "The Apology," *The Apology and Related Dialogues*, ed. Andrew Bailey, trans. Cathal Woods and Ryan Pack. Peterborough, ON: Broadview Press, 2016. "Conversation between Socrates and Callicles in Plato's Gorgias," *The Dialogues of Plato*, trans. Benjamin Jowett. 3rd edition, revised and corrected. Vol. 2. Oxford University Press, 1892. The Online Library of Liberty. http://oll.libertyfund.org/titles/766. "Conversation between Socrates and Gorgias, in Plato's Gorgias," *The Dialogues of Plato*, trans. Benjamin Jowett. 2nd edition. Vol. 2. Oxford: Clarendon Press, 1875. http://classics.mit.edu/Plato/gorgias.html. "Protagoras," from *The Dialogues of Plato*, trans. Benjamin Jowett. 2nd edition. Vol. 1. Oxford: Clarendon Press, 1875. http://classics.mit.edu/Plato/

protagoras.html. "The Rational Self and Tripartite Soul," from *The Republic*, Book IV, *The Dialogues of Plato*, trans. Benjamin Jowett. 2nd edition. Vol. 3. Oxford: Clarendon Press, 1875. http://classics.mit.edu/Plato/republic.html. "The Seventh Letter," trans. George Burges, 1851. Wikisource. https://en.wikisource.org/wiki/Epistles_(Plato)/Seventh_Letter

Rawls, John. Excerpts from *A Theory of Justice: Revised Edition*. Cambridge, MA: The Belknap Press of Harvard University Press. Copyright © 1971, 1999 by the President and Fellows of Harvard College. Adapted from the original by the permission of Harvard University Press.

Sandel, Michael J. Excerpts from *Liberalism and the Limits of Justice*, 2nd edition. Cambridge, UK: Cambridge University Press, 1998. Copyright © Cambridge University Press 1982, 1998. Adapted with the permission of the author and publisher through PLSclear.

Sartre, Jean-Paul. Excerpts adapted from *Existentialism Is a Humanism*, trans. Carol Macomber. Yale University Press, 2007. English-language translation copyright © 2007 by Yale University. *L'Existentialisme est un humanisme* © Editions Gallimard, Paris, 1996. Adapted by permission of Yale University Press.

Excerpts from *The Sayings of The Desert Fathers: The Apophthegmata Patrum: The Alphabetic Collection* by Benedicta Ward, SLG, trans, CS 59. Collegeville, MN: Cistercian Publications, 1975. Used by permission of Liturgical Press. All rights reserved.

Scarborough, William. Adapted from *A Collection of Chinese Proverbs, Translated and Arranged*. Shanghai: American Presbyterian Mission Press, 1875. Archive.org

Schopenhauer, Arthur. "Aphorisms on the Wisdom of Life" ["Aphorismen zur Lebensweisheit"], Vol. 1, Appendices and Omissions [*Parerga und Paralipomena*, 1851], *Counsels and Maxims: Being the Second Part of Schopenhauer's Aphorismen Zur Lebensweisheit*. 2nd edition. London: Swan Sonnenschein & Co., 1891. *The Essays of Arthur Schopenhauer*, ed./trans. T. Bailey Saunders. Project Gutenberg, 2004. http://www.gutenberg.org/files/10715/10715.txt. *The Basis of Morality* [*Über die Grundlage der Moral*, 1840], trans. with an Introduction and Notes by Arthur Brodrick Bullock. London: Swan Sonnenschein & Co., 1903. Project Gutenberg. http://www.gutenberg.org/files/44429/44929-h/44929-h.htm#CHAPTER_I. Selections from "On the Sufferings of the World," from *Parerga und Paralipomena*, trans. T. Bailey Saunders. London: Swan Sonnenschein & Co., 1893. Reprinted in *The Essays of Arthur Schopenhauer: Studies in Pessimism*, trans. T. Bailey Saunders. Project Gutenberg, 2004. http://www.gutenberg.org/cache/epub/10732/pg10732-images.html

Singer, Peter. Excerpts from *Animal Liberation*, 2nd edition. New York, NY: The New York Review of Books. Copyright © 1975, 1990 by Peter Singer. Adapted by permission of the author.

Smith, Arthur H. Adapted from *Proverbs and Common Sayings from the Chinese, together with much related and unrelated matter, interspersed with observations on Chinese things-in-General*. New and revised edition. Shanghai: American Presbyterian Mission Press, 1902. Archive.org

Sojourner Truth. Speech. "Ain't I A Woman?" Delivered at the Women's Rights Convention, Akron, Ohio, 1851. Transcribed by Marius Robinson, *Anti-Slavery Bugle*, June 21, 1851.

Taylor, Charles. Excerpts from *The Malaise of Modernity*. Concord, ON: House of Anansi Press Limited, 1991. Copyright © 1991 by Charles Taylor and the Canadian Broadcasting Corporation. Adapted with the permission of House of Anansi Press Inc., Toronto.

Teresa of Jesus, St. *The Life of St. Teresa of Jesus, of the Order of Our Lady of Carmel*, trans. David Lewis. With additional notes and an introduction by Rev. Fr. Benedict Zimmerman, O.C.D. 3rd edition enlarged. London: Thomas Baker; New York: Benziger Bros., 1904. Project Gutenberg. http://www.gutenberg.org/files/8120/8120-h/8120-h.htm

The Torah. Excerpts from the book of Leviticus and the book of Deuteronomy, from *The Hebrew Bible in English, The Holy Scriptures According to the Masoretic Text: A New Translation with the Aid of Previous Versions and with Constant Consultation of Jewish Authorities*. Philadelphia: The Jewish Publication Society of America, 1917. http://www.mechon-mamre.org/e/et/et0.htm

Excerpts from "Towards a Global Ethic: An Initial Declaration of the Parliament of the World's Religions (updated 2020)." Copyright © Parliament of the World's Religions, Chicago. Adapted by permission of the Parliament of the World's Religions. https://parliamentofreligions.org/documents/towards-global-ethic-initial-declaration

Walters, Gregory J. Excerpts from "Human Rights in Historical Overview." Introduction to *Human Rights. Theory and Practice: A Selected and Annotated Bibliography*. Magill Bibliographies: The Scarecrow Press and Salem Press, 1995.

Wáng Yáng-Míng. Excerpts adapted from "Inquiry on the Great Learning" and others, from *Instructions for Practical Living and Other Neo-Confucian Writings*, trans. Wing-tsit Chan. Number LXVIII of the Records of Civilization: Sources and Studies, UNESCO Collection of Representative Works Chinese Series. New York/London: Columbia University Press, 1963. Heavily adapted with the permission of Columbia University Press.

Wollstonecraft, Mary. *A Vindication of the Rights of Woman: With Strictures on Political and Moral Subjects.* Boston: Thomas and Andrews, 1792. WikiSource. https://en.wikisource.org/wiki/A_Vindication_of_the_Rights_of_Woman

From the Publisher

A name never says it all, but the word "Broadview" expresses a good deal of the philosophy behind our company. We are open to a broad range of academic approaches and political viewpoints. We pay attention to the broad impact book publishing and book printing has in the wider world; for some years now we have used 100% recycled paper for most titles. Our publishing program is internationally oriented and broad-ranging. Our individual titles often appeal to a broad readership too; many are of interest as much to general readers as to academics and students.

Founded in 1985, Broadview remains a fully independent company owned by its shareholders—not an imprint or subsidiary of a larger multinational.

For the most accurate information on our books (including information on pricing, editions, and formats) please visit our website at www.broadviewpress.com. Our print books and ebooks are also available for sale on our site.

broadview press
www.broadviewpress.com

 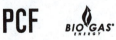